Macroeconomics

Macroeconomics

Robert J. Gordon

Professor of Economics
Northwestern University

Little, Brown and Company
Boston Toronto

Library of Congress Catalog Card No. 77-020435

FIFTH PRINTING

Published simultaneously in Canada
by Little, Brown & Company (Canada) Limited

Printed in the United States of America

with love,
for Julie

Preface:
To the Instructor

Students of the 1970s come to their Macroeconomics class eager to understand why inflation and unemployment have both been so high in the United States and the rest of the world. Too often they leave disappointed and with their high expectations unfulfilled. One of the major reasons for this disappointment is the topic emphasis and abstract theoretical development found in current textbooks. Often two-thirds of the exposition is devoted to the theory of income determination. Readers must digest many chapters of difficult and abstract material before the *IS* and *LM* curves finally are allowed to cross. Other books manage to compress *IS-LM*, but fail to link the analysis of income determination to that of unemployment and inflation. In most books it seems that the treatment of inflation is an afterthought, often left completely unrelated to and separate from the theory of income determination.

Further, major features of the real world are left unexplained. Since 1971, inflation and unemployment in most countries have been *positively* related, making the negative Phillips curve story appear to be a peculiar anachronism. The acceleration of monetary growth since 1965 has *raised* interest rates, leading the reader to wonder whether the *IS-LM* analysis is still relevant.

And, where, the reader asks, is the theory applied directly to dramatic historical episodes? Ironically, current *micro*economics texts have taken the lead in presenting lively case studies, even though macroeconomics is the more topical and potentially more interesting subject.

I have written this book to help readers gain the understanding of today's economy that they seek. The unique topic organization, content features, and pedagogical features reflect this purpose.

UNIQUE CONTENT FEATURES

This intermediate macro text is the first to focus on inflation and unemployment as core topics, rather than treating them as appendages and afterthoughts. The tried-and-true *IS-LM* theory of income determination is presented concisely and then linked clearly to the causes of inflation and unemployment. For the first time there is a modern treatment of the monetarist controversy, or "why economists disagree," that provides a unifying theme for the discussion of policy issues. The real world is brought into the book's every chapter by means of examples and many case studies.

BENEFITS FOR THE READER

INFLATION AND UNEMPLOYMENT

The causes, consequences, and cures of inflation and unemployment constitute this book's five-chapter "core" — Chapters 7–11 — which the reader reaches early in the course, as soon as the essentials of *IS-LM* theory have been developed. The 1970s have taught us that macroeconomics is about aggregate supply, not just aggregate demand. In Chapter 8 the traditional Phillips curve is joined for the first time by an aggregate "budget constraint" (*BC*) line, which depends on the growth of nominal aggregate demand. This makes possible a simple new demand-supply analysis of inflation and unemployment, which translates the puzzles of the 1970s into a single all-purpose graph. Inflation and unemployment are *negatively* related in the conventional way when an acceleration in demand growth shifts the *BC* line upward along the Phillips curve. But inflation and unemployment are *positively* related, as in the 1970s, when the short-run Phillips curve is shifted along the *BC* line by: (a) changing expectations, (b) the introduction or termination of price controls, and (c) oil and food supply shocks. "Inflation Triggers Recession" was announced as a new theory by *The New York Times* in 1975, but will seem an obvious statement to readers of this book.

Attention is given to the causes, consequences, and cures of unemployment. This is the first text to give the welfare economics of unemployment and inflation the prominence they deserve. In Chapter 9 fluctuations of actual unemployment around the natural unemployment rate are distinguished from the separate puzzle — why is the natural unemployment rate so high in the United States? Policy solutions are suggested for mismatch, turnover, and temporary layoff unemployment and sections on the output loss and psychic costs of recessions are included. In Chapter 10 the distinction between real and nominal interest rates is stressed, and students are shown how to integrate the two types of interest rates into *IS-LM* analysis. The redistributive impact of unanticipated inflation is distinguished from the effects of a fully anticipated inflation on money holding. And the impact of our inflation policy on other nations is also examined. Recessions, controls, and institutional reforms including indexation are all discussed in Chapter 11 as cures for inflation.

THE MONETARIST-NONMONETARIST CONTROVERSY

The monetarist-nonmonetarist controversy no longer concerns the slopes of curves, but rather the merits of policy activism and whether economic instability originates in the private sector or the government. The recent drift of opinion in professional writing, conferences, and discussions has identified major areas of consensus, including the theory of income, inflation, and unemployment developed in Chapters 3–11.

What then explains the paradox of convergence without agreement? Monetarists disagree with the nonmonetarist preference for government intervention and an activist stabilization policy, and prefer instead a fixed-growth-rate rule for the money supply. Why? Our analysis in Chapter 12 finds the answer in the monetarists' strong belief that the private economy can remain stable without government help, in their greater distrust of government, and in their belief that the government is capable of doing more harm than good.

This book is neither monetarist nor nonmonetarist in orientation. Instead, the new interpretation of the debate between the two camps provides a unique focus for the last part of the book. Not only the chapters on monetary and fiscal policy, but also those on consumption, investment, and money demand are written with the goal of locating the sources of instability in the economy. A mixed picture emerges with plenty of evidence provided to support both opponents and proponents of an activist stabilization policy.

CASE STUDIES

Almost every chapter of the book contains at least one case study, which analyzes particular historical episodes from the point of view of the theory. In many cases historical data are plotted on the relevant theoretical quadrants to show the adherence of the data to the theoretical prediction and, occasionally, to show puzzles that need to be explained. The case studies help give the student a "breather" from the theory. Once per chapter, and sometimes more frequently, the student is reminded that the theoretical curves do not describe an ivory-tower dream world, but are useful in explaining major episodes of economic history.

Econometrics or statistics are not used at all. Instead of describing the real world in terms of difficult econometric equations, estimated by techniques the student cannot understand, all case studies are based on clear and simple diagrams that plot the data, often in a novel way. Empirical estimates of concepts such as expected rate of inflation, natural unemployment rate, and real interest rate have been created especially for this book. Graphs summarize recent research on the costs of lost output in recessions, the contribution of oil and food prices to the 1974 inflation, and other topics.

UNIQUE ORGANIZATION

The main aim is to introduce the five-chapter core on inflation and unemployment as early as possible to sustain student interest and to allow full attention to these subjects in the ten-week courses taught at many schools on the quarter system. *IS-LM* income determination theory is developed in Chapters 3–6. The conventional long, tedious buildup to *IS-LM* equilibrium is avoided by moving the details of the theory of consumption, investment, and money demand to Chapters 13–15. Instead, the *IS-LM* model is fully developed by the end of Chapter 4 and is used in Chapter 5 to examine the relative potency of monetary and fiscal policy, the crowding-out effect, the endogeneity of the money supply when the Fed tries to stabilize interest rates, and effects of changes in the mix of monetary and fiscal policy. To aid comprehension the price level is fixed throughout Chapters 3–5, but in Chapter 6 prices are allowed to be perfectly flexible.

Chapter 7 is an important bridge chapter linking *IS-LM* to the Phillips curve by developing the concepts of aggregate supply and supply shocks. For the first time policy changes are allowed to alter real output and the price level simultaneously. Then in Chapter 8 the concepts of aggregate demand and supply are converted into an analysis of inflation and unemployment. Chapters 9–11 turn to the consequences and cures of unemployment and inflation.

The role of Chapter 12 is twofold. First, it summarizes the debate on monetarism and policy activism and is a suitable stopping point for short quarter-length courses. Second, it provides a unifying framework, tying the chapters on consumption, investment, and money demand (13–15) with those on monetary and fiscal policy (16–18). Chapters 13–15 discuss the sources of instability in the private economy, while chapters 16–18 determine whether activist policy intervention can do more good than harm.

Some other books introduce the details of monetary and fiscal policy before any mention of inflation or the Phillips curve dilemma. But to discuss policy in isolation from the inflation-unemployment problem is an anachronism dating from the 1960s, with its overemphasis on demand management to the exclusion of supply limitations. Here a general overview of policymaking and of the obstacles to precise fine tuning of demand is presented as part of the monetarist debate in Chapter 12. Detailed features of monetary and fiscal policy are reserved for Chapters 16–18. The decision to discuss consumption, investment, and money demand before the policy chapters reflects the logic of the matter: sources of instability in the private sector need to be understood before assessing the feasibility and desirability of government intervention aimed at offsetting that instability.

Two traditionally peripheral topics – growth theory and international macroeconomics – come at the end of the book. Reflecting the recent well-deserved de-emphasis on growth theory, that topic and the related tradeoff between consumption and investment is treated as an aspect of fiscal policy in Section 18-8. Chapter 19 presents a relatively full treatment of international macroeconomics, with an appropriate emphasis on flexible exchange rates and international policy problems of the late 1970s. Teachers outside the United States should consider assigning Chapter 19 earlier in the course, perhaps after Chapter 8.

PEDAGOGICAL FEATURES

Color. Color is used throughout the book to make the diagrams clear: red lines identify demand curves and black lines identify supply curves. Shading is used liberally to mark off important features of diagrams, such as the area of a Phillips curve diagram where actual inflation exceeds or falls short of expected inflation. In theoretical diagrams involving shifts of curves, new equilibrium points are identified in red on the axes. And color is used frequently for emphasis in tables.

Summary and Look Ahead. Each chapter ends with a summary and then a paragraph called A Look Ahead, which explains how the next chapter is related to the present one.

Diagrams. Except for the standard Keynesian multiplier equations in Chapter 3 (and a few sections of Chapters 13–15), most of the theory is presented graphically, freeing the text from the clutter of algebra. The variables that make each curve shift are always written next to each curve, giving students a firm handle on the old bugaboo – the confusion between movement along a curve and a shift in a curve. In addition, most diagrams tell their own story with verbal labels on each curve. Student review is aided by a concise caption explaining what is going on in every graph and by a headline for each graph that explains the main point in colloquial language. Further, continuity between successive diagrams within a chapter is achieved by using the same letters of the alphabet to denote a given position.

Concept Boxes. There is no separate chapter on concepts. Everything is explained as it is used. Background information is given in separate boxes, such as one explaining why bond prices and interest rates are inversely related and another showing how to read vertical and horizontal lines in economic diagrams.

Footnotes. Rather than a bibliography at the end of each chapter with no indication of the importance, usefulness, or relevance of each item, frequent footnote references are provided to supporting and related literature. Additional suggestions for supplemental reading are provided later in this Preface.

Identifications. For students' benefit the end of each chapter contains a list of important new terms introduced in the chapter, including some that are not in the glossary.

Biographies. Short biographies of four major protagonists – Keynes, Friedman, Tobin, and Modigliani – are included in Chapters 6 and 12.

Numerical Examples. To aid the student's comprehension of the few equations included, each equation is presented twice – in its general form and with a numerical example. A single running numerical example guides the student through Chapters 3–6. All diagrams in these chapters have numbers on the axes and the slopes of all curves correspond to the numerical examples in the text.

Questions and Answers. Each chapter ends with a set of discussion questions of varying difficulty. Answers to all questions are provided in the *Instructor's Manual*.

Glossary. A glossary of terms is included in the back of the book with a cross-reference to the section where the term is first introduced. Terms with glossary definitions are identified in boldface type when first introduced.

Historical Data. Appendix B presents annual data on key variables for 1900–77 and quarterly data for 1947:Q1–1977:Q4. This is intended as a handy reference for instructors and for use in student projects or term papers.

SUGGESTIONS FOR USE

Options for Short Courses. The book is designed to be read straight through, with Chapters 1–12 assigned in quarter-length courses and Chapters 1–18 assigned in semester-length courses. The international chapter (19) is kept separate at the end so that teachers can assign it as they wish. (Teachers of semester courses may wish to substitute it for Chapters 9 or 13–14.) Several other possible 12-chapter course outlines are feasible for short courses.

Option 1: Short course emphasizing theory

1. What Is Macroeconomics?
2. The Measurement of Income and Prices
3. Commodity-Market Equilibrium and the Multiplier
4. Spending, the Interest Rate, and Money
5. Strong and Weak Effects of Monetary and Fiscal Policy
6. Flexible Prices and the Self-Correcting Economy
7. Allowing both Output and Prices to Change Together
8. Determinants of Inflation and Unemployment
12. The Monetarist-Nonmonetarist Debate on Policy Activism
13. Instability in the Private Economy: Consumption
14. Instability in the Private Economy: Investment
15. The Demand for Money and the Choice of Monetary Instruments

Option 2: Short course emphasizing policy

1. What Is Macroeconomics?
7. Allowing both Output and Prices to Change Together
8. Determinants of Inflation and Unemployment
9. Unemployment: Cost, Cures, and Policy Options
10. The Consequences of Inflation
11. Cures for Inflation: Recessions, Controls, and Indexation
12. The Monetarist-Nonmonetarist Debate on Policy Activism
15. The Demand for Money and the Choice of Monetary Instruments
    (could omit sections 15-3 to 15-6)
16. Federal Reserve Monetary Control and Its Limitations
17. The Government Budget and the Public Debt
18. Contributions and Limitations of Fiscal Policy Instruments
19. Policy in an International Setting

An Annotated Guide to Possible Outside Reading Assignments. No book of readings was prepared to supplement this text, because teachers appear to have divergent tastes regarding the desired level of difficulty and the optimal balance of theory and policy. Instead, this section provides a broad menu of possible outside reading assignments. The books listed are *available in paperback* and contain at least two relevant selections, which are keyed to the appropriate section of the text. No instructor would want to assign all of these items. Further, the level of difficulty varies widely and all selections should be examined for level, content, and length well before reading lists are made final.

TITLES CITED

The Challenge of Economics: Readings from Challenge Magazine, Random House, 1977. Very good supplement for its topic coverage and level of difficulty.

R. W. Clower, *Monetary Theory: Selected Readings,* Penguin, 1970. Relatively difficult articles from professional journals.

Economic Report of the President, Government Printing Office, January 1978. Issued each January, contains long but readable chapters on different topics each year.

William Fellner, editor, *AEI Studies on Contemporary Economic Problems 1976,* American Enterprise Institute, Washington, 1976. Also a separate volume with the same title was published in 1977. Medium difficulty.

Milton Friedman, *Dollars and Deficits,* Prentice Hall, 1968. A collection of articles and lectures at a relatively readable level.

John Kenneth Galbraith, *Money,* Bantam Books, 1976. Very readable historical background.

John Maynard Keynes, *The General Theory of Employment, Interest, and Money,* Harcourt Brace, 1965. Most students find this difficult and instructors may have to spend an undesirable amount of time explaining it.

William E. Mitchell, *et al., Readings in Macroeconomics,* McGraw-Hill, 1974. Policy-oriented, somewhat out of date in coverage, wide variation in level of difficulty.

Joseph A. Pechman, ed., *The 1978 Budget: Setting National Priorities,* Brookings, 1977. A new volume each year, often with a different editor. Excellent for an overview of recent policy problems.

M. J. C. Surrey, *Macroeconomic Themes,* Oxford, 1976. Edited readings with helpful commentaries, contains many classic articles, wide variation in level of difficulty.

SUGGESTED ASSIGNMENTS

This lists far too many assignments for a single course — select at will.

Chapters 3–6, Theory of Income Determination
Clower, Part IV
Galbraith, Chapters 13–16 (on the 1920s, the Depression, and the coming of Keynes)
Keynes, Books I, II, IV
Surrey, Chapter 1

Chapters 7–11, Inflation and Unemployment
Challenge, Chapters 1, 2, 5, 6
Economic Report of the President, 1978, Chapter 4
Fellner, 1976, pp. 17–54; 109–182; 255–369
Fellner, 1977, pp. 15–52; 159–202.
Friedman, *Protest,* Chapters 4–6
Friedman, *Dollars,* Part I
Galbraith, Chapter 12 (on German hyperinflation), 19–20 (covers recent history)

ACKNOWLEDGEMENTS

My first and perhaps greatest debt is to those who gave me the opportunity to absorb macroeconomic theory — debates and personalities from widely differing perspectives:

Franco Modigliani, who at M.I.T. in the mid-1960s set up the first large econometric model that merged money properly into the Keynesian framework, and who taught his graduate students equal respect for theory and empirical application.

Milton Friedman, many of whose views seemed outrageous when I came from M.I.T. to join his Money and Banking workshop in 1968, yet appeared remarkably sensible when I left five years later.

Arthur Okun and George Perry, who have given me the opportunity to participate in the Brookings Panel on Economic Activity since its inception and whose talent for constructive criticism is unequaled.

Next, thanks to Basil G. Dandison, former Little, Brown economics editor, the indispensible spark of this project who convinced me to undertake it. And to Darrell Griffin, his successor, whose willingness to invest time and resources and whose marketing wizardry were crucial ingredients in the final product.

A comparison of the initial crude prospectus and the final book underlines the contribution of those who reviewed that prospectus: Michael Babcock (Kansas State), Allen Duehan (Canisius College), L. S. Fan (Colorado State), Carl Gambs (Michigan State), Samuel Gubins (Haverford), George Jensen (California State), Joyce Pickerspill (California State), John Pilgrim (Bradley), Maurice Psannespiel (Wichita State), Richard Smith (Marietta), and Maurice Weinrobe (Michigan State).

I cannot repay the time invested by the reviewers in commenting on the manuscript, except to hope they are pleasantly surprised to see how many of their suggestions have been incorporated into the published version: Charles Cathcart (Pennsylvania State), Richard Caves (Harvard), Robert Clower (U.C.L.A.), Ronald Ehrenberg (Cornell), Michael McElroy (North Carolina State), Ronald Rost (Indiana), John Rutledge (Claremont Men's College), and Paul Worthington (Slippery Rock State).

The comments of Milton Friedman and Arthur Okun helped to make the statement of "why economists disagree" in Chapter 12 a summary with which they both basically agree. Thanks also to Allan Meltzer for his constructive comments on the same chapter.

Undergraduate students at Northwestern, who suggested questions and helped me screen out particularly unintelligible passages, include: G. Marc Bauman, Rosanne Dineen, James Fernald, Tim Gilman, Bradley Ihlenfeld, Bob Klaas, Sally Margolin, James Sommer, and David Waymire.

Fat manuscripts are the bane of any secretary, but Marcey Friedman made her way through the book with incredible speed and accuracy. Thanks go also to Evelyn Goldstein and Karen Ibach for their part in the typing and to Joseph Peek for his help with the data.

The book editor at Little, Brown, Jonathan Baker, contributed a perfect blend of nagging reminders, good judgment, and patience at my nitpicking interventions.

Second-to-last place is reserved for R. A. Gordon, who was willing to scrutinize the outline and contribute his usual merciless criticism of the manuscript, while all the time viewing the project as a needless distraction from more socially useful research.

Finally, thanks to my wife Julie, the chief victim of the twelve-month writing schedule, whose unfailing encouragement and welcome diversions made the book possible.

Evanston, Illinois   Robert J. Gordon
1978

Preface:
To the Student

Macroeconomics is one of the most important topics for college students, because the health of the economy will have an influence on your whole life. The overall level of employment and unemployment will determine the ease with which you find a job after college, and with which you will be able to change jobs or obtain promotions in the future. The inflation rate will influence the interest rate you receive on your savings and pay when you borrow money, and also the extent to which the purchasing power of your savings will be eroded by higher prices.

This macroeconomics text will equip you with the principles you need to make sense out of the conflicting and contradictory discussions of economic conditions and policies in newspapers and news magazines. You will be better able to appraise the performance of the President and Congress, and to predict the impact of their policy actions on your family and business.

WHO SHOULD READ THIS BOOK?

Most college students taking this course will have taken a course in economic principles. But this book has been written to be read by *all* students, even those who have not previously enrolled in an economics course. How is this possible? In Chapters 1–3 we review material which is in every principles course. By the end of Chapter 3, all students will have learned the essential concepts they need to understand the material to be developed.

This book has been carefully designed to look and read like a principles book. The entire presentation is graphic, with simple ninth-grade algebra used only in the review of elementary ideas in Chapter 3. Examples are used frequently. Most chapters have one or more "case studies" to give you a "breather" from the analysis and to show how the ideas of the chapter can be applied to real-world episodes. New words are set off in bold-face type and defined in the Glossary in the back of the book, thus easing vocabulary problems. And the diagrams in the first part of the book, as well as the text description itself, use numerical examples instead of mathematical symbols to show movement of the economy from one situation to another.

HOW TO READ THIS BOOK

Each chapter begins with an introduction, linking it to previous chapters, and ends with a "Summary" and a "Look Ahead" section, which links it to subsequent chapters. When you begin a chapter, first read the introduction to make sure you understand how the chapter differs from the previous ones. Then plan to read each chapter twice, first for the main points. After the first reading, study the summary and then try to answer the questions, marking those points which you do not understand. Finally, go back for a second reading, paying special attention to the discussion of issues which you may not have grasped fully at first.

Always try to write out answers to the questions. Another aid to comprehension is to try to work through the chapter and substitute a different numerical example for the one used in the text. You will find that in Chapters 2–8 you can review the main concepts by looking at the diagram, since each Figure has a descriptive caption.

When you plan your time schedule, don't read this book too rapidly or casually. Time and care devoted to two readings and writing out answers to questions will bring great rewards. Not only will your grades benefit, but more importantly the payoff will be a set of ideas and analytical tools which you can apply in everyday reading. And if your instructor has assigned additional outside readings, approach them by asking yourself whether: 1. the reading applies tools developed in the text; 2. disagrees with a point made in the text; or 3. adds supplementary ideas beyond those in the text.

If you should "get lost" in the course of reading the text, remember that there are built-in study aids to help. If you don't understand a particular section, turn to the Summary at the end of the chapter. If you forget the meaning of a word, turn to the Glossary at the back of the book.

(The Glossary will also help you tackle assigned outside readings.) And immediately following the Glossary is a Guide to Symbols to help you with the alphabetical symbols which are used in equations or in diagrams as labels.

OPTIONAL MATERIAL

Footnotes and chapter appendices have been provided as a place to put more difficult or less important material. Your instructor will decide whether or not an appendix is to be assigned, but even if not assigned, feel free to tackle it on your own when you have mastered the ideas in the body of the chapter. Footnotes contain qualifications, bibliographical references (valuable if you ever need to write a term paper on these topics), and cross-references to related material and diagrams elsewhere in the book.

Finally, notice that tables in the back of the book contain historical data starting with the year 1900 and updated to mid-1977. These figures can help you determine what was going on in periods not covered by the case studies, or can be used in outside assignments and term papers. Don't forget possible applications in history, political science, and sociology courses.

Summary Table of Contents

Detailed Table
of Contents

Part I

Introduction and Measurement

1 What Is Macroeconomics?

The cruel choice between two evils—
unemployment and inflation—has become
the major economic issue of the day.

—James Tobin and Leonard Ross[1]

1-1 PUZZLES TO BE EXPLAINED

Inflation and unemployment are the economic plagues from which the United States has suffered severely in the 1970s. Only in previous wartime periods has inflation raced as rapidly as it did during 1973 and 1974. Only during the Great Depression has unemployment remained as high for as long as it did in the "Great Recession" of 1974 and 1975. In the chapters that follow, we will study the causes, costs, and cures of inflation and unemployment, and will explore the answers to some important questions:

1. Why does the average price level rise, not fall or stay constant? Why has the rate of inflation been so rapid since 1965, and during 1973 and 1974 in particular? Are some people hurt more by inflation than are others? Is inflation worth worrying about if it just makes prices and wages go up faster together without affecting the "real" amount people can buy with their wages?
2. Why is any unemployment necessary at all? Why is unemployment high in some periods and low in others? Why is unemployment consistently lower in most European countries than it is in the United States? Is unemployment worth worrying about in this era when most job losers can qualify for unemployment benefits or welfare payments?
3. Can the private economy be relied upon to manage itself without recurrent bouts of inflation and unemployment? Is government intervention necessary to stabilize the economy, or, on the other hand,

---

[1] "Living with Inflation," *The New York Review of Books,* vol. 16 (May 6, 1971), p. 23.

have government mistakes made things worse? Would we have a more stable economy if the government kept its hands off?

4. Is the fight against inflation incompatible with that against unemployment? Are politicians being realistic when they promise to achieve zero inflation and zero unemployment at the same time? What explains the simultaneous occurrence of inflation and recession (1970–71 and 1973–75), sometimes called **stagflation** or **inflationary recession**? [2]

1-2 REAL AND NOMINAL MAGNITUDES

Economic amounts, or magnitudes—for instance, an individual's income or consumption expenditures—can be expressed as either nominal or real. A **nominal** magnitude is simply the actual value. If I spend $20,000 on consumption in 1977, my nominal consumption is $20,000. Nominal amounts are not very useful for economic analysis because they can increase when people buy more physical goods and services—more cars, steaks, and haircuts—or when prices rise. An increase in my nominal consumption from $15,000 in 1976 to $20,000 in 1977 might indicate that I have become better off and am buying more items or it could simply reflect an increase in prices for the same type and number of items purchased in 1976.

Are we better off? Or have price increases chewed up all our higher

---

[2] Terms set in bold type are defined in the glossary at the back of the book.

The Logarithmic Scale

A notable feature of the vertical axis in Figure 1-1 is its logarithmic scale. One hundred billion dollars uses up more inches in the bottom part of the graph than in the top part. Why? The scale is chosen so that a *proportional* change always consumes the same number of inches. When nominal or real GNP doubles, whether from 200 to 400, from 400 to 800, or from 800 to 1600, we always move upward exactly the same number of inches on the graph. The slope of any line drawn on the graph connecting the level of real output in two years indicates the *proportional* rate of growth between those two years.

Example: Draw straight lines connecting the levels of real GNP in 1905 and 1913 and in 1923 and 1929. Because the slope of the lines (that is, inches of increase in the line up the graph *per year*) is the same between 1905 and 1913 as between 1923 and 1929, you may safely conclude that the rate of growth of real GNP was the same in those two intervals (3.46 percent in each case).

Question: Which era had the fastest rate of real output growth—1905–13, 1923–29, or the more recent period, 1947–55?

Answer: The most recent period experienced the fastest proportional rate of growth (4.28 percent per year). A line connecting 1947 and 1955 is steeper than one connecting the beginning and ending years of the other two periods. It is the job of economic historians to explain accelerations and decelerations of growth during historical epochs.

NOMINAL GNP ALWAYS GROWS FASTER THAN REAL GNP
WHEN PRICES RISE

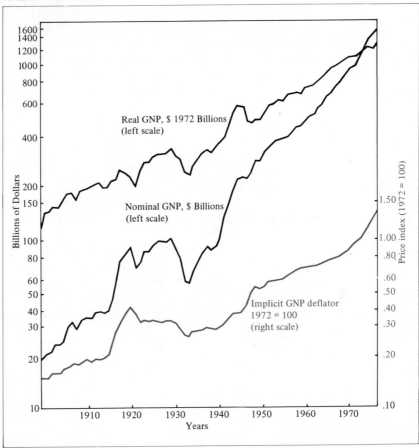

FIGURE 1-1

Nominal GNP, Real GNP, and the Implicit GNP Deflator, 1900-76

Real GNP shows what the United States actually produced measured in the prices of a single year (here, 1972) and thus corrected for inflation. Production boomed during the 1920s, collapsed during the Great Depression of the 1930s, boomed again in the early 1940s during World War II, and grew fairly steadily thereafter. Notice how the implicit GNP deflator has increased in upward jumps, especially during World War I, after World War II, and in the 1970s.

Source: Appendix B

spending, leaving us no better off than before? Changes in nominal magnitudes cannot answer these questions; they hide more than they reveal. So economists concentrate on changes in real magnitudes, which eliminate the influence of year-to-year changes in prices and reflect true changes in the number, size, and quality of items purchased.

A **real** magnitude is the value expressed in the price of an arbitrarily chosen "base year." If the base year is 1972, my real 1977 consumption "in 1972 prices" represents the amount my actual 1977 purchases would have cost if I had been able to buy each item at its 1972 price. For instance, if all prices doubled between 1972 and 1977, then my 1977 purchases of $20,000 would have cost only $10,000 in 1972 prices. Thus my real consumption in 1977 measured in 1972 prices was $10,000.

Any "real" concept measured in the prices of a single **base year** is adjusted for the effects of year-to-year changes in prices. The real **Gross National Product** (GNP) line in Figure 1-1 for each year (for instance, 1910 = $185.6 billion) is measured in 1972 prices and expresses what the production of each year would have cost at 1972 prices. **Real GNP** is sometimes called real **"output"** or "production." Because the prices of most items were higher in 1972 than in 1910, the result of inflation, real 1910 GNP in 1972 prices is a larger number ($185.6 billion) than the number of dollars people actually spent on GNP in 1910 (nominal 1910 GNP = $35.4 billion).

Later on we will discuss other real magnitudes, such as real consumption and the real money supply. Real magnitudes are sometimes expressed in "constant dollars" or in "prices of a single year," in contrast to magnitudes measured in actual current prices, which are usually called "current-dollar" or "nominal magnitudes." In other words:

	Alternate labels for magnitudes
Items measured in prices of a single year	Constant-dollar or Real
Items measured in actual prices paid in each separate year	Current-dollar or Nominal

Any change in nominal GNP can be divided into two parts:

1. Changes in the physical quantities of goods and services that make up real GNP.
2. Changes in the price level.

The black line in Figure 1-1 labeled nominal GNP indicates the actual number of dollars spent on goods and services in 1910 and all other years of this century. Actual nominal spending in 1910 was only $35.4 billion, as compared to real GNP in 1972 prices of $185.6 billion. Because prices in 1910 were so much lower than in 1972, the ratio of nominal to real GNP was the small fraction 0.191.

The red line in Figure 1-1 labeled **implicit GNP deflator** is an aggregate **price index;** it measures the ratio of the price level each year to the price level in 1972. For instance, the deflator in 1910 was 0.191—the ratio of actual gross spending ($35.4 billion) to 1910 spending measured in 1972 prices ($185.6 billion):

$$\text{Implicit GNP Deflator for 1910} = 0.194 = \frac{\$35.4 \text{ billion}}{\$185.6 \text{ billion}} = \frac{\text{Nominal GNP}}{\text{Real GNP}}$$

Be sure you understand why the implicit GNP deflator equals 1.00 in 1972.

During this century real GNP in 1972 prices has increased 10.34 times, from $123.3 billion in 1900 to $1275 billion in 1976. The implicit GNP deflator has increased 8.47 times, from 0.158 in 1900 to 1.339 in 1976. As a result, nominal GNP has increased by an immense 87.5 times, from $19.5 billion of actual spending in 1900 to $1706.5 billion in 1976.

1-3 HISTORICAL REPORT CARD ON INFLATION AND UNEMPLOYMENT

United States experience with inflation and unemployment for this century is illustrated in the top two panels of Figure 1-2.

INFLATION

The top frame illustrates the annual rate of change in the GNP deflator, that is, the **inflation rate.** The inflation rate line in Figure 1-2 shows the percentage rate of change in the implicit GNP deflator line of Figure 1-1. When the deflator rises rapidly, as in 1917–18 or 1973–74 (Figure 1-1), its rate of change is high (Figure 1-2). The inflation rate has fluctuated widely. Some periods have been marked by nearly stable prices—an inflation rate close to zero—as in 1900–14, 1923–29, and 1958–63. Other periods have exhibited short, sharp extremes of price movement, especially during and after World War I (1916–19), before and after World War II (1941–42 and 1946–48), at the outbreak of the Korean War (1951), and, more recently, in 1973–74.

Prices have not always increased. In the postwar years the word "inflation" has rightly come to be used as a synonym for "price change," because the price index has not changed in a *downward* direction in any year since 1949. But the nation experienced an episode of deflation just before World War II, as indicated by gray shading. The deflator also declined sharply in the early years of the Great Depression (1930–33), in 1920–21, and in two periods before World War I.

UNEMPLOYMENT: ACTUAL AND NATURAL

In the middle frame of Figure 1-2 the red line plots the actual unemployment rate. By far the most extreme episode was the Great Depression, when the actual unemployment rate remained above 10 percent for 10 straight years, 1931–40. It is not surprising that the Depression left

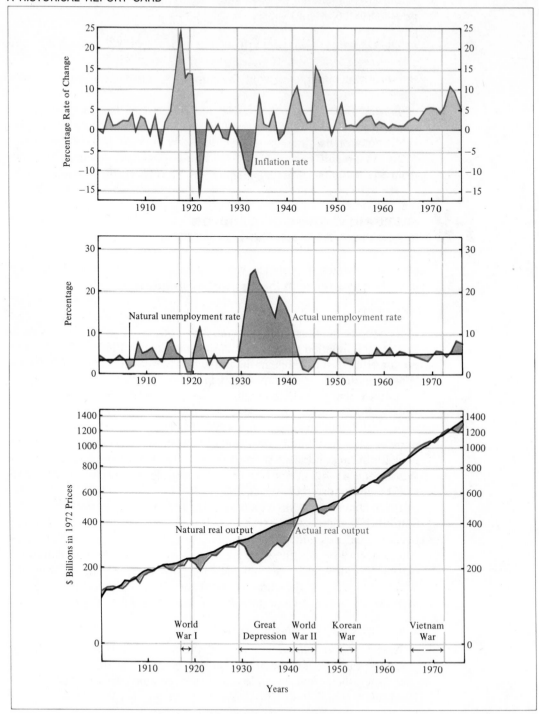

such a profound mark on economic theory, government policy, and political alignments; the masses of unemployed of the 1930s had no welfare programs or unemployment insurance to ease their misery.

The trauma of the Great Depression led Congress to pass the Employment Act of 1946, which pledged to maintain both full employment and stable prices. Since 1946 the **unemployment rate** has never been zero, but it has been lower on the average, and also considerably more stable, than during either the Great Depression or the earlier period 1900–29. Even in the 1974–75 recession, the worst period for unemployment since World War II, the peak rate for any month was 9.0 percent, lower than in recessions occurring between 1900 and 1921. But an unfortunate accompaniment to this relatively favorable level of unemployment has been steady and persistent inflation, especially since 1965.

The black line in the middle frame of Figure 1-2 estimates the **natural rate of unemployment,** the minimum attainable level of unemployment that is compatible with avoiding an acceleration of inflation. The natural unemployment rate is a "danger zone" that sets a lower limit on the level of actual unemployment that can be attained without accelerating inflation. The pink shaded areas mark years when unemployment fell below the natural rate, as in 1917–19 and 1966–69. In most of these periods inflation (see the top frame) accelerated. The gray shaded areas mark years when unemployment exceeded the natural rate. In some of these periods inflation slowed down, as in 1920–21, 1930–33, and 1958–64. But in other periods of high unemployment (particularly in 1974) inflation accelerated, and this presents a puzzle that is examined later in Chapter 8.

REAL OUTPUT: ACTUAL AND NATURAL

How can the ups and downs of the actual unemployment rate be explained? A clue is provided by the bottom frame of Figure 1-2, where the red line shows actual real output, the total dollars of production of goods and services (GNP) each year in constant prices (in this case, 1972 prices). The red actual real output line in Figure 1-2 is identical to the real GNP line in Figure 1-1.

FIGURE 1-2

Inflation, Unemployment, and Real Growth, 1900–76

A historical report card for the three main economic magnitudes during this century. The top frame shows the rate of inflation. The middle frame compares the actual unemployment rate with the natural unemployment rate. In the bottom frame the red line shows actual real output (GNP) and the black

line indicates the natural real output. Notice that high values of actual unemployment relative to the natural rate, indicated by gray shading in the middle frame, occur simultaneously with the gray shortfalls of actual output below natural output in the bottom frame. The largest gray areas mark the Great Depression of the 1930s.

Source: Appendix B

The black **natural real output** line provides an estimate of the amount the economy *could have produced* if it had been operating each year at its natural unemployment rate. Thus actual and natural output are roughly equal in the bottom frame in the same years when actual and natural unemployment are roughly equal in the middle frame (1902, 1927, 1957, and 1972). In years marked by gray shading, actual output fell below natural output. A maximum deficiency occurred in 1933 when actual output was only 64.2 percent of natural, and about 35.8 percent of natural output was wasted. Factories were idle, many workers were unemployed, and even employed workers were less productive because they had less to do. Before 1929 and since 1950 these intervals of substantial output deficiency, shown by gray shading, have been much less serious than in the Great Depression, but nevertheless have added up to billions of dollars in lost output.

In some years actual output exceeded natural output, as marked off by the shaded pink areas. This occurred mainly in wartime periods, particularly during World War I (1917–18), World War II (1942–45), the Korean War (1951–53), and the first half of the U.S. involvement in the Vietnam War (1965–69). In most of these periods of high output, the inflation rate accelerated, as indicated in the top frame of Figure 1-2.

Natural real output in the United States has grown steadily throughout this century for two basic reasons. First, attainable employment has increased as a result of immigration and a birth rate higher than the death rate. Second, each worker has become more productive, thanks to investment in machines, plants, education, and research. Section 18-8 discusses the lag in U.S. growth in the last two decades compared to that of other major industrial nations like West Germany, France, Sweden, and especially Japan. The discussion also covers what government policy can do to stimulate the U.S. growth rate of natural output.

1-4 WHAT IS MACROECONOMICS?

Most topics in economics can be placed in one of two categories: microeconomics and macroeconomics. "Micro" comes from a Greek word meaning "small." Just as a microscope is an instrument for inspecting small things, so microeconomics is devoted to the study of relationships among individual households, firms, and products. Why does a Cadillac cost 10,000 times as much as a package of razor blades? Why is a professor's salary more than that of a secretary but less than that of a university president? Will mandatory pollution control raise the price of steel more than that of milk? Microeconomics is concerned with these and other questions about the interrelationships among individual economic units.

"Macro" comes from a Greek word meaning "large." Just as a

"macrocosm" is the universe itself, **macroeconomics** is the study of the major economic "totals" or **aggregates** — total production (GNP), total employment and unemployment, the average price level of all goods and services, the total money supply, and others. Virtually every quantity discussed in this book has been calculated by taking the sum of all United States households and firms.

Macroeconomics is neither more nor less important than microeconomics and it is not necessary to study one before the other. The main areas of macroeconomic concern — particularly the effects of government policy on inflation, unemployment, and output — are more familiar to the public as a result of continuing political debate and media attention. Although macroeconomics does not primarily consist of deductions from microeconomics, much of macroeconomics nevertheless is based on microeconomic foundations, as we will discover when examining why the demand for money and for investment goods depends on the interest rate and why consumption depends on income.

Macroeconomic analysis has two tasks: to analyze the causes of changes in important aggregates and to predict the consequences of alternative policy changes. In policy discussions the group of aggregates that society cares most about — inflation, unemployment, the long-term growth rate of natural output — are called "goals" or **target variables.** When the target variables deviate from desired values, alternative **policy instruments** can be used in an attempt to achieve needed changes. Instruments fall into three broad categories: **monetary policies,** which include control of the money supply and interest rates; **fiscal policies,** which include changes in government expenditures and tax rates; and a third miscellaneous group, which includes wage and price controls and manpower policy.

1-5 STABILIZATION POLICY AND CONFLICTING GOALS

Modern macroeconomics developed in the aftermath of the traumatic unemployment and wasted output experienced during the Great Depression. The fundamental proposition of macroeconomics is that changes in **aggregate demand** — that is, in total nominal spending on goods and services — are the key to explaining why actual output and unemployment deviated from their natural (best attainable) levels in the periods marked by the gray and pink shaded areas in Figure 1-2. Since *unstable* aggregate demand is the basic macroeconomic problem — with undesired decreases in demand causing excessive unemployment and undesired increases in demand causing excessive inflation — the basic task of macroeconomic policy is to stabilize aggregate demand. The term **stabilization policy** is often used jointly to describe features common to both monetary and fiscal policy.

THE ROLE OF STABILIZATION POLICY

Macroeconomic analysis begins with a simple message: Either type of stabilization policy, monetary or fiscal, can be used to control aggregate demand and to offset undesired changes in private spending. The effects of monetary and fiscal policy on the price level and on real aggregate output (real GNP) are the main subject of Part II. Fiscal policy can raise output and employment by increasing government spending that creates jobs through government hiring. Or fiscal policy can stimulate private spending by cutting tax rates, thus inducing a higher level of private purchases, production, and employment. A monetary policy stimulus to output and employment takes the form of an increase in the money supply, which reduces interest rates and may in turn boost stock prices and make lending institutions more willing to grant credit.

This initial message of macroeconomics, that stabilization policy can smooth undesired fluctuations in aggregate demand, is only part of the story. We can assume that policy stimulus should be applied in a recession when unemployment is high and inflation is absent and that policy restraint is required when inflation is raging and unemployment is low, but we must go further. What is to be done when *both* unemployment and inflation are excessive? The price level increased throughout the recessions of both 1969–70 and 1973–75. In the midst of such stagflation, should stabilization policy adopt a stance of stimulus to fight unemployment or restraint to fight inflation? Why inflation and unemployment coexist and some possible solutions are discussed in Part III. We will learn, for instance, that the natural levels of unemployment and output in Figure 1-2 are neither optimal nor immutable, but can be improved by application of particular policy innovations.

There are further problems in applying stabilization policy. It may not be possible to control aggregate demand instantly and precisely. A policy stimulus intended to fight current unemployment might boost aggregate demand only after a long and uncertain delay, by which time the stimulus might not be needed. The impact of different policy changes may also be highly uncertain. Some economists argue that the lags and uncertainties inherent in stabilization policy are such serious obstacles that policymakers should avoid "fine tuning," which shifts the setting of policy back and forth frequently between stimulus and restraint, and follow a "rule" requiring a constant growth rate of the money supply. The debate between policy "fine tuning" or "activism" on the one hand and a monetary "rule" on the other is a central theme in our consideration of monetary and fiscal policy in Parts IV and V.

CLOSED AND OPEN ECONOMIES

Most of the macroeconomic analysis developed in this book applies to a **closed economy**, which ignores the flow of labor, goods, and money to and from other nations. Although U.S. foreign trade is immense, with exports and imports of close to $200 billion, most U.S. macroeconomic problems can be understood adequately without special consideration of international trade and payments. The domestic part of our economy is so huge that interactions with foreign nations are of secondary importance.[3] The major exception has been the profound influence on the U.S. economy of sharp increases in the prices of imported products, like oil in 1973–74 (less important examples are price increases for sugar in 1974 and coffee in 1976–77). The macroeconomic impact of such events is examined in Chapters 7, 8, and 11.

Our analysis of the closed economy applies not only to the United States but also (in the absence of interplanetary trade) to the world as a whole. If we conclude that inflation in the United States has been caused by excessive growth in the U.S. money supply, we will also have determined that the basic cause of worldwide inflation is excessive growth in the world money supply.

Although international complications play a relatively minor role in U.S. macroeconomics, a discussion of international economic policy can be found in Chapter 19, which examines the determinants of the exchange rate for U.S. dollars, Canadian dollars, British pounds sterling, Japanese yen, and other currencies. We will learn how foreign trade weakens the effects of domestic stabilization policy in an **open economy,** and in some cases may render it completely impotent. Small nations like the Netherlands and Belgium, where more than half of the GNP consists of exports, cannot stabilize their economies as easily as the United States. But U.S. policymakers can benefit from knowledge of international economics. For instance, they can discover that changing foreign exchange rates will alter the impact of both monetary and fiscal policy on real output and on the domestic price level.

1-6 USES OF MACROECONOMIC THEORY

The first third of this book uses economic theory to examine the causes of changes in output, unemployment, and the price level. Why theory? There are an almost limitless number of economic **variables,** or magnitudes, that can and do change. Only five aggregate "macro" variables—inflation, actual unemployment, natural unemployment, actual real output, and natural real output, are plotted in Figure 1-2. Why these five? Why not the production of bricks, the government bond interest rate, the

---

[3] In constant 1972 prices, U.S. exports in 1976 were only 7.6 percent of GNP; imports were an even smaller 6.4 percent.

price of bread, or the nation's total money supply? We are not interested in simply describing a collection of unrelated economic facts. That job can be left for an almanac. To be useful, economic theory must:

1. *Isolate the important economic variables that help explain the behavior of the goals or target variables.* With the help of theory, economists have learned that interest rates and the money supply are much more important determinants of economic conditions than the production of bricks or the price of bread.

2. *Create useful generalizations to describe the relationships among groups of variables.* Examples that will be studied are the relationship between consumption and income and between the rates of inflation and unemployment. A macroeconomic theory is like a simplified picture that shows how a set of important aggregate variables are related, just as a map of the interstate highway system is a simplified picture of the fastest routes between major cities, ignoring the details of every hill, valley, fence post, or telephone booth along the way.

3. *Test whether the generalizations have predictive power.* Economic theories are not unrealistic ivory tower statements but must continuously be adjusted to reflect new information. For instance, the theory of inflation most commonly used in the mid-1960s did not successfully predict the acceleration of inflation in 1968–69, nor the stagflation of 1970–71. Theories that conflict with the facts fade into obscurity and are replaced with new theories that yield better predictions, just as an inaccurate road map would be scrapped if it regularly led travelers to Denver when they were trying to reach Dallas.

USEFULNESS OF THEORY

Economists use theory for two quite separate purposes: for **"positive"** economics — *explaining* the behavior of important variables — and for **"normative"** economics — *recommending* changes in economic policy. Economists have developed theories that explain most of the changes observed in the national unemployment rate or the rate of inflation and why interest rates are now higher than they were 20 years ago. Most disagreements among economists no longer focus on different explanations of these major phenomena; rather they center on the proper conduct of economic policy, a normative issue.

Most policy disagreements stem from the incompatibility of worthy economic goals. Most people would like the price level to be stable and the unemployment rate to be close to zero. But this state of nirvana cannot be achieved instantly, if ever. Macroeconomics, like economics in general, is the science of *choice* in the face of limitations for each of the possible alternatives. Economists differ on the relative importance of reducing inflation versus the alternative of reducing unemployment, because they put different weights on the plight of the unemployed and because they have different views on the relative merits of basing policy decisions on transitory events (e.g., some pay more attention to the costs of a temporary recession created to reduce inflation) as compared to permanent events (e.g., an opposing group emphasizes the benefits of the permanent reduction in inflation that would result from a temporary recession).

In short, economists don their scientific caps when they analyze the consequences of government policies that influence the rates of unemployment and inflation. They take off their scientific caps and don their political caps when they recommend that the government should or should not take measures that would reduce inflation at the cost of a recession and higher unemployment. Similarly, although economists as scientists agree on the general factors that make the nation's economic capacity grow more rapidly, they differ among themselves on the merits of the policy changes necessary to spur faster growth.

1-7 DEVELOPMENT OF MODERN MACROECONOMICS: POST-KEYNESIANS AND MONETARISTS

Most of the analysis in this book has been developed by economists writing since the 1936 publication of John Maynard Keynes' revolutionary *The General Theory of Employment, Interest and Money*. Keynes broke a new trail, discarding obsolete theories that had no explanation for unemployment (a rather glaring defect in the conditions of 1936!).[4] The development of macroeconomic theory since the Keynesian revolution has emphasized the inherent instability of private economy operating free of government control and the need for countercyclical government intervention to stabilize trends toward booms and recessions.[5] The Keynesian revolution was a revolt against an outmoded "classical" (pre-Keynesian) approach. "Classical" thinking led to policy actions in the Great Depression that are presently condemned by economists of all schools of thought. Under Herbert Hoover, fiscal policy aggravated the Depression by *raising* taxes 50 percent, directly opposite to the modern recommendation of fiscal stimulus in a recession.[6] Even worse, the money supply was allowed to decline by 31 percent between 1929 and 1933, and nothing was done to stop the panic and loss of confidence caused by repeated waves of bank failures.

You may well ask: "What has gone wrong? If all this post-Keynesian

---

[4] When the U.S. unemployment rate was 17.0 percent; see Figure 1-2.

[5] Countercyclical applies to anything that moves opposite to the business cycle in total output. A countercyclical policy can be one that stimulates the economy when output is low or one that slows down the economy when output is high.

[6] The share of tax revenues in GNP, calculated at the natural output level, increased from 3.9 percent in 1932 to 6.0 percent in 1933.

economic thinking is so great, why were the problems of unemployment and inflation more serious in the mid-1970s than in any period since World War II? Has economic theory been proved wrong?"

After the tools of post-Keynesian macroeconomic analysis have been explained, you will see that they are powerful instruments for diagnosing the underlying causes of changes in output and spotlighting the effects of changes in government monetary, expenditure, or tax policies on output. The major problems of the 1960s and 1970s were caused not by the inability to understand what determined changes in output, but by three other factors: an overly optimistic approach to inflation, the impact of supply shocks, and policy mistakes.

UNDERESTIMATING INFLATION

In the late 1960s most economists misunderstood the inflationary consequences that alternative paths of output would bring about. They thought unemployment could be pushed down to 3.5 or 4.0 percent with only minor inflationary results. A group of economists called **monetarists** protested against this sanguine assumption of post-Keynesian economists and argued that the acceleration of growth in the **money supply** needed to achieve lower unemployment would cause an acceleration of inflation. A major achievement of the monetarist counterrevolution was to show that any attempt to hold unemployment below the natural rate of unemployment would cause ever-accelerating inflation.[7] Before this contribution of the monetarists had been accepted by most economists, the damage had been done, and inflation was so solidly built into the expectations of firms and workers that it had become almost impossible to eliminate (more on this in Chapters 8 and 11). Oddly enough, today's monetarists and nonmonetarists disagree not on the importance of monetary forces in determining changes in output, but on the importance of fiscal forces. Even these differences have faded with the passage of time, and a broad consensus has emerged. Fiscal policy affects real output in the short run but it only affects the price level in the long run. Changes in the growth rate of the money supply alter real output temporarily, but in the long run they only raise or lower the rate of inflation.

The debate continues, but its focus has shifted from the *consequences* of countercyclical monetary and fiscal policy to the *desirability* of the activist approach. The nonmonetarists favor intervention, whereas the monetarists prefer a "do-nothing" rule fixing the growth rate of the money supply.

---

[7] The phrase monetarist counterrevolution originated with Harry G. Johnson in his "The Keynesian Revolution and the Monetarist Counterrevolution," *American Economic Review,* vol. 61 (May 1971), pp. 1–14. The most important manifesto of the monetarist counterrevolution was Milton Friedman's 1967 Presidential Address to the American Economic Association, "The Role of Monetary Policy," *American Economic Review,* vol. 58 (March 1968), pp. 1–17.

SUPPLY SHOCKS

The **supply shock** was a new phenomenon that sprang up during the 1970s. Most macroeconomic analysis, whether monetarist or nonmonetarist in orientation, concentrates on the determinants of aggregate demand and on the consequences for output and the price level of changes in demand induced by private or government actions. But in 1973–74 two unparalleled events altered producers' willingness to continue to supply goods and services at the previously prevailing prices. Crop failures and other special factors caused farm prices to double in 1973, and the Organization of Petroleum Exporting Countries (OPEC) decided to quadruple the price of oil in late 1973 and early 1974. We will learn that governments faced with a supply shock cannot avoid a temporary worsening of the aggregate rate of inflation or unemployment or, most often, a worsening of both.

POLICY MISTAKES

During both the 1960s and 1970s policy mistakes occurred that many economists had foreseen and warned against. The first was the failure of the Johnson administration to raise taxes to pay for the Vietnam War in 1965–66. The resulting government deficits were the fundamental cause of the inflation that began in 1965–66 and was still going strong more than a decade later. The second mistake was the imposition of price and wage controls in 1971. This policy achieved a temporary slowdown in inflation but had no permanent effect; when controls were lifted in 1974 the price level bounced back up, aggravating the effects of the 1973–74 supply shocks. The third major mistake was the restrictive response of government monetary and fiscal policy to the events of 1973–74. The policies chosen created more unemployment than was necessary and aggravated the 1974–75 recession.

1-8 THE PARADOX OF CONVERGENCE WITHOUT AGREEMENT

Recently some broad areas of consensus have emerged. The material in Parts II and III can be learned without fear that major components will be discarded or contradicted in other courses. The leading monetarist, Milton Friedman, and several of the leading nonmonetarists, particularly Franco Modigliani, have made important recent contributions to the growth of the consensus:

1. The *IS-LM* model of output determination (developed in Chapters 3–6) has long been at the center of nonmonetarist analysis and in all but extreme situations allows both monetary and fiscal policy to influence output in the short run. Although some current textbooks claim

that monetarists deny a role for fiscal policy and assume an extreme vertical slope for the *LM* schedule (see Chapters 4–5), as early as 1966 Milton Friedman adopted the *IS-LM* model and claimed that no fundamental issues depend on whether the *LM* curve is vertical. At the same time he admitted that fiscal policy could alter aggregate demand.[8]

2. Not only have the main protagonists converged in their willingness to use the *IS-LM* model in discussions of the determinants of aggregate demand, but the nonmonetarists have also accepted the major contribution of the monetarist counterrevolution. In the long run, stabilization policy cannot permanently reduce actual unemployment below the natural unemployment rate and permanent changes in inflation must be accompanied by permanent changes in the growth rate of the money supply.[9] Nonmonetarist Modigliani echoed Friedman's early dictum that "We are all Keynesians now" when he admitted that on the central issue of long-run inflation determination "We are all monetarists now."[10]

What then explains the paradox of convergence without agreement? Monetarists and nonmonetarists disagree sharply in their recommendations for stabilization policy. It is possible to agree on the short-run and long-run determinants of output and the price level without agreeing on the desirability of government action to interfere with the operation of the private economy. Monetarists disagree with the nonmonetarist preference for government intervention and an activist stabilization policy. Instead, they prefer a fixed-growth-rate rule for the money supply. Why? Our analysis (Chapter 12) emphasizes the monetarists' greater belief in the ability of the private economy to remain stable without government help, as well as their distrust and lack of confidence that the government is capable of doing more good than harm.

Despite my admitted nonmonetarist sympathies, I provide theories, arguments, and data (Chapters 13–18) relevant for a judgment on the dispute. A mixed picture emerges, with plenty of evidence provided to

---

[8] Milton Friedman, "Interest Rates and the Demand for Money," *Journal of Law and Economics,* vol. 9 (October 1966), reprinted in his *The Optimum Quantity of Money and Other Essays* (Chicago: Aldine, 1969). I have called attention to this and other references in my interpretation of growing convergence in the monetarist-nonmonetarist debate. See Robert J. Gordon, "Comments on Modigliani and Ando," in Jerome Stein (ed.), *Monetarism* (Amsterdam: North-Holland, 1976), pp. 52–66.

[9] The *SP* curve (see Chapter 8), now widely used in empirical and theoretical work by nonmonetarists, is almost identical to Friedman's inflation equation in "A Theoretical Framework for Monetary Analysis," *Journal of Political Economy,* vol. 78 (March/April 1970), equation 45.

[10] Franco Modigliani, "The Monetarist Controversy or, Should We Forsake Stabilization Policies?" *American Economic Review,* vol. 67 (March 1977), p. 1.

support both the opponents and proponents of an activist stabilization policy.

SUMMARY

1. We are mainly concerned with the causes, costs, and cures of inflation and unemployment. A basic problem is that an improvement in inflation may require a temporary worsening of unemployment, or the reverse may be true.

2. Nominal magnitudes, actual recorded values, combine the influence of changing physical quantities and an alteration in the price level. Real magnitudes, expressed in the constant prices of a particular base year, are corrected for the influence of price changes and reflect only changes in physical quantities.

3. In this century, U.S. inflation has fluctuated widely, but has been worst during wars and after 1965. Periods of high unemployment have coincided with those of low output, with the Great Depression clearly scoring worst on both counts. There is no simple relation between unemployment and inflation.

4. Macroeconomic analysis is concerned with broad economic aggregates (inflation, unemployment) and has two tasks. It must analyze the causes of changes in the aggregates and it must predict the consequences of alternative policy changes.

5. Stabilization policy can alter the aggregate demand for goods and services. However, if both inflation and unemployment are too high, stabilization policy by itself cannot improve one without worsening the other. Stabilization policy may operate with a long delay or have effects that are highly uncertain.

6. Theory is a method of simplifying complicated problems to spotlight a few crucial relationships. A macroeconomic theory is useful only if it leads to useful generalizations that have predictive power. Policy recommendations involve not only the predictions of theory but also economic and political judgments.

7. Post-Keynesian economics supports government intervention through stabilization policy to offset the instability of the private economy. Much of the poor performance of the economy in the 1960s and 1970s reflected an overly optimistic (and now obsolete) approach to inflation, the food and oil supply shocks of 1973–74, and the failure of politicians to listen to economists.

8. Much of the book (Chapters 3–11) reflects a broad consensus by monetarists and nonmonetarists on a common economic model for the determination of output, inflation, and unemployment. But an important area of disagreement remains and is the subject of Chapters 12–18. This does not involve the *effects* of monetary and fiscal policy on output or the price level but rather the *desirability* of government intervention in the economy through an activist stabilization policy.

A LOOK AHEAD

Our first task is to develop a simple theoretical model explaining real output (GNP) and the price level. Before we can turn to theory in Chapter 3, however, we must stop in Chapter 2 for a few definitions. What are GNP and the price level? How are they measured? What goods and services are included in or excluded from GNP? How are private saving, private investment, and the government deficit related to each other?

CONCEPTS AND QUESTIONS

IDENTIFICATIONS

The price level versus the inflation rate

The actual unemployment rate versus the natural unemployment rate

Actual real output versus natural real output

Monetary versus fiscal policy

Stabilization policy

Closed versus open economy

Positive versus normative economics

Supply shocks

Target variables versus policy instruments

QUESTIONS FOR REVIEW

1   Is all unemployment harmful? Try to describe a world with zero unemployment. Can you think of reasons why such a world might suffer from substantial inflation?

2   Try to find in Figure 1-2 the most recent year when the price level actually went down. Why do you think that deflation (an actual decline in prices) was a more common event before World War II than afterward?

3   Business firms regularly reach an "all-time high" in nominal sales. Does this always mean that they have sold a larger physical quantity than ever before?

4   In 1976 actual real output exceeded that of 1973. Why then was actual unemployment higher in 1976 than in 1973?

5   Why might two economists share a common economic theory but disagree on their policy recommendations?

6   Ask your instructor whether he or she has any open or hidden bias toward either the monetarist or nonmonetarist position.

2 The Measurement of Income and Prices

True, the statistics are not as good as we want them to be, but what would we do without them?

—Oskar Morganstern[1]

2-1 WHY WE CARE ABOUT INCOME

A basic lesson of Figure 1-2 is that movements in the unemployment rate are closely related to the parallel movements of the gap between actual and natural real GNP. When production drops off, people are laid off and put out of work. When production is very high relative to natural output, job openings will be plentiful and unemployment will be low. So the key to understanding changes in unemployment is the total real *product,* which is equal to total real *income.*

Measures of total real income serve a second purpose. If the total amount of real income is divided by the number of people or the number of families, we obtain a measure of the relative income of one nation compared to another. For example, how well off is the average American compared to the average Englishman or Brazilian? Further, we can chart the growth of income per person over long periods of time and determine whether the rate of increase of our real national product has been accelerating or decelerating and whether other nations are growing faster than the United States.

The subject of this chapter, the definition and measurement of national income—what is included and excluded and why—is an essential prelude to our study of the determinants of changes in real income and output. We will see that many of the rules governing the calculation of national income are arbitrary, that controversial choices must be made as to the proper set of ingredients in the official measure of income, and that the

---

[1] "Qui Numerare Incipit Errare Incipit" *Fortune,* vol. 68 (October 1963).

size of any nation's gross national product is to some degree at the discretion of the economists and government officials who mark off the dividing lines between the included and excluded items. We will also learn how to calculate the price indexes or "deflators" that are used to convert the official current-dollar (nominal) measure of national income and product into a measure of constant-dollar (real) income and product.

2-2 THE CIRCULAR FLOW OF INCOME AND EXPENDITURE

Let us begin with a very simple economy, consisting of households and business firms. We will assume that households spend their entire income, saving nothing, and that there is no government.[2] (This is our first example of the use of theory to simplify an intricate subject by choosing a particular set of assumptions that help focus the discussion on the relevant issues.) Figure 2-1 is a picture of the operation of our simple economy, with households represented by the box on the left and business firms by the box on the right. There are two kinds of transactions between the households and the firms.

First, the firms sell goods and services (product or output) to the households—for instance, bread and bus rides—represented in Figure 2-1 by the lower dashed line labeled "Goods and services." The bread and bus rides are not a gift, but are paid for by a flow of money (C), say $1,000,000 per year, represented by the solid line labeled **"Consumer expenditures."**

Second, households must work to earn the income to pay for the consumption goods. They work for the firms, selling their skills as represented by the upper dashed line labeled "Labor services." Household members are willing to work only if they receive a flow of money, usually called "wages," from the firms for each hour of work. Wages are the main component of income (Q), shown by the upper solid line.

Since households are assumed to consume all of their income, and since firms are assumed to pay out all of their sales in the form of income to households, it follows that income (Q) and consumption expenditures (C) are equal. For the same reason, the labor services provided in return for income are equal to the goods and services (product) sold by the firms to households in return for the money flow of consumer expenditures:

$$\begin{aligned} \text{Income } (Q) &= \text{Labor Services} \\ &= \text{Consumption Expenditure } (C) \qquad (2.1) \\ &= \text{Product} \end{aligned}$$

---

[2] Because households do no saving, there is no capital or wealth, and all household income is in the form of wages for labor services.

A SIMPLE IMAGINARY ECONOMY

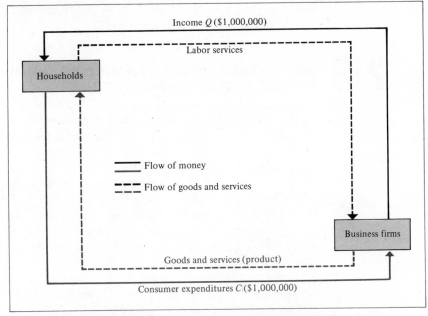

Income Q ($1,000,000)

Labor services

Households

Flow of money

Flow of goods and services

Business firms

Goods and services (product)

Consumer expenditures C ($1,000,000)

FIGURE 2-1

The Circular Flow of Income and Consumer Expenditure

Circular flow of income and expenditure in a simple imaginary economy in which households consume their entire income. There are no taxes, no government spending, no saving, and no investment.

Each of the four magnitudes in equation (2.1) is a **flow magnitude** — any money payment or physical good or service that flows from one economic unit to another. A flow of expenditure, just like a flow of water through a pipe, can only be measured if we first specify the length of time over which the flow is measured. Thus U.S. gross national product (= income = expenditure = factor services) in 1976 was $1707 billion *per year,* or an average of $142.3 billion *per month,* or $4.7 billion *per day.* Most flow magnitudes in the United States are measured at annual rates. If the flow of GNP in a quarter-year ("quarter") is $500 billion, this amounts to $2000 billion at an annual rate.

A flow is distinguished from a **stock,** which is an economic magnitude in the possession of a single unit at a particular moment of time. The stock of money, savings accounts, business equipment, or government debt can be measured by adding up its value at a given point in time, for instance, midnight on December 31, 1977. Measurement of a stock is like taking a flash snapshot, and it does not require specification of a unit of time, as must be done for the measurement of a flow. (What do you guess is the value of the stock of furniture and equipment in the room where you are sitting at the moment?)

2-3 WHAT TRANSACTIONS SHOULD BE INCLUDED IN INCOME AND EXPENDITURE?

The **National Income and Product Accounts** (NIPA) is an official U.S. government accounting of all the millions of flows of income and expenditure in the United States. The basic ideas and methods used in the NIPA were originally developed in the 1930s by economists working at the National Bureau of Economic Research, including Simon Kuznets (one of the first winners of the Nobel Prize in economics.) During World War II, the U.S. Department of Commerce took over the task of computing the NIPA, and it has gradually refined and updated the procedures.[3] The latest NIPA statistics can be found in the monthly periodical, *Survey of Current Business.*

Those responsible for counting up gross national income and product (clerks in the old days, computer programmers now) do not mindlessly add up every figure on every piece of paper mailed to the government by private households and business firms. Instead, they have a set of rules to determine which items to include.

In our free-market economy, the fact that a good or service is sold is usually a sign that it is capable of satisfying certain human wants and needs; otherwise people would not be willing to pay a price for it. So by including in the gross national product only things that are sold through the market for a price, we can be fairly sure that most of the components of GNP do contribute to human satisfaction. (There are important exceptions to this assumption that are discussed in Appendix A in the back of the book.) There are three major requirements in the rule for including items in the total **final product,** or GNP:

> *Final product consists of all currently produced goods and services that are sold through the market but not resold.*

The first part of the rule — *to be included in final product a good must be currently produced* — obviously excludes sales of any used items like houses and cars, since they are not currently produced. It also excludes any transaction in which money is transferred without any accompanying good or service in return (in terms of the circular flow of Figure 2-1 this

---

[3] The latest methodological revisions are described in George Jaszi and Carol S. Carson, "The National Income and Product Accounts of the United States: Revised Estimates, 1929–74," *Survey of Current Business,* vol. 56 (January 1976), pp. 1–38.

would be a counterclockwise money flow without a corresponding flow of goods or services in the opposite direction). Among the **transfer payments** excluded from national income in the United States are gifts from one person to another and "gifts" from the government to persons, like social security, unemployment, and welfare benefits. Also excluded are capital gains accruing to persons as the prices of their assets increase.

The second part of the rule — *goods included in the final product must be sold on the market and are valued at market prices* — means that we measure the value of final product by the market prices that people are willing to pay for goods and services. We assume that a Cadillac gives 10,000 times as much satisfaction as a can of shaving cream for the simple reason that it costs about 10,000 times as much. Of course, it is impossible to compare the satisfaction that an item gives to two people. Presumably a loaf of bread gives more pleasure to a poor Appalachian schoolchild than to a rich New York banker, but if the price of the bread is the same, its contribution to the nation's GNP is considered to be the same no matter who buys it.

The criterion of market price is also a faulty measure of welfare, because it does not take account of the annoyances that are created by some market transactions. Thus the value of a factory's output of goods is included in final product, but we do not subtract from final product the dissatisfaction caused by its output of pollutants into a nearby river.[4] (There are some minor exceptions to the "criterion of market price" in the actual U.S. NIPA that are discussed in Appendix A, and many more exceptions have been proposed by economists.)

The third part of the rule — *to be included in final product a good must not be resold in the current period* — further limits the acceptability of items. The many different goods and services produced in the economy are used in two different ways. Some goods, like wheat, are mainly used as ingredients in the making of other goods, in this case, bread. Any good resold by its purchaser, rather than used as is, goes by the name **intermediate good.** Wheat is mainly purchased by millers who do not consume the wheat themselves, but convert it into flour and then resell it (in its new form) to bakers. Grocers resell bread in the identical form in which it is received from bakers, earning income by providing bread at a convenient location.

The opposite of an intermediate good is a **final good,** one that is not resold. Bread located at the grocery is a final good, used by consumers, as are shoes, clothes, haircuts, and everything else the consumer buys directly.

Why can't we just add up all transactions in the economy and call that

---

[4] Irritants, like water pollution and the noise of jet airplanes, for which no charge is made on the market, are called external diseconomies. An external economy is a benefit for which no charge is made, like the pollen supplied to a honeygrower's bees from a farmer's nearby orchard.

FINAL PRODUCT EQUALS TOTAL INCOME CREATED

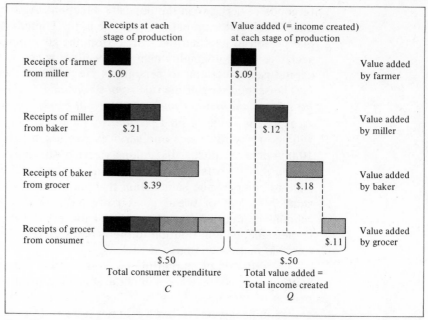

FIGURE 2-2

The Contribution of One Loaf of Bread to Consumer Expenditure and Income Created

The left side shows the amount that each firm—farmer, miller, baker, and grocer—receives in the process of producing one loaf of bread. These total receipts are used for two purposes. First, part of the receipts of each firm are used to pay for the intermediate goods purchased from the firm listed directly above (for instance, the miller pays $.09 to the farmer for the wheat). Second, what is left over —shown on the right side of the diagram—is the income created or value added (such as wages, salaries, profits; $.12 in the case of the miller).

total GNP, instead of taking the trouble to exclude intermediate goods (goods resold in the current period)? Look at Figure 2-2, which shows how the $.50 that a consumer spends for a loaf of bread is divided among the four firms that produce the bread. The bars on the left side of the diagram show the receipts of each of the firms involved in making and selling the bread, and the right side shows the income of the firms' workers, managers, and stockholders *after* the purchase of the intermediate goods.

For instance, the baker adds $.18 of income to the $.21 he pays to the miller for the flour, and the grocer adds $.11 to the $.39 he pays to the baker for the bread. The total paid by the consumer to the grocer, $.50, exactly equals to the total income created by all four firms (.09 + .12 + .18 + .11 = .50). By excluding from final product all goods that are resold (the intermediate goods) and including only the final purchase of $.50 by the consumer who actually uses the bread, we automatically guarantee that final product ($C = \$.50$) equals total income created or **value added** ($Q = \$.50$).

The $.50 paid by the consumer for the bread is an ingredient in the lower loop of consumer expenditure (C) in Figure 2-1. The $.50 of income created is part of the upper loop of income (Q) in Figure 2-1. Now we can see why, by definition, both loops are equal in size.

2-4 INVESTMENT AND SAVING

We know how to handle the bread sold by the grocer, but how do we handle a cash register produced in the current period and purchased by the grocer? The cash register is *not* an intermediate good. Why? Because it is not resold, and since it is currently produced and sold on the market, we know from the rule that it must be included in final product. But surely there must be some difference between bread, which is consumed immediately, and the cash register, which lasts a long time.

The goods and services purchased by business firms that are not resold as intermediate goods to other firms or consumers during the current period qualify by our rule as final product. But the business firm does not consume them. Final goods that business firms keep for themselves are called "private investment" or private capital formation. They add to the nation's stock of income-yielding assets. Private investment consists of:

1. **Inventory investment.** Bread purchased by the grocer but not resold to consumers in the current period stays on the shelves, raising the inventory level. Inventories of raw materials, parts, and finished goods are an essential form of income-yielding assets for businesses, since goods immediately available "on the shelf" help satisfy customers and make sales.

    Example: The grocer has 10 loaves of bread at the close of business on December 31, 1977. His inventory of bread is $3.90 (10 loaves times the wholesale baker's price of $.39). At the close of business on March 31, 1978, he has 15 loaves of bread ($5.85). Inventory investment in the first quarter of 1978 is the *change* in his inventory ($5.85 $-$ $3.90 $=$ $1.95). If the level of inventories had fallen, then inventory investment would have been negative. For example, because the level of total inventories fell sharply in the United States in early 1975, inventory investment in the second quarter of 1975 reached an unprecedented negative figure of $-$\$25.1 billion (at an annual rate).

2. **Fixed investment.** This includes all final goods purchased by businesses other than additions to inventory intended for eventual resale. The

main types of fixed investment are structures (factories, office buildings, shopping centers, apartments, houses) and equipment (cash registers, computers, trucks). Newly produced houses and condominiums sold to individuals are also counted as fixed investment— homeowners are treated in the national accounts as business firms that own their house as an asset and rent the house to themselves.[5]

Figure 2-1 described a simple imaginary economy in which households consumed their total income of $1,000,000. Figure 2-3 introduces investment into that economy. Total expenditures on final product (shown in the lower loops) are once again $1,000,000, but this time they are divided into $750,000 for household purchases of consumption goods (C) and $250,000 for business purchases of investment goods (I). The $1,000,000 of total expenditures flowing to the business firms from the lower loops generates $1,000,000 in income for households shown in the top loop, just as before. Households take their $1,000,000 in income and spend $750,000 on purchases of consumption goods. Where does the remaining $250,000 go?

The portion of household income that is not consumed is called **Personal saving.** What happens to income that is saved? The funds are channeled to business firms in two basic ways:

1. Households buy bonds and stocks issued by the firms, and the firms then use the money to buy investment goods.
2. Households leave the unused income (saving) in banks. The banks then lend the money to the firms, which use it to buy investment goods.

Whether households channel their saving to firms directly (through purchases of bonds and stock) or indirectly (through banks), the effect is the same: business firms obtain funds to purchase investment goods. The box labeled "capital market" in Figure 2-3 symbolizes the transfer of personal saving to business firms for the purpose of investment. Just as total expenditure on final product is equal by definition to income created (see Figure 2-2), investment purchases must be equal to saving. Why? This conclusion follows from the definitions of three concepts just introduced:[6]

---

[5] An individual who owns a house is treated as a schizophrenic in the national accounts: as a business firm *and* as a consuming household. My left side is a businessman who owns my house and receives imaginary rent payments from my right side, the consumer who lives in my house. The NIPA identifies these imaginary rent payments as "imputed rent on owner-occupied dwellings" and they are the most important exception to the rule that a good must be sold on the market to be counted in GNP.

[6] A three-bar equality sign is an identity and means that the relationship is true by definition.

SAVING LEAKS OUT OF THE SPENDING STREAM
BUT REAPPEARS AS INVESTMENT

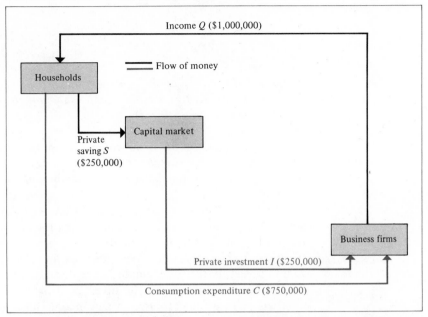

Income Q ($1,000,000)

Flow of money

Households

Capital market

Private saving S ($250,000)

Business firms

Private investment I ($250,000)

Consumption expenditure C ($750,000)

FIGURE 2–3

Introduction of Saving and Investment to the Circular Flow Diagram

Our simple imaginary economy (Figure 2–1) when households save 25 percent of their income. Business firms' investment accounts for 25 percent of total expenditure. Again, we are assuming that there are no taxes and no government spending.

Income $(Q) \equiv$ Expenditure (E) (2.2)

Expenditure $(E) \equiv$ Consumption $(C) +$ Investment (I) (2.3)

Saving $(S) \equiv$ Income $(Q) -$ Consumption (C) (2.4)

It is customary in economics to eliminate unnecessary words by writing equations like these using alphabetical symbols only:

$$Q \equiv E \qquad (2.2)$$

$$E \equiv C + I \qquad (2.3)$$

and $S \equiv Q - C$, or rearranging, $Q \equiv C + S$ (2.4)

Now we can see why saving and investment must be equal. Substitute equation (2.3) for E on the right side of (2.2) and substitute (2.4) for Q on the left side of (2.2). The result:

$$
\begin{array}{rcl}
C + S & \equiv & C + I \\
-C & & -C \\
\hline
S & \equiv & I
\end{array}
\quad \text{(subtracting } C \text{ from both sides)}
$$

(2.5)

Since income is equal to expenditure, the portion of income not consumed (saving) must be equal to the nonconsumption portion of expenditure (investment).

In other words, saving is a "leakage" from the income spent on consumption goods. This leakage from the spending stream must be balanced by an "injection" of nonconsumption spending in the form of private investment.

Why do we bother to distinguish between consumption and investment? One reason is that expenditure plans for the two are made by different economic units. Households decide how much of their incomes they want to consume and save; business firms decide how much they want to invest. In the next chapter we will see that when the saving plans of households do not match the investment plans of business firms, the firms will raise or cut production and income until actual investment is brought in line with their plans. The actual level of investment as measured in the national accounts can differ from business plans if unexpected changes in sales cause involuntary accumulation or decumulation of inventories. In this case the "inventory accumulation" part of total investment differs from the amount business firms had planned to spend. The mismatch between household saving plans and business investment plans has been a major source of instability in U.S. output and income.

A second reason for distinguishing between consumption and investment is the different implications of the two types of spending for the economy's potential to produce output in the future. An economy that consumes a small portion of its income has a large portion left over for saving and investment; that is, for the formation of capital assets. It can build a relatively large number of factories, office buildings, computers, or other business equipment, and those capital assets add to the nation's *potential* output for next year and the years to follow. As Table 2-1 shows, Japan devotes a very high proportion of its income to investment, and its output growth rate has been correspondingly high throughout the postwar period. The United Kingdom and the United States have consumed a greater share of income for present enjoyment (items like food, autos, and haircuts) at the price of a smaller increase in the stock of capital assets. Therefore, they have a smaller increase in output each year.

TABLE 2-1   1970 Investment Shares and Postwar Growth Rates for Major
Developed Countries, 1955–74

	Ratio of investment to GNP, *1970*	*Growth rate of real output, 1955–74*
High-investment countries		
Japan	39	9.58
West Germany	35	4.86
France	32	5.38
Low-investment countries		
United Kingdom	22	3.35
United States	19	3.38

Source: See Appendix C.

2-5 NET EXPORTS AND FOREIGN INVESTMENT

Exports are expenditures for goods and services produced in the United States and sent to other countries. Such expenditures create income in the United States but are not part of the consumption or investment spending of U.S. residents. **Imports** are expenditures by U.S. residents for goods and services produced elsewhere, which thus do *not* create domestic income. For instance, an American-made Chevrolet exported to Canada is part of U.S. production and income but is Canadian consumption. A German-made Mercedes imported to the United States is part of German production and income but is U.S. consumption. If income created from exports is greater than income spent on imported goods, the net effect is an increase in domestic production and income. Thus the difference between exports and imports, **net exports,** is a component of final product and GNP.[7]

Net exports can also be given the name **"net foreign investment,"** and given the same economic interpretation as domestic investment. Why is this? Both domestic and foreign investment raise domestic production and income created. (Foreign investment is an excess in foreign spending

---

[7] Thus equation (2.3) above can be rewritten

$$E = C + I + X - H$$

where X equals exports and H equals imports.

on domestically produced goods and services over *our* spending on foreign goods and services.) Domestic investment creates domestic capital assets; foreign investment creates U.S. claims on foreigners that likewise yield us future flows of income. An American export to Japan is paid for by Japanese yen, which can be used to buy a Japanese asset (a Japanese bank account or part of a Japanese factory).[8]

The main difference between domestic and foreign investment is that the former is primarily determined by what happens in the domestic economy, whereas foreign investment (net exports) depends on events in the outside world as well.

2-6 THE GOVERNMENT SECTOR: TAXES, TRANSFER PAYMENTS, AND PURCHASES

Up to this point we have described the major accounting magnitudes of an economy consisting only of private households and business firms. Now we introduce the government, which collects taxes from the private sector and makes two kinds of expenditures. Like private consumption and investment purchases, government purchases of goods and services (tanks, fighter planes, schoolbooks) generate production and create income. The government can also make payments directly to households without any production of goods and services in return. Social security, unemployment compensation, and welfare benefits are examples of these transfer payments.

Figure 2-4 adds the government (federal, state, and local) to our imaginary economy of Figures 2-1 and 2-3. A flow of tax revenue ($R = \$100{,}000$) flows from the households to the government.[9] The government buys $\$100{,}000$ of goods and services (G), raising total expenditures on GNP and income created from the $\$1{,}000{,}000$ of Figure 2-3 to $\$1{,}100{,}000$ ($E = C + I + G$). So far the government's budget is balanced. But in addition the government sends $\$50{,}000$ back to the households in the form of transfer payments (F), such as welfare payments. Total government spending ($G + F = \$150{,}000$) exceeds tax revenue, leaving a deficit of $\$50{,}000$ that must be financed. The government sells $\$50{,}000$ of bonds to private households through the capital market, just as busi-

---

[8] There is an additional alternative. An American exporter may not want a Japanese asset but may want his payment in U.S. dollars. He can obtain U.S. dollars from the U.S. government in trade for his yen. The increased U.S. government holdings of yen and other currencies can be kept, thus counting as a foreign capital asset, or can be used to pay off U.S. debts, reducing U.S. liabilities to foreigners.

[9] In the "real world" that will be described in Figure 2-6, both households and business firms pay taxes. Here we keep things simple by limiting tax payments to personal income taxes.

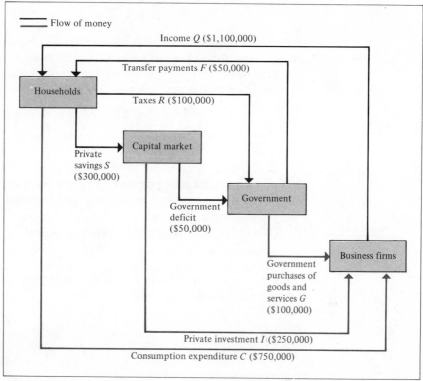

FIGURE 2–4

Introduction of Taxation and Government Spending to the Circular Flow Diagram

Our simple imaginary economy with the addition of a government collecting $100,000 in tax revenue, paying households $50,000 in transfer payments, and purchasing $100,000 of goods and services. Its total expenditures ($150,000) exceed its tax revenues ($100,000), leaving a $50,000 deficit that is financed by selling government bonds to the households.

ness firms sell bonds and stock to households to finance their investment projects.[10]

As before, total income created (Q) is equal to total expenditure on final product (E):

$$Q \equiv E$$

But now there are three types of expenditure on final product: consump-

---

[10] We will see in Section 5-9 that the government can also finance its deficit by printing money.

tion (C); private investment, both domestic and foreign (I); and government purchases of goods and services (G):[11]

$$E \equiv C + I + G \qquad (2.6)$$

The total personal income that households receive consists of the income created from production (Q) and transfer payments from the government (F). This total $(Q + F)$ is available for the payment of taxes (R), saving (S), and the purchase of consumption goods (C):

$$Q + F \equiv C + S + R$$

or, the equivalent expression

$$Q \equiv C + S + R - F \qquad (2.7)$$

In economics, transfer payments (F) can be treated as negative taxes. Thus there is no reason to distinguish tax revenues (R) from transfers (F). Instead, we define **net tax revenue** (T) as taxes (R) minus transfers (F), converting (2.7) into the simpler expression:

$$Q \equiv C + S + T \qquad (2.8)$$

Since $Q \equiv E$, the right side of equation (2.8) is equal to the right side of equation (2.6), and we obtain:

$$
\begin{array}{rl}
C + S + T \equiv & C + I + G \\
-C & \quad -C \\
\hline
S + T \equiv & I + G
\end{array}
\qquad \text{(subtracting } C \text{ from both sides)} \qquad (2.9)
$$

Now we can see that saving and investment do not always have to be equal, as they were in equation (2.5). Instead, we have a more general rule:

> *Since income is equal to expenditure, the portion of income not consumed (saving plus net taxes) must be equal to the nonconsumption portion of expenditure on final product (investment plus government spending).*

In other words, **leakages** out of the income available for consumption goods must be exactly balanced by **injections** of nonconsumption spending.

This rule helps explain how the economy finances government deficits. Subtracting S and G from both sides of equation (2.9) we have:

$$T - G \equiv I - S \qquad (2.10)$$

---

[11] In an open economy with exports (X) and imports (H), equation (2.6) can be replaced with:

$$E \equiv C + I + G + X - H$$

The left side of the equation is the government surplus — net tax revenues (T) minus expenditures (G). Whenever the government runs a surplus, the private economy must adjust to make private investment exceed private saving. When the left side of (2.10) is negative, the government is running a deficit and the private economy must adjust to make private saving exceed private investment.

2-7 CASE STUDY: SAVING, INVESTMENT, AND GOVERNMENT DEFICITS

Figure 2-5 illustrates the workings of equation (2.10) for the postwar period 1946–76. The top section of the illustration shows the annual values of real private investment (I) and saving (S). The bottom section shows the government surplus $(T - G)$. As required by equation (2.10), years in which investment fell short of saving were also years in which the government ran a deficit. But which was the chicken and which was the egg? Did government deficits *cause* investment to decline below saving, or did weak investment spending cause the government deficits? Are government deficits the sign of a spendthrift government that is "crowding out" productive private investment projects or are government deficits simply the passive consequence of weak private investment by business firms? By the end of Chapter 5 you will have explored the answers to both questions.

Deficits imply an excess of saving over investment, as well as the reverse. The history illustrated in Figure 2-5 provides examples of both kinds of causation. In 1967, U.S. federal government spending for Vietnam was high (that is, the federal government was purchasing military weapons at a high rate). As a consequence the private economy had to adjust to reduce private investment below private saving, as indicated by the pink shading for 1967. In this instance, the behavior of government caused private investment to fall below private saving.

But exactly the same situation (low investment with a government deficit) can occur for a different reason. In 1949, 1954, 1958, 1961, 1970, and again in 1975–76, a marked drop in private investment caused the government to run a deficit, by weakening the economy and causing net tax revenue (T) to fall below government expenditure (G).

There is no way to tell from Figure 2-5 whether a government deficit is caused by high government spending, as in the Vietnam war, or by a weak economy, as in years 1975–76. Unfortunately, the economy influences the government budget, and vice versa. A more useful indication of the budget's influence on the economy — the natural employment surplus — is introduced in Section 17-2.

Figure 2-5 can also be viewed as summarizing the relation between household saving and business spending. In years designated by pink

PRIVATE INVESTMENT MINUS PRIVATE SAVING EQUALS
THE GOVERNMENT SURPLUS

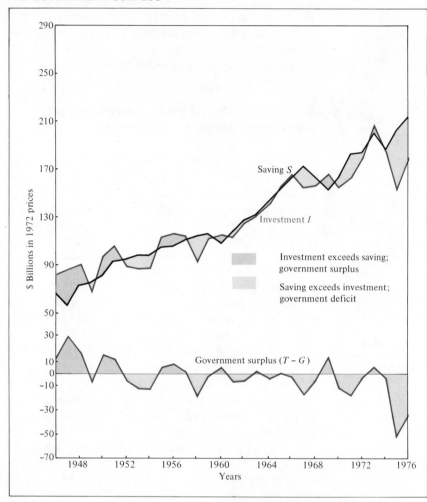

FIGURE 2–5

Private Saving and Investment and the Government Surplus, 1946–76

In the top part of the diagram, the pink shaded area indicates that S exceeds I. In the bottom part, the pink area shows that G exceeds T and that the government is running a deficit. By definition—equation (2.10)—the top and bottom pink areas are equal. The same goes for the gray areas: in the top part I exceeds S, in the bottom part T exceeds G, and in both the government is running a surplus.

Source: Economic Report of the President, January 1977, p. 214.

shading, business firms did not invest all of the funds which the households saved, leaving a remainder available to finance the government deficit. In years designated by gray shading, on the other hand, business firms invested more than households saved, requiring that the government run a surplus to provide the extra funds needed by business. James Tobin sums up the relation this way:

> The moral is inescapable, if startling. If you would like the federal deficit to be smaller, the deficits of business must be bigger. Would you like the federal government to run a surplus and reduce its debt? Then business deficits must be big enough to absorb that surplus as well as the funds available from households and financial institutions.[12]

2-8 A SUMMARY OF TYPES OF SPENDING

The NIPA treatment of the different types of expenditures we have discussed is summarized in Table 2-2. The top part of the table splits total expenditures on final goods and services (GNP) into three basic components: private consumption, private investment (both domestic and foreign), and government spending. It lists the total 1976 amount and gives examples of each.

Private consumption and investment exclude purchases of intermediate goods, which are listed separately at the bottom of the table on line C. The treatment of government spending is different. All government purchases of goods and services, whether intermediate or final, are included in the GNP and on line A.3. Many government purchases, such as wages paid to police officers, do not create assets and are not investment. They are not consumption either, because they are not desired for their own sake. Police protection is an intermediate good, a necessary ingredient in maintaining an orderly society and protecting the value of private property, just as coal and iron ore are necessary ingredients in making steel.

There is an interesting inconsistency in the accounting system. When the crime rate goes up, private businessmen hire more security guards, who are counted as an intermediate good, because they are a business expense. The GNP remains the same, because there has been no increase in expenditures on final product. When the crime rate goes up and the government hires more police, however, GNP goes up by the increase in wages paid to the new government policemen.

Why are government expenditures on fire fighting, police protection,

---

[12] James Tobin, "Deficit, Deficit, Who's Got the Deficit," *National Economic Policy* (Yale University Press, 1966), p. 52.

TABLE 2-2

Items Included in and Excluded from GNP

Type of expenditure	Included in GNP?	1976 spending, $ billions	Examples
A. Final goods and services (GNP)	Yes	1692.4	
1. Consumer expenditures (*C*)	Yes	1078.6	
a. Durable goods	Yes	156.3	Autos, TV sets
b. Nondurable goods	Yes	440.3	Food, clothes, shoes
c. Services	Yes	482.0	Haircuts, airline trips
2. Private investment (*I*)	Yes	248.1	
a. Change in business inventories	Yes	13.5	
b. Producers' durable equipment	Yes	106.1	Computers, tractors
c. Structures	Yes	121.6	
i. Nonresidential	Yes	55.4	Factories, office buildings, shopping centers
ii. Residential	Yes	66.2	Houses, condominiums
d. Foreign (exports minus imports)	Yes	6.9	*Exports:* tractors, computers *Imports:* coffee, bananas, wine
3. Government purchases of goods and services (*G*)	Yes	365.8	
a. Intermediate	Yes	—	Fire fighters, police officers
b. Consumption	Yes	—	City parks, street cleaners
c. Investment	Yes	—	Airports, university dormitories, hospitals
B. Government interest and transfer payments	No	212.2	Social security, welfare, unemployment benefits
C. Private intermediate goods	No	—	Wheat, iron ore
D. Private purchases of used assets	No	—	Purchases of used houses, used cars

Source: *Economic Report of the President* (January 1977). The total level of GNP in this table and in Figure 2–6 differs slightly from that in Appendix B, which takes account of a subsequent revision in the data.

the court system, and other intermediate goods counted as part of GNP? The problem is the difficulty in finding an easy-to-use criterion for the government intermediate goods to be excluded. Private intermediate goods are excluded whenever they are business expenses incurred in making a product that is sold in the current period.[13] But government goods like police and fire protection are not sold; it would be difficult to prevent individuals who do not agree to buy a given government service from receiving the same fire and police protection as everyone else. This is why basic government services are financed by taxes everyone is required to pay.

Although all government spending on goods and services is included in GNP, government expenditures in the form of transfer payments are not included. Government transfer payments (Table 2-2, line B), private intermediate purchases (line C), and private purchases of used assets (line D) are three of the most important exclusions of expenditures from the final product as defined in the NIPA accounts.

2-9 THE CIRCULAR FLOW IN 1976: LEAKAGES FROM THE SPENDING STREAM

Figure 2-6 is a more realistic version of Figure 2-4, showing the relation of the spending streams between households, business firms, the capital market, and the government. Unlike Figure 2-4, this figure uses actual data on spending and income from 1976. The width of the "pipes" flowing among the sectors is scaled to be proportional to the actual 1976 flows of spending, income, taxes, and so on.

Start in the lower right corner, where business firms produce three basic types of final product: consumption goods, investment goods, and government purchases. Expenditures (E) on these three categories are shown as wide pink pipes flowing to the right from households, the capital market, and the government to the business firm box.

Let us look at how the income created from the sale of final output is distributed. The first deduction is for **depreciation (capital consumption allowances)** charged by business firms (*saving* for *depreciation, thus S_D)*, which in 1976 amounted to $179.8 billion. This S_D is shown flowing through a gray pipe from the business firms to the capital market box at the left. (The capital market includes all sources of funds available to finance business investment and government deficits, whether or not a capital-market transaction is actually recorded.)

When new output is produced, a part of the nation's capital equipment is worn out, and business firms deduct a capital consumption allowance from their income to provide funds to replace worn-out equipment. To this extent a part of total output and spending does not represent net income paid to factors of production but is used to *replace* capital goods

---

[13] If the product is not sold in the current period, the business expense incurred in buying raw materials and paying wages is counted as an addition to inventories (a part of final product).

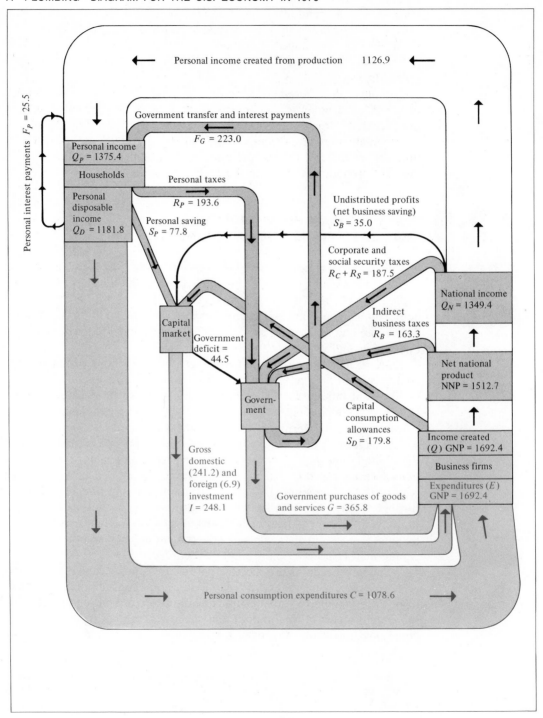

used up in the process of production. This portion of output, capital consumption allowances, must be included in GNP if we are to show the expenditures of final users on the national output. But, at the same time, capital consumption allowances must be excluded from **net national product** (NNP) if we are to show the incomes actually earned by the factors of production.

> *The terms* **gross** *and* **net** *in economics usually refer to the inclusion or exclusion of capital consumption allowances. Thus the difference between "gross investment" and "net investment," or between "gross saving" and "net saving," is exactly the same as that between GNP and NNP.*

The next leakage is the collection by the government (federal, state, and local) of **indirect business taxes** (taxes on business, hence R_B, with a 1976 value of \$163.3 billion). These taxes—for instance, state or city excise and sales taxes—are included in the prices paid by the consumer but are not available for payment as income to workers or firms. Indirect business taxes are shown flowing from the NNP box to the government sector.[14] With the deduction of R_B we move up above NNP to the **national income** (Q_N) of 1349.4 billion, the sum of all net incomes earned by the factors of production (labor and capital) in producing current output.

But not all of the national income is paid out to individuals. Corporations withhold part of their income as **undistributed corporate profits,** shown in Figure 2-6 as a leakage flowing from the national income box to the capital market. This saving by incorporated business (S_B) was valued at \$35.0 billion in 1976. In addition, a substantial amount "leaks out" to the government as corporate income taxes (R_C) and social security taxes (R_S)—both employer and employee contributions. Business

---

[14] Output including R_B is valued at market prices and excluding R_B is valued at factor cost. This terminology is used more often in Europe than in the United States.

FIGURE 2–6

Income, Product, and Transfer Flows in the 1976 U.S. Economy

An elaboration of Figure 2–4 showing that much of the income created in producing GNP (lower right corner) "leaks out" of the white income flow through the gray pipes into saving ($S_D + S_B + S_P$) and into taxes ($R_B + R_C + R_S + R_P$). Government transfer payments (F_G) are a negative leakage adding to personal income. Only the remaining portion of GNP net of all the leakages is available for the pink private consumption pipe. In addition, total expenditures on GNP include the pink expenditure pipes representing private investment and government spending, which are financed by the gray tax and saving leakages.

Source: Economic Report of the President, January 1977. Some minor flows, including the statistical discrepancy, are included as part of R_B, S_B, and F_G to improve legibility.

firms turn over to the government R_C and R_S, which are thus unavailable for consumption expenditure. In Figure 2-6 corporate income taxes and social security taxes $(R_C + R_S)$ are shown together in the one pipe valued at $187.5 billion, which flows from national income to the government sector. Finally, what remains of national income after deducting undistributed corporate profits, corporation income taxes, and social security taxes paid by business ($1126.9 billion) is paid out to persons in the form of wages, salaries, rent, interest dividends, and the profits of unincorporated enterprises (for example, the income of small shopkeepers and farmers).

Some individuals receive incomes that are not a payment for any productive service and therefore are not included in GNP, NNP, or the national income. Part of these payments are government transfers and interest payments on the government debt $(F_G = 223.0 billion), shown flowing from the government sector in the middle of Figure 2-6 to the personal income box at the upper left bypassing GNP, NNP, and national income on the way. Additional "nonproductive" transfer payments of $25.5 billion in installment and mortgage interest payments by consumers (F_P) are shown flowing away from the household sector and then back again.

The total we now arrive at is a **personal income** (Q_P) of $1375.4 billion, the sum of all income payments to individuals. This represents the current flow of purchasing power to individuals through the workings of the productive system plus the transfers from the government and personal sectors. If we now deduct $193.6 billion in personal taxes (R_P), we obtain one of the most important totals in national income accounting. This remainder ($1181.8 billion in 1976) is **Personal Disposable Income** (Q_D), which is the amount of income that individuals as consumers have available to spend or save.

We see three different flows emerging below the personal sector box: personal consumption expenditure (C), which flows around to the right to be spent on GNP; interest paid by consumers (F_P), which is a transfer payment and flows back to households; and the final leakage from the spending stream, personal savings $(S_P = 77.8 billion).[15] The flow of consumption expenditure to the business firms brings us full circle.

Taking an overall view of Figure 2-6, we can see that there are a series of leakages flowing through gray pipes (taxes and saving of various types minus transfer payments) that reduce the amount spent on GNP ($1692.4 billion) to the total disposable income of persons, $1181.8 billion. A further diversion, in the form of personal saving and interest payments, results in consumer expenditures of $1078.6 billion. The total of the leak-

---

[15] The Department of Commerce has labeled consumer expenditures plus interest payments $(C + F_P)$ as "personal outlays." In practice, disposable income and personal outlays are directly estimated, and personal saving is obtained as a residual.

ages, after the necessary adjustments, is exactly equal to the sum of investment (including net exports) and government spending. We can now rewrite equation (2.9) using the specific symbols of the actual U.S. economy as described in Figure 2.6:

$$\underbrace{(S_D + S_B + S_P)}_{\text{Saving}} + \underbrace{(R_B + R_C + R_S + R_P)}_{\text{Taxes}} - \underbrace{F_G}_{\text{Transfers}} \equiv \underbrace{I + G}_{\text{Injections}} \qquad (2.11)$$

or, once again, the more general form (2.9) that combines all the saving terms into one symbol (S) and lets T stand for all tax receipts minus transfers:

$$S + T \equiv I + G \qquad (2.9)$$

Equations (2.11) and (2.9) both summarize the main lesson of Figure 2-6: *Leakages must be equal to injections, by definition.* Transposing (2.9), we have:

$$S - I \equiv G - T \qquad (2.12)$$

The government deficit is written on the right-hand side of (2.12) and is shown as the black line flowing from the capital market down to the government sector at the right. Equation (2.12) illustrates the second lesson of Figure 2-6: *the government deficit must be equal to the difference between total saving $(S_D + S_B + S_P)$ and total investment (including net exports).*

2-10 NOMINAL INCOME, REAL INCOME, AND THE PRICE DEFLATOR

For most problems in economic analysis, we are interested in comparing measurements of income and expenditures at different times. Hence we must measure these magnitudes in "real terms," that is, terms adjusted for the effects of price changes. The illustration of actual and natural GNP in Figure 1-2, and of saving, investment, and the government surplus in Figure 2-5, show these magnitudes in real terms. How do the national income accountants take the recorded nominal income and expenditure (Y) of two years in which prices were very different—say 1972 and 1976—and compute real GNP (Q) adjusted for all effects of price changes?

Real GNP (Q) is the value of expenditures for *each year* (1972 and 1976) when each separate good or service is measured in the prices of a *single year,* say 1972. The implicit GNP deflator, in turn, is the ratio of nominal to real GNP:

$$P = \frac{Y}{Q}$$

TABLE 2-3

Calculation of Nominal GNP, Real GNP, and the Implicit GNP
Deflator in an Imaginary Economy Producing Only Round Steak
and Eggs

	1972	*1976*
1. Prices		
a. Round steak, pound	$ 1.10	$ 1.75
b. Eggs, dozen	.52	.70
2. Production in physical units		
a. Round steak, pounds	500,000	1,000,000
b. Eggs, dozens	1,000,000	1,000,000
3. Production in current prices of each year		
a. Round steak (1a times 2a)	$ 550,000	$1,750,000
b. Eggs (1b times 2b)	520,000	700,000
c. Nominal GNP (3a plus 3b)	1,070,000	2,450,000
4. Real production in constant 1972 prices		
a. Round steak (1a for 1972 times 2a for each year)	$ 550,000	1,100,000
b. Eggs (1b for 1972 times 2b for each year)	520,000	520,000
c. Real GNP (4a plus 4b)	1,070,000	1,620,000
5. GNP deflator, 1972 base (3c/4c)	1.000	1.514

*The implicit GNP deflator (P) is the ratio of nominal GNP (Y)
to real GNP measured in constant dollars (Q).*

Table 2-3 works through an example of the calculation of nominal
GNP, real GNP, and the GNP deflator for a hypothetical economy in
1972 and 1976 producing only round steak and eggs. Nominal GNP
(line 3c) is the sum of expenditures on the two products in the two years
at the actual prices paid. Real GNP (line 4c) is the sum of expenditures
on the two products in the two years in both cases measured at 1972
prices. The GNP deflator (line 5) is the ratio of nominal to real GNP
(1.514), which indicates that the average price level in 1976 was 51.4
percent higher than the level in 1972.[16]

The calculation of the GNP deflator in the imaginary world of Table
2-3 is mere child's play compared to the real world, with its thousands

---

[16] Any year can be used as base year. With 1976 as the base year, the 1976 GNP deflator
is 1.00 and the 1972 deflator is 0.66 (= 1.00/1.514). The choice of base year makes absolutely no difference because the rate of growth of the price level (P) between the two
years is identical with either base:

$$\frac{1.00}{0.66} = \frac{1.514}{1.000}$$

of individual products. This complex job requires not only the use of a large computer for all the arithmetic, but also diligent legwork and many difficult choices. The prices of several thousand products are collected monthly by the U.S. Bureau of Labor Statistics (BLS). Consumer prices are based on reports of 250 price collectors who call or visit about 18,000 stores monthly in 56 cities, collecting about 125,000 prices each month. The prices of investment goods purchased by business firms are recorded on mail questionnaires submitted monthly by thousands of firms that sell these goods. The national income accountants must match the multitudes of BLS price indexes for individual commodities with the different categories of consumption and investment spending. Then choices must be made for expenditures for which no BLS price indexes exist, like computers, jet aircraft, ships, and buildings. (Appendix A in the back of the book explores a few of the main flaws in the present techniques used to estimate the GNP deflator.)

SUMMARY

1. This chapter is concerned with the definition and measurement of national income — what is included and excluded and why. Since many of the rules governing the calculation of national income are arbitrary, the size of any nation's GNP is at the discretion of its economists and government officials who mark off the dividing lines between the included and excluded items.

2. A flow magnitude is any money payment, physical good, or service that flows from one economic unit to another. Examples are income, consumption, saving, and investment. A flow must be distinguished from a stock, which is an economic magnitude in the possession of an individual or firm at a moment of time. Examples are the stock of money, savings accounts, and capital equipment.

3. Final product (GNP) consists of all currently produced goods and services sold through the market (with a few exceptions) but not resold. By counting intermediate goods only once, and by including only final purchases, we avoid double counting and ensure that the value of final product and total income created (value added) are equal.

4. Leakages out of income available for consumption goods are by definition exactly balanced by injections of nonconsumption spending. This equality of leakages and injections is guaranteed by the accounting methods used. In the same way, by definition total income (consumption plus leakages) equals total expenditure (consumption plus injections). Injections of nonconsumption spending fall into three categories — private domestic investment (on business equipment and structures, residential housing, and inventory accumulation); foreign investment or net exports; and government spending on goods and services. The definitions require private investment (including domestic and foreign) to exceed private saving by the amount of the government surplus.

5. Net National Product (NNP) is obtained by deducting depreciation from GNP. Deduction of indirect business taxes from NNP yields national income, the sum of all net incomes earned by factors of production in producing current output. If we deduct corporate undistributed profits, corporate income taxes and social security taxes, and add in transfer payments, we arrive at personal income, the sum of all income payments to individuals. Personal disposable income is simply personal income after the deduction of personal income taxes.

6. The implicit GNP deflator, the economy's aggregate price index (P), is defined as nominal GNP in actual current prices (Y) divided by real GNP measured in prices of a base year (Q).

A LOOK AHEAD

This completes our explanation of the government's measure of total income and product and its measure of the price deflator. The BLS has another branch that computes the monthly figures on employment and unemployment. We examine *its* methods in Section 9-2. In the next chapter we will turn to the elements of the theory of how real GNP (Q) is determined. The causes of changes in the GNP deflator (the price index P) are explored in Chapters 7 and 8. Combining the two theories, we will be able to explain nominal income (Y) through the definition $Y \equiv PQ$. Before turning to the next chapter, interested readers are invited to study Appendix A (in the back of the book), which explores some conceptual problems in the measurement of income and prices.

CONCEPTS AND QUESTIONS

IDENTIFICATIONS

GNP, NNP, national income, personal income, personal disposable income
GNP deflator
Nominal income
Real income
Circular flow of income and expenditure
Value added
Final and intermediate goods

Transfer payments
Consumption expenditures
Inventory investment and fixed investment
Net foreign investment
Leakages and injections
Capital consumption allowances
Gross and net magnitudes
Undistributed corporate profits

QUESTIONS FOR REVIEW

1. Why is double counting a problem? How is the problem avoided in the U.S. national accounts (NIPA)?

2. How could a major disaster appear to make the economy seem better off under our current national accounts system?

3. How are government purchases treated differently from purchases by firms?

4. What is the difference between GNP and NNP? Between gross investment and net investment? Why are we interested in net magnitudes?

5. For a hypothetical country, the implicit GNP deflator for 1980 on a 1970 base is 1.50, and GNP in current dollars for 1980 is $750 million. What is real GNP for 1980 in constant 1970 dollars?

6. Indicate whether or not each of the following items is included in GNP, national income, and personal income:
   a. Social security contributions.
   b. Capital consumption allowances.
   c. The increase in value of a house brought about by general inflation.
   d. Salary of a city police officer protecting against vandalism.
   e. Payment by a consumer for guards to protect against vandalism.
   f. 5 percent Illinois state sales tax.

7. Which flow pipe in Figure 2-6 contains dividends paid by corporations to households?

8. Three loaves of bread are produced by a bakery on December 31, 1977, and sold to a grocery store for 39 cents each. They are not sold until January 1, 1978, when consumers purchase them for 50 cents each. How much do the three loaves contribute to 1977 GNP? 1978 GNP?

Part II

Determination of Real Output and the Price Level

3 Commodity-Market Equilibrium and the Multiplier

Any fluctuation in investment not offset by a corresponding change in the propensity to consume will, of course, result in a fluctuation in employment.

—John Maynard Keynes[1]

3-1 INCOME DETERMINATION AS AN EXPLANATION OF UNEMPLOYMENT

Figure 1-2 shows that unemployment is closely related to the gap between actual real income and natural real income. Since natural real income tends to grow steadily and smoothly, but actual real income does not, understanding the causes of movements in actual real income is the key to understanding movements in the unemployment rate. This chapter will set out the elementary theory of how actual real income is determined and helps us explain modern recessions, the Great Depression of the 1930s, and the operation of fiscal policy. In subsequent chapters the elementary theory will be supplemented by elements that add to its realism without destroying its basic validity.

The theory is very simple. The division of disposable income (Q_D) between consumption (C) and saving (S) follows a regular and predictable pattern. Both consumption and saving can be treated as *passive* — induced by changes in disposable income. The *active* components of spending are assumed to be private investment (I) and government spending (G). We assume that, unlike consumption, both investment and government spending are independent of income, that is, *autonomous*. Both autonomous investment (I) and government spending (G) raise income, and part of that income (Q) is spent on consumption goods (C). Following a \$1.00 change in I or G, the increase in GNP is generally greater than \$1.00, because the passive consumption level (C), part of GNP, is dragged up or down by changes in I or G. The ratio of the change in GNP to the initiating change in I or G is called the **multiplier**.

---

[1] *General Theory*, p. 314.

This is a "tail wags the dog" theory of income determination. The tail consists of I and G. The body is private consumption (C). In this chapter, any movement of the tail (I and G) moves the dog's body (C) and changes total GNP ($C + I + G$) by a multiple of the original alteration in I or G.

In this chapter, we will make two important assumptions. First, the interest rate (and thus monetary policy) is not allowed to influence desired spending. We will focus on "equilibrium" in the **commodity market,** the market for goods and services. In the next chapter a more complete theory will introduce an additional market for money—currency and demand deposits—and changes in private spending will be linked to the interest rate, allowing us to establish a connection between monetary policy and both investment and output.

The second assumption is that the price level is constant. Thus all changes in real income are also changes in nominal income of the same amount. For Chapters 3–5 we will maintain the assumption of "rigid" prices. Not until Chapter 6 will we begin our examination of the effects of private spending decisions and government policy on the price level.

3-2 THE DIVISION OF DISPOSABLE INCOME BETWEEN CONSUMPTION AND SAVING

In this section we begin by examining the division of household disposable income after taxes (Q_D) between consumption purchases (C) and saving (S). We want to determine how much of consumption and saving is autonomous, independent of income, and to what extent consumption and saving react passively to changes in income.

How do households divide their disposable income between consumption (C) and personal saving (S_P)? As we saw in Figure 2-6,

$$Q_D \equiv C + S_P \qquad (3.1)$$

For the rest of this chapter other types of saving are ignored, and so we shall label personal saving simply as S. Figure 3-1 illustrates three possible relations between Q_D, C, and S.

First Possibility. In the top frame of Figure 3-1 the horizontal axis measures disposable income (Q_D) and the vertical axis measures personal consumption expenditure (C). The 45° line shows the first possibility, consumption equals disposable income ($C = Q_D$). Since all disposable income is consumed, saving is zero.

> **Example:** Find point L along the horizontal axis at a disposable income of $1600 billion. Now run your eye up to point B. The vertical distance between L and B is the consumption level of $1600 billion if $C = Q_D$.

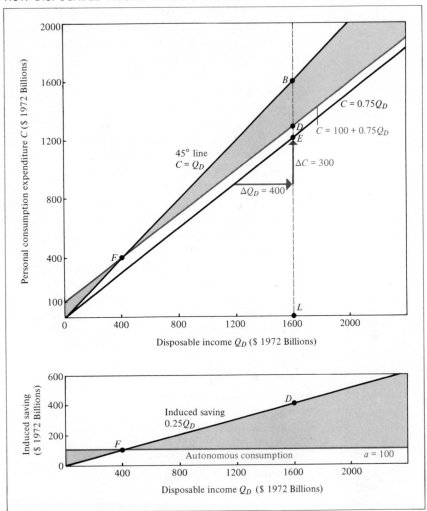

FIGURE 3–1

Three Alternative Hypotheses of Consumption Behavior

Along the 45° line in the upper frame, consumption equals disposable income. The black line passing through point *E* illustrates a second possibility, that consumption is always 75 percent of disposable income. The red line passing through *F* and *D* illustrates the third and more realistic possibility, that consumption is 75 percent of disposable income plus an "autonomous" component of $100 billion that is spent regardless of the level of disposable income. The gray and pink shaded areas in both frames measure saving, that is, disposable income minus consumption. Total saving is positive in the pink area and negative in the gray area.

Second Possibility. What happens if some income is saved? Assume that households always spend 75 percent of their disposable income on consumption purchases and save 25 percent. This is illustrated in the top frame of Figure 3-1 by the line labeled $C = 0.75\,Q_D$, which runs from zero through point E.

> **Example:** Find point L on the horizontal axis at a disposable income level of $1600 billion. Now run your eye up to point E. The vertical distance between L and E is the consumption level of $1200 billion, or 0.75 times the disposable income of $1600 billion ($C = 0.75Q_D$). What happens to the rest of the disposable income? The remainder, $400 billion, is saved ($S = 0.25Q_D$). This is indicated by the vertical distance from E to B.
>
> In economics the fraction of any change in disposable income that is consumed — 0.75 in our example — is called the **marginal propensity to consume.** The symbol "Δ" is used to designate the "change in" any variable, so ΔC is the "change in consumption" and ΔQ_D is the "change in disposable income." The ratio $\Delta C/\Delta Q_D$ is the marginal propensity to consume, equal in our example to 0.75. For instance, the red arrows under point E show that if disposable income changes by $400 billion in a horizontal direction (from 1200 to 1600), then consumption rises in a vertical direction by $300 billion (from 900 to 1200). And 300/400 equals 0.75.

Third Possibility. Assume the same marginal propensity to consume as in the second possibility — 75 percent of each dollar of disposable income is spent on consumption purchases. But in addition assume that consumers spend $100 billion extra no matter what Q_D happens to be. This $100 billion is **autonomous,** completely independent of the level of income. The third possibility is illustrated in Figure 3-1 by the red line going from $100 billion on the vertical axis to points F and D. Consumption is:

$$C = 100 + 0.75Q_D \qquad (3.2)$$

Saving is simply disposable income minus consumption:

$$\begin{aligned} S &= Q_D - C \\ &= Q_D - 100 - 0.75Q_D \\ &= -100 + (1 - 0.75)Q_D \\ &= -100 + 0.25Q_D \end{aligned} \qquad (3.3)$$

> **Example:** Once again find point L on the horizontal axis at a disposable income of $1600 billion. Consumption is $100 + 0.75Q_D = 100 + 0.75(1600) = 100 + 1200 = 1300$. Look above L to D, at a ver-

tical level of $1300 billion. The remainder of disposable income is saved, as indicated by the remaining vertical distance from D to B, $300 billion indicated by the pink shading.

In the next section we will see that the third possibility is the most realistic description of actual consumption and saving behavior, so let us examine more closely the implications of the red line.

1. The red line is called a **consumption function.** It shows the amount of consumption spending for each level of disposable income.
2. Along the red line, the marginal propensity to consume, that is, the change in consumption spending per dollar of extra disposable income, is 0.75.
3. Along the red line the ratio of total consumption to total income (C/Q_D), the **average propensity to consume,** is greater than 0.75, because of the $100 billion of autonomous consumption purchased regardless of the level of disposable income. For instance, at D the average propensity to consume is $C/Q_D = 1300/1600 = 0.8125$.
4. At point F disposable income is $400 billion and consumption equals disposable income. Thus at F saving is zero. To the left of F consumption exceeds income and saving is *negative,* indicated by the gray area between the red line and the 45° line. How can saving be negative? Individuals can consume more than they earn, at least for a while, by withdrawing funds from a savings account, by selling stocks and bonds, or by borrowing.
5. To the right of F the red consumption line lies below the 45° disposable income line and saving is positive, indicated by the pink area.

The bottom frame of Figure 3-1 plots saving behavior separately. The change in saving (ΔS) induced by a change in disposable income (ΔQ_D) is called the **marginal propensity to save** $(\Delta S/\Delta Q_D)$. The black line labeled $0.25Q_D$ in the bottom frame plots the part of saving that is induced by changes in disposable income; its slope is 0.25.

Total saving, however, is less than $0.25Q_D$, because $100 billion is consumed independent of the level of disposable income. Imagine people withdrawing $100 billion from their bank accounts and then redepositing 0.25 of their disposable income. If disposable income is $400 billion, as at F in the lower frame, the withdrawal of $100 billion just balances the deposit of $100 billion (0.25 times $400 billion), and total saving is zero. To the right of F saving is positive, indicated by the pink shading, because the black induced saving line $(= 0.25Q_D)$ lies above the red autonomous consumption line $(a = 100)$. The a stands for autonomous consumption. To the left of point F saving is negative, indicated by the gray shading, because the red autonomous consumption line lies above the black induced saving line.

3-3 CASE STUDY: ACTUAL U.S. CONSUMPTION AND SAVING BEHAVIOR

When disposable income falls very low, as it did during the Great Depression, households take money out of their savings accounts or borrow in order to buy the basic necessities of life.[2] Saving is negative (dissaving), because consumers must draw on their savings accounts and other assets in order to purchase the consumption goods that their disposable income alone can no longer purchase.

Figure 3-2, arranged exactly like the top frame of Figure 3-1, shows the actual values of disposable income, consumption, and saving in the United States during the years 1929–76. Three major conclusions can be drawn from the evidence. First, both consumption and saving have increased as disposable income has grown during the years since World War II. Second, in the worst year of the Great Depression, households consumed more than their incomes, so that saving was slightly negative in 1933. Third, these usual peacetime relationships were interrupted during World War II (1942–45) when consumer goods were unavailable or rationed. In that period households were forced to consume much less and save much more than is normal in peacetime.

3-4 DETERMINATION OF EQUILIBRIUM INCOME

THE CONSUMPTION FUNCTION

Figure 3-2 clearly indicates that the third possibility for the division of disposable income between consumption and saving, illustrated by the red line drawn through point D in Figure 3-1, is the most realistic alternative. Any hypothesis about the relation between consumption and disposable income is called a consumption function. Ours can be written either in the specific form of equation (3.2) or in a more general form that replaces the specific numbers with lowercase letters:

GENERAL FORM   NUMERICAL EXAMPLE
$$C = a + cQ_D \qquad\qquad C = 100 + 0.75Q_D \qquad\qquad (3.4)$$

---

[2] Be careful to distinguish between "savings" (with a terminal "s"), which is the *stock* of assets that households have in savings accounts or under the mattress, from "saving" (without a terminal "s"), which is the *flow* per unit of time that leaks out of disposable income (see Figure 2-6) and is unavailable for purchases of consumption goods. It is the flow of *saving* that is designated by the symbol S.

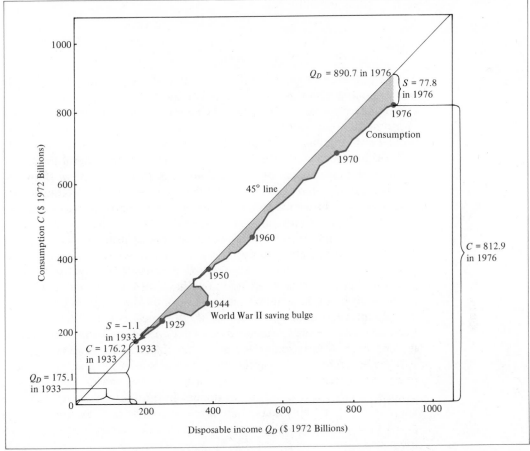

FIGURE 3–2 U. S. Consumption, Saving, and Disposable Income in Constant 1972 Prices, 1929–76

The vertical axis measures consumption, and the horizontal one measures disposable income. The pink shading between the 45° line and the red consumption line measures saving. Notice that in 1933 saving was negative. In 1976 saving was positive and amounted to 8.7 percent of disposable income, leaving the remaining 91.3 percent for consumption. Saving was unusually high during World War II, because consumer goods were rationed.

Source: *Economic Report of the President* (January 1977), and Supplements to the *Survey of Current Business*.

Here *a* stands for the autonomous portion of consumption, $100 billion in the numerical example. And *c* stands for the marginal propensity to consume, 0.75 in the numerical example.

Saving, the difference between disposable income and consumption, can be written either as the specific numerical example of equation (3.3), or in a more general form.

GENERAL FORM   NUMERICAL EXAMPLE

$$S = -a + (1 - c)Q_D \qquad S = -100 + 0.25Q_D$$
$$\text{or } S = -a + sQ_D \tag{3.5}$$

The marginal propensity to save, 0.25 in the numerical example, can be designated in the general form either by $(1 - c)$ or s.[3] The quantity s can be any number between 1.0 (all income saved) and zero (all income consumed).

The autonomous component of consumption, independent of income, is \$100 billion in the numerical example and a in the general form. The autonomous component of saving is *minus* \$100 billion or $-a$. If disposable income was zero, consumption would be \$100 billion (a) and saving would be the difference between disposable income and consumption, zero minus \$100 billion, or $-\$100$ billion $(-a)$.[4]

Our consumption function (3.4) becomes a central component of the theory of income determination. How much can we trust its implication that households alter their consumption purchases by exactly the same fraction of any increase in income? In Chapter 13 we will find that households base their consumption purchases not on their current income, but on their perception of "permanent" or "lifetime" income. They prefer to maintain a fairly stable standard of living consistent with their average income over a fairly long interval, rather than raising or lowering their spending (perhaps requiring the purchase or sale of a house or car) with every short-term fluctuation in income. For this reason, a temporary change in income (caused, for instance, by an income tax rebate or a short-term layoff) may cause only a minor change in consumption compared to a change in income perceived to be permanent (for instance, a job promotion).

In this chapter we ignore the distinction between temporary and permanent changes in income to simplify the theory. The marginal propen-

---

[3] All of any dollar of disposable income must be either consumed or saved. Thus the marginal propensity to save (s) is equal to the fraction of a dollar not consumed ($s = 1 - c$).

[4] Economists sometimes refer to the **average propensity to save** or average saving rate. This is the ratio of saving to disposable income S/Q_D. Dividing (3.5) by Q_D, we obtain the following expressions for the average saving rate:

	GENERAL FORM	NUMERICAL EXAMPLE
Average saving rate or average propensity to save	$\dfrac{S}{Q_D} = \dfrac{-a}{Q_D} + s$	$\dfrac{S}{Q_D} = \dfrac{-100}{Q_D} + 0.25$

Similar expressions for the average propensity to consume (C/Q_D) can be obtained by dividing (3.4) by Q_D.

Example: Calculate the average propensity to consume and to save for the numerical example when disposable income is \$400 billion, \$1200 billion, and \$1600 billion.

sity to consume (c) is assumed to be the same for all changes of disposable income, regardless of their source or expected duration. This exaggerates the effects of temporary changes in investment, government spending, and tax rates on consumption and total income.

WHEN IS THE ECONOMY IN EQUILIBRIUM?

Let us first examine the determination of total income (GNP) in a simple economy in which both government purchases and tax revenues are equal to zero. Total expenditures consist only of consumption plus investment. In the top frame of Figure 3-3 our basic consumption function, the red line labeled $C = 100 + 0.75Q$, is copied directly from Figure 3-1.[5] We assume that the investment purchases that business firms plan to make are autonomous, that is, do not depend on the level of income. The value of planned investment spending (I_p) is assumed to be a fixed number, say $200 billion:

$$I_p = 200 \qquad (3.6)$$

The total of household and business purchases, or planned expenditures (E_p), is the amount of household consumption (C) plus business planned investment (I_p):

$$E_p = C + I_p \qquad (3.7)$$

Substituting the consumption function (3.4) for C (3.7) becomes:

GENERAL FORM NUMERICAL EXAMPLE

$$E_p = a + cQ + I_p \qquad E_p = 100 + 0.75Q + 200 \qquad (3.8)$$

In Figure 3-3 the red planned expenditure (E_p) line plots the numerical example in equation (3.8). The E_p line lies above the red consumption function line by exactly $200 billion, the amount of planned investment. When income is zero, the E_p line intersects the vertical axis at $300 billion, the sum of autonomous consumption $(a = \$100$ billion) and planned autonomous investment $(I_p = \$200$ billion).

A main principle of this chapter is: The economy is in **equilibrium** when income is equal to planned expenditures (as at point B in the top of Figure 3-3). Households and business firms want to spend $1200 billion when income is $1200 billion. That $1200 billion of income is created by $1200 billion of production, all of which can be sold to the households and firms.

Equilibrium is simply a situation in which there is no pressure for change. At point B in Figure 3-3 all production can be sold. There is no pressure on businessmen to cut production, as there would be if planned expenditures fell short of current production. Similarly, they are not pres-

---

[5] The consumption function depends on total income (Q) in Figure 3-3. This makes no difference, and disposable income (Q_D) in Figure 3-1 because $Q = Q_D$ in the absence of taxes and business savings.

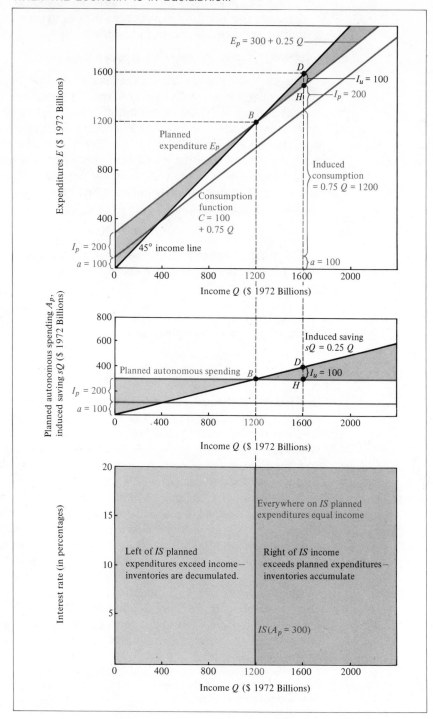

$E_p = 300 + 0.25\ Q$

$I_u = 100$

$I_p = 200$

Planned
expenditure E_p

Induced
consumption
$= 0.75\ Q = 1200$

Consumption
function
$C = 100$
$+ 0.75\ Q$

$I_p = 200$

$a = 100$

45° income line

$a = 100$

Expenditures E (\$ 1972 Billions)

Income Q (\$ 1972 Billions)

Planned autonomous spending A_p,
induced saving sQ (\$ 1972 Billions)

Induced saving
$sQ = 0.25\ Q$

Planned autonomous spending B

D

$I_u = 100$

H

$I_p = 200$

$a = 100$

Income Q (\$ 1972 Billions)

Interest rate (in percentages)

Everywhere on IS planned
expenditures equal income

Left of IS planned
expenditures exceed income—
inventories are decumulated.

Right of IS income
exceeds planned expenditures—
inventories accumulate

$IS\,(A_p = 300)$

Income Q (\$ 1972 Billions)

60 Commodity-Market Equilibrium and the Multiplier

sured to increase production, as they would be if planned expenditures exceeded current production.

The economy is out of equilibrium at all other points along the 45° income line. For instance, at point D, income (which always equals production) is $1600 billion. How much do households and business firms want to spend? Directly beneath D the three components of planned expenditures are marked off in red:

$$
\begin{array}{rl}
\text{Planned investment } (I_p) = & 200 \\
\text{Induced consumption } (0.75Q) = & 1200 \\
\underline{\text{Autonomous consumption } (a) =} & \underline{100} \\
\text{Planned expenditures } (E_p) = & 1500
\end{array}
$$

Thus at an income level of $1600 billion, planned expenditures (E_p) are only $1500 billion (point H on the E_p line). Only $1500 billion of the total production (= income) level of $1600 billion can be sold, leaving business firms with $100 billion of unsold merchandise.

The $100 billion of unsold production is counted as inventory investment, but businessmen do not desire this inventory buildup (if they did, they would have included it in their planned investment, I_p). To bring inventories back to the original desired level, businessmen react to the situation at D by cutting production and income, which moves the economy left toward point B. In the diagram, the distance between points D and H, amounting to $100 billion, is labeled I_u, which stands for **unintended inventory investment.**

The gray area between B, D, and H measures the excess of income over planned expenditures; that is, the positive value of I_u. Production and income will be cut until the gray area disappears and the unwanted

---

FIGURE 3–3

How Equilibrium Income Is Determined

The economy is in equilibrium in the top frame at point B, where the red planned expenditures (E_p) line crosses the 45° income line. At any other level of income, the economy is out of equilibrium, causing pressure on business firms to increase or reduce production and income. For instance, at point D, E_p falls $100 billion short of production, so $100 billion of output piles up on the shelves unsold $(I_u = 100)$. In the middle frame equilibrium occurs at point B, where induced saving (sQ) equals planned autonomous spending (A_p). The red IS line in the bottom frame shows that equilibrium income is the same for all possible values of the interest rate, because planned autonomous spending has been assumed to be independent of the interest rate. In all three frames, the gray areas indicate situations when the economy is out of equilibrium, because income exceeds planned expenditures, causing inventories to accumulate. The pink areas indicate that planned expenditures exceed income, causing inventories to be decumulated.

inventory buildup ceases $(I_u = 0)$. This occurs only when the economy arrives back at B, the only level of income where no force operates to push the economy elsewhere. Only at B are businessmen producing exactly the amount that can be sold.

> **Example:** In late 1974, consumer purchases of automobiles declined, and industry found itself producing more cars than consumers wanted to buy. The Chrysler Corporation had so many unsold cars in stock that it ran out of room to store them and actually rented space at the Michigan State Fair grounds to park unsold cars. Since this inventory accumulation by Chrysler was unplanned and undesired, the company's reaction was a drastic cut in production and substantial layoffs of employees, which meant a cut in Chrysler's contribution to national income and national product. The whole auto industry's contribution to GNP fell from $44.1 billion in the third quarter of 1974 to $32.7 billion in the first quarter of 1975, a decline of 26 percent.[6]

> **Exercise:** What happens in the top frame of Figure 3-3 when income is only $800 billion? Describe the forces that move the economy back to equilibrium at B (assume $I_p + a$ remains at $300 billion).

At point D, as in every situation, income and actual expenditures are equal by definition:

$$\text{Income } (Q) \equiv \text{Expenditures } (E)$$
$$\equiv \text{Desired spending } (E_p = C + I_p) +$$
$$\text{Unintended inventory accumulation } (I_u) \quad (3.9)$$

By contrast, the economy is in equilibrium only when unintended inventory accumulation or decumulation is equal to zero $(I_u = 0)$. Equation (3.9) can be rewritten to describe the economy's equilibrium situation:[7]

$$Q = E_p \quad\quad\quad\quad (3.10)$$

Economists sometimes use the Latin phrase **ex post** to describe the total expenditure that is actually made "after the fact" $(E_p + I_u)$. **Ex ante** describes the expenditure that is desired or planned "before the fact" (E_p). In Table 3-1 the definitional requirement of equation (3.9) — that income is always equal to *ex post* spending — is compared with the statement of equation (3.10) — that the economy is in equilibrium only when income is equal to *ex ante* spending.

---

[6] Seasonally adjusted totals at annual rates in constant 1972 prices.

[7] Another requirement for equilibrium, assumed throughout this chapter, is that there is no unintended consumption or saving. In other words, households are always "on" their consumption function, consuming exactly the fraction of saving that they desire.

TABLE 3-1 Comparison of the Economy's "Always True" and Equilibrium Situations

	Always true by definition	True only in equilibrium
1. What concept of expenditures is equal to income?	Actual *(ex post)* expenditures including unintended inventory accumulation	Planned *(ex ante)* expenditures
2. Amount of unintended inventory accumulation (I_u)?	Can be any amount, positive or negative	Must be zero
3. Which equation is valid, (3.9) or (3.10)?	(3.9) $Q = E = E_p + I_u$	(3.10) $Q = E_p$
4. Described by which point in top frame of Figure 3-3?	Any point on 45° income line (example: point D)	Point B
5. Numerical example in Figure 3-3?	At point D, $Q(1600) = E(1600)$ $= E_p(1500) + I_u(100)$	At point B, $Q(1200) = E_p(1200)$

AUTONOMOUS PLANNED SPENDING EQUALS INDUCED SAVING

The middle frame of Figure 3-3 illustrates the determination of equilibrium income in a slightly different way. It subtracts induced consumption from both income and planned expenditure. The lower horizontal red line in the middle frame is autonomous consumption ($a = 100$). The upper red horizontal line is total planned autonomous spending (A_p), which includes the $100 billion of autonomous consumption (a), plus the $200 billion in planned investment (I_p).

Take the definition of equilibrium in equation (3.10) and subtract induced consumption (cQ) from both sides of that equation:

$$Q - cQ = E_p - cQ$$

Since E_p includes induced consumption (cQ) plus planned autonomous spending (A_p), we can replace $E_p - cQ$ on the right-hand side by its equivalent, A_p:[8]

$$(1 - c)Q = A_p \tag{3.11}$$

---

[8] Because $E_p = a + cQ + I_p$ in equation (3.8), it follows that $E_p - cQ = a + I_p$. When we define total planned autonomous spending (A_p) as equal to $a + I_p$, we obtain the right-hand side of (3.11).

Because the marginal propensity to save equals 1.0 minus the marginal propensity to consume $(s = 1 - c)$, we can rewrite (3.11) as:

GENERAL FORM	NUMERICAL EXAMPLE	
$sQ = A_p$	$0.25Q = 300$	(3.12)

Thus the definition of equilibrium requires induced saving (sQ) to equal planned autonomous spending (A_p). The black sloped induced saving line in the middle frame of Figure 3-3 rises by $0.25 per $1.00 of income and crosses the red A_p line at point B, which is at an income level of $1200 billion and lies directly beneath the top frame's point B. The economy is in equilibrium at B in the top frame because production (Q) equals planned spending (E_p). When this occurs, point B in the middle frame shows that the induced leakage out of the spending stream into saving (sQ) just balances the planned autonomous spending (A_p) injected back into the spending stream by autonomous consumption (a) and planned investment (I_p).

The equilibrium level of income is always equal to planned autonomous spending (A_p) divided by the marginal propensity to save (s), as we can see when both sides of (3.12) are divided by s:

GENERAL FORM	NUMERICAL EXAMPLE	
$Q = \dfrac{A_p}{s}$	$Q = \dfrac{300}{0.25} = 1200$	(3.13)

Equilibrium income must be high enough to generate enough induced saving to balance planned autonomous spending. In our numerical example, $1.00 of income generates $0.25 of induced saving. This means $1200 billion of income is required to generate the $300 billion of induced saving needed to balance $300 billion of planned autonomous spending.

GENERAL METHOD FOR DETERMINING EQUILIBRIUM INCOME

The middle frame of Figure 3-3 and equation (3.13) both illustrate the two-step method used throughout the chapter for determining income. To represent this in a graph, first draw a horizontal line at a height equal to planned autonomous spending (A_p). Then plot a line with a slope equal to the marginal propensity to save (s). The point where the horizontal A_p line crosses the sloped sQ line indicates the equilibrium level of income. At any other point, for instance, D, sQ does not balance A_p, indicating an unplanned increase or decrease in inventories.

Income equilibrium can be determined using the same technique with the symbols in equation (3.13). The numerator is A_p and corresponds to the horizontal A_p line in the figure. The denominator is the fraction of income that leaks out of the spending stream into saving, corresponding to the slope of the induced saving in the figure.

The IS line in the bottom frame of Figure 3-3 plots all the different combinations of the interest rate and income at which the economy is in equilibrium. The *IS* line is vertical at an income level of $1200, because when $A_p = 300$ and $s = 0.25$ the economy is in equilibrium only when $Q = 1200$, regardless of the level of the interest rate. In the gray area to the right of the *IS* line, the economy is out of equilibrium because income exceeds planned expenditures. In the pink area to the left of the *IS* line, planned expenditures exceed income. Later we will show that if the level of planned autonomous spending depends inversely on the interest rate, the *IS* line relating the interest rate to equilibrium income has a negative slope.[9] In the next chapter the *IS* equilibrium line becomes a crucial ingredient in the more general theory which allows monetary factors to influence equilibrium income.

3-5 THE MULTIPLIER EFFECT

The conclusion of section 3-4, that equilibrium income equals $1200 billion, is absolutely dependent on the assumption that planned autonomous spending (A_p) equals $300 billion. It is clear that any change in autonomous spending will cause a change in equilibrium income. To illustrate the consequences of a change in A_p, assume that businessmen become more optimistic, raising their guess as to the likely profitability of new investment projects. They increase their investment spending by $100 billion, boosting A_p from $300 billion to $400 billion.[10] In each situation where a change is described, a numbered subscript is used to distinguish the original from the new situation. Thus A_{p0} denotes the original level of A_p ($300 billion), and A_{p1} denotes the new level ($400 billion).

Economic theorists typically examine the effects of a change in an element on the assumption that all other things are equal. This technique of analysis is sometimes described by the Latin phrase, *ceteris paribus,* abbreviated *cet. par.,* which means "other things being equal." Therefore, in equation (3.13) where the only "other thing" besides A_p determining income is s (the marginal propensity to save) we assume in this section

---

[9] The *IS* line was invented by Sir John Hicks in a classic article, "Mr. Keynes and the 'Classics': A Suggested Interpretation," *Econometrica* (April 1937). Its name comes from the fact that when there is no government the economy is in equilibrium when planned investment (I_p) equals planned saving (S). Rearranging equation (3.11), we have

$$(1 - c)Q = I_p + a$$
$$\text{or} \quad -a + (1 - c)Q = I_p$$
$$\text{or} \quad S = I_p$$

[10] Increased business investment raises I_p from $200 billion to $300 billion. Since autonomous consumption (a) is unchanged at $100 billion, A_p, the sum of the two, increases by $100 billion from $300 billion to $400 billion.

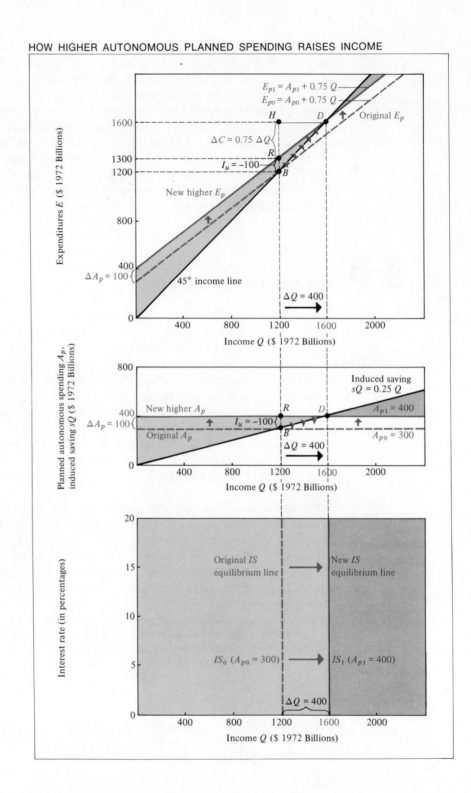

that s is constant. The equilibrium level of income in the new and old situations can be immediately calculated from equation (3.13):

	GENERAL FORM	NUMERICAL EXAMPLE
Take new situation	$Q_1 = \dfrac{A_{p1}}{s}$	$Q_1 = \dfrac{400}{0.25} = 1600$
Subtract old situation	$Q_0 = \dfrac{A_{p0}}{s}$	$Q_1 = \dfrac{300}{0.25} = 1200$
Equals change in income	$\Delta Q = \dfrac{\Delta A_p}{s}$	$\Delta Q = \dfrac{100}{0.25} = 400$ (3.14)

The top line of the table calculates the new level of income when $A_{p1} = 400$. The second line calculates the original level of income when $A_{p0} = 300$. The change in income, abbreviated ΔQ, is simply the first line minus the second. The autonomous spending multiplier (k) is defined as the ratio of the change in income ΔQ to the change in planned autonomous spending (ΔA_p) that causes it:

	GENERAL FORM	NUMERICAL EXAMPLE
Multiplier (k) =	$\dfrac{\Delta Q}{\Delta A_p} = \dfrac{1}{s}$	$\dfrac{\Delta Q}{\Delta A_p} = \dfrac{1}{0.25} = 4.0$

In Figure 3-4 we can see why the multiplier (k) is $1/s$, or 4.0. Each frame of 3-4 reproduces from Figure 3-3 the "original situation," with A_p at its original value of $300 billion. In the top frame the original equilibrium occurs at point B, where the original planned expenditure (E_p) line crosses the 45° income line. Now a new red E_p line is drawn exactly $100 billion above the original E_p line. Point B clearly no longer represents equilibrium, since planned expenditures have risen to $1300, exceeding income at B by $100 billion. The $100 billion excess of desired spending, distance RB, causes an undesired $100 billion drop in inventories $(I_u = -100)$. In order to restock their shelves businessmen raise production and income until they equal spending. The economy moves right from B to D, which ends unintended inventory decumulation (represented by the pink triangle between the E_{p1} and 45° income lines).

FIGURE 3–4

The Change in Equilibrium Income Caused by a $100 Billion Increase in Autonomous Planned Spending

Increasing planned autonomous spending (A_p) by $100 billion raises the planned expenditures line in the top frame vertically by $100 billion. The economy's equilibrium position (where $Q = E_p$) shifts from point B to point D. Thus the change in A_p has a multiplier effect, raising income by $400 billion. In the middle frame the A_p line shifts up by $100 billion, moving the equilibrium position from B to D. The bottom frame illustrates as before that equilibrium income is not sensitive to changes in the interest rate and that the $100 billion increase in A_p shifts the IS equilibrium line right by $400 billion.

HOW HIGHER A_p SPURS CONSUMPTION SPENDING

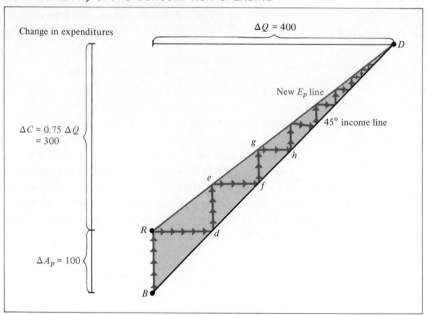

FIGURE 3–5

The Effect of a $100 Billion Increase in A_p on Consumption and Income

The table below provides a detailed

explanation of each line segment, starting with the inventory decumulation of $100 billion (the segment RB) caused by the initial $100 billion boost in planned autonomous spending.

(1) Line segment	(2) ΔA_p	(3) $\Delta E_p = \Delta A_p + c\Delta Q$	(4) $I_u = -\Delta E_p$	(5) $\Delta Q = -I_u$
B to R	100	$100 = 100$	-100	–
R to d	–	–	–	100
d to e	0	$75 = 0 + 0.75(100)$	-75	–
e to f	–	–	–	75
f to g	0	$56.25 = 0 + 0.75(75)$	-56.25	–
g to h	–	–	–	56.25
Cumulative from B to D	100	$400 = 100 + 0.75(300)$	–	400

The middle frame of Figure 3-4 shows the same $400 billion increase in income caused by the $100 billion increase in A_p. The A_p line shifts upward by $100 billion and intersects the fixed induced saving line at point D. Since in equilibrium — see equation (3.12) — induced saving (sQ) equals A_p, induced saving must increase by $100 billion. Because only

25 percent of extra income is saved, income must rise by $400 billion to generate the required $100 billion increase in induced saving. In terms of the line segments in the middle frame:

$$\text{Multiplier } (k) = \frac{\Delta Q}{\Delta A_p} = \frac{RD}{RB} = \frac{1}{s}, \text{ since } s = \frac{RB}{RD}$$

The bottom frame of the figure shows that the IS equilibrium line shifts right, a full $400 billion increase in equilibrium income as a result of the $100 billion increase in A_p. The new IS_1 line, with $A_{p1} = 400$, is at $1600 billion, in contrast to the original IS_0 line at $1200 billion, for $A_{p0} = 300$.

What actually happens in the real world when the multiplier effect is in operation? Figure 3-5 magnifies the triangle RBD in the top frame of Figure 3-4 in order to show what happens during the transition between the original equilibrium at B and the new equilibrium at D. The vertical line segment extending from B to R shows the initial $100 billion increase in A_p. Because production and income have not yet been increased to satisfy the higher sales, all added autonomous spending must be supplied by drawing down inventories. Thus the segment BR also represents inventory decumulation of $100 billion ($I_u = -100$).

To adjust, business firms must increase production and income (ΔQ) by just enough to restock their inventories. Along the line segment from R to d the horizontal movement (ΔQ) is exactly the same distance as the previous inventory decumulation. The consumption function states that 0.75 of the extra income, or $75 billion, will be spent on consumption purchases, which is indicated by the vertical expenditure increase along line segment de. But production has gone up only by enough to supply the initial extra demand for A_p. The $75 billion of extra consumption spending can only be supplied by drawing inventories again by $75 billion.

At the next stage the adjustment continues. Once again business firms increase production (the segment ef) to restock their inventories, once again consumption spending is induced (f to g), and once again inventories are decumulated. Notice that the amount of inventory decumulation becomes less and less at each stage, until finally at D it stops, and the economy returns to equilibrium. The total horizontal movement is the change in production and income, and the vertical movement is the sum of ΔA_p plus the induced consumption at each stage.[11] Higher investment starts off the multiplier expansion and the induced consumption

---

[11] It is possible to use an algebraic trick to prove that the sum of ΔA_p plus the induced consumption at each stage is exactly equal to the multiplier ($1/s$) times ΔA_p. The first round of consumption is $c\Delta A_p$. The second is c times the first, $c(c\Delta A_p)$, or $c^2 A_p$. Thus the total ΔQ is the series:

$$\Delta Q = \Delta A_p \quad + c\Delta A_p + c^2\Delta A_p + \cdots + c^n\Delta A_p \qquad \text{(a)}$$

"Factor out" the common element ΔA_p on the right-hand side of equation (a):

$$\Delta Q = \Delta A_p(1.0 + c \quad + c^2 \quad + \cdots + c^n \quad) \qquad \text{(b)}$$

(continued)

expenditures of income recipients keep the expansion going until total income and production once again equal planned expenditures.

3-6

RECESSIONS AND FISCAL POLICY

Is a multiplier expansion or contraction of output following a change in planned autonomous spending desirable or not? The answer depends on the desired level of total real income. In section 1-3, we defined natural real output as the highest level of real output attainable without causing an accelerating inflation. A multiplier expansion or contraction of output is favorable if it moves the economy closer to its natural output and is unfavorable if it pushes the economy away from natural output.

Assume that the level of natural real output is $1600 billion. In the middle frame of Figure 3-4 a level of planned autonomous spending (A_p) of $400 billion would be perfect, for it would bring about an equilibrium level of actual real output of $1600 billion at point D, the desired level. On the other hand, a decline in A_p by $100 billion would cut equilibrium income to $1200 billion at point B and would open up a gap of $400 billion between actual and natural output. The gap would equal 25 percent of natural output. The last time a gap of 25 percent occurred in the United States was in 1938, when the actual unemployment rate was 19.1 percent.

What might cause actual output to decline below natural output? A drop in planned investment (I_p), a major component of A_p, can be and has been a major cause of recessions and depressions. In the Great Depression, for instance, fixed investment dropped by 74 percent, and this contributed to the 29 percent decline in actual real GNP between those years.[12] But the changing plans of business firms are not the only possible cause of a change in planned autonomous spending. Changes in household autonomous consumption (a) can cause exactly the same kinds of effects on income as changes in the level of planned investment.

Subtract c times both sides of equation (b):

$$-c\Delta Q = \Delta A_p(\quad - c \quad - c^2 \quad - \cdots - c^n - c^{n+1}) \tag{c}$$

The difference between line (b) and (c) is:

$$(1 - c)\Delta Q = \Delta A_p(1.0 \qquad\qquad - c^{n+1}) \tag{d}$$

Since c^{n+1} is almost zero (because c is a fraction and $n + 1$ is large), we can neglect it. Dividing both sides of equation (d) by $(1 - c)$, we obtain the familiar:

$$\Delta Q = \frac{\Delta A_p}{1 - c} = \frac{\Delta A_p}{s}$$

[12] These figures are discussed further and their sources are identified in Figure 3-7.

The top frame of Figure 3-6 is a copy of the middle frame of Figure 3-4. Begin at point B, with A_p at only $300 billion (rather than the $400 billion achieved in Figure 3-4), due to a decline in consumption and planned investment totaling $100 billion. What can the government do to raise actual real income from $1200 billion, at B, to the desired $1600 billion level of natural output?

Government spending and taxation alter the economy in two ways. Let us see how an increase in government spending can raise total income through the multiplier effect, and how an increase in tax revenue has the opposite impact. First, government spending on goods and services (G) is part of planned expenditures. Thus equation (3.7) is modified:

$$E_p = C + I_p + G \qquad (3.15)$$

Second, a positive level of tax revenues (T) reduces disposable income (Q_D) below total actual income (Q):

$$Q_D = Q - T \qquad (3.16)$$

Inserting (3.16) into the consumption function makes the level of consumption spending depend on tax revenues:

$$C = a + cQ_D = a + c(Q - T) \qquad (3.17)$$

We have previously developed a simple theory stating that equilibrium income equals planned autonomous spending (A_p) divided by the marginal propensity to save (s). What is A_p in an economy influenced by the government? Substituting the definition of consumption in (3.17) into the definition of planned spending in (3.15), we have:

$$E_p = a + cQ - cT + I_p + G \qquad (3.18)$$

Planned autonomous spending (A_p) is simply E_p minus induced consumption (cQ), if total tax revenues (T) can be treated as autonomous:

$$A_p = a - c\bar{T} + I_p + G \qquad (3.19)$$

We have converted (3.18) into (3.19) by subtracting cQ and by writing a "bar" on top of $\bar{T}$. The bar reminds us that tax revenues are assumed to be *autonomous*, that is, they do not change automatically with income. Examples of autonomous taxes are local dog licenses and property taxes.[13]

Now we are equipped with a complete theory of income determination that takes into account government spending (G) and autonomous tax revenue ($\bar{T}$). Equation (3.19) says that the change in planned autonomous spending (ΔA_p) equals the change in four components:

---

[13] The value of property subject to taxation does not increase immediately as income goes up because most local governments perform the laborious task of property assessment only at infrequent intervals.

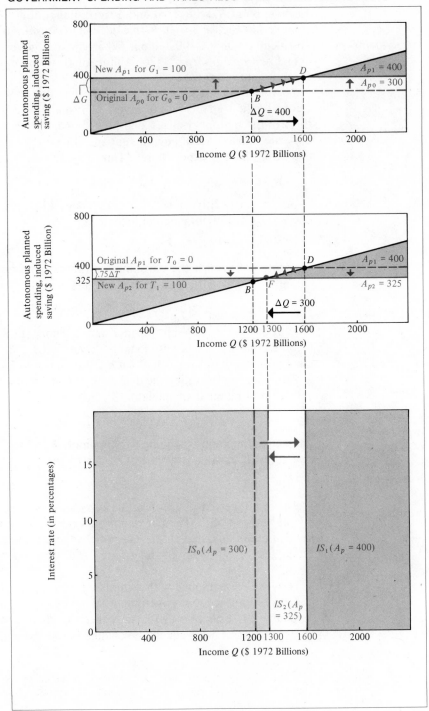

$$\Delta A_p = \Delta a - c\Delta\bar{T} + \Delta I_p + \Delta G \qquad (3.20)$$

In other words, the four causes of changes in A_p are:

1. A $1.00 change in autonomous consumption (a) changes A_p by $1.00 in the same direction.
2. A $1.00 change in autonomous tax revenue ($\bar{T}$) changes A_p by c (the marginal propensity to consume) times $1.00 in the opposite direction. For example, a $100 billion increase in $\bar{T}$ would reduce A_p by $75 billion if c were 0.75. How do households pay for the other $25 billion in higher tax revenue? They obtain the $25 billion by reducing their saving.
3. A $1.00 change in planned investment (I_p) changes A_p by $1.00 in the same direction.
4. A $1.00 change in government spending (G) changes A_p by $1.00 in the same direction.

> **Summary:** Real income can be raised or lowered by a change in autonomous consumption (a), tax revenues ($\bar{T}$), planned investment (I_p), or government spending (G). The job of government fiscal policy is to control tax revenues and government spending to offset undesired changes in private spending (a and I_p).

Once the change in A_p has been calculated from this list, our basic multiplier expression from (3.14) determines the resulting change in equilibrium income:

$$\Delta Q = \frac{\Delta A_p}{s}$$

Now it is clear that in the top frame of Figure 3-6 the government can move the economy from the unsatisfactory initial point B, where real

---

FIGURE 3-6

Effect on Income of a $100 Billion Increase in Government Spending Followed by a $100 Billion Increase in Autonomous Tax Revenue

The top frame is identical to the middle frame of Figure 3-4. It shows that a $100 billion increase in government spending moves the economy from B to D, having the same multiplier impact on equilibrium income as a $100 billion increase in A_p caused by alterations in private spending decisions. In the middle frame the $100 billion tax increase only reduces A_p by $75 billion, since the remaining $25 billion of tax revenue is paid for by higher saving. The economy moves from point D down to point F. In the bottom frame the initial equilibrium position when $A_p = 300$, the intermediate position when $A_p = 400$, and the final equilibrium position when $A_p = 325$ are shown by three separate vertical IS curves. Once again equilibrium income in each situation is independent of the interest rate.

output is too low, to the desired point D by any action that can raise A_p by \$100 billion. Two possibilities are: a \$100 billion increase in G (government spending on goods and services), and a \$133 billion reduction in autonomous tax revenue.[14]

The \$100 billion change in government spending ($\Delta G = 100$) in Figure 3-6 has exactly the same effect on income as any other \$100 billion increase in A_p. The economy reaches a new equilibrium at point D, just as it did in Figure 3-4. The multiplier (k) for ΔG is also the same:

GENERAL FORM

NUMERICAL EXAMPLE

$$k = \frac{\Delta Q}{\Delta G} = \frac{\Delta Q}{\Delta A_p} = \frac{1}{s} \qquad k = \frac{\Delta Q}{\Delta G} = \frac{1}{0.25} = 4.0 \qquad (3.21)$$

In the top frame of Figure 3-6 the government manages to push total income up from \$1200 billion at point B to \$1600 billion at point D by making \$100 billion of purchases. Since its tax revenues remain at zero, the government's purchases cause a government deficit of \$100 billion:

Government deficit $= G - T = \$100$ billion.

How is this deficit financed? A relationship in Chapter 2 sets the difference between private saving and investment $(S - I)$ equal to the government deficit.

$$S - I \equiv G - T \qquad (2.12)$$

The change in the left side of (2.12) must balance the change in the right side:

$$\Delta S - \Delta I \equiv \Delta G - \Delta T \qquad (3.22)$$

The movement in the top frame of Figure 3-6 from point B to point D assumes that investment is fixed ($\Delta I = 0$) and that tax revenue remains at zero ($\Delta T = 0$). Thus the only elements of (3.22) that are changing are ΔS and ΔG:

$$\Delta S - \Delta I \equiv \Delta G - \Delta T$$
$$s\Delta Q - 0 \equiv 100 - 0$$
$$0.25(400) \equiv 100$$

The \$400 billion increase in output induces \$100 billion of extra saving, but there is no extra private investment for the extra saving to finance

---

[14] Why \$133 billion? Because, according to equation (3.20), a reduction in taxes raises A_p by c times the reduction, where c is the marginal propensity to consume. If $c = 0.75$, as in our numerical example, then

$$\Delta A_p = -c\Delta T = -0.75(-133) = 100$$

Recall that transfer payments are equivalent to negative taxes, so that a \$133 billion reduction in taxes has the same impact on A_p as a \$133 billion increase in transfer payments (welfare, social security, or such).

$(\Delta I = 0)$. Thus each extra dollar of saving is available for households to purchase the $100 billion of government bonds that the government must sell when it runs its $100 billion deficit.

3-7 TAX INCREASES AND THE BALANCED BUDGET MULTIPLIER

The government may prefer not to run a deficit. If equilibrium was at point D, with $G = \$100$ billion, what happens if autonomous tax revenues $(\bar{T})$ are raised from zero to $100 billion $(\Delta \bar{T} = 100)$ and everything else remains the same *(ceteris paribus)*? Once again we use our basic two-step method to calculate the change in income. First, the change in A_p in equation (3.20) is:

$$\Delta A_p = \Delta a - c\Delta T + \Delta I_p + \Delta G$$
$$= 0 - c\Delta T + 0 + 0$$
$$= -0.75(100) = -75$$

A $100 billion increase in autonomous tax revenues $(\Delta \bar{T} = 100)$ reduces autonomous planned spending by only $75 billion because households "pay" the remaining $25 billion of higher taxation by saving less than they otherwise would.

The effect of the tax increase on income is illustrated in the middle frame of Figure 3-6. Autonomous spending drops by $75 billion from $400 billion to $325 billion, and equilibrium income drops from $1600 billion to $1300 billion (point F). The corresponding equation is:

GENERAL FORM   NUMERICAL EXAMPLE

$$\Delta Q = \frac{\Delta A_p}{s} = \frac{-c\Delta \bar{T}}{s} \qquad \Delta Q = \frac{-(0.75)\,100}{0.25} = -300 \qquad (3.23)$$

The multiplier for an increase in taxes is the income change in equation (3.23) divided by $\Delta \bar{T}$:

GENERAL FORM   NUMERICAL EXAMPLE

$$\frac{\Delta Q}{\Delta \bar{T}} = \frac{\Delta A_p}{s\Delta \bar{T}} = \frac{-c\Delta \bar{T}}{s\Delta \bar{T}} = \frac{-c}{s} \qquad \frac{\Delta Q}{\Delta \bar{T}} = \frac{-0.75}{0.25} = -3.0 \qquad (3.23)$$

The top and middle frames of Figure 3-6 show that the government can influence total income even if it maintains a balanced budget. In the top frame the $100 billion increase in G moves the economy from B to D; in the middle frame the $100 billion increase in $\bar{T}$ that balances the budget moves the economy from D to F (but *not* all the way to B). Why? The **balanced budget multiplier** is the government spending multiplier $(1/s)$ in (3.21) plus the autonomous tax multiplier $(-c/s)$ in (3.24):

$$\text{Balanced budget multiplier} = \frac{\Delta Q}{\Delta G} + \frac{\Delta Q}{\Delta \bar{T}} = \frac{1}{s} - \frac{c}{s} = \frac{1-c}{s} = 1 \qquad (3.24)$$

Caution: The balanced budget multiplier is $(1 - c)/s$. If all taxes are autonomous the balanced budget multiplier is 1.0. Thus in Figure 3-6 a $100 billion increase in G balanced by a $100 billion increase in tax revenues leads to a $100 billion increase in income as the economy moves from B to F. But, as demonstrated in the appendix to this chapter, when the government collects part of its revenue in the form of an income tax, the denominator of all multipliers is higher than it is in this section, reducing all the multipliers. Thus in general the balanced budget multiplier is less than 1.0.

Exercise: Notice that, starting from point B in Figure 3-6, a balanced budget expansion of $100 billion in both G and $\bar{T}$ is too small to cure the recession. The economy moves only to F, and it fails to reach the desired level of natural output at $1600 billion (point D). What is the size of the balanced budget expansion in both G and $\bar{T}$ that would be necessary to raise income from $1200 to $1600 billion without causing a government deficit?

Our analysis of fiscal policy has been conducted by holding other things constant, including the marginal propensity to save (s). But changes in s can cause major changes in equilibrium income. If $A_p = 400$ and $s = 0.25$, equilibrium income is at the desired level of $1600 billion. If all households were to save more, raising their marginal propensity to save from 0.25 to 0.40, equilibrium income would drop from $1600 to $1000 billion:

$$Q = \frac{A_p}{s}$$
$$= \frac{400}{0.4} = 1000$$

With $s = 0.4$, the multiplier for any change in A_p is $1/s$ or 2.5. The larger is s, the smaller is the spending multiplier.

Thus households through their spending and saving decisions can alter equilibrium income in two ways, by changing autonomous consumption (a) or the marginal propensity to save (s). Consumer attitudes, then, are a major source of economic instability, and a sufficient degree of consumer pessimism can bring about a recession.

The appendix to this chapter contains a more complete model which shows that the denominator of the multiplier is the fraction of income that leaks out of the spending stream (the **marginal leakage rate**), whether into saving, income tax revenue, or imports. The higher the leakage rate grows, the lower the multiplier for changes in A_p and the lower the equilibrium income for any given A_p. Thus the government can influence spending by raising or lowering the income tax rate, which is part of the leakage rate and hence influences equilibrium income.

CASE STUDY: SPENDING, LEAKAGES, AND THE MULTIPLIER IN THE GREAT DEPRESSION

The most traumatic economic event in U.S. history was the Great Depression. Actual real GNP, roughly equal to natural real GNP in 1929, fell precipitously to a level almost 40 percent below natural output in 1933. The unemployment rate rose from a modest 3.2 percent in 1929 to an unprecedented 25.2 percent in 1933.[15] When Franklin D. Roosevelt was inaugurated as president on March 4, 1933, the U.S. economy was almost at a standstill. One of every three workers was unemployed. Almost every bank in the country was closed. And, to make matters worse, no unemployment compensation, national welfare, or social security were available to cushion the blow of lost jobs and income.[16]

Figure 3-7 summarizes the main features of the first phase of the Great Depression (1929–33) in terms of the analytical framework of this chapter. The main components of planned autonomous spending are listed under Figure 3-7. Clearly the cause of the problem was investment, which declined by 85 percent, or $49.5 billion in 1972 prices. Investment was 18.7 percent of natural GNP in 1929, but only 2.5 percent of natural output in 1933. We do not yet have a clue as to the possible causes of the decline in investment, because we have been assuming that planned investment is autonomous. But we can analyze the effects of the investment collapse on GNP.

First we must calculate the change in planned autonomous spending.[17] Although autonomous consumption did not change, government spending increased between 1929 and 1933 and offset part of the decline in investment.[18] But this was offset by an increase in taxation; as a

---

[15] See Figure 1-2.

[16] A vivid, detailed, and exciting narrative of daily life in the 1930s, and of the first attempts of the New Deal to cope with the Great Depression, is contained in William Manchester, *The Glory and the Dream: A Narrative History of America, 1932–1972* (Boston: Little, Brown, 1974), pp. 3–171. A thorough immersion in these pages is almost guaranteed to "turn the student on" to macroeconomics as an important and relevant subject. It will also explain why the Keynesian solution to mass unemployment, first published in J. M. Keynes, *The General Theory of Employment, Interest, and Money* (London: Macmillan, 1936), was so revolutionary in comparison to the doctrines then in vogue.

[17] This discussion simplifies the true situation in 1933 by ignoring the substantial amount of unintended inventory change in that year and thus treats all investment in 1933 as planned.

[18] Actually, the decline in consumption during the Great Depression, although mainly induced, appears partly to have been autonomous, particularly in 1930. See Peter Temin, *Did Monetary Forces Cause the Great Depression?* (New York: Norton, 1976), especially pp. 68–75.

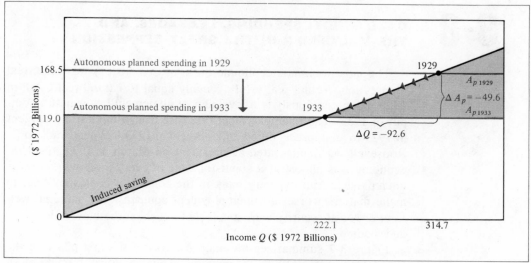

FIGURE 3–7   An Interpretation of Induced Leakages and Autonomous
Planned Spending in the Great Depression

INGREDIENTS IN FIGURE 3–7

	Q	A_p =	I_p +	a +	G	$-c\bar{T}$	Deficit $G - T = S - I$
1929	314.7	168.6	58.1	103.0	40.9	−33.4	−4.6
1933	222.1	119.0	8.6	103.0	42.8	−35.4	7.3
Δ = 1933 −29	−92.6	−49.6	−49.5	0.0	+ 1.9	− 2.0	11.9

Source: *Economic Report of the President,* January 1977. I_p includes foreign investment.
$-cT$ is 95 percent of real state and local government receipts.

result planned autonomous spending declined by $49.6 billion, about
the same as the decline in investment. The decline in A_p amounted to
29.4 percent of the level of A_p in 1929. Assuming that total income was
in equilibrium in both 1929 and 1933, induced saving must have equaled
A_p in both 1929 and 1933, and thus it must have fallen by the same
amount in the interim.[19]

---

[19] Another simplification in Figure 3-7 is that all tax revenues during this period were
autonomous. The bulk of tax revenues during this period was collected from state and local
property taxes, which actually increased in real terms between 1929 and 1933.

The net result of the $49.6 billion collapse in planned autonomous spending was a $92.6 billion decline in real GNP. The multiplier in this case was 1.9 (92.6/49.6). The government may be able to prevent recessions and depressions by regulating G and T to offset reductions in private planned autonomous spending. Figure 3-7 plainly shows that the government deserves a grade of "D−" for its performance in the first four years of the Great Depression. First, although government spending increased by $1.9 billion between 1929 and 1933, this amount was only 4 percent of the increase that would have been necessary to offset the effect of the $49.5 billion collapse in private investment. Second, the total amount of tax revenue collected actually increased, adding to the depressing effect of the investment collapse.

Why did the government make matters worse in this way? The accepted doctrine of the day, later made obsolete by the Keynesian revolution, claimed that a balanced government budget was necessary to "restore investor confidence." Thus tax rates were raised, although not enough to prevent the government deficit from increasing by $11.9 billion (see the far-right column of the table with Figure 3-7). Furthermore, the government allowed the money supply to decline substantially between 1929 and 1933, which compounded and aggravated the collapse in investment. In Chapter 4 we will examine how planned spending is influenced by monetary policy.

SUMMARY

1. This chapter presents a simple theory for determining real income. Important simplifying assumptions include the independence of planned spending from the interest rate and the rigidity of the price level.

2. By definition we divide disposable income between consumption and saving. Throughout the chapter consumption is assumed to be a fixed autonomous amount, $100 billion in the numerical example, plus 0.75 of disposable income. Saving is the remaining 0.25 of disposable income minus the $100 billion of autonomous consumption.

3. During the 1929–76 period, U.S. consumption was a roughly constant fraction of disposable income. Exceptions were during the worst year of the Great Depression, when consumption exceeded income, and during World War II, when rationing prevented households from obtaining the goods they desired and forced them to save an abnormal fraction of their income.

4. Output and income (Q) are equal by definition to total expenditures (E), which in turn can be divided up between planned expenditures (E_p) and unintended inventory accumulation (I_u). We convert this definition into a theory by assuming that business firms adjust production whenever I_u is not zero. The economy is in equilibrium, with no pressure for production to change, only when there is no unintended inventory accumulation or decumulation $(I_u = 0)$.

5. Planned autonomous spending (A_p) equals total planned expenditures minus induced consumption. The four components of planned autonomous expenditures are autonomous consumption (a), planned investment (I_p), government spending (G), and the effect on consumption of autonomous tax revenue $(-c\bar{T})$. Any change in planned autonomous spending (ΔA_p) has a multiplier effect; an increase raises income and induces consumption over and above the initial boost in A_p. Income must increase until enough extra saving has been induced $(s\Delta Q)$ to balance the injection of extra planned autonomous spending (ΔA_p). For this reason the multiplier, the ratio of the change in income to the change in planned autonomous spending $(\Delta Q/\Delta A_p)$, is the inverse of the marginal propensity to save $(1/s)$.

6. The same multiplier is valid for a change in any component in A_p. Thus if private spending components of A_p are weak, the government can raise its spending (G) or cut taxes $(\bar{T})$ to maintain stability in A_p and thus in real output.

7. The multiplier for a balanced-budget government operation that raises spending and tax revenues by the same amount is positive, because the impact of government spending on A_p outweighs the effect of higher tax revenue, since only a fraction (c) of the change in tax revenue influences expenditures.

A LOOK AHEAD

Throughout this chapter we have assumed that planned autonomous spending is not influenced by changes in the interest rate and that the price level is fixed. The first section of the next chapter allows private planned spending to be influenced by the interest rate (a high interest rate causes a reduction in spending). In order to determine simultaneously both equilibrium income and the interest rate, we must introduce an additional "market," that for money. Through its control over the money supply, the government gains an additional method of simultaneously influencing equilibrium real income and the interest rate.

CONCEPTS AND QUESTIONS

IDENTIFICATIONS

Consumption function

Saving function

Marginal propensity to consume and to save

Average propensity to consume
and to save
Planned expenditures
Unintended inventory accumulation
Marginal leakage rate
Equilibrium
Ex ante and *ex post*

Autonomous planned spending
Induced saving
The multiplier
Ceteris paribus
Autonomous tax revenue
Government deficit
Balanced budget multiplier

QUESTIONS FOR REVIEW

1 Under what condition are the average and marginal propensities to consume equal to each other?

2 An increase in government spending causes a government deficit when tax revenues are fixed. How is the deficit financed in the new equilibrium (that is, who buys government bonds issued as a consequence of the deficit)? How is the deficit financed after the increase in spending but before income has had time to adjust?

Assume the following model of the economy:

$$C = 60 + 0.8Q_D \qquad I_p = 100$$
$$Q_D = Q - \bar{T} \qquad G = 200$$
$$\bar{T} = 200$$

3 What is the saving function implied by this model?

4 When $Q_D = 300$, what are the marginal and average propensities to save and consume?

5 With no government sector ($G = \bar{T} = 0$), what is the equilibrium level of income? If I_p increases to 200, what is the new equilibrium level of income? What is the value of the multiplier for a change in I_p? Do the same for an increase of 100 in the autonomous component of consumption. Compare.

6 Now, with the government sector included ($G = \bar{T} = 200$) and $I_p = 100$, what is the equilibrium level of income? What is the value of the multiplier for the introduction of the government sector?

7 How do you account for the difference between the multipliers in question 5 and question 6?

8 Suppose that the government wants to stabilize income at the equilibrium level you calculated in question 6. If I_p were to increase by 40 (to 140), the government must then offset this increase. It may change G or $\bar{T}$ or both to do this. If the government wants to change one policy instrument to offset the increase of 40 in I_p, what will be the required change in G? in $\bar{T}$? Describe how the economy will move back to equilibrium in each case.

APPENDIX TO CHAPTER 3
Income Taxes, Foreign Trade, and the Multiplier

EFFECT OF INCOME TAXES

When the government raises some of its tax revenue (T) from an income tax, in addition to the autonomous tax $(\bar{T})$, its total tax revenue is:

$$T = \bar{T} + \bar{t}Q \tag{1}$$

The first component, as before, is the autonomous tax (revenue from the property tax, dog licenses, and other revenue sources that do not vary automatically with income). The second component is income tax revenue, the tax rate $(\bar{t})$ times income (Q). Disposable income (Q_D) is total income minus tax revenue:

$$Q_D = Q - T = Q - \bar{T} - \bar{t}Q = (1 - \bar{t})Q - \bar{T} \tag{2}$$

Following any change in total income (Q), disposable income changes by only a fraction $(1 - \bar{t})$ as much. For instance, if the tax rate $(\bar{t})$ is 0.2, then disposable income changes by 80 percent of the change in total income. Any change in total income (ΔQ) is now divided into induced consumption, induced saving, and induced income tax revenue. The fraction of ΔQ going into consumption is the marginal propensity to consume disposable income (c) times the fraction of income going into disposable income $(1 - \bar{t})$. Thus the change in total income is divided up as follows:

Fraction going to:	GENERAL FORM	NUMERICAL EXAMPLE
1. Induced consumption	$c(1 - \bar{t})$	$0.75(1 - 0.8) = 0.6$
2. Induced saving	$s(1 - \bar{t})$	$0.25(1 - 0.8) = 0.2$
3. Income tax revenue	$\bar{t}$	0.2
Total	$(c + s)(1 - \bar{t}) + \bar{t}$	1.0
	$= 1 - \bar{t} + \bar{t} = 1.0$	

As before, the economy is in equilibrium when income equals planned expenditures:

$$Q = E_p \tag{3}$$

We found it useful in Chapter 3 to subtract induced consumption from both sides of the equilibrium condition. According to the table above, income (Q) minus induced consumption is the total of induced saving plus induced tax revenue. Planned expenditures (E_p) minus induced consumption is planned autonomous spending (A_p). Thus the equilibrium condition is:

$$Q - \text{induced consumption} = E_p - \text{induced consumption}$$

and is equivalent to:

Induced saving + induced tax revenue =

planned autonomous spending (A_p) $\quad$ (4)

From the above table, (4) can be written in symbols as:

$$[s(1-\bar{t})+\bar{t}]Q = A_p \qquad (5)$$

The term in brackets on the left-hand side is the fraction of a change in income that does not go into induced consumption, that is, the sum of the fraction going to induced saving $s(1-\bar{t})$ and the fraction going to the government as income tax revenue $(\bar{t})$. The sum of these two fractions within the brackets is called the **marginal leakage rate.** Equilibrium income is determined when we divide both sides of (5) by the term in brackets:

GENERAL FORM $\qquad$ NUMERICAL EXAMPLE

$$Q = \frac{A_p}{s(1-\bar{t})+\bar{t}} \qquad Q = \frac{400}{0.25(0.8)+0.2} = \frac{400}{0.4} = 1000 \qquad (6)$$

The numerical example shows that if planned autonomous spending (A_p) is $400 billion, income will only be $1000 billion, rather than $1600 billion (at point D in Figures 3-4 and 3-6 for the same level of A_p). Why? A greater fraction of each dollar of income now leaks out of the spending stream — 0.4 in this numerical example — than occurred due to the saving rate alone, 0.25 in Figures 3-4 and 3-6. This allows the injection of planned autonomous spending $(A_p = 400)$ to be balanced by leakages out of the spending stream at a lower level of income.

How can the government raise equilibrium income from $1000 billion in equation (6) to the desired level of $1600 billion? One alternative would be to cut the income tax rate from 0.2 to zero. Then income would be simply A_p/s, or $400/0.25 = 1600$. Another alternative would be to maintain the income tax rate at 0.2, but to raise A_p by higher spending (G) or reduced autonomous tax revenue $(\bar{T})$. How much must A_p be raised to achieve the desired $600 billion increase in income, from $1000 to $1600 billion? The multiplier is no longer $1/s$ (4.0), but rather:

$$\text{Multiplier} = \frac{\Delta Q}{\Delta A_p} = \frac{1}{s(1-\bar{t})+\bar{t}} = \frac{1}{0.4} = 2.5 \qquad (7)$$

Thus A_p must be increased by $240 billion to achieve the desired income increase of $600 billion, since $600/240 = 2.5$, the new multiplier. When A_p is increased to $640 billion, equilibrium income is determined by equation (6).

$$Q = \frac{A_p}{s(1-\bar{t})+\bar{t}} = \frac{640}{0.25(0.8)+0.2} = \frac{640}{0.4} = 1600$$

Summary: Introducing the income tax has two implications for the theory in Chapter 3:

1. Introducing the income tax increases leakages out of the spending stream and reduces the multiplier (from 4.0 to 2.5 in our example). With an income tax, changes in A_p have a weaker effect on income than without it. This feature of the income tax is sometimes called **automatic stabilization,** because the lower multiplier insulates the economy from the adverse effects of fluctuations in A_p.

2. The government gains a new tool for stabilizing income. Changes in the income tax rate can alter equilibrium—in equation (6) an increase in $\bar{t}$ raises the denominator and reduces income. Thus the government can cut the tax rate when it wants to stimulate the economy (as occurred in 1975), and it can raise the tax rate when it wants to restrain the economy (as occurred in 1968).

Exercise: If $s = 0.2$, and $A_p = 400$, all of which is government spending, is the government's budget balanced?[a] If not, how is the surplus or deficit financed?

EFFECT OF FOREIGN TRADE

Our more general theory of income determination in equation (6) states that equilibrium income equals planned autonomous spending (A_p) divided by the marginal leakage rate. When we trade with nations abroad, U.S. producers sell part of domestic output as exports. Households and business firms purchase imports from abroad, so part of U.S. expenditures do not generate U.S. production.

How do exports and imports affect the determination of income? Since the demand for exports depends on the income level of foreign nations, not the income level of the United States, we can treat exports as a part of planned autonomous spending (recall that "autonomous" means "independent of U.S. income").[b] Thus in place of equation (3.19) we can define A_p as:

$$A_p = a - c\bar{T} + I_p + G + X \tag{8}$$

where X is the abbreviation for the real value of exports.

The level of imports does depend on total U.S. income. When U.S. income is high, households and firms purchase more imported goods than

---

[a] $A_p = G = 400$, and $a = I_p = \bar{T} = 0$.

[b] Since the United States has such a large economy and buys from other countries, the level of income in the rest of the world is partly dependent on the level of U.S. income.

when it is low. Assume that the total level of imports (H) is a fixed fraction (h) of total U.S. income (Q):

$$H = hQ \qquad (9)$$

Imports have exactly the same effect on equilibrium income and the multiplier as does the income tax. Imports represent a leakage from the spending stream, a portion of a change in income that is not part of the disposable income of U.S. citizens and thus not available for consumption. The fraction of a change in income that is spent on imports (h) is part of the economy's **marginal leakage rate.**

Types of leakages	Marginal leakage rate
Saving only	s
Saving and income tax	$s(1 - \bar{t}) + \bar{t}$
Saving, income tax, and imports	$s(1 - \bar{t}) + \bar{t} + h$

When we combine (6), (8), and the table, equilibrium income becomes:

$$Q = \frac{A_p}{\text{Marginal leakage rate}} = \frac{a - c\bar{T} + I_p + G + X}{s(1 - \bar{t}) + \bar{t} + h} \qquad (10)$$

Exercise: In Belgium both exports and imports are a much higher fraction of income than in the United States. Which country has the higher multiplier for changes in government spending, Belgium or the United States? Do you think that the city of Chicago has a high or low multiplier for changes in Chicago income induced by changes in Chicago city government spending?

4

Spending, the Interest Rate, and Money

I still feel that the (*IS–LM*) diagram gives the most convenient summary of the Keynesian theory of Interest and Money which has yet been produced.

—J. R. Hicks[1]

4-1 INTRODUCTION

The basic theme of the last chapter was that income and production change by a *multiple* of any change in planned autonomous spending. But changes in planned autonomous spending (ΔA_p) were assumed to be already known and were not explained. In this chapter we accept everything in Chapter 3 as valid. But we go further by relating the level of private planned autonomous investment and autonomous consumption $(I_p + a)$ to the level of the interest rate. Business firms pay interest when they finance investment projects by borrowing from banks and by selling bonds to households and other business firms. Banks pay interest to households to induce them to hold deposits. We will simplify the discussion by assuming that there is only one interest rate paid on loans and bonds, though in the real world interest rates differ.

If private planned spending depends partly on the interest rate, what determines the interest rate? First we will explore the connection between the interest rate and the supply of money the government provides in the form of currency and checking accounts. Then we will see how the government uses its control over the money supply to influence the interest rate, and thus the equilibrium level of income.

This chapter adds to our understanding of the process of income determination, and begins our investigation of the key questions at the heart of recent economic debates:

1. What factors make the interest rate for borrowing higher in some

---

[1] *A Contribution to the Theory of the Trade Cycle* (Clarendon Press, 1950), Chapter 11.

periods than in others? Why, for instance, did the interest rate on short-term loans reach 12.9 percent in July 1974 and then fall to 4.8 percent in February 1976? Why was the same rate as low as 0.5 percent in early 1958?[2]

2. Is it correct to consider planned investment (I_p) and government purchases (G) as being determined independently of each other, as in Chapter 3? Or does an increase in government spending partially or totally "crowd out" planned investment, leaving no net effect on the total of planned autonomous spending (A_p)? What determines the size of this crowding-out effect?

3. Which is more advantageous: a stimulus to the economy provided by fiscal policy, that is, an increase in government spending (G) or a reduction in tax revenues (T); or a stimulus provided by monetary policy, that is, an increase in the supply of money?

In this chapter, as in Chapter 3, we will assume that the price level is fixed. All changes in real income are accompanied by the same change in nominal income. All effects of spending on inflation, and of inflation on the interest rate, are postponed for treatment later.

4-2 THE RELATION OF PRIVATE AUTONOMOUS PLANNED SPENDING TO THE INTEREST RATE

Why should private planned investment and autonomous consumption ($I_p + a$) depend on the interest rate? Business firms attempt to profit by borrowing funds to buy investment goods — office buildings, shopping centers, factories, machine tools, computers, airplanes. Obviously, firms can stay in business only if the earnings of investment goods are at least enough to pay the interest on the borrowed funds.

> **Example:** United Airlines calculates that it can earn $3 million per year from one additional DC-10 jet airliner after paying all expenses for employee salaries, fuel, food, and airplane maintenance, that is, all expenses besides interest payments on borrowed funds. If the DC-10 costs $20 million, that level of earnings represents a 15 percent **rate of return** ($3,000,000/$20,000,000 = 0.15$), defined as annual dollar earnings divided by the dollar cost of the airplane. If United must pay 10 percent interest to obtain the funds for the airplane, the rate of return of 15 percent is more than sufficient to pay the interest expense.
>
> In the top frame of Figure 4-1, point A shows that the 15 percent rate of return on the first DC-10 exceeds the 10 percent interest

---

[2] Figures refer to the federal funds rate, the rate on overnight loans of bank reserves between one bank and another.

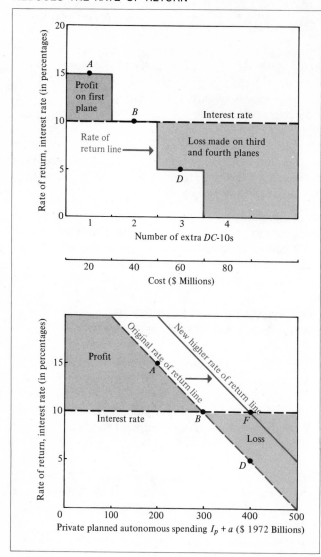

FIGURE 4–1

The Payoff to Investment for an Airline and the Economy

The red step-like line in the top frame shows the rate of return to United Airlines for purchases of additional DC-10s. If the interest rate is 10 percent, a profit is made by purchasing the first plane, and the company breaks even by buying the second plane. Purchase of a third or fourth plane would be a mistake, because the planes would not generate enough profit to pay for the cost of borrowing the money to buy them. The bottom frame shows the same phenomenon for the economy as a whole. An increase in business and consumer confidence can shift the entire rate of return line to the right, increasing spending at any given interest rate.

rate on borrowed funds. The step-like red line in the top frame of Figure 4-1 shows the rate of return on the first, second, third, and fourth planes. The gray area between point A and the 10 percent interest rate represents the annual profit rate made on the first plane. Point B shows that purchase of a second extra DC-10 earns only a 10 percent rate of return or $2 million in extra earnings after payment of all noninterest expenses. Why does the second plane earn less than the first? The first plane is operated on the most profitable routes; the second must fly on routes that are less likely to yield full passenger loads. A third plane (at point D) would have an even lower rate of return, insufficient to pay the interest cost of borrowed funds. A fourth plane earns nothing, because its passenger loads are even lighter. The pink area between the interest rate and rate-of-return line shows the loss made on the third and fourth plane.

How many planes will be purchased? The second can pay its interest expense and will be purchased, but the third will not. If the interest cost of borrowed funds were to rise above 10 percent, purchases would be cut from two planes to one, but if the interest rate were to fall to or below 5 percent, then three planes would be purchased.

The interest rate not only influences the level of business investment, but also affects the level of household consumption. For instance, households deciding whether to purchase a dishwasher or a second automobile are influenced by the size of the monthly payment, which depends on the interest rate.[3] In the bottom frame of Figure 4-1 the original rate of return line shows that the return on planned investment and autonomous consumption spending $(I_p + a)$ decline as the level of spending increases. As for United Airlines, each successive investment good purchased by business firms is less profitable than the last. Similarly, each successive consumption good purchased by households provides fewer services than the last (for instance, a family's second car is less essential and useful than its first car).

The rates of return for three alternative quantities of $I_p + a$ are plotted along the original rate of return line in the bottom frame of Figure 4-1. The three are:

Point	$I_p + a$	Rate of return
A	200	15
B	300	10
D	400	5

The gray area shows that if the interest rate is 10 percent, a profit will be made on the first $300 billion of $I_p + a$. However, the rate of return of further spending is below the interest rate and creates the losses indicated by the pink area.

The rate of return line shows how profitable firms expect additional investment to be, and how useful households expect additional consump-

---

[3] The interest rate also influences households who pay "cash" for the automobile or dishwasher, since they lose the interest that they would have earned if they had refrained from buying and had instead kept the funds in a savings account.

tion goods to be. How much will actually be spent? The answer depends on the interest rate, since firms will not be willing to incur losses by entering the pink-shaded region where the rate of return is below the interest rate.

Thus, determination of the level of $I_p + a$ is a two-step process. First we plot the rate of return line representing firms' and consumers' expectations of the benefit of additional purchases. If business and consumer optimism should increase, the rate of return line shifts to the right. If United Airlines becomes more optimistic and raises its estimate of future passenger loads, it will raise its estimate of the rate of return on each additional plane. Second, we find the level of $I_p + a$ at the point where the rate of return line crosses the interest rate level.

When the interest rate is 10 percent as in Figure 4-1, $I_p + a$ spending will be $300 billion at point B, as long as the level of business and consumer optimism remains constant (*ceteris paribus*), which would maintain the original rate of return line. A decrease in the interest rate will increase purchases $(I_p + a)$; for instance, a decrease from 10 percent to 5 percent moves purchases from $300 billion at B to $400 billion at D. Can purchases ever change when the interest rate is held constant at 10 percent? Certainly—an increase in business and consumer optimism about the expected payoff of additional purchases can shift the entire rate of return line to the right, as indicated by the red new higher rate of return line. This shifts to the right (to point F) the intersection of the rate of return line with the fixed horizontal interest rate line.

Summarizing, we can show the amount of $I_p + a$ spending that would occur at different interest rates and different levels of confidence.

	Demand for $I_p + a$	
Interest rate	Original rate-of-return line (expectations pessimistic)	New higher rate-of-return line (expectations optimistic)
15	200 (at A)	300
10	300 (at B)	400 (at F)
5	400 (at D)	500

This table shows the demand for private planned autonomous spending $(I_p + a)$ for different levels of confidence and different interest rates. The left-hand column (expectations pessimistic) is plotted as the original A_p line (red dashes) in the left frame of Figure 4-2, which is identical to the left-hand dashed line in the bottom frame of Figure 4-1.

Although A_p is negatively related to the interest rate, it is still completely autonomous, that is, independent of income. Why is private investment unaffected by the level of income? This is a restriction we have

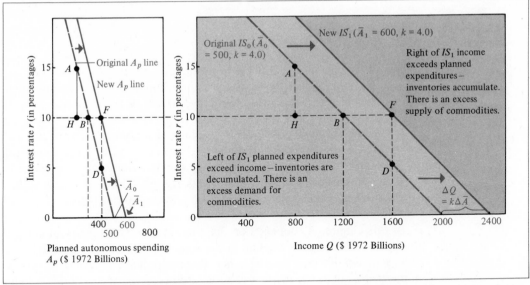

FIGURE 4–2

Relation of the *IS* Curve to the Demand for Autonomous Spending

In the left frame the original A_p line plots the amount of planned autonomous spending that will occur at alternative interest rates. Corresponding to that line is the IS_0 line in the right frame, which is always at a horizontal distance equal to the multiplier $(k = 4.0)$ times the original A_p line. $\bar{A}_0$ is the amount of autonomous spending that occurs at a zero interest rate ($500 billion), so IS_0 intersects the horizontal axis at $2000 billion.

If businessmen and consumers become more optimistic, they demand more A_p at each interest rate, and the A_p line shifts right to the new A_p line. Along this line, spending is $600 billion $(\bar{A}_1)$ at a zero interest rate. The IS curve now shifts right by exactly 4.0 times as much, and it intersects the horizontal axis at $2400 billion $(\bar{A}_1$ times 4.0). The gray area to the right of IS_1 indicates an area of disequilibrium where income exceeds planned expenditures and inventories are accumulated. The pink area indicates the reverse.

imposed to simplify the analysis, but it is not completely realistic. The A_p line in the left frame of Figure 4-2 shifts right or left as expectations of profitability are altered, and those expectations are surely influenced by actual production and income. Later, when we take a closer look at investment in Chapter 14, we will see that it is the desired stock of capital (airplanes, machines) that depends on the interest rate and expected income; investment spending depends on the speed with which businessmen choose to adjust their actual capital stock to the desired level.

4-3 THE *IS* CURVE

We know that total income is a multiple of A_p. In Chapter 3 we used several vertical *IS* lines to show that equilibrium income was independent of the interest rate because A_p was independent of the interest rate.

> **Review:** Equilibrium income is planned autonomous spending divided by the marginal propensity to save, $Q = A_p/s$. In the numerical example in Chapter 3, $s = 0.25$, so $Q = 4.0$ times A_p. The value of the multiplier (k) in this example is $1/s = 4.0$, but it could be higher or lower, depending on saving behavior and other factors.

In this chapter A_p depends on the interest rate, so equilibrium income does also. The original IS_0 line in the right frame of Figure 4-2 plots the values of equilibrium income when the multiplier (k) is 4.0, as in the numerical example in the last chapter. Points A, B, and D along the line IS_0 are all plotted at a horizontal distance exactly 4.0 times the value of the original A_p line in the left frame.

> **Example:** If the interest rate is 10 percent, then A_p in the left frame is \$300 billion at point B, so that equilibrium income is 4.0 times as much, or \$1200 billion at B in the right frame.[4] If the interest rate is zero, then the level of A_p is designated $\bar{A}_0$ and equals \$500 billion, so that equilibrium income in the right-hand frame is \$2000 billion, where the IS_0 curve intersects the horizontal axis.

The *IS* curve shows all of the different combinations of the interest rate (r) and income (Q) at which the economy's market for commodities (goods and services) is in equilibrium, which occurs only when income equals planned expenditures, with no unintended inventory accumulation or decumulation. At any point off the *IS* curve the economy is out of equilibrium. The region to the left of the *IS* curve, for instance at point H, shows unintended inventory decumulation, resulting from output too low for the amount of spending induced by a 10 percent interest rate.

In Chapter 3, each *IS* curve was labeled with a constant value of A_p. But now we need another label, since A_p can take on many different values along any *IS* curve. *We define $\bar{A}$ as the value of planned autonomous spending that would take place at an interest rate of zero.* In the left frame the original A_p line intersects the horizontal axis, where the

---

[4] Thus point B in Figure 4-2 corresponds to point B in Figure 3-4. Point D here corresponds to point D in Figure 3-4.

interest rate is zero, at $A_p = 500$, so $\bar{A}_0$ is \$500 billion. The corresponding IS_0 curve in the right frame is thus labeled $\bar{A}_0 = 500$.

Whenever $\bar{A}$ changes, both the A_p line and the IS curve shift. When business and consumer confidence increases, the expected rate of return on spending goes up, and the demand for A_p rises at each interest rate. This is indicated by the higher new A_p line in the left frame. At a zero interest rate $\bar{A}$ increases from $\bar{A}_0 = 500$ to $\bar{A}_1 = 600$, so the IS curve shifts right by the multiplier (4.0) times the \$100 billion shift in $\bar{A}$. The IS curve that is relevant when $\bar{A}_1 = 600$ is labeled IS_1 in Figure 4-2.

4-4 LEARNING TO SHIFT AND TILT THE *IS* CURVE

Since the IS curve is so important and useful, we need to pause here and study the curve more closely.[5]

1. WHY DOES THE *IS* CURVE SLANT DOWN TO THE RIGHT?

A lower interest rate raises A_p, and a higher level of A_p raises equilibrium Q by k times as much. This is the multiplier process discussed in Chapter 3.

2. WHAT SHIFTS THE *IS* CURVE?

Figure 4-2 demonstrates that the horizontal intercept of the IS curve is always equal to the multiplier (k) times $\bar{A}$, the amount of planned autonomous spending that would occur at a zero interest rate. For instance, the IS_0 curve has a horizontal intercept at \$2000 billion, equal to 4.0 (k) times \$500 billion $(\bar{A}_0)$. Anything that changes the multiplier (k) or $\bar{A}$ will shift the IS curve.

The Multiplier. The position of the IS curve will shift relative to that of the A_p demand curve in Figure 4-2 if the multiplier (k) changes. In Chapter 3 the multiplier is the inverse of the marginal propensity to save $(k = 1/s)$, so that obviously an increase in the desired saving rate will reduce the multiplier, shifting the IS curve to the left. A decrease in the saving rate will have the opposite effect. The appendix to Chapter 3 introduced other elements that reduce the multiplier and shift the IS curve left — an increase in the income tax rate or an increase in the share of GNP that is imported. Opposite changes, for example, an income tax reduction or rebate, shift the IS curve to the right.

Business and Consumer Confidence. Both the A_p demand curve and the IS curve will shift if businessmen and consumers become more opti-

---

[5] Despite its name, the IS curve has no unique connection with investment (I) or saving (S). It shifts whenever $\bar{A}$ changes, which can be caused by a change in government spending or in tax rates.

mistic and raise the amount they desire to spend for any given interest rate. For instance, bank failures in the Great Depression may have shifted the *IS* curve to the left, and the inauguration of President Roosevelt in March 1933 may have helped to restore confidence and shift the *IS* curve to the right.

Government Actions. In Chapter 3 total planned autonomous spending (A_p) included two private components, autonomous consumption (a) and planned investment (I_p), as well as two government components, government spending (G) and autonomous tax collections ($-c\bar{T}$). Although the government components do not depend on the interest rate, they are nevertheless part of A_p, and so any change in government spending or autonomous tax collections will shift the A_p and *IS* curves together.[6]

Each event in Chapter 3 that shifted the *IS* line shifts *IS* now by the same *horizontal* distance. The only difference is that *IS* is a sloped line rather than a vertical one.

Because the position of the *IS* line depends on both k and $\bar{A}$, the value of both is always given next to each *IS* line, as in Figure 4-2. Does a change in the interest rate (r) cause *IS* to shift? No. When there is a change in a variable already plotted on the axes, Q and r in this case, we move along the line, as between B and D along IS_0. If a change occurs in an element relevant to the graph but *not* on the axes, the line shifts. This is true of any graphic line or curve.[7]

3. WHAT IS TRUE OF POINTS THAT ARE OFF THE *IS* CURVE?

The entire area to the left of each *IS* curve, for example point H, is characterized by an *excess demand for commodities.* All points in the region to the right of an *IS* curve are characterized by purchases below production, which means undesired inventory accumulation and an *excess supply of commodities.* For instance, when $\bar{A}_1 = 600$ and the IS_1 line is relevant, the pink shading shows the area where there is an excess demand for commodities. The gray shading shows where there is an excess supply of commodities.

4. WHAT CHANGES THE SLOPE OF THE *IS* CURVE?

How is the responsiveness of spending related to changes in the interest rate? **Spending responsiveness** or "A_p responsiveness" refers to the change in autonomous spending (A_p) divided by the change in the interest rate (Δr) that causes it. Along the original ΔA_p line in the left

---

[6] The appendix to Chapter 3 showed that the multiplier itself depends on income tax rates, giving the government a third way to shift the *IS* curve.

[7] The line shifts only if the change is in a variable not on the axes that matters for the relationship being plotted. Here, for instance, a change in $\bar{A}$ or k will shift *IS*, but a change in the money supply will not.

Funds held in the form of stocks, bonds, or saving accounts pay interest but cannot be used for transactions. Before the invention of the credit card, individuals had to carry currency in their pockets or have money in their bank accounts to back up a check before they could buy anything. Because rich people make more purchases, they generally need a larger amount of currency and larger bank deposits. Thus the demand for real money balances increases when everyone becomes richer, that is, when the total of real income increases.

The credit card allows some purchases to be made without currency, although bank deposits must still be held to allow payment of the credit-card bills. Furthermore, credit cards are not accepted by many stores, including most supermarkets, dry cleaners, barbers, and movie theaters. This requires the continued use of some currency. Credit cards have not eliminated the positive association between the demand for real balances and the level of real income, even if they have reduced the demand for money per dollar of income.

It is customary to discuss the demand for money in real terms, that is, adjusted for changes in the price level. Assume that the demand for nominal money (M) — currency and checking deposits — is always equal to half of nominal income (PQ).[9] We divide both money and income by the price level (P), which is the same as saying that the demand for real money balances (M/P) equals half of real income (Q):

$$\left(\frac{M}{P}\right)^d = 0.5Q$$

The superscript d means "the demand for."

If real income (Q) is at \$1600 billion, the demand for real money balances $(M/P)^d$ will be \$800 billion, as shown in Figure 4-3 by the vertical line (L') drawn at \$800 billion. The line is vertical because we are assuming that the demand for real balances $(M/P)^d$ does not depend on the interest rate (r). A decline in income simply shifts L' to the left, to a position equal to half of the new level of income. An increase in income shifts L' to the right.

THE INTEREST RATE AND THE DEMAND FOR MONEY

The L' line is unrealistic, however, because individuals will not hold as much money at a 10 percent interest rate as at a zero interest rate. Why? Because the interest rate plotted on the vertical axis is paid on assets other than money, like bonds and savings accounts. The higher the reward (r) for holding bonds and savings accounts, which are not money, the less money will be held, because money does not pay interest.

If the interest rate (r) paid by these nonmoney assets (bonds, savings accounts) was zero, there would be no point in holding them. Individuals

---

[9] Remember that nominal income (Y) is the GNP price deflator (P) times real income (Q), so that $Y = PQ$.

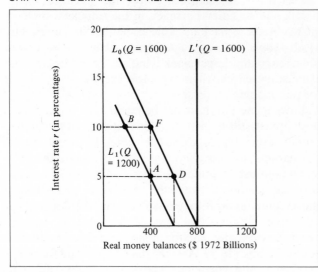

FIGURE 4–3

The Demand for Money, the
Interest Rate, and Real Income

The vertical line L' is drawn on the
assumption that the demand for real
balances is equal to half of real income ($1600 billion in this case), but
does not depend on the interest rate.
The L_0 curve maintains income at
$1600, but it allows the demand for
real balances to fall by $200 billion
for each 5 percent increase in the interest rate. If income falls from $1600
to $1200 billion, the L_0 schedule
shifts left to L_1.

would hold all of their financial assets in the form of money to take advantage of its convenience. But if the interest rate on them was 10 percent,
individuals would be willing to inconvenience themselves by cutting down
on their average money holding in order to earn the higher interest available on alternative assets. Sufficient money would be available for transactions, even if smaller average balances of currency and demand deposits were held, only if individuals are willing to suffer the inconvenience
of more frequent trips to the broker or the bank to obtain money from
sales of stocks and bonds and from transfers out of savings accounts.
This inconvenience would be judged worthwhile if the interest earnings
on the alternative assets were high enough to compensate individuals for
the nuisance of periodically converting these assets into money.

In Figure 4-3 the downward slope of L_0 through points F and D indicates that when real income is $1600 billion and the interest rate is zero,
the demand for real balances is $800 billion. But when the interest rate
rises from zero to 5 percent, people suffer inconvenience to cut down
their money holdings from $800 billion to $600 billion (point D). When
the interest rate is 10 percent, only $400 billion is demanded (point F)
because individuals are willing to suffer the inconvenience of converting
their money into savings accounts, stocks, and bonds even more often.
The new L_0 line can be summarized as showing that the real demand for
money $(M/P)^o$ is half of income $-$ $40 billion $\times$ the interest rate:

$$\left(\frac{M^s}{P}\right) = 0.5Q - 40r$$

A change in the interest rate moves the economy up and down its real money demand schedule. But if real output (Q) falls, for instance, from $1600 billion to $1200 billion, then the curve shifts left from L_0 to L_1. People with a lower level of real income hold less money at any given level of the interest rate. The distance of the leftward horizontal shift between L_0 and L_1 is $200 billion, exactly half of the assumed decline in real income.

THE *LM* SCHEDULE

To have equilibrium in the money market the real supply of money (M^s/P) must equal the demand for real balances $(M/P)^d$:

$$\left(\frac{M^s}{P}\right) = \left(\frac{M}{P}\right)^d = 0.5Q - 40r \qquad (4.1)$$

If the amount of money supplied by the government is $400 billion, and the price index (P) is set at a constant value of 1.0, then (M^s/P) equals $400 billion. Since the supply of money does not depend on the interest rate, (M^s/P) is drawn in the left frame of Figure 4-4 as a vertical line at a level of $400 billion for every interest rate. The two demand schedules, L_0 and L_1, are copied from Figure 4-3.

The sloped demand line L_0, drawn for an income of $1600 billion, crosses the M^s/P line at point F, where the interest rate is 10 percent. The demand for money at F is $400 billion, and the supply of money is also $400 billion. Because the two are equal and thus the money market is in equilibrium when $Q = 1600$ (assumed in drawing the L_0 line) and $r = 10$ percent. This equilibrium combination of values is plotted at point F in the right frame of Figure 4-4.[10]

If income is $1200 billion instead of $1600 billion, the demand for money is smaller at every interest rate, as indicated by the parallel schedule L_1 passing through points B and A.[11] When the income level is only $1200 billion, the demand for real money balances can be equal to the fixed $400 billion real supply of money only at point A, where the interest rate is 5 percent. Thus $Q = 1200$ and $r = 5$ is another combination consistent with equilibrium in the money market and is plotted at point A in the right frame of Figure 4-4. Although the lower income level of $1200 billion cuts the money needed for transaction purposes, the lower

---

[10] Thus in equation (4.1)

$$400 = 0.5(1600) - 40(10)$$
$$= 800 - 400$$
$$= 400$$

[11] Since the demand for real balances falls by $.50 for every dollar decline in real income, the demand schedule through A drawn for an income level of $1200 billion lies everywhere exactly $200 billion to the left of the demand schedule through D drawn for an income level of $1600 billion.

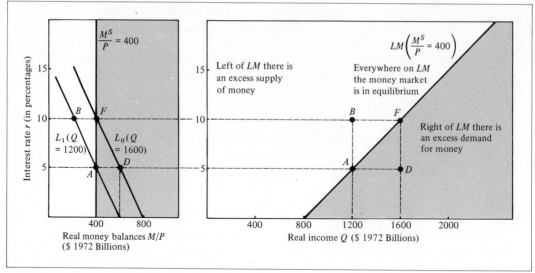

FIGURE 4–4   Derivation of the *LM* Curve

In the left frame the L_0 schedule is copied from the previous figure and assumes that $Q = 1600$, showing that the demand for real balances falls further below $0.5Q$ as the interest rate rises. The L_1 schedule shows the demand for money when income is at the lower level of $1200 billion. The vertical M^s/P line shows the available supply of money provided by the government. The money market is in equilibrium where the supply line (M^s/P) crosses the demand line (L_0 or L_1). When income is $1600 bil-

lion, equilibrium occurs at point F, plotted again in the right frame. When income is $1200 billion, equilibrium occurs where L_1 crosses M^s/P at point A, also plotted in the right frame. The *LM* curve or schedule shows all combinations of Q and r consistent with equilibrium in the money market. The pink shading shows all points (like D) where there is an excess demand for money. In the white area left of *LM* are points (like B) where there is an excess supply of money.

interest rate at A counteracts this by raising the portion of financial assets that people choose to hold in the form of money.[12]

The line connecting points A and F in Figure 4-4 is called the *LM* **curve.** The *LM* curve represents all combinations of income (Q) and interest rate (r) where the money market is in equilibrium, that is, where the real supply of money equals the real demand for money.

---

[12] Thus in equation (4.1)

$$400 = 0.5(1200) - 40(5)$$
$$= 600 - 200$$
$$= 400$$

Points on the lower left portion of the *LM* curve have a low level of income and a correspondingly low demand for money for transaction purposes. The only way the total demand for money can be kept equal to the fixed supply is for a low interest rate to induce individuals to hold most of their assets in the form of money and to abstain from frequent trips to buy and sell stocks and bonds. The upper right portion of the *LM* curve shows a high transaction demand for money caused by high income with a high interest rate inducing individuals to keep only a small share of their assets in the form of money.

At any point off the *LM* curve, say point *D*, the money market is not in equilibrium. The problem at *D* and all other points in the pink area is that the demand for real money exceeds the available supply. Point *D* is located at an income level of $1600 billion and an interest rate of 5 percent, which creates a money demand of $600 billion (see *D* in the frame on the left). This exceeds the available $400 billion supply by $200 billion. Similarly, point *B*, at an income level of $1200 billion and an interest rate of 10, generates too small a demand for money, only $200 billion instead of the required $400 billion. At point *B* and all other points in the white area there is an excess supply of money which exceeds the demand.

How does the economy adjust to guarantee that the given supply of money created by the government is exactly equal to the demand when the money market is out of equilibrium, as at point *D*? One possible adjustment, a reduction in the price level, will be considered later. In this chapter we assume the price index (*P*) to be equal to 1.0. Without changing prices, the economy might achieve money market equilibrium from point *D* by increasing the interest rate from 5 to 10 percent. This would move it to point *F*, cutting the demand for money from $600 to $400 billion. Or, instead, income might fall from $1600 billion to $1200 billion while the interest rate remains fixed. This would cause a movement to point *A*, and would cut the demand for money from $600 billion to $400 billion. Or some other combination might occur, with a partial drop in income and partial increase in the interest rate balanced so as to achieve a money demand equal to $400 billion, the fixed supply of money.

4-6 LEARNING TO SHIFT AND TILT THE *LM* CURVE

1. WHY DOES THE *LM* CURVE SLOPE UP?

When the real money supply (M^s/P) is fixed, an increase in the interest rate leads people to put up with the inconvenience of carrying less money per dollar of income. The higher interest rate has the effect of "stretching" the available real money supply to support a higher level of real income.

For instance along the *LM* line in Figure 4-4 the real money supply is assumed to be $400 billion. If the interest rate is zero, real income is only $800 billion. But each percentage point increase in the interest rate stretches the available money and makes possible an extra $80 billion of income. Thus an increase in the interest rate from zero to 5 percent at point A makes possible an increase in real income by $400 billion, from $800 to $1200 billion. A further increase in the interest rate to 10 percent raises real income by another $400 billion, to $1600 billion at point F.

Along any given LM curve the level of real money balances (M^s/P) is fixed, but real income (Q) varies. The ratio of real income to real balances is called the **velocity** of money (V).

$$\text{Velocity } (V) = \frac{Q}{M^s/P} = \frac{PQ}{M^s}$$

The right-hand expression states that velocity is also equal to nominal income (PQ) divided by the nominal supply M^s. The higher the interest the higher is the velocity as the available money is stretched to support a higher level of income and transactions. Anything that can cause the economy to move back and forth along a fixed LM curve achieves a change of velocity by altering Q while M^s/P is fixed. Later we will find that anything that can shift the IS curve (the multiplier and the components of $\bar{A}$) can change velocity.

2. WHAT MAKES THE *LM* CURVE SHIFT?

The Fed can make a monetary policy decision to alter M^s, the money supply. If the price level P is fixed, this will alter the real money supply (M^s/P). In Figure 4-5, for instance, a $200 billion increase in the money supply from $400 to $600 billion shifts the LM curve from the left-hand dashed line LM_0 to the right-hand solid line LM_1. Since each dollar of extra available money makes possible 2.0 extra dollars of income, the LM curve shifts horizontally by $400 billion.

Point D was not an equilibrium position previously, because it was off the original LM_0 curve, but now it represents a possible equilibrium on the new LM_1 curve. If income was constant, the higher money supply would just reduce the interest rate. Thus a government that finds the current interest rate too high, as at F, can reduce the interest rate to D by expanding the money supply.

3. WHAT ALTERS THE SLOPE OF *LM*?

The slope of LM measures the extra dollars of income made possible by a higher interest rate, $80 billion per each one-percent increase in the interest rate in our example. This is the product of two components, the money-demand responsiveness to a higher interest rate ($40 billion per percentage point) along either the L_0 or L_2 line in Figure 4-4, and the number of dollars of extra income made possible by each dollar of money

HOW A HIGHER REAL MONEY SUPPLY CAN REDUCE
THE INTEREST RATE

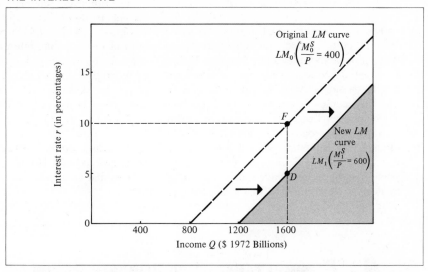

FIGURE 4–5

The Effect on the *LM* Curve of an Increase in the Real Money Supply from $400 Billion to $600 Billion

The dashed LM_0 line in the figure is identical to *LM* in the previous figure. When the money supply is increased, the money available to support output increases, and the *LM* curve shifts rightward by 2.0 dollars per dollar of extra money to the new line LM_1.

released by the higher interest rate (2.0). Thus a change in either factor will tilt the *LM* curve.

Particularly interesting is the extreme case when the demand for money does not depend on the interest rate at all, which would cause the *LM* curve to be vertical.[13] We will see in the next chapter that fiscal policy loses its potency when the *LM* curve is vertical. The slope of *LM* depends on the responsiveness of money demand to a higher interest rate in the following way:

Responsiveness of money demand to a higher interest rate	Slope of LM schedule
0	Vertical
small	Steep
large	Flat
infinity	Horizontal

---

[13] In the numerical example the *LM* curve would be a vertical line at a horizontal position exactly two times the current real money supply (M^s/P).

The *LM* curve by itself cannot tell us the level of both income and the interest rate. Why? You cannot find a city like Des Moines on a map if you are given only the number of a road passing through it, say Interstate 80. The city could be anywhere between New York and San Francisco! Instead, one needs to know two roads that intersect at Des Moines, say Interstate 80 and Interstate 35. In exactly the same way, the *LM* curve is a single line, like a highway, and is not enough by itself to determine the two unknown magnitudes (Q and r).

The other line relating the interest rate and income is the *IS* curve of section 4-3. Together, the *IS* and *LM* curves can determine both income and the interest rate, just as two crossing highways can determine a location on a two-dimensional map. In more formal language, it takes two schedules—the *IS* curve and the *LM* curve—to determine two unknowns (Q and r). If there were three unknowns, three schedules on a three-dimensional graph would be necessary, just as it is necessary to know latitude, longitude, and altitude to find an airplane in a three-dimensional sky.

4-7 SIMULTANEOUS EQUILIBRIUM IN THE COMMODITY AND MONEY MARKETS

Equilibrium in the commodity market for any given value of $\bar{A}$, occurs only at points on the *IS* curve. Figure 4-6 copies the IS_0 schedule from Figure 4-2, drawn for a value of $\bar{A} = 500$. At any point off the IS_0 curve, for instance, A and F, the economy is out of equilibrium. At F production is too high, and unintended inventory accumulation occurs. At A production is too low, and unintended inventory decumulation occurs.

Equilibrium in the commodity market occurs at points B, D, and E_0. These three points represent different combinations of income and the interest rate, all of which are compatible with commodity-market equilibrium. At which equilibrium point will the economy come to rest? The single IS_0 schedule does not provide enough information to determine *both* income and the interest rate. An additional schedule is needed, since *two* schedules are needed to pin down the equilibrium values of *two* unknown variables. The necessary additional information is provided by the *LM* curve, showing all combinations of income and the interest rate at which the money market is in equilibrium for a given real money supply, for instance $400 billion. Figure 4-6 copies the LM_0 schedule from Figure 4-5 drawn for a value of $M_0^s/P = 400$. At any point off the LM_0 curve, for instance, points B and D, the money market is out of equilibrium. At D income is too high and the real demand for money exceeds the real supply. At B income is too low and the real demand for money is below the real supply. Equilibrium in the money market occurs only at points A, F, and E_0, each representing combinations of income and the interest rate at which the real demand for money is equal to a real money supply of $400 billion.

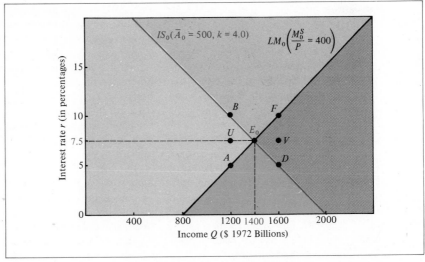

FIGURE 4-6

The *IS* and *LM* Schedules Cross at Last

The IS_0 schedule is copied from Figure 4–2; the LM_0 schedule from Figure 4–5. Only at the red point E_0 is the economy in a "general" equilibrium, with the conditions for equilibrium attained in both the commodity market (along *IS*) and the money market (along *LM*). At points U, V, A, and F the commodity market is out of equilibrium. Can you describe which way – excess demand or supply? At points U, V, B, and D the money market is out of equilibrium. Is the problem too much supply of money or too much demand for money?

At what point is the entire economy, consisting of the commodity and money markets together, in equilibrium? Equilibrium occurs only at the point where the *IS* and *LM* curves cross, point E_0 in Figure 4-6. Why is the economy out of equilibrium at every other point? Consider these examples:

At B the commodity market is in equilibrium, but the demand for real money balances is below the real supply of money.

At D the commodity market is in equilibrium, but the demand for real money balances exceeds the real supply of money.

At A the money market is in equilibrium, but the demand for commodities exceeds production, so that unintended inventory decumulation is occurring.

At F the money market is in equilibrium, but the demand for commodities falls short of production, so that unintended inventory accumulation is occurring.

Exercise: Describe the situation in both the commodity and money markets at U and V in Figure 4-6.

Simultaneous Equilibrium in the Commodity and Money Markets **105**

Interest Rates and Bond and Stock Prices

Whenever individuals have more money than they desire to hold at the present income and interest rate level, they are likely to use the extra unwanted money to buy stocks and bonds and other assets. Any increase in the demand for stocks and bonds drives up their prices. This simultaneously reduces the interest rate. Why? The interest rate on a stock is its dividend yield, the dollar dividend divided by the stock's price. Let us assume that initially the price of a stock paying a $5 dividend is $50, so that the dividend yield is 0.10, or 10 percent (= 5/50). If, however, an increase in the demand for stocks drives the stock price up to $100, the dividend yield drops from 0.10 (= 5/50) to 0.05 (= 5/100), because the $5 dividend payment in this example is unaffected by movements in stock prices.

Similarly, the annual dollar payment of interest on a long-term bond, say $5 per year, is unaffected by movements in bond prices. If the bond's price is initially $50, the bond pays a 0.10 interest "yield" or interest "rate." When the bond price is driven up to $100, the interest yield or rate drops from 0.10 (5/50) to 0.05 (5/100).

In short, if there is an excess real supply of money — a supply beyond the needs of individuals at the present level of income and interest rate — stock and bond prices are likely to be rising and interest rates falling. The reverse occurs if the real supply of money is below the needs of individuals.[14]

How does the economy arrive at its **general equilibrium** at point E_0 if it starts out at the wrong place, as at points U or V? If the commodity market is out of equilibrium and involuntary inventory decumulation or accumulation occurs, firms will step up or cut production, pushing the economy in the direction needed to reach E_0. If the money market is out of equilibrium, there will be pressure on interest rates to adjust. For instance, at point D the real demand for money is higher than the real supply. Individuals cannot obtain enough money to satisfy their demand at an interest rate of 5 percent and an income level of $1600 billion, so that they sell stocks and bonds to obtain the needed money. This drives down stock and bond prices, increasing the interest rate. Similarly, if there is too little demand for money, as at B, people will use the extra unwanted portion of the real supply of money to buy bonds and stocks, thus driving up bond and stock prices and driving down the interest rate. Either way, the economy arrives at E_0 — from above if it starts at point B and from below if it starts at point D.

The *IS* and *LM* curves are the basic tools that allow us to study the effects of fiscal and monetary policy when both the commodity market and money market are in equilibrium. Can the Fed by its monetary policy decisions offset or cancel the stimulative impact of higher government spending or lower tax rates? What difference does it make if the govern-

---

[14] Later we will see that an excess supply of money reduces the interest rate only in the short run. Once prices are allowed to change, an excess supply of money can create inflation and raise the nominal interest rate.

ment decides to stimulate the economy by means of fiscal or monetary policy? As we will see, both fiscal and monetary policy can effect income, but the level of the interest rate will depend on which policy instrument is used.

SUMMARY

1. Private planned autonomous spending (A_p) depends partly on the interest rate. We cannot know the total level of A_p, hence the level of income (A_p times the multiplier k), until we know the level of the interest rate. The higher the interest rate, the lower is A_p.

2. Private planned autonomous spending (A_p) depends also on the profitability firms expect from additional investment and the utility households expect from additional consumption goods. When firms and consumers become more optimistic about the payoff of additional purchases, A_p tends to increase for any given level of the interest rate.

3. The *IS* curve indicates all the combinations of the interest rate and income at which the economy's market for commodities is in equilibrium. At any point off the *IS* curve the economy is out of equilibrium: to the right of the *IS* curve, purchases lag behind production and unintended inventory accumulation is occurring; to the left, purchases exceed production and inventory decumulation is occurring.

4. The real quantity of money that people demand depends both on total real income and on the interest rate. Equilibrium in the money market requires that the real supply of money equal the demand for real money balances. The *LM* curve represents all the combinations of real income and of the interest rate where the money market is in equilibrium. To the right of the *LM* curve money demand exceeds the money supply; to the left, the money supply exceeds money demand.

5. Neither the *IS* nor the *LM* schedule alone provides enough information to determine the equilibrium values for both income and the interest rate. Since there are two unknown variables, the situation of "general equilibrium" must be determined using both schedules simultaneously. This simultaneous equilibrium occurs only at the point where the *IS* and *LM* curves intersect. At any other point, one or both markets are out of equilibrium.

A LOOK AHEAD

Now we have determined simultaneously the levels of equilibrium income and the interest rate. Both depend on the variables that establish the positions of the *IS* and the *LM* curves: the multiplier, business and consumer confidence, fiscal policy, and monetary policy. But can monetary and fiscal policy maintain control over the economy under all conditions? In Chapter 5 we examine the effects of changes in policy and establish several extreme situations in which either fiscal or monetary policy is impotent.

CONCEPTS AND QUESTIONS

IDENTIFICATIONS

Rate of return
Interest rate
Business and consumer confidence
IS curve
LM curve
Federal Reserve control over the money supply

Demand for real money balances
Equilibrium in the commodity market
Equilibrium in the money market
Simultaneous general equilibrium for the entire economy

QUESTIONS FOR REVIEW

1   Why do private planned investment and autonomous consumer spending depend on the interest rate? What types of purchases would be most sensitive to interest rate changes? Why?

2   What are the costs of holding money? Given these costs, why do people hold money?

3   Which factors shift the position of the *IS* curve and which change the slope?

4   Which factors shift the position of the *LM* curve and which change the slope?

5   To achieve maximum responsiveness of income to changes in the money supply, what should the *LM* curve look like? What does this imply about the underlying money demand curve?

6   Would the response of income to a change in the money supply be greater if the *IS* curve were completely vertical or completely horizontal?

7   How can the Federal Reserve Board use monetary policy to offset the impact on income of higher government spending? Of higher tax rates?

8   To raise output toward the full employment level, either a monetary or a fiscal policy stimulus may be used. While both can raise total output to the same level, other variables may not be the same. Which variables would you expect to be different? The interest rate? The share of private sector spending in total GNP?

5 Strong and Weak Effects of Monetary and Fiscal Policy

First, let me explain what *I* thought the main issue was. In terms of the Hicksian language of Friedman's article, I thought (and I still think) it was the shape of the *LM* locus.

—James Tobin[1]

5-1 INTRODUCTION

The last chapter introduced the *IS* and *LM* curves, the tools necessary to determine the economy's level of equilibrium real income and its interest rate, as well as the effect of monetary and fiscal policy on both real income and the interest rate. We will now use these tools to find the strength or weakness of monetary and fiscal policy, still assuming that the price level is fixed. Under some circumstances monetary policy may be powerful, creating large changes in real income with relatively small shifts in the real money supply. But under other circumstances, real income may get "stuck" at an unsatisfactory level, and even massive increases in the real money supply may not be able to raise real income. Similarly, fiscal policy (changes in government purchases or tax rates) may or may not be a potent instrument for controlling real income.

As we have learned, the *IS* curve shows all the combinations of real income and the interest rate that keep the commodity market in equilibrium, with production equal to planned expenditures and with no involuntary accumulation or decumulation of inventories ($I_u = 0$). The *IS* curve slopes downward because a lower interest rate raises planned investment and consumption spending, requiring higher production to avoid involuntary inventory decumulation. The slope of the *IS* curve is relatively flat, that is, a given reduction in the interest rate requires a larger increase in production when the interest responsiveness of planned investment and

[1] "Friedman's Theoretical Framework," in Robert J. Gordon, ed., *Milton Friedman's Monetary Framework* (Chicago, 1974), p. 77.

consumption spending is relatively great and when the multiplier (k) is large. The position of the IS curve shifts whenever there is a change in the autonomous spending planned at a zero interest rate ($\Delta \bar{A}$); this could occur because of a change in consumer or business optimism *or* because of a change in government purchases or autonomous tax revenue. In addition, the IS curve can shift whenever the multiplier (k) is changed by an alteration in the household saving rate or in the income tax rate.

The LM curve shows all the combinations of real income and the interest rate that keep the money market in equilibrium, with the demand for real money balances equal to a given real money supply (M^s/P). The LM curve slopes upward because an increase in the interest rate reduces the demand for money by inducing people to shift more of their funds into savings accounts. This shift requires an offsetting increase in real income to generate a higher demand for money for transactions, thus keeping the total demand for money equal to a fixed supply. The slope of the LM curve is relatively steep when the interest responsiveness of the demand for money is small, because an increase in the interest rate that reduces the demand for money by only a small amount requires only a small offsetting increase in real income to maintain a constant total demand for money. The LM curve shifts its position whenever there is a change in the real money supply, requiring a corresponding change in real money demand to maintain equilibrium in the money market. Each LM curve is labeled with the value of the real money supply that fixes its position.

5-2 STRONG EFFECTS OF AN INCREASE IN THE REAL MONEY SUPPLY

In Figure 4-5, we saw that an increase in the real money supply reduces the interest rate. Our more general analysis, which combines the money market and the commodity market, shows that most increases in the real money supply not only reduce the interest rate but also cause an increase in real income. The top frame of Figure 5-1 repeats the LM_0 curve of Figures 4-5 and 4-6, drawn on the assumption that the real money supply is $400 billion. Also repeated is the IS curve of Figures 4-2 and 4-6, which assumes that $\bar{A} = 500$ and $k = 4.0$. The economy's general equilibrium, the point where both the money and commodity markets are in equilibrium, occurs only at point E_0.

Let us look at the effects of a move by the government to raise the nominal money supply from $400 billion to $600 billion. As long as the price level stays fixed at 1.0, the real money supply increases by the same amount. As in Figure 4-5, the LM curve shifts horizontally to the right by $400 billion and vertically down by 5 percent. At the initial position E_0, with an income level of $1400 billion, and an interest rate of 7.5 percent, the real demand for money remains equal to the initial real money supply

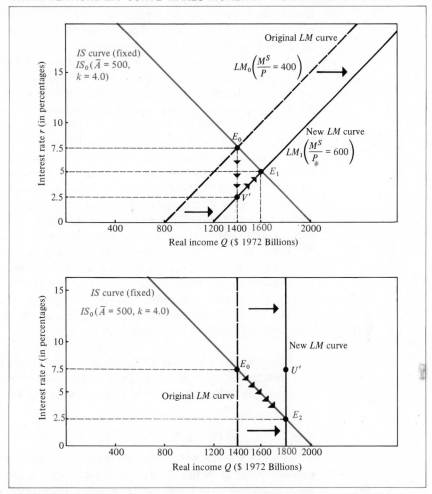

FIGURE 5-1

The Effect of a $200 Billion Increase in the Money Supply with a Normal *LM* Curve and a Vertical *LM* Curve

The top frame repeats the $200 billion increase in the money supply that was shown in Figure 4–5. In order to maintain equilibrium in both the commodity and money markets here, two effects occur; equilibrium income rises and the interest rate declines, as indi-cated by the movement from E_0 to E_1. In the bottom frame, the *LM* curve is vertical and the same $200 billion increase in the money supply shifts the *LM* curve to the right by $400 billion, and leads to a greater drop in the interest rate and a greater increase in equilibrium income.

of \$400 billion. Now, with the new higher real money supply of \$600 billion, there is an "excess supply of money" of \$200 billion. How can the economy generate the \$200 billion increase in the real demand for money needed to balance the new higher supply?

Finding themselves with more money than they desire, individuals do not merely let it rest idle in their pockets or in checking accounts that pay no interest. Instead, they transfer some into savings accounts and use some to buy stocks, bonds, and commodities. In the top frame of Figure 5-1, we assume that individuals take time to decide on the commodities they wish to purchase and that their initial reaction is to put all the extra \$200 billion of excess money into financial assets. This new higher demand raises the prices of bonds and stocks and reduces the interest rate, from 7.5 percent at point E_0 to 2.5 percent at point V'.

Only at point V' has the interest rate dropped enough to make people willing to hold \$600 billion of money voluntarily, because of the low 2.5 percent interest rate paid on other financial assets. But point V', although it represents equilibrium in the money market, is off the IS curve. The lower interest rate raises the desired level of autonomous consumption and investment spending, requiring an increase in production if undesired inventory decumulation is to be avoided. Only at point E_1, with an income level of \$1600 billion and interest rate of 5 percent, are both the money and commodity markets in equilibrium.

> **Summary:** Compared to the starting point E_0, the increase in the real money supply has caused both an increase in real income and a reduction in the interest rate to the new equilibrium point E_1.

THE PULL OF HIGHER INCOME ON THE INTEREST RATE

Why does the new equilibrium point E_1 occur at an interest rate of 5 percent rather than the 2.5 percent interest rate at point V'? Because the increase in production and output would raise the real demand for money above \$600 billion at a constant interest rate of 2.5. To avoid this, a 5 percent interest rate is required to keep money demand equal to the \$600 billion supply of money.[2]

The size of the initial drop in the interest rate, from E_0 to V' in Figure 5-1, depends on the interest responsiveness of the demand for money. For instance, if this is very small, then it takes a very large drop in the interest rate to induce individuals to hold the higher money supply voluntarily. An extreme case is illustrated in the bottom frame of Figure 5-1, where we assume that the demand for money depends only on real income and does not depend on the interest rate at all (as signified by the

---

[2] If the price level were flexible, a higher price level could cancel the increase in the real money supply. But in this chapter, we continue to assume a fixed price level.

vertical *LM* curve). Here no interest rate will raise the demand for money
even one cent above its initial level at E_0 in response to a $200 billion
increase in the real money supply. Because the demand for money depends only on income, then the only way for the demand for money to rise
by the necessary $200 billion is for real income to rise by $400 billion
(recall that the demand for money increases by half of the increase in real
income).

But the interest rate cannot stay constant at the initial level of 7.5 percent at the higher income level, as at point U', because that point is off
the *IS* curve. If involuntary accumulation of inventories is to be avoided,
the interest rate must decline enough to induce $1800 billion of desired
expenditures, which requires that we move down the *IS* curve to a new
equilibrium at point E_2.

Now compare the top and bottom frames of Figure 5-1. In both the real
money supply increases by $200 billion. Yet in the top frame income in-
creases by only $200 billion, whereas in the bottom frame income in-
creases by $400 billion, or twice as much. Why? The supply of money
has increased by the same amount, $200 billion, in both cases, and the
demand for money must increase the same $200 billion in both dia-
grams. In the top diagram the responsibility for increasing the demand
for money by $200 billion between equilibrium points E_0 and E_1 is shared
—half is accomplished by the drop in the interest rate from 7.5 to 5 percent, and the remaining half is accomplished by the $200 billion increase

---

[3] Only a remote coincidence would make money supply and demand have positive and
negative interest responses of exactly the same amounts.

in income. But in the bottom diagram the interest rate cannot contribute to raising money demand because the demand for money is completely independent of the interest rate, requiring that the entire responsibility for raising money demand be shouldered by an increase in income.

Summary: If the demand for money is independent of the interest rate, the *LM* curve is vertical and an increase in the money supply has a potent effect on real income. When the demand for money is responsive to the interest rate, the *LM* curve is flatter, and the impact of the money supply on real income is less potent.

5-3 WEAK EFFECTS OF MONETARY POLICY: UNRESPONSIVE EXPENDITURES AND THE LIQUIDITY TRAP

If, as we assumed in Chapter 3, natural real GNP (Q^*) equals $1600 billion, then the initial position at E_0 in Figure 5-1, with an income level of only $1400 billion, would be considered unsatisfactory by government policymakers. The **GNP "gap"** would be $200 billion (1600 − 1400), and the unemployment rate would be high. The previous section demonstrated that the Federal Reserve would be able to raise real income by raising the real money supply if:

1. The price level is fixed,
2. The *IS* curve is negatively sloped, and
3. The *LM* curve is positively sloped or vertical. The comparison of the top and bottom frame of Figure 5-1 demonstrated that a given increase in M^s/P, say $200 billion, is more potent if the interest-responsiveness of money demand is zero than if it is positive.

Now we examine two situations in which the Federal Reserve *cannot raise the level of actual real income*. The first, illustrated in Figure 5-2, occurs if planned expenditures do not respond to the interest rate. In this case the *IS* curve is vertical (parallel to the vertical interest rate axis). The position of the *IS* curve and the level of income in this case depend *only* on the level of $\bar{A}$ (autonomous expenditures planned at a zero interest rate), and of k (the multiplier). Since income is *independent* of the interest rate, changes in the real money supply have no effect on real income.

In Figure 5-2 an increase in the money supply from $400 to $600 billion has absolutely no effect on real income, which remains "stuck" at $1400 billion. The equilibrium position does shift down vertically from E_0 to E_3, because at E_0 the higher money supply throws the money market out of equilibrium. A $200 billion increase in money demand is required, and the interest rate must drop from 7.5 percent at E_0 to 2.5 percent at E_3 to induce households to shift funds out of stocks, bonds, and savings ac-

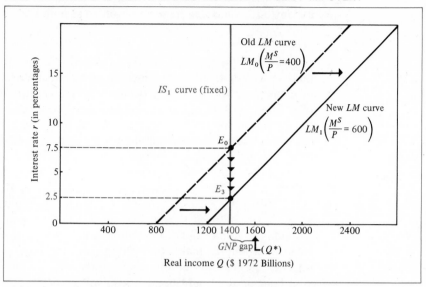

FIGURE 5–2

Effect of a $200 Billion Increase in the Real Money Supply When the Interest Responsiveness of A_p Is Zero

The shift right from LM_0 to LM_1 is the same as in Figure 4–5 and the top frame of Figure 5–1. But now a reduction in the interest rate, required to achieve equilibrium in the money market, does nothing to stimulate more expenditures. Autonomous planned spending (A_p) is independent of the interest rate, as indicated by the vertical IS_1 schedule. Thus the lower interest rate does not raise A_p or Q. Notice that the interest rate must fall more here than in top frame of Figure 5–1. Why?

counts into money (cash and checking accounts). The movement from E_0 to E_3 is exactly the same as from E_0 to V' in the top frame of Figure 5-1. The difference is that in Figure 5-1 the lower interest rate stimulates planned expenditures, so that V' is not a position of commodity market equilibrium, and production is increased. But here in Figure 5-2, since planned expenditures are not stimulated by the lower interest rate at E_3, there is no change in planned expenditures, and no change in production or income.

Thus, even if the Federal Reserve wants to raise the level of income above $1400 billion to Q^*, $1600 billion, it is powerless to do so in the situation of Figure 5-2, with a zero interest response of planned expenditures. This does *not* mean that the fiscal branch of government is powerless to raise output, however. It can increase Q either by raising $\bar{A}$ with higher government purchases or lower autonomous tax revenues, or it can lower income tax rates, increasing the multiplier. Only monetary expansion is rendered impotent, not fiscal policy.[4]

THE LIQUIDITY TRAP

Even with the normal, negatively sloped *IS* curve, the Federal Reserve may be unable to push real income as high as natural output. This case of monetary impotence may occur if there is a lower limit to the interest rate. The Fed does not control the interest rate directly; it influences only the supply of money. An increase in the money supply usually reduces the interest rate, because individuals try to get rid of their excess holdings of money by buying stocks and bonds, which drives up stock and bond prices and drives down the interest rate.[5] But if this effect is to work, some individuals must be willing to buy stocks and bonds. If, on the other hand, *every* individual were convinced that stock and bond prices were so far above "normal" that they could not rise further, and could only fall, no individuals would hold or be willing to buy stocks or bonds. The Federal Reserve would be unable to push up stock and bond prices (or reduce the interest rate), no matter how much money it was willing to create.[6] People who believe stock and bond prices will go down are often called bears. As Keynes remarked, the minimum interest rate is reached when all investors have joined the "bear brigade."

The theory of the minimum interest rate requires for its validity both a constant "normal" interest rate and agreement among all individuals that the current interest rate is so far below normal that the holding of stocks and bonds can lead only to capital losses. Some writers have held that the **liquidity trap,** a phrase sometimes used to describe the minimum interest rate situation, is an essential part of Keynes' case for downgrading monetary policy and emphasizing fiscal policy. But, as we will see, the liquidity trap did not occur in the 1930s, Keynes never claimed that it did occur, and there is no reason why individuals would ever maintain

---

[4] An exception is discussed in Section 5-5, where it is shown that under certain circumstances changes in M^s/P engineered by the Federal Reserve can directly affect planned expenditures and shift the *IS* curve.

[5] Throughout we adopt the simplification of referring to the interest yield on bonds and the dividend yield on stocks as "the interest rate." To review the reasons for the inverse relationship between stock and bond prices and the interest rate, turn back to the boxed explanation in section 4-7.

[6] If individuals refuse to hold or buy bonds, who holds all the existing bonds? The logic of the situation requires that the Fed have bought up all the stocks and bonds, paying for them with money that individuals prefer to hold because it carries with it no risk of capital loss. Notice that this "speculative" motive for the holding of money cannot be valid if savings deposits exist, because they pay interest and thus are preferable to money, but at the same time they are free from the risk of capital loss. The theory of the speculative motive for money demand was developed by Keynes in the *General Theory* and is compared with postwar developments in the theory of money demand in Axel Leijonhufvud, *On Keynesian Economics and the Economics of Keynes* (New York: Oxford, 1968), pp. 354–86.

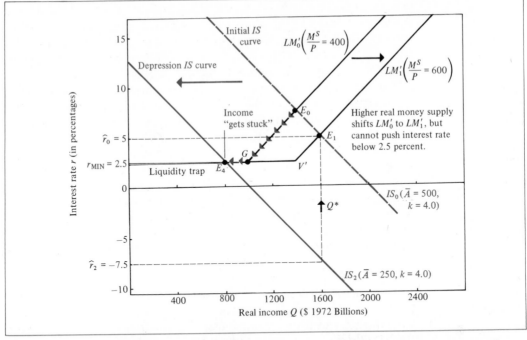

FIGURE 5–3

Effect of a $200 Billion Increase in the Real Money Supply When the Economy Is in a Liquidity Trap

Two elements are necessary. First, businessmen and consumers must be very pessimistic, so that the IS curve shifts far to the left. Second, the point at which the IS curve crosses Q^* ("target" or "natural" output) must fall at an interest rate ($\hat{r}$) below the minimum interest rate attainable along the LM curve (r_{min}). The economy "gets stuck" at point E_4, and no increase in the money supply, no matter how large, can get it unstuck.

a constant immutable view of the normal interest rate in the face of the massive economic changes that occur in a depression.

The liquidity trap illustrated in Figure 5-3 is an academic exercise, not a description of any real-world depression. The LM_0' curve is drawn for a fixed real money supply of $400 billion and is identical to the LM_0 curve of Figures 5-1 and 5-2 everywhere to the right of point G, where $Q = 1000$, but everywhere to the left LM_0' is a flat horizontal line, reflecting the assumption that the minimum interest rate is 2.5 percent. This minimum interest rate level occurs because individuals consider 2.5 too far below normal. It is marked off by the abbreviation r_{min} in the left margin.

Now let the real money supply grow to $600 billion, as before. The LM_1' curve is identical to LM_1 of Figure 5-2 everywhere to the right of

Weak Effects of Monetary Policy **117**

point V', where $Q = 1400$. But to the left of V', LM_1' is a flat horizontal line at the minimum interest rate of 2.5 percent. The consequences of the liquidity trap, the flat portion of the LM_0' and LM_1' schedules, depend entirely on the position of the IS curve. The IS_0 curve, drawn for a value of $\bar{A} = \$500$ billion, poses no problems. The Fed can raise real income from E_0 to E_1 just as in the top frame of Figure 5-1.

But consider another situation in which business and consumer optimism have collapsed, as in the Great Depression, and $\bar{A}$ has fallen from $\$500$ billion to $\$250$ billion. This $\$250$ billion decline in $\bar{A}$ causes the IS curve to move horizontally to the left by $\$1000$ billion.[7] The new depressed IS_2 curve intersects the initial LM_0' money-market curve at point E_4. Now notice that the Fed cannot end the depression. In fact, it cannot raise income by even one dollar. For instance, an increase in M^s/P from $\$400$ billion to $\$600$ billion cannot reduce the interest rate, which is already at its minimum value of $r_{min} = 2.5$ percent, so that there is nothing to stimulate added planned expenditures. Real income is "stuck" at point E_4 at $\$800$ billion, unless fiscal policy comes to the rescue.

GENERAL RULE FOR MONETARY IMPOTENCE

The situation in Figure 5-3 can be summarized. Let us define the interest rate where each IS curve intersects natural real output ($Q^* = \$1600$ billion), as $\hat{r}$. For instance, the initial "trouble-free" IS_0 curve intersects the $\$1600$ billion natural output level at point E_1 so that $\hat{r}_0$ for the IS_0 curve is 5 percent. Monetary policy has no problem pushing income up to its potential of $\$1600$ billion, because $\hat{r}_0$ is greater than r_{min}. There is plenty of room for an expanded money supply to push the economy from E_0 to E_1 without encountering the barrier of the minimum interest rate.

Along IS_2 in contrast, the interest rate $\hat{r}_2$ required to induce planned expenditures equal to natural output is *minus* 7.5 percent. Because monetary policy cannot push the interest rate below *plus* 2.5 percent, it is incapable of stimulating planned expenditures by enough to achieve natural output. The general rule that applies is:

> When $\hat{r}$ is greater than or equal to r_{min}, the monetary authority (the Fed) is capable of stimulating the economy by enough to return actual real income to the level of natural real income if IS is not vertical. But when $\hat{r}$ is less than r_{min} (as is true along IS_2), the monetary authority is incapable of stimulating the economy by enough unless it can find some way to raise $\hat{r}$ directly.

Notice that the general rule applies even if there is no liquidity trap. It is impossible for the interest rate to be negative. (Why? Banks would

---

[7] Why? Movement in a horizontal direction keeps the interest rate constant and moves IS by the multiplier ($k = 4.0$) times the $\$250$ billion decline in $\bar{A}$.

pay you interest to borrow money, so that you would instantly borrow infinity dollars.) Thus the lowest possible value of r_{min} is zero. In this case, the general rule says that monetary policy cannot achieve natural output (Q^*) if $\hat{r}$ is negative. Monetary policy can succeed only if it can operate directly on $\hat{r}$ and raise it above r_{min}.

Belief in the weakness of monetary policy reached its peak of popularity among economists in the 1940s and 1950s, summarized in the saying "You can take a horse to water but you can't make it drink." The Fed can create all the money it wants, but it can't force the economy to use it for consumption and investment purchases.

5-4 CASE STUDY: WAS THERE A LIQUIDITY TRAP DURING THE GREAT DEPRESSION?

In Figure 5-4 the interest rate is once again drawn on the vertical axis. Instead of plotting the real money supply by itself on the horizontal axis, we have plotted data for the real money supply divided by real income (M^s/PQ).[8] This technique makes a rough correction for the effect on money demand of changing real income, and it allows us to concentrate on the relationship between money demand (holding income constant) and the interest rate.

The annual data for (M^s/PQ) and for the interest rate on long-term government bonds have been plotted for each year between 1929 and 1940. A line connecting the 1929 and 1940 points has been added. The points for most of the years lie fairly close to the line, although between 1931 and 1934 they are too high, suggesting that in the darkest days of the Great Depression individuals were so pessimistic that they held more money, particularly in the form of cash, than would normally have been warranted at the prevailing interest rate.

But certainly the observations between 1935 and 1940 are consistent with the hypothesis that the demand for money depends inversely on the interest rate (compare the line in Figure 5-4 with the money demand schedules drawn in Figure 4-3). There is no sign at all that the interest rate hit a minimum level at any time during the latter half of the Great Depression. If the Fed had created more money, it is likely that the long-term interest rate would have fallen further and provided at least some additional stimulus to planned expenditures.

The verdict taken from these data did not surprise Keynes, who was not an apostle of the liquidity trap. As of the publication of his book in 1936, Keynes knew "no example of it hitherto," although he was willing to concede that the trap "might become important in the fu-

---

[8] M^s/PQ is the inverse of the velocity of money. See Section 4-6. The data refer to $M1$, which includes currency and checking accounts at commercial banks.

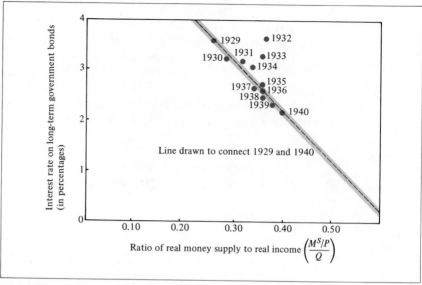

FIGURE 5–4

The Effect of a Higher Money Supply Relative to Income on the Long-Term Interest Rate, 1929–40

For a liquidity trap to have occurred during the Great Depression, we should find evidence that the Fed was unable to push down the interest rate by raising the money supply. Although the relationship between money and the interest rate does not fall along the pink line in every year, most of the years do fall quite close to the line except for 1932 and 1933, the worst years of economic collapse. This suggests that the liquidity trap did not occur during the Great Depression, so that monetary policy was not rendered impotent.

Source: M^s/PQ from Appendix B. Interest rate is Series B–73 in *Long Term Economic Growth 1860–1965* (U.S. Department of Commerce, 1966).

ture."[9] He recognized that the logical assumptions necessary for the liquidity trap were unlikely to occur, primarily because the "normal" expected interest rate was likely to drift downward in a continuing state of depression.[10] In fact, the long-term government bond rate drifted even lower in 1941, despite the increase in output connected

---

[9] J. M. Keynes, *The General Theory of Employment, Interest and Money* (London: Macmillan, 1936), p. 207.

[10] Leijonhufvud, *op. cit.,* pp. 202–03.

TABLE 5-1

Money, Output, and Unemployment in the Great Depression, 1929–40

Year	Real money supply ($ billions, 1972 prices)	Real output ($ billions, 1972 prices)	GNP gap (in percentages)	Unemployment rate (in percentages)
1929	81.1	314.7	−1.4	3.2
1930	81.0	285.2	10.5	8.9
1931	83.5	263.3	19.6	16.3
1932	82.1	226.8	32.6	24.1
1933	79.2	222.1	35.8	25.2
1934	80.1	239.4	32.6	22.0
1935	93.1	260.8	28.5	20.3
1936	105.8	296.1	21.0	17.0
1937	105.6	309.8	19.6	14.3
1938	106.7	297.1	24.9	19.1
1939	120.2	319.7	21.5	17.2
1940	136.2	343.6	17.8	14.6

Sources: See Appendix B.

with the beginning of World War II, suggesting that investors had substantially revised downward the interest rate they considered normal.

Although there does not appear to have been a liquidity trap during the 1930s, the beneficial effects of a higher real money supply were quite weak. As illustrated in Table 5-1, the real money supply was increased between 1929 and 1939 by 48 percent, and yet real output in the latter year was only 1.6 percent higher than in the former.[11] Because natural output had grown in the meantime, the GNP gap between actual and natural output grew from −1.4 to 21.5 percent and the unemployment rate from 3.2 percent to 17.2 percent. Output began to grow rapidly only in 1940, when the *IS* curve was shifted to the right by the beginning of government military purchases and by heavy exports of war supplies to the United Kingdom. All in all, most movements of output in the Great Depression appear to have reflected changes in planned expenditures ($\Delta \bar{A}$) rather than changes in the real money supply ($\Delta M^s / P$).

[11] The sources of the 1929–39 increase in the money supply are identified in the case study in section 16-5. For a recent statistical study which finds no evidence of a liquidity trap, see John L. Scadding, "An Annual Money Demand and Supply Model for the U.S.: 1924–1940/1949–1966," *Journal of Monetary Economics,* vol. 3 (January 1977), pp. 41–58. See also Karl Brunner and Alan Meltzer, "Liquidity Traps for Money, Bank Credit, and Interest Rates," *Journal of Political Economy,* vol. 76 (January/February 1968), pp. 1–35.

5-5 WEAK MONETARY EFFECTS: QUALIFICATIONS TO THE GENERAL RULE

The general rule in Section 5-3 states that monetary policy cannot by itself push the economy out of a recession or depression when $\hat{r}$, the interest rate at which the IS curve crosses the level of natural output, is below r_{min}. Even when there is no liquidity trap, and hence the minimum interest rate (r_{min}) is zero rather than a positive number, the Fed may be incapable of achieving higher output if $\hat{r}$ is negative, as when businessmen and consumers are very pessimistic. Businessmen may refuse to build new factories and buy new machines when their present ones are running at only half capacity, as in the Great Depression, or at only three-quarters capacity, as in some postwar recessions. Consumers may be less willing to assume more debt to buy automobiles, appliances, furniture, and vacations on the installment plan when they are worried that a layoff may prevent them from paying off present debts. When this kind of pessimism is pervasive, it may well take a negative interest rate to induce more spending by businessmen and consumers.

The negative value of $\hat{r}$ does not mean that the entire government is incapable of ending the depression or recession; it is just that the Fed by shifting the LM curve has no power. The fiscal policymakers (Congress and the President) are still able to raise $\bar{A}$ and hence shift the IS curve to the right as far as necessary to bring the economy back to its natural level of output (Q^*) and full employment. In Figure 5-3 the fiscal authority can raise $\bar{A}$ back to \$500 billion by raising government expenditures, autonomous taxes can be cut, or autonomous transfer payments can be raised. This action would shift the IS curve back rightward to IS_0 and at the same time raise $\hat{r}$ back to 5 percent, well above r_{min}. Another technique for shifting the IS curve to the right would be a cut in the income tax rate.

Another possibility is that the Fed can directly influence $\hat{r}$ without help from the fiscal branch of government. It can do so if planned autonomous expenditure depends not just on the interest rate, but also on the current value of real balances (the real money supply $-M^s/P$). In this case the IS curve shifts not only when $\bar{A}$ changes, as in Figure 4-2, but also whenever the Fed changes M^s/P. Why? Because an increase in the real money supply increases household wealth, which in turn induces households to purchase more consumption goods. Imagine two households, A and B, with exactly the same real income but with household A owning ten times as much money (cash and checking accounts) as household B. It is likely that household A would consume more than household B because its "cushion of cash" would free it from the need to save as much for a "rainy day" (unexpected calamities) as household B.

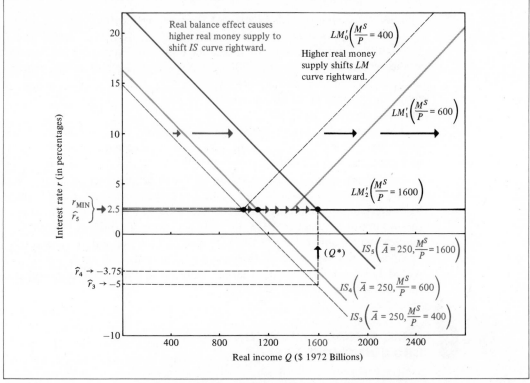

FIGURE 5–5

The Effect of an Increase in the Real Money Supply by $200 Billion and by $1200 Billion When Autonomous Planned Spending Depends Directly on the Real Money Supply

Until now the changes in the real money supply (M^s/P) have shifted only the LM curve, not the IS curve. But now we assume that each $100 billion increase in M^s/P raises auton-

omous planned spending by $12.5 billion, shifting the IS curve to the right by $50 billion (the multiplier is still 4.0). Thus a $200 billion increase in the real money supply shifts the IS curve right by $100 billion, from IS_3 to IS_4. It takes a massive increase in the real money supply, from $400 billion to $1600 billion, to return the economy to its desired $1600 billion income level. (What causes the problem in the first place? The low level of $\bar{A}$, only $250 billion.)

The addition of the real money supply to the list of determinants of the IS schedule (along with $\bar{A}$ and k) is usually called the **real balance effect** or the **Pigou effect,** after the British economist who first recognized its implications.[12] The real balance effect rescues monetary policy in situ-

---

[12] A. C. Pigou, "The Classical Stationary State," *Economic Journal,* vol. 53 (1943), pp. 353–51.

ations when $\hat{r}$ is less than r_{min} by giving the monetary authority a direct lever to control $\hat{r}$.

Figure 5-5 shares with Figure 5-3 the assumption that r_{min} is 2.5 percent, but it allows the monetary authority to shift the IS curve and $\hat{r}$ through the operation of the real balance effect. In Figure 5-3 an increase in the real money supply by $200 billion was incapable of raising real income by even $1.00. But now in Figure 5-5 the IS curve is governed by a new assumption: A $1.00 increase in the real money supply shifts the IS curve to the right by $.50.

The lesson of Figure 5-5 is simple. In principle, the real balance effect gives the monetary authority the power to achieve natural output (Q^*) and eliminate the GNP gap ($Q^* - Q$), but to do this a massive increase in the money supply may be required, much larger than anything ever attempted. Table 5-1 shows, for instance, that during the Great Depression the real money supply had been raised by 1940 by 68 percent above the minimum reached in 1933, but this achievement did not prevent unemployment from staying at the high rate of 14.6 percent. To reach true prosperity in 1940, with an unemployment rate as low as that of 1929, would have required a much larger increase in the real money supply than actually occurred.[13]

5-6 PURE FISCAL EXPANSION AND THE CROWDING-OUT EFFECT

We have so far examined **pure monetary policy shifts,** those which hold fiscal variables constant. Now we turn from pure monetary to pure fiscal policy. Because our purpose is to study the effects of monetary and fiscal policy separately, our subject here is **pure fiscal policy shifts,** that is, changes in government spending or taxes while the money supply is held constant. Once we understand pure monetary and fiscal operations separately, we can easily carry out combined monetary-fiscal changes.

Under what circumstances are the effects of a pure fiscal stimulus strong or weak? The normal situation is depicted in Figure 5-6, where we begin at the original equilibrium point E_0, the crossing point of the LM_0 and IS_0 curves. A $100 billion increase in government purchases (ΔG) raises $\bar{A}$ by the same amount and shifts the IS curve to the right by $400 billion, from the old IS_0 schedule drawn for $\bar{A} = \$500$ billion to the new IS_1 schedule drawn for $\bar{A} = \$600$ billion. The details of the rightward IS shift were described in Figure 4-2, which shows why the $100 billion increase in $\bar{A}$ causes real income to rise by $400 billion (the $100 billion of ΔG times the full multiplier, $k = 4.0$).

---

[13] By 1947, after World War II, full employment had returned and the real money supply in 1972 prices was $224.9 billion, an increase of 177 percent above 1929.

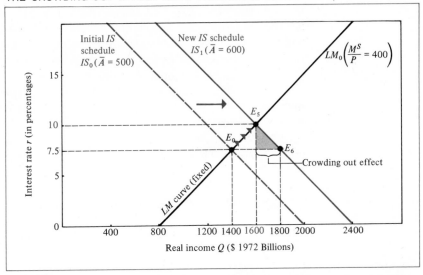

FIGURE 5-6

The Effect on the Interest Rate and Real Income of a $100 Billion Increase in Government Spending

Along the original IS_0 schedule autonomous spending desired at a zero interest rate $(\bar{A})$ is 500, and the economy's equilibrium occurs at point E_0, the crossing point of the IS_0 line and the fixed LM_0 line. A $100 billion increase in government spending boosts $\bar{A}$ from 500 to 600, and shifts the IS curve rightward to IS_1. The economy's equilibrium slides up the LM curve from point E_0 to point E_5. In contrast to Chapter 3's multiplier of 4.0, now the government spending multiplier is only 2.0 (the $200 billion increase in real income between E_0 and E_5 divided by the $100 billion boost in government spending which causes it).

But Figure 4-2 described the conditions necessary for equilibrium in the commodity market only. The money market was ignored. In Figure 5-6 we see that the fiscal policy multiplier is reduced when the money market is taken into consideration. The full fiscal multiplier of $k = 4.0$ would move the economy horizontally from the initial equilibrium position at E_0 to point E_6, where income is $400 billion higher. But at E_6 the money market is not in equilibrium. Income is higher than at E_0, raising the transaction demand for money, but the money supply remains unchanged, so that there is an excess demand for money. To cut the demand for money back to the level of the fixed supply, the interest rate must rise. But an increase in the interest rate makes point E_6 untenable by reducing planned consumption and investment expenditures. Only at point E_5 are both the commodity and money markets in equilibrium. Real income does not increase by the fully multiplied $400 billion, but only by half as much, $200 billion.

There is another way to describe the reason for the increase in the interest rate. The $100 billion increase in government spending is financed by sales of government bonds to the public. If the public was willing to hold the preexisting government debt at the original interest rate (7.5 percent), an increase in the interest rate is now necessary to "bribe" the public voluntarily to purchase the new government bonds.

The higher interest rate accounts for the reduction in the fiscal policy multiplier from 4.0 to 2.0. The increase in the interest rate from 7.5 to 10 percent cut private autonomous planned consumption and investment spending by $50 billion, fully half of the $100 billion increase in government spending. Thus fully half of the original multiplier of 4.0 is "crowded out."

COMPARISON OF EQUILIBRIUM POSITIONS E_0 AND E_5

	Initial E_0	New E_5
Interest rate (r)	7.5	10.0
Private autonomous spending $(I_p + a = 500 - 20r)$	350	300
Government spending (G)	0	100
Total autonomous spending $(A_p = I_p + a + G)$	350	400
Income $(Q = 4.0A_p)$	1400	1600

Some economists and journalists have begun to use the phrase **crowding-out effect** to compare points such as E_0 and E_5 in Figure 5-6. If the interest rate were to remain constant, the higher government spending would shift real income from $1400 billion at point E_0 to $1800 billion at point E_6. But the interest rate cannot stay fixed so long as the unchanged $400 billion real money supply pins the economy to the LM_0 curve and leads to an equilibrium position with a $1600 billion level of real income at point E_5. The difference, the $200 billion difference in real income between points E_6 and E_5, represents the investment and consumption spending "crowded out" by the higher interest rate. In Figure 5-6 notice the gray triangle beneath E_5. The base of the triangle shows the amount of income crowded out by the increased interest rate measured by the height of the gray triangle.

Point E_6, used in calculating the size of the **crowding-out effect**, is a purely hypothetical position that the economy cannot and does not reach. Actually, far from being crowded out, total private spending is higher in the new equilibrium situation at E_5 than at the original situation at E_0— real income has increased by $200 billion, of which only $100 billion represents higher government purchases, leaving the remaining $100 billion for extra private expenditures. The composition of private spending changes, however, as a result of the higher interest rate. Induced consumption spending increases, but autonomous spending decreases. Expenditures are divided up as follows in the two situations:

	At E_0	At E_5
Government purchases	0	100
Autonomous private spending $(I_p + a)$	350	300
Induced consumption	1050	1200
Total real expenditures	1400	1600

Summary: Higher government spending raises real output, but not by as much as implied by the simple multiplier of Chapter 3. The steeper the *LM* curve, the more powerful the crowding-out effect, and the smaller the fiscal policy multiplier.

5-7 CASE STUDY: INTEREST RATES AND THE EXPANSION OF VIETNAM SPENDING

The 1965–67 period, during which U.S. government spending was expanding rapidly as our involvement in the Vietnam War deepened, provides an unusual case study of the consequences of fiscal expansion while the real money supply remains fixed. In the fourth quarter of 1966 (October through December), which we write as 1966:Q4, the real money supply was almost exactly the same as five quarters earlier, in 1965:Q3. A *LM* curve corresponding to this fixed level of M^s/P is drawn in Figure 5-7 and is labeled LM_0. During this five-quarter interval the level of real government purchases grew by 12.9 percent, represented in Figure 5-7 by the rightward shift in the *IS* curve from IS_0 to IS_1.

How did real income and the interest rate behave over the five-quarter interval? Real income increased by $60.4 billion, more than the $27.3 billion increase in government spending, because of the multiplier effect.[14] And the higher transaction demand for money forced an increase in the interest rate from 4.2 to 4.7 percent to keep the total demand for money equal to the fixed real money supply.

The real world is always a bit more complicated than our simple *IS-LM* model. Here the *IS-LM* model ignores the delay between the increase in the interest rate and subsequent decline in investment. As shown in the data in the table accompanying Figure 5-7, the higher interest rate did not cut investment immediately. In fact, in 1966:Q4 investment was higher than in the original situation in 1965:Q3. But

---

[14] The real-world multiplier is slightly larger than the 2.0 multiplier assumed in the hypothetical example of Figure 5-6.

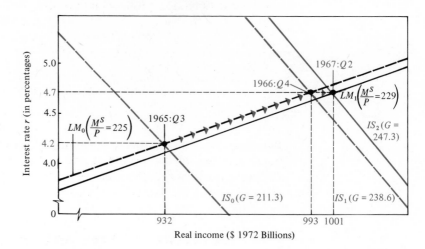

FIGURE 5–7

Real Income and the Interest Rate During a Period of Expanding Government Expenditures, 1965:Q3 to 1967:Q2

In both 1965:Q3 and 1966:Q4 the economy was on the same *LM* curve because the real money supply was identical in both periods. But govern-

ment spending was much higher in the second period, so that the *IS* curve was much farther to the right. One consequence of the rightward shift of the *IS* curve was to raise the interest rate in order to release extra money to support the higher level of transactions in 1966:Q4. In early 1967 the real money supply began to rise again.

	Real income	Real government expenditures	Real gross investment	Real money supply	Interest rate, (long-term government bonds, in percentages)
1965:Q3	932.3	211.3	152.5	224.9	4.20
1966:Q4	992.7	238.6	160.2	225.4	4.70
1967:Q2	1001.3	247.3	147.1	228.7	4.71

Note: All Real Magnitudes in 1972 Prices.
Source: Supplement to the *Survey of Current Business; Business Statistics: 1975 Biennial Edition.*

then over the next two quarters the delayed effect of the higher interest rate caused a decline in gross investment of $13.1 billion. Without the massive increase in government spending, there is little doubt that the level of investment would have been higher in 1967:Q2 than the actual figure; in this sense the crowding-out effect was in operation.

Notice that no further increase in the interest rate resulted from the $8.7 billion increase in government spending in the interval 1966:Q4 to 1967:Q2. Why? The real money supply was allowed to grow, providing room for the transaction demand for money to grow without any need for an increase in the interest rate.[15]

5-8 STRONG AND WEAK EFFECTS OF FISCAL POLICY

The effect of a fiscal policy stimulus on real income may be either greater or less than in our numerical example of Figure 5-6, depending on the assumed values of the multiplier and the interest responsiveness of money demand and of autonomous private spending. Fiscal policy is strong when demand for money is highly interest responsive, as illustrated in the top frame of Figure 5-8, where we choose the largest possible responsiveness, infinity. This makes the *LM* curve horizontal, so that the multiplier becomes just the simple multiplier (4.0) of Chapter 3. Just as in Chapter 3 we ignored the effect of a changing interest rate, we can ignore the interest-rate effect in exactly the same way here so long as the interest responsiveness of money demand is infinity, because this means that the interest rate is fixed.

The opposite situation occurs when the interest responsiveness of money demand is zero, which makes the *LM* curve vertical (compare with the bottom frame of Figure 5-1). An increase in government spending by $100 billion shifts the *IS* curve to the right in the bottom frame of Figure 5-8 exactly as in the top frame, but real income cannot increase without throwing the money market out of equilibrium. Even $1.00 of extra income above $1400 billion raises money demand, but because of the zero interest responsiveness of money demand, there is no increase in the interest rate that can bring money demand back into balance with the fixed money supply. In this case, the only effect of a fiscal stimulus is to raise the interest rate. The crowding-out effect is complete, with the higher interest rate cutting autonomous private spending by exactly the amount by which government spending increases, so that the net effect on income of the higher government spending is zero.

In recent years, the possibility of a vertical *LM* curve has received considerable attention as a result of the claim by some monetarists that the stimulative effect of fiscal policy on real output is negligible or even

---

[15] The curious reader will notice that real GNP grew between 1966:Q4 and 1967:Q2 by a modest amount, $8.6 billion, despite the fact that the sum of government spending and gross investment did not grow at all. This growth suggests that autonomous planned consumption, or the marginal propensity to consume, must have grown during the interval, perhaps partly induced by the higher real money supply through the real balance effect and perhaps partly reflecting an increase in consumer optimism.

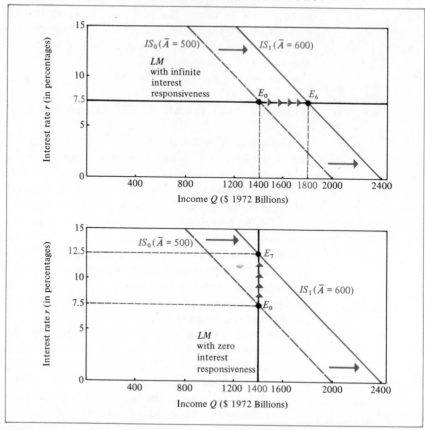

FIGURE 5-8

Effect of a $100 Billion Fiscal Stimulus When Money Demand Has an Infinite Interest Responsiveness and When Money Demand Has Zero Interest Responsiveness

In the top frame an increase in government spending has exactly the same effect as in Figure 3–6, with the full multiplier effect of 4.0. An infinite interest responsiveness means only that the interest rate is fixed, and no crowding out can occur. In contrast, the same fiscal stimulus has no effect on income when the interest responsiveness is zero (bottom frame), because then a higher interest rate releases no extra money to support higher income, and the income level is completely determined by the size of the real money supply.

zero.[16] All recent statistical studies are unanimous in concluding that the interest responsiveness is not even close to zero.[17] As will be seen in the next chapter, fiscal effects could be weak despite a positively sloped *LM* curve if the fiscal stimulus raises the price level and causes the real money supply to shrink, shifting the *LM* curve to the left. Thus the demonstration that the *LM* curve is positively sloped is not by itself a logical proof that fiscal policy can raise real income.[18]

5-9 FISCAL EXPANSION WITH AN ACCOMMODATING MONEY SUPPLY

We have been considering the effects of a pure fiscal expansion that involves no change in the money supply. Because both the money supply and the price level have been held fixed, the various *LM* curves in Figures 5-6 and 5-8 have remained stationary as the *IS* curve has shifted rightward. But there may be a possibility of interaction between fiscal and monetary expansion. If the sole policy goal of the monetary authority is to hold the interest rate constant, then the fiscal branch of government automatically gains indirect control of the money supply. Any type of fiscal expansion, whether an increase in government expenditures or a cut in tax rates, will lead to monetary accommodation—the monetary authority increases the money supply to prevent an increase in the interest rate.

Figure 5-9 illustrates again the same rightward shift in the *IS* curve caused by a $100 billion increase in real government purchases. Previously, however, the real money supply was kept constant and as a result the interest rate was forced to rise to keep the demand for money equal to the fixed supply. If the goal of the monetary authority is not to keep the money supply fixed but to keep the interest rate fixed, the money

---

[16] One source of this assertion is the empirical result obtained in L. C. Andersen and J. L. Jordan, "Monetary and Fiscal Actions: A Test of Their Relative Importance in Economic Stabilization," *Review—Federal Reserve Bank of St. Louis* (November 1968), pp. 11–23, that the fiscal effect vanishes after four quarters. For a summary of the debate on this issue, and some different results, see Robert J. Gordon, "Perspectives on Monetarism," in Jerome L. Stein (ed.), *Monetarism: Studies in Monetary Economics* (Amsterdam: North-Holland, 1976), and other papers in the same volume. The best analysis of the methodological defects of the Andersen-Jordan approach is Stephen M. Goldfeld and Alan S. Blinder, "Some Implications of Endogenous Stabilization Policy," *Brookings Paper on Economic Activity,* vol. 3 (1972, No. 3), pp. 585–640.

[17] See, for instance, Stephen Goldfeld, "The Demand for Money Revisited," *Brookings Papers on Economic Activity,* vol. 4, no. 3 (1973), pp. 577–646.

[18] On this issue, see the exchange between James Tobin and Milton Friedman in Robert J. Gordon (ed.), *Milton Friedman's Monetary Framework: A Debate with His Critics* (Chicago: University of Chicago Press, 1974). Because of the possibility of changing prices the Tobin quote that begins this chapter is not strictly valid.

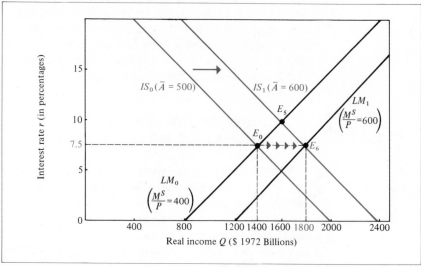

FIGURE 5–9

Effect on Real Income of a $100
Billion Fiscal Stimulus When the
Monetary Authority (the Fed)
Acts to Keep the Interest Rate
Constant

If the money supply were to remain
constant in the face of the $100 billion
fiscal stimulus, the economy would
move from E_0 to E_5, just as in Figure

5–6. Now, however, the monetary
authority (the Fed) attempts to keep
the interest rate constant. The money
supply must be increased by exactly
enough to support the higher level of
income. Because $1.00 of extra money
is needed for each $2.00 of extra in-
come, the money supply must be
raised $200 billion to allow income to
grow $400 billion in response to the
fiscal stimulus.

supply must be allowed to change automatically whenever there is a
shift in the *IS* curve.

The result of any fiscal change when the monetary authority acts to
stabilize the interest rate is exactly the same as the result of the same
fiscal change when the interest responsiveness equals infinity. No increase in the interest rate occurs, and the economy's equilibrium moves
directly to the right from point E_0 to point E_6. The multiplier for the fiscal
change is the simple multiplier of Chapter 3, $k = 4.0$.

It was not clearly recognized by all economists in the mid-1960s that
the full fiscal policy multipliers of Chapter 3 required the tacit cooperation or accommodation of the monetary authority. If the Fed refuses to
allow the money supply to be influenced by the position of the *IS* curve,
and instead holds the money supply constant, the fiscal policy multipliers
(as in Figure 5-6) are smaller than if the monetary authority accommo-

dates the fiscal change by holding the interest rate constant (as in Figure 5-9). Policymakers were surprised by the relatively small effect on spending of the temporary income tax increase of 1968 because they had judged the effect of the 1964 tax cut to be quite substantial. But the tax cut in 1964 was accompanied by an accommodating monetary policy that held the interest rate constant between late 1963 and mid-1965, whereas in the 1968 tax surcharge case the Fed counteracted the fiscal change, moving the *LM* curve opposite to the *IS* curve instead of in the same direction.[19]

Summary: An accommodating monetary policy eliminates the crowding-out effect and leads once again to the simple fiscal-policy multiplier of Chapter 3.

5-10 THE MONETARY-FISCAL POLICY MIX

Throughout this chapter, we have taken the starting point to be an unsatisfactorily low level of real output, $1400 billion instead of the desired natural output (Q^*) level of $1600 billion. Two methods of reaching $1600 billion have been examined, a pure expansion of the money supply to point E_1 in the top frame of Figure 5-1 and a pure fiscal expansion to point E_5 in Figure 5-6. Does the choice between these two alternatives for the monetary-fiscal mix make any difference?

Figure 5-10 compares points E_1 and E_5. In both cases, the total level of real income is identical and equal to Q^*, $1600 billion. We can assume that the total level of employment and unemployment would also be identical. What are the differences? Point E_5 has a lower money supply and, in order to keep money demand equal to money supply, also has a higher interest rate. This can be described as the "tight money, easy fiscal" position. Point E_1, on the other hand, is the "easy money, tight fiscal" position, with a higher money supply and a lower interest rate to stimulate a demand for money equal to the supply. The higher interest rate at point E_5 cuts planned private autonomous spending, both investment and consumption, below that at point E_1, to make room for the government spending. Induced consumption is the same at both E_1 and E_5.

Which position, E_1 or E_5, should society prefer? At point E_1 investment is higher, and thus the economy's rate of natural output growth is likely to be higher.[20] This growth does not benefit us today, but will help us in future years and future generations as well. At point E_5, government

---

[19] These two episodes are considered in more detail in the case studies of Sections 13-6 and 16-6. In 1969 the Fed reversed itself and allowed M/P to decline.

[20] We return to this point and examine some evidence in Section 18-8.

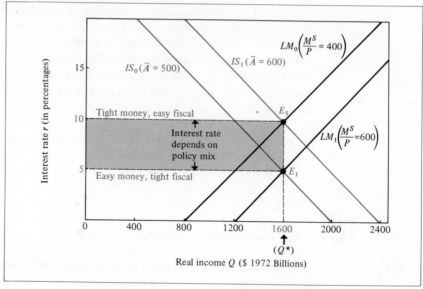

FIGURE 5–10

Two Alternative Methods of Achieving the Natural Level of Output ($Q^* = \$1600$ Billion)

The IS_0, IS_1, LM_0, and LM_1 schedules are the same as we have encountered earlier in this chapter. The combination at E_1 achieves target income with a low interest rate by avoiding a government deficit. At E_5 the same income level requires a higher interest rate because the government deficit requires sales of bonds to households and a higher interest rate to "bribe" them to buy the bonds. The table shows that E_5 can be achieved either by raising government spending (line 2) or by raising consumption expenditures through higher government transfer payments (a reduction in net autonomous taxation).

Line	Position	Real money supply	Real money demand	Real income	Real government spending	Real investment	Real autonomous consumption	Induced consumption
1.	E_1	600	600	1600	0	300	100	1200
2.	$\}E_5\{$	400	400	1600	100	225	75	1200
3.		400	400	1600	0	225	175	1200

spending is higher than at point E_1. The government purchases may be currently consumed government services (national defense, police and fire protection, education, or health) or government investment (school buildings, hospitals). Should society prefer the faster output growth of point E_1 to the higher level of public services of point E_5? This is a difficult problem to which we will return (Chapters 14 and 18). Its solution depends partly on society's preference for public versus private goods and partly on its taste for present goods and services versus those obtained in the future.

The fiscal stimulus that takes the economy to the tight money, easy fiscal point E_5 is assumed in line 2 of the table accompanying Figure 5-10 to take the form of $100 billion of government purchases. But we learned in section 3-7 that a $133 billion cut in autonomous tax revenue, or a $133 billion increase in autonomous government transfer payments, has exactly the same effect on autonomous planned spending ($\bar{A}$) as a $100 billion increase in government purchases. Line 3 of the table gives the consequences of achieving point E_5 by means of a $133 billion transfer payment, such as Social Security payments, instead of by $100 billion in government purchases.[21] The interest rate and money demand are identical at point E_5 whether achieved by higher government purchases or by transfer payments. The difference is that under the transfer payment scheme, $100 billion is spent on private consumption purchases rather than on government purchases. The debate between fiscal stimulus in the form of government spending or transfer increases has been going on for a long time, at least since the 1958 publication of J. K. Galbraith's *Affluent Society*, and is mainly political, not economic.[22]

SUMMARY

1. In most cases, an increase in the real money supply not only reduces the interest rate but also causes an increase in real income. That increase is large for *small* values of the interest- and income-responsiveness of money demand and a *large* value of the multiplier (k), and of the interest responsiveness of planned private spending.

2. The monetary authority (Federal Reserve or Fed) can increase real income by raising the money supply if the price level is fixed, the *IS* curve is negatively sloped, and the *LM* curve is positively sloped or vertical. Two situations in which the Fed cannot raise the level of actual real income are (1) if planned expenditures do not respond to the interest rate (a vertical *IS* curve) and (2) if the economy is operating in a liquidity trap.

3. When $\hat{r}$ (the interest rate where the *IS* curve intersects natural output) is greater than or equal to r_{min} (the lower limit to the interest rate), the Fed is capable of stimulating the economy by enough to return actual real income to the level of natural real income. But when $\hat{r}$ is less than

---

[21] Why does the lump sum transfer payment have to increase by $133 billion to raise $\bar{A}$ by $100 billion? The $133 billion transfer raises autonomous consumption spending by $100 billion [$c\Delta T = 0.75(133) = 100$]. **Review:** Section 3-7.

[22] Galbraith argued that a basic weakness of the United States was "private affluence and public squalor," too much spending on personal automobiles and dishwashers with too little spending on public parks, schools, and other government programs.

$r_{\min}$, the Fed is incapable of stimulating the economy by enough unless it can find some way to directly raise $\hat{r}$.

4. In the latter case, monetary stimulation succeeds only if planned autonomous expenditure depends not just on the interest rate but also on the current value of real money balances. This real balance effect rescues monetary policy in situations where $r_{\min}$ exceeds $\hat{r}$, because the monetary authority can now shift the IS curve by altering the real money supply.

5. Large fiscal policy multipliers are associated with small values of the interest responsiveness of spending and the income responsiveness of money demand and with large values of the multiplier and of the interest responsiveness of money demand. At one extreme, when the LM curve is horizontal, the fiscal multiplier becomes the simple multiplier of Chapter 3. At the other extreme, when the LM curve is vertical, the fiscal multiplier is zero and the crowding-out effect is complete; the higher interest rate cuts private planned spending by exactly the same amount as the increase in government spending.

6. The size of the fiscal policy multipliers depends on whether the monetary authority holds the money supply constant or accommodates the fiscal changes by holding the interest rate constant. In the first instance, the crowding-out effect can occur, but in the latter instance, output is raised by the full multiplier effect.

7. The composition of total expenditures depends on the mix of monetary and fiscal policy. The tight money, easy fiscal policy combination has a low money supply and a high government deficit and the easy money, tight fiscal combination has the reverse. The interest rate is lower in the second combination, and investment is stimulated by the lower interest rate raising the economy's rate of natural output growth. In the first combination, government spending or private consumption purchases crowd out investment, cutting the growth of natural output. The choice between the two policy combinations depends on the relative attractiveness of investment, consumption, and government spending.

A LOOK AHEAD

In the last three chapters the price level has been assumed to be fixed. Several determinants of the level of real output, and hence employment and unemployment, have been identified—business and consumer confidence, government spending and taxation, and the money supply. But as yet we have not begun to deal with inflation. Nor can we answer a critic who claims "government policy is not necessary, because the economy can get itself out of a recession without help through the stimulating effects on aggregate demand of a declining price level."

Now we switch hats and examine the consequences for the price level of changes in the demand for commodities, assuming that the price level adjusts to keep real output constant. We will find that under some conditions, but not others, the private economy can maintain target output through price flexibility without help from the government. Only in Chapter 7 will we be ready to wear both hats at once and to allow the price level and real output to change simultaneously.

CONCEPTS AND QUESTIONS

IDENTIFICATIONS

Interest responsiveness of demand for money

Interest responsiveness of planned expenditures

Liquidity trap

$\hat{r}$ and $r_{\min}$

The "normal" interest rate

Real balance effect

Pigou effect

Crowding-out effect

Monetary accommodation

Monetary-fiscal policy mix

QUESTIONS FOR REVIEW

Are the following statements true, false, or uncertain? Be sure you can give a clear explanation of your answer.

1   The size of the increase in real income resulting from a given increase in the real money supply depends only on the slope of the *LM* curve.

2   An increase in government expenditures results in an increase in the equilibrium level of real income and of the interest rate.

3   A fiscal multiplier of the simple form of Chapter 3 requires that the economy must be operating in a liquidity trap.

4   Crowding out refers to the decline in total private spending that occurs when government expenditure is increased.

5   Monetary policy is impotent when the *LM* schedule is a horizontal line.

6   If $\hat{r}$ is below $r_{\min}$, the monetary authority is incapable of stimulating the economy back to the level of real potential output.

7   An increase in the real money supply results in a lower equilibrium level of real income and a lower rate of interest.

APPENDIX TO CHAPTER 5
The Elementary Algebra of Equilibrium Income

When you see an *IS* curve crossing a *LM* curve, as in Figure 4-6 and in all of Chapter 5, you know that the equilibrium level of income (Q) and the interest rate (r) occurs at the point of crossing, as at point E_0 in

Figure 4-6 or 5-1. But how can the equilibrium level of income and the interest rate be calculated without going to the trouble of making careful drawings of the *IS* and *LM* curves? Wherever you see two lines crossing to determine the values of two variables, such as Q and r, exactly the same solution can be obtained by solving together the two equations describing the two lines.

In Chapter 3 we found that equilibrium income was equal to autonomous planned spending (A_p) divided by the saving rate (s), so that the multiplier (k) was $1/s$. Then in the appendix to Chapter 3, we found that more generally the multiplier (k) is equal to 1.0 divided by whatever fraction of income leaks out of the spending stream into saving, the government's income tax revenue, and imports. Once we have determined Chapter 3's multiplier (k), income can be written simply as:

GENERAL FORM   NUMERICAL EXAMPLE

$$Q = kA_p \qquad\qquad Q = 4.0A_p \tag{1}$$

At the beginning of Chapter 4 (Figures 4-1 and 4-2), we introduced the assumption that autonomous planned spending (A_p) declines when there is an increase in the interest rate (r). If the amount of A_p at a zero interest rate is written as $\bar{A}$, then the value of A_p can be written:

GENERAL FORM   NUMERICAL EXAMPLE

$$A_p = \bar{A} - br \qquad\qquad A_p = \bar{A} - 20r \tag{2}$$

where b is the interest responsiveness of A_p, in our example \$20 billion of decline in A_p per one percentage point increase in the interest rate. Substituting (2) into (1), we obtain the equation for the *IS* schedule:

GENERAL FORM   NUMERICAL EXAMPLE

$$Q = k(\bar{A} - br) \qquad\qquad Q = 4.0\bar{A} - 80r \tag{3}$$

Thus if $\bar{A}$ is 500 and $r = 0$, the IS_0 curve intersects the horizontal axis at 2000, as in Chapters 4 and 5.

The *LM* curve shows all combinations of income (Q) and the interest rate (r) where the real money supply (M^s/P) equals the real demand for money $(M/P)^d$, which in turn depends on Q and r. This situation of equilibrium in the money market was previously written as equation 4.1 in the text:

GENERAL FORM   NUMERICAL EXAMPLE

$$\left(\frac{M^s}{P}\right) = \left(\frac{M}{P}\right)^d = eQ - fr \qquad\qquad \left(\frac{M^s}{P}\right) = 0.5Q - 40r \tag{4}$$

where e is the responsiveness of real money demand to higher real income, 0.5 in our example, and f is the interest responsiveness of real money demand, in the example a \$40 billion decline in real money demand per one percentage point increase in the interest rate. Adding fr (or $40r$) to both sides of (4), and then dividing by e (or 0.5), we obtain the equation for the *LM* schedule:

$$Q = \frac{\dfrac{M^s}{P} + fr}{e} \qquad\qquad Q = \frac{400 + 40r}{0.5}. \qquad\qquad (5)$$

We are assured that the commodity market is in equilibrium whenever Q is related to r by equation (3) and that the money market is in equilibrium whenever Q is related to r by equation (5). To make sure that both markets are in equilibrium, both equations must be satisfied at once.

Equations (3) and (5) together constitute an **economic model.** Finding the value of two unknown variables in economics is very much like baking a cake. One starts with a list of ingredients, the **parameters,** or knowns, of the model: $\bar{A}$, M^s/P, b, e, f, and k. Then one stirs the ingredients together using the "instructions of the recipe," in this case equations (3) and (5). The outcome is the value of the unknown variables, Q and r. The main rule in economic cake-baking is that the number of equations, the instructions of the recipe, must be equal to the number of unknowns to be determined. In this example there are two equations and two unknowns (Q and r). There is no limit on the number of ingredients known in advance, the parameters. Here we have six parameters, but we could have seven, ten, or any number.

To convert the two equations of the model into one equation specifying the value of unknown Q in terms of the six known parameters, we simply substitute (5) into (3). To do this, we rearrange (5) to place the interest rate on the left side of the equation, and then we substitute the resulting expression for r in (3). First, rearrange (5) to move r to the left side:[1]

$$r = \frac{eQ - \dfrac{M^s}{P}}{f} \qquad\qquad (5a)$$

Second, substitute the right side of (5a) for r in (3):

------

[1] First multiply both sides of (5) by e:

$$eQ = \frac{M^s}{P} + fr$$

Then subtract M^s/P from both sides:

$$eQ - \frac{M^s}{P} = fr$$

Now divide both sides by f:

$$\frac{eQ - \dfrac{M^s}{P}}{f} = r$$

Equation (5a) is then obtained by reversing the two sides of this equation.

$$Q = k(\bar{A} - br) = k\left[\bar{A} - \frac{beQ}{f} + \frac{b}{f}\left(\frac{M^s}{P}\right)\right] \qquad (6)$$

Now (6) can be solved for Q by adding $kbeQ/f$ to both sides and dividing both sides by k:

$$Q\left(\frac{1}{k} + \frac{be}{f}\right) = \bar{A} + \frac{b}{f}\left(\frac{M^s}{P}\right)$$

Finally, both sides are divided by the left term in parentheses:

$$Q = \frac{\bar{A} + \frac{b}{f}\left(\frac{M^s}{P}\right)}{\frac{1}{k} + \frac{be}{f}} \qquad (7)$$

Equation (7) is our master general equilibrium income equation and combines all the information in the IS and LM curves together; when (7) is satisfied both the commodity market and money markets are in equilibrium. It can be used in any situation to calculate the level of real income by simply substituting into (7) the particular values of the six known right-hand parameters in order to calculate unknown income.[2] Because we are primarily interested in the effect on income of a change in $\bar{A}$ or M^s/P, we can simplify (7):

$$Q = k_1\bar{A} + k_2\left(\frac{M^s}{P}\right) \qquad (8)$$

All we have done in converting (7) into (8) is to give new names, k_1 and k_2, to the multiplier effects of $\bar{A}$ and M^s/P on income. The definitions and numerical values of k_1 and k_2 are:

GENERAL FORM   NUMERICAL EXAMPLE

$$k_1 = \frac{1}{\frac{1}{k} + \frac{be}{f}} \qquad\qquad \frac{1}{\frac{1}{4.0} + \frac{20(0.5)}{40}} = 2.0 \qquad (9)$$

$$k_2 = \frac{b/f}{\frac{1}{k} + \frac{be}{f}} = \left(\frac{b}{f}\right)k_1 \qquad\qquad \frac{20(2.0)}{40} = 1.0 \qquad (10)$$

Using the numerical values in (9) and (10), the simplified equation (8) can be used to calculate the value of real income illustrated by E_0 in Figure 4-6 and in several figures of Chapter 5.

---

[2] A parameter is taken as given or known within a given exercise. Parameters include not just the small letters denoting the multiplier (k), and the interest and income responsiveness of planned autonomous expenditures and money demand $(b, e,$ and $f)$, but also planned autonomous expenditures at a zero interest rate $(\bar{A})$ and the real money supply (M^s/P). Most exercises involve examining the effects of a change in a single parameter, as in $\bar{A}$ or in M^s/P.

$$Q = k_1\bar{A} + k_2\left(\frac{M^s}{P}\right) = 2.0(500) + 1.0(400) = 1400 \qquad (11)$$

With this equation it is extremely easy to calculate the new value of Q whenever there is a change in $\bar{A}$ caused by government fiscal policy, or by a change in business and consumer confidence, and whenever there is a change in M^s/P caused by a change in the nominal money supply.[3] Remember, however, that the definitions of k_1 and k_2 in (9) and (10) do depend on particular assumptions about the value of parameters $b, e, f,$ and k.

The main point of Chapter 5 is that changes in fiscal and monetary policy may have either strong or weak effects on income, depending on the answers to these questions.

1. How does the effect of a change in $\bar{A}$ on income, the multiplier k_1, depend on the values of b and f (the interest responsiveness of the demand for commodities and money)?
2. How does the effect of a change in M^s/P on income, the multiplier k_2, depend on the values of b and f?

You should work through Chapter 5 to see if you can derive each of the diagrammatic results by substituting the appropriate definition of k_1 and k_2 into the simplified general equilibrium equation (8).

Example: If we work through Figure 5-1, the value of k_1 is, using (9):

$$k_1 = \frac{1}{\dfrac{1}{k} + \dfrac{be}{f}} = \frac{1}{\left(\dfrac{1}{4}\right) + \left(\dfrac{20}{40}\right)(0.5)} = 2.0$$

The value of k_2 is, using (10):

$$k_2 = \frac{b}{f}k_1 = \left(\frac{20}{40}\right)(2.0) = 1.0$$

Thus income in the new situation at point E_1 in the top frame of Figure 5-1, using equation (8), is:

$$Q = k_1\bar{A} + k_2\left(\frac{M^s}{P}\right) = 2.0(500) + 1.0(600) = 1600$$

In the bottom frame, $f = 0$, and so:

---

[3] The equilibrium interest rate illustrated in Figure 4-6 can be calculated in the same way by substituting the numerical values into equation (5a):

$$r = \frac{0.5(1400) - 400}{40} = \frac{300}{40} = 7.5 \text{ percent}$$

$$k_1 = \frac{1}{\dfrac{1}{k} + \dfrac{be}{f}} = \frac{1}{\dfrac{1}{4} + \dfrac{20(0.5)}{0}} = 0$$

$$k_2 = \frac{b}{\dfrac{f}{k} + be} = \frac{20}{0(0.25) + 20(0.5)} = 2.0$$

Thus in the bottom frame of Figure 5-1, the new equilibrium situation at point E_2 is as follows when the real money supply rises from 700 along the left-hand LM line to 900 along the right-hand LM line.[4]

$$Q = k_1\bar{A} + k_2\left(\frac{M^s}{P}\right) = 0(500) + 2.0(900) = 1800$$

Exercise: Assume the following simple model with the price level fixed at 1.00.

$$IS \text{ curve:} \quad Q = k(\bar{A} - br)$$

$$LM \text{ curve:} \quad Q = \frac{\dfrac{M^s}{P} + fr}{e}$$

With the following parameter values:

$$\bar{A} = 600 \qquad \frac{M^s}{P} = 600$$

$$b = 20 \qquad f = 20$$

$$k = 5.0 \qquad e = 0.40$$

1. Plot the IS and the LM curves. What are the equilibrium values for Q and r? Why do these values of Q and r differ from those in Figure 4-6?
2. Now suppose $\bar{A}$ declines from 600 to 450. What are the new equilibrium values for Q and r? What kind of event might cause $\bar{A}$ to decline in this way?
3. Suppose that the Federal Reserve wanted to offset this decline in $\bar{A}$ by using monetary policy. To regain the initial income level, what is the required real money supply? What will be the new equilibrium interest rate?
4. Assuming the initial set of parameters, describe the situation at a point such as $Q = 1500$, $r = 8$. Which market or markets is out of equilibrium? Describe the adjustment to the equilibrium point.
5. Describe what happens when the Federal Reserve uses monetary policy to raise the equilibrium real income level back to its original value.

---

[4] These assumed numerical values for the real money supply were not used as labels for the bottom frame of Figure 5-1 to avoid complicating the exposition in the text.

6 Flexible Prices and the Self-Correcting Economy

It is, therefore, on the effect of a falling wage- and price-level on the demand for money that those who believe in the self-adjusting quality of the economic system must rest the weight of the argument.

—John Maynard Keynes[1]

6-1 INTRODUCTION

Today's aggregate price index or **deflator** is simply an economywide weighted average of the prices of goods today compared to the prices of the same goods in a base year, say 1967 or 1972. When the prices of most goods are rising, the aggregate deflator (P) increases and we have inflation, whereas **deflation** describes a situation in which the prices of most goods and hence the aggregate deflator are falling. During a period of aggregate price stability, like that achieved briefly from 1959 to 1964, the prices of some goods increase, some decrease, but the average of all prices (P) stays approximately steady.

Throughout Chapters 3, 4, and 5 all our analysis has held the price level fixed for simplicity. Now that we are ready to allow the price level to vary, we find that the basic tools developed so far retain their usefulness. When we allow the price level to be perfectly (instantly) flexible in this chapter, we find that shifts in monetary and fiscal policy that previously caused real income to vary now cause the price level to change in the same direction. Increases in government expenditure or reductions in tax rates shift the IS curve to the right, and this tends to raise the aggregate price level (P) rather than the level of real income (Q). Similarly, increases in the money supply raise P rather than Q when we allow for price variation.

During the first part of this chapter we assume that P is perfectly flexible and examine the conditions under which that flexibility automatically maintains a stable level of real output, making monetary and

---

[1] Keynes, *General Theory*, p. 266.

fiscal policy unnecessary. When can the governors of the Federal Reserve "go fishing," confident that any change in business and consumer confidence will be automatically counteracted by the economy's **self-correcting forces?** Can a shift in the price level maintain the stability of real output and employment? We will see now that a decline in the price level plays the same role as an increase in the money supply in Chapter 5 and that our general rule from Chapter 5 remains valid. Just as under the fixed price conditions of Chapter 5 an expansion in the nominal money supply can raise output whenever $\hat{r}$ equals or exceeds $r_{\min}$,

> *a decline in the price level can automatically push the economy back to its natural output level whenever prices are flexible and $\hat{r}$ equals or exceeds $r_{\min}$. In short, whenever monetary policy was weak in Chapter 5 under fixed prices, so too flexible prices in Chapter 6 are a weak stabilizing rudder incapable of automatically holding the economy on a steady course.*

In the previous chapters we artificially held P constant to examine the forces that can vary real income (Q). Through much of this chapter we do just the opposite, holding Q constant and examining the same forces that can vary P. Only in the next chapter will we be ready to enter fully into the real world in which Q and P can and do change together.

6-2 FLEXIBLE PRICES, THE REAL MONEY SUPPLY, AND THE *DD* CURVE

In this section we develop a new tool, the aggregate demand (DD) curve, which summarizes the stimulating effect of lower prices on the level of real output. It can be used to illustrate the operations of the economy's self-correcting forces which operate to stabilize the level of real output when prices are flexible.

The LM curve shifts its position whenever there is a change in the real money supply. Until now every LM shift has resulted from a change in the nominal money supply, while the price level has been held fixed at a constant level. The price level has been treated as a **parameter,** or a known variable, allowing us to concentrate on the determination of the two unknowns, real income (Q) and the interest rate (r).

There is no reason, however, why the LM curve could not shift in exactly the same way when a change in the real money supply M^s/P is caused by a change in the price level P, while the nominal money supply M^s remains fixed at a single value, say \$400 billion. The top frame of Figure 6-1 illustrates three LM curves drawn for three values of P and M^s/P, each assuming that $M^s = 400$. For instance, the middle curve LM_0 is identical to LM_0 in the previous chapter. The price index is 1.0, and

THE AGGREGATE DEMAND CURVE SHOWS THAT A DECLINE IN THE
PRICE LEVEL STIMULATES REAL OUTPUT, AND VICE VERSA

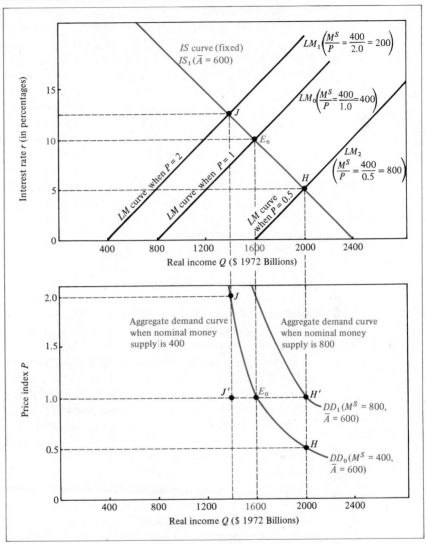

FIGURE 6-1

Effect on Real Income of Different Hypothetical Values of the Price Index and the Nominal Money Supply

In the top frame three different *LM* curves are drawn for three different hypothetical values of the price index. Corresponding to the three levels of the price index are three positions of equilibrium, *J*, E_0, and *H*. These three points are drawn again in the lower frame with the same horizontal axis (real output), but the price index for the vertical axis. A drop in the price index from point *J* to E_0 and then to *H* raises the *real* money supply and stimulates real output along the aggregate demand curve DD_0. When the *nominal* money supply is doubled from 400 to 800, the aggregate demand curve shifts rightward to DD_1.

because $M^s = 400$, M^s/P also equals 400. A doubling of the price level to $P = 2.0$ would cut the real money supply in half to $M^s/P = 400/2.0 = 200$. For the real demand for money to stay equal to the smaller real supply of money, some combination of lower real income and a higher interest rate is needed, as along the left-hand curve LM_1. Similarly, if the price level is very low, only 0.5, the real money supply is a large $M^s/P = 400/0.5 = 800$, and equilibrium in the money market occurs along the right-hand curve LM_2.

What is the level of real income if the nominal money supply remains fixed at $400 billion? The answer depends not only on which price level and LM curve is valid, but also on the position of the IS curve. Once again, we need two schedules to determine two unknowns (r and Q), just as a driver needs to know which two highways intersect in a city toward which he is driving. When $\bar{A} = 600$, the commodity market is in equilibrium anywhere along the IS_1 curve copied from Chapters 4 and 5. When $P = 1.0$ and the LM_0 curve describes money-market equilibrium, the economy's general equilibrium occurs at point E_0, where LM_0 crosses IS_1 and equilibrium real output (Q) is $1600 billion.[2]

To show the relationship between equilibrium Q and the assumed price index P, a new diagram is drawn in the bottom frame of Figure 6-1. The horizontal dimension once again is real output, and so point E_0 in the bottom frame lies just below E_0 in the upper frame. The vertical dimension in the lower bottom frame measures the price index P, and so E_0 is plotted at the assumed value $P = 1.0$.

Other values of real income occur if the assumed price level is higher or lower than 1.0. A price level of 2.0 cuts the real money supply in half, as shown along LM_1 in the top frame, and it reduces real output to $1400 billion at point J. Point J is plotted in the lower frame again at a vertical height $P = 2.0$. Similarly, a lower price index of $P = 0.5$ boosts the real money supply, shifts the LM curve to LM_2, and raises output to $2000 billion, as plotted at point H.

The curved line in the bottom frame connecting points J, E_0, and H shows all the possible combinations of P and Q consistent with a nominal money supply of $400 billion and a value of $\bar{A}$ of $600 billion.[3] If the assumed value of P is high, then Q is low, and vice versa. The curved line is called the **aggregate demand curve** and is abbreviated DD. The main characteristics of DD are:

1. The DD curve shows all the possible crossing points of a single IS commodity market equilibrium curve with the various LM money market equilibrium curves drawn for each possible price level. In

---

[2] E_0 is the same as E_5 in the last chapter. We now take the opportunity to renumber the equilibrium points.

[3] Recall that the definition of $\bar{A}$ is the level of autonomous planned real spending that would occur if the interest rate were zero.

contrast to the *IS* curve, along which only the commodity market is in equilibrium, and a single *LM* curve, along which only the money market is in equilibrium, everywhere along the *DD* curve both the commodity and money markets are in equilibrium.

2. The *DD* curve slopes downward because a lower price index (P) raises the real money supply and stimulates planned expenditures, requiring an increase in actual real output (Q) to keep the commodity market in equilibrium. The steeper the *IS* curve, the steeper the *DD* curve. The *DD* curve embodies what we call (section 6-6) the Keynes effect.

> **Exercise:** Try to determine whether a steeper *LM* curve would make the *DD* curve steeper or flatter without peeking at the footnote.[4]

3. Because it describes the economy's general equilibrium, the position of the *DD* curve depends on all the factors that can shift the *IS* and *LM* curves except the price level.[5] Since a shift in either M^s or in $\bar{A}$ will shift *DD*, the assumed values of both M^s and $\bar{A}$ are always written next to each *DD* curve. In the lower frame of Figure 6-1, for instance, the assumed values $M^s = 400$ and $\bar{A} = 600$ are written next to the DD_0 curve, because these are the values assumed in drawing the *LM* and *IS* curves in the upper frame.

4. An increase in either M^s or $\bar{A}$ will shift the *DD* curve to the right and a decrease in either will shift the curve to the left.

> **Examples:** Begin at point E_0 in the upper frame and assume for the moment that the price level equals 1.0. If the nominal money supply were raised from \$400 to \$800 billion, then M^s/P would rise to $800/1.0 = 800$ and the money market would be in equilibrium along LM_2, not LM_1. General equilibrium would occur at point H in the top frame, where LM_2 crosses the fixed *IS* curve, at $Q = \$2000$ billion.
>
> Looking directly below, point H' is plotted for $Q = \$2000$ billion and $P = 1.0$, the assumed value. Thus H' lies on a higher aggregate

---

[4] **Answer:** Compare the top and bottom frames of Figure 5-1. Notice that a steep *LM* curve amplifies the effect on output of a higher real money supply. Thus a reduction in the price level that raises M^s/P and shifts the *LM* curve will raise output more and make the *DD* curve flatter when the *LM* curve is steep (the interest responsiveness of the demand for money is zero or very small).

[5] The equation of the *DD* curve is the master income equation (7) in the Appendix to Chapters 4 and 5. The simplified equation of the *DD* curve is (8), in which a change in either $\bar{A}$ or M^s clearly alters the relationship between Q and P:

$$Q = k_1 \bar{A} + k_2 \frac{M^s}{P}$$

demand curve DD_1, which shows the various possible combinations of real output with various assumed price levels when $M^s = \$800$ billion. Curve DD_1 lies to the right of the original DD_0 curve drawn for $M^s = \$400$ billion. By the same reasoning, a low assumed nominal money supply value of \$200 billion would shift the DD curve leftward to a new curve (not drawn) running through point J'.

Notice that the aggregate demand schedule DD shifts up vertically in Figure 6-1 by exactly the same proportion as the nominal money supply. Along DD_1 the nominal money supply (\$800 billion) is exactly double its value along DD_0 (\$400 billion), and at H' the DD_1 curve is exactly twice as high (where $P = 1.0$) as the DD_0 curve at H (where $P = 0.5$). This occurs because a doubling of money and a doubling of prices from point H to H' leads to the same real money supply, hence the same LM curve, the same interest rate, and hence the same demand for commodities.

Exercise: Experiment in Figure 6-1 to see how the IS and DD curves would be shifted by an increase in $\bar{A}$ from \$600 to \$750 billion. By an increase in Chapter 3's multiplier (k) from 4.0 to 5.0.

6-3 THE SELF-CORRECTING ECONOMY: DEFLATION AS A CURE FOR RECESSION

The study of countercyclical monetary and fiscal policy began in the dark days of the Great Depression and was initiated by the publication of Keynes' *The General Theory of Employment, Interest, and Money.* Why did pre-Keynesian economists minimize the need for policy? It was generally believed that the economy had sufficiently powerful self-correcting forces to guarantee full employment and to prevent actual real output (Q) from falling below natural output (Q^*) for more than a short time.[6]

The flexibility of the price level was the automatic mechanism that was believed capable of regulating real output without help from government policymakers. In the bottom frame of Figure 6-2 the vertical line marked QQ is plotted at an income level of \$1600 billion and shows the level of natural output (Q^*) that the economy is capable of producing with its present population and stock of structures, equipment, education, and research knowledge. Any vertical line is independent of the variable plotted on the vertical axis, so that in this case the vertical QQ schedule represents the assumption that the economy's natural output $(Q^* = 1600)$ does not depend on the price index (P).

When actual real output (Q) is to the left of the QQ line, firms are producing less than the capacity for which their factories and equipment are

---

[6] See the epigraph which begins this chapter.

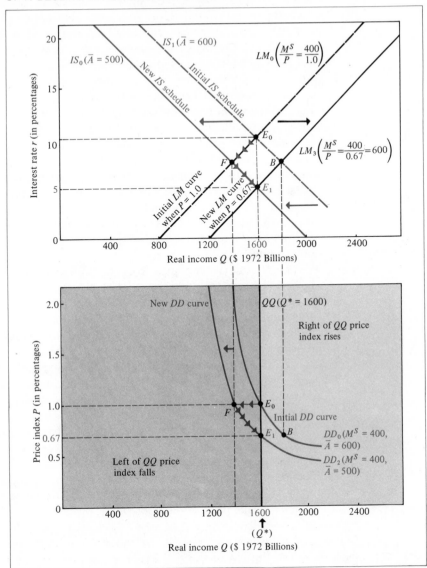

FIGURE 6–2

Effect of a $100 Billion Decline in Planned Autonomous Spending

Initially the economy is at E_0 in both frames. If the price index were to remain constant, a $100 billion drop in $\bar{A}$ from $600 billion to $500 billion would move the economy to point F, where real output has declined by $200 billion. But anywhere to the left of the QQ line in the bottom frame (as at point F) the price level declines. A drop in the price index from 1.0 to 0.67 raises the real money supply from $400 billion to $600 billion, shifting the LM curve in the upper frame rightward from LM_0 to LM_3. The economy's equilibrium moves rightward in both frames from F to E_1, where real output has returned to its initial value.

designed and prices will tend to be reduced in order to stimulate fuller use of plant capacity. During the 1975 recession, for instance, automobile manufacturers offered $200 and $300 rebates, or price reductions, to stimulate auto purchases and retail stores offered higher than usual discounts and more frequent than usual sales. In the bottom frame of Figure 6-2, the price level (P) declines continuously whenever low demand pushes the economy to the left of the QQ natural output line.

When high demand raises actual real output to the right of the QQ line, on the other hand, firms are working overtime to produce more than their optimal capacity. Overtime wage rates and shift differentials must be paid to obtain the necessary hours of work from employees; employees are less efficient because old, obsolete machinery must be pressed into service; and firms must pay more to suppliers to obtain extra raw materials. Thus firms have extra costs in periods of high production that induce them to raise prices. The high level of demand and sales makes the price increases "stick." Thus in the bottom frame of Figure 6-2 the price level (P) increases whenever real output is to the right of the QQ potential output line.

The DD_0 curve is copied from the bottom frame of Figure 6-1 and as before assumes $M^s = 400$ and $\bar{A} = 600$. Now a decline in business and consumer confidence occurs, and planned autonomous investment and consumption spending ($I_p + a$) falls by $100 billion, reducing $\bar{A}$ from $600 billion to $500 billion. The IS curve shifts leftward from IS_1 to IS_0 in the top frame, and the economy's general equilibrium shifts southwest from E_0 to F if the price index stays constant. Similarly, the position of the DD curve depends on $\bar{A}$, and the $100 billion decline in $\bar{A}$ shifts the aggregate demand curve left from DD_0 to DD_2. The economy's equilibrium shifts from E_0 to F in the lower diagram as well.

This is not the end of the story, however, because point F in the lower diagram lies to the left of the QQ curve and is in the region where P falls. The price level declines continuously as long as Q lies below Q^*. But the decline in the price level raises the real money supply and allows the economy to move southeast to point E_1, where income has reached $1600 billion and the price level stops falling.

Summary: Whenever the initial price level crosses the DD curve to the left of the QQ curve, as at point F, the price level declines and the economy "slides down" the DD curve to the crossing point of DD and QQ, as at point E_1. The reverse is also true, that when the initial price level crosses the DD curve to the right of the QQ curve, the price level rises and the economy "slides up" the DD curve to the crossing point of DD and QQ at E_0.

Thus when we allow for price flexibility we see that the economy can be in equilibrium, with no tendency for the price level to either rise or fall, only at the single point where DD and QQ cross. Anything that cuts aggregate demand, whether a drop in business and consumer confidence, a cut in government expenditures or the nominal money supply, or an increase in taxes, will shift the DD curve left and reduce the price level. In the example of Figure 6-2 the loss of business and consumer confidence causes the price level to decline from 1.0 at point E_0 to 0.67 at point E_1.

There is no need for stimulative monetary or fiscal policy, because the economy has managed to correct the drop in real output without government interference.

6-4 FLEXIBLE PRICES AND FISCAL POLICY: REAL VERSUS NOMINAL CROWDING OUT

A positively sloped LM curve does not guarantee that a fiscal policy stimulus can raise real output. An illustration is provided by Figure 6-2. Imagine that $\bar{A} = \$500$ billion and that the economy starts at point E_1, with a real income level of $\$1600$, an interest rate of 5 percent, and a price level of 0.67. Now let us assume that the government raises its purchases by $\$100$ billion, boosting $\bar{A}$ to $\$600$ billion and shifting the IS curve from IS_0 to IS_1. At the same time the DD curve shifts from DD_2 to DD_0.

If the price level were fixed, the economy's equilibrium would move from point E_1 to B. The $\$100$ billion increase in government spending would increase real income by $\$200$ billion, exactly as in Figure 5-6. But in this chapter we are assuming that the price level does not stay fixed. Instead, the price level rises whenever the DD schedule moves rightward relative to the vertical QQ schedule. P rises from B to E_0 in the lower frame of Figure 6-2 and stops rising only when real equilibrium income arrives back on the QQ curve at its starting level of $\$1600$ billion. In the upper diagram, the increase in P cuts the real money supply (M^s/P) and shifts the LM curve left, moving the economy's general equilibrium position northwest from B to E_0.

Now, allowing for price flexibility, the $\$100$ billion expansion of government spending has a zero multiplier. Real income at E_0 is not $\$1.00$ higher than at the initial position E_1. Crowding out has become complete. With total real income unchanged, and government purchases increased by $\$100$ billion, fully $\$100$ billion of autonomous investment and consumption spending ($I_p + a$) must have been crowded out by the fiscal expansion. Complete crowding out, therefore, is not ruled out as a logical possibility by the demonstration that the LM curve is positively sloped.[7]

---

[7] In 1966, Milton Friedman understood this point completely when he wrote that "... no fundamental issues in either monetary theory or monetary policy hinge on whether" the

(continued)

Summary: When prices are completely flexible, shifts in the *IS* curve—whether caused by fiscal policy or changes in business or consumer confidence—have no effect on real output. Rightward shifts in the *IS* curve move *DD* rightward and raise the price level, whereas leftward shifts in *IS* have the opposite effect.

6-5 THE FAILURE OF DEFLATION IN EXTREME CASES: THE GENERAL RULE REVISITED

Price deflation can automatically equate equilibrium real output (Q) to its natural level (Q^*) in all situations in which a change in the real money supply is capable of raising equilibrium output. In Chapter 5 we learned a general rule that this capability of the real money supply requires $\hat{r}$, the interest rate at which the *IS* curve crosses Q^*, to be equal to or greater than r_{min}, the minimum interest rate along the *LM* curve. Figure 5-3 examined a case when monetary expansion failed, when $\hat{r}$ was well below r_{min}.

This case is illustrated again in Figure 6-3. The diagram is drawn on the assumption that the minimum interest rate (r_{min}) is 2.5 percent. The LM'_0 curve in the top frame is drawn for a real money supply of $400 billion, consisting of a nominal money supply of $400 billion and an initial assumed price level of 1.0. It is identical to LM_0 in Figures 6-1 and 6-2 everywhere to the right of point G. But everywhere to the left of point G, LM'_0 is a flat horizontal line, reflecting the assumption that the minimum interest rate is 2.5 percent. The interest rate cannot fall below r_{min} because individuals consider 2.5 percent too far below normal and refuse to purchase bonds or stocks at this level. There is a liquidity trap, and all investors have joined the bear brigade.

As before, there are different *LM* curves corresponding to different values of the real money supply. Curves LM'_0, LM'_1, and LM_4 all lie on top of each other to the left of G, because the interest rate cannot fall below 2.5 percent. The consequences of the liquidity trap (as in Figure 5-3) depend entirely on the position of the *IS* curve. When $\bar{A}$ is $500 billion, the position of the *IS* curve is IS_0 and of the *DD* curve is DD_2. Deflation of the price level can automatically raise real output from $1400 billion at point F to $1600 billion at the level of E_1 in both the top and

---

interest-responsiveness of the demand for real money balances is zero or a positive number, so long as it is "seldom capable of being approximated by infinity." But as late as 1972 James Tobin wrote that "First, let me explain what *I* thought the main issue was. . . . I thought (and I still think) it was the shape of the *LM* locus." Quotations and context may be found in Robert J. Gordon (ed.), *Milton Friedman's Monetary Framework: A Debate with His Critics* (Chicago: The University of Chicago Press, 1974), pp. 138 and 77, respectively. The second quote began Chapter 5.

bottom frames of Figure 6-3. Point $\hat{r}_0$ along the IS_0 curve is 5 percent, well above r_{min}.

But the situation may be entirely different when business and consumer optimism have collapsed, as in the Great Depression, and $\bar{A}$ has fallen from \$500 billion to \$250 billion. The new depressed IS_1 curve intersects the initial LM'_0 money market curve at point Z. Point $\hat{r}_1$ along IS_1 is at the depressed level of -7.5 percent. Now notice that a drop in the price level cannot raise real income by even \$1.00. A decline in the price level from 1.0 to 0.67 shifts the LM curve from LM'_0 to LM'_1, but real income stays stuck at \$800 billion. In the bottom frame we drop down directly below Z to Z', plotted at $P = 0.67$. The DD curve between Z and Z' is completely vertical because the equilibrium level of income is completely independent of the price level (P). No matter how far the price level drops, even to 0.25 (illustrated at point Z'' in the bottom frame), real income does not budge.

As in Figure 6-2, the price level declines continuously whenever we are to the left of the vertical QQ potential output schedule. But now the DD curve does not intersect QQ. The price level never stops falling and real output cannot equal Q^*. No equilibrium is possible because there is continuous and unending pressure on P to fall. Our general rule is amended:

> *Whenever $\hat{r}$ is less than r_{min}, and the position of the IS curve does not depend on the price level, then the DD curve becomes a vertical line to the left of QQ. There is no point of intersection between DD and QQ and thus no possibility of a stable-price, full-employment equilibrium where actual and natural output are equal.*

Once again, the general rule can prevent full employment even without the liquidity trap. When r_{min} is at its normal level of zero, $\hat{r}$ may still be negative if business and consumer confidence is low.

6-6   TWO SOLUTIONS TO CONTROL $\hat{r}$: FISCAL POLICY AND THE REAL BALANCE EFFECT

In Chapter 12 we will study more closely the differences between the modern economic Keynesians, or nonmonetarists, who support active government use of policy tools, particularly fiscal policy, to stabilize the economy, and the monetarists, who support fixed settings for the policy tools and trust the economy's self-correcting forces to keep private output on target. The present-day Keynesian position originates in the dilemma of Figure 6-3, where the private economy cannot cure a depression by itself through price deflation because $\hat{r}$ falls short of r_{min}. It was Keynes who first pointed out the possibility that $\hat{r}$ might be negative and

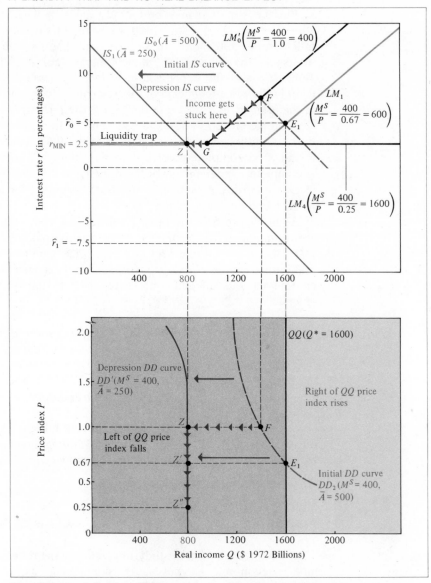

FIGURE 6–3

The Effect of Falling Prices on Real Output When Planned Autonomous Spending Has Fallen to $250 Billion and r_{min} Is Fixed at 2.5 Percent

The drop in planned autonomous spending shifts the IS curve leftwards from IS_0 to IS_1. At the initial price level of 1.0, the position of the LM curve is indicated by LM_0, and the economy's equilibrium is at Z in the top and bottom frames. The price in-that r_{min} might (but was not likely to) be some positive number.[8] And it was Keynes who pointed to fiscal policy as a way out of the dilemma.

The crucial problem in Figure 6-3 is not the liquidity trap, the positive value of r_{min}. The dilemma would persist even if there were no liquidity trap and r_{min} were at zero, its normal level. Instead, the dilemma arises because the IS curve is too far to the left and $\hat{r}$ is negative, due to the low level of $\bar{A}$ caused by a collapse in business and consumer confidence.

How can estimates of the future rate of return be raised to revive the economy? All problems disappear if $\bar{A}$ can be raised back by enough to make $\hat{r}$ equal or exceed r_{min}. For this reason fiscal policy, which can shift $\bar{A}$ through increases in government expenditure and transfer payments and reductions in tax rates, is the obvious antidepression tool to use. In fact, fiscal policy might avert the depression entirely if government policymakers could accurately forecast the drop in business and consumer confidence and could instantly raise $\bar{A}$ by $1.00 for each dollar decline in $\bar{A}$ caused by reduced confidence.

In fact, however, government action may not be necessary. A. C. Pigou originally pointed out (as we learned in section 5-5) that the Keynesian dilemma illustrated in Figure 6-3 is not a dilemma at all if the demand for commodities depends directly on the level of real money balances. The IS curve would then shift not only when $\bar{A}$ changes, as in Figure 6-3, but also whenever the price level changes. Thus a sufficient drop in the price level could raise real balances as high as necessary to move the IS curve rightward and raise $\hat{r}$ up to r_{min}.

Figure 6-4 illustrates the power of the real balance effect to boost real output when $\hat{r}$ is too low at the initial price level.[9] We start from an initial situation in which business and consumer confidence has collapsed, as in Figure 6-3, reducing $\bar{A}$ to 250 and making $\hat{r}$ negative. At the initial price

---

[8] Neither of the diagrams in Figure 6-3 appeared in Keynes' book. The IS and LM curves were invented soon afterward by John Hicks and published as part of his article "Mr. Keynes and the Classics," *Econometrica* (1937).

[9] All the details of the top frame of Figure 6-4 are the same as Figure 5-5, which illustrated the power of the monetary authority to raise $\hat{r}$ when the price level is fixed. Once again a $1.00 increase in the real money supply is assumed to shift the IS curve right by $0.50.

---

dex declines (because the economy is to the left of the QQ line) but the interest rate is "stuck" at 2.5 percent in the liquidity trap. Real output does not rise, so that in the top frame the economy's equilibrium stays at point Z. In the bottom frame real output also remains constant but the price index declines steadily, so the equilibrium moves downward from Z to Z' to Z'' and beyond.

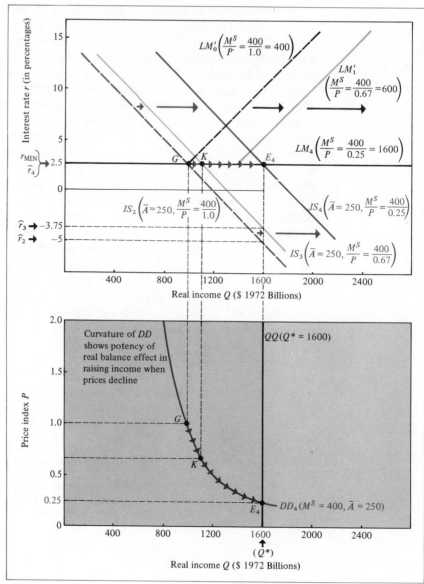

FIGURE 6-4 The Effect of Falling Prices on Real Output When Planned Autonomous Spending Has Fallen to $250 Billion, r_{min} Is Fixed at 2.5 Percent, and the Real-Balance Effect Is in Operation

level ($P = 1.0$) the economy rests at point G, well below the desired natural output target (Q^*) of $1600 billion.[10]

As in Figures 6-2 and 6-3, the price level falls whenever the economy lies to the left of the vertical QQ schedule, that is, whenever real output (Q) is less than natural output (Q^*). In Figure 6-2 a decline in the price level by one-third, from 1.0 to 0.67, was enough to achieve $Q = Q^*$. But now, because the initial situation is worse, a much more substantial price deflation is necessary. A price index of 0.67 brings real output up only to $1100 billion, at point K, and this is not enough. Only when the price level has fallen to 0.25, and the real money supply has increased to $1600 billion, is the demand for commodities stimulated sufficiently to raise real output to the desired level. In the bottom frame of Figure 6-4, point E_4 is the economy's resting place at the crossing point of DD_4 and QQ, where the price level has fallen enough to achieve $Q = Q^*$.

> **Summary:** The real balance effect completely changes the slope of the DD curve: in Figure 6-3 the DD curve is vertical below point Z because price deflation has no stimulative effect on real output, but with the real-balance effect in Figure 6-4 a price deflation can achieve any desired output level if prices fall far enough.

Why is the real balance effect so powerful when the price level is flexible? Imagine yourself owning only a $5.00 bill. You would not be able to consider purchasing a $12,000 Cadillac. But there is some price level at which your money would have more impressive buying power. If the price index were to decline from 1.0 to 0.0001, the price of the Cadillac would fall from $12,000 to $1.20, and your $5.00 would be more than ample to buy the Cadillac, leaving $3.80 in change! Although the numbers in this illustration are extreme, they forcefully illustrate the logic of the real balance effect. A fixed nominal amount of money buys more when the price level falls, so that individuals are bound to find

---

[10] With an initial price level of 1.0 the economy in Figure 6-4 is at G, with income $200 billion higher than at point A in Figure 6-3. This occurs because we have now introduced the assumption that each $1.00 of real money shifts the IS schedule by $0.50, so that the $400 billion of money along LM'_0 generates $200 billion more income at G than in Figure 6-3.

In contrast to Figure 6–3, now the higher real money supply created by falling prices not only shifts the LM curve to the right, but also shifts the IS curve. As a result, $\hat{r}$ (the interest rate at which IS crosses the natural output level of $1600 billion) rises until it reaches the level of r_{min}, or 2.5 percent. This occurs at point E_4 in both frames, where the price level has dropped from 1.00 to 0.25, thus boosting the real money supply by a factor of four.

John Maynard Keynes
(1883–1946)

The Bettmann Archive, Inc.

John Maynard Keynes' *The General Theory of Employment, Interest, and Money* (1936) is one of the two or three most influential economics books of the twentieth century. It sets out explicitly the story that has been called the Keynesian Revolution.

The book ended the reign of the prevailing classical orthodoxy, which viewed the economy as having an automatic self-correcting mechanism that maintained prosperity and full employment. Instead, Keynes argued, the propensity of firms to invest may be too low compared to that of households to save, leading to endemic depression. Lacking forces sufficiently powerful to restore full employment, the private sector may need help from government fiscal policy in the form of lower taxes and higher government spending.

Keynes was a distinguished economist, intellectual leader, and member of the upper crust of England's literary and artistic establishment long before 1936. He was born into economics, the son of Neville Keynes, a Cambridge don who specialized in economics and logic. By the time World War I broke out, young Keynes had written most of two books,

Indian Currency and Finance (1913) and *A Treatise on Probability* (1921). During the war, he rose rapidly as an official in the British Treasury handling external finance, and eventually resigned from the British negotiating team at the 1919 Paris Peace Conference in protest against the stiff reparation payments the victors were demanding from the Germans. He put his objections into writing in

some portion of their previous money balances excessive and to spend more on real commodities.

When the price level is perfectly flexible and the real balance effect is in operation, no monetary or fiscal policy is necessary. The Federal Reserve Governors and the Chairman of the President's Council of Economic Advisers can "go fishing," confident that the *DD* curve crosses the *QQ* curve and that price flexibility will automatically maintain actual real output to equal natural output.

We have now identified two stimulative effects of price deflation:

1. The **Keynes effect** is the stimulus to aggregate demand (both consumption and investment) due to a decline in the rate of interest, which in turn is brought about by an increase in the real money supply (M^s/P) caused either by an increase in the nominal money supply or by price deflation. The Keynes effect brings the economy from point F to E_1

The Economic Consequences of the Peace, one of the finest pieces of polemic writing of his generation.

The first postwar decade was Keynes' heyday as a multifaceted financier, journalist, academic, editor, socialite, and farmer. He spent half an hour in bed each morning making investment decisions and was able to convert a small loan from members of his family into a fortune of half a million pounds, largely by speculating in foreign exchange. He was Bursar of King's College, Cambridge, increasing its endowment by a factor of ten. He wrote frequent essays for newspapers and magazines, and published collections in *Essays in Biography* and *Essays in Persuasion.* Married to a famous Russian ballerina, he was a member of the "Bloomsbury Circle," a group of England's best-known and most colorful artists and authors, including E. M. Forster, Virginia Woolf, and Lytton Strachey. He spent much of his time on a small country farm that he worked to improve, and—as if all this were not enough—found time to be the editor of the prestigious *Economic Journal* (England's equivalent of the *American Economic Review*) from 1911 to 1945.

In addition to the *General Theory,* Keynes wrote two earlier and more orthodox books on monetary economics, *A Tract on Monetary Reform* (1923), and *A Treatise on Money* (1930). Since 1936, however, the word "Keynesian" has been synonymous with support of an activist government policy that intervenes to offset the economy's tendency to slip into episodes of depression and inflation. Until the mid-1960's, the Keynesians ruled macroeconomics, but more recently the Monetarist Counterrevolution has gained many adherents to the view that partly returns to the pre-Keynesian orthodoxy—that the private economy's self-correcting forces have been underestimated, and that government intervention may do more harm than good.[a]

[a] Monetarism is the subject of Chapter 12. For more reading on Keynes, see R. F. Harrod's *The Life of John Maynard Keynes* (New York: St. Martins, 1951). A short but brilliant comparison of the two revolutions is Harry G. Johnson, "The Keynesian Revolution and the Monetarist Counter-Revolution," *American Economic Review,* vol. 61 (May 1971), pp. 1–14. For the recent state of the debate among prominent economists on what Keynes really meant, see Robert J. Gordon, ed., *Milton Friedman's Monetary Framework* (Chicago: University of Chicago Press, 1974).

in Figure 6-2. It is the Keynes effect that is cut off and rendered ineffective when $\hat{r}$ falls below r_{min}, because the interest rate (r) cannot drop enough to return actual output (Q) to the natural level (Q^*), as illustrated in Figure 6-3.

2. The **Pigou effect (real balance effect)** is the direct stimulus to consumption spending, which occurs when a price deflation causes an increase in the real money supply; this stimulus does not require a reduction in the interest rate. The real balance effect accounts for the curvature of the DD_4 schedule in Figure 6-4, as compared to the vertical portion of DD' in Figure 6-3, and it allows the economy to glide smoothly down DD_4 from G to E_4.

Unfortunately, the stimulative effects of price deflation are not always favorable, even when the Pigou effect is in operation. The two major unfavorable effects of deflation are:

1. The **expectations effect.** When people expect prices to continue to fall, they realize that goods will cost less to buy next week and next year, and they will tend to postpone purchases as much as possible to take advantage of lower prices in the future. This decline in the demand for commodities may be strong enough to offset the stimulus of the Pigou effect, although most economists agree that at a sufficiently low level of prices the huge increase in real balances would eventually swamp the expectations effect.

2. The **redistribution effect** may be more important. Deflation causes a redistribution of income from debtors to creditors. Why? Debt repayments are usually fixed in dollar value, so that a uniform deflation in all prices causes an increase in the real value of mortgage and installment repayments from debtors to creditors (banks, and ultimately, savers).

> **Example**: Imagine an individual who originally earns $100 per week and pays $25 per week in debt repayment (not an unusual situation). A drop in the price level from 1.00 to 0.25 will cut his earnings from $100 to $25 per week (assuming the deflation reduces all prices and wages uniformly). All his $25 earnings will be required for the fixed $25 debt repayment, reducing to zero the income available for current consumption. The debtor's consumption may be cut by far more than the increase in the consumption of the creditor who receives the debt repayment, because rich creditors may consume less of their incomes than do poor debtors. The net effect on total economy-wide spending may be negative, further depressing $\hat{r}$.[11]

During the Great Depression deflation of 1929–33, for instance, the GNP price deflator fell from an initial 0.329 to 0.251 in 1933 (1972 = 1.0), a decline of 23.7 percent. Yet the interest income of creditors hardly fell at all, from $4.7 to $4.6 billion (current dollars). Farmers were hit worst by falling prices—their current-dollar income fell by two-thirds, from $6.2 to $2.1 billion—and many lost their farms through foreclosures as a result of this heavy debt burden. Although many factors were at work in the collapse of real autonomous spending during the Great Depression, it appears that the negative redistribution effect of the 1929–33 deflation may have dominated the stimulative Keynes effect and Pigou effect.

---

[11] A relatively advanced discussion of the consequences of these effects on the economy's self-correcting mechanism is contained in James Tobin, "Keynesian Models of Recession and Depression," *American Economic Review*, vol. 65 (May 1975), pp. 195–202. See also Axel Leijonhufvud, *On Keynesian Economics and the Economics of Keynes* (New York: Oxford 1968), pp. 315–31.

6-7 SUMMARY AND EVALUATION OF DEPRESSION ECONOMICS

The main thrust of the mid-1930s Keynesian revolution in economics was a denial that the economy's self-correcting forces unleashed by a price deflation are always strong enough in every situation to maintain full employment $(Q = Q^*)$. Beyond that, at least two interpretations of Keynes' position are possible:

1. *Hard-line fiscalists*. Not only is a price deflation incapable in every situation of raising Q to Q^*, but monetary policy is ineffective as well. This position is summarized by the saying that "You can take a horse to water but you can't make it drink," meaning that the Fed can make money available but can't force businessmen to spend it on new investment projects. The only salvation is fiscal policy, which can add $1.00 to $\bar{A}$ for every dollar subtracted during a decline in business and consumer confidence.
2. *Soft-line Keynesians*. A price deflation might raise output enough if prices were sufficiently flexible to fall instantly and steeply, but in fact prices decline relatively slowly, if at all. Government action is necessary to counteract the inflexibility of prices, but either monetary or fiscal policy is capable of achieving the natural level of employment $(Q = Q^*)$.

Table 6-1 helps to sort out the assumptions necessary for either the hard-line or soft-line view to be valid. The hard-liners must believe in the assumptions listed under item 3, that there is no real balance effect and that it is possible for $\hat{r}$ to fall below $r_{\min}$. Those who take this position find fiscal policy necessary whether or not the price level is flexible. A price deflation under conditions of price flexibility and a monetary expansion under conditions of fixed prices are equally ineffective.

Soft-liners do not find the universal denial of the real balance effect, as in line 3, to be an appealing assumption, and they regard lines 1 and 2 to be more accurate. But they reject perfect price flexibility as unrealistic, and, though not willing to claim that the price level is completely fixed, they find the assumption of price fixity closer to reality than that of perfect price flexibility. The implications of their view are listed in the two identical items in column (b), lines 1 and 2. Since instantaneous price deflation does not occur, the economy can get stuck with real output (Q) well below potential (Q^*) and substantial unemployment, unless a monetary or fiscal stimulus is applied.

A large number of U.S. economists today, probably a majority, holds views that can be described as "soft-line Keynesian." Both monetary

TABLE 6-1

Summary of Depression Economics: Starting from a Low Level of Output, Can Actual Real Income (Q) Be Raised Back to Equal Natural Real Income (Q^*)?

Case	(a) Price level perfectly flexible	(b) Price level fixed
1. Normal case: $\hat{r}$ equal to or greater than r_{min}	Yes: government policy-makers can go fishing.[a] (Example: Figure 6-2)	No: without government action. Yes: with enough monetary or fiscal stimulus. (Examples: Monetary: Figure 5-1 Fiscal: Figure 5-6)
2. $\hat{r}$ less than r_{min}; real balance effect exists	Yes: government policy-makers can go fishing.[a] (Example: Figure 6-4)	No: without government action. Yes: with enough monetary or fiscal stimulus. (Example: Figure 5-5)
3. $\hat{r}$ less than r_{min}; but no real balance effect	No: without government fiscal action; monetary policy ineffectual (Example: Figure 6-3)	No: without government fiscal action; monetary policy ineffectual (Example: Figure 5-3)

[a] Ignores expectation and redistribution effects of a price deflation.

and fiscal policy are considered important, and the private economy cannot keep itself on course without help from the government. Most of the remaining U.S. economists are monetarists, who generally attribute more flexibility to the price level and who tend to oppose countercyclical policy activism as undesirable and unnecessary. We will return to the Keynesian-monetarist debate and identify some issues where the two schools of thought have converged, and others where disagreement continues today (Chapter 12).

6-8 CASE STUDY: PRICES AND OUTPUT DURING THE GREAT DEPRESSION

It is an outstanding characteristic of the economic system in which we live that . . . it seems capable of remaining in a chronic condition of sub-normal activity for a considerable period without any marked tendency either towards recovery or towards complete collapse.

Keynes, *General Theory*, p. 249

Does the behavior of output and the price level in the Great Depression tend to support the hard-line fiscalists, the soft-line Keynesians, or neither? For neither to be correct we should be able to find evidence of the economy's self-correcting forces at work through price deflation. Turning back to Figure 6-2, we notice that when price deflation works in a stabilizing direction, the economy slides down a DD curve to the southeast toward the QQ output curve, as from point F to natural point E_1. Similarly, in Figure 6-4 the economy slides southeast from point G to point E_4.

Now compare these theoretical diagrams to a graph of the actual data plotted in the top frame of Figure 6-5. To eliminate the effect of growth in natural output (Q^*), the horizontal axis is measured as the ratio of actual to natural real output (Q/Q^*). Starting on the vertical QQ schedule at natural output in 1929, with a price index of 1.0 (on a 1929 base), the economy moved rapidly to the southwest until 1933. Then a recovery to the northeast began, interrupted briefly in 1938. In terms of our analysis of section 5-4, we can view the decline of output up to 1933 as caused by several factors that shifted DD to the left: a collapse in confidence, a major decline in the money supply, and an ineptly timed move to fiscal restraint in 1932.[12]

In 1933 a recovery began, under the combined influence of an increase in the real money supply, a fiscal stimulus, and a revival of confidence. The recovery got stuck around 1936, with no progress between 1936 and 1939, and the massive monetary and fiscal expansion induced by the outbreak of World War II was required before the economy was able to regain its starting position in early 1942.

The story of the Great Depression appears to lie in shifts in the DD curve to the left and then back to the right. There is no evidence at all of a movement southeast along a given DD curve, as would have occurred had price deflation played a major role in stimulating the recovery. The economy moved southeast only between 1938 and 1939, and then only slightly. Particularly important is the fact that there was no deflation at all between 1936 and 1940, even though the economy remained at or below 80 percent of its natural output throughout that five-year interval. Thus the evidence appears quite conclusive that the government cannot rely on rapid and massive price deflation to revive the economy, at least if the price level today is as sluggish as it was in the late 1930s.

---

[12] We have not yet attempted to explain why confidence fell so low. Monetary policy and the collapse of the banking system played a role after autumn 1931, but it is difficult to explain the initial 1929–31 period as a monetary phenomenon. See Peter Temin, *Did Monetary Forces Cause the Great Depression?* (New York: Norton, 1975). Details of the 1932 tax increase are presented in section 17-7.

THE PRICE LEVEL WAS NEITHER PERFECTLY FIXED NOR PERFECTLY
FLEXIBLE DURING THE GREAT DEPRESSION

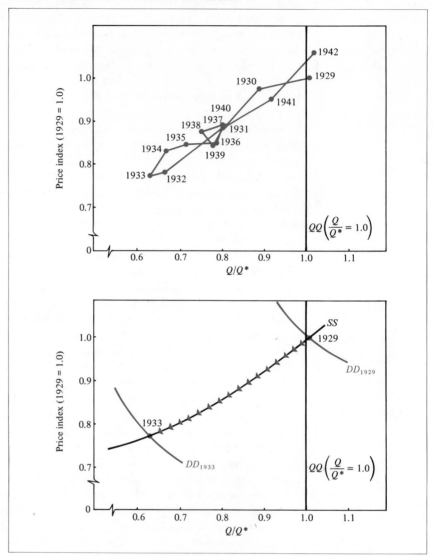

FIGURE 6–5 The Price Level (P) and the
Ratio of Actual to Natural Out-
put (Q/Q^*) during the Great
Depression, 1929–42

The upper frame illustrates the actual
values of the implicit GNP deflator
(P) and an estimate of the ratio of
actual to natural output during the
Great Depression era, 1929–42. The

Despite the absence of perfect price flexibility, however, it is also clear from the top frame of Figure 6-5 that the price level was not rigid at all during the Great Depression and did drop 24 percent between 1929 and 1933. The path from northeast to southwest to northeast reflects a regularity, as if the DD curve were following a well-marked highway. The bottom frame of Figure 6-5 represents a hypothetical interpretation of what happened. The DD curve in 1929 was close to the vertical natural output (QQ) schedule, but by 1933 it had moved well to the left as business and consumer confidence collapsed. The DD_{1933} schedule provides a menu of possible combinations of the price level and real output. An additional curve is necessary to pin down the economy's 1933 location along the DD_{1933} schedule.

Just as elementary economic principles place great emphasis on demand and supply curves, in intermediate macroeconomics we employ the aggregate demand curve DD and an **aggregate supply curve** SS. Curve SS slopes upward to reflect the fact that firms can and do charge higher prices in a prosperous year such as 1929 than they do in a depressed year such as 1933. If the price level were always fixed, the SS curve would be a horizontal line. If the price level were instantly flexible, SS would be a vertical line, just like the QQ schedule. The SS curve drawn in the bottom frame of Figure 6-5 is intermediate between these two extremes: When demand declines and the DD curve shifts leftward, the price level falls, but not continuously and without limit.

The SS curve is the major new tool introduced in Chapter 7. As we will see, SS is a supply curve for the short run and assumes that business and consumer expectations of the normal price level are fixed. Whenever expectations change, the SS curve shifts its position. A chief puzzle of the Great Depression is why the SS curve remained so stable, and why expectations of the normal level of prices did not decline in light of the prolonged reduction in prices that actually occurred.

---

remarkable fact in the top frame is that the economy returned to natural output in 1942 with a price level that was actually higher than in 1929, despite the intervening decade that should have pushed the price level down. The bottom frame illustrates a hypothetical interpretation of what happened. A drop in the economy's aggregate demand curve (DD) moved the economy along its aggregate supply curve (SS), a concept to be discussed fully in the next chapter. The puzzle of the Great Depression is the failure of the supply curve to shift downward during that long decade of wasted output and high unemployment.

SUMMARY

1. In the previous chapters we assumed that the price level (P) is constant and that any change in aggregate demand is completely reflected in a change in real income. When the price level is allowed to be perfectly flexible in this chapter, we find that shifts in monetary and fiscal policy that previously caused real income to vary now cause the price level to change in the same direction.

2. A decline in the price level plays the same role as an increase in the money supply in Chapter 5. Price deflation can automatically return real output to its natural level in any situation in which a change in the real money supply is capable of raising output. Perfect price flexibility automatically maintains a stable level of real output, making changes in monetary and fiscal policy unnecessary.

3. The aggregate demand curve (DD) shows all the possible combinations of the price deflator (P) and of real output (Q) consistent with a fixed nominal money supply and a fixed autonomous spending schedule ($\bar{A}$). Everywhere along the DD curve both the commodity and money markets are in equilibrium.

4. The DD curve is steep when the IS curve is steep and the LM curve is flat. An increase in either the nominal money supply or in the autonomous spending schedule shifts the DD curve to the right.

5. The price level declines whenever real output is less than natural output (Q^*) and rises when real output exceeds natural output. With flexible prices the economy can be in equilibrium with no tendency for price level movements only at the point where DD intersects the vertical natural output line (QQ), that is, when actual output (Q) equals natural output (Q^*).

6. Whenever $\hat{r}$ is less than r_{min} and the position of the IS curve does not depend on the price level, the DD curve becomes a vertical line, allowing no possibility of a stable-price, full-employment equilibrium when the IS curve is depressed. But with a real balance effect a sufficient drop in P can move the IS curve to the right and raise $\hat{r}$ to r_{min}. Thus when the price level is perfectly flexible and the real balance effect is in operation, no monetary or fiscal policy is necessary.

7. The Keynes effect is the stimulus to aggregate demand that occurs when price deflation raises the real money supply and reduces the rate of interest. It is this effect that is rendered ineffective when $\hat{r}$ falls below r_{min}.

8. The Pigou effect or real balance effect is the direct stimulus to autonomous consumption spending of an increase in the real money supply. The stimulative effects of price deflation may not always be favorable, even when the Pigou effect is in operation, if the expectations effect and the redistribution effect are sufficiently weak.

9. Hard-line fiscalists find fiscal policy necessary whether or not the price level is flexible. Soft-line Keynesians reject perfect price flexibility as unrealistic, and, although not willing to claim that the price level is completely fixed, they find the assumption of short-run price fixity closer to reality. In this case the economy can get stuck with a low level of real and substantial unemployment unless a monetary or fiscal stimulus is applied.

A LOOK AHEAD

The case study of the Great Depression in section 6-8 suggests that in reality the price level is neither perfectly fixed nor perfectly flexible. Thus the real world cannot be adequately described by our theory in Chapters 3–5, which assumes that the price level is completely fixed, nor by that in Chapter 6, which assumes that the price level is perfectly and instantly flexible.

Our next task is to maintain intact our theory of the determinants of the aggregate demand curve *(DD)* and add a theory of the supply curve that explains how a shift in aggregate demand is divided between output and price changes in the short run. We will find that under most conditions an increase in aggregate demand is accompanied by both higher prices and higher output. Eventually, as expectations adjust to the initial price increase, most or all of the effect takes the form of higher prices; changes in aggregate demand have little if any effect on real output.

CONCEPTS AND QUESTIONS

IDENTIFICATIONS

Implicit price deflator	Pigou effect
Aggregate demand curve	Expectations effect
Self-correcting forces	Redistribution effect
Perfect flexibility	$\hat{r}$ and r_{min}
Keynes effect	

QUESTIONS FOR REVIEW

Are the following statements true, false, or uncertain? Be sure you can give a clear explanation of your answer.

1   A liquidity trap always prevents a natural output equilibrium from being attained even if prices are perfectly flexible.

2   The Keynes effect is operative except when the economy is in a liquidity trap.

3   A fall in the rate of interest is necessary for the operation of the Pigou effect.

4   A change in prices shifts the *IS* curve, but not the *LM* curve, when the real balance effect is in operation.

5   A fiscal stimulus always raises real output as long as the *LM* curve is positively sloped.

6   The price level fell continuously during the Great Depression in response to a large output gap and high unemployment.

7   Evidence from the Great Depression supports the proposition that any unexpected demand shock — that is, drop in demand growth relative to expected demand growth — has its main short-run impact on output behavior rather than on price behavior.

Part III

Inflation and Unemployment

7 Allowing Both Prices and Output to Change Together

Inflation is always and everywhere a
monetary phenomenon.

—Milton Friedman[1]

7-1 INTRODUCTION

In the last two chapters we have explored the determinants of the
economy's general equilibrium in which both the commodity market and
money market are simultaneously in equilibrium. We have been particularly interested in the effect on aggregate demand of shifts in autonomous spending, whether caused by changes in business and consumer
confidence or in government fiscal variables, and of shifts in the real
money supply. We were able to link changes in aggregate demand to
changes in real output only by assuming that the price level was fixed
(Chapter 5). Exactly the opposite assumption, that changes in aggregate
demand influence the price level while maintaining real output fixed, was
made in Chapter 6. Now it is time to allow the price level and real output
to change at the same time.

Neither the fixed price approach of Chapter 5 nor the fixed output
approach of Chapter 6 is adequate. Why? Neither extreme assumption
is derived from any basic theoretical analysis, and neither is valid in
reality. Our assumption in Chapter 6 that output is fixed at the level of
natural output (Q^*) may be valid for studying long-run economic movements over 20 or 30 year intervals, but it is not valid for any shorter
period, as you see clearly from the historical data in Figure 1-2. The
fixed price assumption of Chapters 3–5 is completely arbitrary and in-
defensible. No allowance is made for the price hikes that firms commonly
introduce in response to booming demand or to increases in costs. By

---

[1] "Inflation: Causes and Consequences" (Asia Publishing House, 1963), reprinted in
Dollars and Deficits (Prentice-Hall, 1968), p. 39.

assuming away the entire phenomenon of price change an economist is kept from saying anything about inflation.

As we here allow real output and the price level to change together in the short run, we take into explicit account the effect on output and prices of the anticipations workers and firms hold about the price level. This analysis, however, shares with previous chapters the approach of **comparative statics.** Our basic diagram measures the level, not the rate of change, of real output and the price level. Our analysis is just like a show of photographic slides—we show one slide in the form of a single static equilibrium position, we turn out the lights, and, when the lights come back on, the economy has moved to a new static equilibrium position. Our comparative static slide-show method of analysis cannot tell us anything about economic dynamics—how long does it take output and the price level to change? What is the rate of price change (the inflation rate) per year or per month? Only in Chapter 8 will we be able to examine the dynamic relationship between the rate of inflation and the GNP gap or unemployment rate.

7-2 BEHAVIOR OF FIRMS AND WORKERS IN THE LABOR MARKET

A basic tool of microeconomics, introduced in every elementary economics course, is the supply curve for the individual business firm. The producer, say a farmer, observes the current price he can obtain on the market where he sells his output and produces until that market price equals his marginal cost of production. If the farmer's price per dozen eggs is 50 cents, he will produce until marginal cost is 50 cents, say 1000 dozen eggs per week, but no further. Why not? Because the extra cost of additional production, say an extra 100 dozen eggs, is likely to be greater than 50 cents. Whenever the marginal cost of producing added output exceeds price, then the firm makes a loss on the extra items and refuses to produce them.

Will the farmer ever be willing to produce more than 1000 dozen eggs, when currently his marginal cost equals the market price of 50 cents? Certainly, but only if the market price should rise will he be able to produce additional eggs without suffering a loss. Thus the microeconomic supply curve for the firm plots a positive relation between price and output, since a higher price will induce firms to produce more goods and services.

Here we develop the macroeconomic equivalent of the firm's supply curve, the aggregate supply curve. It plots a positive relation between the aggregate economy-wide price index (P) and aggregate output (Q). Our purpose is to determine why the aggregate supply curve has a positive slope, with a higher price required to induce firms to produce more output.

HOW FIRMS MAXIMIZE PROFITS BY HIRING MAN-HOURS
UNTIL THE MARGINAL PRODUCT OF LABOR EQUALS
THE REAL WAGE

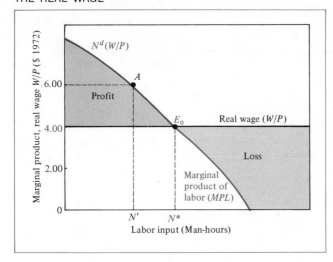

FIGURE 7–1

Derivation of the Demand Curve for Labor

The sloping red line measures the marginal product of added man-hours. Man-hours hired beyond N^* create losses for the firm, as indicated by the pink area, so long as the real wage is fixed at $4.00. To hire less than N^* means giving up part of the gray profit triangle. Profits are maximized by hiring up to the right edge of the profit triangle at E_0, while avoiding contact with the pink loss area. If the real wage were to increase from $4.00 to $6.00, the amount of labor hired would drop from N^* to N'.

Three basic features of the economy combine to yield a positive connection between the aggregate price level and output:

1. Firms are in business to make a profit. They will not produce extra units of output on which they incur a loss because their profits are higher when they abstain from producing the loss-making units.
2. To produce additional output, firms must obtain a higher input of labor, either new employees or added hours of work by current employees. But the law of diminishing returns suggests that the marginal product (extra output added) will decline as extra labor input is added, causing the marginal cost of the extra output to rise. Thus to avoid losses firms will need to raise their price to compensate for the higher marginal cost, even if the wage rate paid to labor remains constant.
3. But the wage rate will not remain constant, because workers must be "bribed" by a higher wage if they are to be willing to work longer hours, assuming that initially the economy is in an equilibrium where workers are supplying all the hours they desire at the original wage.

PROFIT MAXIMIZATION AND DIMINISHING RETURNS TO LABOR

The first two elements on this list are illustrated in Figure 7-1. The vertical axis measures two equivalent magnitudes, the **marginal product of labor** and the **real wage**. The marginal product of labor is the value in constant prices of the extra output that one additional **man-hour** of labor can produce.[2] If a farmer hires an additional worker who can raise production 8 dozen eggs in an hour, and if the price of eggs in some base period, say 1972, was 50 cents a dozen, then the marginal product of the additional labor (MPL) is 8 dozen eggs, worth $4.00 in the base period:

$$\text{Marginal product of labor} = MPL = \frac{\text{Dozens}}{\text{Man-hour}} \frac{\text{Base price}}{\text{Dozen}}$$

$$= 8 \, (\$0.50) = \$4.00$$

The real wage is the actual nominal wage (W) paid per man-hour divided by the price index (P) relating today's price to the base-period price. If initially workers are paid $4.00 per hour, and the price of eggs remains at the base period price (P = 1.0), the real wage (W/P) can be written:

$$\text{Real wage} = W/P = \frac{\text{Nominal wage } (W)}{\text{Price index } (P)} = \frac{\$4.00}{1.00} = \$4.00$$

Any business producer, like the egg farmer, maximizes profits if he hires labor up to the point where the marginal product of the last man-hour hired (MPL) is exactly equal to the real wage (W/P). Compare the following alternatives when the real wage is fixed at $4.00:

Man-hours hired	Hypothetical marginal product (dozens)	Hypothetical marginal product (MPL), ($ 1972)	Real wage (W/P), 1972 base	Profit added by hiring this man-hour (MPL − W/P)
One too few	8.5	$4.25	$4.00	$0.25
Equilibrium (N*)	8.0	$4.00	$4.00	$0.00
One too many	7.5	$3.75	$4.00	−$0.25

The business firm will always hire workers up to the point where labor's marginal product equals its real wage. To hire one too many man-hours, as in the table, is to make a loss, by paying that extra man-hour $0.25 more than it produces. To hire too few man-hours means forgoing profits on man-hours that produce more than they are paid. Only when exactly the right equilibrium amount of labor is hired do business firms maximize profits, as when in the example they hire the amount of labor that produces a marginal product of 8.0, with $4.00.

Figure 7-1 illustrates the same relationship as the table. The red line labeled marginal product of labor slopes downward, reflecting the diminishing marginal product of additional man-hours. The horizontal line at $4.00 is the assumed value of the real wage (W/P). Only if the firm hires workers up to point E_0, but no further, will profits be maximized.

Would the firm ever hire a different number of man-hours than N*?

---

[2] A man-hour is one person (man or woman) working one hour. A firm obtains an additional man-hour of labor input either by hiring an additional worker for an hour or by adding one hour's overtime for a worker already employed.

Any change in the real wage alters the profit-maximizing level of labor input. If the real wage were to rise from $4.00 at point E_0 to $6.00 at point A, then firms would find themselves making a loss on the man-hours between N' and N^*, which have a marginal product below $6.00. Man-hour labor input will be reduced from N^* to N' as a result. Thus the red downward sloping marginal product curve is also a demand curve for labor, showing the number of man-hours that will be hired at different levels of the real wage.

What events might change the real wage (W/P)? First, workers might obtain a nominal wage rate above $4.00 as a result of wage increases in competing firms or industries. Or, second, the price index might decline if the price of eggs were to decline. A $6.00 real wage could reflect any of numerous possible combinations:

	Nominal wage (W)	Price index (P) $(1972 = 1.00)$	Real wage (W/P)
Initial situation at E_0	$4.00	1.00	$4.00
Alternatives at A	1. $6.00	1.00	$6.00
	2. $5.00	0.83	$6.00
	3. $4.00	0.67	$6.00

Notice that in Figure 7-1, for the first time, we have discontinued writing specific numerical values on the horizontal axis. We do not indicate the number of man-hours hired, but label points only by general designations, N^* and N'. Why? From here on, with only a few exceptions, specific numbers on the axes would add unnecessary arithmetic without contributing anything essential to understanding. The main thing to notice about a diagram such as Figure 7-1 is the direction of the relation being discussed. The demand for labor depends negatively on the real wage. Exactly how much man-hour input falls between N^* and N' is not important; it is necessary to observe only that N' is to the left of N^*.

As with any schedule or curve, we move along the firm's labor demand curve if the variable indicated on the vertical axis changes, the real wage (W/P). A change in anything not indicated on either axis will shift the labor demand curve, including changes in the inputs of other factors of production (capital, land, energy supplies) and changes in the level of technology and knowledge. These factors cause the labor demand curve for individual firms and for the economy as a whole to shift as time passes. In this discussion, devoted to short-run changes in output and prices, we will ignore these sources of long-run economic growth and will assume that the labor demand curve remains fixed in place.

How does the economy's aggregate labor demand curve relate to the individual firm's curve? We will assume that all firms are identical, so that the economy's labor demand curve has exactly the same shape as that for the individual firm in Figure 7-1. The economy-wide labor demand curve can be labeled $N^d(W/P)$, which states that the demand for labor man-hours (N^d) depends on the real wage (W/P). The only difference between the economy-wide and individual curves is the number of man-hours represented on the horizontal axis (thousands or millions for firms, but billions for the whole economy).[3]

LABOR SUPPLY AND THE VALUE OF HOME TIME

The labor demand curve (N^d) shows the amount of labor firms want to hire. But how much labor will individuals be willing to provide to the firms? Twenty hours per person per week? Forty hours? Sixty hours? Most people work to obtain income for the purchase of consumer goods and services. Their reward for working consists of the goods and services that their income will buy, the wage per hour divided by the price index that they expect to be in effect in the future when they make their consumption purchases. In late February a worker might be considering a wage offer for March. If he is paid for the first time at the end of March, he will want to evaluate his wage offer at the prices he expects to be in effect in early April.

Thus the worker adjusts the nominal wage offer he receives for any changes in prices expected between now and the time consumption purchases will be made with the income from work. Starting with a price index $P = 1.0$, a nominal wage offer of $4.00 is expected to be worth $4.00 in the future if the expected future price index (P^e) remains unchanged $(P^e = 1.0)$. But if the price level were expected to double to $P^e = 2.0$, then the expected real wage implied by a nominal $4.00 wage offer would be much lower:

$$\text{Expected real wage} = \frac{W}{P^e} = \frac{\$4.00}{2.0} = \$2.00$$

Will workers be more willing to work at an expected real wage of $4.00 or $2.00? Microeconomic analysis concludes that the answer is ambiguous, because of two offsetting effects. On the one hand, the higher $4.00 expected real wage (W/P^e) raises the reward for working as compared to staying at home. At the higher real wage some people currently at home might be induced to seek work and other people might be tempted to take a second job (this is the microeconomic substitution effect). On the other hand, the higher real wage makes people better off and induces them to consume more of all goods and services, including leisure or home time, thus cutting back on their time at work (this is the microeconomic income effect). Will the substitution or income effect dominate? We will assume throughout this chapter that the higher real expected wage raises the

---

[3] In 1976 aggregate U.S. man-hours for the year as a whole summed to about 160 billion, about 1875 annual hours for each of 87.5 million employees.

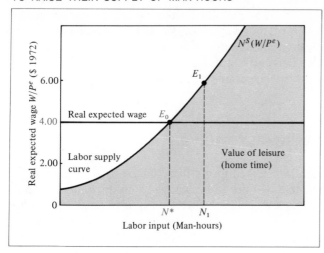

FIGURE 7-2

The Economy's Labor Supply Curve

The economy's labor supply curve slopes upward, reflecting our assumption that the substitution effect of a higher expected real wage dominates the income effect, at least for the short-run changes in labor input we consider in this chapter. The area under the labor supply curve represents the value of leisure or home time. At a real expected wage of $4.00, why won't individuals provide more man-hours than N^*? Because their time at home for extra man-hours is more valuable to them than $4.00.

supply of labor, inducing extra man-hours to be provided as individuals give up leisure to obtain a higher expected real wage.[4]

In Figure 7-2 the upward sloping black line is the economy's labor supply curve. At a real expected wage of $4.00, point E_0 on the supply curve indicates that individuals will provide a total supply of man-hours of N^*. Why won't more be provided? The area under the labor supply curve represents the value of leisure or home time. Individuals refuse to work more than N^* man-hours because the leisure provided by extra man-hours is regarded as more valuable than the goods and services that people could buy with the $4.00 real expected wage obtained from the extra work. The upward slope of the labor supply curve suggests that hours of leisure become more valuable as people give up more of them. How much would you require before you were willing to raise your hours of work per week from 40 to 60? From 60 to 80? Few people are willing to work more than 100 hours per week at any price, because that leaves them with little time for anything but sleeping and eating. When would they find time to spend their income?[5]

---

[4] In more complete theories, individuals distinguish between (1) increases in the expected real wage that are thought to be permanent—which may lead to reduced man-hours through more liberal vacations and sick-leave rules—and (2) increases that are thought to be temporary, which may lead to a temporary spell in the labor force or a temporary extra moonlighting job.

[5] The amount of leisure is measured on Figure 7-2 from right to left. At the "0" origin there is no work; all the week is spent in leisure-time activities. Looking at the curve from

(continued)

Would individuals ever be willing to work more than N^* man-hours? If the real expected wage were to rise from \$4.00 to \$6.00, for instance as a result of a higher \$6.00 wage offer combined with no change in the expected price level, the labor supply curve indicates that individuals would raise their desired man-hours of work from N^* to N_1. Homemakers and teenagers currently at home or in school might seek work, and other people might seek second or third jobs.

7-3 THE AGGREGATE SUPPLY CURVE

Now we have been introduced to the three factors that require an increase in price if businessmen are to be willing to produce more output. A higher price (P) is required because (1) business firms maximize profits and are unwilling to hire extra man-hours without a reduction in the real wage (W/P) by enough to compensate for the (2) diminishing marginal product of labor. The higher price would be necessary to achieve a lower real wage (W/P) even if the nominal wage rate (W) were constant. But (3) the nominal wage will have to rise to induce workers to increase their supply of labor.

How can the real wage fall (as required by firms to produce more output) and rise (as required by workers) at the same time? The answer is that the firms and workers define the price level differently. Firms are interested in the current price of their output (P), because they can sell immediately the worker's daily output. But workers are interested in the future expected price level (P^e), because they are paid after two weeks or a month of work and they spread out the spending of their wage income for several weeks or months after they are paid. In reality, wage offers are made for a substantial period, a year or even three years, and workers evaluate such long-term wage offers by the average price level they expect over the duration of the contract.

The essential element necessary to achieve higher output is an increase in the price level (P) above the level workers expect (P^e). The real wage expected by workers (W/P^e) deviates from the current real wage calculated by firms (W/P) if the price level (P) differs from the expected price level (P^e).

$$\text{Expected real wage} = \frac{W}{P^e} \equiv \frac{W}{P} \frac{P}{P^e}$$

Imagine that the price level were to rise from $P = 1.0$ to $P = 2.0$. If the

---

right to left, we can treat it as a demand curve for leisure, and its downward slope toward the zero origin reflects the diminishing marginal productivity or enjoyment provided by each additional hour of leisure.

nominal wage rate were to rise from $4.00 to $6.00, and workers had not yet adjusted their expectations of future prices above $P^e = 1.0$, then simultaneously the real wage would fall while the real wage expected by workers would rise. Both parties would voluntarily desire an increase in output and labor input. In this example:

$$\text{Real wage calculated by firms} = \frac{W}{P} = \frac{\$6.00}{2.0} = \$3.00$$

$$\text{Real wage expected by workers} = \frac{W}{P} \frac{P}{P^e} = \frac{\$6.00}{2.0} \frac{2.0}{1.0} = \$6.00$$

The top frame of Figure 7-3 combines the labor demand curve from Figure 7-1 and the labor supply curve from Figure 7-2. The vertical axis is the actual real wage (W/P), the same variable upon which the labor demand curve depends, so that the labor demand curve can be copied directly from Figure 7-1.

As always, the position of a curve is fixed if we change a variable already represented on one of the axes in a diagram. The ratio of the actual price to the expected price (P/P^e) is not on the axes, and thus any change in P/P^e shifts the labor supply curve.

In the example in the top frame of Figure 7-3 we start at point E_0, with the fixed labor demand curve and a labor supply curve drawn for correct expectations ($P_0/P_0^e = 1.0$). The original level of labor input is N^*, which we will see is always the level of man-hours demanded and supplied when worker expectations are correct. But when worker expectations are incorrect, labor input can vary from N^*.

For instance, if the price level rises from P_0 to some higher level P_1, and if at the same time workers are unaware of the higher price and maintain their expectations at the original P_0^e, the ratio of actual to expected price rises to P_1/P_0^e. This shifts the labor supply curve to the right, and the economy moves from the initial point E_0 in the top frame to the new position E_1. Firms are willing to hire more labor because the real wage has actually declined (P has risen more than W). But workers are willing to provide more labor, because they are attracted by the higher nominal wage (W) and do not realize that the price level has risen, and thus they evaluate the higher W at the original unchanged P_0^e.[6]

---

[6] Economists have built more detailed models to explain why the workers fail to "catch on" to the higher price. Workers may notice that their firm has raised the price of the product it produces, but they may believe that this is a special local phenomenon rather than a nationwide aggregate phenomenon. The simple model described in Figure 7-3 is precisely that of Milton Friedman's Presidential Address. "The Role of Monetary Policy," *American Economic Review*, vol. 58 (March 1968):

> Because selling prices of products typically respond to an unanticipated rise in nominal demand faster than prices of factors of productions, real wages received have gone down—though real wages anticipated by

(continued)

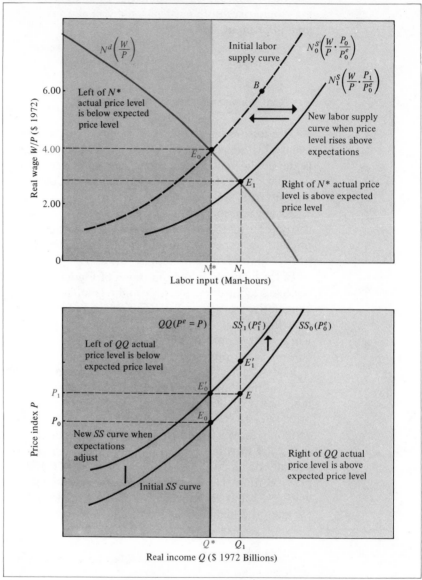

FIGURE 7–3   Deriving the Aggregate Supply
Curve

In the upper frame the labor demand
curve (N^d) is fixed. The labor supply
curve can shift right only when the
actual price level (P) rises above the
expectations of workers (P^e). The
economy moves from E_0 to E_1 in both

The bottom frame of Figure 7-3 plots the price level (P) on the vertical axis and the level of output (Q) on the horizontal. We make the simplifying assumption that output and employment increase in proportion, so that output in the bottom frame is always drawn directly below the man-hour labor input in the top frame which produces that output.[7]

The line connecting points E_0 and E_1 in the bottom frame is the **aggregate supply curve,** and it plots the relationship between output (Q) and the price level (P), on the assumption that the expected price level is constant at P_0^e. The aggregate supply curve is abbreviated SS and has these characteristics:

1. The SS curve slopes up, because when the expected price level is constant at P_0^e, a higher actual price level will reduce the real wage and induce firms to hire more workers and produce more output.
2. Everywhere along any SS curve, the expected price level is fixed. For SS_0 in Figure 7-3, the expected price level is P_0^e.
3. At the initial output level Q^*, expectations of the price level are correct. The expected price level (P_0^e) is exactly the same as the actual price level (P_0). Thus the price level that workers are anticipating along an SS curve is always measured by the vertical height of the intersection of that SS curve with the vertical QQ line.
4. When workers catch on that the price level has in fact risen, they will adjust their expectations (P^e) upward. The SS curve will shift upward whenever P^e rises.

---

employees went up, since employees implicitly evaluated the wages offered at the earlier price level. Indeed, the simultaneous fall *ex post* in real wages to employers and rise *ex ante* in real wages to employees is what enabled employment to increase.

[7] This simplification is, of course, inconsistent with the assumption of diminishing returns to labor used in drawing the labor demand curve. Thus, in reality, output responds by a smaller and smaller amount to a given increase in labor input as we move rightward in Figure 7-3. The simplification of drawing Q^* directly below N^* and Q_1 directly below N_1 avoids the necessity of including an extra quadrant on the diagram to represent the economy's production function. No conclusions are changed by this simplifying device, since we are interested that output rises whenever P/P^e exceeds 1.0, not by how much it rises.

---

diagrams when the price level increases from P_0 to P_1 while worker expectations remain at P_0^e. Once expectations adjust upward to reality, and $P_1^e = P_1$, then output falls back to its initial level. In the upper frame the economy returns to point E_0, and in the lower frame it moves to E_0', which lies above the initial position by the amount by which actual and expected prices have increased.

Let us examine the new situation after workers have raised their expectations from the initial P_0^e to the new P_1^e, equal to the new higher price level P_1. Since the actual price level no longer exceeds the expected price level, which has now increased from P_0^e to P_1^e, the labor supply curve in the upper frame shifts back to its initial position. Firms can no longer afford to hire more man-hours than N^*, so that labor input is cut back to point E_0 in the top frame. Output falls from Q_1 to Q^* at point E_0' in the bottom frame.

The new SS_1 curve drawn through point E_0' lies above the original SS_0 curve by exactly the amount by which the expected price level has risen. As always, the expected price level that workers anticipate along the SS curve (P_1^e) is measured by the vertical distance of that SS curve above natural output Q^*, a vertical distance equal to P_1. The black vertical QQ line running up above Q^* through E_0 and E_0' shows the different points where expectations are correct ($P^e = P$). Only if the price level once again increases above P_1, while expectations remain at P_1^e, can output increase along the SS_1 curve to the right of the vertical QQ line.

> **Summary:** When worker expectations of the future price level are correct ($P^e = P$), there is only one possible natural level of employment (N^*) and one possible natural level of output (Q^*). Only when the actual price level exceeds expectations, everywhere in the pink area to the right of Q^*, can actual output exceed natural output. Only when the actual price level is below expectations in the gray area can output fall below natural output. An output level differing from Q^* is not a long-run equilibrium situation, since there is upward or downward pressure on the price level caused by the inevitable adjustment of expectations toward reality.

7-4 FORMING EXPECTATIONS

So far we have learned that the output can rise above its natural level (Q^*) only when workers are "fooled" by an increase in the price level above what they expect.

But one ingredient is missing. We cannot determine the position of the SS curve until we know what price level workers expect. How are their expectations formed? One particularly simple hypothesis, described in Figure 7-4, plots the path of the expected price level (P^e) along the black line on the assumption that workers always set P^e at last period's actual value of the price level (P_{-1}):

$$P^e = P_{-1}$$

Thus when the price level follows the hypothetical path plotted by the

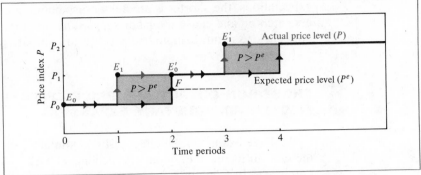

FIGURE 7–4

The Path of the Expected Price Level When Expectations Lag One Period behind Actual Events

The behavior of the actual price level (P) is assumed to follow the red line. The black line shows the behavior of the expected price level (P^e), if the latter is always set equal to last period's actual price level. If errors in forecasting the price level are not completely made up in each period, then expected prices do not rise by the full amount of the previous error, as indicated by the dashed line at point F.

red line starting from the initial position E_0, the expected price level "tags along" one period later.

The hypothesis that the expected price level is based on past values of the actual price level is called **adaptive expectations**. In general, expectations do not necessarily adjust fully to an increase in the price level because workers may believe that some part of a price increase is temporary. For instance, they might adjust their expectations by only a fraction (g) of any change in the price level from what they previously expected:

$$P^e - P^e_{-1} = g(P_{-1} - P^e_{-1})$$

Example: Assume that $g = 0.5$. What will be the expected price level in period 2 in Figure 7-4? In the previous period the actual price level (P_{-1}) exceeded the expected price level (P^e_{-1}) by the vertical distance indicated by the first pink box. If the current expected price level were to adjust upward by half of that pink expectational error, then the new level of the expected price in period 2 would be indicated by the dashed line at point F. When $g = 1.0$, as assumed in Figures 7-3 and 7-4, the expected price in period 2 rises by the full amount of the pink error to point E'_0, correcting the full amount of the previous error.

In general, the higher the value of g, the coefficient of adjustment of expectations, the shorter is any temporary boom in output before workers catch on and cause the labor supply and SS curves to shift the economy back to natural employment (N^*) and output (Q^*).

7-5 SHORT-RUN OUTPUT AND PRICE EFFECTS OF FISCAL AND MONETARY EXPANSION

We have examined the effect of fiscal stimulus, such as a $100 billion increase in planned autonomous spending caused by higher government purchases. In Chapter 5 we assumed that the price level was fixed, and that the fiscal stimulus raised real output; in Chapter 6 we assumed that real output was fixed, and that the fiscal stimulus simply raised the price level. Now we find that both output and the price level are increased simultaneously in the short run.

In Figure 7-5, we begin in equilibrium at point E_0 with an actual price level equal to P_0.

Now a fiscal stimulus is introduced, in the form of an increase in government purchases that raises autonomous planned spending from $\bar{A}_0$ to $\bar{A}_1$. Where do we find the new equilibrium levels of output and the price index? If the price level were to remain constant, we would move straight to the right in Figure 7-5 from point E_0 to point K. But the price level cannot remain fixed because firms will insist on an increase in the price level to cover the higher costs of the increased production. In short, point K is off the short-run supply curve SS_0 and is not a point at which firms will be willing to produce.

Point E_1 is the crossing point of the SS_0 schedule with the new DD_1 schedule, where businessmen are willing to produce. The increase in government purchases has raised the price level and increased output at the same time. But output has not increased by the full Chapter 5 multiplier based on a fixed price level, the horizontal distance between E_0 and K. Instead, point E_1 lies northwest of the constant price point K, because the higher price level at E_1 reduces the real money supply and hence the demand for commodities.

The situation illustrated in Figure 7-5 at point E_1 would result from any stimulative factor that raises aggregate demand, not only an increase in government purchases, but also from:

1. An increase in autonomous transfer payments or a reduction in autonomous taxes that raises $\bar{A}$.
2. An improvement in business and consumer confidence that raises $\bar{A}$.
3. A reduction in the income tax rate that raises the multiplier.
4. An increase in the nominal money supply.

A FISCAL EXPANSION RAISES BOTH THE
PRICE INDEX AND REAL INCOME IN THE SHORT RUN

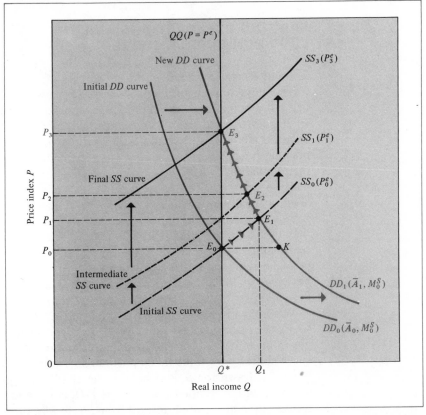

FIGURE 7–5

Effects on the Price Index and Real Income of an Increase in Planned Autonomous Spending from $\bar{A}_0$ to $\bar{A}_1$

Higher planned autonomous spending shifts the economy's equilibrium position from the initial point E_0 to E_1, where both the price level and real output have increased. Point E_1 is not a sustainable position, however, be-cause the actual price level P_1 exceeds the expected price level P_0^e, and soon the expected price level will adjust upward to the new reality of higher actual prices. Then the SS curve shifts upward from SS_0 to SS_1. But again the actual price level exceeds expectations at point E_2. Only at point E_3 does the expected price level finally catch up to the actual price level.

As long as the short-run supply curve SS slopes upward to the right, any of the changes on this list will shift the DD curve rightward and raise both output and prices simultaneously.

7-6 SHIFTING EXPECTATIONS AND THE LONG-RUN SUPPLY CURVE

Point E_1 is not the end of the adjustment of the economy to the higher level of government purchases, however, because business firms are satisfied but workers are not. The price level has risen from P_0 at point E_0 to P_1 at point E_1, but point E_1 assumes that the expected price level is unchanged (P_0^e). Why should workers still be willing to work for the same nominal hourly wage as before when the higher price level has reduced their actual real wage?

Each SS (short-run supply) curve assumes that the expected price level is fixed at a particular value; P_0^e for the supply curve SS_0. Once workers learn that the actual price deflator has risen higher than the level they originally expected, they will revise their expectations upward. One reasonable assumption, illustrated in Figure 7-4, is that the new expected price level in the current pay period (P_1^e) is estimated by workers to be equal to the actual price level reached at the end of the last pay period (P_1).

When the price level rises from P_0 at point E_0 to P_1 at point E_1, workers revise the price level expected for the next period upward to P_1^e. Since the position of the SS curve depends on the expected price level, the SS curve shifts up from the initial position SS_0, drawn for P_0^e, to the new position SS_1, drawn for P_1^e. As before, the equilibrium price level occurs at the point of intersection between the DD_1 curve and the SS curve. Since the SS curve has shifted upward from SS_0 to SS_1, the point of intersection has shifted upward from point E_1 to point E_2.

But once again, the workers have been fooled! They expected the price level to be P_1, and it turns out to be P_2 at point E_2. What is the problem? The actual price level along any SS curve equals the expected price level (P^e) on which that SS curve is based only when actual output equals natural output ($Q = Q^*$), that is, only at points on the vertical QQ curve. Since the SS curve slopes up to the right of the QQ curve, the actual price level is higher than expected whenever the economy is to the right of the QQ schedule.

The only place where the economy can be on its DD curve and simultaneously where workers are not fooled is at the point of crossing of DD and QQ. For instance, initially in Figure 7-5 the economy was in equilibrium at point E_0. Now, however, with the rightward shift in the DD_1 curve, the full "no fooling" equilibrium can occur only at point E_3, where DD_1 intersects the vertical QQ schedule. At any lower price level the economy will be to the right of QQ, workers will be fooled, and they will revise upward their expectation of next period's price level. Only at point E_3 does the price level turn out to be just what workers expect, so that they no longer are forced to revise their expectations, and the economy can stay put.

SHORT-RUN AND LONG-RUN EQUILIBRIUM

The economy is in **short-run equilibrium** when two conditions are satisfied. First, the level of output produced must be enough to balance the demand for commodities, without any involuntary accumulation or decumulation of inventory—this first condition is satisfied at any point along the appropriate DD curve. Second, price level P must be sufficient to make firms both able and willing to produce the level of output specified along the DD curve; this can happen only along a short-run supply curve (SS) specified for a particular set of expectations about the price level (P^e). The equilibrium at the crossing point of the DD and SS curves, however, is not permanent if actual real output is either above or below natural output (Q^*), since the actual price level will then differ from that which had been expected, leading to a revision of expectations.

The economy is in **long-run equilibrium** only when all the conditions for a short-run equilibrium are satisfied, and, in addition, the actual price level turns out to be exactly equal to what individuals expect for the current period. Since expectations are realized, there is no need for the expected price level to be revised any further, and thus there is no pressure for any further change in the price level as long as aggregate demand (the DD curve) remains constant. In Figure 7-5, long-run equilibrium occurs only where all three schedules (DD, SS, and QQ) intersect.

> **Summary:** In the long run, any change in aggregate demand (shift in the DD curve), whether caused by monetary, fiscal, or confidence factors, changes the price level without causing any change in real output. Real output can change in short-run equilibrium but not in long-run equilibrium.

The effect of a shift in aggregate demand in long-run equilibrium in this chapter is thus exactly the same as the perfectly flexible price case of Chapter 6. The difference now is that we have carefully specified an intermediate step, short-run equilibrium, and we have introduced the state of expectations of the future price level as a central element in the process of price adjustment that takes the economy from point E_0 to point E_3.

7-7 CONDITIONS REQUIRED FOR A CONTINUING DEMAND-PULL INFLATION

Inflation is an upward movement in prices that is (1) shared by all components of the price deflator, and (2) is sustained. Thus an increase in the price of haircuts and other services during the early years of the

1960s was not considered as an episode of inflation, because at the same time other prices (particularly television sets and other durable goods) were falling. The average price index, the GNP deflator, hardly increased at all. Part (1) of our definition of inflation was violated; the relative price of haircuts increased, but the upward movement in this price was not shared by all components of the price deflator. Since 1965, however, almost all prices have increased in the United States and we have had what almost everyone describes as an inflation.

Part (2) of the definition requires that a general upward movement of prices be sustained to be called an inflation. An upward movement in prices is not generally classified as inflation if it lasts for only six months or a year and then stops or is followed by a general decline in prices. If the price index were to increase in some years and decrease in others, ending the decade roughly where it began, there would be no serious consequences and no one would describe the situation as an era of inflation.

The price increase caused in Figure 7-5 by a rightward shift in the DD curve takes the economy from a long-run equilibrium at point E_0 to another long-run equilibrium at point E_3. But there is no sustained inflation. Once the price level has arrived at point E_3, it rises no further, and both the actual (P) and expected price deflator (P^e) are constant and equal to each other.

A shift in the DD curve caused by an increase in autonomous spending $(\bar{A})$ while the nominal money supply remains constant can cause the price level to increase substantially, as in Figure 7-5, but it cannot cause a sustained continuing increase in P. Why? Imagine that the government continues to increase its purchases (G), raising the price level higher and higher. The total level of income cannot increase in long-run equilibrium; the economy must stay on the vertical QQ curve where real income is constant. Thus the ever-growing level of government purchases must crowd out private investment and consumption purchases, eventually reaching the point where all production is purchased by the government and none remains for private households or firms. Here, when it has purchased 100 percent of total GNP, the government cannot increase its purchases any further in long-run equilibrium, and so the price level must stop growing.

This is an extreme example to make the picture clear; in reality the share of government purchases in real GNP stays in a relatively narrow range, and thus it cannot be a source of a continuing inflation as long as the nominal money supply (M^s) remains constant.[8]

Just as a fiscal stimulus can shift the DD curve, and raise the price level, so too can a monetary stimulus. The top frame of Figure 7-6 de-

---

[8] The share of real federal, state, and local government purchases in real GNP was as follows:

picts an initial long-run equilibrium situation at point E_0, just as in Figure 7-5, with an initial level of $\bar{A}_0$ and M_0^s. The DD curve is now shifted to the right by an increase in the money supply from M_0^s billion to M_1^s. The results are just the same as when a fiscal stimulus is applied in Figure 7-5: first both output and the price level increase as the economy moves northeast of point E_0 to point E_1. But then, as workers notice that the price level has risen above the level of 1.0, which they initially expected, they revise upward the expected price level (P^e), and the actual price level (P) is pushed upward until the economy attains long-run equilibrium at point E_3.

EVERY INFLATION HAS A MONETARY CONNECTION

So far our conclusion is exactly the same as in Figure 7-5. A demand-pull increase in the price level can be initiated by any event that shifts aggregate demand and the DD curve to the right, thus pulling upward on the price level. A one-shot monetary stimulus, an increase in real government spending, a cut in taxes, or an increase in business and consumer confidence are all capable of shifting DD and so are capable of initiating a demand-pull increase in the price level. But for a demand-pull inflation to occur, that is, a sustained continuous increase in the price level, something more is necessary. A continuous rightward shift in DD is necessary. Since there is a natural limit on the size of a fiscal stimulus, only a continuous increase in the nominal money supply can fuel a sustained inflation.

This is illustrated in the top frame of Figure 7-6, where the money supply grows first from M_0^s to M_1^s. If the nominal money supply were to grow further to M_2^s and even higher amounts, it would shift the DD curve continuously rightward and carry the price level with it from P_0 at point E_0 to P_3 at point E_3 to P_4 at point E_4 and so on to points further north of E_4. A sustained, continuous inflation requires the continuous expansion of the nominal money supply. This is what Milton Friedman meant when he issued his famous dictum that "inflation is always and everywhere a monetary phenomenon."[9] This does not mean that an increase in M^s is the cause of every one-shot increase in the price level, because a fiscal stimulus or a change in business and consumer confidence can shift the DD curve as well. But these stimuli have natural limits that prevent them

---

1950	18.3%	1965	22.6%
1953	27.3	1968	24.6
1955	23.0	1970	23.3
1960	23.5	1975	21.7

Peak rates were reached when wartime activities were at their highest, during the Korean War (1953, 27.3%) and the Vietnam War (1968, 24.6%).

[9] See the epigraph which began this chapter.

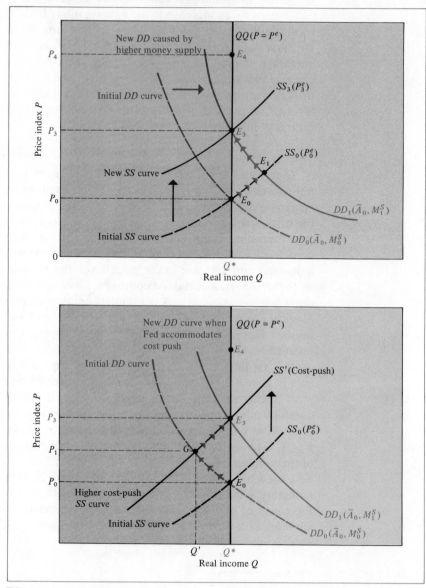

FIGURE 7-6 Effects in the Short Run and Long Run of an Increase in the Money Supply and of a Labor Union Cost-Push Ratified by a Higher Money Supply

In the top frame the economy's adjustment to a higher money supply (M^s) follows the same path as its adjustment in Figure 7–5. At first output increases above Q^*, but then the expected price level adjusts, shifting the short-run supply curve upward from

from shifting the *DD* curve to the right continuously, whereas there is no natural limit to an increase in the money supply.

The word "inflation" carries with it the idea of a "blowing up" of prices, as when one blows up a balloon. And, just as air is required to blow up a balloon, so an inflation requires that prices be "blown up" by a continuous increase in the nominal money supply.

Every sustained inflation has a monetary connection. But this does not mean that the branch of government responsible for the creation of money, the Federal Reserve Board, always initiates every episode of inflation. Instead, the Fed may be induced to raise the money supply if it attempts to keep the interest rate constant when the administration and Congress provide a fiscal stimulus, a situation illustrated in Figure 5-9. The Fed may also be induced to raise the money supply by other events, such as the behavior of labor unions, as we will see next.

COST-PUSH AND SUPPLY SHOCKS

All shifts in the short-run supply curve *SS* have resulted as the price level (P) was pulled above the expected price level (P^e) by an increase in aggregate demand, forcing a revision of expectations. But an increase in the price level can also be caused by a spontaneous upward shift in *SS* caused by **cost-push,** a decision by workers to demand a higher real wage, or by firms to raise their profit margins, even when the expected price level is constant.

Let us imagine that workers suddenly demand that their nominal wage rate be doubled, requiring a price increase if firms are to be willing to produce the same output as before. In the bottom frame of Figure 7-6 the initial equilibrium is as before at point E_0, where the SS_0 and DD_0 curves cross the vertical *QQ* schedule. The aggressive cost-push pressure by workers for a doubling of nominal wages causes the supply curve to shift up vertically to SS'. If the levels of $\bar{A}$ and the nominal money supply (M^s) remain constant, the aggregate demand curve remains at DD_0, and the economy arrives at a short-run equilibrium at point G, where the price level has increased and the level of output has fallen. Why? The higher price level decreases the supply of real balances (M^s/P), forc-

SS_0 to SS_3. In the bottom frame higher nominal wage demands by workers shift the supply curve upward from SS_0 to SS'. If the Federal Reserve keeps the money supply constant, and if there is no further adjustment of the nominal wage, the economy moves to point G, where output has fallen from Q^* to Q'. But if the Fed raises the money supply from M_1^s to M_2^s, the economy winds up at point E_3, just as in the top frame.

ing a reduction in output along the DD_0 curve in order to reduce the real demand for money.

Thus, if the Fed stands firm and holds the money supply at its initial level, the aggressive cost-push by the workers actually makes some workers worse off, because output declines as the economy moves from point E_0 to G, production is cut, and some workers are laid off. The price level increases, but not by the full extent of the upward shift in the supply curve. The cut in production allows firms to discharge low productivity workers, so that marginal cost increases by less than the twofold increase in nominal wage rates.

Why would a labor union demand such an increase in wages at the cost of unemployment for some of its workers? Part of the answer may reflect internal union politics: the workers most likely to be laid off as the economy moves from point E_0 to point G are usually the youngest ("last hired, first fired"), and the majority of union members may be older workers who have sufficient seniority to be free from concern about the possibility of a layoff.

But the union leaders may be able to escape without any unemployment whatsoever. Federal Reserve policy may choose to maintain full employment by adjusting the money supply. The economy can be pushed northeast from point G to point E_3 if the Fed allows the money supply to double from M_0^s to M_1^s. At point E_3 the price level and the money supply have doubled, leaving the real money supply unchanged and avoiding the need for any decline in the demand for money and output. The Fed, by allowing the union cost-push action to raise the price level without the penalty of unemployment, is said to have accommodated or ratified the cost-push.

Point E_3, however, is not likely to be the end of the story. The problem is that the workers have not accomplished anything. They have achieved a doubling of their *nominal* wage (W), but the price level (P) has doubled, and so the *real* wage (W/P) has not increased at all. If workers again attempt to achieve a doubled real wage, the SS curve will shift up again. The result will be the same—higher prices and unemployment if the Fed holds the money supply constant, or even higher prices without extra unemployment if the Fed accommodates the wage demands.[10]

PASSIVE MONETARY ACCOMMODATION

In moving from point E_0 to point E_3, both the price level and the money supply have doubled. But does this mean that the Fed has caused the inflation by irresponsible monetary policy? The ultimate cause of the inflation is the cost-push by workers, and the Fed's role is passive "ratifier" of the higher prices by allowing the money supply to increase. In the same way, an inflation may be initiated by a fiscal action that shifts

---

[10] If the unions insist on a permanent increase in the real wage, the natural output level Q^* declines permanently as firms cut back on low marginal product man-hours.

the DD curve when government purchases increase; if the Fed wants to keep the interest rate from rising, it allows the money supply to increase and thus accommodates or ratifies the fiscal stimulus. An increase in government purchases, creating a continuous deficit financed by printing money, can cause a continuing inflation unless the Fed refuses to print the money. Similarly, a cost-push by workers or firms can cause a continuing inflation if ratified by the Fed, but only unemployment and a one-shot increase in the price level if not ratified.

Thus, the distinction between cost-push and demand-pull inflation is largely spurious. A shift in either SS or DD moves the equilibrium position of the economy from point E_0 to E_3 to E_4 and further points north. The only difference is that initially a demand-pull inflation raises output along path $E_0E_1E_3$ in the top frame of Figure 7-6 if expectations are slow to adjust, and a cost-push inflation reduces output along path E_0GE_3 in the bottom frame if the Fed is slow to raise the level of the nominal money supply. But to be sustained and continuous, the increase in prices must be accompanied by an increase in the money supply, once again confirming that "inflation is always and everywhere a monetary phenomenon."

A Keynesian demand inflation generated by shifts in fiscal policy or in business or consumer optimism, or a cost-induced inflation generated by autonomous increases in wage or profit demands, has to be validated by the monetary authority. Can one argue, therefore, that a distinction should be made not between demand-pull and cost-push inflation, but rather between inflations in which the role of money is active versus passive? Even this potential basis for classification becomes blurred when one recognizes that, even in most classic wartime or postwar money-fueled inflations, the role of the monetary authority has been passively to finance deficits arising from the unwillingness or inability of politicians to finance expenditures through increases in conventional taxes. Keynesian fiscal-induced money-accommodated inflation and "pure" money-initiated inflation have in almost all historical cases amounted to one and the same thing.

> Thus, a more general view is that inflation results from the passivity of the monetary authority in the face of pressures emanating from all groups in society—workers, firms, and government.[11]

In 1973 and 1974, the United States experienced a new kind of cost-push inflation. Poor harvests and buoyant foreign demand caused the

---

[11] The notion that the Federal Reserve (or any central bank) is operating under a tripartite set of pressures from labor, management, and the fiscal side of government was originated in a classic article by Melvin W. Reder, "The Theoretical Problems of a National Wage-Price Policy," *Canadian Journal of Economics and Political Science* (February 1948), pp. 46–61.

prices of raw agricultural commodities to double in 1973, forcing up the price of food in supermarkets. Then in early 1974 the price of oil was quadrupled by OPEC, forcing up the prices paid by U.S. firms and consumers for gasoline, motor oil, heating oil, chemicals, and other products. A third inflationary impetus was provided by the 1971 and 1973 devaluations of the dollar, which raised the dollar price of goods imported into the United States relative to the foreign currency price of those nations producing the goods. Since the higher prices of foods, oil, and imported goods in general forced businessmen to raise the price deflator (P) above the level of expected prices (P^e), the economy's supply curve SS shifted up, just as in the bottom frame of Figure 7-6. But the outcome differed from the illustration, because the Federal Reserve chose not to accommodate the SS shift, and, in fact, held down the growth of the nominal money supply (M^s) below normal. The economy's real income was allowed to decline, and workers were laid off. By May 1975, unemployment had reached a postwar peak of 9.0 percent.

Many economists now use the phrase supply shocks to refer to crop failures, increases in raw commodity prices caused by collusion among members of a cartel (as in the 1974 oil case), and other unforeseen events that raise the price necessary to induce firms to produce a given amount. The effect of a supply shock is just the same as a cost-push by workers or firms; the price level increases without any initiating action by the government. However, the extent of the increase in the aggregate price deflator and the extent of the decline in output, if any, depend on the response of the Fed.

7-8 CASE STUDY: INFLATION IN HISTORY— DEMAND OR SUPPLY INDUCED?

Comparing the northward movement of the economy from point E_0 to E_3 to E_4 in the top and bottom frames of Figure 7-6, we see that prices, wages, and the money supply all increase together, preventing any easy statement that inflation is caused by a wage push or by overly stimulative Federal Reserve policy. But there is a difference between the top and bottom frames. If expectations are slow to adjust, then a demand-pull inflation initiated by a rightward shift in DD is accompanied by an increase in output from point E_0 to point E_1, followed by a decrease in output from E_1 to E_3 when expectations begin to adjust. The line connecting E_0, E_1, and E_3 can be thought of as a counterclockwise loop:

An inflation initiated by cost-push or a supply shock differs. If the monetary authority either does not accommodate the cost-push, or delays its accommodation, then the increase in prices initiated by a leftward shift in SS is initially accompanied by a decrease in output from point E_0 to point G, followed by an increase in output from point G to E_3 if the Fed raises the money supply. The line connecting E_0, G, and E_3 can be thought of as a "clockwise" loop:

Figures 7-7 and 7-8 plot the data for P and Q/Q^* for the major United States episodes of inflation in the twentieth century. We can examine the economy's path in each case to see whether a counterclockwise (demand-pull) or clockwise (cost-push) route is followed. Figure 7-7 shows the inflations connected with World Wars I and II. In both the increase in prices was initially accompanied by an increase in output, as one would expect in the classic wartime inflation in which the government runs a large deficit and finances the deficit by printing money.[12] In both, the initial increase in Q/Q^* was followed by the inevitable decline as wartime expenditures wound down after the war, and in both cases the price level continued to rise after the termination of hostilities in 1918 and in 1945.

The main differences between the two wartime episodes are, first, that the price level fell substantially between 1920 and 1922 but did not fall at all after World War II. One obvious explanation is that prices were set freely by business firms during World War I, but during World War II prices were tightly controlled by the government Office of Price Administration (OPA). After the termination of controls in mid-1946, prices jumped rapidly and wound up about 70 percent higher than at the beginning of the war, very similar to the 60 percent net increase between 1915 and 1923. This similarity between the two episodes is somewhat surprising, given the much more nearly total production effort in the second war and much higher share of total production purchased by the government.

Figure 7-8 plots data for indexes of P and Q/Q^* in the four major episodes of postwar inflation. The first two episodes (1950–54 and 1954–58) resulted in an increase in the price level of about 10 percent. Both loops are counterclockwise, with the main differences limited to the timing of price and output increases. In the first episode Q/Q^* remained high for three straight years, 1951–53, whereas in the second episode Q/Q^* increased for only one year, 1955, and then fell

---

[12] Thus the wartime economic stimulus is neither pure monetary nor pure fiscal policy. but mixed monetary and fiscal expansion.

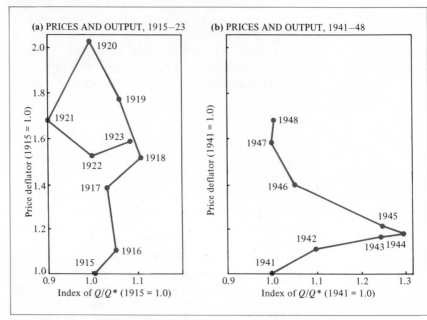

FIGURE 7–7

The Behavior of the Price Deflator and the Ratio of Actual to Natural Real Output (Q/Q^*) in Two Wartime and Postwar Episodes, 1915–23 and 1941–48

In both episodes both the price level and the output ratio increased together, but the timing was different. The increase in the price level during World War II in 1942–45 was moderated by controls on prices and wages, whereas in World War I (1916–18) there were no controls. The postwar experience also differed. There was an overshooting of the price level in 1919–20, followed by a drastic deflation in 1921 and 1922, which returned prices to the 1918 level. In contrast, prices shot up at the end of World War II (1946–48) when price controls were terminated.

for three years. In the first episode, almost all the price increase occurred immediately, whereas in the second episode most of the price increase occurred relatively late, possibly because of a delayed upward shift in the expected price level (P^e).

The third episode, 1964–70, also follows a counterclockwise course, consistent with the hypothesis that the major cause of higher prices was the rightward DD shift caused by the combined monetary-fiscal expansion that began in 1965 when the United States entered active Vietnam combat. The 1964–70 counterclockwise path is very smooth and regular in appearance: The economy in 1970 arrived back at exactly the same Q/Q^* value achieved in 1964, but over the intervening six years the price level had increased by more than 25 percent.

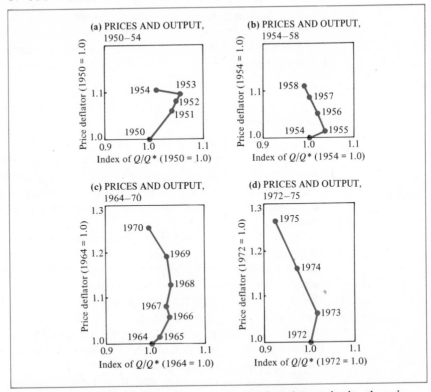

FIGURE 7–8

The Behavior of the Price Deflator and the Ratio of Actual to Natural Real Output (Q/Q^*) in Four Postwar Episodes, 1950–54, 1954–58, 1964–70, and 1972–75

In the first three episodes the price deflator and the output ratio increased together, a sign of demand-pull inflation. But between 1973 and 1975 a dramatic increase in the price level was accompanied by a decline in the output ratio, the result of cost-push in the form of higher oil and food prices.

Only the most recent 1972–75 episode qualifies for a cost-push interpretation. After a brief movement northeast between 1972 and 1973, the economy moved rapidly northwest in 1974 and 1975. The higher prices of food, oil, and imports in general pushed the SS curve leftward, while a tight Federal Reserve monetary policy kept the DD curve approximately constant. The 1973–75 inflation was aggravated by the termination in mid-1974 of the wage and price controls that had been in effect under the different "phases" of the control program between 1971 and 1974. It has been estimated that the removal of price controls subtracted about 3 percent from the price level in 1971 and 1972 but added about the same amount back to the price level in 1974.[13]

Our conclusion is that five of the six major inflationary episodes in the twentieth century were demand-pull in origin rather than cost-push. We will next look further into the causes of inflation and begin to explore the policy options available to fight inflation.

SUMMARY

1. In this chapter real output and the price level are allowed to change together in the short run. We take into account the effect on output and prices of the anticipations workers and firms hold about the price level. Along a single aggregate supply curve (*SS*), actual output exceeds natural output when the actual price level exceeds the expected price level, and vice versa.

2. For output to rise above natural output, the price level tends to rise for at least two reasons: (1) As output is increased the principle of diminishing returns is likely to apply. Reduced product per added worker raises wage cost per unit of output and induces profit-maximizing firms to raise prices; (2) workers must be bribed to work more and firms are likely to raise their prices to cover the higher wage costs. Just as the price level is likely to rise above initial expectations when actual real output increases, the price level will fall relative to the expected price level when aggregate demand declines.

3. A fiscal or monetary stimulus shifts the aggregate demand (*DD*) curve to the right and raises both output and prices simultaneously in the short run as long as price expectations are fixed. Equilibrium at the intersection of the *DD* and *SS* curves is necessarily temporary and unstable if actual real output is either above or below natural output (Q^*). The actual price level then differs from that which has been expected, leading to a revision of price expectations and a shift of the *SS* curve.

4. The economy is in long-run equilibrium only when all the conditions for a short-run equilibrium are satisfied and, in addition, when the actual price level turns out to be exactly equal to what people expect. In the long run, any change in aggregate demand changes the price level without causing any change in real output, the same result as in the perfectly flexible prices case in Chapter 6.

5. Inflation is a sustained upward movement in prices that is shared by all components of the price deflator. A demand-pull increase in the price level results from a rightward shift of the *DD* curve. An auton-

---

[13] Robert J. Gordon, "The Effect of Aggregate Demand on Prices," *Brookings Papers on Economic Activity,* vol. 6, no. 3 (1975), pp. 613–62.

omous decision by workers to demand a higher real wage, or by firms to raise their profit margins, results in a cost-push, which shifts the *SS* curve upward.

6. An upward shift in either the *SS* or the *DD* curve raises prices. The distinguishing difference is that initially a demand-pull inflation raises output if expectations are slow to adjust, whereas a cost-push inflation initially reduces output if the Fed is slow to raise the level of the nominal money supply. But to be sustained and continuous, any increase in prices must be accompanied by a continuous increase in the money supply.

7. Most inflationary episodes in U.S. history, with the exception of 1973–1975, appear to have been initiated by an increase in aggregate demand.

A LOOK AHEAD

We have now been introduced to the basic factors which cause inflation. But what are the causes of the other major macroeconomic problem, high unemployment? In the next chapters we shall learn how inflation and unemployment are interrelated, and about their consequences for society.

CONCEPTS AND QUESTIONS

IDENTIFICATIONS

Comparative statics	Long-run equilibrium
Short-run aggregate supply curve	Inflation
Expected price level	Demand-pull inflation
Actual real wage	Cost-push inflation
Expected real wage	Monetary accommodation
Short-run equilibrium	Supply shock

QUESTIONS FOR REVIEW

1 Explain in words why the *SS* curve slopes up and to the right.

2 How do *you* formulate an expectation of the future price level?

3 What is the difference between short-run and long-run equilibrium?

Are these statements true, false, or uncertain? Be sure you can explain your answer.

4 A sustainable long-run equilibrium is always reached at the point of intersection of the *DD* and *SS* curves.

5 The Fed controls both the nominal money supply and the interest rate and can set them both simultaneously at any desired level.

6 When a large increase in both the price level and the nominal

money supply occurs in the same year, one can correctly conclude that the Fed initiated the inflation.

7   A period of inflation is always initially accompanied by an increase in actual real output.

8   Even at full employment, changes in the nominal money supply will alter the interest rate.

8 Determinants of Inflation and Unemployment

I don't think the President understands why there's high inflation and high unemployment at the same time. But then neither does anyone else.

—Anonymous Treasury Official[1]

8-1 INTRODUCTION

Now we are ready to study the relationship between unemployment and inflation, the two most important macroeconomic problems of modern societies. Why has the rate of inflation been so much more rapid since 1965 than previously? Does the government, through its monetary and fiscal policy, bear the blame for the inflation we have experienced? What keeps the government from providing a job for everyone? Is a slack economy, with frequent layoffs and high unemployment, the only way to bring down the rate of inflation? Finally, how can high unemployment be treated as a "cure" for inflation when in 1974 high unemployment occurred simultaneously with more inflation, not less?

If the price of coffee rises from $1.00 to $4.00 per pound, and no other prices change, we are not experiencing inflation. Inflation describes a sustained continuous upward movement in prices shared by all components of the aggregate price index (or GNP deflator). In Chapter 7 we studied the determinants of the level of the price index. We learned that a jump in the price index from an initial level to a new higher level could be caused by a fiscal stimulus, a monetary stimulus, or an improvement in business and consumer confidence. In short, any event that can cause a single rightward shift in the economy's aggregate demand schedule (DD curve) can cause at the same time a single upward jump in the price index.

But inflation is a continuous increase in the price index, not a single

---

[1] Quoted in *The Wall Street Journal* (September 23, 1977) p. 23.

jump. Thus a sustained inflation requires a continuous increase in aggregate demand. To focus on the determinants of inflation, we now shift from the diagrams of Chapter 7, which measure the level of the price index on the vertical axis, to related diagrams that measure vertically the rate of change of the price index, that is, the inflation rate itself. In Chapter 7, a continuous inflation results in a steady upward movement of the economy's equilibrium position so that the economy eventually moves off the upper edge of the page. Now, as we shift to the rate of inflation, the equilibrium position of an economy experiencing a steady inflation of, say, 6 percent, remains fixed on the page.

In this chapter we study the determinants of inflation and of unemployment as well. In the postwar United States, the **unemployment rate** — the ratio of those seeking jobs to the total labor force — has been highly unstable, hitting a low level of 2.9 percent in the spring of 1953 and a high level of 9.0 percent in May 1975. We will find that movements in the unemployment rate correspond to the changes in real output (Q), which we have studied in Chapters 3 through 7. When the economy is prosperous and output is high, firms hire additional workers from the ranks of the jobless, and the rate of unemployment falls. In a business slump, sales fall off, workers are laid off, and the rate of unemployment rises.

We will first study normal situations in which shifts in aggregate demand are the main cause of swings in inflation and unemployment. Just as we learned in Chapter 7 that an increase in aggregate demand only raises real output temporarily, before worker expectations have time to adjust, so we reach the parallel conclusion here that, starting from an initial equilibrium position, higher aggregate demand only cuts unemployment temporarily. We will see that low unemployment cannot be sustained permanently without an acceleration of inflation. In the last part of the chapter we examine the effects on inflation and unemployment of shifts in aggregate supply. A drought or freeze that causes crops to fail, or a sudden major increase in the price of an important raw material such as oil, can generate higher inflation and unemployment at the same time. In short, we will find that inflation and unemployment sometimes move in the same direction and sometimes in opposite directions.

8-2 THE SHORT-RUN PHILLIPS CURVE

We learned in the last chapter that when aggregate demand increases, because of a stimulative monetary or fiscal policy action or increased business and consumer confidence, there tends to be an increase in both real output and the price level together. Why? First, when real output rises, firms are forced to hire less productive workers and a higher price is required to allow firms to cover the cost of this loss in labor productivity. Second, wage rates tend to go up as firms find that to avoid cost-raising unskilled workers and to obtain skilled workers the latter must be lured from other firms by higher wage rates. Third, some business firms have market power—that is, a lack of effective competitors—and can raise profit margins when the demand for their products is high.

Just as we found in Chapter 7 that a single rightward shift in the economy's aggregate demand schedule can cause a one-time increase in the price level, now we will see that a continuous increase in demand pulls the price level up continuously. This kind of inflationary process is sometimes called demand-pull inflation, describing the role of rising aggregate demand as the factor "pulling up" on the price level.

This type of inflation is depicted in Figure 8-1, where the top frame repeats the last chapter's aggregate supply and demand schedules. Point E_0 represents a position of long-run static equilibrium. The actual and expected price levels (P and P^e) are both equal at point E_0, where $P_0 = P_0^e = 1.00$, and there is no pressure on the price level to change. The vertical line QQ, the long-run supply schedule, shows all the different long-run equilibrium positions such as E_0 that are characterized by equality between the actual and expected price levels ($P = P^e$).

Anywhere to the right of QQ, in contrast, the price level (P) exceeds what people expect. If, for instance, there should be a rightward shift in the aggregate demand curve from DD_0 to DD_1, say because of an increase in the money supply, the economy would move initially to point E_1. There the actual price level has increased from $P_0 = 1.00$ at point E_0 to $P_1 = 1.06$, but the expected price level has temporarily remained at the original level $P_0^e = 1.00$. There is an upward pressure for the expected price level to change at point E_1, rather than a no-change position of equilibrium, since people will shift their expectations in response to what has actually happened. Thus point E_1 and all other points to the right of the QQ line are not positions of long-run equilibrium.

What happens when people "catch on" and raise the expected price level up from the initial $P_0^e = 1.00$ to $P_1^e = 1.06$ in response to the previous increase in the actual price level? The aggregate supply curve shifts upward by exactly 6 percent, from SS_0 to SS_1. But what happens to output and the actual price level depends on the behavior of aggregate demand.

Two possibilities are illustrated in the top frame of Figure 8-1. The first possibility is that aggregate demand stays at the level indicated by the DD_1 schedule. Then the upward shift of the supply curve to SS_1 would shift the economy from E_1 northwest to point E_2, just as occurs in Figure 7-5. What must happen if the level of output is to be prevented from declining? The aggregate demand schedule DD must shift upward by exactly the same amount as the supply schedule SS. Thus if the expected price level increases from 1.00 to 1.06, shifting supply up from SS_0 to SS_1, output can remain fixed only if the demand curve shifts up

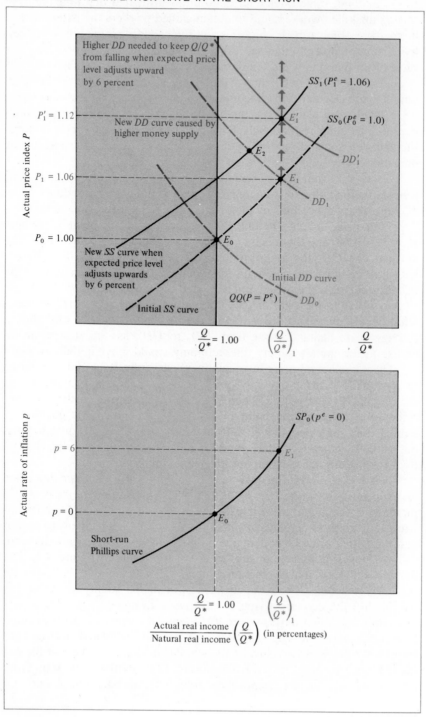

again, this time from DD_1 to DD_1'. Once again people are fooled, because again the price level at E_1' ($P_1' = 1.12$) turns out to be higher than they expected ($P_1^e = 1.06$).

To keep output from declining, aggregate demand must continuously increase; the economy will move straight upward along the path depicted by the red arrows in the top frame. The bottom frame shows the same process in a much simpler way. In the bottom frame the horizontal axis is the same as in the top frame, but now the vertical axis measures not the price level, but its rate of change. Thus in the top frame when the price level is fixed in long-run equilibrium, as at point E_0, the percentage rate of change of prices (or the rate of inflation) in the bottom frame is zero, as at point E_0. Throughout the book we will write percentage rates of change as lowercase letters, p in the case of inflation, and so the vertical axis measures off the zero rate of inflation occurring at point E_0 as $p = 0$.

A higher level of output requires a continuous increase in aggregate demand and in the price level, as depicted by the vertical path followed by the red arrows in the top frame. This same process of continuous inflation in the bottom frame occurs at the single point E_1, where each period the rate of change of the price level is 6 percent (just as in the top frame the price level rises by 6 percent between points E_1 and E_1').

The upward sloping schedule connecting points E_0 and E_1 in the bottom frame of Figure 8-1 is called the **short-run Phillips curve** and is abbreviated SP. The curve is named after A. W. H. Phillips, who first discovered the statistical relationship between the output ratio (Q/Q^*) and

---

FIGURE 8-1

Relationship of the Aggregate Supply Curve (SS) and the Short-Run Phillips Curve (SP)

In the top frame the economy is in long-run equilibrium at point E_0, just as in the bottom frame of Figure 7-3. At any point to the right of E_0 and the vertical QQ line, the economy is out of equilibrium. At E_1, for instance, the actual price level is $P_1 = 1.06$, but the expected price level (everywhere along the SS_0 aggregate supply curve) is only $P_0^e = 1.00$. Once expectations start to adjust, the economy can stay to the right of the QQ line only if aggregate demand shifts up continuously. For instance, along the higher black SS_1 curve expectations have adjusted upward to 1.06, but an additional upward shift in demand from DD_1 to DD_1' again raises the price level, this time to $P_1' = 1.12$. Again the actual price level (1.12) exceeds the expected price level (1.06) at point E_1', and the economy continues to be out of equilibrium.

To keep real output at the high level $(Q/Q^*)_1$, aggregate demand must keep ahead of the upward adjustment of expectations along the vertical path marked by the red arrows. This continuous inflation of 6 percent is represented directly below in the lower frame at point E_1.

the inflation rate (p).[2] Just as each short-run supply curve assumes that the price level people expect is the same everywhere along that curve (for instance $P_0^e = 1.00$ is expected everywhere along the SS_0 curve in the top frame of Figure 8-1), so the short-run Phillips curve assumes a single anticipated rate of inflation (p^e). For instance, people do not anticipate inflation at all along the SP_0 curve drawn in the bottom frame of Figure 8-1, and so the assumption of a zero anticipated inflation rate $(p^e = 0)$ is written next to that curve.

8-3   THE EXPECTED PRICE LEVEL AND THE ANTICIPATED RATE OF INFLATION

The remarkable thing about the inflation process illustrated in Figure 8-1 is that people are continuously fooled. Each period the price level races ahead of the expected price level along the path shown by the red arrows, but people never figure out what is going on. They always adjust the expected price level upward to take account of what happened last period, but they never anticipate a continuing inflation in advance of its occurrence.

The top frame of Figure 8-2 depicts exactly the same relationship between the actual and expected price levels as plotted in the top frame of Figure 8-1. Notice how the price level (P) follows the red line and each period stays ahead of the black line representing the expected price level (P^e). For instance, at point E_1 (which corresponds to E_1 in Figure 8-1) the excess of the price level over the expected price level is indicated by the first pink rectangle.

People are not likely to be continuously fooled by inflation for very long. If a 6 percent inflation has been going on for a while, they will begin to anticipate that it will occur again next period. Their expected price level (P^e) will be adjusted upward from last period's actual price level (P) by the percentage inflation rate they anticipate (p^e). If initially the price level is $P_0 = 1.00$ and people anticipate an inflation of 6 percent $(p^e = 6)$, then the price level expected for the subsequent period is not 1.00, but 1.06. The more reasonable upward adjustment of the expected

---

[2] Phillips showed that over 100 years of British history the rate of change of wage rates was related to the level of unemployment. Because the change in wage rates in turn is related to inflation, and unemployment is related to the output ratio Q/Q^*, the research of Phillips popularized the idea depicted by the SP curve in Figure 8-1, that a high level of output is associated with a high inflation rate. See A. W. H. Phillips, "The Relation Between Unemployment and the Rate of Change of Money Wage Rates in the United Kingdom, 1861–1967," *Economica* (November 1958), pp. 283–99. The curve should actually be called the "Fisher curve," since the relationship between the unemployment and inflation rates had been pointed out much earlier in Irving Fisher, "A Statistical Relation between Unemployment and Price Changes," *International Labour Review* (June 1926), pp. 785–92, reprinted in *Journal of Political Economy* (March/April 1973), pp. 596–602.

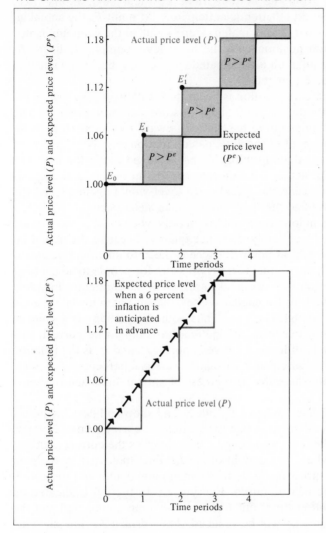

FIGURE 8-2

The Adjustment of the Expected Price Level (P^e) Contrasted to Accurate Anticipation of Inflation (p^e)

The top frame shows the relationship assumed in Figure 8-1 between the actual price level (P), depicted by the red line, and the expected price level (P^e), depicted by the black line. Because P^e always is assumed to adjust upward one period later than P, the pink shaded rectangles indicate the disequilibrium excess of P over P^e at points E_1 and E_1' in the top frame of Figure 8-1. The problem is that a continuing inflation is not anticipated. A contrasting adjustment is illustrated in the bottom frame. Line P^e always keeps up with P, because P^e is always set at last period's value of P plus an extra 6 percent upward adjustment to reflect the anticipated inflation rate of 6 percent ($p^e = 6$).

price level, when the anticipated inflation rate is 6, is illustrated by the black arrows in the bottom frame of Figure 8-2. There the price level (P) follows the same red path as in the top frame, but the expected price level never falls behind. Instead, each period people raise their expected price level in advance and the actual price level always turns out to be exactly what they expect.

Such "smart" behavior shifts the short-run Phillips curve as we can illustrate in Figure 8-3, where the lower SP_0 short-run Phillips curve is copied directly from the bottom frame of Figure 8-1. Everywhere along the SP_0 curve no inflation is anticipated. At point E_0 the actual inflation rate is just what is anticipated — zero — and so the economy is in a long-run equilibrium position with the price level completely fixed. At point E_1 as well no inflation is anticipated ($p^e = 0$), but the actual inflation rate turns out to be 6 percent.

But when a 6 percent inflation is accurately anticipated ($p = p^e = 6$), the long-run equilibrium or "no fooling" position occurs at point E_3. The entire short-run Phillips curve has shifted upward by exactly 6 percent, the degree of adjustment of the anticipated inflation rate. Now an output ratio (Q/Q^*) greater than 1.00 cannot be achieved along the new SP_1 schedule unless the actual inflation rate speeds up further and exceeds 6 percent, in which case the actual price level would again exceed the expected price level and "fooling" would once again occur.

The economy is in long-run equilibrium only when there is no pressure for change. Point E_1 certainly does not qualify, because the actual inflation rate of 6 percent at point E_1 exceeds the zero inflation rate anticipated along the SP_0 curve, and there is pressure for people to adjust their erroneous expectation ($p^e = 0$) to take account of the continuing inflation. At point E_3 the pressure for change ceases, because anticipated inflation has been boosted enough ($p^e = 6$). Thus point E_3 qualifies as a point of long-run equilibrium because anticipations turn out to be correct, just as does E_0. The only difference between points E_0 and E_3 is the inflation rate that is correctly anticipated, zero at E_0 versus 6 percent at E_3; otherwise the two points share the correctness of anticipations and the same output ratio Q/Q^*.

The vertical LP line connects E_0 and E_3 and shows all possible points where the anticipated inflation rate turns out to be correct. The LP stands for Long-run Phillips curve and can be thought of as the correct anticipations line. Everywhere to the right of the LP line (indicated by the pink shading) inflation turns out to be faster than anticipated, and the anticipated inflation rate will be raised. Everywhere to the left (indicated by gray shading) inflation turns out to be slower than anticipated and the anticipated inflation rate will be reduced. The vertical LP line showing all possible positions of long-run equilibrium is completely analogous to the vertical QQ long-run supply schedule of Chapters 6 and 7. Its message is the same: Output (Q) cannot be pushed permanently above its long-run equilibrium level (Q^*), and thus the output ratio Q/Q^* cannot be pushed permanently above 1.0 because eventually people will adjust their expectations to eliminate the "fooling" that makes high output possible.

The message of Figure 8-3 as a whole is simply that the combination of output and inflation that the economy can achieve depends on the anticipated rate of inflation (p^e). For any output ratio, (Q/Q^*), the actual rate of inflation will be higher, the higher is the inflation rate that is an-

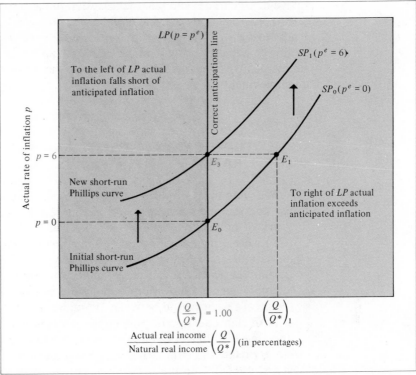

FIGURE 8-3

Effect on the Short-Run Phillips Curve of an Increase in the Anticipated Inflation Rate (p^e) from Zero to 6 Percent

The lower SP_0 curve is copied directly from the bottom frame of Figure 8–1 and shows the relation between output and inflation when no inflation is anticipated ($p^e = 0$). The output ratio (Q/Q^*) is at its long-run equilibrium value of 100 percent when the inflation rate is zero at point E_0, and it is raised higher when inflation is 6 percent at point E_1. But when people be-gin to anticipate fully the 6 percent inflation, the "fooling" necessary for high output no longer occurs, and now the 6 percent actual inflation yields only the equilibrium level of output at E_3. The short-run Phillips curve has shifted upward by exactly 6 percent, the amount by which people have raised their anticipated inflation rate. The vertical LP line running through points E_0 and E_3 shows all the possible positions of long-run equilibrium where the actual and anticipated inflation rates are equal ($p = p^e$).

ticipated. In this sense inflation is self-propelling—if people expect it, it will occur, even if output is at its long-run equilibrium level ($Q/Q^* = 1.0$). A cure for inflation, as we will see in Chapter 11, cannot be successful without cutting the inflation rate that people anticipate.

We have not completed our investigation of inflation, because each SP

curve gives a whole "menu" of possible combinations of output and inflation. What determines where the economy will actually be along the relevant SP curve? And what factors determine the anticipated inflation rate (p^e), which tells us which SP curve is the relevant one? We will be ready to answer these questions as soon as we demonstrate that our family of SP curves not only relates inflation to real output but also simultaneously ties the inflation rate in the short run to the rate of unemployment.

8-4 CASE STUDY: UNEMPLOYMENT AND THE REAL OUTPUT RATIO

We were first introduced to the close relationship between real output and the unemployment rate in Figure 1-2. There we noticed that years of output (Q) below the natural or long-run equilibrium level (Q^*) were also years in which the unemployment rate (U) was above its natural or long-run equilibrium level (U^*). The same close relationship between the ratio of actual to natural output (Q/Q^*) and the unemployment rate is plotted in Figure 8-4, where we examine just the most recent period between 1964 and 1976.

Although one cannot predict the unemployment rate perfectly by knowing the Q/Q^* ratio, nevertheless the unemployment rate is very closely related to Q/Q^*. In Figure 8-4 notice the cluster of prosperous years, 1966–69, in the lower right corner, with values of Q/Q^* well above 1.00 and unusually low unemployment rates. The contrasting situation in the upper left corner occurred in the recession year 1975, when massive layoffs caused record unemployment and the Q/Q^* ratio fell to only .917. The negative slope in Figure 8-4 just reflects common sense. When sales slump, workers are laid off and the jobless rate (U) rises. But when sales boom and Q/Q^* is high, some of the jobless are hired and the unemployment rate (U) goes down.

The close negative connection between U and Q/Q^* was first pointed out in the early 1960s by Arthur M. Okun, now at the Brookings Institution and formerly Chairman of the Council of Economic Advisers in the Johnson Administration.[3] Because it has held up so well, the relationship has been widely dubbed **Okun's law.** Not only does U tend to follow the major movements in Q/Q^*, but in addition the percentage point change in the unemployment rate tends to be

---

[3] Arthur M. Okun, "Potential GNP: Its Measurement and Significance," reprinted in Okun's *The Political Economy of Prosperity* (Washington: Brookings Institute, 1970), pp. 132–45. The most recent study of the relationship is contained in George Perry, "Potential Output and Productivity," *Brookings Papers on Economic Activity,* vol. 8, no. 1 (1977), pp. 11–47.

A HIGH OUTPUT RATIO GOES WITH
LOW UNEMPLOYMENT, AND VICE VERSA

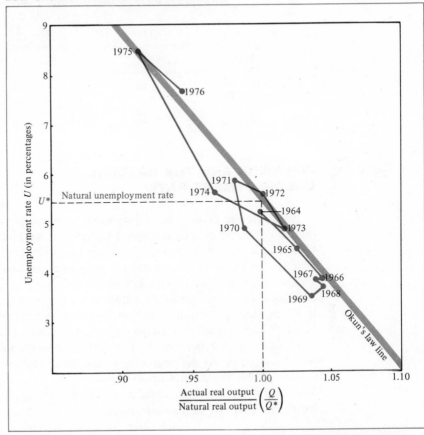

FIGURE 8–4

The U.S. Ratio of Actual to
Natural Real Output (Q/Q^*) and
the Unemployment Rate,
1964–76

This diagram illustrates that unemployment (U) moves inversely with
the output ratio (Q/Q^*). In prosperous years, such as 1966–69, the
observations are in the lower right
corner, with a high output ratio and
low unemployment. The opposite ex-

treme occurred in 1975, the observation plotted at the upper left corner.
A recession occurred, the output ratio
fell, workers were laid off, and the
unemployment rate reached 8.5 percent for the year as a whole (with a
monthly peak of 9.0 percent reached
in May 1975). The line connecting
1966 and 1975 expresses the relation
between U and Q/Q^* sometimes
called Okun's law.

about one-third the percentage change in the Q/Q^* ratio, in the opposite direction. As an example, Q/Q^* fell from 1.016 in 1973 to .917 in
1975, almost exactly a 10 percent decline. The unemployment rate increased between 1973 and 1975 from 4.9 to 8.5 percentage points, for

a 3.6 percentage point jump, a bit more than one-third the percentage decline in real output. Other examples from Figure 8-4 are:

Years	(1) Percentage change in Q/Q^*	(2) Percentage change in U	Ratio of (2) to (1) (%)
1964–66	4.6	−1.4	−30
1966–71	−5.9	2.1	−36
1971–73	3.6	−1.0	−28
1975–76	2.7	−0.8	−30

8-5 INFLATION AND THE NATURAL UNEMPLOYMENT RATE

Naturally the Okun's law relationship between U and Q/Q^*, like any regular relationship, may not hold true forever. And the ratio of one-third between changes in U and Q/Q^* varies from time to time; before World War II, for example, it was usually only one-half or less. But in recent United States history Okun's law has proved to be remarkably accurate.

What is the natural unemployment rate (U^*) that the economy attains in a long-run equilibrium situation when the output ratio Q/Q^* is equal to 1.00? The output ratio was close to 1.00 in 1964, when the unemployment rate was 5.2 percent, and in 1972, when the unemployment rate was 5.6 percent. At the beginning of the next chapter we will see that in the mid-1970s the natural unemployment rate was roughly 5.4 percent.[4] Thus at 5.4 percent the vertical axis in Figure 8-4 is labeled U^*, standing for the **natural rate of unemployment.**

> *The natural unemployment rate (U^*) is the economy's long-run equilibrium level of unemployment that occurs when output (Q) equals its long-run natural level (Q^*) and is a situation, in which the actual inflation rate turns out to be exactly what people anticipate.*

Just as policymakers cannot keep output permanently above its natural level at a single inflation rate such as 6 percent, because anticipations will catch on to that inflation rate, so policymakers cannot keep unemployment permanently below the natural rate of unemployment without setting off a spiraling acceleration of inflation.

The impossibility of attaining zero inflation together with zero unem-

---

[4] The methods used in estimating U^* and Q^* are provided in Appendix C and are based on the author's recent research. Most economists feel that it is impossible to pin down U^* and Q^* precisely, and so it is better to think of U^* not as a figure of precisely 5.4 percent but as a band extending roughly from 5 to 6 percent unemployment.

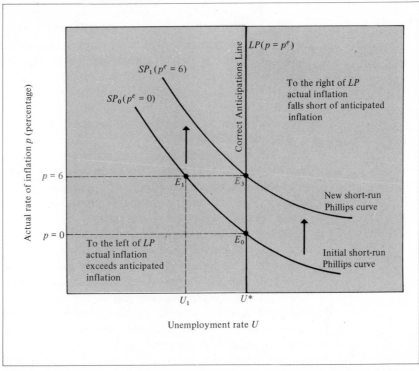

FIGURE 8–5

Derivation of the Phillips Curves Relating Inflation and Unemployment

This diagram is the mirror image of Figure 8–3, but with unemployment rather than the output ratio plotted on the horizontal axis. Now an economic expansion creates jobs, reduces unemployment, and moves the economy along the SP curve. This boosts the actual inflation rate above the anticipated rate.

Point E_1 shows a disequilibrium situation in which the inflation rate of 6 percent exceeds the zero inflation that people anticipate, leading to upward pressure on the anticipated inflation rate and hence a tendency for the SP curve to shift upward.
Points E_0 and E_3 show two long-run equilibrium situations with unemployment at its natural rate, but with two different inflation rates.

ployment is illustrated in Figure 8-5, an important new diagram that plots the inflation rate in the vertical direction, just as occurs in Figure 8-3, and the unemployment rate in a horizontal direction. This allows us to redraw each SP curve as a relation between actual inflation and unemployment.

Point E_0 represents a long-run equilibrium situation with a stable actual and expected price level. Moving left into the pink-shaded region the economy becomes more prosperous and the inflation rate speeds up from point E_0 to E_1 along the initial SP_0 short-run Phillips curve (which assumes $p^e = 0$). But now, with p exceeding p^e, the rate of anticipated inflation will speed up, shifting the SP curve upwards, and moving E_1 to E_3.

In every respect this inflation-unemployment diagram is just the mirror image of Figure 8-3. If unemployment is pushed too low into the pink area, inflation will speed up and the anticipated inflation rate will follow along. Only in long-run equilibrium along the vertical LP long-run Phillips line is there no pressure for change in the anticipated inflation rate because only along LP do expectations turn out to be correct.

The story told by Figure 8-5 is not a happy one. A low unemployment rate in the pink area, much less a zero unemployment rate, cannot be achieved for very long, because soon an upward adjustment of anticipations will shift up the SP curve and cause an upward acceleration of inflation. Only if the natural unemployment rate were zero could an actual zero unemployment rate be maintained.

Why is the natural unemployment rate (U^*) in long-run equilibrium such a high figure, apparently about 5.4 percent in Figure 8-4? We study in Chapter 9 why U^* is so high in the United States and what can be done to lower U^*. There we will find that one of the most important problems is a "mismatch" between job-seekers and unfilled job slots. Because many job openings call for highly skilled workers but many job-seekers are unqualified for the open job slots, an increase in aggregate demand tends to push up wages and prices as employers try to steal skilled employees from each other. If unskilled workers could somehow be made more attractive as potential workers, then aggregate demand could be raised enough to allow some of the unemployed to fill the skilled job openings, and U^* would fall.

Thus the term natural rate of unemployment (U^*) is a misnomer. Rate U^* is neither natural, immutable, nor optimal. The word "natural" for U^* follows the terminology introduced in the 1960s by Milton Friedman, but U^* is not truly natural, or given by nature, because many government policies and institutional restrictions make U^* higher than necessary.[5] Nor is U^* immutable, because changes in government policies and private behavior can raise or lower U^*. In fact, most economists agree that U^* increased between the mid-1950s and the mid-1970s as a result of a shift in the composition of the labor force to groups with relatively high unemployment rates, particularly teenagers and women.[6] Finally, today's U^* is not the optimal or best-possible unemployment rate. Though some

---

[5] Milton Friedman, "The Role of Monetary Policy," *American Economic Review*, vol. 58 (March 1968). Friedman used the adjective "natural" in the tradition of Knut Wicksell, a turn-of-the-century Swedish economist, whose work had led to the widespread adoption of the word for the long-run equilibrium rate of interest.

[6] The shifting structure of the labor force and unemployment is discussed in detail in section 9-3.

unemployment serves a useful function, by allowing people to look a bit without being forced to take the first available job, there is widespread agreement that much unemployment in the present-day United States is unnecessary and excessive.

Figure 8-5 summarizes several of the most important conclusions of this chapter:

1. Anything that stimulates the growth of aggregate demand tends to raise inflation while temporarily reducing unemployment, moving the economy northwest along its initial SP (short-run Phillips) curve. This northwest movement characterized the U.S. economy in the early Vietnam period, 1965–66.
2. Anywhere to the left of the natural unemployment rate (U^*), actual inflation exceeds the anticipated inflation rate, and people will begin to adjust their anticipations of future inflation, thus shifting the SP curve upward. The SP curve will shift upward continuously, and inflation will accelerate continuously, everywhere in the pink area to the left of U^*.
3. Anywhere to the right of U^* actual inflation is below the anticipated rate, and people will begin to reduce their anticipations of future inflation, thus shifting the SP curve down. Thus high unemployment in excess of U^* is a possible cure for excessive inflation, a cure that was used in the United States in 1970–71 and again in 1974–75.
4. Only when actual unemployment is equal to U^*, the natural unemployment rate, does the inflation rate tend to remain stable, equal to the rate that people anticipate.

These conclusions, though important, are only part of the story of inflation and unemployment. Each SP curve predicts a negative association between inflation and unemployment, with inflation falling in years of rising unemployment. But an important feature of the United States economy in the early 1970s was an apparent tendency for inflation and unemployment to be positively correlated. A reduction of inflation in 1972 was accompanied by falling unemployment. Then in 1974 the inflation and unemployment rates increased together. Is it possible to explain why inflation and unemployment sometimes move in opposite directions and sometimes in the same direction? How can we predict which relation will occur?

8-6 AGGREGATE DEMAND GROWTH AND INFLATION

Real GNP (Q) is defined as the ratio of nominal GNP (Y) to the GNP deflator or aggregate price index (P):

$$Q \equiv Y/P \qquad (8.1)$$

The growth rate of real output (q) is therefore defined as the difference between the growth rates of nominal GNP (y) and the GNP deflator (p):[7]

$$q \equiv y - p \qquad (8.2)$$

Example: Imagine that nominal and real GNP are each equal to $1000 billion and the price index equals 1.00. Equation (8.2) states that a 10 percent growth rate of nominal GNP (y), say from $1000 to $1100 billion, while inflation is 10 percent, must by definition be accompanied by a growth rate of real GNP (q) of zero:

GENERAL FORM   NUMERICAL EXAMPLE

$$q \equiv y - p \qquad\qquad 0 \equiv 10 - 10$$

In contrast, if nominal income stays fixed ($y = 0$) while the inflation rate (p) is 10 percent, then real GNP must *shrink* by 10 percent:

GENERAL FORM   NUMERICAL EXAMPLE

$$q \equiv y - p \qquad\qquad -10 \equiv 0 - 10$$

This simple definition ($q \equiv y - p$) provides the missing positive association between inflation and unemployment needed to explain actual events in the 1970s. Imagine that nominal GNP, which we have been calling aggregate demand, is growing at some fixed rate, say $y = 10$ percent. Then this demand growth of $y = 10$ is the sum of inflation (p) and real output growth (q). If a high inflation rate "uses up" lots of the 10 percent of aggregate demand growth, then real output is forced to grow slowly or fall, in turn boosting unemployment. On the other hand, if the inflation rate is low, more nominal GNP growth is available to "pay for" fast real output growth, which in turn creates new jobs and cuts the unemployment rate.

To define this relationship more precisely, let us subtract from y and q in (8.2) the growth of natural long-run equilibrium output (q^*), roughly 3.5 percent per annum in the United States, which occurs as a result of population growth and advances in knowledge:

$$q - q^* \equiv y - q^* - p$$
or
$$\hat{q} \equiv \hat{y} \qquad - p \qquad (8.3)$$

The second line uses a single symbol, topped by a "hat" ($\hat{}$), to represent the deviation of actual from natural output growth ($\hat{q}$) and the deviation of aggregate demand growth from natural output growth ($\hat{y}$). From now on, we will call $\hat{q}$ **adjusted output growth,** that is, the growth rate of actual output minus the growth rate of natural output, and $\hat{y}$ will be called **adjusted demand growth,** the growth rate of aggregate demand (nominal

---

[7] Lowercase letters indicate growth rates of variables whose levels are expressed in uppercase letters.

GNP) minus the growth rate of natural output. Thus $\hat{y}$ rises whenever anything occurs that raises planned spending and shifts Chapter 7's *DD* curve to the right, such as an increase in business and consumer confidence or a monetary or fiscal policy stimulus. We will examine the way policymakers through their choice of $\hat{y}$ (for example, zero, 6 percent, or 12 percent) influence unemployment in the short run and inflation in both the short and long runs.

What do $\hat{q}$ and $\hat{y}$ have to do with unemployment? When the output ratio (Q/Q^*) is fixed, actual output (Q) and natural output (Q^*) must be growing at the same rate, so that the difference between their growth rates, adjusted output growth, must be zero $(\hat{q} = 0)$. But Okun's law in Figure 8-4 suggests that a fixed value of Q/Q^* on the horizontal axis, and hence $\hat{q} = 0$, occurs only when the unemployment rate on the vertical axis is fixed, as on line 1 of the following table.

	Output ratio (Q/Q^*)	Adjusted output growth $(\hat{q} = q - q^*)$	Unemployment rate (U)	Actual U.S. example in Figure 8-4, between years:
1.	Fixed	Zero	Fixed	1966–68
2.	Rises	Positive	Falls	1971–73
3.	Falls	Negative	Rises	1973–75

When adjusted output growth $\hat{q}$ is zero, as on line 1, unemployment is fixed. But equation (8.3) states that when $\hat{q} = 0$, then inflation (p) "uses up" all of adjusted demand growth $(\hat{y})$.

Example: If $\hat{y}$ equals 6 percent per year, then inflation (p) must be 6 percent per year for unemployment to remain constant. In terms of equation (8.3), unemployment can remain constant only in this situation:

GENERAL FORM $\qquad$ NUMERICAL EXAMPLE
$$\hat{q} \equiv \hat{y} - p \qquad\qquad 0 \equiv 6 - 6$$

Figure 8-6 repeats from Figure 8-5 the vertical and horizontal unemployment axis. The situation with $\hat{y} = 6$, $p = 6$ and constant unemployment is plotted as the horizontal **constant unemployment line** CU.[8] No matter what the level of unemployment happens to be, for that unemployment rate to remain constant when $\hat{y} = 6$, inflation (p) must equal 6 percent as well.

Example: Say last period the unemployment rate was 5 percent, indicated along the horizontal axis by the point labeled $U_{-1} = 5$ (the -1 subscript means "last period"). For the unemployment

---

[8] The CU curve is labeled with C for "constant," and U for "unemployment."

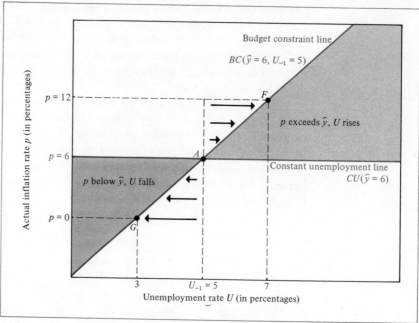

FIGURE 8–6

The horizontal *CU* line marks all the possible positions of constant unemployment, given an adjusted demand growth rate ($\hat{y}$) of 6 percent. The upward sloping *BC* budget constraint line shows all the combinations of inflation and unemployment consistent with $\hat{y} = 6$ and an initial unemployment rate $U_{-1} = 5$ percent. At point *F* an excessive inflation rate ($p = 12$) uses up 6 extra percentage points of nominal income growth, forcing unemployment to rise by 2 percentage points. Point *G* is the opposite situation, with zero inflation freeing up 6 extra percentage points of nominal income growth that allows a boom in real output growth and a 2 percentage point drop in unemployment to occur.

rate to remain fixed at 5 percent this period, the economy must stay on the *CU* constant unemployment line, and so the economy's position must be at point *A*, where the horizontal *CU* line intersects the vertical dashed line rising from $U_{-1} = 5$.

Under what conditions will unemployment change rather than stay constant? The assumed rate of adjusted demand growth, $\hat{y} = 6$, is the economy's **budget constraint,** setting a limit on the sum of inflation (p) plus allowable adjusted output growth ($\hat{q}$). If inflation is greater than 6 percent, the budget constraint of $\hat{y} = 6$ does not provide enough aggregate demand to "pay for" both high inflation and constant unemployment. Instead, the extra inflation, over and above the 6 percent growth rate of $\hat{y}$, must be "paid for" by a negative value of $\hat{q}$. When this occurs, actual output grows slower than natural output, the Q/Q^* ratio falls, and unemployment rises.

The upward sloping BC line in Figure 8-6 illustrates the economy's budget constraint *this period* and shows all the combinations of inflation (p) and unemployment (U) that are consistent with the budget constraint of 6 percent adjusted demand growth ($\hat{y}$) and a starting point, inherited from last period, of 5 percent unemployment. The BC line slopes upward because an increase in inflation uses up more of adjusted demand growth ($\hat{y}$) and leaves less left over for adjusted output growth ($\hat{q}$), forcing unemployment to rise. As an example, an inflation rate of 12 percent would use up not only the 6 percent rate of adjusted demand growth ($\hat{y}=6$), but an additional 6 percent that can come only from negative adjusted output growth ($\hat{q}=6$). In terms of equation (8.3):

$$\text{GENERAL FORM} \qquad \text{THIS EXAMPLE}$$
$$\hat{q} \equiv \hat{y} - p \qquad\qquad -6 \equiv 6 - 12$$

The Okun's law relation plotted in Figure 8-4 implies that $\hat{q} = -6$, that is, a drop in the Q/Q^* output ratio by 6 percent, will cause an increase in unemployment of 2 percentage points. Thus point F along the BC line in Figure 8-6 plots the combination of 12 percent inflation with a 7 percent unemployment rate, the latter representing a 2 percentage point increase from last period's starting point of 5 percent unemployment.

Similarly, a low rate of inflation means that less demand growth is needed to "pay for" inflation and more is available to support a real output boom. For instance, in Figure 8-6 a zero rate of inflation allows all the assumed rate of demand growth, $\hat{y} = 6$, to go into adjusted output growth:

$$\text{GENERAL FORM} \qquad \text{THIS EXAMPLE}$$
$$\hat{q} = \hat{y} - p \qquad\qquad 6 = 6 - 0$$

In turn, when adjusted output growth ($\hat{q}$) is 6 percent, Okun's law indicates that unemployment can fall by 2 percentage points. Thus point G along the BC budget constraint line plots the combination of zero inflation with 3 percent unemployment, the latter representing a 2 percentage point decline from last period's 5 percent unemployment rate.

Summary: Figure 8-6 conveys the message that for any given adjusted growth rate of aggregate demand ($\hat{y}$), an increase in inflation above that rate raises unemployment, while an inflation rate lower than $\hat{y}$ causes unemployment to drop.[9]

[9] Construction of the diagram is straightforward. First, the horizontal CU constant unemployment line is drawn in at the assumed value of $\hat{y}$, then the initial unemployment rate is marked off (as in Figure 8-6 at $U_{-1} = 5$), and finally the positively sloped BC budget con-

(continued)

The pink area in Figure 8-6 between the BC and CU lines represents the excess of inflation above $\hat{y}$, that is, the fact that $\hat{q}$ is negative and unemployment must rise. The greater the inflation rate, the larger the pink distance between the BC and CU lines, the more negative $\hat{q}$, and the more unemployment increases (as shown by the horizontal arrows). Similarly, for situations of low inflation the gray area represents the shortfall of inflation below $\hat{y}$, which allows $\hat{q}$ to be positive and unemployment to fall.

What would make the two lines in Figure 8-6 shift their position?

1. An increase in $\hat{y}$, say from 6 percent to 12 percent, caused by a monetary or fiscal policy stimulus, or by increased business or consumer optimism, would cause both the CU and BC lines to shift upward by exactly the amount of the change, 6 percentage points. The BC line would continue to intersect the CU line at the starting point of last period's unemployment rate.

2. Any change in the unemployment rate from last period to this period, while $\hat{y}$ remains fixed, shifts the BC line rightward or leftward along the fixed CU line. If this period we are at point G in Figure 8-6, and unemployment drops to 3 percent, then next period's starting point will be $U_{-1} = 3$. Next period's BC line will shift leftward to intersect the CU line directly above point G, because next period's initial unemployment rate is 3 percent at point G. Thus when unemployment declines, the BC line shifts left along CU, and when unemployment increases, the BC line shifts to the right along CU.

3. When does the BC line stop moving to the left or right? Only when inflation equals $\hat{y}$, as at point A in Figure 8-6, because only then can the economy simultaneously have constant unemployment (by being on the CU line) and at the same time satisfy its budget constraint (by being on the BC line).

8-7 EFFECTS OF AN ACCELERATION IN AGGREGATE DEMAND GROWTH

The CU constant unemployment line in Figure 8-6 shows that a 6 percent inflation rate is required if the economy's unemployment rate is to remain constant, given a fixed rate of adjusted demand growth, $\hat{y} = 6$. Starting from today's initial unemployment rate, the BC line shows all the other combinations of unemployment and inflation that are compatible with $\hat{y} = 6$. But which of these various combinations along the BC line describes the economy's current position?

---

straint line is drawn through the intersection of the CU line with initial unemployment, as at point A in Figure 8-6. The slope of the BC line depends on Okun's law; if $\hat{q} = -3$ raises unemployment by one percentage point, then the BC rises 3 percentage points vertically for each one percentage point rightward increase in unemployment.

The SP curve from Figure 8-5 is needed to pin down the economy's position along the BC line. In the same way, the BC line is needed to determine where the economy rests on its SP short-run Phillips curve. The two lines, BC and SP, are needed to determine the two variables, inflation and unemployment.

Figure 8-7 shows at point E_0 an initial long-run equilibrium consistent with adjusted demand growth of zero ($\hat{y} = 0$). If policymakers initially set adjusted demand growth at zero, $\hat{y} = 0$, the initial constant unemployment CU_0 line intersects point E_0, as does the initial budget constraint line BC_0.

What happens now if demand growth speeds up, say from $\hat{y} = 0$ to $\hat{y} = 6$, either as a result of buoyant consumer and business confidence or as a result of a monetary or fiscal policy stimulus? Both the CU and BC lines instantly shift upward by 6 percent, so that they intersect the initial unemployment rate at point E_3 rather than E_1. But the economy's short-run temporary equilibrium cannot be at point E_3. Why? Because initially the anticipated inflation rate is $p^e = 0$, so that the initial SP_0 curve remains valid. For the economy to be in short-run equilibrium, it must be on both its BC and SP curves, a situation that occurs only at point H. Thus the faster growth of $\hat{y}$ has both raised the inflation rate and reduced the unemployment rate.

But point H is not the end of the story. Even if everyone continues to be fooled and the anticipated rate of inflation does not adjust, so that the SP_0 curve remains valid, the BC budget constraint line will shift leftward. Why? Because BC always intersects CU directly above last period's unemployment rate. Because the economy's position has shifted from E_0 to H, in the next period the new BC_2 line must cross CU_1 at point K, which lies directly above point H.

What happens next? Again the economy shifts northwestward to the intersection at point J of its fixed SP_0 curve and its new BC_2 line, because the economy must always be on both its SP and BC lines. Once again the unemployment rate has changed, from point H to point J, and so once again the BC line shifts leftward to BC_3. Only when the economy reaches a situation of constant unemployment along the CU line does the BC line stop shifting leftward. This occurs at point E_1 where the CU_1 line intersects the fixed SP_0 curve.

But point E_1 is not entirely satisfactory either. Granted that it lies on both the BC and SP curves, satisfying the requirements for a short-run equilibrium. And it is a point of constant unemployment, lying on the CU line. But, alas, the economy cannot stay at point E_1. Why? Because at E_1 inflation is racing along at 6 percent ($p = 6$), but anticipations of inflation remain at zero along SP_0 ($p^e = 0$). It is inevitable that people will adjust their anticipations of inflation to take account of the unfortunate reality of 6 percent inflation, causing the SP curve to shift upward. And once this occurs, the economy cannot sustain a low unemployment rate. A long-

THE IMPACT ON INFLATION AND UNEMPLOYMENT OF
FASTER DEMAND GROWTH WHEN THE ANTICIPATED
INFLATION RATE FAILS TO ADJUST

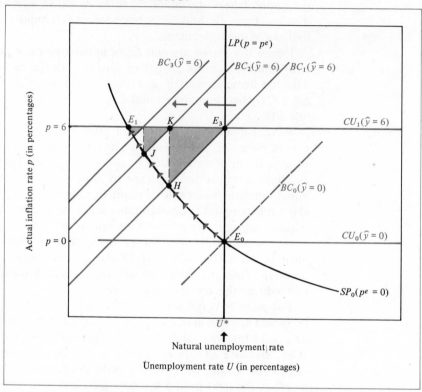

FIGURE 8-7

The Adjustment Path of Inflation and Unemployment to an Acceleration of Adjusted Demand Growth from $\hat{y} = 0$ to $\hat{y} = 6$ Per Year

This diagram combines the Phillips curves from Figure 8–5 with the inflation-unemployment relations from Figure 8–6. At the initial starting point E_0, the economy is in long-run equilibrium at its natural unemployment rate U^*, a zero inflation rate, zero demand growth ($\hat{y}$), and constant unemployment. If demand growth were raised by stimulative policy from $\hat{y} = 0$ to $\hat{y} = 6$, the CU and BC lines would shift straight upward to CU_1 and BC_1. Initially the economy would move to a short-run equilibrium at point H, where the new BC_1 line crosses the fixed SP_0 short-run Phillips curve. Then, in the next period, the economy's starting point would have shifted to point H, and so the BC line would have to cross CU_1 directly above point H (at K), as indicated by the new budget constraint line BC_2. Only when the economy arrives at point E_1, along the constant unemployment line, does the BC line stop shifting leftward.

run equilibrium can be attained only where actual and anticipated inflation are equal, that is, along the LP curve. This happens only when the unemployment rate returns to its original value (U^*).

How low can the unemployment rate be pushed, and for how long? Everything depends on the speed at which expectations are adjusted. If workers and firms do not catch on at all and are completely fooled by the inflation, the economy can reach point E_1 along the original SP_0 curve. At the other extreme, if workers and firms are completely rational and understand the workings of the economy completely, they will realize that the acceleration of $\hat{y}$ from 0 to 6 percent will cause inflation to shift up to 6 percent in long-run equilibrium. Thus they will raise their expectations immediately to $p^e = 6$ percent, and the SP curve will shift up instantly, preventing any decline in unemployment. In between these two situations of no adjustment and instant adjustment we have various intermediate cases in which unemployment declines temporarily, but not so far as point E_1.

8-8 ADAPTIVE EXPECTATIONS AND THE INFLATION CYCLE

A hypothesis of how expectations are formed, which has been widely studied and verified, is called **adaptive expectations**.[10] The idea is simply that when people find that actual events do not turn out as they expected, they adjust their expectations to bring them closer to reality. A simple way of writing the adaptive expectations hypothesis for inflation is that the expected (or anticipated) rate of inflation (p^e) is set as an average of last period's actual inflation (p_{-1}) and last period's expected inflation rate (p^e_{-1}):

$$p^e = gp_{-1} + (1-g)p^e_{-1} \qquad (8.4)$$

Here g represents the weight put on last period's actual inflation; g could be any fraction between zero and 1.0.

Here are examples showing how the expected inflation rate is formed when g takes on different hypothetical values:

Value of g	Calculation of p^e	Example when $p_{-1} = 3$ and $p^e_{-1} = 0$
0	$p^e = (0)p_{-1} + (1)p^e_{-1} = p^e_{-1}$	$p^e = 0$
0.25	$p^e = 0.25p_{-1} + 0.75p^e_{-1}$	$p^e = 0.75$
1	$p^e = (1)p_{-1} + (0)p^e_{-1} = p_{-1}$	$p^e = 3$

[10] The idea of adaptive expectations was first used in macroeconomics in a paper that has become a classic, Phillip Cagan, "The Monetary Dynamics of Hyperinflation," in Milton Friedman (ed.), *Studies in the Quantity Theory of Money* (Chicago: University of Chicago Press, 1956), pp. 25–117.

In the first line of the table, g is zero. People do not adjust their expectations at all to the actual behavior of inflation, but instead they maintain their expectation (p^e) at its value in the previous period (p^e_{-1}). This behavior, which is not very realistic, is the same as in Figure 8-7, where the SP_0 curve remains in effect as a result of the failure by people to raise their anticipation of inflation above $p^e = 0$.

In the second line of the table, g is at the intermediate value of 0.25. People compromise, basing part of their estimate of expected inflation on what actually happened last period (p_{-1}) and the remainder (0.75) on what they previously expected. Why is this compromise approach plausible? Last period's actual inflation may not be a very good guide to what will happen this period. If inflation has been running at a zero rate, and people have been expecting a zero rate $(p^e_{-1} = 0)$, then a sudden acceleration to 3 percent $(p_{-1} = 3)$ might not necessarily continue into the future. A value of g equal to 0.25 indicates that people believe that there is a one-quarter chance that the new rate of inflation will continue and a greater three-quarter chance that inflation will return to what they previously expected.

The third line of the table shows the extreme case of $g = 1.0$, which means that the expected inflation rate is always set equal to what actually happened last period. In Figure 8-7, the acceleration of adjusted demand growth, which raises actual inflation from zero to 3 percent as the economy moves from point E_0 to point H, would cause next period's expected inflation rate to rise by the same amount, to 3 percent. The SP curve would shift upward by 3 percent, and the economy would move next not to point J, as occurs in Figure 8-7, but directly above H to point K (where the BC_2 line would intersect the new higher SP curve resulting from the upward adjustment of expected inflation).

The economy's response to higher demand growth is quite different, depending on g, the coefficient of adjustment of expectations. In Figure 8-8 three responses are plotted, corresponding to each of the three values of g assumed in the table: zero, 0.25, and 1.0. The black line moving straight northwest from point E_0 through points H and J to E_1 duplicates Figure 8-7. Since g is zero, expectations do not adjust at all and the economy remains on its original SP_0 curve.[11]

The other black line shows the opposite extreme of rapid adjustment of expectations when $g = 1.0$. In each period the SP curve shifts upward by exactly the previous period's increase in actual inflation. Because actual inflation increases by 3 percentage points in going from E_0 to point H, in the next period the SP curve shifts upward by 3 percentage points and takes the economy northward from H to K. At point K the economy is on its BC_2 and CU_1 lines (see Figure 8-7), but then expectations adjust upward again from $p^e = 3$ to $p^e = 6$, moving the economy in period 3 north-

---

[11] To simplify the diagram, the SP curve has been drawn as a straight line in Figure 8-8.

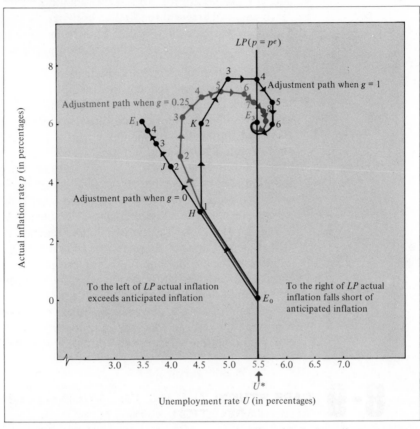

FIGURE 8-8

Effect on Inflation and Unemployment of an Acceleration of Adjusted Demand Growth ($\hat{y}$) from Zero to 6 Percent, Under Alternative Assumptions of Expectation Adjustment

When expectations do not adjust at all, the economy follows the black path northwest from E_0 to E_1, exactly as in Figure 8–7. An adjustment coefficient g of 0.25 causes expectations to shift upward slowly, pushing the economy onto the higher adjustment path indicated in red. When expectations adjust fully to last period's actual inflation ($g = 1.0$), the economy moves upward even faster, as shown by the black path going north from point H to point K and beyond.

east up the budget constraint line. Eventually, after looping around the long-run equilibrium point E_3, the economy arrives there.

When the expected inflation rate adjusts by only part of the difference between last period's actual and expected inflation, in the example of $g = 0.25$, the economy follows the red path in Figure 8-8. This lies between the two black paths and illustrates a slower adjustment. For instance, the black path for $g = 1.0$ crosses the LP line in period 4, but the red path does not arrive at the LP line until period 7.

Both the red path for $g = 0.25$ and the black path for $g = 1.0$ share several basic characteristics of the inflation process:

1. An acceleration of demand growth as in Figures 8-7 and 8-8 raises the inflation rate and reduces the unemployment rate in the short run.
2. In the long run, if expectations adjust even partially to the actual behavior of inflation, the inflation rate rises by exactly the same amount as $\hat{y}$, and the decline in unemployment is only temporary. The economy eventually arrives at point E_3, where the unemployment rate has returned to the natural unemployment rate (U^*) from which it started.
3. Inflation always "overshoots" its final equilibrium value of 6 percent, rising temporarily above 6 percent and then returning to 6 percent. Along the upper black path inflation reaches 7.5 percent in periods 3 and 4. Along the red path inflation reaches a peak of 7.12 percent in period 5. The reason for the overshooting is that the economy initially arrives at its long-run 6 percent inflation rate, as at point K, before expected inflation has caught up with actual inflation. The subsequent points that lie above point K reflect the combined influence on inflation of (1) the upward adjustment of expectations and (2) the continued upward demand pressure that raises actual inflation above expected inflation whenever the economy is to the left of its long-run LP line.

8-9 CASE STUDY: THE U.S. INFLATION CYCLE AND STAGFLATION, 1964–71

For too long in the 1960s, economists preached that there was a trade-off between inflation and unemployment. Along any SP curve, the enjoyment of lower unemployment requires tolerating more inflation. But no SP curve is likely to stay fixed for long if the inflation rate differs substantially from the expected rate of inflation. There is no trade-off between inflation and unemployment in the long run when expectations have adjusted to the actual inflation experience. The natural rate hypothesis states that in the long run the unemployment rate is at a natural value (U^*) independent of the inflation rate.

Some journalists and critics have claimed that "economics is bankrupt" because it could not explain stagflation, the simultaneous occurrence of inflation, recession, and high unemployment in the late 1960s and early 1970s. But stagflation is precisely what we have generated in Figure 8-8! Both the red and upper black adjustment paths display segments in which the inflation rate and unemployment rates are rising at the same time. Along both paths the economy suffers through several periods when inflation is higher than its long-run 6 percent equilibrium value while simultaneously unemployment is higher than the natural rate.

The real world never precisely duplicates any simple textbook model, but the U.S. inflation and unemployment rates during the 1964–71 period provide a classic example of the effects of accelerating demand growth. For the four years 1960–63 the adjusted growth rate of nominal income ($\hat{y}$) was 1.5 percent per year. Coincidentally, the inflation rate at the beginning of 1964 was just the same, 1.5 percent.[12] In the first quarter of 1964 the average unemployment rate was 5.5 percent, as depicted in Figure 8-9 at the lower right-hand point labeled 1964:Q1.[13]

Then $\hat{y}$ accelerated to an average of 4.4 percent per year for the five years 1965–69. Inevitably, inflation had to increase, and the path of adjustment is illustrated in Figure 8-9. At first, in 1965 and 1966, the BC curve moved left along a relatively fixed SP curve, and a very substantial reduction in unemployment was achieved at the price of only a small increase in the inflation rate, from 1.5 percent at the beginning of 1964 to 2.8 percent at the beginning of 1966.[14] After that, however, the expected inflation rate appears to have begun a rapid adjustment upward. Between 1966 and 1969, there was little further reduction in the unemployment rate while inflation accelerated to about 5 percent.

But 1969 was not the end of the story. Expected inflation had not yet caught up with actual inflation, and it continued to push up the SP curve. Inflation "overshot" its long-run equilibrium value and "used up" so much of nominal income growth that the unemployment rate began to rise. The government added to the upward pressure on the unemployment rate, reducing $\hat{y}$ substantially in 1970–71. The economy arrived in early 1971 with an unemployment rate of 6 percent, higher than initially in 1964, but now with an inflation rate of 5 percent instead of the initial 1.5 percent.

Our story ends for now with the middle of 1971, when the Nixon administration introduced wage and price controls. A major topic of Chapter 11 is a reconsideration of the policy options faced in 1971. What would have happened to inflation and unemployment in 1971–72 if controls had not been introduced? What would have been the consequences of "living with" the 5 percent inflation of early 1971? The major point of this section has been the demonstration in Figure 8-9

---

[12] All inflation rate figures in this discussion and in Figure 8-9 refer to the rate of change of the GNP deflator over the previous four quarters.

[13] As noted earlier, 1964:Q1 is an abbreviation for "1964, first quarter of the year."

[14] I estimate that in 1965 the natural unemployment rate was 4.7 percent. See the discussion at the beginning of the next chapter.

INFLATION ACCELERATED IN THE 1960s AS THE
THEORETICAL MODEL WOULD HAVE PREDICTED

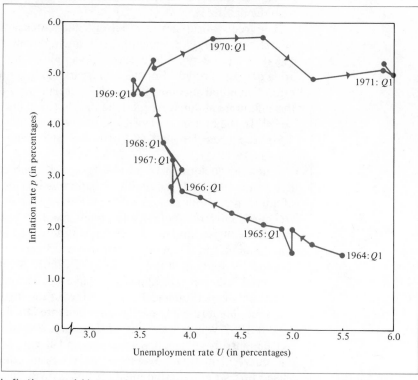

FIGURE 8–9

Inflation and Unemployment in the United States, 1964–71

Notice how faster demand growth initially raised output and reduced unemployment. But then in 1967 and 1968 expectations adjusted upward and the economy moved almost straight up until a reduction of demand growth brought about the recession of 1970–71.

Source: Appendix B

that our simple inflation-unemployment model based on the *SP* and *BC* curves provides an extremely realistic description of the economy's inflation cycle adjustment path in response to an acceleration or deceleration in $\hat{y}$ introduced by government policymakers.

Preview: In Chapter 11 we consider the consequences of a drastic deceleration of $\hat{y}$ as a possible cure for the early-1971 inflation. Can you describe what would happen in Figures 8-7 and 8-8 if the government were suddenly to reduce $\hat{y}$ from 6 percent to zero? Would inflation be eliminated instantly? What would be the costs of the reduction in inflation?

8-10 PRICE CONTROLS AND SUPPLY SHOCKS: MOVING ALONG THE *BC* CURVE

IMPOSITION OF CONTROLS

What will happen to inflation and unemployment if the government introduces wage and price controls that succeed in holding the rate of inflation some percentage amount below the rate that would have occurred without the controls? For instance, at the initial position E_3 in the top frame of Figure 8-10 inflation is at a long-run equilibrium value of 6 percent. Let us assume that the government's price control program succeeds in reducing inflation 3 percent below what it would have been otherwise.

The new element of controls serves as an additional factor (along with changing inflation expectations p^e) that can shift the *SP* curve up or down. When the government's price control agency introduces its program, the *SP* curve shifts vertically downward by 3 percent, from SP_2 to SP_3 in the top frame of Figure 8-10. The effect on the unemployment rate depends on the response of another branch of government, the monetary and fiscal policymakers who control demand growth $\hat{y}$. If adjusted demand growth continues unchanged at 6 percent, the *CU* and *BC* lines will remain fixed and the economy will move southwest from E_3 to *L*. Inflation will decline, making more of $\hat{y}$ available to support a real output boom and a drop in unemployment. But inflation will not fall by the full 3 percent downward shift of *SP*, because the added inflationary pressure caused by lower unemployment will counterbalance some effects of the controls, as shown by the economy's position at point *L* rather than point *N*.

Point *L* is not the end of the story, however. If the price controls continue to hold down inflation for a considerable period, the economy is likely to move away from point *L*. Three factors influence subsequent events, and all three might operate at the same time:

1. Point *L* is off the economy's CU_1 constant unemployment line. In the next period the *BC* line will shift so that it intersects *CU* directly above point *L* (review Figure 8-7). Subsequently the *BC* budget constraint line will shift continuously leftward until the economy arrives at point *M*, if the price controls continue to hold down the *SP* curve.
2. Policymakers might decide that the reduction of unemployment below the natural rate (U^*) is undesirable, and they might pursue a restrictive monetary or fiscal policy to cut adjusted demand growth ($\hat{y}$). This would cause both *CU* and *BC* to shift downward, moving the economy to a point such as *N*, with the same unemployment rate as initially at E_3 but with lower inflation.
3. The effectiveness of the controls might reduce the expected rate of inflation and shift *SP* down even below SP_3. Whether the economy

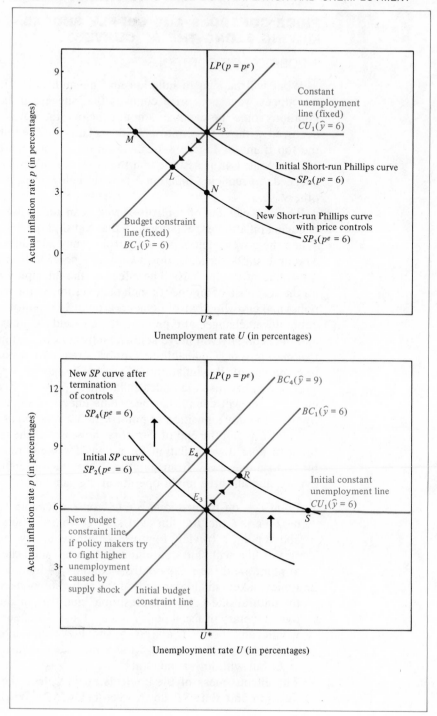

then moves leftward to lower rates of unemployment or downward to lower rates of inflation depends on the rate of demand growth chosen by policymakers. But another possibility is that people will not adjust their expectations at all. They may realize that the controlled behavior of prices is "special" and may believe that when controls are lifted prices will jump back up to the level that would have occurred without the controls. We will see later that this describes the response of the United States economy to the price and wage control program of 1971–74.[15]

TERMINATION OF CONTROLS

These three possibilities assume that the controls continue to hold down the rate of inflation. Yet another possibility, which appears to have occurred in the United States in 1974, is that after the controls are terminated, the price level bounces back up to what it would have been without the controls, and therefore temporarily the inflation rate exceeds its long-run equilibrium value during the "bounce-back" period. This case is illustrated in the bottom frame of Figure 8-10. The effects of the termination of controls are exactly the opposite of the introduction of controls. The economy moves northeast, with rising inflation and unemployment, to a point such as R, as long as policymakers hold the original rate of demand growth ($\hat{y} = 6$). The SP curve is shifted temporarily up from SP_2 to SP_4 for a short period when the controls end, and the economy slides up the fixed BC_1 schedule. When the "bounce-back" or termination effect is over, the SP curve resumes its long-run equilibrium position at SP_2, so long as there has been no adjustment of anticipations of future inflation in response to the controls or their termination.

---

[15] An alternative type of control policy would set $p = 0$ by rigidly fixing all prices, thus both shifting SP down and "rotating" it to a horizontal position. The main point of this section would still be valid; real output growth would be stimulated as the economy moves down the fixed BC_1 curve.

FIGURE 8-10

Effect on Inflation and Unemployment of Price Controls and Supply Shocks

In the top frame the economy starts out at point E_3 in long-run equilibrium with an inflation of 6 percent and unemployment at the natural rate (U^*). A price control program then is introduced that reduces the rate of inflation by 3 percentage points, shifting the economy's SP curve from SP_2 downward to SP_3. The economy slides down its initial BC_1 budget constraint line to point L, and it enjoys a reduction in inflation and unemployment simultaneously.

In the bottom frame exactly the opposite occurs. The termination of price controls, or a supply shock in the form of higher oil or food prices, can shift the SP curve upward from SP_2 to SP_4. Now the economy slides northeast up its BC_1 line, suffering an increase in inflation and unemployment simultaneously.

The inevitable conclusion is that, unless they succeed in permanently changing the expected rate of inflation, controls do more harm than good. The imposition of controls moves the economy from point E_3 to point L in the top frame, creating a temporary output boom and reduction in unemployment, but then the termination of controls creates an output recession and a temporary increase in unemployment. Inflation is held down for only a short time and output is made more unstable than otherwise. One important aim of government policy should be to stabilize output, to help businessmen and workers form accurate expectations and plan efficiently. But in the example of Figure 8-10, imposing controls creates a temporary output boom that leads firms to order new machines and hire new workers. Then the termination of controls ends the boom, causes waste as the new machines go unutilized, and dashes the hopes of low-seniority workers (often teenagers, blacks, and women) who are last hired and then the first fired.

Just as the output boom is temporary, so too is the post-controls recession. The SP curve is shifted up to SP_4 only temporarily, while the price level catches up to its no-controls value. Then the catch-up ends, inflation returns to normal, and the economy returns to its starting place at point E_3. How can the instability of output be prevented when price controls are introduced? If the government had coordinated its price control "department" with its monetary and fiscal "department," the former could use controls to shift SP down, and the latter could slow down money supply growth or introduce fiscal restraint to slow down the rate of adjusted nominal growth ($\hat{y}$), shifting the CU and BC curves down. Similarly, when the controls are terminated and the SP curve shifts back up, $\hat{y}$ could be increased to prevent a recession. Although this accommodative policy would avoid the harmful fluctuations of output, the controls program would nevertheless still fail to reduce inflation permanently unless the expected inflation rate were to decline.

SUPPLY SHOCKS

Between mid-1972 and early 1974, bad harvests and buoyant foreign demand caused farm prices to increase by almost two-thirds.[16] Then, in early 1974, adding to the inflationary pressure, the OPEC oil cartel quadrupled the price of oil, forcing increases in the prices of gasoline, motor oil, fuel oil, electricity, chemicals, and many other components of the GNP deflator. Economists refer to unexpected events that shift the SS curve of Chapter 7 and the SP curve of this chapter as **supply shocks.** These are distinguished from shifts in demand that move the DD curve of Chapter 7 and the CU and BC curves of this chapter.

The effect of a supply shock on the price level and output was explored in Chapter 7. For instance, if the prices of farm products and oil were to

---

[16] On a base of 1971 = 1.00, the index of "prices received by farmers" increased to 1.64.

increase by 60 percent, and these products constituted 5 percent of output, then the GNP deflator would be pushed up 3 percent (= 5 percent of 60) faster than normal. Thus a supply shock has the same effect on inflation and unemployment as the termination of price controls, and it can be illustrated in Figure 8-10 by an upward shift from SP_2 to SP_4. If the monetary and fiscal policymakers maintain adjusted demand growth ($\hat{y}$) unchanged, the CU and BC curves will be unaffected by the supply shock, and the economy will move from point E_3 to point R in the bottom frame of Figure 8-10.

We have now encountered three events that can cause stagflation or an inflationary recession, that is, an increase in inflation and unemployment at the same time:

1. In Figure 8-8 an increase in the growth rate of aggregate demand ($\hat{y}$), although it initially creates an output boom, eventually causes a period of stagflation as expectations adjust and shift the SP curve upward.
2. In Figure 8-10 stagflation occurs during the period in which price controls are terminated.
3. In Figure 8-10 stagflation occurs as the result of a supply shock.

Just as the government can prevent fluctuations in output during a period of price controls by manipulating the CU and BC curves, so the government can prevent an increase in unemployment in Figure 8-10 by shifting the CU and BC curves upward temporarily while the SP curve remains high. Turning back to the bottom frame of Figure 8-10, recall that a supply shock that temporarily pushes the SP curve up from the initial position SP_2 to the new higher position SP_4 raises both inflation and unemployment, as the economy slides northeast from E_3 to R. But point R is reached only if demand growth remains unaffected by the supply shock.

POLICY RESPONSE
TO STAGNATION

Another possibility is that government officials try to avoid the increase in unemployment that would occur at point R. To do this, they must raise demand growth by exactly the amount of the vertical upward shift in the SP curve, 3 percent in this case. When demand growth is raised from $\hat{y} = 6$ to $\hat{y} = 9$, the BC line moves straight up by 3 percentage points to the line marked BC_4. Line CU also moves up (not shown to simplify the diagram). As long as the supply shock holds the short-run Phillips curve at the higher level SP_4, and expectations do not adjust (people believe the effect of the supply shocks on inflation to be temporary), the economy can remain at point E_4.

What is likely to be the response of expectations to the supply shock? At point E_4 expected inflation still remains at its original rate, $p^e = 6$, while actual inflation is racing along at 9 percent. This situation cannot be sustained for long; otherwise expectations will begin to shift upward to $p^e = 9$. But fortunately, supply shocks in most cases lead to only temporary spurts in the inflation rate. Why?

Temporary Supply Shock. One type of supply shock is a crop failure, caused by an untimely freeze or drought. The result is likely to be a temporary increase in the level of prices, followed by a return in the price index to its previous level. This occurred in the winter of 1977, when an unusually severe freeze ruined fruit and vegetable crops in Florida at the end of January, causing an increase in prices in February and March. But then normal weather returned and the price index for these products dropped to its initial level:

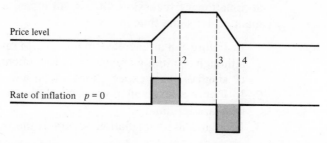

In the diagram, at time 1 the price level begins to rise, increasing the rate of inflation (which is, after all, just the rate of change of the price level). At time 2 the price index levels off, so that the rate of inflation returns to zero. At time 3 the price level begins to fall, so that the rate of inflation becomes negative, and finally both the price level and rate of inflation return at time 4 to their initial values. This type of supply shock is unlikely to cause any adjustment of the expected inflation rate, because most people will correctly view the initial inflation (indicated by the pink-shaded area) as a temporary phenomenon.

Permanent Supply Shock. The OPEC oil price increase of 1974 permanently raised the level of oil prices, but it did not permanently affect the rate of inflation. Increasing energy prices pushed up the rate of inflation as firms adjusted to the higher price of oil, but then no further direct impact was felt on the price level. This type of "permanent" supply shock can be depicted as follows:

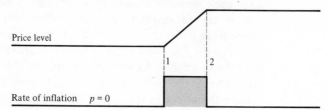

This diagram duplicates the previous one for the first two time periods during which the price index rises to a new higher level. The difference is that no subsequent drop in the price level occurs; the OPEC oil cartel has not allowed the price of oil to return to its pre-1973 level, unlike the cooperative Florida fruits and vegetables that were willing to renew themselves after the freeze of 1977.

Because even the permanent supply shock, such as the OPEC oil cartel, does not permanently raise the inflation rate, there is no reason for the expected rate of inflation (p^e) to adjust upward in response to the temporary inflation that is caused. If there is no shift in p^e, then the short-run Phillips curve shifts up to SP_4 in the bottom frame of Figure 8-10 temporarily and then shifts back to the original SP_2. Policymakers are free to accommodate the supply shock by temporarily raising the growth rate of demand ($\hat{y}$) enough to prevent an increase in unemployment.

In contrast a do-nothing policy of maintaining constant growth in demand will lead to a simultaneous increase in inflation and unemployment, as the economy moves northeast from E_3 to R. The main disadvantage of the accommodative policy that temporarily raises $\hat{y}$ in response to the supply shock is that the rate of inflation is temporarily pushed higher to point E_4 in the diagram. A danger of the accommodative demand raising response to a supply shock is that policymakers may not be able to predict in advance whether workers will cooperatively maintain their previous inflation expectations and accept a drop in the real wage (as the price level rises while wage rates do not) or whether the behavior of workers will make point E_4 unsustainable as rising expectations push the SP curve upward beyond E_4, requiring even faster demand growth if higher unemployment is to be avoided.[17]

8-11 CASE STUDY: INFLATION TRIGGERS RECESSION, 1971–75

In mid-1976 *The New York Times* announced "A New Theory: Inflation Triggers Recession."[18] But this idea is nothing new to readers of the previous section. Any upward shift in SP, whether caused by an upward revision in the expected rate of inflation, by the termination of price controls, or by a supply shock, can both raise the actual inflation rate and trigger a recession as long as the adjusted growth rate of nominal income ($\hat{y}$) is held constant by monetary and fiscal policymakers.

PROSPERITY 1971–73

The story of inflation, unemployment, and recession in the United States in the early 1970s is a dramatic one. In the four quarters of 1974

---

[17] Instructors and advanced students will find a much more complete analysis of the consequences of alternative policies in Robert J. Gordon, "Alternative Responses of Policy to External Supply Shocks," *Brookings Papers on Economic Activity*, vol. 6, no. 1 (1975), pp. 183–206.

[18] *The New York Times*, July 18, 1976, Section F 13.

the GNP deflator for the private business part of the economy increased at an annual rate of 11.1 percent, faster than in any year since 1948. And in the second quarter of 1975 the average unemployment rate was 8.8 percent, the highest since 1941. This interval can be explained mostly by shifts in the SP curve along a fixed CU constant unemployment curve. The adjusted average growth of nominal income ($\hat{y}$) in the five years 1970–74 was 4.9 percent per year, little different from the 4.4 percent average rate of 1965–69, so that the CU curve bears little responsibility for causing the unprecedented instability of inflation and unemployment in the early 1970s. Movements in CU upward in 1972–73 and downward in 1974–75 served mainly to amplify the instability of real output and unemployment primarily caused by price controls and supply shocks.

In Figure 8-11 the inflation and unemployment rates of each quarter between 1971:Q2 and 1976:Q2 are plotted. On August 15, 1971, the Nixon administration imposed comprehensive wage and price controls, which did not prevent all increases in prices but which nevertheless were strict enough to significantly reduce the rate of inflation. We can interpret the effect of the controls with the help of the top frame of Figure 8-10, which shows a leftward movement of the SP curve, moving the economy southwest from point E_3 to point L. The real-world economy behaved similarly, moving southwest from the point marked 1971:Q2 with an inflation rate of 4.5 percent to that marked 1973:Q1 with an inflation rate of only 3.5 percent.[19] The main difference between the theory in Figure 8-10 and the real world of Figure 8-11 is that real-world unemployment reacted to lower inflation with a time lag; the unemployment rate did not begin to drop until early 1972, about six months after the price controls cut the inflation rate.

RECESSION 1973–75

The price controls were terminated in two stages. The rules were loosened in early 1973 and then the controls were taken off completely at the end of April 1974. Now compare the bottom frame of Figure 8-10, where the termination of controls moves the economy from point E_3 to point R, with the actual real-world behavior of Figure 8-11. At first in 1973 inflation increased, but there was no immediate increase in unemployment. Then in early 1974 the combined effect of the termination of controls and the supply shock of the higher relative prices of food, oil, and general imports raised inflation and unemployment simultaneously. The top line in Figure 8-11 shows that inflation doubled from 6 to almost 12 percent between mid-1973 and late 1974, while unemployment almost doubled from 4.8 percent at the end of 1973 to 8.8 percent in the second quarter of 1975.

---

[19] Figure 8-11 shares with Figure 8-9 the device of measuring the rate of inflation over the four quarters ending in the designated quarter.

THE POSITIVE RELATION BETWEEN
INFLATION AND UNEMPLOYMENT IN THE 1970s

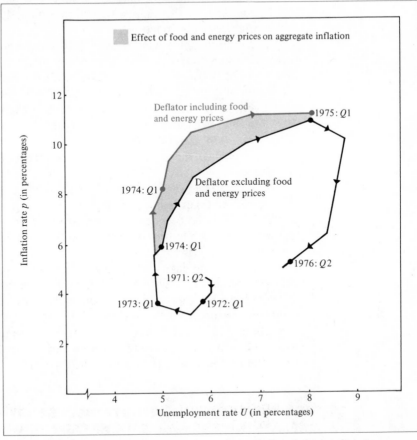

FIGURE 8–11

The Unemployment Rate and the Inflation Rate, Both Including and Excluding Food and Energy Prices, 1971–76

The black line traces the relation between unemployment and the rate of inflation excluding food and energy prices. Notice the southwest movement in 1971–72 when prices were controlled and the northeast movement in 1974 when controls were terminated. Compare with the theoretical diagram, Figure 8–10. The upper red line shows inflation including the prices of energy and food and the pink area measures the effect of the 1973–74 supply shocks.

Source: Appendix B and C.

The black line in Figure 8-11 plots the actual unemployment rate and an adjusted price deflator that excludes the effect of higher food and energy prices. For the period between mid-1973 and mid-1975, the pink area indicates the effect on aggregate inflation of the higher relative prices of food and energy.[20] The lower line indicates that a substantial acceleration of inflation would have occurred in 1974 and 1975 even without the supply shocks in food and energy, mainly because price controls ended in 1974.

The SP curve shifts caused by supply shocks and by the introduction and termination of controls do not explain in full the high inflation rate of 1974. Part of the blame must be shared by the temporary acceleration of $\hat{y}$ during 1972 and 1973 to 7.2 percent (from the 4.4 percent average of 1965–69). This aggravated inflationary pressure in 1973, and the belated response by policymakers who reduced $\hat{y}$ to 3.5 percent in 1974 and 1975 moved the BC curve back suddenly to the right and pushed the unemployment rate higher than was otherwise necessary.

We have treated the CU and BC lines, on the one hand, and the SP curves, on the other hand, as independently determined. Shifts in CU and BC are caused by changes in the adjusted growth rate of nominal income ($\hat{y}$), which in turn depend on all the determinants of aggregate demand and the DD curve of Chapters 6 and 7: business and consumer confidence and monetary and fiscal policy. Shifts in SP are caused by changes in the expected rate of inflation, price controls, and supply shocks. But changing inflation expectations may directly affect business and consumer confidence, and thus shift SP, CU, and BC at the same time. Economists have begun to find evidence that unexpected increases in inflation, caused for example by higher food prices, sometimes cause consumers to cut back their spending.

8-12 ARE GOVERNMENT DEFICITS NECESSARY FOR INFLATION? EXCESSIVE MONETARY GROWTH?

Many interesting questions in economics can be answered if we can determine, in each case, where the relevant demand curve crosses the supply curve and what makes each curve shift. This chapter is another application of the same principle. The dynamic demand curves for the economy, dynamic in the sense that they relate the rate of growth of prices to the growth of aggregate demand, are the CU line, showing the conditions for constant unemployment, and the BC budget constraint line, showing the combinations of current inflation and unemployment consistent with a given growth rate of aggregate demand.

The economy's dynamic aggregate supply curve has been called the SP short-run Phillips curve and shows the combinations of unemploy-

---

[20] We have not excluded the effect on domestic prices of the 1971 and 1973 devaluations of the dollar. Most evidence suggests that only a minor portion of the 1973–74 acceleration of inflation was caused by this factor. See Robert J. Gordon, "The Effect of Aggregate Demand on Price" *Brookings Paper on Economic Activity,* vol. 6, no. 6, (1975), pp. 613–62.

ment and inflation consistent with today's expectations of future inflation. The economy can be in short-run equilibrium only at points where the short-run demand curve (BC) crosses the short-run supply curve (SP).

What insight does this provide on the often heard remark that inflation is caused by excessive government deficits? Anything that can shift the BC or SP curves upward can be said to cause inflation. Because government deficits occur when the government spends more than it takes in from tax revenue, an increase in government spending financed by borrowing (rather than taxation) is likely to cause simultaneously (1) a larger deficit, (2) faster inflation (as the BC curve shifts up along the initial SP curve), and (3) a temporary decrease in unemployment. But government deficits are not special in this regard. A private firm may decide to build a plant or buy a machine. If the firm sells bonds or issues stock to pay for the investment expenditure, it simultaneously causes (1) a larger deficit for itself, (2) faster inflation, and (3) a temporary decrease in unemployment.

Government deficits may appear different from private deficits, because deficits in the government sector can be financed directly when the Federal Reserve decides to print money to cover the deficits. But this action by the Fed occurs only because government deficits push up interest rates, an event the Fed often tries to resist by allowing faster monetary expansion. There is, however, nothing special about Federal government deficits. If AT&T or some other company issues more bonds to finance investment spending, interest rates will be pushed up, and the Fed may try to resist this in exactly the same way by allowing faster monetary expansion.

Thus government deficits are no more inflationary than an equal number of dollars spent on a private investment project financed by borrowing.[21] The popular myth that government deficits always are inflationary stems from the frequent episodes of huge deficits and rampant monetary expansion in wartime. But in principle, if an equally large private investment boom were to develop, private spending financed by borrowing could be equally inflationary.

Recall Milton Friedman's statement that "inflation is always and everywhere a monetary phenomenon." In our analysis in this chapter we agree that an acceleration of monetary growth, which raises $\hat{y}$, can cause an acceleration of inflation in the short run and must cause an acceleration of inflation in the long run. But excessive monetary growth is not necessary for inflation, because inflation can be caused without any change in the rate of monetary growth. Only one example is necessary to contradict a generalization as sweeping as Friedman's: the unusual 1974 events in which inflation accelerated without any similar previous

---

[21] The statement in the text refers to the short run. Later after the private investment project has been completed and is in operation, it will raise the economy's aggregate supply of output, particularly offsetting the initial inflationary effect.

acceleration in monetary growth.[22] In the long run no sustained inflation can persist without support from an acceleration of monetary growth. But in the short run—which may last three, five, or even ten years—shifts in the *SP* curve, or shifts in the *BC* curve not caused by changes in monetary growth rates, can alter the rate of inflation.

In short, the message of this chapter is that both demand factors (monetary and fiscal policy, business and consumer confidence) and supply factors (expectations, controls, supply shocks) are needed to explain the inflation of the seventies. Monetary policy by itself is part of the story, but only part. A complete explanation requires a much broader view than attributing all sins to the Federal Reserve.[23]

SUMMARY

1. The fundamental cause of inflation is excessive growth in aggregate demand, or nominal GNP. In long-run equilibrium, when actual inflation turns out to be exactly what people anticipate, the pace of that inflation depends only on the growth rate of aggregate demand adjusted for the trend growth of natural output. Zero adjusted demand growth $(\hat{y})$ is necessary for the economy to be in long-run equilibrium with zero inflation.

2. Because a high rate of demand growth is sustainable only if it is fueled by a continuous increase in the nominal money supply, in the long run inflation is a monetary phenomenon. The Federal Reserve, by choosing growth rates for the money supply over a decade, determines roughly what the inflation rate will be over that decade.

3. In the short run actual inflation may be higher or lower than expected, and unemployment can differ from the long-run equilibrium natural unemployment rate (U^*). An acceleration of demand growth in the short run goes partially into an acceleration of inflation, but also partly into an acceleration of growth in real output. And when actual real output grows rapidly, the unemployment rate falls. But policymakers cannot keep the unemployment rate below the equilibrium U^* forever; when expectations of inflation catch up to actual inflation, the economy will return to U^*.

4. Inflation and unemployment do not always move in opposite directions. An acceleration of inflation can be accompanied by an increase in unemployment in any situation when the short-run Phillips curve (*SP*)

---

[22] In a recent paper I showed that at most only one-sixth the acceleration of inflation between 1970 and 1974 could be explained by an acceleration of monetary growth. See Robert J. Gordon, "Can the Inflation of the 1970's Be Explained?" *Brookings Papers on Economic Activity*, vol. 8, no. 1 (1977), pp. 253–77.

[23] A well-written literary introduction to the topic of inflation may be a useful supplement to the graphical analysis of this chapter. See Robert M. Solow, "The Intelligent Citizen's Guide to Inflation," *The Public Interest* (Winter 1975), pp. 30–66.

shifts up faster than the growth rate of demand. This could occur when expectations of future inflation are being adjusted rapidly, after the termination of price controls, or as the result of a supply shock.

5. Unless price controls succeed in permanently changing the expected rate of inflation, they do more harm than good by making the path of output more unstable than would occur otherwise. The imposition of controls can create a temporary output boom and reduction in unemployment, but the termination of controls can create the opposite effects; in 1974 it aggravated an inflation already made worse by supply shocks.

6. Supply shocks temporarily shift upward the economy's short-run Phillips curve. The economy's response to the shocks, such as the sudden increases in the price of food and oil in 1973–74, depends on the response of policymakers. If the growth rate of demand is raised in response to the shocks, unemployment can be prevented from rising at the cost of a marked increase in inflation. If the growth rate of demand is reduced in response to the shocks, the inflationary consequences are moderated at the cost of a marked increase in unemployment.

A LOOK AHEAD

If unemployment cannot be permanently pushed below the natural unemployment rate (U^*), then the only way to reduce unemployment is to cut U^* itself. The next chapter asks why U^* is so high in the United States and what can be done to reduce it. Then in Chapter 10 we examine the costs of inflation to society to determine whether inflation is a sufficiently serious problem to warrant the costly process of reducing inflation examined in Chapter 11.

CONCEPTS AND QUESTIONS

IDENTIFICATIONS

Inflation rate
Unemployment rate
Short-run Phillips curve (SP)
Long-run Phillips curve (LP)
Expected rate of inflation
Okun's law
Natural rate of unemployment

Constant unemployment schedule (CU)
Budget constraint schedule (BC)
Adaptive expectations
Supply shocks
Price controls

QUESTIONS FOR REVIEW

Are these statements true, false, or uncertain? Be sure you can give a careful explanation for your answer.

1   Inflation and unemployment always move in opposite directions

because an acceleration of demand growth simultaneously raises the inflation rate and reduces the unemployment rate.

2   If the adjustment coefficient of price expectations (g) is zero, an acceleration of demand growth can reduce the unemployment rate permanently.

3   A boom in output and a reduction in unemployment can be created by price controls, even if demand growth remains unchanged.

4   Policymakers can reduce the United States unemployment rate below 5 percent permanently if they are willing to create faster demand growth.

5   A stable price level and zero unemployment are incompatible.

6   The inflation rate can be reduced, without any effect on the unemployment rate, if the Federal Reserve simply reduces the growth rate of the money supply.

7   It is impossible for policymakers to maintain a stable rate of inflation in the presence of a supply shock.

8   "Inflation is always and everywhere a monetary phenomenon."

Optional. *It is possible to translate the SP and BC curves into simple equations and calculate the economy's inflation and unemployment rate under given conditions. For example:*

SP curve	$p = p^e - 3(U - U^*)$	(a)
BC line	$p = \hat{y} + 3(U - U_{-1})$	(b)
Expectations	$p^e = p_{-1}$	(c)

The economy's starting position is a situation of long-run equilibrium with:

$$\hat{y} = p = p_{-1} = p^e = 0 \quad \text{and} \quad U = U_{-1} = U^* = 5.5$$

The government wishes to reduce the unemployment rate to 4 percent.

1   What rate of change of demand ($\hat{y}$) must the government generate to reach 4 percent unemployment in one period (before expectations have a chance to adjust)?

2   What will be the actual rate of inflation in the new situation?

3   For the government to maintain the 4 percent unemployment rate in the second period, at what value must they set $\hat{y}$? What inflation rate (p) will result?

4   Similarly, what must happen to $\hat{y}$ for unemployment to remain at 4 percent in the third period?

5   What do your answers imply about the attempt by the government to maintain an unemployment rate below U^*?

6   Suppose the government has now become alarmed by the rate of inflation. To keep p from accelerating further, what must be the value of $\hat{y}$ in the fourth period? The fifth period?

7   Suppose the government decides to maintain inflation at a 3 percent rate. What value of $\hat{y}$ must it maintain permanently? Describe the paths of U and p in reaching long-run equilibrium, starting from the situation that you had calculated for the third period in part 4.

Hint: *The answers to several of these questions can be calculated if equations* (b) *and* (c) *are substituted into* (a), *yielding a single equation relating current inflation to past inflation, current and past unemployment, and adjusted demand growth:*

$$p = \frac{p_{-1} + \hat{y} + 3(U^* - U_{-1})}{2} \tag{a'}$$

9 Unemployment: Causes, Costs, and Policy Options

You're never right for anything. At first you're too young; then you don't have experience; by the time you're 35 or 40 years, you're too old. . . . You know, it's everything — job and experience, no experience, no job. To get a job you gotta have money; you gotta have a job to get money. So it's just a vicious circle of nothing. And you're all locked up in this thing, crossed in it all your life. One circle that leads nowhere. That makes you pretty angry. Angry isn't even the word for it. I don't even *know* how to describe that feeling.[1]

9-1 THE DILEMMA OF HIGH UNEMPLOYMENT

The average U.S. unemployment rate in the decade ending in 1976 was 5.4 percent. In 1975 and 1976 the jobless rate soared to 8.5 and 7.7 percent, respectively, both figures higher than in any year since the Great Depression. Why should society tolerate such high levels of unemployment, together with the waste that occurs when machines, factories, stores, and office buildings are underutilized? Should we conclude that there is some simple solution that economists understand but politicians refuse to accept? Or have economists failed to comprehend some aspect of the problem? Or is the problem of high unemployment basically insoluble?

In Chapter 8 we concluded that the government does have the power to reduce the unemployment rate by stimulating aggregate demand through the use of monetary or fiscal policy. Unfortunately, the actual jobless rate can be pushed below the natural rate of unemployment only temporarily, because any attempt to hold the actual unemployment rate permanently below the natural rate causes a continuously accelerating rate of inflation.

The actual unemployment rate can be zero permanently only if the natural rate of unemployment is zero. In this ideal world an acceleration of inflation caused by excess demand stimulation could not occur, if

---

[1] Remarks of Rosie Washington, quoted in "Down and Out in America," *The New York Times Magazine* (February 9, 1975), pp. 9–10.

the actual unemployment rate were maintained at the zero natural unemployment rate.

> *Thus the first and most basic cause of high U.S. unemployment is that the natural rate of unemployment is not zero, but a much higher number, in the vicinity of 5.0 or 5.5 percent.*

We learn in the first part of this chapter why the natural rate of unemployment is not zero. We discover that at least some unemployment is not a complete waste but actually serves a social purpose. Nevertheless, the high level of the natural rate of unemployment in the United States includes a wasteful portion: The natural rate is higher than necessary as a result of discrimination against blacks and women, barriers to mobility and the acquisition of job skills, and even to some extent because of government regulations.

Thus the terminology "natural rate of unemployment" is misleading. The natural rate is not carved in stone, immutable, or desirable. It can change either as the result of actions by private firms and households (for instance, better matching of job requirements and worker skills) or by changes in government policy (for instance, changes in minimum wage rates or unemployment benefits). The rate is natural only in the sense of equilibrium—at the natural unemployment rate, whatever its value in a particular year, there is no pressure on the inflation rate to change. Any attempt to push the unemployment rate lower than this year's natural rate of unemployment causes inflation to speed up, whereas a higher unemployment rate slows inflation.

In many years actual unemployment exceeds the natural rate of unemployment. Thus the causes of the high natural rate provide only part of the explanation for high actual unemployment. During 1949–50, 1954, 1958–64, 1971, and 1975–76, the actual unemployment rate rose above the natural rate.

> *Many periods of high actual unemployment above the natural unemployment rate have been the result of deliberate government anti-inflationary policy designed to decelerate inflation by holding actual unemployment above the natural rate.*

After we examine in the main portion of this chapter why the natural unemployment rate is so high, and what can be done to reduce it, in the last sections we will look closer at the costs to society of policies that allow actual unemployment to exceed the natural rate. We will measure these costs of recessions, and then in Chapter 10 for comparison examine the costs of inflation.

9-2 HOW THE GOVERNMENT MEASURES UNEMPLOYMENT

Many wonder how the government determines facts such as "the teenage unemployment rate in September 1976 was 18.1 percent," because they have never spoken to a government agent about their own experiences of employment, unemployment, and time in school. It would be too costly for everyone in the country to be contacted every month; the government attempts to reach each household to collect information only once each decade when it takes the Decennial Census of Population. On the other hand it would not be enough to collect information just once every ten years, because policymakers would have no guidance for conducting current policy.

As a compromise, the Census Bureau interviews each month about 50,000 households, or about 1 in every 1500 households in the country. Each month one-fourth the households in the sample are replaced, so that no family is interviewed more than four months in a row. The laws of statistics imply that an average from a survey of a sample of households of this size comes very close to the true figure that would be revealed by a costly complete census.[2]

The interviewer first asks, for each separate household member, "What was he (or she) doing most of last week — working, keeping house, going to school, or something else?" The person is counted as employed if he did any work at all for pay during the past week, whether part-time, full-time, or temporary work.

For those who say they did no work, the next question is "Did he have a job from which he was temporarily absent or on layoff last week?" If the reason for job absence is that the person is awaiting recall from a layoff or has obtained a new job but is waiting for it to begin, he is counted as unemployed. If the person neither works nor is absent from a job, the next question is "Has he been looking for work in the last four weeks?" If so "What has he been doing in the last four weeks to find work?" If the person has not been ill and has searched for a job by applying to an employer, registering with an employment agency, checking with friends, or other specified job-search activities, he is counted as unemployed. The remaining people who are neither employed nor unemployed, mainly homemakers who do not seek paid work, students at school, disabled people, and retired people, are counted as not in the labor force.

Despite the intricacy of questions asked by the interviewer, the concept is simple: "People with jobs are employed; people who do not have

---

[2] The facts in this section are taken from *How the Government Measures Unemployment,* BLS Report no. 312 (Washington, D.C.: U.S. Bureau of Labor Statistics, June 1967).

jobs and are looking for jobs are unemployed."[3] The **total labor force** is the total of the employed and the unemployed. Thus the entire population aged 16 and over falls into one of three categories:

1. Total labor force
   a. Employed (civilian employed plus members of the armed forces)
   b. Unemployed
2. Not in the labor force

The actual unemployment rate is defined as the ratio:

$$U = \frac{\text{Number of unemployed}}{\text{Civilian employed} + \text{unemployed}}$$

Example: In September 1977 the BLS reported an unemployment rate of 6.9 percent. This was calculated as the ratio:

$$U = \frac{\text{Number of unemployed}}{\text{Civilian employed} + \text{unemployed}} = \frac{6{,}773{,}000}{91{,}095{,}000 + 6{,}773{,}000}$$

$$\text{or } U = 6.9 \text{ percent}$$

The government's unemployment measure sounds relatively straightforward, but unfortunately it disguises almost as much as it reveals:

1. *The unemployment rate by itself is not a measure of the social distress caused by the loss of a job.* Each person who lacks a job and is looking for one is counted as "1.0 unemployed people," whether he is the head of a household responsible for feeding three, four, or even ten dependents or whether he is a 16-year-old looking only for a 10-hour-per-week part-time job to provide pocket money for milk shakes and rock records. For instance, the unemployment rate of adult males (aged 25 and up) was almost the same in 1974 as in 1955 (after fluctuating in between). But the total unemployment rate increased over the same period from 4.2 to 5.6 percent because of increased unemployment among teenagers and the shifting composition of the labor force. This structural increase in unemployment is not as serious as the increase in total unemployment from 4.2 to 5.6 percent that occurred between February and October 1970, an interval during which the unemployment rate of adult males shot up rapidly.
2. *The government's unemployment concept misses some of the people hurt by a recession.* Some suffer a cut in hours, being forced by their employer to shift from full-time to part-time work. Still counted as employed, they never enter the unemployment statistics.[4]

---

[3] *How the Government Measures Unemployment*, p. 10.

[4] The government does keep separate records on the number of people on part-time work who want to work full-time. In 1974, for instance, there was an average of 1.3 million people who usually worked full-time but instead were working part-time for economic reasons.

3. *A person lacking a job must have performed particular specified actions to look for a job during the past four weeks.* What if he has looked and looked and has given up, convinced that no job is available? He is not counted as unemployed at all. He simply "disappears" from the labor force, entering the category of not in labor force. Those out of the labor force who would like to work but have given up on the job search are sometimes called discouraged workers or the disguised unemployed. They have numbered as many as 1 million in some postwar recessions.[5]

Despite the inadequacies of the government unemployment concept, our graphs and tables emphasize the total official unemployment rate because it is most widely publicized and discussed by the public.[6] To reach a better understanding of the meaning of unemployment, however, we have to probe deeper and look at some of the subtotals and supplementary figures published in government reports.

9-3 CASE STUDY: ACTUAL AND NATURAL RATES OF UNEMPLOYMENT IN THE UNITED STATES

The top frame of Figure 9-1 for the period since 1953 compares the actual unemployment rate with my estimate of the natural rate of unemployment.[7] The period can be divided into several major episodes, a recession in 1954, a boom in 1955–57, a long period of high unemployment and sluggish output growth between 1958 and 1964, a prolonged boom (partly caused by the Vietnam War) between 1965 and 1969, followed in the early 1970s by two recessions (1970–71 and 1973–75) interrupted by a period of prosperity (1972–74). Episodes with actual unemployment above the natural rate are distinguished from episodes with actual unemployment below the natural rate by the shading on the diagram.

The natural rate hypothesis, examined in Chapter 8, tells us that in-

---

[5] Two techniques have been used to estimate disguised unemployment. One is to measure how far the labor force in a recession falls below its normal growth. The second, which yields much smaller estimates of disguised unemployment, is to count those who tell the Census interviewer that their reason for being not in labor force is that they "think they cannot get a job." Why the discrepancy between the two methods? Some discouraged workers may drop out of the labor force and enter school or take up housework, and then they may tell the Census interviewer that those activities are the reason they are not in the labor force.

[6] A recent attempt to correct some of these inadequacies is Sar A. Levitan and Robert Taggart III, *Employment and Earnings Inadequacy: A New Social Indicator* (Johns Hopkins, 1974).

[7] Details of my method of estimation are presented in Appendix C. The procedures are similar to those used in Michael L. Wachter, "The Changing Cyclical Responsiveness of Wage Inflation," *Brookings Papers on Economic Activity*, vol. 7, no. 1 (1976), pp. 115–159.

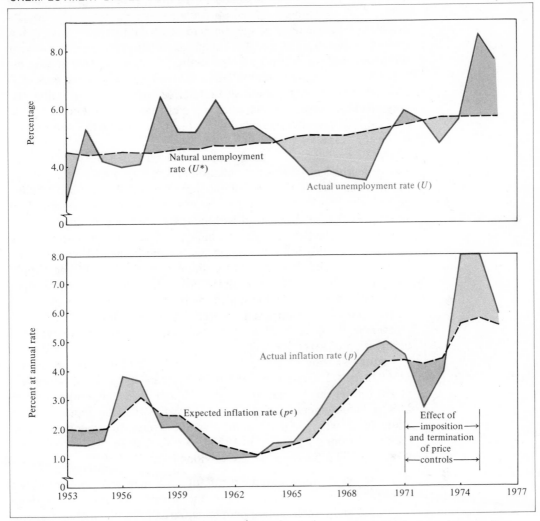

FIGURE 9–1   The Actual (U) and Natural (U^*) Unemployment Rates and the Actual (p) and Expected (p^e) Inflation Rates in the United States, 1953–76

Notice that before 1971 during the two main intervals of low unemployment (1955–57 and 1965–69) the inflation rate accelerated ahead of what people expected. During the long period of high unemployment between 1958 and 1963, the inflation rate decelerated. Supply shocks and the effects of controls caused the relationship to break down after 1971.

Source: Details in Appendix C. Official unemployment rate figures before 1967 are adjusted for changes in the method of measurement that occurred in 1967.

flation increases faster than people expect when actual unemployment falls below the natural rate. Figure 9-1 illustrates the workings of the natural rate hypothesis. The top frame, as we have seen, plots the actual rate and estimated natural rate of unemployment. During the interval between 1953 and 1971, periods of low actual unemployment (pink shading) were also periods, denoted by pink shading in the bottom frame, when the rate of inflation exceeded the estimated expected rate.[8] In contrast to the pink-shaded periods of price acceleration, the gray shading shows periods when price change slowed. During all the gray periods the actual unemployment rate was above the natural rate in the top frame of Figure 9-1.

Notice in Figure 9-1 that the relation breaks down after 1971. Why? As we learned in Chapter 8, inflation and unemployment can change in the same direction if something shifts the *SP* or short-run Phillips curve. In 1971–75 two major factors interfered: (1) the food and oil supply shocks resulting from bad harvests and from the formation of the OPEC oil cartel, and (2) the imposition and termination of price controls. The inflation rate data in the bottom frame of Figure 9-1 exclude energy and food prices to eliminate the effects of the supply shocks. In this way the effects of the price controls become more apparent. We can see the reduction of inflation below what was expected when controls were imposed, as well as the following acceleration of inflation as the price level jumped back to its no-controls level with the termination of price controls.

Figure 9-1 shows a gradual increase in the natural employment rate (U^*) from 4.2 percent in 1953 to 5.4 percent in 1976.[9] This gradual upward creep in U^* has resulted from a shift in the composition of U.S. unemployment. Compared to 1955, the 1974 unemployment of adult males was about the same, but the overall unemployment rate increased from 4.2 percent in 1955 to 5.6 percent in 1974. How could it do that? The two reasons are obvious from Table 9-1:

1. Although the unemployment rate of adult men and women did not change between 1955 and 1974, the other two groups, male young people and female young people, suffered from much higher unemployment rates in 1974.
2. The labor force was dominated in 1955 by adult men, but by 1974 less than half the labor force consisted of adult men. Because the composition of the labor force shifted over to other groups, each

---

[8] The expected rate of inflation is estimated by using information on the response of interest rates to inflation. The methodology is described in Appendix C.

[9] Where did these numbers come from? No data on the natural unemployment rate are printed in any government document. We have not picked the numbers out of a glass jar but have used an electronic computer to find the values of U^* that achieve the closest possible relationship between $(p - p^e)$ in the bottom frame and $(U - U^*)$ in the top frame for the 1954–74 period.

TABLE 9-1 The Structural Shift in the Composition of Unemployment, 1955 and 1974

	Unemployment rates			Shares in the labor force		
	1955*	1974	1955–74 change	1955	1974	1955–74 change
1. Males aged 25 and over	3.0	3.0	0.0	59.8	47.4	−12.4
2. Females aged 25 and over	4.6	4.6	0.0	25.2	28.6	+ 3.4
3. Males aged 16–24	8.7	11.4	+2.7	8.6	13.2	+ 4.6
4. Females aged 16–24	7.4	12.4	+5.0	6.4	10.8	+ 4.4
5. Total, all groups	4.2	5.6	+1.4	100.0	100.0	0.0

* The 1955 figures have been adjusted to reflect changes in the methods of measuring unemployment introduced in 1967. See Robert L. Stein, "New Definitions for Employment and Unemployment," *Employment and Earnings* (Washington, D.C.: U.S. Bureau of Labor Statistics, February 1967), pp. 3–27.
Source: Handbook of Labor Statistics 1975 — Reference Edition (Washington, D.C.: Bureau of Labor Statistics, 1975), BLS Bulletin 1865.

having higher unemployment rates, the average unemployment rate would have increased even if the separate unemployment rates of each of the subgroups had remained absolutely unchanged. (This is true of any average: if a baseball player begins to suffer a higher fraction of bad hitless days than good two-hit days, his batting average will go down.)

Why should a shift in the composition of unemployment toward adult women and teenagers change the natural rate of unemployment? An unemployment rate of 5.0 percent in the mid-1950s included a substantial fraction of skilled and experienced adult males who were available to fill job vacancies. But in the mid-1970s the same unemployment rate includes mainly adult women and teenagers, *many of whom lack the job skills required by employers.* Although some teenagers and adult women are hired and trained to fill job vacancies, other firms find it cheaper to bribe an experienced male away from another firm by offering him a higher wage rate. This upward wage bidding plays a part in the acceleration of inflation that occurs in tight labor markets when actual unemployment (U) is below the natural rate (U^*).

9-4 WHY IS THE NATURAL UNEMPLOYMENT RATE SO HIGH?

We gain a better understanding of the natural unemployment rate (U^*) if we think of an imaginary society in which U^* is zero. All jobs are completely identical in their skill requirements, and all are located

A MISMATCH BETWEEN WORKERS AND JOB
OPENINGS CAN CAUSE VACANCIES AND UNEMPLOYMENT
TO EXIST AT THE SAME TIME

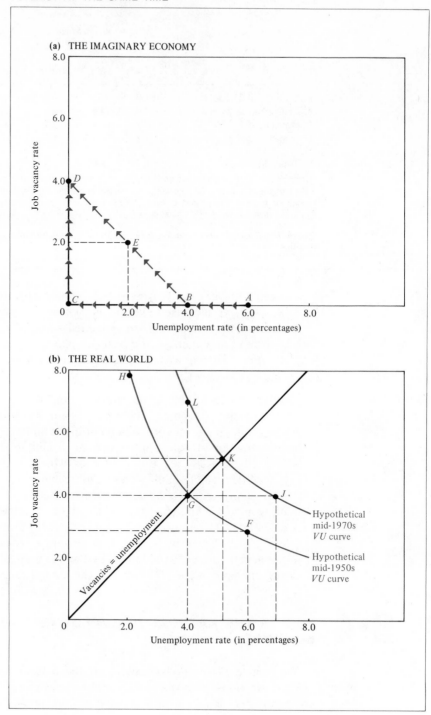

(a) THE IMAGINARY ECONOMY

(b) THE REAL WORLD

at exactly the same place. All workers are completely identical, with skill requirements perfectly suited for the identical jobs, and all workers live in the same location as the jobs. We can imagine a 10-mile-high combined factory-office-apartment skyscraper with very fast elevators at the corner of State and Madison Streets in Chicago.

In this imaginary economy it is impossible for vacancies and unemployment to exist simultaneously. Why? Find point *A* in the top frame of Figure 9-2. Point *A* is along the horizontal axis at an unemployment rate of 6 percent, and there are no job vacancies.

> The **job vacancy rate** *is the ratio of total job vacancies to the civilian labor force.*

The phrase "vacancy rate" is a concept that unfortunately has no empirical counterpart in the United States, which does not collect comprehensive job vacancy data. Now we can examine the effects of expansive monetary and fiscal policies that stimulate aggregate demand. Additional jobs open up, but the unemployed workers are in exactly the right place and possess the right skills, so that they instantly zoom up or down the speedy elevators in the 10-mile-high skyscraper to the job's location. The job vacancy disappears immediately, and unemployment declines, moving up leftward with the arrows from point *A* to *B* to *C*.

At point *C* all the unemployed have found jobs. The unemployment rate is zero. Any further job vacancies caused by an additional aggregate demand stimulus will not disappear because there are no available jobless people to fill them. The economy will move up toward point *D,* as the aggregate demand stimulus expands the number of job vacancies.

To be slightly more realistic, let us now assume that there are two types of jobs and workers in the 10-mile-high skyscraper, typists and computer programmers. As the economy expands from *A* leftward to *B* in the top frame of Figure 9-2, it gradually uses up its supply of trained computer programmers. At point *B* all the computer programmers have jobs; all the 4 percent unemployment rate consists of unemployed

---

FIGURE 9-2

The Relationship between the Vacancy and Unemployment Rates in an Imaginary Economy (top frame) and in the Real-World Economy (bottom frame)

In the top frame the arrows going through point *C* show the path the economy would follow with expanding aggregate demand if all jobs and workers were identical and in the same place. The diagonal path through point *E* shows that vacancies and unemployment can exist at the same time if firms refuse to hire unemployed workers for available openings, because they lack skills or are in the wrong location. In the bottom frame the two *VU* curves show that the mismatch between job openings and workers became more serious between the mid-1950s and mid-1970s.

typists. If the government further stimulates aggregate demand, we assume that an equal number of job vacancies is created for programmers and typists. The typist vacancies disappear immediately as available typists are carried by elevator to fill the job openings. But there are no computer programmers left, and so the programmer job openings remain. In expanding from point *B* to point *E,* the economy creates vacancies equal to 2 percent of the labor force for programmers and another 2 percent for typists. The programmer vacancies remain unfilled at point *E,* which is at a vertical height of 2 percent, but 2 percent of the unemployed are capable of filling the typist vacancies, moving us leftward by 2 percent along the horizontal unemployment axis.

At point *E* vacancies and unemployment exist simultaneously because firms refuse to hire typists to fill programmer vacancies. The costs of training are just too high. If training were costless, typists could fill the programmer vacancies, there would be no remaining vacancies or unemployment, and the aggregate demand stimulus would have taken us to point *C* instead of point *E*.

In reality the actual economy is divided into numerous separate labor markets differing in location, working conditions, and skill requirements. If aggregate spending increases when the overall unemployment rate is 20 or 30 percent, then unemployed workers are available in almost every skill category and location and firms do not have to raise wage rates to attract applicants. But in our economy at a 5 or 6 percent unemployment rate, any increase in aggregate spending generates job openings in some labor markets while many people remain unemployed in other markets. Some unemployed are able to fill developing job vacancies. But others are prevented from qualifying by the cost of moving to the locations of the job openings, by the cost of acquiring the required skills, and even by the "cost of information" involved in finding out what jobs are available. More machine-tool operators and computer programmers may be needed, but only unskilled bootblacks or retail salesclerks may be available among the unemployed. Or the new jobs may be created in Houston or Chicago, while the unemployed may be in Boston, New York, San Francisco, or Appalachia.

IMBALANCE BETWEEN VACANCIES AND UNEMPLOYMENT

The bottom frame of Figure 9-2 is a more accurate description of the real world than is the top frame.[10] First, examine the lower curve labeled Hypothetical mid-1950s *VU* curve (*VU* stands for vacancies-unemployment). The curve shows all the possible combinations of vacancy and unemployment rates in the mid-1950s that could be achieved by different

---

[10] Use of this diagram was introduced in J. C. R. Dow and L. A. Dicks-Mireaux, "The Excess Demand for Labour: A Study of Conditions in Great Britain, 1946–56," *Oxford Economic Papers,* vol. 10 (February 1958), pp. 1–33.

degrees of monetary and fiscal stimulus. Although at point F the unemployment rate is 6 percent, there are still job vacancies in a few occupations and locations. As the economy expands northwest from F to G in response to a demand stimulus, new job openings are created. Some are filled by the unemployed, reducing unemployment from 6 to 4 percent, but others remain unfilled, raising the vacancy rate. At point G the vacancy and unemployment rates are equal, whereas any further demand stimulus, say to point H, would raise the vacancy rate above the unemployment rate.

What does the VU curve have to do with the natural rate of unemployment? In jobs with vacancies, the wage rate is pushed up as firms attempt to steal workers from each other by making higher wage offers. In jobs with available unemployed workers, the wage rate may rise less than usual because the unemployed stand ready to replace any workers who might quit in reaction to an unsatisfactory wage offer.

If the upward wage pressure created by the 4 percent vacancy rate at point G exactly balanced the downward wage pressure created by the 4 percent unemployment rate, then 4 percent would be the natural rate of unemployment. Any attempt to push the economy northwest of point G, with vacancies greater than unemployment, would result in a net upward pressure on wages and, because firms pass on their higher wage costs to consumers in the form of higher prices, would result in an accelerating inflation.[11]

In the mid-1970s the economy no longer operates along the mid-1950s VU curve. When the vacancy rate is 4 percent, the unemployment rate is no longer 4 percent, as at G, but a higher number at point J, perhaps 7 percent. Why do so many more people remain unemployed in the face of plentiful job vacancies? As shown in Table 9-1, the unemployed now consist much more of relatively inexperienced women and teenagers, whom business firms do not consider qualified for the job openings available. Under the conditions of the mid-1970s, vacancies equal unemployment when an aggregate demand stimulus brings the economy to point K.

The natural rate of unemployment, which can be approximately described as the unemployment rate at which vacancies equal unemployment, has shifted upward from G to K because there is now a greater mismatch than 20 years ago between the skill requirements of jobs and the skill endowments of the unemployed.

Any attempt to achieve an unemployment rate of 4 percent in the mid-1970s would take the economy northwest of K to point L, where the va-

---

[11] Normally, wages increase at a rate equal to the rate of expected inflation, plus the growth rate of output per worker-hour. The increase in the real wage thus equals the increase in the amount each worker produces. "Net upward pressure on wages" in the text sentence means a circumstance that raises the wage rate faster than the sum of the growth rates of expected inflation and output per worker-hour.

cancy rate exceeds the unemployment rate by the distance LG. There would be upward pressure on wage rates, and inflation would accelerate. Policymakers want to prevent inflation from accelerating, and so they attempt to keep the economy from passing to the left of point K. But one can ask why aggregate demand was restrained by so much in 1975–77 to keep the economy far to the right of point K and even point J, despite the absence of any danger of accelerating inflation when the unemployment rate is so far above the natural rate. One also wonders why the economy is constrained to operate on the high mid-1970s VU curve and what actions the government could take to get us back on the mid-1950s VU curve. Why are job vacancies and unemployed workers so badly mismatched at points K and J that high vacancies and high unemployment can exist at the same time?

9-5 THE MISMATCH OF JOBS AND WORKERS

Our analysis has been very much oversimplified. The natural rate of unemployment does not automatically occur when unemployment and vacancies are equal because the upward pressure put on wages by job vacancies may be different from the downward pressure put on wages by the existence of unemployed workers. We cannot perform careful tests of the location of the current VU curve in the United States because we lack comprehensive vacancy statistics suitable for comparison with our comprehensive unemployment data. Nevertheless, the VU curve for the 1970s in Figure 9-2 does summarize our basic problem, that a demand stimulus creates job openings that are not necessarily suitable for the skill endowments or locations of the unemployed, and these job slots remain unfilled and create inflationary pressure.

In early 1975, despite an unemployment rate that exceeded 8 percent, numerous jobs were vacant in the U.S. economy. *Business Week* reported:

> Help Wanted: machinists, welders, nurses, traveling salesmen, computer repairers, and many, many others. Help Wanted? With unemployment at 8.2 percent . . . jobs going begging? In brief, yes. They always do, in every recession. The unemployed do not have the right skills for the unfilled jobs. A jobless auto worker cannot step into a nurse's white shoes.[12]

Among the occupations with unfilled jobs at the depth of the 1975 recession were some that always have had job openings in recent years—secretaries, draftsmen, X-ray technicians, machinists, television and hi-fi re-

---

[12] "A Million Jobs Go Begging," *Business Week* (March 17, 1975), p. 44.

pairmen, and electronics engineers. The 1973–74 increase in the price of oil had created a boom in oil exploration and drilling, opening up unfilled vacancies in a wide range of occupations related to energy: rig builders, dehydration plant operators, oil well drillers, piping designers, and welders. Environmental legislation had also created openings for industrial hygienists and lab technicians.[13]

Not only do most of the teenage and adult female unemployed fail to qualify for these jobs but in a recession many adult males have the wrong skills or are in the wrong location. Why does the job-worker mismatch occur? The explanations fall into at least seven categories:

1. INFLEXIBILITY OF RELATIVE WAGES

A basic principle of elementary economics is that a shortage of a commodity develops when its price is held too low and is prevented from rising. A surplus develops when its price is held too high. Similarly in labor markets, high unemployment for a group such as teenagers is a sign that its wage rate is too high relative to the wage rates of skilled adult men. A reduction in the teenage wage rate would induce firms to create more job openings teenagers could fill. Government minimum wage legislation is one factor that keeps the relative wage of high unemployment groups from declining.

Inflexible relative wages mean that some members of disadvantaged groups are unemployed while others are employed at higher wage rates than would occur with flexible wage rates. But this factor provides no explanation at all why teenagers, women, blacks, and other groups are disadvantaged in the first place. The remaining factors help to explain the disadvantaged status that leads to high unemployment.

2. LACK OF INCENTIVES FOR FIRMS TO TRAIN WORKERS

Many skills are not taught in school. Firms must train workers on the job. When workers are new and inexperienced, their productivity often falls short of their wage so that the firm loses money on them. After they become experienced, the firm would like to recoup its losses by making a profit on the workers. It can do so when their skills are "firm-specific," that is, when the skills are useful only to that firm. The worker cannot quit in protest when the firm pays him a wage below his productivity because he cannot carry his job skills with him to a rival firm. In contrast, when the worker's skills are general and can be used at several companies, the training firm loses all its investment in his training if he should quit. Many jobs that were vacant in the 1975 recession, such as electronics engineers and welders, require general skills. Firms are under-

---

[13] Examples from the *Business Week* story.

standably unwilling to hire and train inexperienced workers who might reward the firm by a slap in the face — quitting to join a rival firm.[14]

3. "RATIONAL" EMPLOYER DISCRIMINATION

Many managerial and white-collar occupations do provide workers with specific training that makes them more valuable to their firm than to rivals. Because a firm takes losses on new employees, and begins to make profits only as they become experienced, it is understandable that firms try to hire only those job applicants who can be predicted to stay with the firm a long time. Any member of a group with an above-average tendency to quit will be excluded. Personnel managers steer away from hiring adult women and teenagers for "good jobs" that lead to lifelong careers and regular promotions. Young women, it is predicted, are likely to stay on the job only a short time before they quit to have children. Older women may already have grown children but are in their 40s and 50s, too near to retirement age to allow a heavy training investment to pay off.

Teenagers face even greater problems. They take jobs for short periods either to make money for further schooling or to experiment with several possible occupations. Because it is impossible for job interviewers to guess which women or teenagers will be stable workers and which will quit early, they take the easy way out and brand all applicants with the undesirable characteristics of the group to which they belong. The real losers are the young applicants who are serious in wanting to stick with a job and learn a skill and the women who plan to keep working while they have children (or not to have children at all).

4. "PURE" DISCRIMINATION

Some employers will not hire women, blacks, or young workers, even if some members of these disadvantaged groups are actually more capable than some of the adult white males who are favored. Much "pure" discrimination stems from long-standing customs and from social pressure. Because some occupations are considered better suited for women or blacks by custom, we observe that almost all secretaries, telephone operators, elementary school teachers, nurses, and typists are women, and black workers are pushed into relatively unpleasant occupations. Although women and blacks made significant progress in the decade after

[14] The distinction between general and specific training, or human capital, was introduced by Gary Becker, *Human Capital* (New York: Columbia University Press, 1964, 2nd ed. 1975). Other important contributions include Jacob Mincer, "On-the-Job Training: Costs, Returns, and Some Implications," *Journal of Political Economy,* vol. 70 (October 1962 supplement), pp. 40–79; and Sherwin Rosen, "Learning and Experience in the Labor Market," *Journal of Human Resources,* vol. 7 (Summer 1972), pp. 326–42. A recent survey of the state of this literature is Mark Blaug, "The Empirical Status of Human Capital Theory: A Slightly Jaundiced Survey," *Journal of Economic Literature,* vol. 14 (September 1976), pp. 827–55.

1964, many of the gains were limited to those who completed college. Less educated blacks and women are still prevented in many cases from entering unions in blue-collar trades.[15] As for teenagers, government regulations may do more harm than good, particularly the high minimum wage that makes many teenagers too expensive to hire and regulations that set age minimums for particular occupations or require bureaucratic red tape for teenage hires but not for adults.[16]

5. HIT-AND-MISS AVAILABILITY OF TRAINING IN SCHOOL

If firms are unwilling or unable to provide training, why can't the schools and community colleges equip their students with the skills needed in today's job markets? Often the curriculum lags years behind changes in skill requirements. Sometimes school systems are unwilling to spend the money for expensive equipment. High school counselors still advise teenagers to go into specialties that became obsolete long ago. Sometimes the students themselves are the problem, hoping to go to college in order to enter a "prestigious" professional field and refusing to take courses to become the technicians and skilled tradesmen that society needs.

6. DIFFICULTY OF BORROWING

Many young people would be willing to learn useful skills in community colleges or private trade schools but they cannot afford to go, either because their families are poor or because they have married early and need an immediate job to support their family. Because schooling is an investment that yields a return in the form of higher future earnings, young people should be able to borrow for their schooling and pay back the loans out of future income. State university systems are a form of borrowing, allowing a student to pay a low tuition subsidized by tax collections from state residents. The student "repays" part of the subsidy in the future as the state collects sales and income taxes from him. But state university systems are unfair, because the whole population is taxed but only the most able students with high school grade records that qualify them for entry are subsidized.

---

[15] The progress of blacks is documented in Richard B. Freeman, "Changes in the Labor Market for Black Americans, 1948–72," *Brookings Papers on Economic Activity,* vol. 4, no. 1 (1973), pp. 67–120. The earnings of women have fallen relative to those of men, as is shown in Robert J. Gordon, "Structural Unemployment and the Productivity of Women," *Journal of Monetary Economics* (January 1977 supplement), pp. 181–229.

[16] A high estimate of the job losses from the minimum wage is presented by Jacob Mincer, "Unemployment Effects of Minimum Wages," *Journal of Political Economy,* vol. 84, part 2 (August 1976), pp. S87–S104. A more modest effect is measured by Edward Gramlich, "The Impact of Minimum Wages on Other Wages, Employment and Family Incomes," *Brookings Papers on Economic Activity,* vol. 7, no. 2 (1976), pp. 409–451.

7. LONG ADJUSTMENT LAGS IN EDUCATION

In 1966, when the demand for engineers was buoyant, many students entered college and decided to major in engineering. But they found upon graduation that the demand for engineers had been dried up by the recession and the decline in government spending for the Vietnam War and for space exploration. Because college takes four years to complete, information that may have been perfectly valid when students entered as freshmen became obsolete by the time they were seniors. The long educational lag may create cycles of feast and famine. The depressed market for engineers cut the number of engineering majors in the early 1970s and created some of the shortages of engineers that surfaced in the 1974–75 recession.[17] In the mid-1970s the problem appeared to be more general—the number of people graduating from college substantially exceeded the creation of new jobs of the type that had traditionally required a college degree.[18]

9-6 TURNOVER UNEMPLOYMENT AND JOB SEARCH

In the preceding section we developed the mismatch view that the natural rate of unemployment is high because the requirements of job openings and the qualifications of the unemployed do not mesh. Another view—partly a competing explanation and partly complementary—is that the major force maintaining a relatively high natural rate of unemployment is turnover in the labor force. In this view there is no long-run imbalance between job requirements and worker qualifications, but instead jobs and workers are highly differentiated so that unemployed workers require time to find the job that is best for them.

An individual is counted as unemployed when he lacks a job and, if not on temporary layoff, has made specific efforts to find one within the last month. Anyone who quits his old job before finding a new one, as well as any teenager entering the labor market for the first time, or any older woman reentering after her children have left home, will quite sensibly spend some time trying to find the best possible job and will be counted as unemployed while doing so.

If, for instance, every teenager left school on June 1, searched for a job for two weeks, and worked at a summer job for 12 weeks thereafter, the average annual teenage unemployment rate would be 14 percent

---

[17] Richard B. Freeman, *The Market for College-trained Manpower* (Cambridge, Mass.: Harvard University Press, 1971).

[18] Richard B. Freeman, *The Over-educated American* (Washington, D.C.: Academic Press, 1976).

TABLE 9-2

Unemployment Rates by Reason, Sex, and Age, in 1974

	1974 unemployment rate				Percentage of 1974 group unemployment			
	Males, 20 and over	Females, 20 and over	Teenagers, 16–19 years	All groups	Males, 20 and over	Females, 20 and over	Teenagers, 16–19 years	All groups
1. Lost job	2.5	2.1	3.1	2.4	65.8	38.2	19.4	43.6
2. Left job	0.5	1.0	2.0	0.8	13.2	18.2	12.5	14.6
3. Reentrant	0.7	2.1	4.9	1.6	18.4	38.2	30.6	29.1
4. New entrant	0.1	0.3	6.0	0.7	2.6	5.4	37.5	12.7
5. Total for group	3.8	5.5	16.0	5.5	100.0	100.0	100.0	100.0

Source: Handbook of Labor Statistics 1975 – Reference Edition (Washington, D.C.: Bureau of Labor Statistics, 1975), Table 62.

(0.14 = 2/14, the number of weeks unemployed divided by the number of weeks in the labor force).

Table 9-2 divides up the unemployed by the major reason for their unemployment: (1) people who have lost their job, mainly because of layoffs, (2) people who have left their job by quitting it, (3) people who have reentered the labor force after a period out of the labor force at school or at home, and (4) new workers, mainly teenagers, who have never held a job before. The year illustrated in Table 9-2 is 1974, when the economy was quite close to the natural rate of unemployment (see Figure 9-1). A glance at the table reveals several important differences that help to explain the higher unemployment of adult women and teenagers. The three groups are very close together on the percentage of the labor force out of work through job loss (line 1). Adult women and teenagers suffer by their higher "left job" (quit) rates and by their more frequent unemployment due to reentry. On line 4, 6 percentage points of the total 16 percent teenage unemployment rate appears to be due to the extra unemployment experienced by teenagers when they search for their first job ("new entrant"). Overall, perhaps the most striking contrast is between the large percentage of adult male unemployment caused by "lost job" (65.8 percent on line 1) as opposed to the small share of teenage unemployment caused by job loss (19.4 percent).

The most important novelty in the theory of "search" unemployment is the idea that an unemployed person may sometimes do better to refuse a job offer than accept it! Why? Imagine a teenager who quits school and begins to look for his first job. He walks down the street and soon encounters a restaurant displaying a sign "Dishwasher Wanted." An inquiry provides the information that the dishwasher opening is available immediately and pays $2.00 per hour. Will the teenager accept the job without further search? Refusal may benefit the teenager if he is able to locate a job with higher pay or better working conditions. But, on the other hand, refusal imposes two immediate costs: (1) the loss of the dish-washer wage during the extra days spent searching, and (2) the costs of telephone calls, bus fares, and other extra search expenses. At first the benefit of refusing a job offer may outweigh the costs, but as time goes on the advantages of job refusal decline. Either a better job does turn up which is too good to be refused or the failure to find a better offer causes the searcher to "lower the odds" on eventual success.[19]

The turnover view treats unemployment as a socially valuable, pro-ductive activity. Unemployed individuals "invest" in job search. The cost of their investment is the cost of search itself plus the loss of wages that could be earned by accepting a job immediately. The payoff to their investment is the prospect of earning a higher wage for many months or years into the future. Because people do not always want the first avail-able job and prefer to search, the only way for the government to bring down the natural rate of unemployment is either (1) to lessen entry into job search by reducing the reasons behind quitting, reentry, and initial entry, or else (2) to change the economic incentives that unnecessarily prolong the search, particularly unemployment benefits and high taxes on the income of the employed, both of which cut the net earnings of taking a job immediately.

9-7 POLICY SOLUTIONS: THE MISMATCH AND TURNOVER DEBATE

There are striking similarities between the mismatch and turnover explanations of the high U.S. natural unemployment rate. Both explain why adult women and teenagers have higher unemployment rates than do adult men. The assumption shared by both explanations is that job openings and workers are diverse. The main difference between the two views lies in the height and size of the barriers separating jobs and work-ers. The barrier in the turnover theory, the absence of perfect information, which makes search necessary, is eroded automatically by the passage of

---

[19] Many of the original papers on the theory of job search are collected in Edmund S. Phelps *et al., Microeconomic Foundations of Employment and Inflation Theory* (New York: Norton, 1970). Another important early reference is Dale T. Mortensen, "Job Search, the Duration of Unemployment, and the Phillips Curve," *American Economic Review*, vol. 60 (December 1970), pp. 847–862. Unfortunately for undergraduate students, much of the early work in this field, including these two references, is quite mathematical. More comprehensible introductions to the subject are Martin S. Feldstein, "The Eco-nomics of the New Unemployment," *The Public Interest*, no. 33 (Fall 1973), pp. 3–42; Robert E. Hall, "Why Is the Unemployment Rate So High at Full Employment?" *Brookings Papers on Economic Activity*, vol. 1, no. 3 (1970), pp. 369–402; and Robert E. Hall, "Turn-over in the Labor Force," *Brookings Papers on Economic Activity*, vol. 3, no. 3 (1972), pp. 709–756.

time. The barriers between jobs and workers in the mismatch theory, the absence of required skills and the locational concentration of the unemployed in the wrong places, are much more serious and do not necessarily fade away as time passes.

In an economy with no government regulations and no unions or other institutional barriers to flexible wages, there should be no unemployment caused by mismatch. Unskilled workers would simply earn low wages and skilled workers would earn high wages. Indeed, the U.S. economy succeeded in creating jobs for millions of unskilled immigrants before 1929, although the wage rates for these jobs were usually very low (in 1907 the average wage rate for "helpers and laborers" in the building trades was $0.22 per hour, about $1.36 in 1976 prices). Part of the problem of unemployment among unskilled workers in the modern economy is due to government regulations, including the minimum wage laws that hold up the wage rates of unskilled workers and thereby cut the number of unskilled job openings, creating unemployment among unskilled workers who cannot improve their skills. Other barriers include legislation that limits employment in many industries and regions to union workers whose high wage rates cut job availabilities. Without these barriers to the flexibility of relative wage rates, the mismatch problem would gradually cure itself through a reduction in the relative wages of unskilled workers. But flexibility in relative wages is a superficial solution, in the sense that it converts an unemployment problem of unskilled workers into a poverty problem. Any true solution requires an upgrading of skills.

EFFECTS OF UNEMPLOYMENT COMPENSATION

The turnover view also blames the government for making unemployment higher than necessary and advocates measures to reduce the duration in weeks of an average episode ("spell") of unemployment, as well as reducing the number of episodes per worker. In a series of articles, Martin S. Feldstein of Harvard University has focused on how the unemployment compensation system extends the duration of unemployment. A job with a before-tax wage of $200 per week may yield a worker only $146 in take-home pay. With no unemployment compensation or welfare benefits to sustain him, the worker would have an incentive to search many hours per day and take a new job quickly. But the opportunity to receive an unemployment benefit of $120 per week, as in our economy today, obviously cuts drastically the worker's incentive to search for a new job. The combination of taxes on income from work together with unemployment compensation imposes a tax rate of 87 percent — that is, the drop in take-home pay during unemployment ($146 − $120 = $26) is only 13 percent of the before-tax original wage. Many workers on layoff do not search at all, but simply wait to be recalled to their old job.[20]

---

[20] Martin S. Feldstein, "The Importance of Temporary Layoffs: An Empirical Analysis," *Brookings Papers on Economic Activity,* vol. 6, no. 3 (1975), pp. 725–744.

The unemployment compensation system not only lengthens an episode of unemployment, it also increases the number of individuals experiencing an episode by giving employers an incentive to lay off workers during periods of slack demand. Why should a business firm keep unneeded workers on the payroll when the government stands ready to subsidize the workers to stay at home? Not only are individual businessmen more prone to lay off workers at the slightest sign of declining demand, but in addition the unemployment compensation system subsidizes businesses with strong cyclical or seasonal fluctuations in demand.

The incentive for temporary layoffs given by the unemployment compensation system occurs not only in recessions but also when the economy is operating at its natural rate of unemployment. The economy may be in equilibrium, with no tendency for inflation to accelerate or decelerate, and yet a firm may find that its sales have dropped temporarily. The unemployment compensation system provides an incentive for the firm to adjust by laying off workers rather than by cutting hours per employee or simply by allowing inventories to grow. Even in a relatively prosperous economy such as that of 1973, each month roughly 1 percent of manufacturing workers were laid off.[21] This is a third factor contributing to the high natural unemployment rate (U^*) in the United States. To summarize, the three factors are:

1. *Mismatch unemployment.* The economy can be at U^* with unfilled job slots for which the presently unemployed do not qualify or cannot fill because they are in the wrong location.
2. *Turnover (or search) unemployment.* When the economy is at U^*, people are unemployed because they are unwilling to take the first available job, hoping by further search to find a job with higher pay or better working conditions.
3. *Temporary layoffs.* An economy at U^* still contains firms that desire to trim production temporarily, and it is often most economical for them to reduce their labor input by laying off workers.

REFORM OF UNEMPLOYMENT COMPENSATION

Feldstein's remedy for the artificial incentive given to turnover and temporary layoff unemployment is not to eliminate the unemployment compensation system but to reform it by making the unemployment benefit check taxable, just as income from work is taxable. In the above numerical example this would cut take-home unemployment benefits from $120 per week to $100 or less and would increase the incentive for workers to search. Perhaps, more important, Feldstein would penalize

---

[21] In his recent unpublished paper, "The Effect of Unemployment Insurance on Temporary Layoff Unemployment," October 1976, Martin S. Feldstein has estimated that fully half of temporary layoff unemployment can be attributed to the current average level of unemployment insurance benefits.

the worker for long periods of unemployment. When he finally returns to the job, the worker would find his take-home pay reduced by an extra "unemployment tax" proportional to the length of time spent unemployed. A man who spent 4 weeks on layoff might face a 1 percent unemployment tax, whereas a man out of work for 26 weeks might face a 10 percent unemployment tax. This would obviously cause many workers to seriously consider accepting a new job rather than waiting for recall to their old job.

Some economists criticize Feldstein's ideas as failing to remedy the underlying causes of unemployment. First, the entry and reentry portions of turnover unemployment are not stimulated by unemployment compensation, for which only former employees are eligible. Second, curing the unemployment problem by imposing an unemployment tax on the long-term unemployed, they reply, is like trying to cure a disease by imposing an illness tax on those who report symptoms to their doctor. The clash brings us back to the contrast between the turnover and mismatch views of unemployment. Both emphasize that numerous unfilled job openings are available when the economy is at its natural rate of unemployment (as at point K in Figure 9-2). But then the views diverge:

The *turnover view* assumes that the job vacancies would be filled by the unemployed if only there were not such great incentives for the unemployed to refuse to accept the jobs. The two main incentives are (1) the government's unemployment compensation system, as criticized by Feldstein, and (2) the "crummy" and "dead-end" nature of many of the available jobs (restaurant dishwashers, laundry and household work, and such).

The *mismatch view* in contrast minimizes the importance of voluntary job refusal by the unemployed. Most job vacancies simply have skill requirements that the unemployed cannot meet. The unemployed do not refuse job offers because they have such a hard time finding a job opening for which they qualify.

As in many areas of economics, the truth is not as simple as either extreme view, but in fact both diagnoses are correct. Some job vacancies have high skill requirements, as emphasized by the mismatch view, but some do not, as pointed out by the turnover view. A recent *Wall Street Journal* story began with four sample job vacancies, the first three of which were skilled openings and the fourth a relatively "crummy" job:

A construction outfit putting up a soda-ash plant in Wyoming is having trouble finding enough experienced pipe fitters. NCR Corporation in Dayton, Ohio, is looking for experts in developing the software for computer systems. General Dynamics Corporation's shipbuilding division, in Quincy, Mass., needs at least 200 more welders of heavy steel plates to help build eight big liquefied-natural-gas tankers. And Mike's Cafe in Strongsville, Ohio, near Cleveland, wants a short-order cook to work from 6 A.M. to 2 P.M. But none of this helps Ernest Gardner one bit. The young Cleveland native was laid off two months ago and hasn't been able to find a job since.[22]

Feldstein may be right: Ernest Gardner might be forced to take the job at Mike's Cafe if unemployment benefits were taxed and if Ernest would eventually face an extra unemployment tax by refusing to accept the cook's job. But the mismatch view is also right: changes in the unemployment compensation system would contribute nothing to filling the three remaining skilled job openings in the *Wall Street Journal* story and would leave plenty of unemployed workers in a worse plight after the "crummy" jobs have been filled.

9-8 POLICY SOLUTIONS: BETTER MATCHING BETWEEN JOBS AND JOBLESS

The mismatch view emphasizes two factors that prevent the unemployed from filling job openings: (1) lack of skills and (2) being in the wrong location.

LACK OF SKILLS

First Solution: Training Subsidies. At present firms lack profit incentives to train unskilled workers. Because much training is best acquired on the job, many schemes have been proposed to subsidize firms to train new workers. One idea, also proposed by Feldstein, would be to give teenagers a training voucher redeemable by employers who hire them and provide them with job skills. The main weakness of the proposal is the difficulty of monitoring the firms to make sure that they actually use the voucher money for training and to make sure that they do not fire the teenagers after the voucher money is received.[23] Other subsidy schemes would apply to adults as well as to teenagers and would give money to firms willing to hire workers with low skills and train them to fill high-wage jobs. Once again, enforcement is the biggest problem. Also, firms would tend to hire the most able individuals possible within the rules of the program, leaving the least capable individuals without help.

Second Solution: The Teenage Minimum Wage. Some European countries have a lower minimum wage for teenagers than for adults, and, at least partly as a result, have a lower excess of the teenage unemployment rate over the adult unemployment rate. To some extent a lower

---

[22] Ralph E. Winter, "Over 400,000 Jobs Go Begging in an Era of 8.5 Million Jobless," *Wall Street Journal* (June 10, 1975), p. 1.

[23] An excellent recent discussion of several of Feldstein's ideas is contained in Walter Guzzardi, Jr., "How to Deal with the 'New Unemployment,'" *Fortune* (October 1976), pp. 132ff. See also "Carter's Job Policy: A Key Role for Business," *Business Week* (December 13, 1976), pp. 63–66.

teenage minimum wage simply increases the number of available "crummy" jobs and cuts the time necessary for a teenager to find such a job. But in addition a lower minimum wage encourages firms to train teenagers and to develop apprenticeship systems. A training subsidy scheme has two main advantages relative to a cut in the teenage minimum wage: (1) direct encouragement for firms to train teenagers and (2) greater political feasibility, given the iron-hard opposition of U.S. labor unions to any cut in the minimum wage for teenagers.

Third Solution: Better Schooling. Much vocational training is obsolete, partly because individual school systems do not have the funds or talent to keep up with changing training needs. Government subsidies to local school systems might help, as well as provision by the federal government of better information on occupations with ample job openings that need trained people. It seems unlikely, however, that schools are better suited than private firms to train welders and pipefitters. Extra dollars might be more efficiently spent on subsidies to unskilled individuals than to school systems. Government manpower training programs appear to suffer many of the same disadvantages as training in public schools.

Fourth Solution: Training Loans. Some occupations with job openings, such as television repairers, can be entered by graduates of private training schools. Some of these schools, unfortunately, are disreputable. But a more important problem is that many students from lower-income homes cannot afford to attend them. Nor can they borrow the tuition money, because banks do not trust them. The government could bridge this shortage of loan money by lending to students who would then be billed for the repayment on their federal income tax forms (eliminating any problem of enforcing repayment). At present our society discriminates against vocational training and encourages too many young people to attend college because government loans are limited to college students and because state governments subsidize state colleges but not private vocational training institutions.[24]

Fifth Solution: Reduce Discrimination. Teenagers, blacks, and women suffer from low wages and high unemployment rates, often through no fault of their own. The basic difficulty is the economic and social barriers that keep them from entering career jobs with opportunities for promotion. Several Western European nations have helped reduce discrimination against women by subsidizing maternity leaves and providing subsidized child care, allowing women with children to maintain more stable job records. A case could be made for similar subsidies in the United

---

[24] The bias in our system against vocational training is the theme of Edward F. Denison, "Some Reflections," *Journal of Political Economy,* vol. 80, part 2 (May/June 1972), pp. 290–92.

States to members of minority groups who have been cheated in the past by segregated school systems, low expenditures on inner-city schools, and outright job discrimination. Some barriers, particularly the limitation of many blue-collar craft unions to white males, may require legal rather than economic remedies.

WRONG LOCATION

First Solution: A Better Employment Service. Some economists criticize the Feldstein turnover emphasis on the unemployment compensation system by pointing to West Germany and other countries that enjoy a much lower natural unemployment rate despite generous unemployment benefits. Part of the German success is due to the migrant workers from Italy, Greece, Turkey, and other countries, who fill the "crummy" jobs and are quietly shipped back home without entering the unemployment statistics whenever a recession strikes. But another favorable factor in Germany and other European countries is a very efficient government employment service, which has much more complete records of job openings (because employers are forced to list openings) and is able to direct workers quickly to those firms most likely to hire them. The employment service also minimizes job refusals, not by any Feldstein type of unemployment tax, but by the simple threat that unemployment benefits will be stopped should the worker refuse to accept a job. In the German and Swedish systems officials in the employment service have considerable power; they can decide whether the refusal by a laid-off steelworker to take a job as a short-order cook is sufficient grounds to remove his unemployment benefits.

Second Solution: Moving Subsidies or Loans. If the unemployed workers are concentrated in one part of the country and the unfilled job openings in another part, the government could cut the natural rate of unemployment by giving or lending money to jobless individuals to enable them to move. The same problem occurs within many metropolitan areas, with excess unemployment of central-city residents who lack adequate transportation to allow them to fill job openings in the suburbs. Although moving subsidies would cost money, the government would save on unemployment benefits and would collect taxes from the newly employed workers. This idea has actually been introduced in West Germany in the form of a plan to pay moving costs and a direct subsidy to encourage unemployed workers to accept job offers in distant locations. A major disadvantage of this proposal would be to accelerate the decline of central cities and the U.S. northern states and the rise of the suburbs and sunbelt. Many critics argue that too much federal government money already goes to subsidize the suburbs and sunbelt. An alternative would be a solution already attempted in Britain and France: government subsidies to induce firms to locate in areas of high unemployment.

9-9 ARE GOVERNMENT JOB PROGRAMS A SOLUTION?

If people are unemployed, why can't the government simply create jobs for them? During the Great Depression, the Roosevelt administration created millions of jobs in the Civilian Conservation Corps, the Works Progress Administration, and other agencies that put unemployed individuals to work building post offices, roads, public housing projects, improving national parks, and many other activities. The modern counterpart is Public Service Employment (PSE), a program under which the federal government pays the salaries of a specified number of workers added to state and local government payrolls. These workers include teachers' aides, clerks, janitors, security guards, bus drivers, and recreation instructors. To the outside observer they appear identical to other state and local government employees doing the same tasks; the only difference is that their paychecks are covered by federal funds, rather than local funds.

Advocates have endorsed PSE as (1) a method to cure cyclical unemployment, when the actual unemployment rate exceeds the natural rate (U^*), and as (2) a method that can reduce U^* itself:

1. As a cyclical remedy PSE does not accomplish anything to raise aggregate demand that cannot be achieved by the normal monetary and fiscal policy tools of Chapters 3–7. Any type of policy stimulus in a large enough dose can raise aggregate demand and lower the actual unemployment rate to the natural rate of unemployment. The main difference between the alternative methods of stimulating the economy lies in the composition of the extra output they create. Tax reductions stimulate personal consumption; increases in the money supply mainly stimulate business investment, residential construction, and consumer purchases of durable goods; whereas increases in government expenditures naturally expand the share of government spending in GNP. Public Service Employment simply concentrates the extra government expenditures on activities that hire employees in the state and local government sector, in contrast to a general increase in government spending that also adds employees in defense factories, military bases, and federal government employees in Washington office buildings. The main argument in favor of PSE is that it creates more jobs per dollar of spending and it creates jobs faster than do alternative methods of fiscal stimulus.

2. PSE can lower the natural rate of unemployment only if it succeeds in hiring unemployed individuals who presently cannot qualify for

available job openings or who refuse offers of "crummy" jobs. Clearly, a massive PSE program limited to blacks, teenagers, and adult women would reduce the natural rate of unemployment. But such "reverse discrimination" might not be politically acceptable, and a general PSE program might well hire some skilled adults who would then be unavailable for an unfilled job in the private sector. Further, many of the PSE jobs would be "crummy" dead-end jobs without training programs or possibilities for promotion or career.

If PSE simply pays a high wage for unskilled work in local government, only a portion of the PSE expenditures will go to those presently employed. Some dollars will be paid by local governments to new employees who replace local government workers and shift the burden of unemployment to someone presently employed. Recent studies have concluded that up to half the federal funds used for PSE so far have been used to pay for local government employees who would have been hired anyway. Other dollars will be paid to new employees who are not presently employed but who are in school or doing housework. Still others will be paid to those working in low-paid private jobs, forcing an increase in wages and prices in private restaurants and laundries.

In sum, PSE funds may involve substantial waste. The natural rate of unemployment might be lowered more if government funds were spent directly on programs that directly raise the skills or change the locations of unemployed workers and enable them to qualify for job openings. The actual effect of a permanent PSE program would be to raise the proportion of the labor force working in the government sector, as opposed to private firms, at any actual unemployment rate. Discussion of PSE must therefore concentrate on the familiar debate between the Galbraithites who want cleaner parks, more paramedical personnel, more police, and more of other public services, and the Friedmanites who want to reduce the share of the government sector. Ultimately, this choice must be made on political rather than purely economic grounds.

A more traditional type of federal job program is expenditures on public works — schools, post offices, and roads. Critics of the use of public works programs for creating jobs point to the long delay required before plans can be drawn, bids can be let, and construction can begin. Some defenders of public works spending claim that the delay has been exaggerated because private construction firms will begin to hire workers once a program is signed into law even though the actual funds have not been disbursed. But a still more serious problem remains: judged strictly as a job-creation program, public works projects are flawed because they create few jobs. Only a small fraction of the funds are used to pay wages, often to skilled craftsmen. Between half and three-quarters of the funds go to purchase contruction materials and equipment.

9-10 CASE STUDY: THE COSTS OF RECESSIONS

So far we have examined the factors that make the natural rate of unemployment so high in the United States. Although some unemployment performs a valuable function, by allowing individuals to explore without being forced to accept the first available job, which may pay little or have unattractive working conditions, nevertheless much of the unemployment that occurs at the natural rate reflects social waste. Far from refusing a wide variety of job offers, many unemployed people never have a job offer to consider.

During a substantial part of the postwar era actual unemployment has exceeded the natural rate, raising the share of the unemployed who find that unemployment involves waiting for even one opportunity to appear, not a continuous search for and refusal of jobs. But the costs of a recession far exceed the value of the wages lost by the individuals who become unemployed. Recall that the empirical relationship called Okun's law, plotted in Figure 8-4, states that real output changes relative to natural output by roughly three times the change n the unemployment rate.

Thus a recession that raises the unemployment rate by one percentage point above the natural unemployment rate cuts actual output 3 percent below natural output, for an output loss of $51 billion at 1976 prices.

Why does output decline by so much?

1. The unemployed lose their wages. Although they receive unemployment benefits, taxes must still be paid to finance these benefits, and so society as a whole suffers the loss of all the earnings of the unemployed.[25]
2. Some of the unemployed become discouraged and drop out of the labor force, so that society loses the value of their wage even though they are not counted as among the unemployed.
3. Overtime hours are cut substantially, reducing the take-home pay of many of those still employed.

---

[25] If the unemployed person previously earned a wage W, and if his unemployment benefit is B, then society loses the taxes levied to pay for the benefit B plus the taxes levied on the previous wage (tW) plus the loss in take-home pay of the unemployed individual himself $[(1 - t)W - B]$:

$$\text{Total loss} = B + tW + [(1 - t)W - B] = W$$

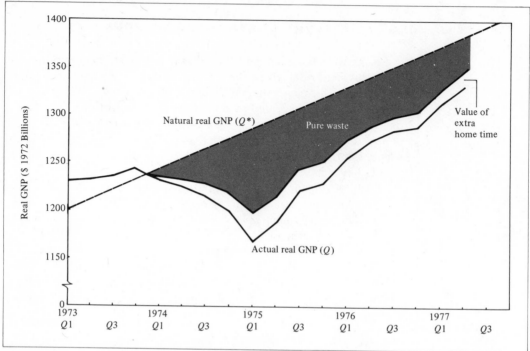

FIGURE 9–3

Natural Output (Q^*), Actual Output (Q), and an Estimate of the Value of Extra Home Time during 1974–76 in the U.S. Economy

The steadily growing line represents natural output (Q^*), the amount the economy can produce when unemployment is equal to the natural rate of unemployment. The solid line repre-sents actual output (Q), and it falls below Q^* at the end of 1973. The maximum loss of output, the differ-ence between Q^* and Q, occurred in the first quarter of 1975. The red area labeled Pure waste reflects the estimate, explained in the text, that about 75 percent of the loss of output in a recession is not balanced by a compensating gain of leisure or home time.

4. Many employees are needed to keep a business firm functioning even when its sales decline, and they must be paid (janitors, execu-tives, maintenance workers, people with valuable skills whom the firm is afraid to lose). Because the recession cuts a firm's sales with-out reducing its wage bill proportionately, its profits (part of GNP) drop precipitously.

5. All branches of government lose a substantial amount of tax revenue—sales, excise, income, payroll, and corporation taxes.

Figure 9-3 presents a magnified view of the GNP gap during the long recession of the mid-1970s.

During a recession, almost all the GNP gap is pure waste. When the actual unemployment rate is one percentage point above the natural rate, it is almost as if a $51 billion tax had been imposed on everyone (about $680 per household) without providing a single service in return.

Why is "almost all" the GNP gap pure waste, rather than "all"? Unemployed individuals, as well as the discouraged workers who drop out of the labor force, as well as those who work less overtime, have the partial compensation of more hours to enjoy at home. Hours of home time are valuable, but not nearly as valuable as the GNP that an hour of time produces at work. Why not?

Imagine that GNP per worker is $8.00 per hour on average. Before the workers are paid, some money must be left aside for sales, excise, and property taxes, for replacing worn-out capital equipment, for corporate profits, for corporate profits taxes, and for employer contributions to social security and unemployment payroll taxes. Only about $4.00 may be left over for payment as gross before-tax wages to workers. But then workers do not get $4.00 per hour, but only around $3.00, after deductions for social security and federal and state income taxes. Most workers must pay something for the expenses of working and getting to work (uniforms, bus fares, child care, lunches that cost more than eating at home), leaving perhaps $2.00 per hour "net spendable pay" when they finally arrive home at night.

The extra hours of time at home that people give up when they go to work cannot be worth more than net spendable pay, or about $2.00 per hour. Yet society gains $8.00 per hour when an individual goes to work. Thus the extra time at home "enjoyed" by the unemployed and by discouraged workers has only a small value and offsets only part of the GNP gap lost during a recession.[26] The dollar value of the GNP gap needs only a slight adjustment, say a downward revision of 25 percent, to be a reasonably accurate measure of the social waste society suffers during a recession.[27]

---

[26] On average, the home time regained during a recession is worth less than $2.00 per hour. Why? Because an individual going to work compares the value of the net spendable pay from work with the value to him of the last most valuable hour given up to go to work, say the 40th hour when the job involves 40 hours per week. The first hour given up to go to work is the least valuable and is probably worth much less than $2.00 per hour.

[27] The analysis of this section follows Robert J. Gordon, "The Welfare Cost of Higher Unemployment," *Brookings Papers on Economic Activity,* vol. 4, no. 1 (1973), pp. 133–95.

9-11 PSYCHIC COSTS OF RECESSION UNEMPLOYMENT

Numerical calculations of the cost of job loss may seem mechanical, and they are. The GNP gap underestimates the trauma of a recession, because it does not include:

1. The time wasted waiting in line at the unemployment office, when an individual neither works nor enjoys home activity.[28]
2. The insecurity caused by the loss of medical insurance by laid-off employees whose premiums were covered by their companies.[29] The dollars of lost premiums are included in the GNP gap, but not the nervousness and insecurity of families who suddenly face the danger of health expenses without coverage.
3. The strain and tension faced by children who find their parents suddenly preoccupied by worries about money, debts, and job seeking.[30]
4. The psychological anguish faced by adults: embarrassment passing local merchants who cannot be paid, "disintegration of your confidence as a man," adding "a crushing dimension to the natural self-doubts that are part of the process of growing older."[31] "After a while, it becomes a question of personal worth. You ask yourself, 'What am I worth?' and the answer comes back, 'Apparently nothing.'"[32]
5. A deterioration in both physical and mental health. Heart disease, deaths from cirrhosis of the liver, suicide, and homicide have all been found to rise in a regular way between one and three years after the onset of a national recession. One recent study claims that a one-percentage-point permanent increase in the unemployment rate ultimately causes 30,000 extra deaths each year.[33]
6. The increase in crime as unemployed workers turn to illegal activity, imposing on society higher expenses for police, courts, and prisons.

---

[28] Charlayne Hunter, "Tension, Disappointment Strain West Side Unemployment Office," *The New York Times* (July 27, 1976), p. 35.

[29] William K. Stevens, "For the 'Hidden' Jobless, a Drastic Impact," *The New York Times* (February 8, 1975), p. 1.

[30] "Down and Out in America," *The New York Times Magazine* (February 9, 1975), p. 9.

[31] Edward B. Furey, "The Fear, the Numbing Fear," *The New York Times* (April 1, 1975), p. 35.

[32] *Newsweek* (January 20, 1975), p. 56.

[33] See M. Harvey Brenner, "Estimating the Social Costs of National Economic Policy: Implications for Mental and Physical Health, and Criminal Aggression," prepared for the use of the Joint Economic Committee, U.S. Congress (Washington, D.C.: Government Printing Office, October, 1976). See also M. Harvey Brenner, *Mental Illness and the Economy* (Cambridge, Mass.: Harvard University Press, 1973).

All these factors together have a substantial consequence. The total welfare cost of cyclical unemployment may not be an amount 25 percent less than the GNP gap, as concluded in the last section, but an amount equal to or larger than the GNP gap.

SUMMARY

1. A primary concept in this chapter, as well as in the last, is the natural rate of unemployment, abbreviated U^*. The term natural rate does not mean immutability or desirability but natural in the sense of equilibrium, the unemployment rate at which there is no pressure for the inflation rate to change.

2. The most important cause of high unemployment in the United States is that the natural rate of unemployment is not zero but in the vicinity of 5.5 percent.

3. A gradual increase in the natural rate of unemployment over the 20 years between the mid-1950s and mid-1970s was caused by a shift in the composition of U.S. unemployment. The unemployment rate of young people has increased relative to that of adults. At the same time the composition of the labor force has shifted away from adult males toward groups that suffer higher unemployment rates, especially teenagers and adult women.

4. One explanation of a high natural rate of unemployment is called the mismatch view. It emphasizes the mismatch between the high skill requirements of available jobs and the low skills possessed by many of the unemployed. In an economy with flexible relative wages, the unskilled would be able to find jobs more easily but would receive lower wage rates. Any real cure for the problems of the unskilled—whether high unemployment, or low wages, or both—requires an increase in their skills and better matching of their locations with the locations of available job openings.

5. Among the policy proposals that have been recommended to cure mismatch unemployment are training subsidies and loans, better schooling, a lower minimum wage for teenagers, a reduction in discrimination, a better employment service, and moving subsidies or loans.

6. Another explanation of the high natural rate of unemployment emphasizes job turnover. The barrier that maintains a high natural rate is the absence of perfect information, making necessary an investment in job search to locate job openings that offer higher wage rates or better working conditions.

7. Policy solutions to reduce turnover unemployment include an improved employment service to provide better information; also changes in the present system of unemployment compensation, which provides a subsidy to workers who turn down job offers and continue to search or to remain at home awaiting recall to their old job.

8. The increase in the official unemployment rate during a recession understates the cost to society of the recession. Typically the gap between natural output (Q^*) and actual output (Q) grows by three percentage points for every one percentage point by which the actual unemployment rate rises above the natural unemployment rate. Only a small fraction of this gap is offset by the enjoyment of time at home by the unemployed; the rest is pure waste.

9. The output gap itself may understate the true costs of a recession, because mental and physical health are not included in official measures of gross national product.

A LOOK AHEAD

We have seen that unemployment imposes major costs on society. Yet to reduce inflation, the government must slow down the growth of aggregate demand and must raise the unemployment rate temporarily. Is the benefit of lower inflation worth the cost of higher unemployment? The next chapter examines the nature of the harm done by inflation, which groups in society are losers from inflation, and how government regulation of interest rates can alter the impact of inflation on savers. Then in Chapter 11 we consider the merits of the three main methods of dealing with the costs of inflation — higher unemployment, price controls, and indexation.

CONCEPTS AND QUESTIONS

IDENTIFICATIONS

Actual rate of unemployment
Natural rate of unemployment
Disguised unemployment
Job vacancy rate
VU curve
Firm-specific skills versus general skills

"Pure" versus "rational" discrimination
Mismatch versus turnover views of unemployment
Compositional (structural) shift in unemployment
Public service employment

QUESTIONS FOR REVIEW

1   Are government policymakers able to lower the actual unemployment rate below the natural unemployment rate? Explain.

2   Discuss what you feel are the major defects in our current measures of unemployment. Which defects do you feel are worth improving upon? Why?

3   Why is the natural rate of unemployment higher than zero? Suggest at least two explanations.

4   Compare the mismatch and turnover views of unemployment. Which do you feel more accurately describes current unemployment in the United States? Can you suggest another nation where the balance between the two views differs from the United States?

5   Should turnover unemployment be reduced? What policy prescriptions would you suggest to reduce it? .

6   What is the welfare cost of a recession? Is the welfare cost greater or less than the average wage rate multiplied by the lost hours of work that would otherwise have been performed by an unemployed individual?

7   If an economy had unemployment exceeding its natural rate by 100,000 unemployed, would a policy to create 100,000 new jobs by stimulating aggregate demand solve the problem? Explain.

8   Can you suggest any reasons why Japan and the United Kingdom have on average experienced lower teenage unemployment rates than the United States?

9   Comment on these statements:
     a "Policymakers may reduce temporarily the *natural* rate of unemployment by pursuing an expansionary monetary policy."
     b "As long as there are approximately the same number of job vacancies as of unemployed, there will be no upward pressure on wages other than from productivity increases."

10

The Consequences of Inflation

Inflation is the time when
those who have saved for a rainy day
get soaked.

10-1 INTRODUCTION

The U.S. economy in the mid-1970s has a "built-in" inflation because individuals and firms alike expect inflation to continue. One basic method of cutting the inflation rate is deliberately to create a *recession*. How hard should the government try to eliminate the inflation? Is the benefit of lower inflation worth the cost of layoffs, unemployment, and lower incomes during the transition period? This and the previous chapter provide the raw material for our evaluation in Chapter 11 of this great policy problem. How much difference does inflation make?

At first glance, worry about inflation may appear misplaced. When inflation is zero, wages may increase at 3 percent a year. When inflation proceeds at 6 percent annually, wages may grow at 9 percent annually. Workers have little reason to be bothered about the inflation rate (p) if the growth in their wages (w) always stays the same distance ahead, as in this example:

	No inflation	6 percent annual inflation
Growth rate of nominal wages (w)	3	9
Growth rate of price deflator (p)	0	6
Growth rate of real wages ($w - p$)	3	3

The main point in this chapter is that inflation is felt primarily by owners of financial assets, not by workers whose only income is earned

278

in the form of wages and who spend their entire wage income on consumption goods.[1] An unexpected "surprise" inflation hurts "ordinary people" by cutting the real value of individual saving accounts and hits particularly hard at the savings and to some extent at the pension funds of those who are retired or are about to retire. Even when inflation is fully anticipated and is no surprise, everyone notices the shrinkage in the value of the cash in their pockets and the dollars in their checking accounts, and people invest extra effort in managing their cash that would not be necessary in the absence of inflation.

10-2 NOMINAL AND REAL INTEREST RATES

As Americans have become accustomed to inflation, they have learned that the interest rates charged by banks and finance companies are not as onerous as they seem. Without any help from economics textbooks, many people understand the difference between nominal and real interest rates, even if they have not been taught the economist's jargon.

> *The* **nominal interest rate** (*i*) *is the rate actually quoted by banks and negotiated in financial markets. The* **expected real interest rate** (*r^e*) *is what people expect to pay on their borrowings or earn on their savings after deducting expected inflation* ($r^e = i - p^e$). *The expected real interest rate is what matters for investment and saving decisions.*

The nominal interest rate can be very different in two countries with different inflation rates, or in one country at different moments in history. But investment and saving decisions will be the same in the two situations as long as the expected real interest rate is the same. Let us consider the example of Pete Puritan and Sam Spendthrift, two boys who are both broke but both want a new ten-speed bicycle. Both plan to earn $100 at part-time jobs over the next year, exactly the price of a new bicycle, but Sam impatiently buys his bike immediately with borrowed money, whereas Pete patiently waits until the end of the year. When there is no inflation, the price of the bicycle remains constant at $100:

---

[1] The statement that workers do not lose refers to a normal inflation fueled by increasing aggregate demand. When the economy experiences a supply shock, as did the United States in 1974 at the time of the oil price increase, inflation experiences a temporary acceleration while real wages simultaneously decline.

	Pete Puritan	Sam Spendthrift
1. Sam purchases bicycle on January 1 with borrowed money	–	100
2. Earnings during year, put into savings account	100	100
3. Savings account on December 31, including 3 percent interest	103	103
4. Sam repays loan, including 3 percent interest	–	103
5. Pete buys bicycle	100	–
6. Balance at end of year (line 3 minus 4 and 5)	3	0

At the end of the year, each boy has his bicycle, but Pete has $3.00 left and Sam has nothing. Why? Pete has received a reward for his patience, the interest on his savings account. Sam has spent his interest earnings to pay the interest cost of his loan; he was not patient, and so he receives no reward for patience as does Pete.[2]

Now we consider the example again in a second situation in which inflation proceeds at a 6 percent annual rate instead of zero. If the expected real interest rate is to remain at 3 percent as in the first situation, the nominal interest rate on both savings accounts and bicycle loans must rise from 3 to 9 percent:

GENERAL FORM   NUMERICAL EXAMPLE

$$r^e = i - p^e \qquad r^e = 9 - 6 = 3$$

With a 6 percent rate of inflation, the price of the bicycle rises from $100 to $106 by the end of the year, but the higher interest rate exactly compensates, and both boys wind up in exactly the same situation as before:

	Pete Puritan	Sam Spendthrift
1. Sam purchases bicycle on January 1 with borrowed money	–	100
2. Earnings during year, put into savings account	100	100
3. Savings account on December 31, including 9 percent interest–	109	109
4. Sam repays loan, including 9 percent interest	–	109
5. Pete buys bicycle on December 31, which now costs $106	106	–
6. Balance at end of year (line 3 minus 4 and 5)	3	0

---

[2] Notice the simplifying assumptions introduced to keep this example manageable. First, neither boy pays taxes on his wages. Second, we pretend that interest is earned on the $100

As before, Pete receives a $3.00 reward for his patience, while Sam is compensated not by money but by the nonmonetary benefit of an extra year's enjoyment of his bicycle. The extra $6.00 that Sam earns on his savings account is exactly eaten up by the extra interest on his loan, whereas the extra $6.00 that Pete earns on his savings account is exactly eaten up by the $6.00 increase in the price of the bicycle.

Summary: This example was designed to illustrate an artificial situation in which inflation has no effect on economic well-being. Our current inflation would have no adverse consequences, and there would be no need for policymakers to try to reduce or stop inflation if these basic characteristics of the example were universally true in the United States:

1. Inflation is universally and accurately anticipated.
2. Inflation raises the prices of all goods by the same percentage rate (that is, any changes in the relative prices of goods are just the same as would have occurred in the absence of inflation).
3. An inflation of p_0 percent raises the market nominal interest rate (i) for both saving and borrowing by exactly p_0 percent above the no-inflation interest rate.
4. All savings are held in bonds, stocks, or savings accounts earning the nominal interest rate (i); no one holds money in accounts with an interest rate held below the market nominal interest rate. We will see that this condition is violated in the United States, where the interest rate on cash and checking accounts is maintained at zero and the interest rate on savings accounts is held down by the Regulation Q ceiling.

10-3 REDISTRIBUTIVE EFFECTS OF AN INFLATIONARY SURPRISE

Now let us violate condition (1), that inflation is accurately anticipated. In several postwar episodes, such as 1966–69 and 1973–74, the actual inflation rate accelerated well above the rate expected by most people. We now assume that in the bicycle example both the savings and borrowing rate stay at 3 percent, because banks expect a zero rate of inflation. Then, as a total surprise to everyone, the price of all goods jumps 6 percent on December 30, forcing Pete to pay $106 for his bicycle:

---

of wage earnings throughout the year, whereas, in fact, if work is distributed evenly in each month the average balance in the savings account is only $50. Third, the borrowing interest rate and savings account interest rate are both 3 percent, whereas in the real world borrowing rates are higher to compensate banks and other lenders for risk and for administrative costs. Fourth, we disregard the depreciation on Sam's bicycle, which is one year older than Pete's.

	Pete Puritan	*Sam Spendthrift*
1. Sam purchases bicycle on January 1 with borrowed money	–	100
2. Earnings during year, put into savings account	100	100
3. Savings account on December 31, including 3 percent interest	103	103
4. Sam repays loan, including 3 percent interest	–	103
5. Pete buys bicycle on December 31, which now costs $106	106	–
6. Balance at end of year (line 3 minus 4 and 5)	−3	0

Poor Pete's hopes have been dashed. He would never have bothered to save if he had known that his money would lose value during the year. Pete is the classic loser from inflation, the individual who has his savings eroded by an **unanticipated inflation,** but who does not (like Sam) have debts to match. Because most people start out in life with relatively few assets, and then gradually build up savings in preparation for retirement, those hurt most by an unanticipated inflation are those who have retired or who are about to retire.

When actual inflation ($p = 6$ percent in the example) turns out to be different than expected ($p^e = 0$ in the example), the actual **real interest rate** differs from that which was expected. In the example a 3 percent real interest rate was expected ($r^e = 3$), but after the fact (*ex post*) the actual real interest (r) turned out to be much less:

GENERAL FORM   NUMERICAL EXAMPLE

$$r = i - p \qquad r = 3 - 6 = -3$$

Who gains from inflation? Sam does not gain, because he has a debt and an asset to match when the price increase occurs. His bicycle has gained in value. But because all prices have increased together, his capital gain on the bicycle does him no good. If he wanted to sell his bike and buy schoolbooks, the higher price of schoolbooks would prevent him from buying any more schoolbooks than would have been possible in the absence of inflation. The real gainers from unanticipated inflation are those who are heavily in debt, but who have no financial assets, only physical assets whose prices rise with inflation. Private individuals who have just purchased houses with small down payments are among the classic gainers from an unanticipated inflation. Here is an example for

Harold Homeowner, who purchases his $100,000 house on January 1 with a 10 percent down payment.[3] His financial statement appears as follows on January 1 and December 31, when an inflationary surprise increases the price of his house by 6 percent on December 30.

Harold Homeowner's Financial Statement, January 1 and December 31, when an inflationary surprise increases the price of his house by 6 percent on December 30

	January 1	December 31
Assets		
House	$100,000	$106,000
Liabilities		
Mortgage debt	90,000	90,000
Net worth		
= Assets − liabilities	10,000	16,000
Real net worth		
$= \dfrac{\text{Net worth}}{\text{Price index}}$	$\dfrac{10,000}{1.00} = \$10,000$	$\dfrac{16,000}{1.06} = \$15,094$

Other classic gainers are corporations, whose outstanding stocks and bonds are the counterpart of household assets. The government also gains from inflation, because its outstanding liabilities are money (currency and bank reserves) and government bonds. A steady inflation can continue only if the nominal money supply grows steadily, and these extra dollars of money that the government "prints" can be used to pay for government purchases without the legislative strife required to raise tax rates. The extra revenue the government gains by increasing its liabilities (money) in response to higher prices is often called the **inflation tax.**

The best known extreme of the redistributional consequences of unanticipated inflation occurred during the German hyperinflation of 1922–23, at the end of which the inflation rate was 600 percent per month. In 1919 a farmer sold a piece of land for 80,000 marks as a nest egg for old age. All he got for the money a few years later was a woolen sweater. Elderly Germans can still recall the days in 1923 when:

> People were bringing money to the bank in cardboard boxes and laundry baskets. As we no longer could count it, we put the money on scales and weighed it. I can still see my brothers coming home Saturdays with heaps of paper money. When the shops reopened after the weekend they got no more than a breakfast roll for it. Many got drunk on their pay because it was worthless on Monday.[4]

---

[3] The repayment of mortgage debt is ignored.

[4] Alice Siegert, "When Inflation Ruined Germany," *Chicago Tribune* (November 30, 1974).

The basic case against unanticipated inflation, then, is that it redistributes income from creditors (savers) to debtors without their knowledge or consent. Conversely, a deflation does just the opposite, redistributing income from debtors to creditors. Throughout history, farmers have been an important group of debtors who have been badly hurt by deflation. The interest income of savers hardly fell at all between 1929 and 1933, but farmers, badly hurt by a precipitous decline in farm prices, saw their nominal income fall by two-thirds, from $6.2 to $2.1 billion.

Another example of deflation occurred in the late nineteenth century, when the price level fell fairly steadily, by a total of 64 percent, between 1865 and 1896. A main issue in U.S. economic history during this period was the "free coinage of silver," which would have added a great amount of silver to the predominantly gold-based money supply, raising the growth rate of money and moderating or even ending the decline in prices. Savers and the "Eastern monied interest" benefited from deflation and wanted the money supply strictly tied to gold. William Jennings Bryan, speaking for farmers and other debtors, decried this "cross of gold" in a famous speech delivered to the Democratic National Convention in 1896:

> You shall not press down upon the brow of labor this crown of thorns. You shall not crucify mankind on a cross of gold.

10-4 CASE STUDY: REDISTRIBUTION IN U.S. POSTWAR INFLATIONS

Inflation redistributes income from creditors and savers to debtors when there is a surprise, that is, when inflation proceeds faster than creditors and savers expected when they put their money into the bank or bought bonds. If savers were willing to buy a four-year certificate at a savings bank yielding 5 percent when they expected a 2 percent inflation, then their expected real rate of return was 3 percent ($r^e = i - p^e = 5 - 2 = 3$). They lose if the inflation rate exceeds their expectation, because their actual real rate of return ($r = i - p$) is cut below the interest rate they expected. If inflation actually turns out to be 5 percent, not the 2 percent that savers expected, the actual real interest rate will turn out to be zero ($r = i - p = 5 - 5 = 0$).

What return did savers expect in recent years in the United States, and how badly has inflation treated them? This is a complicated question not yet adequately treated in a scholarly paper in economics. But we can explore some of the elements of the problem in Figure 10-1. Our first task is to determine the average expected real return (r^e) that savers demanded on their savings. The top black line displays the nominal interest rate (i) for the period 1949–76.[5]

---

[5] This is the interest rate on top-grade (Aaa) corporate bonds.

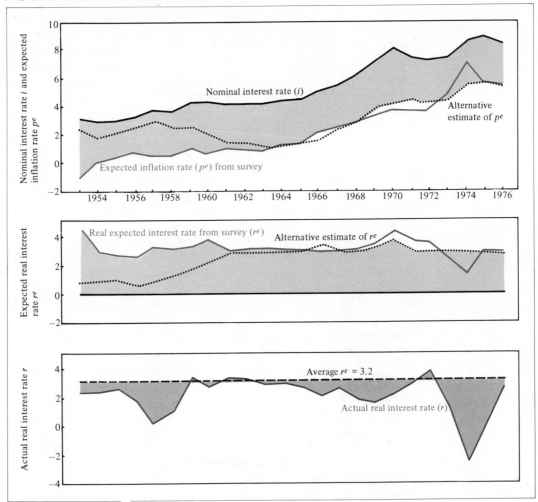

FIGURE 10-1   The Nominal Interest Rate (i),
Expected Inflation (p^e), and the
Actual (r) and Expected (r^e)
Real Interest Rates, 1953–76

In the top frame the black line is the
nominal interest rate (i) on top-grade
(Aaa) corporate bonds. Below it the
red and dotted black lines are two
estimates of expected inflation (p^e).
The pink area between is our suggested estimate of the expected real
interest rate (r^e). The middle frame
displays the expected real interest rate
directly, with the red and dotted lines
corresponding to the two estimates of
expected inflation in the frame above.
The bottom frame displays the actual
(*ex post*) real interest rate, which in
most years fell short of the 3.2 percent real rate that was expected.

Directly below the nominal interest rate in the top frame are plotted two alternative estimates of the expected inflation rate. The first, indicated by the red line, is based on a survey of economists' expectations. The second estimate, indicated by the black dotted line, is identical to that plotted in Figure 9-1; it is a weighted average of recent rates of inflation, based on the idea of adaptive expectations.[6] Which estimate is relevant for calculating the expected real interest rate? A compromise solution, explained in detail in the accompanying box, is to choose the red survey line before 1970 and the dotted adaptive expectations line since 1970. The difference between the black nominal interest rate (i) line and the compromise expected inflation estimate (p^e) is marked off by pink shading and indicates an estimate of the real interest rate.

In the middle frame the two alternative estimates of the real interest rate are plotted directly, and the compromise is indicated again by pink shading. In each year, the height of the pink shading in the middle frame is identical to that in the top frame; the two frames show different ways of plotting the same compromise estimate of the expected real interest rate (r^e). The compromise estimate of r^e fluctuates in a narrow range around 3 percent and averages out at 3.2 percent for the 24 years plotted. By coincidence, the compromise real expected interest rate was exactly 3.00 percent for four straight years, 1972–75.[7]

The redistributive effect of inflation depends on the actual real interest rate (r), that is, the interest return people actually receive after the fact (*ex post*) on their saving minus the inflation that actually has occurred ($r = i - p$), because it is actual inflation that determines the quantity of goods people can consume with their savings at today's prices. The bottom section of Figure 10-1 shows that the actual real interest rate fell below its 3.2 percent average in the three periods when inflation accelerated, during 1956–58, a long interval between 1966 and 1970, and a shorter but sharper period in 1973–75.[8] These periods of low real returns on saving were compensated only a little by a higher-than-expected return during the 1971–72 period when price controls were imposed.

Although inflation redistributes income away from all savers, some have suffered more than others. Low-income families who lack the

---

[6] The hypothesis of adaptive expectations is explained and applied to the analysis of the inflation-unemployment cycle in section 8-8.

[7] This series overstates the expected real return for all savers: (1) because the income tax liability on the nominal interest receipts is neglected, and (2) because many savers kept their money in savings accounts and received nominal yields considerably below the Aaa corporate bond rate plotted as i.

[8] The actual inflation rate is the annual change in the consumer price index, which includes the prices of food and energy, unlike the expected inflation rate for 1970–76, which excludes them.

funds and expertise to buy bonds place most of their money in savings accounts, which have experienced nominal interest yields (i) considerably below the corporate bond rate displayed in Figure 10-1. Some savers have even kept their money in cash under the mattress or in cookie jars and have lost every year, because cash has a nominal interest rate of zero.

The losses displayed in Figure 10-1 are measured in percentages. How much have people lost in billions of dollars? G. L. Bach and James B. Stephenson have estimated that the postwar inflation through 1971 redistributed about $500 billion away from households.[9] For every percentage point of unanticipated inflation that occurs now, savers lose an additional $40 billion, so that roughly another $450 billion was lost in the 1973–75 episode alone.

If the redistribution of an inflationary surprise causes savers to lose, who gains? Roughly half the gain goes to the government, and the rest

---

[9] G. L. Bach and James B. Stephenson, "Inflation and the Redistribution of Wealth," *Review of Economics and Statistics,* vol. 61 (February 1974), pp. 1–13.

is split between corporations and small businesses. Government gains because it can finance some of its spending by the revenue gained by printing the money people need to conduct their transactions at the new higher prices. But this revenue from the inflation tax reduces the government's need for conventional (income, sales, social security) taxes, benefiting all of us who pay federal taxes.

Inflation has an additional effect on government finance caused by the present practice of stating tax brackets, exemptions, and the standard deduction in nominal rather than real terms. Inflation raises the nominal income of individuals without raising their tax exemptions or standard deduction and without changing the nominal boundaries of tax brackets at which the percentage rate of tax increases.

Example: A family of four making $20,000 per year pays $2816 in tax (at 1976 rates). If inflation raises both the price level and their before-tax income by 10 percent, their income goes up to $22,000 and their tax goes up to $3323. Their real after-tax income has gone down by 1.2 percent, because an 18 percent increase in their tax has held their nominal income gain to only 8.8 percent, not enough to keep up with the 10 percent inflation.

Many economists have recommended that the nominal amounts of exemptions and the standard deduction, as well as the boundaries between tax brackets, be escalated each year by the rate of inflation.

Why does Congress resist repeated recommendations to escalate the tax system? The present situation automatically redistributes money each year from taxpayers to the government without any Congressional action because tax revenue rises faster than income. If Congress fails to reduce tax rates, the share of tax revenues in total GNP increases automatically, and Congressmen have the pleasant task of dividing up the "loot" on their favorite projects. Or, if Congressmen feel that the share of government spending in GNP should not be increased, they can demonstrate their "generosity" to their constituents by voting a reduction in tax rates. Either way, Congress gets the credit without the blame because many voters do not understand that the present system automatically boosts revenues faster than income.

The effects of an inflationary surprise can be summarized:

1. Retired individuals lose if they own more in bonds and savings accounts than they owe in debts. Very poor people also lose if they have small cash holdings but do not qualify for loans. Middle-aged and middle-income earners who carry heavy debts tend to gain, particularly if they are homeowners. These same people also gain in their status as taxpayers, because inflation reduces the government's need to raise tax rates.
2. To the extent that the government spends its revenue from the in-

flation tax on increased transfer payments (welfare, social security), the low-income groups are aided. This appears to have happened in 1973–74.

3. Within the group of savers, rich individuals have access to higher interest rates than do small savers. But rich individuals also hold most of the outstanding corporate stock and were badly hurt by the poor performance of stock prices in the decade after 1966. Although inflation raises the nominal value of corporate earnings and dividends, and thus should have raised stock prices during the 1966–76 decade, economic instability offset this and held stock prices down by increasing investors' perceptions of the riskiness of holding stocks.[10]

10-5 ANTICIPATED INFLATION AND AGGREGATE DEMAND

The redistributional effects of inflation disappear if the actual inflation rate (p) remains equal to the expected rate of inflation (p^e) and all contracts are written in real terms. Are there any adverse consequences for society in allowing a 6 percent inflation rate to continue, as long as everyone accurately anticipates that rate? If the government refrains from placing restrictive ceilings on savings accounts that prevent small savers from receiving a sufficiently high nominal return to compensate them for inflation, the remaining losers from a fully anticipated inflation are holders of cash and checking accounts, which still pay no interest in the United States.

An increase in the expected rate of inflation tends to reduce the average household demand for real money balances, a reduction that imposes a welfare cost by making everyday transactions more inconvenient. Figure 10-2 illustrates the adjustment of nominal interest rates and real money balances in response to an increase in the expected inflation rate from zero to 5 percent. Consumption, saving, and investment decisions all depend on the real interest rate r, as in the Pete Puritan-Sam Spendthrift example, so that the red IS line labeled IS_r is drawn with reference to the real interest rate (r). The IS_r curve is identical to the IS_0 curve in Chapters 4 and 5.[11] It shows all possible combinations of the real interest

---

[10] Another reason for the poor performance of corporate stocks has been the government rules that impose taxes on corporate profits after allowing deductions for depreciation at too-low historical costs. The replacement costs of machines and factories are much higher (in most cases) than the historical purchase price, making true depreciation higher than allowable for tax purposes. Thus true profits are lower than taxable profits. In short, inflation raises the ratio of corporate tax collections to true corporate profits.

[11] The position of the IS curve depends on $\bar{A}$, the value of planned autonomous spending (A_p) when the interest rate is zero, and on the multiplier (k). Review section 4-3.

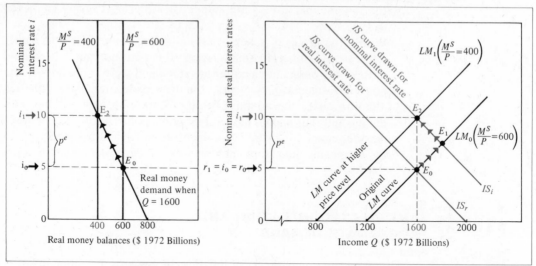

FIGURE 10–2

The Response of Real Money Demand and the Nominal Interest Rate to an Increase in Expected Inflation from Zero to 5 Percent

The economy starts at point E_0, at the crossing of the initial red IS_r line and the initial black LM_0 line. An increase in expected inflation from zero to 5 percent causes the nominal interest rate to rise 5 percentage points above the real interest rate. Thus, corresponding to the initial unchanged IS_r curve drawn for the real interest

rate, there is a second IS_i curve drawn exactly 5 percentage points higher in the vertical direction. Initially the economy moves from E_0 to E_1. But the higher nominal interest rate causes individuals to reduce their holdings of real balances, indicated the movement along the money demand schedule in the left frame of the diagram. Only when money demand has been reduced to $400 billion, and the LM curve in the right frame has shifted left to LM_1, can both the commodity and money markets again be in equilibrium.

rate (r) and real output that keep the commodity market in equilibrium, with output and income equal to planned expenditure.

The demand for money does not depend on the real interest rate, as does the demand for commodities. Instead, because government regulations hold the nominal interest rate on money equal to zero, individuals shift out of money into bonds and saving accounts whenever there is an increase in the *nominal* interest paid on these alternative assets. In 1947 the nominal interest rate was about 3 percent; holdings of money amounted to a very large 48 percent of GNP. In 1975, when the nominal interest rate on bonds was a much higher 8.5 percent, people economized on their holdings of money to earn the lucrative interest paid on bonds; holdings of money in that year amounted to only 19 percent of GNP.

The left side of Figure 10-2 shows a negatively sloped real money demand curve, indicating a decline in the demand for real money balances as the nominal interest rate on bonds increases. The LM_0 curve in the right frame shows the different combinations of output and the nominal interest rate consistent with equilibrium in the money market. The economy's general equilibrium occurs at the crossing point of LM_0 and IS_r at point E_0 if expected inflation is zero. Up to this point, everything is the same as in Chapters 4 and 5.

Now, however, let us assume that the Fed announces a policy of raising the money supply at 5 percent per annum, causing people to raise their expectation of future inflation from zero to 5 percent. Now the nominal interest rate rises by 5 percent. Point E_0 is no longer an equilibrium, because the inflation makes consumers and firms want to borrow and spend more money.

The solution in the new situation of positive expected inflation is to draw a new IS curve in terms of the nominal interest rate (i), labeled IS_i, lying parallel to the unchanged IS_r line and above it by exactly 5 percent, the rate of expected inflation. The new IS_i curve crosses the original LM_0 curve at point E_1, where the nominal interest rate has risen to 7.5 percent and real output has risen from \$1600 billion to \$1800 billion.

Point E_1 is not the end of the story, because the 5 percent expected inflation reduces the real money balances which people want to hold, shown in the left-hand frame by the north-west movement from point E_0 to E_2, and in the right-hand frame by the leftward shift in the LM curve to the new LM_1 line drawn for a supply of real balances (M^s/P) equal to \$400 billion, down from \$600 billion in the initial situation.

The economy is in a dynamic long-run equilibrium at point E_2, with output constant at \$1600 billion, the real interest rate constant at 5 percent, the nominal interest rate constant at 10 percent, and both money and the price level growing at a steady fully anticipated rate of 5 percent. The only consequence of the fully anticipated inflation has been to raise the nominal interest rate from 5 to 10 percent and to reduce the real money supply from \$600 billion to \$400 billion.[12]

10-6 SHOE-LEATHER COSTS AND THE OPTIMUM QUANTITY OF MONEY

Why should anyone care about a reduction in real balances? Although the nominal interest rate has risen, the anticipated real interest rate has remained constant at 5 percent. By assumption, inflation actually turns

---

[12] If the initial money supply is \$600 billion and grows 5 percent to \$630 billion in one year, the required level of real balances of \$400 billion can be achieved only if the price level rises to 1.575. An increase from 1.00 to 1.50 is required to reduce the real money supply enough to keep real output at \$1600 billion, whereas the extra increase in P from 1.500 to 1.575 incorporates the 5 percent anticipated rate of inflation.

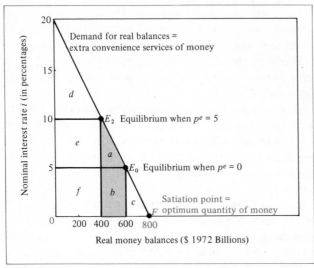

FIGURE 10-3   The Effect on the Demand for Real Money Balances of an Increase in the Expected Inflation Rate (p^e) from Zero to Five Percent

At E_0 the inflation rate is expected to be zero, the nominal interest rate on bonds is five percent, and \$600 billion of real balances are held. If instead the inflation rate is expected to be a faster five percent, the nominal interest on bonds shoots up to 10 percent, causing people to economize on their holdings of money to bring real money balances down to \$400 billion at point E_2. The pink area under the money demand schedule shows the cost to society of losing the convenience provided by holding the extra \$200 billion of money. The best situation of all is point F, where the nominal interest rate is zero (and the expected inflation rate is −5 percent). At F people hold all the money they can possibly use to facilitate their transactions (given the size of their real incomes).

out to be exactly what people expect, and so the accurately anticipated inflation has absolutely no effect on consumption, saving, and investment decisions in the commodity market. But nevertheless there is a change in the money market because the reduction in real balances induces people to make an extra effort to manage their cash. They use up "shoe leather" taking extra trips to the bank, and the welfare cost of an anticipated inflation is sometimes called the shoe-leather cost.

In Figure 10-3, we have made an exact copy of the money demand schedule from the left frame of Figure 10-2. At point E_2 real balances are \$400 billion, and the interest rate is 10 percent. People are voluntarily willing to hold \$400 billion of money that pays no interest and know perfectly well that they are giving up 10 cents of interest income ($i = 10$) that they could earn for every dollar switched out of money into bonds. They are willing to give up the interest return on bonds to obtain the convenience of money for conducting transactions. Money, unlike bonds, can be used directly for purchases without the nuisance of time-consuming and shoe-leather consuming trips to the bank.

At point E_2, for instance, people are willing to hold \$400 billion of real balances when the nominal interest rate is 10 percent, *but no more than that.* The 401 billionth dollar must be judged to provide **extra convenience services** worth less than the 10 percent paid on bonds, so that it is not held. Thus we can interpret the money demand curve as showing the extra convenience services provided by each successive dollar of money held. The first dollar, second dollar, and so on down to the 400 billionth dollar of money holdings all provide extra convenience services (*ECS*) worth more than the nominal interest rate sacrificed by holding money instead of bonds (*i*). The 401 billionth dollar and all further dollars provide *ECS* less than *i*. People hold money up to the point E_2 where the last dollar held provides *ECS* equal to *i*:

$$i = ECS$$

When inflation is zero and the nominal interest rate on bonds (*i*) is 5 percent, then $ECS = 5$ percent. The money market is in equilibrium at point E_0. The switch to an expected inflation rate of 5 percent and a nominal interest rate of 10 percent at point E_2 causes people to give up $200 billion of real balances, each dollar of which provides *ECS* between 5 and 10 percent. What is the total value of this loss? The value of all services provided by money is the area under the demand curve for money to the left of the initial equilibrium point E_0. Comparing the old and new situations:

	Total ECS *provided by all money held*
Old situation at E_0 with $p^e = 0$	Areas labeled $a + b + d + e + f$
New situation at E_2 with $p^e = 5$	Areas labeled $d + e + f$
Difference = convenience value of money lost	$a + b$

The total value of the convenience services lost by the increase in anticipated inflation from 0 to 5 percent is represented by the shaded areas $a + b$.

Area of b	= 5 percent × $200 billion	= $10 billion
Area of triangle $a = \frac{1}{2}$ of 5 percent × $200 billion		= $ 5 billion
Total area $a + b$		$15 billion

The real-world counterpart of this loss is the extra effort made by corporations and households to maintain lower cash balances when inflation occurs. Corporations try harder to synchronize cash inflows and outflows. Individuals try harder to keep their bank balances as close to zero as possible, paying all their bills on the day their paycheck arrives. The funds that otherwise would be kept in checking accounts and cash are kept in savings accounts and bonds, requiring the inconvenience of more frequent trips to deposit and withdraw cash and to transfer funds into checking accounts to cover checks just written. All these inconvenient shoe-leather consuming activities are not a transfer from one person to another, but *a real net loss to society.*

In diametric contrast to the inconvenience caused at point E_2 would be an alternative situation at point F, with a zero interest rate on bonds and savings accounts. When there is no incentive to own alternative assets to money, there would be no effort expended on trips to the savings bank nor any need to pay brokers fees for sales of bonds. All that wasted time would be available either for working longer hours or for the enjoyment of leisure. Society is genuinely better off at point F than at point E_2, and this situation at F is called the **optimum quantity of money.** The total area of the sections labeled $a + b + c$ ($20 billion) measures the benefit to society of moving from point E_2 to the optimum quantity of money at point F.

How can society achieve the zero nominal interest rate necessary to induce people to give up savings accounts and hold all their money in cash and checking accounts? At point F:

$$i = ECS = 0$$

Consumption, saving, and investment decisions require a real expected interest rate of 5 percent, so that achieving a zero nominal interest rate (r^e) requires a 5 percent yearly deflation:

$$p^e = i - r^e = 0 - 5 = -5$$

When no interest is paid on money and other taxes collected by the government are neglected, the optimum inflation rate is equal to minus the expected real interest rate (optimum $p = -r^e$).

10-7 OTHER DETERMINANTS OF THE OPTIMUM INFLATION RATE

The achievement of the optimum quantity of money in Figure 10-3 appears to require a 5 percent continuous and fully anticipated deflation. This outcome would be very difficult for U.S. policymakers to achieve, seeing that they have had a hard enough time ending inflation, much less creating deflation. The last time the U.S. experienced continuous deflation was a century ago, between 1865 and 1896.

But there is another possibility that avoids the necessity of falling prices. This possibility would allow individuals to live with inflation without suffering any cost at all from a fully anticipated inflation. The demand for money in Figure 10-3 depends on the nominal interest rate paid on alternative assets, such as bonds and savings accounts, *only because government regulations prohibit the payment of interest on currency and checking accounts*. If banks were allowed to pay any interest they choose on checking accounts, the competition between banks would drive the interest paid on those deposits to a value equal to or close to the interest rate on bonds (i). Savings accounts would tend to disappear, since people could earn interest and conduct transactions with a single asset, their checking accounts.

In one area of the United States the payment of interest on checking accounts has already arrived in fact if not in name. Although banks in New England are still prohibited from paying interest on checking accounts, they now can let customers write checks on special savings accounts. If this arrangement were allowed throughout the United States, and this is currently being considered, we would have to count all savings accounts as money, and the interest paid on that money would be close to the nominal interest rate on bonds (i), achieving the optimum quantity of money without a deflation. When the interest rates on money and bonds are equal, there is no optimum rate of inflation because the economy can avoid all shoe-leather costs at any inflation rate as long as the two interest rates are equal.

The only hitch in the payment of interest on money is the impracticality of paying interest on currency, which makes up about one-quarter of the money supply. But modern technology may eventually be able to solve even this problem. Each dollar bill could have a magnetic strip containing information on its true value; at an interest rate of 1 percent per month, a dollar bill would be worth $1.00 on January 1, $1.01 on February 1, $1.02 on March 1, and so on. Electronic currency reading machines could read the magnetic strips and credit purchasers with the true value of their dollar bills, including interest.

Aside from the payment of interest on money, there is a second factor that can make the optimum inflation rate higher than minus the value of the expected real interest rate ($-r^e$). An increase in the inflation rate generates more inflation tax revenue for the government. The government must print 5 percent extra money each year to keep real balances (M^s/P) constant if there is a 5 percent inflation. In Figure 10-3 a $400 billion total of real balances can be maintained at point E_2 in the coming year (with a 5 percent inflation) only if the government prints $20 billion more money, an amount equal to the size of the square labeled e. This is the government's revenue from the inflation tax. If the government keeps its real expenditures constant, *it can reduce conventional income, sales, and payroll taxes by $20 billion.* Because the effort people invest in rearranging their activities to avoid conventional taxes is thereby reduced, it is not at all clear that a little inflation is a "bad thing." In the jargon of economists, the economy reaches an optimum inflation rate when the extra inconvenience caused by the effort invested in cash management just balances the extra convenience of the smaller effort invested in avoiding conventional taxes.[13]

---

[13] A more scholarly but still short and readable presentation of this section is contained in Edward Tower, "More on the Welfare Cost of Inflationary Finance," *Journal of Money, Credit, and Banking,* vol. 3 (November 1971), pp. 850–60.

10-8 INFLATION, THE BALANCE OF PAYMENTS, AND FLEXIBLE EXCHANGE RATES

Because of its size and the minor importance of its foreign trade, the United States can be treated as a closed economy with no international trade as we analyze the determinants of real income, inflation, and unemployment. But the consequences of inflation do include effects on U.S. economic relations with the rest of the world. Most nations are much smaller and trade comprises a much larger part of their GNP.

The consequences of domestic economic policy depend on the system of **exchange rates** that rules the price of our currency relative to other currencies. Throughout most of our history the United States has been on a system of fixed exchange rates, in which the dollar exchange rate was fixed for a long period at a single value in terms of foreign currencies, particularly the British pound sterling. Between 1949 and 1967 one American dollar would buy 0.357 of a British pound. Since 1973, however, the value of the U.S. dollar has floated, changing in its relation to other currencies from day to day. In the summer of 1973 the dollar was very weak, with $1.00 buying only 3.9 French francs. In the summer of 1976 the dollar was much stronger, with $1.00 buying 5.0 French francs. As for the British pound, it has continually lost value, with the dollar strengthening until in mid-1977 $1.00 could buy 0.60 of a British pound, 65 percent more than in 1967.

When the dollar strengthens, or **appreciates,** in terms of other currencies, as in the 1973–76 period, an import from abroad with a price fixed in pounds or francs takes fewer dollars to buy, and the price of our imports declines. United States consumers benefit. The losers are U.S. exporters who find that a given pound or franc price for U.S. tractors or computers, set to compete with local companies selling their tractors and computers in Britain and France, brings home fewer dollars. A U.S. tractor selling in France for 50,000 francs brought home $12,820 in mid-1973 when the exchange rate was 3.9 francs per dollar, but brought home only $10,000 in mid-1976 when the exchange rate was 5.0 francs per dollar.

Conversely, a **depreciation** of the dollar, like the one between 1970 and 1973, raises the price of imports into the United States, hurting the U.S. consumer. The gainers are U.S. exporters who find that they receive more dollars for a price set in pounds or francs. The U.S. depreciation or devaluation in the 1970–73 period raised the U.S. rate of inflation, even though the price of imports is not included in the deflator for U.S. production (GNP). The deflator was raised because the depreciation of the dollar increased the prices of goods produced in the United States by inducing price increases in dollars by U.S. exporters, who found that they could maintain fixed prices in foreign currencies while still receiving a higher price in dollars. Also, U.S. producers whose goods compete closely with imports found that they could match the price increases posted by imported goods. Many will recall the rapid price increases of Volkswagens, Mercedes, and other imported cars during the 1971–74 period, which induced U.S. auto manufacturers to raise very markedly the prices of their small cars.[14]

Other countries are profoundly affected in a system of fixed exchange rates by a decision by U.S. policymakers to raise our rate of monetary growth and hence our rate of inflation. Our inflation travels abroad by several routes. First, price increases by U.S. exporters create an incentive for price increases by foreigners producing exports and import-competing goods. Second, U.S. price increases will induce foreigners to shift to other suppliers and as well will create an incentive for U.S. residents to buy more foreign goods. Our exports will fall and our imports will rise, creating a deficit in our **balance of trade** with other countries.[15] Our deficit is their surplus, and the high demand for their exports represents an injection of aggregate demand into their domestic economies. Now, one of two reactions can occur:

1. Foreigners now hold an extra supply of dollars received as revenue on sales of goods to U.S. residents. They turn the dollars in to their central banks for domestic currency, say West German marks. If foreign central banks then attempt to sell the dollars on the foreign exchange market in exchange for their own currency, the excessive supply of dollars will drive the price of dollars down, violating our initial assumption that the exchange rate is fixed.
2. Foreign central banks can refuse to sell the excessive dollars and can hold them. Then the domestic currency — marks — remains in circulation. That is how U.S. inflation can indirectly cause an acceleration of the growth of the domestic money supplies of foreign nations, an increase in their own rates of inflation, and, ultimately, an increase in the world rate of inflation.

Both of these reactions, (1) and (2), occurred within the past decade. At first in 1968–71, foreigners allowed their holdings of dollars to build up as U.S. inflation accelerated, substantially raising the growth rate of the world money supply and the world rate of inflation as in reaction (2). But by 1971 the situation had become untenable, dollar holdings had become excessive, and foreigners attempted to sell dollars. For a while the U.S. attempted to hold the value of the dollar up, but a succession of crises in the foreign exchange markets eventually led to a major devalua-

---

[14] Many of these price increases were delayed until the May 1974 expiration date of the U.S. price control program.

[15] Balance of trade = exports − imports. See the Glossary and Section 19-2.

tion of the dollar in late 1971, followed by another in February 1973. By early 1973 most countries had given up the attempt to peg their currencies to the dollar and had allowed their exchange rates to float up and down.

Summary: A decision by a large country such as the United States to raise the rate of inflation in a system of fixed exchange rates forces other countries to inflate along with us, usually against their will. The longer-run consequences of excessive domestic inflation are balance-of-trade deficits and, eventually, a devaluation of the dollar. Small foreign countries have no ability to control their domestic inflation rate. So much of their national production is sold abroad, or competes with imports, that the national price level is like a small boat that rises automatically with the tide of world inflation.

Flexible exchange rates make a substantial difference, both for the United States and for small countries. If the United States chooses a faster or slower inflation rate than other countries, it can reach this decision purely on the basis of the domestic considerations reviewed earlier in this chapter. An acceleration of U.S. inflation has no lasting consequences for U.S. export sales or import purchases. A depreciation of the dollar will offset the acceleration in domestic inflation and keep the foreign prices of U.S. goods unaffected. This in turn will prevent any direct effect on higher U.S. prices of foreign prices, as well as any indirect effect of U.S. dollar outflows into foreign central bank reserves. Small foreign nations can choose their own inflation rate irrespective of world inflation when their exchange rate is free to float.

There is much more to say about the floating exchange rate system than simply "domestic inflation rates are insulated from foreign repercussions." The balance between monetary and fiscal policy is shifted, because a monetary stimulus will tend to push down our exchange rate and raise prices, whereas a fiscal expansion will do the opposite. Conversely, a monetary expansion under floating exchange rates will have a higher multiplier than under fixed exchange rates, whereas a fiscal expansion will have a lower multiplier. We return to these issues in Chapter 19.

SUMMARY

1. Inflation is felt primarily by owners of financial assets. The basic case against unanticipated inflation is that it redistributes income from creditors to debtors unfairly without their knowledge or consent. The gainers from unanticipated inflation are those who are heavily in debt and whose assets are primarily physical rather than financial. Roughly half the net gain goes to the government with the rest split between corporations and small businesses.

2. The redistributional effects of inflation disappear if the inflation is accurately anticipated, the prices of all goods are affected by the same percentage rate, and nominal interest rates are raised by exactly the inflation rate.

3. An increase in the expected rate of inflation tends to reduce the average holdings of real money balances as the cost of holding these balances, the nominal interest rate paid on alternative financial assets, increases. The extra effort made by corporations and households to maintain lower real money balances is a cost imposed on them by inflation.

4. The optimum inflation rate is reached when the extra inconvenience caused by the increase in the inflation tax is just balanced by the extra benefits of the reduction in conventional taxes.

5. The consequences of domestic policy depend on the system of exchange rates that rules the price of our currency relative to other currencies. In a system of fixed exchange rates, an increase in a large country's inflation rate forces smaller countries to inflate along with it. But when exchange rates are free to float, small countries can choose their own inflation rate irrespective of world inflation, because the acceleration of a country's domestic inflation will be offset by a depreciation of its currency.

A LOOK AHEAD

We have examined the costs to society of high unemployment and inflation and the programs that might enable the government to reduce the natural (equilibrium) rate of unemployment. Now it is time to turn to the possibility of ending inflation. If this had been a simple or costless task, it would have been accomplished long ago. Obviously there are costs, but what are they? Are they sufficiently onerous to warrant giving up in the fight against inflation?

CONCEPTS AND QUESTIONS

IDENTIFICATIONS

Nominal and real interest rates
Anticipated and unanticipated
   inflation
Costs of unanticipated inflation
Costs of fully anticipated inflation
The inflation tax

Expected real return (r^e)
Extra convenience services of
   money (ECS)
Optimum quantity of money
Optimum inflation rate
Fixed and floating exchange rates

QUESTIONS FOR REVIEW

A. Are the following statements true, false, or uncertain?

   1   When inflation is fully anticipated, it imposes no welfare costs on any group in society.

2 It is the expected real rate of interest, not the nominal rate, that is important in determining economic behavior.

3 Inflation redistributes income from creditors and savers to debtors only when the actual inflation rate exceeds the expected inflation rate.

4 If payment of interest were allowed on all checking accounts, the optimum rate of inflation would be increased.

5 An increase in a large country's rate of inflation will be exported to smaller countries, raising their rates of inflation.

6 It is unwise for the government to attempt to reduce the rate of inflation, for this would redistribute income to savers from debtors, hurting those who have recently paid high mortgage interest rates to obtain new or used homes.

B. Discuss the following: What interest rate do you receive on your savings? (If you don't have a savings account, answer this for someone you know.) What inflation rate to you expect over the next few years? Calculate your expected real interest rate (r^e). Do you consider your r^e an adequate reward for saving? If not, why do you bother to save at all?

APPENDIX TO CHAPTER 10
Inflation and Economic Growth

Very high rates of inflation generally disrupt economic growth, as in the German hyperinflation of 1923, during which labor productivity dropped as workers exhausted themselves running from the payroll window to the grocery store with wheelbarrows of almost worthless mark notes. But there is little evidence that moderate inflation rates interfere with growth. In the 1960s both Japan and France experienced about 6 percent annual inflation in consumer prices, a more severe inflation than in the United States or the United Kingdom, yet both experienced growth in natural output much faster than in the United States or the United Kingdom. Brazil had the same combination of even higher inflation and rapid growth between 1967 and 1973.

Most of the presumption that inflation and growth are connected is based not on real-world evidence, but on theoretical analysis. In Figure 10-4 the money demand curve has been copied from Figure 10-2 and 10-3, but it has been relabeled. At a fixed level of output of $1600 billion, this schedule, now called LM_i, shows all the possible combinations of the nominal interest rate (i) and the supply of real balances (M^s/P) that will keep the money market in equilibrium. As we saw in Figure 10-2, the money market can be in equilibrium both at point E_0, with a nominal in-

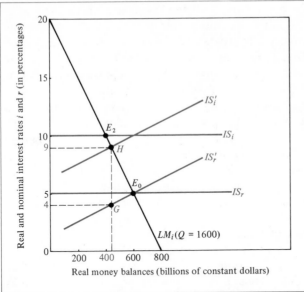

FIGURE 10-4   The Effect of a Five-Percent Increase in the Expected Inflation
Rate on Interest Rates and Holdings of Real Balances, with and
without a Real Balance Effect

When there is no real balance effect, equilibrium in the commodity market can occur only at the fixed 5 percent real interest rate. An increase in the expected inflation rate shifts the economy from point E_0 to point E_2, just as in Figure 10-3. But with a real balance effect the IS curve becomes positively sloped, because a reduction in real balances caused by inflation must be offset by the stimulus of a lower real interest rate, if the commodity market is to remain in equilibrium. As a result, the same increase in expected inflation moves the economy from point E_0 to point H (for the nominal interest rate) and point G (showing the associated real interest rate).

terest rate of 5 percent and real balances of $600 billion, and at point E_2, with a nominal interest rate of 10 percent and real balances of $400 billion.

It is possible to draw an IS curve on this diagram as well. The red flat IS_r line shows all the combinations of the real interest rate and real balances that keep the commodity market in equilibrium. Because M^s/P does not influence the position of the IS line, the equilibrium real interest rate in the commodity market at an output level of $Q = 1600$ is 5 percent as in Figure 10-2, regardless of the level of real balances. When the expected inflation rate increases from zero to 5 percent, the nominal rate rises 5 percent above the real rate, and a new IS_i curve must be drawn five percentage points above IS_r in order to find the new general equilibrium of the economy at point E_2 where IS_i crossses LM_i.

So far we have added absolutely nothing in Figure 10-4 to the story of Figure 10-2. But the result does change if we now incorporate the real balance effect of Chapters 5 and 6, which allows autonomous consumption to be influenced directly by higher real money balances. With a real balance effect, the demand for commodities does depend directly on the level of real balances (M^s/P). When M^s/P increases, there is an increase in the demand for commodities. To keep the demand for commodities equal to the fixed supply, a condition that is satisfied on any IS line, something else has to occur to create an offsetting decrease in the demand for commodities. That something is an increase in the real interest rate, which cuts both planned consumption and investment spending. Thus an increase in M^s/P requires an increase in the real interest rate—that is, an upward sloping IS curve like IS'_r in Figure 10-4—to maintain commodity market equilibrium in the presence of a real balance effect. Corresponding to IS'_r is the parallel IS'_i line drawn at a position 5 percent higher to correspond to the nominal interest rate.

The economy's general equilibrium now occurs at point H where the LM_i curve, which is the same as before, crosses the new positively sloped IS_i curve. The nominal interest rate in the new situation is 9 percent compared to 10 percent before, and the real interest rate is 4 percent at point G. The increase in the expected rate of inflation has reduced the quantity of real balances as the economy has moved from E_0 to H, and this in turn has reduced the demand for commodities through the workings of the real balance effect. The demand for commodities falls short of the assumed \$1600 billion level of production unless something happens to boost the demand for commodities back to the original level. That something is the decline in the real interest rate between points E_0 and G, which stimulates investment and consumption spending by exactly as much as the drop in M^s/P has restricted consumption spending.

But point G for the real interest rate, and point H for the nominal interest rate, are not the end of the story. An increase in investment spending stimulated by the lower real interest rate at G will add to the nation's stock of plants, machines, and other factors of production and will stimulate faster output growth. Inflation causes the economy to substitute real physical capital (plants, machines) for financial capital in the form of real money balances. The higher rate of output growth will continue until the real interest rate has returned to its original position.[a]

---

[a] The economy reaches the original level of the real interest rate through the effect of growth in raising the real demand for money, shifting LM to the right, and the effect of growth in raising nonmonetary wealth, which stimulates consumption and forces up the IS curve to keep the commodity market in equilibrium. The details are worked out in Edi Karni, "Inflation and Real Interest Rate: A Long-Term Analysis," *Journal of Political Economy*, vol. 80, no. 2 (March/April 1972), pp. 365–74.

11 Cures for Inflation: Recessions, Controls, and Indexation

You can get accustomed to almost anything. A 6 percent rate of inflation 20 years ago would have knocked out your mind, but today I guess people are getting conditioned to price increases.

—Thomas Murphy, Chairman of General Motors[1]

11-1 INTRODUCTION

Chapters 8 through 11 explain why it is so difficult for governments to achieve zero unemployment and zero inflation. In Chapter 9 we learned why all unemployment cannot be eliminated. Only if all jobs and workers were identical and at one location would it be possible for the government to expand aggregate demand enough to create a job opening for which every unemployed person could qualify. In the real world too much aggregate demand creates job vacancies that the unemployed cannot fill, forcing firms to fill job slots by raising wages in order to "steal" workers from each other. The higher wages help set off an inflationary spiral when aggregate demand creates too many job vacancies.

Monetary and fiscal policy can stimulate aggregate demand enough to push actual unemployment below the natural rate of unemployment temporarily, but any attempt to hold unemployment below the natural rate permanently causes an accelerating inflation. Thus the natural unemployment rate, presently between 5 and 6 percent in the United States sets a lower limit on the unemployment rate that monetary and fiscal policy can achieve. Further reductions in actual unemployment below this level require government manpower policies to cut the natural rate of unemployment itself.

Unfortunately, government monetary and fiscal policies that prevent actual unemployment from going below the natural unemployment rate do not necessarily achieve the second major goal of macroeconomic

---

[1] *Chicago Tribune* (October 17, 1977), Section 4, p. 11.

policy—a zero rate of inflation (that is, a stable average price level). We learn in this chapter that there is no instant and costless way to cut the inflation rate to zero. We are victims of past events, primarily the long period of excess demand in the late 1960s that kept the actual unemployment rate below the natural rate for five years, 1965–69.

What options are available to a government that inherits an inflation caused by past events? The major choices are three, each with pros and cons to be reviewed in this chapter:

1. *Recession.* Just as inflation speeds up when unemployment is low, maintenance of high unemployment (above the natural unemployment rate) tends to slow the rate of inflation. The U.S. government has deliberately used recessions to fight inflation in the late 1950s, in 1970–71, and during the long period of high unemployment that began in 1975. The advantage of this approach is that it eventually succeeds in achieving lower inflation. The main disadvantages are two. First, society suffers a large loss of output by leaving men and machines idle, which is a pure waste. Second, the recession cuts investment spending and reduces society's capital stock and hence its future standard of living.

2. *Controls.* The government can attempt to eliminate inflation by imposing direct controls on wages and prices. The advantage of this option is that some output losses of a recession are avoided. But the disadvantages are very serious. First, the controls may not work. Second, if they do work, they are likely to create a misallocation of resources, causing shortages of some goods and types of workers.

3. *Indexation.* This third option does not cut the inflation rate to zero but instead attempts to reduce the costs of inflation, which we studied in Chapter 10. If the adverse consequences of inflation on holders of assets can be eliminated, then some economists argue that there is no need to impose on society the agony of recession or the inefficiency of controls.

11-2 RECESSION AS A CURE FOR INFLATION

In this section we will examine how a government can eliminate inflation by deliberately creating a recession. As an example we consider a nation that has inherited from the past a 6 percent inflation rate that everyone expects to continue at the same 6 percent rate. The negatively sloped SP_2 (short-run Phillips) curve in Figure 11-1 shows the various combinations of inflation and unemployment that are possible as long as everyone expects an inflation rate of 6 percent ($p^e = 6$). For instance:

1. At point E_3 the unemployment rate (U) is equal to the natural unemployment rate (U^*), about 5.5 percent. Whenever $U = U^*$, as at point E_3, then actual inflation (p) is exactly equal to the average inflation rate people expect $(p^e = 6)$.
2. At point D stimulative monetary and fiscal policy reduces unemployment below U^* to 4 percent. The excess demand for goods and workers pushes the inflation rate (p) above the 6 percent rate people expect, to a bit less than 8 percent.
3. At point A just the opposite occurs. Restrictive monetary and fiscal policies cut output and raise unemployment above U^* to 8 percent. The excess supply of goods and workers drops the inflation rate below the 6 percent rate people expect, down to about 4.5 percent.

The choice of restrictive policies that move the economy from point E_3 to A is only the beginning of the process by which high unemployment cuts inflation. The economy will not stay at point A. Why? The SP_2 curve running from D to E_3 to A is valid only as long as people expect inflation to continue at a 6 percent rate $(p^e = 6)$. Whenever actual unemployment is raised above U^*, however, as at point A, inflation turns out to be less than people expect and they will revise their expectations downward. The SP curve shifts down continuously whenever actual U exceeds U^*. For instance, the SP' curve shows the various combinations of inflation and unemployment that are possible when the inflation rate people expect (p^e) has fallen to 5 percent.[2] Point B indicates that if the inflation rate people expect drops to 5 percent, and monetary and fiscal policy maintain the high unemployment rate of 8 percent, then actual inflation will drop further to about 3.5 percent. Then expectations will adjust further. Eventually maintenance of unemployment above U^* can reduce inflation by any desired amount, to zero or even to a negative number.

When does the process end? The LP curve shows all the different combinations of actual inflation (p) and expected inflation (p^e) that are possible in the long run, after expectations have time to adjust fully to changing events. One such long-run position is point E_0, with both actual and expected inflation equal to zero. To reach point E_0, actual unemployment must be kept above U^* until actual inflation has slowed enough to make expected inflation fall to zero.

How should policymakers reach point E_0? One possible route is for unemployment to be held at 8 percent until the adjustment cuts inflation to zero at point C, and then for unemployment to be dropped rapidly to the natural rate U^* at point E_0. Another possibility would be to allow

---

[2] The SP' curve, drawn for the assumption that $p^e = 5.0$, must intersect the vertical LP curve at a height of $p = 5.0$ percent, just as SP_0 intersects LP at $p = 6.0$ percent. Why? Because when $U = U^*$ (as it does everywhere along the LP schedule), the inflation rate (p), the variable plotted along the vertical axis, equals $p^e = 5$ percent, the rate of inflation expected everywhere along SP'.

unemployment to fall gradually even before inflation reaches zero, as illustrated by the sloped dashed line descending leftward from B toward E_0. Inflation will continue to slow down even when unemployment is falling as long as the economy stays to the right of the vertical LP line, that is, as long as the actual unemployment rate (U) exceeds U^*.

11-3 ALTERNATIVE ROUTES TO STABLE PRICES

The extreme difficulties faced by policymakers who want to end inflation by moving the economy down from point E_3 to point E_0 can be illustrated by some simple examples. In each we assume that the policymakers can achieve perfect control of adjusted demand growth ($\hat{y}$), the growth rate of nominal income (y) adjusted for the natural or trend growth of output (q^*). This underlying assumption, that the government can achieve perfect "fine tuning" of $\hat{y}$, is called into question in Chapters 12–18.

At first glance the control of inflation might appear a very simple task. In the long run the inflation rate (p) is simply equal to adjusted demand growth ($\hat{y}$). A new president inheriting a 6 percent inflation, as at point E_3 in Figure 11-1, might conclude that the best way to cut inflation to zero would be to drop $\hat{y}$ immediately to zero. "After all," reasons the new president, "in the long run, inflation must equal $\hat{y}$, so that setting $\hat{y} = 0$ appears on the surface to be a straightforward solution to the inflation problem."

Unfortunately, the effect on the economy of a sudden drop in $\hat{y}$ may be to create a deep recession lasting a decade or more. This possibility is illustrated in Figure 11-2. Unlike Figure 11-1, which fails to specify the number of years needed for the economy to reach zero inflation, here we make the example more specific by marking off the passing years on the diagram. We assume that in 1977 the new president inherits an economy that has a 6 percent inflation rate, which everyone expects to continue at 6 percent, a $\hat{y}$ also equal to 6 percent, and actual unemployment equal to the natural unemployment rate of 5.5 percent. Thus the point marked 1977 in Figure 11-2 is exactly equivalent to point E_3 in Figure 11-1.

As the first possibility presented by the route 1 path, in 1978 policymakers drop $\hat{y}$ from 6 percent to zero by restrictive monetary and fiscal policy. Furthermore, they succeed in holding $\hat{y}$ at zero forever afterward. Just as in Figure 11-1, where the economy responds to a cut in demand by initially moving from point E_3 to point A, here in Figure 11-2 the economy moves down from the point marked 1977 southeast to 1978. What happens after 1978? The outcome depends on how fast the short-run Phillips curve (SP) shifts downward.

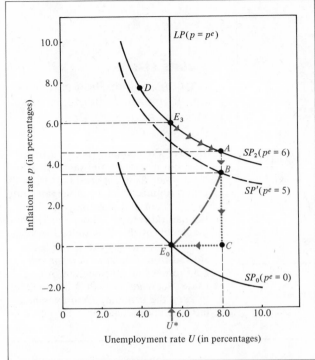

FIGURE 11–1 The Response of Inflation and Unemployment to a Restriction in the Growth Rate of Aggregate Demand

Initially the economy is at point E_3, with a fully anticipated inflation of 6 percent and unemployment (U) equal to the natural unemployment rate (U^*). A reduction in the growth rate of aggregate demand will cut output growth and raise unemployment, moving the economy down its initial SP_2 curve to point A. At point A actual inflation, about 4.5 percent, is less than the 6 percent inflation expected along the SP_2 curve ($p^e = 6$). Gradually people will adjust their expectations downward in line with actual inflation, and the SP curve will shift down, first to SP', and then to even lower levels. Eventually, when expected inflation has reached zero the economy can attain point E_0 with zero inflation and unemployment equal to the natural rate.

The more rapidly expectations adjust downward in response to lower inflation, the sooner the economy can reach its desired long-run equilibrium point E_0. Along route 1 we assume that each year people correct all their error in predicting inflation made in the previous year; that is, this year's expected inflation rate (p^e) is set exactly equal to last year's actual inflation rate (p_{-1}).[3]

But 1978 is not the end of the story. The high level of unemployment

---

[3] Following the discussion of adaptive expectations in section 8-8, we have set the adjustment coefficient g equal to 1.0. Route 1 reflects exactly the same assumptions about the adjustment of expectations as the $g = 1.0$ path in Figure 8-8. The only difference is that in the earlier chapter the economy adjusted gradually to an *acceleration* in demand growth from zero to 6 percent, and here the economy adjusts slowly to a *deceleration* in demand growth from 6 percent to zero.

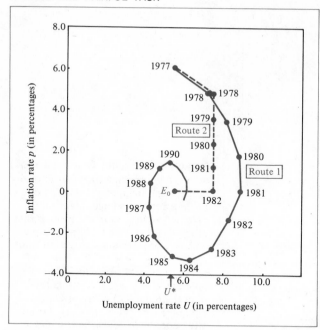

FIGURE 11-2

Response of Inflation and Unemployment to Alternative Restrictive Aggregate Demand
Policies

In 1977 the economy is assumed to
start out in exactly the same situation
as at point E_3 in Figure 11-1. Inflation is running at a fully anticipated rate
of 6 percent and unemployment is at
the natural rate of 5.5 percent. Then
demand growth ($\hat{y}$) is slowed. Along
route 1 demand growth is suddenly
slowed from 6 to zero percent and
held forever at zero percent. Along
route 2 demand growth is manipulated
to keep the economy from overshooting as it does along route 1.

causes inflation to keep slowing further, eventually becoming negative.
When the inflation rate is negative, the level of prices actually falls. Only
in 1985 after the economy passes the natural rate of unemployment,
assumed to be 5.5 percent, does the inflation rate start to rise back toward zero.[4] When inflation exceeds zero in 1988, unemployment starts
to rise again, and eventually, after the year 1995, the economy finally
reaches the desired point E_0 (where inflation is zero and unemployment
settles down at U^*).

The more slowly expectations adjust downward in response to lower
inflation, the more slowly the economy reaches its desired point E_0. If
only part of an error in predicting inflation is corrected each year, the
economy takes even longer to adjust than along route 1.[5]

Even along route 1, unemployment remains above the natural unemployment rate (U^*) for the entire period between 1978 and 1984. The
fundamental cause of the recession's length is the slowness in the downward adjustment of inflation, which in turn stems from the slow adjust-

---

[4] Recall that actual inflation (p) exceeds the expected rate (p^e) whenever actual unemployment (U) sinks below the natural unemployment rate (U^*).

[5] Compare the different paths of adjustment in Figure 8-8 in the opposite situation of an
increase in aggregate demand.

ment of expectations. People refuse to adjust their expectations of inflation downward until they actually experience a reduction in inflation. In contrast, no recession would be necessary at all if people were to realize that the drop in $\hat{y}$ from 6 percent to zero implies a reduction in the equilibrium inflation rate by the same amount and if people were instantly to drop their expectation of inflation from 6 percent to zero.

Why is instant adjustment of price expectations unrealistically optimistic? Why do price expectations adjust only gradually in the real world, requiring the nation to endure a recession if inflation is to be eliminated?

1. People do not instantly adjust their expectations with every change in demand growth ($\hat{y}$) because they do not believe that businessmen set their prices according to $\hat{y}$ alone. An automobile firm, for instance, bases its current price mainly on the current prices of materials it purchases from suppliers and on the current wages of its workers.
2. Materials prices and wages, in turn, do not adjust instantly in response to government policy but are often fixed in advance by long-term contracts lasting one to three years.

Thus, since long-term contracts prevent a decline in $\hat{y}$ from cutting wages and materials prices instantly, the prices of products such as automobiles will not fall instantly. And, since individuals in the economy know this, they do not adjust their expectations downward completely by the full amount of the drop in $\hat{y}$. Instead, because policymakers and ordinary people really are quite uncertain about the pace of downward adjustment of actual inflation, they hold off any adjustment of their expectations until they see for themselves the inflation slowing down.[6] Their motto is "Show Me."

The gradual adjustment of expectations makes a recession inevitable if a 6 percent inflation is to be brought completely to a halt. But the policy chosen along route 1, a steady zero percent growth rate in adjusted nominal income ($\hat{y}$), is an extremely inefficient way to achieve zero inflation. Compare route 1 in Figure 11-2 with a new and much more direct route 2. Along route 2 the recession ends abruptly in 1983 when the economy has reached zero inflation, in contrast to the 20-year adjustment required along Route 1.

The difference between routes 1 and 2 has nothing to do with the adjustment of expectations. Indeed exactly the same adjustment assumption is made along both routes, that people correct all their error in predicting prices made during the previous year. Then what is the difference? Along route 1 policymakers keep adjusted nominal income growth ($\hat{y}$)

---

[6] The widespread disagreement among politicians and economists during 1976 about the consequences for inflation of alternative economic policies simply stresses the great uncertainty faced by ordinary people. No wonder people say "show me the drop in inflation first and only then will I lower my guess of next year's inflation."

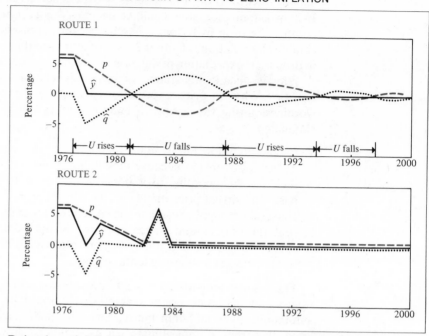

A SOPHISTICATED DEMAND MANAGEMENT POLICY
CAN SHORTEN THE ECONOMY'S PATH TO ZERO INFLATION

FIGURE 11-3

Behavior of Adjusted Demand Growth ($\hat{y}$), Inflation (p), and Adjusted Output Growth ($\hat{q}$) along Two Alternative Paths of Adjustment toward Zero Inflation

Along route 1 adjusted demand growth ($\hat{y}$) slows from 6 to zero percent immediately and remains fixed forever thereafter. In 1981, when inflation reaches zero, there is nothing to keep inflation from dropping further, because unemployment is still so high. Thus the economy overshoots. The overshooting is prevented by a policy that causes a one-time drop in output growth to raise unemployment in 1978, followed by a one-shot acceleration in output in 1983 to end the recession.

rigidly and inflexibly at zero, even though the economy suffers from this policy by going through a long period of high unemployment. But along route 2, $\hat{y}$ is moved around carefully to guide the economy to its destination (point E_0) in the minimum possible time.

A new diagram, Figure 11-3, illustrates more clearly the exact source of the superiority of route 2 over route 1. In the upper frame for route 1 the solid black line shows the sudden drop in $\hat{y}$ from 6.0 to 0.0 percent in 1978. By definition, $\hat{y}$ is divided up between inflation (p) and the deviation of actual output growth from natural or trend output growth

$\hat{q}$.[7] Thus the red p line and dotted black $\hat{q}$ line always add up to $\hat{y}$. In 1981 the inflation is over, but policymakers waste the opportunity to stabilize the economy! Instead they produce a roaring economic boom that causes the economy to overshoot its destination, the natural unemployment rate (U^*).

The strategy along route 2 is much more flexible and sensible. In 1978 a sudden drop in $\hat{y}$ pushes $\hat{q}$ down and causes unemployment to rise. Up to here the two routes are identical. But then in 1979 any further increase in U is prevented by moving $\hat{q}$ back up to zero, which requires that $\hat{y}$ be raised into equality with p. Inflation (p) continues to drop, because high unemployment continues to slow the growth of wages and prices. Finally in 1982 inflation hits zero, and $\hat{y}$ is then suddenly accelerated to raise $\hat{q}$ by exactly enough to move U back down to 5.5 percent, the natural unemployment rate. The major problem with route 2 is that it is dubious whether it is possible to control demand growth ($\hat{y}$) so precisely.

Summary: Inflation can't be ended without a recession unless expected inflation can be caused to drop suddenly. This is unlikely to happen because people will wait for evidence that inflation is actually slowing down. The reduction of inflation below what people expect requires a recession and high unemployment in order to reduce actual inflation. Only then will expectations of future inflation begin to be adjusted downward. The process of ending inflation can be shortened by a flexible policy as along route 2, which varies the growth of adjusted nominal income $\hat{y}$ to prevent the economy from overshooting its desired inflation and unemployment targets.

11-4 CASE STUDY: THE BEHAVIOR OF WAGES IN POSTWAR RECESSIONS

A major point in the previous section was that the inflation rate is prevented from dropping suddenly in response to restrictive monetary and fiscal policy because the downward adjustment of wage rates is inhibited by previously negotiated long-term labor contracts. Firms may not be able to afford to keep their prices stable if they have previously signed a labor contract calling for wage increases of 7 percent annually. Any attempt to maintain a stable price under these circumstances would cause labor costs to outpace sales revenue, at first cutting profits, then causing losses, and finally driving the firm out of business.

If the growth rate of nominal wages (w) is no higher than the growth of output per worker or **productivity** ($q - n$), then the extra output

---

[7] The relationship between $\hat{y}$, $\hat{q}$, and p is first introduced in section 8-6.

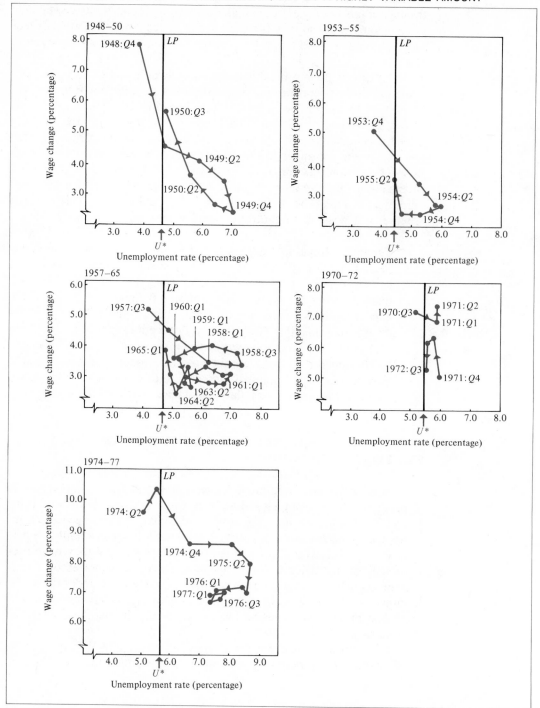

produced by each worker exactly pays for his higher wage without requiring that firms raise prices:

GENERAL FORM	NUMERICAL EXAMPLE	
$p = w - (q - n)$	$p = 2.5 - 2.5 = 0$	(11.1)

In the numerical example, both wages and productivity are rising at 2.5 percent per annum, allowing the inflation rate to be zero. A higher growth rate of wages, say 5.5 percent, would require inflation of 5.5 − 2.5, or 3.0 percent.

Inflation does not follow in the footsteps of wage rates every quarter. But over several years inflation does not deviate very far from the value suggested by the equation, that is, wage growth (w) minus productivity growth. Thus

A good test of the ability of a recession to cause a lasting drop in inflation is to examine whether actual postwar recessions succeeded in cutting wage growth.

Figure 11-4 consists of five separate diagrams showing the adjustment of wage growth in each of the five postwar recessions. Before examining each episode closely, let us stop and ask ourselves how we would expect wages to behave, on the basis of the previous sections.

1. In a short, sharp recession we would expect higher unemployment (U) to cut wage growth (w) as the economy moves southeast along its initial SP curve. But if policymakers end the recession before expectations have begun to adjust downward, the economy will move back up to the northwest along its original SP curve and wind up with as much wage growth as before the recession. The first two episodes in Figure 11-4, the 1948–50 and 1953–55 recessions, appear to have been too short to result in a substantial permanent downward movement of wage growth. Instead, w dropped temporarily and then jumped back up as the economy neared the natural unemployment rate (U^*).
2. In a long recession, we should expect to see a steady reduction in wage growth as price expectations gradually decline. During the

FIGURE 11-4   Relationship between Wage Growth and Unemployment in Five Postwar Recessions

Each of the five frames of this diagram plots the rate of change of wages against the unemployment rate. The five frames correspond to the five postwar recessions. The conclusions are simply that wage change responds in a highly variable manner to recessions. Compare the rapid slowdown in wage change in 1975 with the absence of any slowdown in 1971.

long period between late 1957 and early 1965 the economy remained above the natural unemployment rate (U^*); a recovery during 1958–60 aborted and a second recession occurred in 1960–61. There appears to have been some decline in expectations of inflation. For instance, wage growth (w) in the 1960–61 recession in Figure 11-4 appears to have been about 0.7 percentage point lower than in the same stage of the 1957–58 recession. By early 1964 w was only about 2.5 percent, compared to 5.2 percent in 1957. The most notable aspect of the 1957–65 episode is the amazing slowness of the downward adjustment, less than 3 percentage points in seven years. This pace was even slower than route 1 in Figure 11-2.

3. The fourth episode in 1970–72 was different. Inflation expectations continuously increased during the 1965–71 period. Thus in the 1970–71 recession wage growth actually increased, apparently indicating that the SP curve was still shifting up in response to higher inflation expectations, as people attempted to adjust to the acceleration of inflation that had surprised them in the previous five years.[8] Unfortunately we do not know what would have happened to wage growth in 1971–72 if the economy had been left alone to adjust by itself because the Nixon administration introduced wage and price controls on August 15, 1971. The data for late 1971 and 1972 show a sudden drop in w, suggesting that the primary cause was the control program.

4. 1974–76 was another period of high unemployment. Actual unemployment (U) rose above the natural rate (U^*) about as much as had occurred in 1958 and 1961. But wage growth (w) slowed much more rapidly than in the earlier recessions. Why? We examined part of the reason in the case study of this period in section 8-11. Inflation (p) and wage change (w) were both abnormally high in 1974 because of the coincidence of two unprecedented events: the oil and food supply shocks and the termination of the Nixon wage-price control program in May 1974. In short, the 1974–76 slowdown in inflation expectations, which allowed the SP curve and wage growth both to drop substantially, can be partly explained by the realization of ordinary people that the supply shocks were over, abnormal times had ended, and more normal times were ahead.

Summary: Wage growth has behaved differently in each postwar recession, mainly because inflation expectations responded to the special circumstances of each episode. In 1948–50 and 1953–55,

---

[8] Although there are no definitive data on the expected rate of inflation (p^e), it is possible to construct an estimated series in various ways. Two candidates for p^e are displayed in Figure 10-1.

the recessions were too short to allow enough time for a substantial downward adjustment in expectations. In 1970–71, expectations were still adjusting upward to the previous years of accelerating inflation caused by too-low unemployment. In 1974–76 expectations dropped rapidly, mainly because of the abnormal wage and price behavior in 1974. Thus we are left with the long, slow adjustment of 1957–65 as perhaps the best evidence of the potential for curing inflation by deliberate creation of high unemployment. That episode suggests that inflation can be cured only by causing many years of high unemployment and lost output.

11-5 WAGE AND PRICE CONTROLS AS A CURE FOR INFLATION

High unemployment is likely to be a long and painful cure for inflation. For this reason some economists have continued to recommend wage and price controls as a "quick fix" to cut inflation without the pain of a recession. Many other economists oppose controls on the grounds that (1) they won't work, (2) even if they achieve a temporary cure, they cannot work permanently, and (3) any cure, no matter how limited, does more harm than good by interfering with the efficiency of the private economy's operation.

Controls are not a new idea. The Roman Emperor Diocletian imposed a comprehensive control program in 301 A.D. Offenders who violated the edict by charging prices or paying wages differing from those decreed by the emperor were sentenced to death! The program was abandoned as a failure after 13 years.[9] More recently, the United States had a comprehensive and compulsory system of wage and price controls during World War II, a more limited system during the Korean War, a period of voluntary wage-price guidelines in the Kennedy-Johnson administrations during 1962–66, and, finally, a full-fledged control program in the Nixon administration between August 1971 and April 1974.

The basic argument in favor of controls is that the duration of the transition to lower inflation can be shortened. Our hypothetical examples in Figures 11-1 through 11-3, and the actual real-world episodes in Figure 11-4, suggest that without controls the transition can take many years, perhaps more than a decade. Workers and firms are slow to adjust expectations downward because they refuse to believe inflation has subsided until they actually see it happening. On the basis of past evidence people

---

[9] This and other examples are reviewed in C. Jackson Grayson, "Controls Are Not the Answer," *Challenge* (November/December 1974), pp. 9–12, which contains a good introduction to the major arguments against controls. See also the debate between David Lewis and Myron E. Sharpe, "The Great Debate on Wage-Price Controls," *Challenge* (January/February 1975), pp. 26–32.

are unlikely to believe that the government will actually maintain the restrictive policies long enough to achieve price stability. Imposition of controls, however, may cut the rate of inflation immediately, causing people to respond by reducing their expectations of inflation and hence accepting lower rates of wage increase.

If controls could reduce the growth rate of all wages and prices by the same percentage, without having any effect on the flexibility of relative prices or relative real wages, the widespread criticisms would be less convincing. Unfortunately, the relative prices of different products and the real wages of different groups of workers are continually changing as the private marketplace uses the price system to allocate resources. Because government officials running the control program cannot possibly know how relative prices and real wages would be moving each day in the absence of controls, they have no way to *decree* exactly the same changes in relative prices and real wages by the use of controls. Instead, all actual control programs tend to impose simple rules, particularly on the growth of wage rates.

Imagine that the control officials attempt to set the inflation rate (p) to zero. Then they calculate the required growth rate of wages (w) from equation (11.1) as equal to the growth of productivity:

GENERAL FORM   NUMERICAL EXAMPLE

$$w = p + (q - n) \qquad w = 0 + 2.5 = 2.5$$

For instance, the numerical example indicates that if the productivity trend is 2.5 percent per year, then wage rates can grow at the same 2.5 percent per year without causing inflation.

The attempt to impose the same 2.5 percent wage rule on all employees may create shortages of some employees in growing occupations. Firms may be unable to attract computer programmers without an above-average wage offer, but that is prohibited by the controls. As a result firms selling computer programming services will be unable to supply the demand for their product, causing a shortage, and they will be unable to increase the price to eliminate the shortage.[10] The danger of shortages of products or labor skills is the chief argument against controls. The United States does not have a massive planning bureaucracy to allocate resources, like that of the USSR, and it must use the price system to allocate resources. Controls inevitably interfere by changing relative prices and misallocating resources.

Some economists agree that controls would be harmful in a competi-

---

[10] In the Kennedy-Johnson guidelines era, w was to be limited to the growth rate of productivity over the previous five years, calculated to be 3.2 percent, and price changes were to be held to 3.2 percent minus the rate of productivity increase on each product. This allowed the prices of haircuts (with no productivity increase) to rise at 3.2 percent but forced the prices of computers to fall.

tive economy. But they claim that prices and wages are jacked up by powerful large corporations and large unions.[11] In this view the enforced control of union wages would be beneficial even if real wage rates were reduced, because the supply of workers would still exceed the demand and firms could hire more unemployed workers. Enforced control over the prices of large corporations would be beneficial even if corporate profits were reduced, by reducing misallocation of resources caused by corporate monopoly profits.

A control program limited to large unions and corporations would be easier to administer than a universal program. But large corporations produce thousands of products. Some relative prices would surely be pushed out of line. Corporations offering buyers a product, say an automobile, are promising to deliver a given quality, warranty, and financing terms at the original uncontrolled price. Controls may cause quality to be reduced, warranties to be shortened, or financing terms to be stiffened. Controls by themselves do not create the new firms whose entry into production would cut monopoly profits. A more efficient method of reducing monopoly profits would be for the government to encourage competition by better enforcement of the antitrust laws.

Concentrating controls on large corporations also leaves the large service sector uncontrolled. A price lid on General Motors' automobiles will not automatically prevent the television repairer from raising his charge. This leaves us with wage controls on large unions as the least harmful system, but labor unions are unlikely to welcome being selected as the sole victim of the control program. They will protest against the erosion of wage differentials separating skilled plumbers and electricians from unskilled busboys and dishwashers. "Where are the controls," they will ask, "on the rent, interest, and dividend checks that rich people receive and on executive stock options and bonuses?"

11-6 CASE STUDY: EFFECTS OF THE U.S. CONTROLS PROGRAM, 1971–74

The Nixon administration's wage-price control program did temporarily reduce the rate of inflation, but it does not appear to have had lasting influence. The control program cut the rate of inflation and made more of the growth of nominal income available to support real output expansion. As a result output growth zoomed ahead in late 1971 and throughout 1972, and unemployment fell steadily (see Figure 8-11). By failing to restrain the expansion of output, monetary and fiscal policy allowed unemployment to fall below the natural unem-

---

[11] See especially John Kenneth Galbraith, *The New Industrial State* (Boston: Houghton Mifflin, 1967).

ployment rate, and ultimately inflationary pressures built up that forced abandonment of the controls in early 1974.[12]

Several sources are available that measure how the 1971–74 controls affected inflation.[13] One recent calculation, summarized in Table 11-1, suggests that the initial effect of controls was exactly offset by subsequent price increases exceeding the rates that would have been expected if the controls had never been put into effect! If these estimates are correct, then the termination of controls in 1974 made inflation worse. The inflation, in turn, made the subsequent recession worse.

Summary: The termination of price controls is like a crop failure, an increase in the price of imported oil, or any other supply shock in that inflation is made temporarily worse than it would have been. More of existing nominal income growth is "used up" to pay for the inflation, and as a result real output may fall.

But the miscarriage of the 1971–74 controls program extends far beyond its failure to reduce inflation permanently and its destabilizing effects that aggravated the economic boom of 1971–72 and deepened the economic recession of 1974–75. Shortages of several products developed during the control period, partly because the United States, despite its great size, is actually an open economy that trades with other nations.

Controls on the price of lumber in 1972 began to curtail the supply of lumber and cause sawmills to shut down operations. Shortages of molasses, fertilizer, and logs appeared because higher world prices pulled domestic supplies abroad while domestic producers were forbidden from raising prices within the United States. Reinforcing steel bars fell under the controls, but the steel scrap used in making the bars was excluded from the controls and shot up in price, squeezing the profits of the makers of steel bars, causing their production to shrink, and interfering with construction projects. Baling wire used by farmers to bundle crops also was in short supply because steel companies found

---

[12] In the analysis of section 8-10, controls shifted the *SP* curve down the *BC* curve. Policymakers could have prevented unemployment from falling too low by accommodating the controls, that is, by reducing the rate of nominal income growth to moderate the high growth rate of real output.

[13] See Robert J. Gordon, "Wage-Price Controls and the Shifting Phillips Curve," *Brookings Papers on Economic Activity,* vol. 3, no. 2 (1972), pp. 385–421. See also "The Response of Wages and Prices to the First Two Years of Controls" and "The Impact of Aggregate Demand on Prices," in the same journal (1973, vol. 4, no. 3) and (1975, vol. 6, no. 3), respectively. Additional papers and a general discussion of methodological issues are contained in K. Brunner and A. Meltzer (eds.), *Conference on Wage and Price Controls, Journal of Monetary Economics* (April 1976 supplement).

TABLE 11-1   The Effect of the 1971–74 Control Program on the Private GNP Deflator (Excluding Food and Energy Prices)

| | | Percentage Price Change over Interval | | |
	Period	Actual	Predicted without controls	Difference
Initial effect	1971:Q2–1973:Q3	7.79	11.27	−3.48
Subsequent effect	1973:Q3–1975:Q3	15.40	11.88	3.52
Total effect	1971:Q2–1975:Q3	23.19	23.15	0.04

Source: Robert J. Gordon, "The Impact of Aggregate Demand on Prices," *Brookings Papers on Economic Activity,* vol. 6, no. 3 (1975), Table 5, p. 641.

that they were losing $100 on every ton of baling wire at the low controlled price.[14]

The control officials can attempt to deal with some of these problem areas by devising exceptions and special rules, but soon producers of similar products protest that they have been treated unfairly. The Nixon controls exempted raw farm products, which normally exhibit volatile ups and downs in prices and would have been almost impossible to control without creating havoc in the nation's wholesale and retail food markets. But then problems of definition arose. What is a raw farm product?

Was honey a "raw" food – or processed by the busy bees? What if the honey were strained or drained? What about fish and other seafood when "shelled, shucked, skinned, or scaled"? Cucumbers went up but pickles were controlled; popped corn was controlled, raw corn was not. Since chicken broilers were cut up and packaged before being sold, they were considered a processed food, and their price was frozen. When the price of feed went up, the farmer simply discontinued production; the nation was shocked at pictures of thousands of chicks being drowned.[15]

Overall, the 1971–74 U.S. wage-price control program can be judged a failure on at least four counts:

1. Controls had no long-run effect on inflation or the price level.
2. The removal of controls caused an extra catch-up inflation in mid-1974 at the most awkward possible time, when the economy was

---

[14] These examples are from C. Jackson Grayson, "Controls Are Not the Answer," *Challenge* (November/December 1974), pp. 9–12; and Walter Guzzardi, Jr., "What We Should Have Learned about Controls," *Fortune* (March 1975), p. 105.

[15] Guzzardi, *op. cit.*

reeling from higher farm and oil prices. There is little question that the control program made the recession of 1974–75 worse.

3. Controls caused shortages and a misallocation of resources.

4. Finally, the controls consumed large amounts of time, in the form both of extra government employees hired by the control agency and extra hours diverted by businessmen from constructive projects to the tasks of implementing, fighting, and evading the controls.

This negative evaluation for the United States is not contradicted by European experience. In fact a recent study concluded that European wage controls or "incomes policies" either did not work at all or broke down after a short-lived success.[16] And in some countries controls have been imposed on prices but not wages, with prices held down by government subsidies. In Chile, Argentina, Britain, and other countries, the end result has been an inflation that was worse than before because the subsidies caused government deficits that had to be financed by printing more money, and because prices shot up when finally the large government deficits forced abandonment of the controls.

11-7 CASE STUDY: CONTROL OF INFLATION IN COMMUNIST COUNTRIES

> We do not have inflation — we just have high prices.
> — Anonymous Soviet economist[17]

Visitors to the USSR and other Communist countries are often told that Communist central planning has succeeded in eliminating inflation, in contrast to the accelerated inflation in Western countries in the 1970s. Indeed, a visitor cannot deny that prices of many staple commodities have remained unchanged for a long time. As of 1975, the price of sugar in Prague was the same as in 1937. Moscow subway fares were the same in 1976 as in 1935. Russian meat and dairy prices have remained unchanged since 1962, and bread prices and rents have remained level since the 1940s.

Economic control by central planners allows maintenance of high aggregate demand and low unemployment without accelerating inflation. In the Western countries such a situation is characterized by an upward bidding of wages and prices as firms attempt to obtain scarce products and workers. But in the USSR controls prevent wages and prices from going up, so that the firms are simply forced to do without the workers and products they need. Unlike the surplus of workers in

---

[16] Lloyd Ulman and Robert J. Flanagan, *Wage Restraint: A Study of Incomes Policies in Western Europe* (Berkeley: University of California Press, 1971).

[17] Quoted in *Time* (August 5, 1974), p. 64.

high-unemployment countries such as the United States, Communist countries have a perpetual shortage of workers. We too could have a shortage of workers if all wages were suddenly cut by half while prices and aggregate demand were left at their present level!

Three main criticisms can be made of the Communist claim that inflation has been eliminated. First, techniques for measuring prices in those countries are deceiving. Many instances of price increases are left out of the official price indexes. Second, these economies are characterized by widespread shortages of consumer goods, as evidenced by flourishing black markets in which citizens can purchase illegally the desirable goods that are unavailable in the stores. Third, governments are forced to devote a substantial part of their budgets to subsidizing low consumer prices of necessities, forcing the postponement of government investment projects.[18]

Price Measurement. Although most major economic activities in Communist countries are carried out in government-owned factories, offices, and shops selling price-controlled goods, a substantial fraction of GNP consists of privately produced goods and services that are excluded from the official price indexes. For instance, the Soviet system for distributing food produced on state-owned farms is inefficient and often leaves state-owned stores short of basic commodities. Consumers are willing to pay prices as high as $4.50 a pound for fresh tomatoes, creating an incentive for farmers to carry tomatoes in suitcases and fly from agricultural regions to Moscow to sell the tomatoes on the street (an activity partly made possible by low state-subsidized airline fares)! Another measurement technique is to limit the price index only to "old" varieties of goods. This allows the introduction of "new" varieties differing from the previous models in only trivial ways at sharply higher prices. For instance, in 1974 when the GAZ-21 model of the Volga car was replaced by its not very different successor, GAZ-24, the price jumped from $7,500 to $12,630.[19]

Shortages of Goods. Western economists criticize price controls for causing shortages. The USSR has no mechanism to adjust demand

---

[18] A much more sanguine view by an Eastern economist is Bela Csikos-Nagy, "The Re-Evaluation of the Theory of Repressed Inflation in the Light of the Experience of Some Socialist Countries," in D. C. Hague (ed.), forthcoming proceedings of International Economic Association Conference on Inflation, held in Saltsjobaden, Sweden, in August 1975.

[19] The specific examples in this case study were obtained from the following sources: "Inflation is Not a Russian Word," *Economist* (April 24, 1976), pp. 77–78; "No Inflation? Well, Not Exactly," *Economist* (December 7, 1974), pp. 50–55; "Black Markets Bloom in Eastern Europe Behind Façade of Strait-Laced Marxism," *The New York Times* (September 9, 1975), p. 8; "Polish Price Crisis Reflects Inflation Ills," *The New York Times* (June 29, 1976), p. 6; "Inflation, Communist Style," *Time* (August 5, 1974), p. 64; "The Communist World: 'Sneaking' up on Inflation," *Newsweek* (November 25, 1974), pp. 100–104.

to supply, so that in one part of a store desirable goods are sold out almost as soon as they are unpacked, while in another part of the same store unwanted low-quality goods stay on the shelves unpurchased, with no clearance sale to get rid of them. Goods are rationed by the time spent standing in lines, and frustrated consumers are sometimes forced to turn to the black market where Western watches, blue denims, and other products are sold at prices three to ten times higher than in the West.

Special stores in the USSR sell higher-quality goods unobtainable in regular stores, but only for Western currencies, and eager Russians are willing to accept as little as 30 U.S. cents for one ruble, compared to the $1.40 official exchange rate. One recent example of a shortage occurred in 1976, when coffee prices in the West almost doubled as a result of a freeze that killed much of the Brazilian coffee crop. Russian officials were unwilling to raise the price of coffee in the shops, so that the government was faced with the choice between providing massive subsidies to allow coffee to be sold at the old price or allowing coffee to disappear. They compromised, continuing to sell coffee in restaurants but allowing coffee to vanish from the retail food stores.[20]

Subsidies. Maintenance of stable food prices is a costly policy on which the Russian government spends about $25 billion per year. Some smaller Eastern European governments have attempted to reduce the subsidies by instituting sudden jumps in food prices, but the population has protested. Poland in particular experienced food riots in 1970, and food price increases of up to 100 percent in 1976 were withdrawn after workers went on strike and ripped up railway lines. In Western countries the government deficits caused by subsidies are often financed by money creation, but in the Eastern countries subsidies tend to crowd out government investment projects. Subsidies have been described as "chewing up capital that would otherwise be invested in new plants and machines." Perhaps the main benefit of food subsidies is to lessen the inequality between rich and poor members of society. Food subsidies help the poor most, because they spend a larger fraction of their incomes on food, and in addition the long waiting lines experienced in the Soviet Union are less onerous for poor people, whose time is less valuable.[21]

Yugoslavia is the Communist nation that has gone furthest in allowing the price system to allocate resources, but it has also experienced a severe Western-style inflation. During 1971–73 Yugoslavian infla-

---

[20] In August 1976, when I visited Leningrad, coffee had been unobtainable in Leningrad stores for four months and could be obtained for home use only by bribing workers who had access to the coffee cabinet in restaurants and canteens.

[21] In the USSR there is much more equality than in the West in the space, quality, and location of housing occupied by factory workers as compared with managers and officials. But high-ranking officials often have access to special privileges, including foreign travel and the use of the foreign-currency stores, which are denied to ordinary citizens.

tion averaged 16.8 percent annually, and in 1974–75 the average rate rose to 22.8 percent. These figures exceed the inflation rates of any of the industrialized countries of Western Europe, even those of Britain and Italy, the two inflationary "problem children" of the mid-1970s.

11-8 INDEXATION AND OTHER REFORMS TO REDUCE THE COSTS OF INFLATION

So far in this chapter we have examined two cures, recessions and controls, which would attempt to reduce the costs of inflation by ending inflation itself. Unfortunately, recessions impose a huge cost in higher unemployment and lost output, while controls may not work, and, if they do work, they tend to interfere with the efficient operation of the economy. A third cure for the costs of inflation is quite different. Instead of attempting to get rid of the inflation itself, **indexation** and other reforms have been proposed to cut substantially the costs imposed by inflation.

A fully anticipated inflation of 6 percent, as depicted in Figure 11-1 at point E_3, does not harm savers if the nominal interest rate has increased by exactly enough to compensate them for the loss in the purchasing power of their savings accounts caused by inflation. If the real interest rate in an inflation-free economy were 3 percent, then the nominal interest rate in an economy with a 6 percent inflation should be 9 percent.[22] In other words, a 9 percent nominal interest rate incorporates a full "inflation premium" that leaves savers just as well off as they would be without the inflation. And borrowers can afford to pay this inflation premium because their assets purchased with the proceeds from the loans will rise in value 6 percent faster than if there were no inflation. The capital gain enjoyed by a homeowner will be larger in an economy with a 6 percent inflation than in one with zero inflation, and this capital gain would be balanced by a higher interest rate on mortgages.[23]

REGULATION Q AND VARIABLE-RATE MORTGAGES

In the U.S. economy the major barrier that causes inflation to erode savings accounts while enriching borrowers is the fixed-rate home mortgage. Many homeowners are still paying off 4 and 5 percent mortgages, while the value of their homes in many cases is increasing at 8 or 10 percent per year.[24] Savings and loan institutions are receiving a low level of interest income on the portion of their mortgage loans that were taken

---

[22] This example, repeated from section 10-2, neglects the taxation of interest earned on the savings account. If the average tax rate is t, then the nominal interest rate i must rise to equal $r + p^e/(1 - t)$, where r is the real interest rate. If the tax rate is 0.33, in the text example i must rise to 12 percent $(3 + 6)/(1 - 0.33)$.

[23] Numerical examples are given in sections 10-2 and 10-3.

[24] A well-publicized example involves ex-President Ford, whose house in Arlington, Virginia, appreciated from $35,000 in 1955 to $137,000 in 1976.

out a decade ago, and for this reason they cannot afford to pay an interest rate on savings deposits that fully compensates savers for inflation. Why don't savers switch their savings to commercial banks, which have very few mortgages in their asset portfolios? The federal government protects savings and loan associations against the loss of their deposits by setting a legal **Regulation Q** ceiling on the interest rate that commercial banks can pay to holders of time deposits. In 1976 these ceiling rates ranged from 5.0 percent on passbook deposits to 7.5 percent on long-term certificates.

Thus the first major reform that would help redress the imbalance between borrowers and savers in an inflationary economy would be variable interest-rate mortgages. An acceleration of inflation would cause mortgage interest rates to increase, allowing financial institutions to pay a higher interest rate to savers. The major disadvantage of this plan is that homeowners, while they would enjoy higher capital gains as a result of inflation, might not have enough money in their household budgets to pay the higher monthly payments required at the new higher mortgage interest rate.[25]

But even if savers were to be fully compensated for inflation by receiving a nominal interest rate that includes a full inflation premium on their savings accounts, everyone will still suffer an erosion of purchasing power on their checking accounts and pocket cash. Inflation causes everyone to work harder to keep their checking account balances at a minimum, but most of this extra effort (Chapter 10's shoe-leather cost of inflation) could be eliminated if the government were to allow banks to pay interest on checking accounts. Already progress has been made in this direction: bank customers in New England can write checks on interest-bearing "NOW" accounts. Although inflation would still erode the value of pocket cash, this would be a minor cost of inflation when balanced against the enormous benefits of avoiding the need to cure inflation through recessions and controls.

INDEXED BONDS

Even though introducing variable rate mortgages and lifting government interest rate ceilings on savings and checking accounts would substantially cut the costs of inflation, many economists have recommended that the government go further and issue an **indexed bond** that would fully protect savers against any unexpected movements in the inflation rate. An indexed bond simply pays savers a fixed real interest rate (r_0), say 2 percent, plus the actual inflation rate (p). Thus the saver's nominal interest rate (i) would be:

---

[25] One possibility would be to allow homeowners to pay the higher interest rate by stretching their mortgage, for example, from 30 to 35 years. If the homeowner should die before his mortgage is repaid, his home can be sold at the high inflated price to provide funds to repay the mortgage.

GENERAL FORM	NUMERICAL EXAMPLE

$$i = r_0 + p$$

(a) $\quad 2 = 2 + 0$

(b) $\quad 12 = 2 + 10$

In the first numerical example (a), savers would receive a 2 percent return if the inflation rate were zero. If inflation suddenly accelerated to 10 percent, as in example (b), savers would find that the nominal return (i) rises to 12 percent, and they would be just as well off as without the inflation.[26]

The main disadvantage of the indexed bond proposal is that savers might find it too attractive! Banks and savings institutions might experience a flood of withdrawals by savers eager to buy the indexed bonds. At present, banks could not compete because of the Regulation Q interest-rate ceilings. Thus the indexed bond proposal must be linked with the reforms of bank and savings institution regulations that would allow banks to issue their own indexed bonds.

INDEXED TAX SYSTEM

The government should not stop with indexed bonds. It should fully index the tax system, that is, raise the dollar amounts of tax credits, exemptions, the standard deductions, and tax rate brackets each year by the amount of inflation that has been experienced. A 10 percent inflation would thus cause the $750 personal exemption to rise to $825 in the following year.[27] Without an indexed tax system, inflation raises individual incomes and pushes taxpayers into higher tax brackets. A typical taxpayer might pay 15 percent of his income in income tax in 1977 but 15.5 percent at his higher 1978 wage, even if all his wage increase between 1977 and 1978 is eaten up by inflation. This system has been called "taxation without representation," because the share of personal income flowing to the federal government automatically is pushed up by inflation without Congressional legislation to authorize the increase.

WAGE INDEXATION AND SUPPLY SHOCKS

The final and most controversial type of indexation (or escalation) involves wage rates. Many wage contracts already contain provisions that automatically raise the wage by a fraction (rarely 100 percent) of the inflation rate.[28] Should the government require that all wages be fully indexed, that is, should rise by 1 percentage point faster for each 1 percentage point of inflation? Although this idea was embraced with some

---

[26] At present, savers pay taxes on all interest received. To leave them untouched by inflation, the government would have to make the inflation part of the interest return exempt from taxation.

[27] $825 is 10 percent higher than $750.

[28] Such contracts are said to contain **COLA's**, *cost-of-living-adjustments*.

enthusiasm by economists a few years ago,[29] subsequent analysis has pointed out a major difficulty.

Imagine that a supply shock, for instance an oil price increase, raises the consumer price index and that all wages are indexed to the consumer price index. If domestic firms have experienced no increase in the demand for their products, they will not be able to raise prices to pay for the higher wages. Thus supply shocks can cause business bankruptcies when wages are fully indexed.[30] To prevent bankruptcies, the central bank may step in and raise the growth of aggregate demand, thus endowing indexed economies with a permanent increase in inflation resulting from a temporary supply shock.

In the early 1970s Brazil appeared to have settled down to a steady 20 percent inflation rate that was fully incorporated into expectations. Savers were protected by indexed assets, and workers were protected by indexed wages. Instead of creating a recession to get rid of the 20 percent inflation, the Brazilians were content to live with the inflation under their system of indexation, which substantially reduced inflation's costs. Many nations envied the steady 10 percent annual real output growth experienced by Brazil between 1968 and 1973. Unfortunately, Brazil's indexing system made it particularly vulnerable to the supply shocks of 1973–74, and by late 1975 inflation was running at an annual rate of 37 percent.[31]

11-9 CONCLUSION TO PART III: THE INFLATION AND UNEMPLOYMENT DILEMMA

The inflation advanced industrialized countries have experienced in the mid-1970s originated in an excessive monetary and fiscal stimulus to aggregate demand, particularly in the mid- and late 1960s. Too much

---

[29] This was one of many ideas in economics first popularized by Milton Friedman. See his "Monetary Correction," in *Essays on Inflation and Indexation* (Washington, D.C.: American Enterprise Institute, 1974), pp. 25–61.

[30] Numerical examples of the instability created by wage indexing are contained in Robert J. Gordon, "Alternative Responses of Policy to External Supply Shocks," *Brookings Papers on Economic Activity*, vol. 6, no. 1 (1975), pp. 183–206. A simple theoretical model is provided by Joanna Gray, "Wage Indexation: A Macroeconomic Approach," *Journal of Monetary Economics*, vol. 2 (April 1976), pp. 221–36.

[31] Unfortunately space limitations preclude a full-fledged case study of the Brazilian attempt to "live with inflation." The following are suggested as good introductions to the Brazilian economy and its indexation procedures: The survey of the Brazilian economy in the *Economist* (July 31, 1976); Stefan H. Robock, "Anti-inflation Lessons from Abroad: The Brazilian Experience," *Proceedings of the Academy of Political Science*, vol. 31, no. 4 (1975); Albert Fishlow, "Indexing Brazilian Style: Inflation without Tears?" *Brookings Papers on Economic Activity*, vol. 5, no. 1 (1974), pp. 261–82. N. I. Nadiri and Alfonso C. Pastore, *Inflation: The Brazilian Experience*, Explorations in Economic Research, Occasional Papers of the National Bureau of Economic Research, vol. 4 (Winter, 1977).

aggregate demand growth, as we learned in Chapter 8, causes inflation to accelerate above the pace people expect whenever unemployment is allowed to dip below the natural unemployment rate. Governments must limit the growth in aggregate demand to keep unemployment at the natural unemployment rate, but in the 1960s the wartime financing needs of the Vietnam War pushed aggregate demand too high and unemployment too low for too long.

Monetary and fiscal policy are of little use in providing jobs to the unemployed, once the economy has reached the natural rate of unemployment. Instead structural and manpower programs must be instituted to cut the natural unemployment rate itself by better matching of workers with job openings and by reforms to reduce present incentives that favor long extended periods of low-intensity job search.

A monetary and fiscal policy that maintains actual unemployment at the natural unemployment rate will keep inflation from accelerating further if the economy is spared from supply shocks, but such a policy will do nothing to curb the expectations of further inflation that are so crucial in the persistence of actual inflation from year to year. Instead, policymakers are faced with three options. They can try to cut the inflation rate by deliberately using restrictive monetary and fiscal policy to create a recession, causing a massive waste of men and machines. They can try to control the inflation rate, but they stand little chance of succeeding without causing shortages of some products and of skilled workers. Finally, the government can loosen present financial regulations that cause inflation to erode the value of savings accounts, redistributing income from savers to debtors, and it can issue an indexed bond to insulate savers from the effects of inflation.

The main danger is that, like Brazil, an indexed economy may suffer further accelerations of inflation. Even if policymakers generate the aggregate demand growth compatible with today's inflation, they cannot prevent every situation that might shift the *SP* curve upward. Crop failures, oil price increases, and excessive union wage demands can all raise both inflation and unemployment. Strong political pressure will be placed on the government to accommodate these shocks by raising aggregate demand growth; widespread indexation makes these pressures worse. Failure to accommodate will make unemployment worse, and a government afraid of electoral defeat will not want to incur the wrath of the unemployed and their allies.[32] But the availability of indexed assets will lessen the opposition of creditors and savers to the higher inflation that would accompany demand accommodation and in turn makes accommodation more likely.

---

[32] The allies are everyone who loses from the drop in output during a recession, employed workers with fewer overtime hours, businessmen who fear bankruptcy if their profits erode too far, salespeople who lose commissions, and many others.

What should we conclude? As we will see in Chapter 12, monetarists prefer fixed rules for demand growth that (as in Figures 11-1 through 11-3) create high unemployment to cure inflation. Their opponents, the nonmonetarists, are much more ready to interfere with the economy by monetary and fiscal policy to expand demand while relying on controls to control inflation. The choice between these two approaches ultimately is more political than purely economic. A lower unemployment rate aids poor people and young people disproportionately, while lower inflation benefits rich people and old people (who are the main holders of assets). Conservatives typically worry more than liberals about the government interference required to institute a control program. Liberal nonmonetarists are eternally optimistic about their ability to dream up new methods of controlling wages that will bribe union leaders to cooperate by tying wage increases to tax changes.[33]

SUMMARY

1. Three major alternatives are available to an economic policymaker who wishes to counteract the costs of a continuing inflation. The first two, recessions and wage and price controls, attempt to reduce the costs of inflation by eliminating or reducing inflation itself. The third, indexation, instead of attempting to eliminate inflation, attempts to eliminate the adverse consequences of inflation imposed on the holders of assets.

2. Although recessions eventually achieve lower inflation rates, their success is achieved at a cost. Society suffers a large loss of current output and, through the resulting reduction in investment spending, also imposes on future generations a lower standard of living.

3. The fundamental cause of the length of the recession required to reduce inflation to the desired level, say zero percent, is the slowness in the downward adjustment of inflation in response to high unemployment. The more rapidly expectations of inflation adjust downward in response to lower actual inflation, the more rapidly the economy can reach its desired goal.

4. Controls, on the other hand, avoid the output losses of a recession. But the very serious objections to controls are that they may not work, and if they do work, they are very likely to create shortages and a drastic

---

[33] Arthur Okun and other liberal economists favor wage restraints that would offer payroll tax reductions to unions that cooperate and tax increases for those who fail to cooperate. This type of control is easier to administer in some European countries (for example, Germany and Sweden) where wage bargaining is centralized and simultaneous, as compared to the decentralized and staggered wage bargains common in the United States. See "Government-Prescribed Wage Restraints to Squeeze Worldwide Inflation," *Business Week* (July 26, 1976), pp. 62–68 and "Hunting New Remedies," *Newsweek* (May 17, 1976), pp. 77–81.

misallocation of resources. Furthermore, most economists feel that although controls may temporarily reduce the rate of inflation, they cannot achieve a similar reduction permanently.

5. The basic economic argument in favor of wage-price controls is that the transition to lower inflation rates can be shortened, because imposition by the government of controls may cause an immediate drop in the rate of inflation. Experience, however, has shown that the termination of price controls bears important similarities to a supply shock, worsening inflation temporarily as the economy goes through a catch-up period.

6. The advocates of indexation, on the other hand, have suggested a number of reforms that would ease the costs of living with inflation, in contrast to the approach that attempts to eliminate inflation. Among the most productive reforms would be the introduction of variable-rate mortgages and the lifting of government interest rate ceilings on savings and checking accounts. Reformers have also supported the issuance of indexed bonds by the government and would allow banks to issue their own indexed bonds. A fully indexed tax system has also been suggested.

7. Wage indexing, or cost-of-living escalators, should be only partial, not complete, because full wage indexation interferes with the economy's flexibility to adjust to a supply shock such as the 1974 oil price increase.

A LOOK AHEAD

Throughout the book to this point it has been assumed that aggregate demand can be controlled exactly. Monetary and fiscal policy have been assumed to be capable of setting demand growth ($\hat{y}$) at any desired value. But in the real world, life is more difficult for the policymaker: $\hat{y}$ reacts to policy changes with a lag and by an uncertain amount. As a result, many economists argue that activist government policy intervention is unwise. The next chapter sets out the main issues in the great debate on policy activism.

CONCEPTS AND QUESTIONS

IDENTIFICATIONS

Wage and price controls
Indexation
Growth rate of productivity
Relative prices

Inflation premium
Variable interest-rate mortgages
Indexed bonds
Regulation Q

QUESTIONS FOR REVIEW

1   What are the advantages and disadvantages of creating recessions as a means of reducing inflation?

2 Evaluate wage and price controls as a method of reducing inflation.

3 Why do you feel that controls are continually suggested as a remedy, in spite of our unproductive experience with controls?

4 Lowering inflationary expectations is an essential prerequisite to reducing the actual rate of inflation, and vice versa. What policy prescriptions would you propose to speed the adjustment of expectations and shorten the recession required to reduce the inflation rate to zero?

5 In selecting the desired inflation-unemployment position, what should the policymakers weigh as their major considerations?

6 "Inflation cannot accelerate in a recession when the economy remains above the natural rate of unemployment." Comment.

7 What are the primary dangers introduced by indexation?

8 Give some reasons why the U.S. government fails to offer an indexed savings bond.

9 At present full cost-of-living adjustments (wage indexation) cover only a small fraction of the U.S. labor force. If you were the president of a large U.S. manufacturing firm, would you favor introducing full cost-of-living adjustments for your own employees? What risks would you take by this action?

10 Which (or what combination of) the three options of handling inflation presented in this chapter would you prefer? Explain your answer carefully.

Part IV

Sources of Instability in the Private Economy

12 The Monetarist— Nonmonetarist Debate on Policy Activism

This month I've seen authoritative economic reports predicting:
(1) that the entire world is about to go into recession, (2)
that a boom is just around the corner, (3) that a mild slowdown
has already set in, (4) that things will be about the same
next year as they were this year.
—Eliot Marshall[1]

12-1 LINK TO PREVIOUS CHAPTERS: THE CENTRAL ROLE OF AGGREGATE DEMAND

In Part II (Chapters 3–7) we studied the determinants of the level of aggregate demand. Aggregate demand can be raised by a monetary or fiscal stimulus or by an increase in business or consumer optimism. When the private demand for consumption and investment spending falls off, an offsetting monetary or fiscal stimulus can keep aggregate demand from dropping. In the same way, a boom in private spending can be balanced by monetary or fiscal restraint.

The level of aggregate demand does not by itself tell us the level of prices or output, but rather how much nominal spending is available to be divided between the price level and real output. The division that actually occurs depends on the conditions of aggregate supply. How much output are firms willing to produce at different price levels?

Part III, especially Chapters 8 and 11, provided a dynamic analysis of aggregate demand and supply. The growth of aggregate demand $(\hat{y})$ can be controlled by the monetary and fiscal policymakers, but the division of that demand growth between inflation and output growth depends on the position of the short-run Phillips curve. A cut in demand growth $(\hat{y})$ may at first mainly affect output growth and only later mainly take the form of lower inflation. Policymakers can reduce inflation by restricting the rate of growth of aggregate demand $(\hat{y})$, but the slow downward adjustment of inflation expectations may require a long recession during the transition to a lower inflation rate.

---

[1] "False Prophets," *New Republic* (October 1, 1977), p. 50.

In Part III, however, we unrealistically assumed that the growth of aggregate demand could be controlled precisely. Policies to end inflation that required short, sharp variations in the growth of nominal income ($\hat{y}$) were illustrated. Unfortunately, policymakers cannot act as if the economy is an automobile that can quickly be steered back and forth. Rather, the procedure of changing aggregate demand is much closer to that of a captain navigating a giant supertanker. Even if he gives a signal for a hard turn, it takes a mile before he can see a change, and ten miles before the ship makes the turn. In the same way, the real-world economy has a momentum of its own, and policy shifts cannot control aggregate demand instantly or precisely.

The main subject of Part IV is the control of aggregate demand. First we ask an obvious question: Why bother? Just as the classical economists assumed that the economy has powerful self-correcting mechanisms that continuously act to steer it back to full employment without government interference (Chapter 6), so the modern school of thought called monetarism denies that the benefits of active government control of aggregate demand are worth the cost. Stabilization policy is not necessary, the monetarists claim, because steady output growth and a satisfactory rate of unemployment can be achieved by raising the money supply every year at a relatively constant rate. In fact, it is a basic tenet of the monetarist position that government interference does more harm than good and actually destabilizes the economy. Constant monetary growth eliminates one source of uncertainty and allows plans to be made with more confidence.

In this chapter we examine the monetarist case that stabilization policy (active government control of aggregate demand) is not necessary. There is substantial evidence that the economy's self-correcting forces are weak and take a long time to operate. Shifts in private spending behavior do not tend to be canceled out immediately by changes in the opposite direction; instead, destabilizing movements in private spending tend to persist. Despite these factors indicating a need for an activist stabilization policy, the government may not be capable of carrying out such a policy promptly or efficiently.

In the next two chapters we look more closely at the determinants of private spending. In the first part of the book our discussion of private aggregate demand was highly simplified. In Chapter 3 consumption was assumed to depend only on consumer disposable income (after taxes) and on consumer confidence. Investment in Chapter 4 was assumed to depend only on the interest rate and on business confidence. In fact, consumption spending may be considerably more stable than we assumed earlier, but investment spending may be less stable. Lasting swings in investment spending can destabilize the economy and constitute a major justification for government interference to push aggregate demand back to the desired level. Thus the first major defense of nonmonetarists against the monetarist critique of stabilization policy emphasizes the built-in instability of private spending.

Next, in Chapters 15 and 16, we examine the determinants of the demand for money, and the procedure by which the Federal Reserve (Fed) controls the supply of money. In the short run the Fed finds it difficult to achieve precise control of money, in part because it attempts to stabilize the interest rate. We learn that instability in the private demand for money adds a second element, in addition to the instability of private spending plans, which may call for a variable rather than constant growth policy in the money supply. But these arguments in favor of an activist monetary policy are tempered by consideration of the weak points of monetary control. For example, a tight monetary policy designed to offset buoyant private spending has the disadvantage that its effects may be felt only with a long lag, perhaps too late to achieve the desired stability. Furthermore, its effects may be disruptive to financial markets, to the housing industry, and to state and local governments.

The pros and cons of fiscal policy come next. Should the government run a balanced budget? What burdens does deficit spending impose on the economy? Should a fiscal stimulus take the form of higher government expenditures or lower tax rates? Which types of tax changes should play the main role in the government's fiscal stabilization policy? Does an activist fiscal policy share the limitations of an activist monetary policy, calling instead for a nonactivist fiscal policy rule?

12-2 THE MONETARIST CONTROVERSY IS NOT ABOUT THE POTENCY OF MONETARY POLICY

In almost every episode of the past decade, monetarists offered policy recommendations that differed from their nonmonetarist opponents. In essence the monetarists usually said "Do nothing" while their opponents said "Do something." (The only exceptions to this statement were periods when the "do something" monetarist recommendations involved slowing the growth rate of the money supply to a lower number more consistent with what the monetarists believed the "do nothing" constant growth-rate target should be.) But the reasons for the differing policy recommendations had little to do with the relative potency of monetary or fiscal policy. The great irony of the debate between the monetarists and nonmonetarists is that the effect of money on unemployment and inflation is not the central issue![2]

---

[2] Traditionally, macro textbooks have interpreted the monetarist debate as the strength of policy multipliers. An extended statement that attempts to reorient the monetarist debate is Franco Modigliani, "The Monetarist Controversy, or, Should We Forsake Stabilization

(continued)

The adjectives monetarist and nonmonetarist are confusing and deceptive labels, but we are forced to use them because of their widespread usage and acceptance by economists and journalists. The term monetarist carries the misleading implication that "only monetary policy matters."[3] Yet as early as 1966 the chief monetarist, Milton Friedman, admitted in writing that fiscal policy could affect real output in the short run and the price level in the long run. The term nonmonetarist is even worse. As early as 1944 one of the chief nonmonetarists, Franco Modigliani of MIT, gave monetary policy a key role in his theoretical writing. None of the current leading nonmonetarists ever claimed that "money does not matter at all" for the determination of income and output.

Chapter 5 contains all the elements needed for an old-fashioned interpretation of the monetarist debate. Monetary policy is potent and fiscal policy weak when the *LM* curve is steep and the *IS* curve is flat. In the extreme case of a completely vertical *LM* curve, a fiscal expansion completely crowds out an equivalent amount of private investment and leaves total real GNP unaffected. The opponents of the monetarists could not understand how it could be claimed that fiscal policy is impotent because the required vertical *LM* curve occurs only when the demand for money is unresponsive to changes in the interest rate, a condition that has been rejected by almost all economic research on the real world. The new interpretation of the monetarist debate in this chapter places no emphasis at all on the slope of the *LM* curve because none of the major monetarist conclusions depend on that slope.[4]

The real dispute between monetarists and nonmonetarists has little to do with the relative potency of monetary versus fiscal policy. Instead, their main clash concerns the location in the economy of the principal source of instability. Monetarists believe that the private economy is basically stable and that fixed policy rules are necessary to protect the economy against ill-conceived and poorly timed government actions that in the past have caused economic instability. In contrast, the nonmone-

---

Policy?" *American Economic Review,* vol. 67 (March 1977), pp. 1–19. An earlier paper is Milton Friedman, "Why Economists Disagree," in *Dollars and Deficits* (Englewood Cliffs, N.J.: Prentice-Hall, 1968), pp. 1–16. Friedman on pp. 6–9 shares the same orientation as this chapter, although on pp. 10–16 he places considerably more weight than we do here on the influence of money on inflation. Our orientation reflects Friedman's own influence. There remain very few economists who disagree with him that in the long run inflation is a monetary phenomenon.

[3] The term "monetarism" was introduced in Karl Brunner, "The Role of Money and Monetary Policy," *Review of the Federal Reserve Bank of St. Louis,* no. 50 (1968), pp. 9–24.

[4] **Review:** Return to Figure 6-2. An increase in government spending starting from point E_1 has no effect on real output if the price level is flexible. The price level rises, moving the *LM* curve left from LM_3 to LM_0. Thus the real question affecting the multiplier of government or private spending on real output is not the slope of the *LM* curve (which is positively sloped in Figure 6-2), but the speed and extent of the price increase following the fiscal expansion, and the effect on private spending of that price increase.

tarists pinpoint private spending decisions as the main source of instability and generally support an activist government countercyclical policy (both monetary and fiscal) to achieve economic stability.

To add one irony to another, both the monetarist and nonmonetarist camps regard the period of the Great Depression as providing the most dramatic example of instability originating from, respectively, the government and the private sectors. Monetarists show how the Depression was made more severe by the 31 percent decline in the money supply that the Fed allowed to occur between 1929 and 1933, whereas nonmonetarists emphasize the 85 percent decline in private investment during the same interval.[5] Nonmonetarists add that even in the years 1936–39, when the money supply had substantially surpassed its 1929 level, real private investment was on average still 40 percent below 1929.

12-3 A MONETARIST PLATFORM

The continuing disagreements between monetarists and nonmonetarists can be traced to several basic assumptions of the monetarist platform with which nonmonetarists disagree.[6]

> **Plank 1:** *Without the interference of demand shocks introduced by erratic government policy, private spending would be stable.* The stability of private spending stems from the **permanent income hypothesis** of consumption explored in Chapter 13. Consumption, the largest component of private spending, changes only gradually as households adjust their estimate of their long-run or permanent income. Another basic stabilizing factor is the flatness of the *IS* curve due to the broad range of assets whose demand depends on the interest rate.

> **Plank 2:** *Even if private planned spending is not completely stable, flexible prices create a natural tendency for it to come back on course.* The equilibrium to which flexible prices guide the economy

---

[5] The money supply concept (*M*1) declined by 25 percent, and *M*2 by 31 percent. See Appendix B for the actual data, and the glossary for definitions of *M*1 and *M*2.

[6] The monetarist platform is not copied directly from any monetarist publication but is my own invention suggested by the recent drift of the continuing policy debate. It is, however, similar to the overall interpretation of Modigliani in "The Monetarist Controversy," cited in footnote 2. Early drafts of this section have benefited from the detailed constructive suggestions of Milton Friedman in conversation and correspondence during the spring of 1977, and from correspondence with Allan Meltzer. Almost all their suggestions have been adopted, and in some cases their own suggested wording, in an effort to make this chapter an accurate and unbiased reflection of the current status of the monetarist-nonmonetarist debate.

is the natural rate of unemployment (U^*). Not only is U^* compatible with steady inflation, but the inflation expectations of individuals are realized when the economy is at U^*. Furthermore, many demand shocks are transitory, and as their destabilizing influence on output disappears before any offsetting government policy could possibly be put into effect.

Plank 3: *Even if private planned spending is not completely stable, and prices are not completely flexible, an activist monetary and fiscal policy to counteract private demand swings is likely to do more harm than good.* All policy changes affect the economy with a long and uncertain lag, so that the effect of policy may be felt after it is needed and in some cases may occur so late that it pushes the economy in the wrong direction. Economists' forecasting abilities are too limited to short-circuit this lag in the effect of policy. Further, uncertainty in the effect of policy changes adds an additional source of disturbance which makes the economy less stable than would occur with rules which limit changes in policy.

Plank 4: *Even if prices are not completely flexible, so that the economy can wander away from U^* in the short run, there can be no dispute regarding the flexibility of the price level in the long run.* Furthermore, it is unwise to base policy changes on short-run considerations, because the long run is a succession of short runs. It is best to set a growth rate for the money supply compatible with steady inflation or even zero inflation in the long run and avoid the temptation to tinker with the economy in the short run. In economic jargon, monetarists have a relatively low rate of "time preference," putting little emphasis on short-run events and paying primary attention to the consequences of present actions in the future.

Some critics have accused monetarists of heartless disregard of unemployment, since their policy recommendations oriented to a gradual slowdown in the inflation rate appear to imply a long period of high unemployment.[7] Indeed, Milton Friedman and other monetarists have argued that the unemployment data, properly interpreted, show unemployment to be a much less serious problem than the raw numbers suggest and show that a substantial portion of unemployment is voluntary (a position explored in section 9-6).[8] Nevertheless, monetarists generally

---

[7] The duration of high unemployment required to reduce the inflation rate depends on the slope of the short-run Phillips curve, the speed of adjustment of expectations, and the type of demand management policy that policymakers pursue. Two examples are illustrated in Figure 11-2.

[8] A classic monetarist attempt to reinterpret the meaning of an increase in unemployment is Milton Friedman, "Unemployment Figures," *Newsweek,* October 20, 1969,

The Monetarist Platform and the Nonmonetarist Response

The Monetarist Platform

Plank 1: Without the interference of demand shocks introduced by erratic government policy, private spending would be stable.

Plank 2: Even if private planned spending is not completely stable, flexible prices create a natural tendency for it to come back on course.

Plank 3: Even if private planned spending is not completely stable, and prices are not completely flexible, an activist monetary and fiscal policy to counteract private demand swings is likely to do more harm than good.

Plank 4: Even if prices are not completely flexible, so that the economy can wander away from U^* in the short run, there can be no dispute regarding the increased flexibility of prices, the longer the period of time allowed for adjustment.

The Nonmonetarist Response

Plank 1: Shifts in business and consumer attitudes and expectations represent a substantial source of economic instability that should be countered by offsetting monetary and fiscal policy actions.

Plank 2: Prices are relatively inflexible downward, as illustrated by the failure of prices to decline during the last half of the the decade of the 1930s despite extraordinarily high unemployment.

Plank 3: Although there is no denying that monetary and fiscal policy have been destabilizing in particular past episodes, economic knowledge is now sufficiently advanced to allow countercyclical monetary and fiscal policy actions to stabilize the economy in the face of destabilizing swings in private demand.

Plank 4: The period of time required for flexible prices to bring the economy automatically back to U^* is intolerably long, and there is no reason for government policymakers to tolerate the persistence of high unemployment and low levels of output that occur in the meantime.

refuse to accept as a characterization either disregard for unemployment or excessive concern for inflation.[9]

In some recession situations of high unemployment, as occurred in 1975 in the United States, the monetarist distaste for activist policy would appear to condemn the economy to a longer recession than the alternative nonmonetarist approach of monetary or fiscal stimulation. Yet monetarists deny that their recommendation reflects a choice be-

reprinted in his *An Economist's Protest,* Second Edition (Glen Ridge: Thomas Horton, 1975), pp. 105–07. An extended answer to Friedman's article is Robert J. Gordon, "The Welfare Cost of Higher Unemployment," *Brookings Papers on Economic Activity,* vol. 4, no. 1 (1973), pp. 133–95.

[9] The first draft of this book did contain such a characterization as a fifth plank of the monetarist platform. When Milton Friedman read that draft, he agreed with the first four planks but objected to the fifth. The interpretation in the next paragraph is based on a conversation with him in March 1977, and some of the wording is adapted from suggestions in a letter from him written in June 1977.

tween more or less unemployment now, but only between a lesser reduction in unemployment now and a greater increase in unemployment later. Why? They distrust the political process, which is said to throw up great obstacles to the achievement of sensible economic policy. The economy is bound to overshoot any target, they would argue, and politicians are unlikely to have the courage to apply the brakes to the economy soon enough to allow a "soft landing" at the target unemployment rate. Instead, the economy will be allowed to expand too far and too rapidly,

Milton Friedman

"If Milton Friedman had not existed, it would have been necessary to invent him," wrote his fellow *Newsweek* columnist, Paul Samuelson. For many years, Friedman was a brilliant and outspoken gadfly who challenged from the outside many of the most cherished propositions of establishment economics and helped to keep economics a lively and controversial subject. In the last decade, Friedman has had the satisfaction of seeing many of his long-held beliefs adopted as part of the mainstream.

Friedman's scholarly activity as a professor has centered in monetary economics. Starting his work in the late 1940's when fiscal policy was in its prime and monetary policy was viewed as impotent, Friedman almost single-handedly restored money to the center of the macroeconomic analysis. In his 850 page treatise (co-authored with Anna J. Schwartz) *A Monetary History of the United States* (1963), he argued that United States business cycles were attributable to excessive fluctuations in the supply of money, and that the Federal Reserve was responsible for the severity of the Great Depression because it allowed the money supply to drop by almost one-third between 1929 and 1933. Almost as influential was Friedman's *A Theory of the Consumption Function* (1957), which held that short-run changes in income had a much smaller impact on consumption spending than in Keynesian theory, implying that the economy's inherent stability was greater than had been realized

Camera Press from NYT Pictures

(see Chapter 13). In his Presidential address to the American Economic Association, Friedman introduced the then heretical natural rate hypothesis of unemployment, which has since been accepted by most economists (see Chapter 8).[a]

Much of the scholarship responsible for the renaissance of money took place in Friedman's Money and Banking workshop at the University of Chicago, where for 25 years (1952–1976) graduate students and visitors presented papers to receive Friedman's suggestions, approval, or disapproval. The work-

[a] "The Role of Monetary Policy," *American Economic Review*, vol. 58 (March 1968), pp. 1–15.

inflation will accelerate, and the Federal Reserve will be forced to cause another recession and bout of unemployment to fight the renewed acceleration of inflation.

In the end the basic conflicts in policy recommendations by economists do not originate in irreconcilable analytical differences that call into question the scientific claims of economics. Most economists now accept the basic theoretical framework summarized in the *IS-LM* analysis of income determination (Chapters 3–6) and the Phillips curve analysis

shop was almost always stimulating, even if the paper being presented was not, in which case Friedman would explain to confused participants what they had really meant to say, what the issues of dispute really were, and what he thought about aspects of present policy and past history.

Unlike many economists of his brilliance and reputation, Friedman chose not to participate in active policymaking in Washington. Nevertheless, his policy proposals, particularly his emphasis on maintaining steady growth in monetary aggregates, have gradually won adherents in Washington, including his old undergraduate teacher Arthur Burns, Chairman of the Board of Governors of the Federal Reserve Board during 1972–1978. One of the regional Federal Reserve Banks in St. Louis has been dominated by Friedman's disciples and has contributed much of the empirical work to support his emphasis on monetary policy as a source of economic instability.

But Friedman is no narrow monetary specialist. His broader aim has been to support individual liberty and oppose every aspect of government intervention in individual affairs, from the military draft, to compulsory social security and public education, to auto safety and drug regulations, chaotic welfare systems, fixed exchange rates, and controls on wages, prices, rents, and interest rates. His libertarian and antigovernment position is an outgrowth of themes emphasized by his teachers in graduate school in the 1930's at the University of Chicago. Since his return there as a teacher in the late 1940's, he has been a leader of the

"Chicago School" of economics, which stands in opposition to the activist government intervention espoused by most leading economists at eastern universities, largely on the grounds that many government policies hurt those they were designed to help and vice versa.

The best introduction to Friedman's views on government regulation is his classic *Capitalism and Freedom* (1962). His basic position is applied to a wide range of current problems in a collection of his *Newsweek* columns, *An Economist's Protest* (Second Edition, 1975). Born in 1912, Friedman decided to retire from the University of Chicago in early 1977. In his last quarter at Chicago, he received the Nobel Memorial Prize in economics, a tribute that many thought should have come earlier. He lives now for half the year in Vermont in a beautiful mountaintop home called "Capitaf" (for "Capitalism and Freedom"), and for the rest of the year in San Francisco, where he continues scholarly work on U.S. and U.K. monetary history at Stanford's Hoover Institute. Wherever he is, he is kept busy answering a flood of correspondence and writing the columns that grace the pages of *Newsweek* every third week.[b]

---

[b] Friedman has not been immune to criticism. See the essays by Tobin and Patinkin in Robert J. Gordon, ed., *Milton Friedman's Monetary Framework* (Chicago: University of Chicago Press, 1974). Also, see several of James Tobin's collected essays, cited in his biography in this chapter.

Franco Modigliani

Born in Rome in 1918, Modigliani emigrated to the United States at the outbreak of World War II. Nevertheless, it did not take him long to make his mark. In his classic article, "Liquidity Preference and the Theory of Interest and Money," he presented the first formal theoretical analysis that integrated monetary factors into Keynesian analysis.[a] In retrospect it is ironic that Modigliani, now considered one of the two or three leading "nonmonetarists," presented the first modern analysis of the role of money in the Keynesian system.

Several of Modigliani's other articles rank among the most influential of the postwar era. He invented (with R. Brumberg) the "life-cycle" hypothesis of consumption, which shares with Friedman's "permanent income hypothesis" the ability to explain why the marginal propensity to consume is inversely proportional to income at any given moment, but remains steady over long historical periods as society becomes richer (see Chapter 13). With various co-authors he wrote several seminal articles and a book on a mathematical approach to production and employment scheduling in business. With Merton Miller of the University of Chicago, he proved the controversial "Modigliani-Miller" theorem of corporate finance, which states that the value of a corporation is independent of its ratio of debt to equity. More recently his interests have spread even wider into international finance and capital theory.

Modigliani's career shifted from a theoretical to an empirical orientation with the advent of rapid electronic computers and with his move to MIT in 1962. Aided by a succession of bright MIT students, Modigliani, together with Albert Ando of the University of Pennsylvania, designed and built an elaborate computer model of the U.S. economy, in which he attempted to incorporate empirical estimates

of the several channels by which money influences income. Recently Modigliani and others have used the model, now renamed "MPS," to attack the pro-monetarist conclusions of Friedman's monetarist disciples, and to confirm that both monetary and fiscal policy changes influence the level of real GNP.[b]

Unlike many emigrants, Modigliani has retained his connection with his home country. Many of his articles have been written in Italian, and he has recently studied the latest evidence on wage behavior and the consumption function in Italy.

Modigliani is almost unique among contemporary economists in the contagious enthusiasm he conveys to his students about a wide range of topics in economics, and his generosity in granting co-authorships to those who help him investigate them. Although many of his nonmonetarist contemporaries have been kept on the defensive by the Monetarist Counterrevolution, Modigliani has succeeded in increasing his stature by his feverish energy in scrutinizing a wide range of propositions— whatever their origin.

---

[a] *Econometrica,* vol. 12 (January 1944), pp. 45–88.

[b] MPS=MIT-Penn-Social Science Research Council. Quarterly forecasts with the model are produced by Albert Ando and others at the University of Pennsylvania.

James Tobin

Born in 1918, James Tobin became a superstar in the economics firmament soon after he emerged with his Ph.D. from Harvard in 1947. Noted for his role in opening up new areas of research and discussion in monetary economics, Tobin in recent years has become the outspoken arch-opponent of Milton Friedman's analysis of monetary problems and of his opposition to activist government intervention.

Tobin, who has been a professor at Yale throughout his career, differs from Keynes and Friedman in that he has never been sole author of a book. His fame stems from his articles written for a wide range of publications, and particularly his scholarly papers. After beginning his career with a series of articles on issues in the Keynesian theory of consumption and wages, and on problems in estimating statistical demand functions for food, he turned to monetary theory. Among his most noted articles are three written in the 1950's: "The Interest-Elasticity of Transactions Demand for Cash," which showed that the interest-sensitivity of the demand for money could be de-

Camera Press from NYT Pictures

rived independently of Keynes' speculative motive; "Liquidity Preference as Behavior Towards Risk," which introduced the crucial idea of risk aversion into the economic analysis of asset management and the demand for money; and "A Dynamic Aggregative Model," one of the first models of economic growth.

(continued)

of Chapter 8 based on shifting expectations of inflation. The dispute over planks 1 and 3 is not a matter of right or wrong but of differences in emphasis, perhaps the most important of which is the greater nonmonetarist willingness to trust the government to follow the advice of economists, as contrasted to the fundamental distrust of the political process exhibited by monetarists.[10] Plank 2 on the flexibility of prices remains in dispute because the historical data do not send strong signals that would allow economists to predict the speed of adjustment of inflation to higher unemployment. Finally, the disagreement over plank 4, on the importance of the short run as opposed to the long run, reflects not only differing value judgments but also differing degrees of optimism regarding the pay-off of short-run policy shifts.

---

[10] What is the fundamental cause of this contrast? There is a chicken-and-egg problem of determining which of these statements is closer to the truth: (1) Does the preponderance of nonmonetarists in important policymaking posts in Washington lead them to greater faith in the ability of the government to do the right thing? (2) Or does the absence of monetarists in leading policy positions reflect their own unwillingness to associate themselves with policymaking functions that they feel are inherently destabilizing.

In the 1960's Tobin continued to convert economic loose ends into brilliantly concise analysis. He wrote classic articles on how the government debt should be managed and how the government debt affects the demand for money; what makes commercial banks different from other financial institutions; how government policy should attempt to influence the nation's output growth rate; and how money affects the long-run growth of the economy.

Tobin has not confined his attention to the narrow area of monetary economics. Unlike Friedman, he went to Washington and participated in the economic policymaking process as a member of the President's Council of Economic Advisers in 1961–62, and as a consultant to the Council for many years thereafter. He took a particular interest in the economic status of black Americans and in the poverty problem in general. Though he disagrees with Milton Friedman on many issues in monetary economics, he shares with Friedman early support for the idea of a guaranteed annual income in the form of the negative income tax.

As an articulate exponent of government activism to achieve economic stability and one of the original designers of the Kennedy-Johnson economic philosophy, Tobin has been placed on the defensive in the last decade by the Monetarist Counterrevolution. Several of his scholarly articles during this period have been critiques of the work of Milton Friedman. Tobin's comments and Friedman's rejoinders make lively reading, but it is hard to avoid the impression that the consensus within the economic profession has been drifting in Friedman's direction. Tobin continues to have faith, perhaps too much, in the wise and omniscient government that would solve most problems if it would only do the right thing.[a]

---

[a] A collection of Tobin's essays is contained in *Macroeconomics—Volume 1* (Chicago: Markham Publishing Company, 1971). See also his exchange with Friedman in the volume cited in Friedman's biography, and also a critical review essay, Herschel I. Grossman, "Tobin on Macroeconomics," *Journal of Political Economy,* vol. 83 (August 1975), pp. 829–48.

12-4 SOURCES OF INSTABILITY IN PRIVATE PLANNED SPENDING

The basic aim of stabilization policy is to keep the actual unemployment rate equal to the natural rate of unemployment (U^*), that unemployment rate which is consistent with a continuation of inflation at its present rate without any acceleration or deceleration. Real output should be kept equal to the economy's natural output level, the amount of output that the economy can produce each year when its unemployment rate is kept equal to U^*. Natural output, or GNP, illustrated as the black line at the top of Figure 12-1, grows each year by about 3.5 percent, as technological progress, capital accumulation, and growth in the labor force all work together to raise the amount the economy can produce when unemployment is equal to U^*.

How successfully has actual real GNP (Q) been kept equal to natural GNP (Q^*)? The postwar record illustrated in Figure 12-1 is decidedly mixed. Although mass unemployment has been avoided, and no repetition of the Great Depression has been experienced, nevertheless Q has diverged repeatedly from Q^*, sometimes for many years in the same direction. Between 1957 and 1964, Q was continuously below Q^*, reaching shortfalls of almost 6 percent in the recessions of 1958 and 1961. On the other hand, between 1966 and 1969 the reverse was true. For four straight years Q overshot and remained 3 percent or more too high. The worst year of all was 1975, when Q dropped more than 8 percent below Q^*.

GOVERNMENT SPENDING

Three expenditure components that contributed to unstable actual output growth are illustrated in Figure 12-1. Monetarists are correct that much of the postwar instability has been contributed by uneven changes in real government expenditures on goods and services (G). Any component of total real spending tends to destabilize total GNP if it grows appreciably faster or slower than the 4 percent annual growth of natural output.[11] But real government spending (G) has grown in fits and starts. The most notable episode of erratic growth occurred during the Korean War, when G increased by 74 percent in the interval 1950–53. The Vietnam War buildup caused another period of rapid growth, 24 percent between 1965 and 1968. On the other hand, G did not grow at all between 1968 and 1975.

Nonmonetarists protest any attempt by the monetarists to discredit stabilization policy by pointing to erratic growth in G in Figure 12-1. "Erratic G growth is just one of many reasons why we need activist stabilization policy," reply the nonmonetarists. "Wartime bursts in defense spending result from political decisions, not economic ones, and it is the job of stabilization policy to recommend offsetting actions that will keep the wartime expenditures from causing total actual output to overshoot Q^*. Tax increases and tight monetary policy are appropriate activist actions to be taken in wartime situations."

PRIVATE SPENDING

Nonmonetarists then point to the behavior of the other two series plotted in Figure 12-1, fixed investment (I) and consumer purchases of durable goods (C_D), as evidence against plank 1 of the monetarist platform. Private spending does not tend to grow steadily each year at 3 or 4 percent, but tends to exhibit periods of a few years of boom followed by

---

[11] A $1.00 change in government spending may cause GNP to change by more or less than $1.00, depending on how the government spending is financed (by taxes, borrowing, or money creation) and on the slopes of the IS and LM curves. See section 5-6.

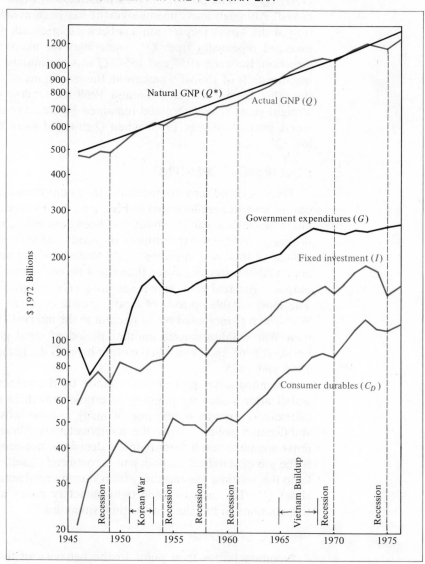

FIGURE 12–1 Actual and Natural Real GNP, and the Real Values of Government Spending, Fixed Investment, and Consumer Durable Expenditures, 1946–76

Fluctuations in government spending (G) were about as important as shifts in fixed investment (I) and consumer durable expenditures (C_D) in contributing to economic instability. The scale is logarithmic (Section 1–2), so the steeper increases and decreases in the G, I, and C_D lines than in the

several years of slump. Fixed investment (I) grew 13.4 percent between 1954 and 1956, but then increased only 3.7 percent between 1956 and 1961. Then came an investment boom that pulled I up by 44 percent between 1961 and 1966. Another boom and bust cycle occurred between 1970 and 1975, with I first rising by 27 percent in 3 years and then falling right back to 1975 by its 1970 level.

But businessmen who make investment decisions are not uniquely to blame for the instability of private spending. There is very little difference in Figure 12-1 between the behavior of the fixed investment series (I) and that plotted directly below, consumer expenditures on durable goods (C_D, about half automobiles, the remaining half appliances, furniture, and other products). The most notable instance of instability occurred in 1955, when C_D grew by exactly 20 percent in one year! After that year C_D growth became stagnant until 1962. It is true, as monetarists may argue, that at least some of the fluctuations in I and C_D are due to disturbances introduced by the government. For instance controls on consumer credit held down C_D during the Korean War, and their elimination partly caused the 1955 spending boom.

The instability of fixed investment and consumer durable spending lies at the heart of the nonmonetarist case in favor of an activist stabilization policy. Short, sharp fluctuations in private planned spending would not be terribly serious if they lasted only six or nine months. But the behavior of I and C_D in Figure 12-1 indicates that periods of boom or bust tend to persist. Both I and C_D were weak between 1958 and 1961 and both were strong through most of the 1960s.

Plank 2 of the monetarist platform states that even if private spending is unstable, flexible prices will come to the rescue. When private demand is too high, prices will rise to choke off undesirable spending, and when private demand is weak, prices will fall (or at least rise slower) to stimulate spending. This monetarist proposition was examined quite carefully in Chapter 11, where we found that it takes many years for inflation to slow down when private demand is weak. Figure 11-5 showed that in the

actual output line indicate that the three spending components were more unstable than total real spending. The major component left out, consumer spending on nondurables and services, was a stabilizing factor during the period.

Sources: Actual and Natural Real Output, see Appendix B. Spending Components (G, I, and C_D). U.S. Department of Commerce, *Survey of Current Business,* various issues.

seven years between 1957 and 1964 when actual output was below natural output, the inflation rate fell by only three percentage points at an annual rate. Nonmonetarists ask, "Why should we patiently wait for five years for the slowdown in inflation to stabilize real output? Even if stimulative monetary and fiscal policy take as long as one year to affect spending, that time lag sure beats the monetarist recommendation that we play a long waiting game."

12-5 STABILIZATION TARGETS AND INSTRUMENTS IN THE ACTIVISTS' PARADISE

THE NEED FOR MULTIPLE INSTRUMENTS

When the driver of a car has a destination to reach on a map, he is trying to hit two targets, a particular latitude (north-south position) and a specific longitude (east-west position). To reach these two targets, he needs two basic instruments in his car, an engine to move him forward or back and a steering wheel to move him left or right. Similarly, an airplane pilot attempts to maintain three targets, latitude, longitude, and altitude. In addition to an engine and a steering wheel, he needs a third instrument (his elevators) to move him up or down. An airplane lacking any device to move up or down might achieve the desired longitude and latitude, but it would fail miserably in achieving its desired altitude.

Stabilization policy attempts to achieve several targets. Just as for an automobile or an airplane, each target requires at least one instrument of stabilization policy. Several examples of this principle have become evident in earlier chapters. We learned in Chapter 5 that the money supply instrument could not simultaneously achieve both a target level of output and a target interest rate. Both monetary and fiscal policy must be manipulated together to achieve an intersection of the IS and LM curves at a given combination of the interest rate and real output. Then in Chapter 8 we learned that monetary and fiscal policy together cannot achieve any desired level of real output after all. The long-run level of natural output Q^* is limited to the output the economy can produce at the natural rate of unemployment (U^*). Any higher level of output achieved by monetary and fiscal policy will result in higher prices rather than higher output after a transition period.

Monetary and fiscal policy acting together are the two main instruments that control adjusted demand growth ($\hat{y}$) and the interest rate.[12]

---

[12] The nominal interest rate (i) consists of an inflation component (p) and a real interest rate component (r): $i = r + p$. In the long run, inflation must be equal to adjusted demand growth. The real interest rate can be influenced by fiscal policy; high deficits tend to raise the real interest rate, and vice versa.

In the long run the unemployment rate target is beyond the control of monetary and fiscal policy. A permanent reduction in unemployment requires a permanent drop in the natural rate of unemployment, which requires in turn a separate instrument. That instrument is the mixture of manpower policy tools discussed in Chapter 9 — reform of unemployment compensation, training subsidies to firms, and so on.

But we are not finished yet. Fiscal policy really consists of two types of policy instruments: government spending and tax rates. A given government deficit can be achieved with high spending and high tax rates or low spending and low tax rates. Thus within fiscal policy the mixture between spending and tax rates determines yet another target of policy, the division of total real output between public and private spending.

So far we are up to four instruments and four targets:

Instruments	*Targets*
Manpower policy	Unemployment rate
Monetary policy	Inflation rate
Government spending	Interest rate
Tax rates	Division of real output between public and private spending

A more complete illustration of the principles of economic policy is Figure 12-2. The goal of economic policy is economic welfare, represented by the box in the upper right corner of Figure 12-2. Social welfare can be thought of as simply happiness, the things that individual members of society want — stable prices, full employment, and a high standard of living.

TARGETS, INSTRUMENTS, AND STRUCTURAL RELATIONS

Looking left from the social welfare box in Figure 12-2 we find a box that lists the main policy target variables that influence social welfare. Some are more important than others. The health of the balance of payments or the level of the foreign exchange rate is not very interesting in itself unless foreign factors begin to prevent the achievement of other domestic goals, as in the 1970s in Britain, Italy, and other countries. The distribution of income is a target quite different from the others; any policy shift that raises the income of one group at the expense of others (rich versus poor; creditors versus debtors) is bound to be controversial and lead to political conflict. Almost every proposal for a change in tax rates excites disagreement because of its implications for the distribution of income. The interest rate is not listed separately as a target variable because its level is mainly relevant for growth in natural output. Low in-

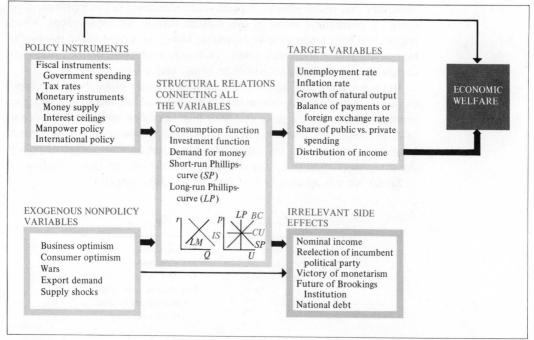

FIGURE 12-2   A Flow Chart Showing the Relation Between Policy Instruments, Policy Targets, and Economic Welfare

Both policy instruments and exogenous nonpolicy variables are ingredients fed into the structural relations that connect the exogenous (policy and nonpolicy) variables with the endogenous (target and nontarget) variables. Total economic welfare at the upper right depends on the achieved values of the target variables, and thus it depends in turn on the decisions of policymakers on the settings of the policy instruments.

terest rates stimulate investment and the growth of capital inputs, in turn raising the growth rate of output.[13]

   In the upper left corner of Figure 12-2 is a list of some of the policy instruments that the government can use to try to achieve the targets. The upper left instrument box is linked with the upper right target box through the large central box containing the structural relations that link the variables. The CU, BC, SP, and LP curves of Chapter 8 summarize the main relations that link money, taxes, and government spending to unemployment and inflation. But those curves can be shifted as well by

---

[13] An introduction to these and other targets is Arthur M. Okun, "Conflicting National Goals," in Eli Ginsberg (ed.), *Jobs for Americans* (Englewood Cliffs, N.J.: Prentice-Hall, 1976).

several exogenous factors not under the direct control of policymakers, as by a burst of business or consumer optimism or higher export sales (shifting the CU and BC curves upward) or a supply shock (shifting the SP curve upward). Wars have also been listed in the exogenous rather than the instrument box, because the level of government spending in wartime is almost always set in accord with the goals of military strategy rather than economic stabilization, and in fact wars almost always represent an undesirable interference with the goals of stabilization policy.

Exogenous and instrument variables are ingredients in the structural economic relations in the middle box and yield particular values of the target variables — unemployment, inflation, and the others. Other variables are also affected, called irrelevant in the lower right rectangle because they are not major determinants of social welfare. No one cares about the level of nominal income ($Y = PQ$), but people do care about the inflation rate and unemployment rate that a particular level of nominal spending in part determines. Other irrelevant side effects may be the victory or defeat of politicians, of economic theories, and of academic institutions; these are irrelevant consequences for society as a whole, even if the individuals involved may care a lot about the outcome.

MONETARISM AND THE ACTIVISTS' PARADISE

Monetarists oppose activist countercyclical swings in the money supply and think that the economy will be better off with a **Constant Growth Rate Rule** ($CGRR$) for the money supply.[14] They have also argued for a constant rule for fiscal policy, a flexible exchange rate to meet the international target, and numerous measures to raise the economy's efficiency (eliminating minimum wages, tariffs, and other forms of government price-fixing and intervention).

What do monetarists respond when faced with the instability of government and private real spending plotted in Figure 12-1? This looks like fairly convincing evidence of the weakness of planks 1 and 2 of the monetarist platform (the stability of private spending and the ability of flexible prices to correct any instability). At this stage monetarists move on to plank 3, which says that stabilization policy may do more harm than good. "Nonmonetarist economists," they claim, "require a utopian set of assumptions about the economy if they expect an activist stabilization policy to do more good than harm."

---

[14] When he received his Nobel Prize in December 1976, Milton Friedman remarked that it was no thanks to him that the Central Bank of Sweden, which donated the money for his prize, still exists. "My monetary studies have led me to the conclusion that central banks could profitably be replaced by computers geared to provide a steady rate of growth in the quantity of money. Fortunately for me personally, and for a select group of fellow economists, that conclusion has had no practical impact . . . else there would have been no Central Bank of Sweden to have established the award I am honored to receive. Should I draw the moral that sometimes to fail is to succeed?" (Quote from the mimeographed text of the remarks, provided by the author.)

The utopian "activists' paradise" is a hypothetical world in which activist policy could achieve almost perfect control over total aggregate demand. It has these main characteristics:[15]

1. Ability by policymakers to forecast perfectly future changes in the private demand for and supply of goods and services.
2. Ability by policymakers to forecast perfectly the future effect of current changes in monetary and fiscal policy.
3. Possession by policymakers of policy instruments that powerfully affect aggregate demand.
4. Absence of any costs of changing policy instruments.
5. No political constraints on using the policy instruments for the desired purposes.

In the following sections we will find that there is reason to doubt the validity of several of the characteristics necessary for activist stabilization policy to achieve perfect control over aggregate demand. The argument for activist government intervention must be that imperfect activist control is better than the monetarist approach, not that activist control is perfect.

12-6 CASE STUDY: THE PERFORMANCE OF U.S. FORECASTERS IN THE 1970s

The first characteristic of the activists' paradise is the ability of forecasters to foresee perfectly future changes in demand and supply. The ability to look into the future is required by the time lag in the effect of policy changes. An increase in the money supply in December 1979 may not have its main influence on spending until the fall of 1980. Thus policymakers must be able to look ahead to determine whether private demand in the fall of 1980 is likely to be too high or too low.

United States forecasters experienced some dramatic failures in the early 1970s, as illustrated in Figure 12-3. The diagram compares the actual growth rate of nominal income (y), real output (q), and the GNP price deflator (p) with the change predicted one year in advance of the illustrated date by five well-known forecasting organizations. Most of these forecasters sell their forecasts to business firms and have every incentive to take account of all relevant factors that might affect the economy in the coming year.

As an example, in the upper left corner of the diagram we see that in the year ending in the first quarter of 1971 (1971:Q1) nominal GNP

---

[15] The term "activists' paradise" and its major characteristics originate in Arthur M. Okun, "Fiscal-Monetary Activism: Some Analytical Issues," *Brookings Papers on Economic Activity,* vol. 3, no. 1 (1972), pp. 123–63. The rest of this chapter relies heavily on Okun's analysis of the arguments for and against activism.

actually increased by 7.2 percent (the actual y line), whereas the median (middle) forecast made one year earlier (in 1970:Q1) had been for an increase of 6.2 percent (this is the value for predicted y plotted for 1971:Q1). Through the middle of 1972 forecasts of nominal income growth (y) made a year earlier were fairly accurate, but then began a five-quarter period when actual y substantially exceeded the previously forecasted values. The maximum error occurred in the year ending in 1973:Q1, when actual y was 12.2 percent compared to a forecast growth of 9.9 percent.

Was poor forecasting responsible for the excessive aggregate demand growth that pushed the actual unemployment rate in the bottom frame well below the natural rate of unemployment between late 1972 and early 1974? Although the high growth rate of y was not predicted well, much of the error in the first three quarters of 1973 was accounted for by the failure to foresee the acceleration of inflation. The portion of nominal income growth (y) left over after taking out inflation — real output growth (q) — was fairly well predicted for the year ending in 1973:Q3, as was the unemployment rate for that quarter. Thus the overshooting of the economy in 1973, as reflected in the decline of actual unemployment (U) well below the natural rate (U^*), was caused not by bad forecasting, but by the unwillingness or inability of policymakers to restrain aggregate demand growth.

FAILURE OF FORECASTING

The real failure of forecasting occurred in early 1974. At that time the year-ahead forecasts for 1975:Q1 overpredicted y and q by record amounts. As a result, inflation was the only major problem that was forecast as requiring policy action. Unemployment was predicted to rise only slightly. Because inflation was predicted to be high, the forecasts suggested to policymakers that restraint rather than stimulation of aggregate demand was appropriate. In fact the early fall of 1974 witnessed President Ford's WIN (Whip Inflation Now) program in which the main emphasis was on restraining demand.

Yet what happened? Real output growth turned out to be −5.6 percent in the year ending in 1975:Q1, as opposed to the +2.2 percent forecast, and unemployment soared during that year from 4.9 percent in 1974:Q1 to 8.7 percent in 1975:Q2. Although there is no way to prevent a supply shock from raising both unemployment and inflation simultaneously, most nonmonetarist economists feel in retrospect that some policy stimulus should have been applied in 1974.

Why did these serious forecasting errors occur? Any economic forecast that is more than a simple guess requires three main ingredients, all of which are depicted in Figure 12-2:

1. First, a guess must be made about the settings of the various policy instruments. Often forecasters make several forecasts. An initial

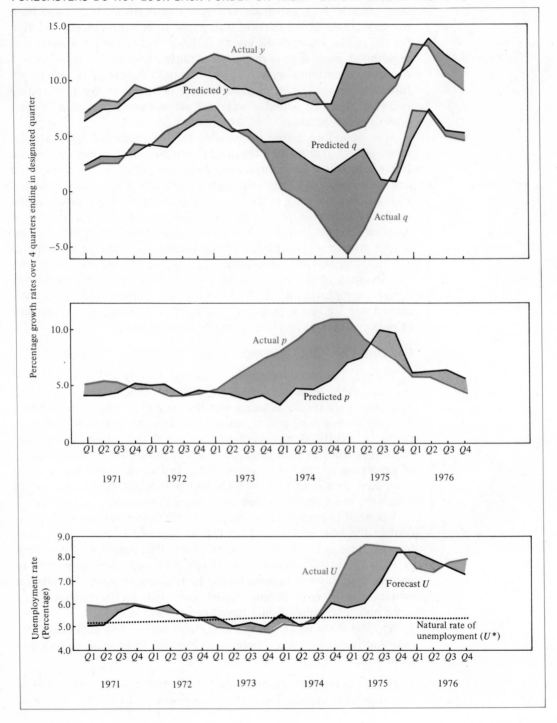

control forecast is made that assumes that policy remains unchanged, for instance, that tax rates remain fixed, that government spending equals the most recent administration estimate for the federal government budget, and that the growth rate of the money supply is the same over the following year as it has been during the past year. Then additional forecasts may be made that vary these policy assumptions in specified ways.

2. Second, a guess must be made about the values of the nonpolicy exogenous variables. Among these, as depicted in Figure 12-2, are export demand, supply shocks, and any special aspects of business and consumer optimism that might invalidate the consumption function and investment function of the forecasting model.

3. Third, there must be a structural model that ties together the structural exogenous variables, the policy instruments, and target variables. In the first part of this book we developed a simple version of such a model. Modern forecasting uses **econometric models** that estimate the values of the parameters by statistical study on electronic computers of past historical episodes.

Example: If the computer calculates that on average in past postwar history a $1.00 increase in after-tax disposable income increased consumption spending by $0.90, then the estimated marginal propensity to consume is 0.90.

FIGURE 12-3

Actual and Predicted Values of the Unemployment Rate (U) and of the Growth Rates of Nominal Income (y), Real Output (q), and the GNP Price Deflator (p)

For each of the four variables plotted, the pink areas show the periods when the economy did worse than forecasters had predicted four quarters earlier, with higher inflation and unemployment and lower growth in nominal income and real output. The gray shading designates those periods when the economy did better than forecast. The most important forecasting error was an underprediction of inflation throughout 1973 and 1974. Because nominal income was predicted with fair accuracy before 1975, most of the errors in forecasting inflation caused errors in forecasting real output growth (q) in the opposite direction.

Sources: Actual values are from Appendix B. Forecast values are calculated as the actual values plus the forecast errors reported in Stephen K. McNees, "The Forecasting Performance in the 1970s," a revised 1977 reprint of an article originally appearing in the *New England Economic Review* (July/August 1976). McNees calculated the median error from the four-quarter-ahead forecasts of these forecasters: (1) U.S. Bureau of Economic Analysis; (2) Chase Econometric Associates, Inc.; (3) Data Resources, Inc.; (4) Wharton Econometric Forecasting Associates, Inc.; (5) Median forecast from the Economic Research Survey by the American Statistical Association and the National Bureau of Economic Research.

Econometric models must estimate numerical values for a large number of parameters: the response of money demand to changes in the interest rate and income (the *LM* curve); the response of consumption spending to changes in disposable income and wealth and the response of investment to changes in output and various financial variables (the *IS* curve); the response of inflation to unemployment given expected inflation (the *SP* curve); and other relationships as well.

In the 1974–75 episodes, each of these three elements contributed to the failure of forecasters:

1. Forecasters failed to predict accurately the main instrument of monetary policy, the growth rate of the money supply. The money supply grew scarcely at all between June and December 1974, an event that was not foreseen.[16]

2. As shown in Figure 12-3, forecasters failed miserably in predicting the unprecedented acceleration of inflation in 1974. Part of this error resulted from the surprise nature of the 1974 supply shocks that raised the prices of oil and food. But another part resulted from the failure to foresee that the termination of price controls in April 1974 would lead to a period of large price increases as firms attempted to boost their prices back to the levels that they would have charged in the absence of controls.

3. How flawed were the econometric structural models? So far there has been little systematic research that would answer this question.[17] My guess is that the forecasters' models would have been reasonably adequate if the tight setting of the monetary instruments and the 1974 acceleration of inflation had been accurately foreseen. But in every postwar recession forecasters have failed to foresee the sharpness of the recession drop in real GNP, primarily because they do not have accurate methods of forecasting the exact timing of the involuntary inventory accumulation and subsequent production cuts by businessmen when their sales fall.[18]

FORECASTING AND ACTIVISM

Does the forecasting record of the 1970s support the nonmonetarist case for activism or the monetarist case for a monetary rule? Despite the large errors made, forecasters almost always managed to forecast

---

[16] This statement refers to $M1$, the total of currency and demand deposits.

[17] An early paper that reviews the first stages of the 1974–75 recession is Arthur M. Okun, "A Postmortem of the 1974 Recession," *Brookings Papers on Economic Activity,* vol. 6, no. 1 (1975), pp. 207–21. Okun's paper does not perform any restrospective tests that would reveal the sources of errors in econometric forecasts. See also F. M. Mishkin, "What Depressed the Consumer: The Household Balance Sheet in the 1973–75 Recession," *Brookings Papers on Economic Activity,* vol. 8, no. 1 (1977), pp. 123–64.

[18] The role of involuntary inventory accumulation and decumulation in a simple economic model is the subject of section 3-4.

correctly one year in advance whether unemployment would be above or below the natural unemployment rate (U^*). A nonmonetarist policymaker who slowed the growth of aggregate demand during the quarters when unemployment was forecast to fall below U^* and stimulated the economy when unemployment was forecast to be above U^* would have stabilized unemployment, as compared to an alternative monetarist policymaker who simply maintained a fixed predetermined growth rate of aggregate demand (y).[19] The major flaw in this argument is that there was no agreement in the early 1970s on the value of U^*. Most policy discussions assumed that it was safe to push unemployment down to the range of 4.5 percent, a rate that now appears to have been too low.

Another feature of the 1970s record is that the forecast values of unemployment almost always deviated less from U^* than the actual unemployment outcomes. Thus an activist stabilization policy that always acted to push unemployment back to U^* would have pushed the economy in the correct direction. But it is not enough to say that activist policy could have pushed the economy in the right direction. The crucial question is precisely by how much should policy have been changed? If a policy move was in the right direction but was overdone, the result might have been a more unstable unemployment rate than with a steady monetarist policy.

More generally policymakers should conduct stabilization policy as if their forecasts are correct. As Arthur Okun makes the case, "so long as forecast errors are distributed symmetrically on the up side and the down side, the middle of the target is the place to aim even though the bull's eye will not always be hit."[20] But again uncertainty about the effects of policy actions temper this conclusion; policymakers should not attempt to close the entire gap between current income and the target level.

12-7 UNCERTAINTY ABOUT THE INFLUENCE OF POLICY

Chapters 3–5 developed a set of multiplier formulas indicating the size of the change in real GNP that would result from a change in a policy instrument, such as tax rates, government spending, or the money supply. But the *IS-LM* models summarized in those chapters were very simple.

---

[19] We will see in Chapter 15 that the monetarist prescription that calls for stabilization of the growth rate of money does not automatically lead to stabilization of the growth of aggregate demand.

[20] Okun, "Fiscal-Monetary Activism: Some Analytical Issues," *Brookings Papers on Economic Activity,* vol. 3, no. 1 (1972), summary, p. 8.

In practice, each builder of **econometric models** chooses a different way of elaborating the *IS-LM* textbook model to make it more realistic. Some estimate separate equations for several components of consumption spending; others for only one. Each model differs on many other choices, for instance, which interest rate to relate to the demand for money and to the demand for investment goods. These small differences add up to quite substantial disagreement about the multipliers for changes in different policy instruments.

In the early chapters of this book we also simplified the exposition of income determination by ignoring the time lag between changes in policy instruments and the resulting effect on the target variables. An essential part of the monetarist case against activism is that the lags in the effects of policy changes are likely to be both long and variable.[21]

Figure 12-4 illustrates several sets of **dynamic multipliers** calculated from various econometric models of the economy. The horizontal axis is successive quarters after the policy change. For each model the graph shows the cumulative total change in real GNP (Q) caused by a sustained $1 billion increase in real government spending. For instance, the MPS model yields a multiplier that starts out only a bit above 1.0. Because government spending is part of GNP, the multiplier would be exactly 1.0 if there was no stimulus at all to consumption or investment spending in the initial quarter of the increased government spending. Then the MPS multiplier rises to a peak of about 2.4 after seven quarters, reflecting the stimulus of higher income to both consumption and investment. Later, however, the multiplier begins to fall.

What should policymakers do if they predict that the economy needs $15 billion of stimulus to aggregate demand four quarters from now because unemployment is forecast to be higher than desired at that time? The Brookings multiplier for the four-quarter effect is 2.8, implying that an increase in government spending of 15/2.8 or $5.38 billion is needed. At the other extreme, the St. Louis model says that the multiplier after four quarters is only 0.5, implying that an increase in government spending of 15/0.5 or $30 billion is needed. The other models produce multipliers between these extremes.

Although leading nonmonetarists claim to have discredited the St. Louis techniques, the other models still leave policymakers highly uncertain about the size of the policy stimulus needed.[22] Multipliers for other policy instruments, not shown in Figure 12-4, also indicate considerable divergence between the econometric models. Though **multiplier**

---

[21] The most extensive discussion of the monetarist position is Milton Friedman, "The Lag in Effect of Monetary Policy," *Journal of Political Economy,* vol. 69 (October 1961), reprinted in *The Optimum Quantity of Money and Other Essays* (Chicago: Aldine, 1969), pp. 237–60.

[22] The best analyses of the St. Louis multiplier controversy are unfortunately not very comprehensible for undergraduates unless they have taken an introductory course in econometrics. See Alan S. Blinder and Robert M. Solow, "Analytical Foundations of Fiscal

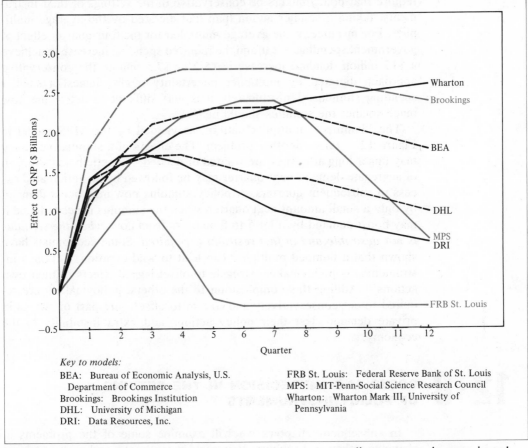

Key to models:

BEA: Bureau of Economic Analysis, U.S.
   Department of Commerce
Brookings: Brookings Institution
DHL: University of Michigan
DRI: Data Resources, Inc.

FRB St. Louis: Federal Reserve Bank of St. Louis
MPS: MIT-Penn-Social Science Research Council
Wharton: Wharton Mark III, University of
   Pennsylvania

FIGURE 12–4   Change in Real GNP Induced by a Permanent $1 Billion Increase in Real Government Nondefense Spending, Estimates of Seven Econometric Models

Each line corresponds to the estimate of a different econometric model. For instance, the line labeled Brookings indicates that, according to the Brookings model, a $1 billion increase in real government nondefense spending causes an increase in real GNP by $1.8 billion in the first quarter, $2.4 billion in the second quarter, and so on. A peak is reached at $2.8 billion in quarters 4–7, after which the impact declines.

Source: Gary Fromm and Lawrence R. Klein, "A Comparison of Eleven Econometric Models of the United States," *American Economic Review,* vol. 63 (May 1973), Table 5, p. 391.

Policy," in *The Economics of Public Finance* (Washington, D.C.: Brookings, 1974), pp. 63–78. Also Franco Modigliani and Albert Ando, "Impacts of Fiscal Actions on Aggregate Income and the Monetarist Controversy: Theory and Evidence," in Jerome Stein (ed.), *Monetarism* (Amsterdam: North-Holland, 1976), pp. 17–42.

uncertainty does not make activist policy intervention impossible, it does require that policymakers be conservative in the settings of their instruments, taking a smaller action than that dictated by the average multiplier. For instance, if the average multiplier for the four-quarter effect of government spending is 2.0, and the required spending increase to achieve a $15 billion demand increase is 15/2 or $7.5 billion, the conservative approach dictated by multiplier uncertainty might suggest a smaller spending stimulus. Unfortunately it is very difficult to determine how much smaller the stimulus should be.[23]

The "humped" multiplier pattern, as yielded by the MPS model in Figure 12-4, raises another problem. The effects of a stimulative policy may linger long after they are wanted or needed. An anticipated shortfall of aggregate demand next quarter may be followed by an anticipated excess in subsequent quarters. A policy stimulus now may boost demand by only a small amount next quarter, when the stimulus is needed, and it may boost demand by a lot 5 to 8 quarters from now, *when the stimulus is not desirable and in fact restraint is required.* Some economists have shown that a humped multiplier can lead to wild gyrations in policy instruments, as policymakers struggle to offset lagged effects of their own actions![24] Adding this complication to the others, policymakers are required to act conservatively and to aim to offset only part of swings in private demand, lest their policy actions add extra instability to the economy.

12-8 COSTS AND IMPRECISION IN THE SETTING OF POLICY INSTRUMENTS

In subsequent chapters we will examine some of the problems in changing policy instruments. It is easy in textbooks and undergraduate examinations to speak loosely about changing government spending, tax rates, and the money supply. But actual policymakers operate in a more complicated world. "Government spending on *what?*" they will ask. Leaf raking? Jet fighter planes? If we need more leaves raked or fighter planes now, why didn't we need them yesterday separately from the requirements of stabilization policy? Almost by definition, the use of spend-

---

[23] See William Brainard in his "Uncertainty and the Effectiveness of Policy," *American Economic Review,* vol. 57 (May 1967), pp. 411–25. Brainard's formula suggests that the expected gap between actual and target GNP should be closed by only a fraction of the gap, but that fraction depends on correlations that we are most unlikely to know. An earlier analysis is Milton Friedman, "The Effects of a Full-Employment Policy on Economic Stability: A Formal Analysis," *Essays in Positive Economics* (Chicago: University of Chicago Press, 1953), pp. 117–32.

[24] Robert S. Holbrook, "Optimal Economic Policy and the Problem of Instrument Instability," *American Economic Review,* vol. 62 (March 1972), pp. 57–65.

ing increases or decreases to stabilize the economy means introducing government programs that were not previously thought to be justified on their own merits or, when policy restraint is required, cutting back on programs that were previously thought desirable.

These disadvantages lead most activist economists to espouse tax changes as the main fiscal instrument of stabilization policy. But there are still details to be resolved. Should taxes be changed for rich people, poor people, or both? Should corporate taxes be altered as well? Should tax changes be temporary or permanent?

The use of monetary policy for stabilization purposes raises problems as well. Some of these problems are faced even by monetarists. Their recommendation that policymakers do nothing by stabilizing the growth rate of the money supply raises the question—which definition of the money supply? Activists need also to remember that a slowdown in monetary growth introduced when aggregate demand is forecast to be too high is likely to raise interest rates and possibly disrupt financial markets, drastically cut home-building expenditures, and even bankrupt building contractors.

Policymakers in Washington do not have levers in their offices that can be turned to precise settings for the level of government spending, tax rates, and the money supply. Thus, added to uncertainty about the size and lags of policy multipliers is further uncertainty about the levels of the policy instruments themselves. In the fall of 1976 economists both inside and outside the administration were puzzled by an apparent shortfall of government spending of $10 billion below the budgeted level. In 1974 effective income tax rates turned out to be higher than forecast, and real disposable income turned out to be lower than forecast, because unexpected inflation pushed taxpayers into higher tax brackets. Finally, the money supply ($M1$) during 1974–75 repeatedly fell below the Federal Reserve's stated policy objectives.

12-9 ACTIVISM, POLITICS, AND THE TIME HORIZON

So far, the proponents of activism concede that the artificial assumptions of the activists' paradise are unrealistic. But they argue that forecasting uncertainty, multiplier uncertainty, lags, and costs and imprecision in the setting of policy instruments call for caution in setting stabilization policy, not its outright abandonment. They feel that the monetarist emphasis on a fixed rule for monetary growth creates too much danger that the economy will be allowed to drift away from policy targets over substantial periods of time. Monetary growth was actually quite stable during the 1970s, but this fairly close adherence to a monetarist rule did not prevent the unprecedented instability in inflation and unemployment that occurred between 1971 and 1976.[25]

Here the debate between monetarists and nonmonetarists turns to the relationship between planks 3 and 4 of the monetarist platform. The inherent obstacles to an effective activist policy combined with the political realities that often cause irrational government behavior (plank 3) lead monetarists to prefer to leave the private economy alone. Even though sluggish price adjustment may imply that the private economy will take a very long time to correct deviations of actual unemployment from the natural unemployment rate, monetarists are willing to wait. Their long time horizon leads them to emphasize long-run consequences and to deemphasize short-run flaws in the performance of the economy (plank 4). Milton Friedman has written most explicitly on the relationship between the long-time horizon of monetarists and their distaste for government intervention:

> The man who has a short time perspective will be impatient with the slow workings of voluntary arrangements in producing changes in institutions. He will want to achieve changes at once, which requires centralized authority that can override objections. Hence he will be disposed to favor a greater role for government. But conversely, the man who favors a greater role for government will thereby be disposed to have a shorter time perspective. Partly, he will be so disposed because centralized government can achieve changes of some kinds rapidly; hence he will feel that if the longer term consequences are adverse, he — through government — can introduce new measures that will counter them, that he can have his cake and eat it. Partly, he will have a short time perspective because the political process demands it. . . . In the political process, an entrepreneur must first get elected in order to be in a position to innovate. To get elected, he must persuade the public in advance. Hence he must look at immediate results that he can offer the public. He may not be able to take a very long time perspective and still hope to be in power.[26]

The monetarists are correct that in some past episodes the absence of fixed rules allowed government actions to destabilize the economy. Perhaps the most famous episode was the failure of President Johnson to recommend a tax increase to finance the upsurge of government expenditures during the Vietnam War buildup. A rule that required a balanced budget would have forced Johnson to recommend the tax increase he

---

[25] Between December 1969 and December 1976 the average growth rate of $M2$ (currency and deposits at commercial banks) was 9.7 percent per year; the maximum deviation in the average December-to-December growth rate in any one year was only 1.5 percent above or below the 9.7 percent average. My own econometric research suggests that at most one-sixth of the acceleration of inflation in 1974 can be attributed to rapid monetary growth in 1971–73. See Robert J. Gordon, "Can the Inflation of the 1970's Be Explained?" *Brookings Papers on Economic Activity*, vol. 8, no. 1 (1977), pp. 253–77.

[26] Milton Friedman, "Why Economists Disagree," in Friedman, *Dollars and Deficits* (Englewood Cliffs, N.J.: Prentice-Hall, 1968), p. 8.

resisted in 1966 for political reasons. Similarly, the economy was allowed to reach too low an unemployment rate in 1966–69, partly because the Federal Reserve accommodated the tax cuts of 1964–65 by creating enough extra money to moderate the higher interest rates that the tax cuts would otherwise have caused. A monetary rule would in retrospect have prevented the creation of the extra money and thus avoided much of the acceleration of inflation in the late 1960s. There would have been a short-run leap in interest rates that would have created a political outcry in 1964–65, but less than the outcry which accompanied the even greater leaps of 1966 and 1969.

Activists agree with the proponents of rules that monetary accommodation in the 1950s and 1960s caused money to move in the same direction as undesired movements in demand and aggravated economic instability. They agree that in some (not all) episodes a rule would have been better. But then they part company with the monetarists by supporting an activist countercyclical policy, the exact opposite of accommodation. Activists would move money in the opposite direction to undesired swings in aggregate demand.

At this point in the debate many economists are willing to turn the floor over to the politicians and their "bosses," the voters. Will the government usually act irresponsibly, as the monetarists predict, overlooking the careful prescriptions of activist advisers in order to win votes in the next election even at the cost of destabilizing the economy? This is a motive many feel was responsible for the undesirable acceleration in monetary growth that occurred in 1972 during President Nixon's reelection campaign. Or can activist economists trust politicians to place economic welfare first, even at the cost of lost votes that may be caused by a timely tax increase or monetary squeeze? There can be no final victor in the monetarist-nonmonetarist debate, because ultimately the nonmonetarists must stake their confidence on the willingness of politicians to do what is needed to stabilize the economy rather than what is politically expedient, a confidence that some politicians may deserve and others may not.

SUMMARY

1. In earlier chapters we assumed that the growth of aggregate demand could be controlled precisely by the monetary and fiscal policymakers. We now recognize that in the real-world economy, policy shifts cannot control aggregate demand instantly or precisely.

2. Most economists recognize the possibility of slippage between policy shifts and the response of demand, but they disagree on the merits of an activist stabilization policy as compared to a policy based on fixed rules.

3. The monetarist-nonmonetarist debate centers on the location in the economy of the principal source of economic instability. Monetarists believe that the private economy is basically stable and that fixed policy rules are necessary to protect the economy from ill-conceived and poorly timed government actions that in the past have caused economic instability. In contrast, the nonmonetarist group considers private spending to be the primary source of instability and hence supports an activist government countercyclical policy to achieve economic stability.

4. Although they recognize the problems introduced by forecasting uncertainty, multiplier uncertainty, lags, and costs and imprecision in the setting of policy instruments, the proponents of activism nevertheless favor caution in setting stabilization policy rather than its outright abandonment. Some monetarists admit that sluggish price adjustment may prolong the adjustment of the economy to insufficient or excess demand, but they are more interested in long-run consequences than short-run transition periods.

5. Both sides agree that monetary accommodation aggravated economic instability in the 1950s and 1960s, when the Fed allowed money to move in the same direction as undesired movements in demand. The monetarists point out that in most of these episodes a rule would have been better than actual policy; the nonmonetarists counter by claiming that an activist countercyclical policy (the opposite of accommodation) would have outperformed both what actually happened and the proposed monetarist fixed rules. But the nonmonetarists have yet to prove that such an activist policy would have been politically feasible.

A LOOK AHEAD

Do decisions made in the private sector stabilize the economy, insulating it from instability stemming from government actions or outside events? Or do private decisions add additional instability that establishes a need for an activist government policy? In the next three chapters we will examine the theory of consumer spending, private investment, and the demand for money. We will find support for the proposition that consumer spending on nondurable goods adds stability to the economy, but that consumer and business spending on durable goods introduces instability.

CONCEPTS AND QUESTIONS

IDENTIFICATIONS

Stabilization policy
Monetarists
Nonmonetarists
Policy targets
Policy instruments

Dynamic multipliers
Econometric forecasts
Multiplier uncertainty
Long and variable lags

1 When the economy is experiencing slack demand, monetarists are usually not willing to accept the long-run costs of higher inflation for the short-run gains in the form of lower unemployment that would result from an expansionary policy. Are the gains from temporary increases in output limited to the short run? Are the costs of inflation limited to the long run? Explain.

2 How can both the monetarists and the nonmonetarists find support for their positions in the erratic growth of government expenditures? Which side do you feel has the stronger case? Why?

3 Must econometric forecasts be precisely correct to be useful for activist countercyclical policy? Why or why not?

4 What problems do long and variable lags present to the policymaker? If lags are long and fixed (rather than long and variable), do any problems remain?

5 For policymaking, is the shape of the dynamic multiplier path of monetary and fiscal changes important or only the size of the total cumulative effect? Explain.

6 There are numerous instances in the postwar economy during which a monetarist rule would have been superior to the policy actually carried out. Can we therefore conclude that we should follow the monetarists' prescription and forget activist policy? Explain.

7 During the first half of the 1970s monetary growth was relatively stable, yet at the same time the inflation and unemployment rates experienced an unprecedented instability. Can we therefore conclude that we should follow the nonmonetarist prescription of activist policy and forget the monetarist rule?

13

Instability in the Private Economy: Consumption

Economists become upset when they learn
that we aren't spending money as they've
planned for us.
—Eliot Marshall[1]

13-1 CONSUMPTION AND ECONOMIC STABILITY

The dispute between monetarist rules and nonmonetarist activism was summarized in Chapter 12 as a monetarist platform. That platform says in essence that (1) the private economy would be basically stable if the government would only leave it alone and (2) government intervention does more harm than good. In this and the next chapter we carefully study the validity of the first part of the monetarist platform. Here we ask, "Does personal consumption spending contribute to economic stability by damping down instability in other forms of spending or does consumption add extra instability of its own?" In Chapter 14 we study the sources of instability in private investment spending.

In the elementary theory of income determination of Chapter 3, consumption spending is a purely passive element. The level of consumption spending was assumed there to be some fixed amount plus a fixed fraction of personal disposable income. In that simple theory did consumption add to economic stability or make stability harder to achieve? In one sense consumption behavior made GNP more unstable, because any $1.00 change in autonomous planned spending had a multiplier effect as extra consumption was induced by higher income, leading to a total change in GNP of several dollars. On the other hand, the passively induced changes in consumption were always completely predictable. If a decrease in private investment had a multiplier of 3.0, so that a $1.00 decrease in investment caused a $3.00 total decrease in GNP (the extra $2.00 consisting of a passively induced drop in consumption), a stable

---

[1] "False Prophets," *New Republic* (October 1, 1977), p. 50.

level of spending could be achieved by an exactly offsetting $1.00 increase in government spending. Consumption did not add to instability in this case, because the multiplier effect of private investment was exactly offset by the multiplier effect of government spending.

This chapter introduces a major amendment to the simple consumption theory developed in Chapter 3. Individuals do not base their consumption solely on their disposable income at each instant of time. A farmer, who may have a high income in years of good harvests and a low income in years of bad harvests, is likely to desire a fairly even average consumption pattern over the years. He will save an above-average fraction of his income in good years and a below-average fraction (or perhaps nothing) in bad years. More generally, individuals who want to achieve an even consumption spending pattern over a period of years, or over their lifetime, will not consume much of a transitory income increase that they expect to disappear next year. They will raise their consumption spending much more if they receive an increase in income that they expect to be permanent.

This hypothesis, called the **permanent income hypothesis** (PIH) of consumption spending, is of major importance. Since consumption does not respond completely to every short-run "blip" in income caused by movements in investment or government spending, the PIH cuts the multipliers of Chapter 3 down below the values calculated there and helps to insulate the economy from destabilizing shocks. Thus the PIH helps to bolster plank 1 of the monetarist platform, supporting the monetarist case that the economy can be trusted to stabilize itself. Unfortunately, however, the PIH is not the whole story of consumption behavior. Several additional ingredients must be added before we can gain a complete understanding of fluctuations in consumption.

13-2 THE CONFLICT BETWEEN THE TIME-SERIES AND CROSS-SECTION EVIDENCE

One of the major innovations in Keynes' *General Theory* was the multiplier, which followed directly from the assumption that consumption behaved passively. Keynes' description of consumption behavior begins with the idea that there is a positive marginal propensity to consume that is less than unity: "The fundamental psychological law . . . is that men are disposed, as a rule and on the average, to increase their consumption as their income increases, but not by as much as the increase in their income."[2]

---

[2] See John Maynard Keynes, *The General Theory of Employment, Interest, and Money* (New York: Macmillan, 1936), Book III. The idea of the multiplier was first introduced by R. F. Kahn, "The Relation of Home Investment to Unemployment," *Economic Journal* (June 1931), but Keynes was the first to fit the multiplier into a general economic model of the commodity and money markets.

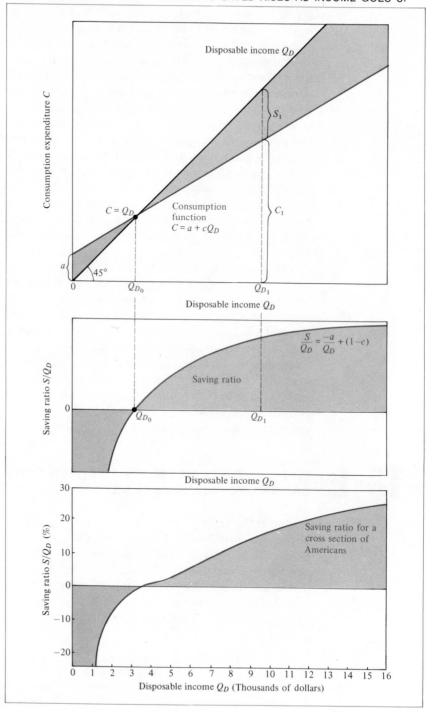

Keynes' second main idea is that there is a specific amount that individuals will consume independent of their income, so that it is possible for saving actually to be negative if disposable income is very low. Denoting consumption as C, and disposable income as Q_D, the Keynesian consumption function can be written:

$$C = a + cQ_D \qquad (13.1)$$

The hypothetical Keynesian consumption function and saving ratio are plotted in the top two frames of Figure 13-1. In the top frame, look to the lower left corner and find the value of consumption (a) that occurs when disposable income is zero. Then move your eye from left to right up the red $C = a + cQ_D$ line. Consumption (C) rises less rapidly than disposable income (Q_D), since the marginal propensity to consume (c) is less than 1.0. Consumption starts out greater than Q_D, equals Q_D at the income level Q_{D_0}, and then is less than Q_D. Everywhere to the right of Q_{D_0} the shortfall of consumption below disposable income allows room for a positive amount of saving. For instance, the income level Q_{D_1} is divided into the consumption level C_1 and the saving level S_1.

Moving down to the middle frame of Figure 13-1, we find plotted the saving/income ratio, S/Q_D. To the left of the income level Q_{D_0} saving is negative; to the right of Q_{D_0} saving is positive.[3] As people become richer, according to the hypothetical Keynesian relation in the middle frame, they save a larger share of their disposable income.

The actual data plotted in the bottom frame of Figure 13-1 confirm Keynes' hypothesis for a **cross section** of Americans who were polled on their income, saving, and consumption behavior. Very poor people do

---

[3] The shape of the saving/income curve depends on the relative values of parameters a and c.

FIGURE 13-1

The Relation between Disposable Income (Q_D), Consumption Spending (C), and the Ratio of Saving to Income (S/Q_D)

The top frame repeats the consumption function introduced in Chapter 3. At levels of disposable income below (to the left of) point Q_{D_0}, people consume more than their income. To the right of Q_{D_0} consumption is less than income, and the shaded pink difference between income and consumption, the amount of saving, is a steadily growing fraction of disposable income.

In the middle frame the share of saving in disposable income is plotted, a negative fraction to the left of point Q_{D_0} and a positive and growing fraction to the right. The bottom frame plots actual data on the relation of saving to disposable income from a survey of consumers. Notice the close correspondence between the theoretical diagram in the middle frame and the actual data in the bottom frame.

Source (for bottom frame): I. Friend and S. Schor, "Who Saves?" *Review of Economics and Statistics*, vol. 41 (May 1959), p. 217, Table 2, columns 5 and 6.

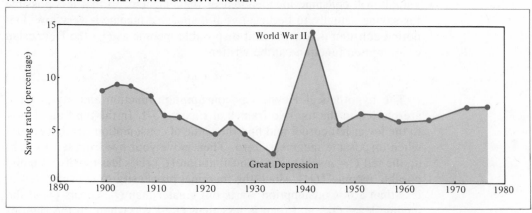

FIGURE 13–2 Ratio of Saving to Disposable Income (S/Q_D), Averages over Business Cycles, 1898–76

The low level of saving during the Great Depression is consistent with our theory (Compare Figure 3–2). The high level of saving during World War II was a special event caused by the unavailability of consumer goods. Leaving out these two extreme periods, the ratio of saving to disposable income was fairly constant.

Notice that the ratio in 1975–76 was very close to its value at the turn of the century. Note that observations plotted are averages over complete business cycles.

Sources: 1898–29 and 1949–69: Paul A. David and John L. Scadding, "Private Savings: Ultrationality, Aggregation, and 'Denison's law,' " *Journal of Political Economy,* vol. 82 (March/April 1974), Table 4. 1930–48 and 1970–76: Bureau of Economic Analysis, U.S. Department of Commerce.

not save at all but instead "dissave," consuming more than they earn by drawing on accumulated assets in savings accounts. As we move rightward from the poor to the rich, we find that the saving/income ratio increases, just as in the hypothetical relationship of the middle frame.

Figure 13-1 raises a potentially serious problem for the economy. If people save more as they become richer, then one presumes that society will save more as economic growth raises average incomes. According to the figures in the bottom frame, the doubling of real family incomes that occurred between 1948 and 1972 from about $6500 to $13,000 (in 1974 prices) should have increased the saving rate from only 6 percent to more than 20 percent. Because saving in equilibrium must equal investment plus the government deficit, the increase in the saving ratio appears to require a massive increase in the ratio of investment to income or in the ratio of the government deficit to income. In the late 1930s it was feared that the economy might stagnate with high unemployment forever if saving leakages from high-employment income were to exceed investment plus the government deficit at that level of income.

Turn now to Figure 13-2, which plots the actual historical **time-series** data on the saving rate achieved on average during each of the major business cycles of this century. Between 1898–99, the first observation plotted, and 1975–76, the last observation, income per family increased by a factor of more than four, from roughly $3300 to $14,000 at 1974 prices.[4] And yet the feared increase in the saving ratio has not occurred! The saving ratio in 1975–76 was actually below that in 1898–99. In fact, the saving ratio in Figure 13-2 was amazingly stable in the range of 4.5–7.5 percent during the 1910–1976 period, with the two main exceptions of low saving during the Great Depression and high saving during World War II.

Clearly Keynes' assumption that the saving ratio increases as society becomes richer must be modified in a way that retains the observed cross-section increase in the saving ratio when poor people are compared to rich people at a given time. The two most important hypotheses that resolve the apparent conflict between the historical time-series evidence of a fairly constant saving ratio and the cross-section evidence of a steadily increasing saving ratio with higher income are (1) the permanent income hypothesis developed in the 1950s by Milton Friedman and (2) the **life cycle hypothesis** developed at about the same time by Franco Modigliani and collaborators.

13-3 THE PERMANENT INCOME HYPOTHESIS

Imagine that you have a job and your take-home pay of $800 is received on the first day of each month. Strictly speaking, your income on the first day of each month is $800, and your income on each of the remaining days of the month is zero. According to the simple Keynesian consumption function, you should do all your consumption spending on the first day of the month and consume absolutely nothing during the rest of the month!

Of course people do not consume their entire income on their payday, but set aside part of their pay to buy groceries and other items during the rest of the month. Why? People can eat only so much on one day and prefer to eat more or less the same amount each day of the month instead of cramming in a whole month's food in one day. This rather obvious point is illustrated in Figure 13-3, where the horizontal axis measures dollars of consumption spending and the vertical axis measures the total

---

[4] Average family income from the *Economic Report of the President,* (January 1977) (Table B–20) is extrapolated backward by the growth in real GNP per capita.

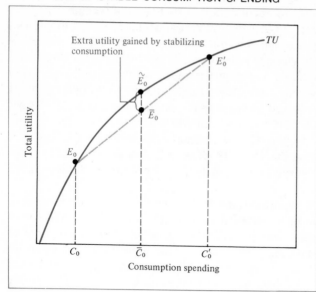

FIGURE 13-3

The Hypothetical Relation between Total Utility and Consumption Spending

The red TU line shows the amount of total utility in the vertical direction that is obtained from different amounts of consumption spending in the horizontal direction. If consumption were to fluctuate between C_0 and C_0', total utility would fluctuate between points E_0 and E_0', for an average utility level shown at $\bar{E}_0$. But if consumption is held stable at point $\bar{C}_0$, the average of C_0 and C_0', then total utility would be higher, as indicated by point $\tilde{E}_0$ plotted along the TU line directly above $\bar{C}_0$.

"utility" (happiness or satisfaction) yielded by an individual's consumption spending at a particular time.

Why does the red TU line relating utility to consumption have a curved shape, rising rapidly at first and then more and more gradually? The first dollar of consumption allows an individual to stave off hunger and buy basic foodstuffs, so that clearly the avoidance of hunger adds a great deal to utility. But at the other extreme, after many thousands of dollars have been spent on a single day, one more dollar does not make much difference. If Elizabeth Taylor already has ten diamond rings, how much can she possibly increase her utility if she is told that she can spend one more dollar?

The shape of the TU curve implies that individuals who have an unstable income pattern will be happier if they consume a constant amount each day rather than allowing their consumption to change each day with their changing income. The utility yielded by consumption spending C_0 in Figure 13-3 is shown directly above at E_0, and the utility yielded by spending C_0' is shown directly above at E_0', because points E_0 and E_0' both lie on the total utility curve (TU). The average utility yielded by a spending pattern that alternates between C_0 and C_0' is indicated by the point marked $\bar{E}_0$, which lies along the pink line drawn between E_0 and E_0'.[5]

---

[5] Why is $\bar{E}_0$ the point representing average utility? Look at the consumption level marked off as $\bar{C}_0$ on the horizontal axis. This point is halfway between C_0 and C_0'. Thus when a straight line is drawn between E_0 and E_0', the point marked as $\bar{E}_0$, which lies directly above

In contrast, a steady unchanging consumption pattern at the average of C_0 and C_0', marked off as $\bar{C}_0$ on the horizontal axis, will yield the higher level of utility $\tilde{E}_0$ that lies directly above $\bar{C}_0$ on the TU curve. In real life people are happier if they achieve a relatively stable consumption pattern than if they live high on the hog during days (or years) of high income and starve during days (or years) of low income.

People can achieve the desirable stable consumption pattern if they consume a fraction not of their actual income but rather of their expected income over a period of time. A farmer may have experienced an annual income in recent years of $3000, $17,000, $9000, and $11,000. Because his income has averaged out at $10,000, his best guess for his expected income next year is $10,000.[6] Let us assume on average that he wants to spend 90 percent of his expected income and save the remaining 10 percent. Then his planned consumption will be $9000 and saving $1000. If the harvest turns out to be bad and his actual realized income falls to a paltry $5000, achieving the $9000 consumption plan would require withdrawing $4000 from savings, to be returned in years of good harvests.

Milton Friedman first proposed the hypothesis that an individual (represented by superscript i) consumes a constant fraction (k^i) of his expected income, which Friedman called **permanent income** (Q^{pi}):[7]

GENERAL FORM	NUMERICAL EXAMPLE FOR THE FARMER	
$C^i = k^i Q^{pi}$	$C = 0.9(\$10,000) = \$9000$	(13.2)

The individual marginal propensity to consume out of permanent income (k^i) depends on individual tastes and on the variability of income (farmers and others with variable income need higher savings accounts to support them during bad years). In addition k^i depends on the interest rate, since people should be willing to save more on average if they receive a higher rate of interest on their savings accounts.

The permanent income hypothesis summarized in equation (13.2) does not say that individuals consume exactly the same amount year after year. Every year new events occur that are likely to change each individual's guess about his average expected or permanent income. For instance, the individual represented in Figure 13-3, after several years in which his expected income turned out to be a correct guess, might find that in good years his income has increased. Gradually he will revise his estimate of his average expected income and will find that he can increase his stable consumption level above $\bar{C}_0$.

$\bar{C}_0$, must be halfway between the two ends of the dashed straight line, not only in the horizontal (consumption) direction but also in the vertical (utility) direction.

[6] It is easy to construct examples in which inflation and real economic growth cause people to expect a higher income next year than their average income of the last few years.

[7] Milton Friedman, *A Theory of the Consumption Function* (Princeton, N.J.: Princeton University Press, 1957), especially Chapters 1–3, 6, and 9.

Friedman's permanent income hypothesis consists of the assumption in equation (13.2) that individuals consume a constant portion of their permanent income. But this is not enough, because an additional assumption is required to indicate how individuals arrive at a guess about the size of their permanent income. Friedman proposed that individual estimates of permanent income for this year (Q^{pi}) be revised from last year's estimate (Q^{pi}_{-1}) by some fraction (g^i) of the amount by which actual income (Q^i) differs from (Q^{pi}_{-1}):

GENERAL FORM

$$Q^{pi} = Q^{pi}_{-1} + g^i(Q^i - Q^{pi}_{-1})$$

NUMERICAL EXAMPLE

$$Q^{pi} = 10,000 + 0.2\,(15,000 - 10,000)$$
$$= 11,000 \qquad (13.3)$$

The behavior described in equation (13.3) is sometimes called the "error learning" or "adaptive" hypothesis of expectation formation. If actual current income and last year's permanent (expected) income are the same, no change is made in the estimate of permanent income for this period. If, on the other hand, actual income (Q^i) exceeds Q^{pi}_{-1}, then this period's estimate (Q^{pi}) will be raised. In the numerical example an actual income outcome of $15,000, compared to Q^{pi}_{-1} of $10,000, causes this period's Q^{pi} to be raised to $11,000.[8] A person who has a widely fluctuating income (farmers, door-to-door salespeople) will pay little attention to his actual income (Q^i) and will thus have a smaller value of g^i than a college professor or government worker who has a relatively stable income.

Now we can see that an individual will allow his consumption to respond modestly to changes in actual income, because consumption depends on permanent income, and in turn permanent income in equation (13.3) depends only in part on this period's actual income. When we substitute (13.3) into (13.2), we obtain the following relationship between an individual's current consumption (C^i), this period's actual income (Q^i), and last period's estimate of permanent income (Q^{pi}_{-1}):

$$C^i = k^i Q^{pi}_{-1} + k^i g^i(Q^i - Q^{pi}_{-1}) \qquad (13.4)$$

For instance if k^i is 90 percent and g^i is 20 percent, as in the above numerical examples, then the marginal propensity to consume out of a change in actual income is $k^i g^i$, or 18 percent (0.9 times 0.2 equals 0.18). In contrast, the marginal propensity to consume out of permanent income is k^i, the much higher value of 90 percent.

---

[8] Exactly the same hypothesis for the formation of expectations was introduced in Chapter 8 in the discussion of inflation expectations (see section 8-8). Equation (13.3) can be rewritten in the form used in Chapter 8:

$$Q^{pi} = g^i Q^i + (1 - g^i) Q^{pi}_{-1}$$

This says that permanent income in this period is a weighted average of actual income and last period's permanent income.

Figure 13-4 illustrates how the permanent income hypothesis can reconcile the apparent conflict between the cross-section data in Figure 13-1, where rich individuals have a higher saving ratio than poor people, and the time-series data in Figure 13-2, where society does not appear to have raised its saving ratio as it has become richer. The solid red line running up through point A and point F lies everywhere at a vertical position equal to k^i times disposable income (Q^i). But consumption can equal $k^i Q^i$ only if permanent income Q^{pi} were exactly equal to actual income (Q^i), given the permanent income hypothesis that individuals consume the fraction k^i of their permanent income. Thus the line running through A and F is labeled the long-run schedule, because it indicates the level of consumption only when actual income has remained at a particular level long enough for individuals to have adjusted fully their estimated permanent income to the same level.

What happens in the short run, when actual income can differ from permanent income? The flatter dashed red schedule running between D, A, and B is the short-run schedule and plots equation (13.3). When current income (Q^i) is exactly equal to last period's permanent income (Q^{pi}_{-1}), the short-run schedule intersects the long-run schedule at point A. But during a good year when an individual's income is at the high level Q^i_0, his current estimate of permanent income (Q^{pi}) rises above last period's estimate (Q^{pi}_{-1}) by a fraction (g^i) of the excess of actual income over last period's estimate $(Q^i_0 - Q^{pi}_{-1})$. And the higher value of Q^{pi} raises consumption by k^i times the increase in permanent income. Thus consumption at point B lies vertically above point A by the fraction $k^i g^i$ (18 percent in the numerical example) times the horizontal distance between Q^{pi}_{-1} and Q^i_0.

With the short-run marginal propensity to consume $(k^i g^i)$ so far below the long-run propensity (k^i), any short-run increase in income goes disproportionately into saving and raises the saving-income ratio, as illustrated in the bottom frame of Figure 13-4 at point B. And any shortfall decrease in income below Q^{pi}_{-1} cuts consumption by only a small amount, requiring a sharp cut in saving or even dissaving, as illustrated at point D in both the upper and lower frames.

Milton Friedman used a diagram similar to Figure 13-4 to illustrate why wealthy people on average save more than poor people. Among the wealthy are many people (including, perhaps, some people who on average are poor), who are having a good year, farmers with bumper crops, executives in profitable firms who have just received high bonuses, movie stars who have just completed a popular film, and this year's champion used-car salesman. Because a disproportionate number of wealthy individuals report incomes above their own individual estimates of their permanent income, they save more than average.

Among the poor, however, are many people who are having a bad year, including farmers with diseased crops, executives who have just been fired, and show business people whose popularity has waned. These individuals formerly had estimated that their permanent income level was

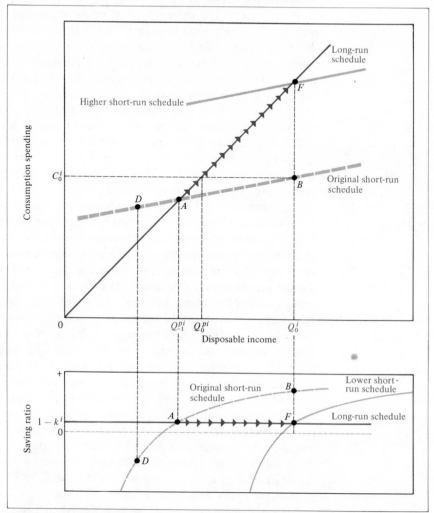

FIGURE 13–4

The Permanent Income
Hypothesis of Consumption
and Saving

In both frames the long-run schedule
shows that consumption and saving
are fixed fractions of income in the
long run, when actual and permanent
income are equal. But short-run gains
in actual income, as at point B, are
not fully incorporated into permanent
income. Thus consumption increases
only a small amount (compare points
B and A) and at B most of the short-
run increase in income is saved. The
same gain in income maintained
permanently causes the short-run
schedule to follow the arrows along
the long-run schedule to point F.

high; now they try to maintain relatively high consumption by saving little or even dissaving.

As for the observed time-series behavior of the nationwide savings ratio over this century, the Friedman permanent income hypothesis has the following explanation. We can now interpret Figure 13-4 as the relation between actual consumption and actual income for the whole economy, rather than for one individual.[9] When income increases temporarily, the saving ratio goes up, as from A to B in the bottom frame; when income declines below normal, the saving rate drops or even becomes negative, as at point D. Thus in booms the saving ratio is predicted to be high on average and in recessions low on average.

> **Review:** In the worst years of the Great Depression income had dropped so much in relation to individuals' permanent incomes that the nationwide saving rate became negative. This is illustrated for 1933 in Figure 3-2. As we will see, the prediction that the saving ratio drops in recessions has not turned out to be universally valid in recent years.

The long-run constancy of the saving ratio can be explained by the gradual upward adjustment of permanent income as actual income grows. When a high income level such as Q_0^i occurs only once, as at point B, it is considered unusual, and saving is high. But when the high income level Q_0^i has persisted for a long time, individuals gradually raise their estimates of their permanent income, shifting upward the short-run consumption schedule in the top frame of Figure 13-4 and shifting down the saving schedule in the bottom frame. When estimated permanent income finally reaches Q_0^i, the short-run consumption schedule in the top frame will have shifted upward, following the arrows, to the flat short-run schedule line through point F. The saving schedule in the bottom frame will have shifted downward, following the arrows, to the new line through point F.

> **Summary:** Estimates of permanent income are continually raised, as actual income outstrips previous levels, causing the saving ratio and the relationship between consumption and income to follow along the long-run schedules, as marked by the arrows in Figure 13-4. Thus in the long run the saving ratio is roughly constant. But in the short run a temporary increase in income raises the saving ratio and a temporary decrease reduces the saving ratio because permanent income does not adjust completely to each change in actual income.

---

[9] Variables for the whole economy (C, Q, Q^p) are identical to the abbreviations for individuals (C^i, Q^i, Q^{pi}), but with the i superscripts dropped.

13-4 THE LIFE CYCLE HYPOTHESIS

About the same time that Friedman wrote his book on the permanent income hypothesis, Franco Modigliani of MIT and collaborators devised a somewhat different way of reconciling the positive relation between the saving ratio and income observed in cross-section data and the constancy of the saving ratio observed over long periods in the historical time-series data.[10] Modigliani and Friedman both began from the argument summarized in Figure 13-3: Individuals achieve a higher level of total utility when they maintain a stable consumption pattern than when they allow consumption to rise or fall with every transitory oscillation of their income. But Modigliani carried the stable consumption argument further than Friedman and suggested that people would try to stabilize their consumption over their entire lifetime, as shown by the red consumption level C_0 that is held fixed at each age in Figure 13-5.

Because people tend to earn relatively low wages when they are young, high wages when they are middle-aged, and low incomes again after retirement, the saving ratio fluctuates regularly with age. Young people dissave, middle-aged people repay the debts of their youth and then save for retirement, and then after retirement again dissave, drawing down their accumulated assets. Figure 13-5 is drawn to have the total shaded area of saving equal the total shaded area of dissaving, so that over an individual's lifetime saving averages out to zero.[11] In real life most individuals are afraid to run down their savings too far when they are in retirement, because they need to be prepared for heavy medical expenses and other unforeseen events, and thus most people die with positive amounts of assets to bequeath to their children.[12]

---

[10] Franco Modigliani and R. E. Brumberg, "Utility Analysis and the Consumption Function," in K. K. Kurihara (ed.), *Post-Keynesian Economics* (New Brunswick, N.J.: Rutgers University Press, 1954). Also A. Ando and F. Modigliani, "The 'Life Cycle' Hypothesis of Saving: Aggregate Implications and Tests," *American Economic Review*, vol. 53 (March 1963), pp. 55–84.

[11] Even if an individual's accumulated saving has been run down to zero when he dies, he can consume more during retirement than the total of his earlier saving, because he has earned interest in the meantime. Similarly, during middle-age he must repay more than he borrowed in his youth, as a consequence of interest charged on the borrowings.

[12] I believe that most people, other than the very rich, bequeath money to their children because they cannot insure themselves completely against every eventuality of their old age. Another main source of bequests is the value of farms and small businesses that cannot be "consumed" without first selling them. For the alternative interpretation that the only reason for bequests is that parents want to make their children better off, see Robert J. Barro, "Are Government Bonds Net Wealth?" *Journal of Political Economy*, vol. 82 (November/December 1974), pp. 1095–1117.

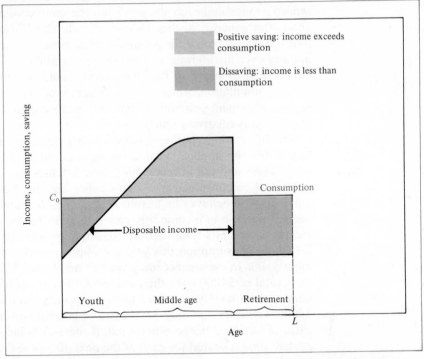

FIGURE 13–5 **The Behavior of Consumption and Saving under the Life Cycle Hypothesis**

Saving is positive in the middle-age region as indicated by the pink shading. This period of saving initially goes to pay off debts (the gray area) incurred in youth. The remaining saving is spent in retirement.

The Modigliani theory, the life cycle hypothesis of consumption and saving, easily explains the observed cross-section increase of the saving ratio with higher income plotted in Figure 13-1.

> *The group of individuals with high incomes includes a disproportionate share of middle-aged people who have above average saving ratios as they prepare for retirement. The group of individuals with low incomes and low saving ratios includes young people who are borrowing heavily and old retired people who are living off their accumulated assets.*

How does the life cycle hypothesis explain the long-run constancy of the saving ratio observed in historical data? If the population of each historical era is divided into the same shares of young, middle-aged, and retired people, and each age group has the same saving behavior in generation after generation, then the saving ratio should remain unchanged as time passes. In fact, if the population is constant, and if each person saves nothing over his lifetime as a whole, the nationwide average saving ratio would tend to be zero. Positive saving would be observed only with a growing population, which cuts the fraction of the population in the dissaving retirement generation, and only if dissaving in the large younger generation is relatively small.

The life cycle hypothesis shares with Friedman's permanent income hypothesis the implication that the saving ratio should rise in economic boom years and fall in recession years. A temporary increase in income today will be consumed over one's entire lifetime. For instance, imagine a person who believes he has 40 years left to live and receives an unexpected increase in income this year of $4000 that he does not expect to receive again. His total lifetime consumption goes up by the $4000 and his actual consumption this year goes up by only 1/40 of that amount, a mere $100. In each succeeding year an additional $100 would be spent, for a total of $4000 over the remaining 40 years of life. Thus, in an economic boom widely expected to be temporary, an unexpected bonus of $4000 would lead to only $100 extra of current consumption and $3900 extra of saving. On the other hand, if the $4000 income increase is expected to be repeated for each of the next 40 years, then $4000 extra can be consumed this year and again in each of the next 39 years and the saving ratio will not rise.

THE ROLE OF ASSETS

The Modigliani theory provides an important role for assets as a determinant of consumption behavior. Imagine that life lasted only two years. In the first year let us say that a worker's income is $10,000, divided into $5000 of consumption and $5000 of saving. Then in the second year the worker retires, consumes $5000, and earns nothing, dissaving $5000 and winding up with no assets when he dies. In any one year in this imaginary world half the population is retired, half working, and the nationwide total of consumption spending ($10,000) is exactly equal to income. After the workers have earned their income in the first year, any event that raises the value of assets will allow them to raise their consumption level during their retirement. A boom in the stock market that raises the value of accumulated saving from $5000 to $6000 at the beginning of the second year would allow the old people to consume $6000 during retirement instead of $5000.

In his empirical studies of consumption behavior, Modigliani has found a substantial positive effect of asset values or net wealth on consumption. Consumption may be stimulated by any of several events that raise the value of assets: an unexpected inflation that raises the value of housing prices; a stock market boom; or an increase in the supply of money.[13] Unlike the simple example of the previous paragraph, in which only retired people have assets, in the real world people accumulate assets throughout their working life. When the real value of assets goes up, lifetime consumption can be raised. A $1.00 increase in real asset values therefore raises consumption by a few cents this year, a few cents next year, and so on. Modigliani has estimated that a $1.00 increase in asset values raises consumption this year by about $.06.

We learned in Chapter 6 that the economy's self-correcting forces are enhanced when real consumption spending depends on real assets or real wealth. If a drop in spending cuts the price level, the level of real wealth is raised, and this helps to arrest the decline in spending.[14] In the other direction, if an increase in spending raises the price level, the level of real wealth declines, which helps to dampen the original stimulus to spending.

Thus, ironically, nonmonetarist Modigliani's life cycle hypothesis helps to support plank 1 of the monetarist platform of Chapter 12. Private spending is stabilized because transitory increases in disposable income that are not expected to last a lifetime have only a modest influence on current consumption. In addition, the real asset effect stabilizes the economy through the effect of higher prices in cutting real assets and dampening spending. Overall, the life cycle hypothesis helps to reduce the current marginal propensity to consume, cut the multiplier, and insulate the economy from unexpected changes in investment, exports, or other types of spending.

13-5 CASE STUDY: PERMANENT INCOME, RECESSIONS, AND CONSUMER DURABLES

Both the permanent income and life cycle hypotheses (PIH and LCH) provide an explanation of the positive cross-section relation between the saving ratio and income. Both predict that a short-run drop in total income, as during a recession, will cause the saving ratio to drop, and a short-run increase in income will cause the saving ratio to increase. Over the long run, both predict that the short-run consumption schedule will shift upward, maintaining an approximately constant saving ratio.

The behavior of the saving ratio in postwar business cycles is plotted

---

[13] Several issues that are usually discussed in more advanced courses in economics are relevant here. First, is all the money supply part of the public's net wealth or only the portion of the money supply that is a liability of the central bank? Second, is part or all of the public debt a part of the public's net wealth?

[14] Review the Pigou effect discussed in section 6-6.

in Figure 13-6 for the entire period between 1946 and 1976. The data are quarterly, so that the short-term wiggles in the saving ratio are clearly evident. Each postwar recession is marked off by gray shading between a pair of vertical lines, with the left vertical line of each pair labeled P to designate the *peak* quarter marking the beginning of the recession and the right vertical line of each pair labeled T to designate the *trough* quarter marking the end of the recession.[15]

Several wiggly lines are plotted in Figure 13-6. At first let us concentrate on the bottom line set off by pink shading, the saving ratio itself.[16] Both the permanent income and life cycle hypotheses predict that in recessions and the early stages of recoveries, when actual income is low relative to permanent income, the saving ratio should be *below average*. Then in boom periods when actual income is high, the saving ratio should be *above average*. But in Figure 13-6 this predicted **procyclical** fluctuation in the saving ratio does not emerge clearly.[17] The only recessions in which there was a clear drop in the saving rate occurred in 1948–49 and 1960–61. The exceptions to the theoretical predictions of the PIH and LCH appear to be much more numerous than the confirming episodes. Among the exceptions are these:

1. The saving ratio reached lower levels during both 1947 and 1950 than at any time in the 1948–49 recession.
2. The lowest saving ratios experienced between 1951 and 1959 occurred neither during the 1953–54 nor 1957–58 recessions but during two successive quarters in 1955 when personal disposable income had far exceeded previous values.
3. The saving ratio was much lower in the expansion years of 1959 and 1963 than during the recession of 1957–58.
4. The saving ratio increased dramatically during the recession year 1970 as compared to the average ratio during the last six quarters of the preceding expansion in 1968–69.
5. Perhaps the most glaring contradiction occurred quite recently. The saving ratio in every quarter of 1972, when real per person disposable income grew by 5.8 percent, was lower than in every

---

[15] The high saving rate of World War II cannot be used to test theoretical predictions because consumer goods were rationed, preventing individuals from consuming as large a share of their income as they would have otherwise desired.

[16] In this diagram the saving ratio is calculated as personal saving (S) divided by personal income (Q^P). Personal income is in turn equal to disposable income—the normal denominator of the saving ratio—plus personal tax payments. This slightly different definition of the saving ratio is used here because we will be interested in the next section in the division of personal income between personal taxes, saving, and consumption.

[17] A procyclical variable is one that fluctuates in the same direction as total income over the business cycle, rising in booms and falling in recessions. **Countercyclical** behavior is just the opposite; a countercyclical government spending policy would raise spending during recessions and reduce spending in boom years.

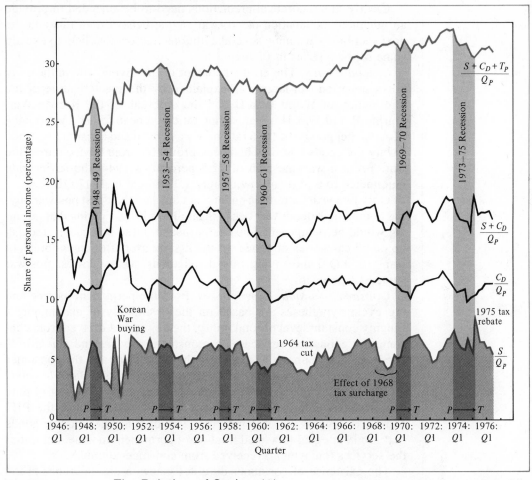

FIGURE 13-6

The Relation of Saving (S), Consumer Durable Purchases (C_D), and Personal Tax Payments (T_P) to Personal Income (Q_P), 1946–76

The bottom line marked off by pink shading is the ratio of saving (S) to personal income (Q_P). Although predicted by theory to drop during recessions and increase in expansions, the S/Q_P ratio does not do so. Part of the reason is that consumers do part of their saving by purchasing consumer durable goods (C_D). Thus the $(S + C_D)/Q_P$ ratio shows more of a tendency to decline in recessions. The red line at the top is described in the next section.

Source: Survey of Current Business, various issues.

quarter of the 1973–75 recession, when real per person disposable income fell by 2.1 percent.[18]

Clearly, the theoretical predictions need to be amended to provide an adequate explanation of postwar saving behavior. In this and the next section we examine several additional factors that help to explain some of the puzzles in Figure 13-6.

Special Events. The erratic behavior of the saving ratio in the early postwar period can largely be explained by the special nature of the termination of World War II and the outbreak of the Korean War. During World War II a high saving ratio had been forced by rationing of consumer goods. In 1946 rationing was ended and consumers rushed to buy the goods that they had been prevented from buying during the war. From a wartime high of 25.5 percent in 1944, the saving rate plummeted to a postwar low of only 1.3 percent in 1947:Q2.

Only two years after consumers had finished their first postwar buying boom, the Korean War began in late June 1950. Fearing that rationing would be reimposed, consumers rushed out to buy again, stocking up on all categories of goods. In the first quarter after the outbreak of war (1950:Q3) the saving rate dived to its second lowest postwar value, 2.1 percent.

Consumer Durable Expenditures. Both the permanent income and life cycle hypotheses are based on the desirability of maintaining a roughly constant level of total utility, the enjoyment derived from consumption goods and services. For consumer *services* and *nondurable* goods such as haircuts and donuts, the enjoyment and the consumer spending occur at about the same time. But consumer *durable goods* are different. A television set is purchased at a single instant of time but produces enjoyment for many years thereafter. Thus, the PIH and LCH suggest that it is not purchases of consumer durable goods that are kept equal to a fixed fraction of permanent income, but rather the services (enjoyment) received from consumer durables.

The existence of consumer durables makes a big difference in the predictions of the behavior of the saving ratio made by proponents of the PIH and LCH. Now it is possible for the saving ratio actually to rise in recessions rather than to drop. This possibility is illustrated in Table 13-1 for a hypothetical Smith family. Successive periods of time are read from left to right in the table. Initially the Smiths' actual income and permanent income are both equal at $10,000, but then a business cycle raises their actual income to $12,000 in period 2, fol-

---

[18] Data from the Bureau of Economic Analysis, U.S. Department of Commerce. The 1972 figures in the text refer to the interval 1971:Q4 to 1972:Q4. Recession figures refer to the six-quarter interval 1973:Q4 to 1975:Q2.

TABLE 13-1

A Hypothetical Example for the Smith Family That Allows the Permanent Income Hypothesis to Generate a Countercyclical Saving Ratio

		Periods			
Variable	0	1	2	3	4
1. Actual income (Q^i)	10,000	10,000	12,000	9,000	10,000
2. Permanent income $(Q^{pi} = 0.5Q^{pi}_{-1} + 0.5Q^i)$	10,000	10,000	11,000	10,000	10,000
3. Nondurable consumption spending $(C^i_{ND} = 0.6Q^{pi})$	6,000	6,000	6,600	6,000	6,000
4. Desired stock of consumer durables $(K^i_D = 1.5Q^{pi})$	15,000	15,000	16,500	15,000	15,000
5. Expenditures on consumer durables $(C^i_D = 0.2K^i_{D_{-1}} + \Delta K^i_D)$	3,000	3,000	4,500	1,800	3,000
6. Total consumer expenditures $(C^i = C^i_{ND} + C^i_D)$	9,000	9,000	11,100	7,800	9,000
7. Personal saving $(S^i = Q^i - C^i)$	1,000	1,000	900	1,200	1,000
8. Saving ratio (S^i/Q^i)	.10	.10	.075	.133	.10
9. Ratio of saving plus consumer durable expenditures to actual income $\left(\dfrac{S^i + C^i_D}{Q^i}\right)$	.40	.40	.45	.333	.40

lowed by a recession that drops actual income to $9,000 in period 3, followed by a return to the original $10,000 in period 4.

The Smiths estimate their permanent income as equal to the average of last period's permanent income and this period's actual income.[19] Thus permanent income on line 2 rises to $11,000 in period 2 but thereafter falls back to $10,000.

The Smiths' nondurable consumption expenditure follows the PIH and is always set at 60 percent of permanent income, as shown in line 3 of the table. As for durable goods, the Smiths are not directly concerned about their expenditures, but rather about the size of their total stock of durable goods – the total value of their automobile(s), appliances, furniture, tools, and so on. The table assumes that the Smiths attempt to keep their total stock of durable goods at exactly 1.5 times their permanent income, as is shown in line 4.

Spending by the Smiths on new durable goods occurs for two reasons. First, the Smiths have to replace old automobiles and ap-

[19] In terms of equation (13.3), we have set $g^i = 0.5$:

$$Q^{pi} = 0.5Q^{pi}_{-1} + 0.5(Q^i - Q^{pi}_{-1}) = 0.5Q^{pi}_{-1} + 0.5Q^i$$

pliances that wear out; on line 5 the table assumes that the average durable good lasts for five years, requiring annual replacement of 20 percent of the stock of durable goods. Second, new goods must be purchased when there is a change in the desired stock (ΔK_D^i).[20] On line 5 in the table, in periods 0 and 1, durable purchases are limited to replacement (20 percent of the $15,000 stock is $3,000). But in period 2 the desired stock increases by $1,500, requiring expenditures of the original $3,000 for replacement plus an additional $1,500 to raise the stock to the desired level. In period 3 permanent income falls, the desired stock declines back to the original level, and so consumer durable spending falls drastically. Not only is no spending needed to add to the stock, but only $1,800 of replacement spending is needed rather than the original $3,000 of replacement.

In lines 6 and 7 of Table 13-1 total consumption expenditures and saving are calculated. Then in line 8 we see the surprising conclusion.

Result: Even though both desired nondurable spending and the desired stock of durables were calculated according to the permanent income hypothesis (PIH), the saving ratio on line 8 does not exhibit the procyclical behavior that occurred in Figure 13-4. Instead of rising with higher income in period 2, saving actually falls. The reverse occurs when income drops in period 3.

We can look more closely at the table to see why this surprising result occurs. In period 2 the total income left over for saving and durable purchases — after purchases of nondurables have been made — is $5,400, or 45 percent of income, a higher left-over ratio than in periods 0 and 1.[21] But the big jump in durable purchases needed to raise the stock of durables to the desired level completely swamps the increase in saving, both using up extra saving and cutting into the previous saving level as well.

Thus countercyclical fluctuations in the saving ratio do not contradict the PIH or LCH but confirm them. Both theories predict that the sum of saving and consumer durable purchases should increase in relation to personal income in booms and fall in recessions, as indeed occurs in the example on line 9 of Table 13-1. But notice that consumer durable purchases on line 5 in the table are highly unstable, rising in period 2 when actual income is high and falling precipitously when ac-

---

[20] The symbol Δ was introduced in Chapter 3. It stands for "change in" a variable between period -1 and the current period. Here in period 2, for example:

$$\Delta K_D^i = K_D^i - K_{D_{-1}}^i = 16,500 - 15,000 = 1,500$$

[21] In periods 0 and 1, $4,000, or 40 percent of income, is left over after purchases of nondurables.

tual income declines. Thus durable purchases (1) are simultaneously consistent with the PIH and LCH but (2) constitute a source of demand fluctuations in the private economy.

Turning back now to Figure 13-6, we notice that the upper black wiggly line plots the ratio of the sum of saving and consumer durable purchases to personal income $(S + C_D)/Q_P$. In each recession, with the single exception of 1969–70, there appears to have been at least some drop in this total ratio, as predicted by the PIH and LCH. The main remaining puzzles to be explained are the low level in the total ratio in 1968–69 relative to the 1969–70 recession and the short, sharp drop in the total ratio in 1972.[22]

13-6 CASE STUDY: TEMPORARY TAX CHANGES AND THE SAVING RATIO

According to the permanent income hypothesis, a drop in this month's actual income does not cut consumption unless people believe that the decline in actual income will persist, in which case permanent income declines. In the life cycle hypothesis such a drop in current income does not cut consumption unless a person has some reason to conclude that his lifetime income has declined. For this reason a change in actual current disposable income caused by a tax change announced by the government to be *permanent* should cause a bigger change in consumption than a tax increase announced as *temporary*.

What would happen to consumption and to the saving ratio if a temporary tax surcharge was assumed by individuals to be a short-lived event with no effect at all on permanent income? Then consumption spending (C) would stay the same, because according to the PIH, consumption depends only on permanent income. People would pay for the temporary tax surcharge entirely by saving less, and so the ratio of saving to personal income (S/Q_P) would fall by exactly the increase in the ratio of taxes to personal income (T/Q_P).

We can begin to understand several puzzling episodes of saving behavior if we compare the movements of the ratios S/Q_P and T/Q_P, as in Figure 13-7. Several episodes plotted there illustrate sharp movements in the tax ratio (T/Q_P) that are almost totally offset by movements of the saving ratio (S/Q_P).

The two most important examples occurred in mid-1968, when Congress passed the temporary tax surcharge belatedly proposed by President Johnson to finance Vietnam War spending, and in mid-1975,

---

[22] In the recessions of 1948–49, 1953–54, 1957–58, 1960–61, and 1973–75, the lowest value of $(S + C_D/Q_P)$ occurred either during the recession or within a quarter or two afterward. The 1969–70 recession was the exception.

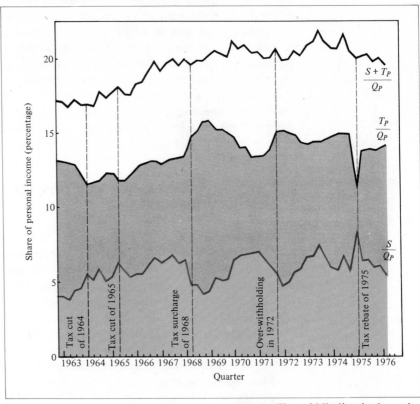

FIGURE 13–7

The Relation of Saving (S) and Personal Tax Payments (T_P) to Personal Income (Q_P), 1963–76

The lower line shaded in pink is identical to that in the previous figure, the ratio of saving to personal income

(S/Q_P). The middle line is the ratio of personal tax payments to personal income (T_P/Q_P). Notice how the movements of the S/Q_P ratio are almost a mirror image of T/Q_P.

Source: Survey of Current Business, various issues.

when a temporary tax rebate was declared to help revive the economy.[23] Individuals must have been led by the term "temporary surcharge" in 1968 to hold unchanged their estimates of their permanent income. Thus the mid-1968 increase in the T/Q_P ratio in Figure 13-7 is

---

[23] The word "belatedly" refers to the long delay between the acceleration of Vietnam spending in late 1965 and the proposed tax increase that President Johnson finally introduced in 1967.

completely offset by a drop in the S/Q_P ratio. Because the sum of the saving and tax ratios remained constant, we can conclude that the tax surcharge totally failed to achieve its aim of dampening consumption. In fact there was very little further movement in the sum of the saving and tax ratios (the top line in Figure 13-7) during the 10 quarters following the imposition of the surcharge. The saving ratio fell suddenly in 1968 and then gradually rose in the next two years as the surcharge was removed.

Another dramatic example of the effect of a temporary tax change occurred in early 1975, when individuals received a rebate of up to $200 per family on their income tax liability. Much of the rebate went into saving, at least initially, as indicated by the upward blip in the S/Q_P ratio in 1975:Q2, the same quarter as the downward blip in the T_P/Q_P ratio. The 1975 tax changes also included some permanent elements, which individuals may have treated as calling for an adjustment in their permanent income rather than in their saving ratio. In the last half of 1975 the saving ratio returned to the average level of 1973 and 1974, so that the permanent portion of the 1975 tax cut appears to have succeeded in stimulating consumption.[24]

Another episode occurred in 1964 and 1965, when permanent tax cuts were introduced in two stages. The saving rate did not remain unaffected. An increase in saving almost completely offset the tax cuts when they occurred (in 1964:Q2 and 1965:Q3), and there was only a minor subsequent decline in the saving ratio.[25]

The effects of tax changes and consumer durable purchases are combined in the red line at the top of Figure 13-6. This ratio of saving plus consumer durable purchases plus personal taxes to personal income $(S + C_D + T_P)/Q_P$ is predicted by the PIH and LCH to rise in expansions and to decline in recessions. Its behavior is smoother than the black line directly below because, by adding in personal taxes, we have eliminated erratic ups and downs in saving caused by changes in tax rate. The top red line displays marked declines in each postwar recession except 1969–70, when the drop was moderate.

---

[24] A recent study indicates that all personal income tax changes, whether temporary or permanent, require about two years before the initial saving bulge is spent on consumption purchases. See F. Modigliani and C. Steindl, "Is a Tax Rebate an Effective Tool for Stabilization Policy?" *Brookings Papers on Economic Activity,* vol. 8, no. 1 (1977), pp. 175–203.

[25] One final episode marked in Figure 13-7 is not discussed in the text. At the beginning of 1972 the Internal Revenue Service issued new withholding tables that resulted in a substantial increase in the amounts withheld from paychecks, without any accompanying change in tax liability. The PIH would have expected all the effect of this event to be soaked up by a drop in the saving ratio, since people could look forward to larger refunds in early 1973. Indeed, the saving ratio did drop substantially in mid-1972, although the lack of response of saving at the beginning of 1972 differs from the simultaneity of the offset that occurred in the 1968 and 1975 episodes.

$(S + C_D + T_P)/Q_P$ RATIO

Recession	Trough quarter	Percentage point decline, peak to trough
1948–49	1949:$Q2$	−2.7
1953–54	1954:$Q3$	−2.8
1957–58	1958:$Q2$	−2.2
1960–61	1961:$Q1$	−1.8
1969–70	1970:$Q4$	−0.8
1973–75	1975:$Q2$	−2.5

13-7 CONCLUSION: CONSUMPTION AND THE CASE FOR ACTIVISM

If all consumption spending consisted of nondurable goods and services, the permanent income hypothesis and life cycle hypothesis both would strengthen the case of monetarists that the private economy is basically stable if left alone by the government. Consumption would respond only partially to temporary bursts of nonconsumption spending, so that the economy's true short-run multipliers would be smaller than those calculated in Chapters 3–5. Both the PIH and LCH predict that consumers dampen the decline of the economy in a recession by cutting their saving rate and dampen the subsequent expansion by raising their saving rate. Both the PIH and LCH are able to reconcile the observed cross-section increase in the saving ratio that occurs with higher incomes with the long-run historical constancy of the aggregate saving ratio.

Our study of the historical data began with several puzzles that the PIH and LCH did not appear able to explain. The saving ratio in the postwar United States has not fallen in every recession, and it has declined in some prosperous periods. In addition to special events connected with the end of World War II and the outbreak of the Korean War, two major factors help to reconcile the actual behavior of the saving ratio with the PIH and LCH. First, the share of consumer durable expenditures in disposable income falls in recessions and can offset part or all of the drop in the saving ratio that one would otherwise expect. The sum of the saving ratio and the consumer durable expenditures ratio exhibits the expected decline in almost all postwar recessions.

The second source of puzzling shifts in the saving ratio is the effect of temporary changes in tax rates. If temporary tax changes fail to alter permanent income, then the tax changes will be offset by movements in the saving ratio. It is ironic that the PIH, first developed by the chief monetarist, and the LCH, first developed (in collaboration with others) by one of the principal nonmonetarists, both imply that temporary tax changes introduced to implement an activist fiscal policy may be ineffective. From our study of saving behavior, the widespread nonmonetarist faith in the efficacy of temporary tax changes as a central tool of an activist stabilization policy does not appear to be warranted. On the other hand, the nonmonetarist case for policy activism is strengthened by the procyclical fluctuations in consumer durable purchases, because this source of instability in the private economy may need to be offset by countercyclical government policy.

SUMMARY

1. A major area of dispute between monetarists and nonmonetarists is the stability of private spending decisions. Friedman's permanent income hypothesis (*PIH*) and Modigliani's life cycle hypothesis (*LCH*) are based on the assumption that individuals achieve a higher level of total utility (well-being) when they maintain a stable consumption pattern than when they allow consumption to rise or fall with every transitory fluctuation in their actual income. Individuals can achieve the desirable stable consumption pattern by consuming a stable fraction of their permanent or lifetime income.

2. If all consumption consisted of nondurable goods and services, both the PIH and the LCH would strengthen the case of monetarists that the private economy is basically stable if left alone by the government. Consumption would respond only partially to temporary fluctuations of nonconsumption spending, so that the economy's short-run multipliers would be smaller than the simple theoretical multipliers of Chapters 3–5. Consumers would dampen the decline of the economy in a recession by reducing their saving rate, and they would similarly moderate the subsequent economic expansion by raising their saving rate.

3. Both hypotheses can reconcile the observed cross-section increase in the saving ratio that occurs for higher incomes with the observed long-run historical constancy of the aggregate saving ratio.

4. Both hypotheses have important implications for fiscal policy. For example, a tax change announced as permanent should cause a bigger change in permanent income, and hence in consumption expenditures, than another equal-sized tax change announced as temporary. Thus temporary tax changes introduced to implement an activist fiscal policy may be rendered ineffective by offsetting movements in the saving ratio.

5. An additional consideration in explaining observed consumption and saving behavior is that consumer durable expenditures should be treated as a form of saving, not as current consumption. Sharp increases in income tend to go mainly into saving, which means that consumer durable expenditures treated as a form of saving may be very responsive to transitory income changes. Thus the PIH and LCH may be valid, but still consumer durable purchases are a source of instability in the private economy.

A LOOK AHEAD

If consumers purchased only nondurable goods and services, the PIH and LCH theories would predict that consumer behavior stabilizes the economy. An offsetting factor is the procyclical movement of consumer durable purchases. Although this is consistent with the PIH and LCH, nevertheless it tends to aggravate booms and recessions. In the next chapter we will find that business fixed investment fluctuates procyclically, for reasons very similar to those used in this chapter to explain consumer durable spending. Both durable purchases by consumers and investment purchases by businessmen thus introduce instability into the private economy, leading nonmonetarists to claim that an activist stabilization policy is justified.

CONCEPTS AND QUESTIONS

IDENTIFICATIONS

Transitory versus permanent income

Permanent income hypothesis of consumption (PIH)

Life cycle hypothesis of consumption (LCH)

Consumer durable expenditures

Desired stock of consumer durables

Time-series (historical) versus cross-section evidence

Temporary versus permanent tax changes

QUESTIONS FOR REVIEW

1   Reconcile the positive cross-section relationship between income and the saving ratio with the observed historical constancy of the saving ratio.

2   How would you expect the short-run marginal propensity to consume to differ for farmers and university professors?

3   The growth rate of the U.S. population has declined in the past two decades. What effect would you expect this slowing to have on the aggregate saving ratio under the life cycle hypothesis?

4   Why are estimates of permanent income continually changing?

5   Under the LCH, individuals try to smooth out their consumption over their lifetimes, yet we continually observe large positive bequests given by people to their children. Can you explain why most individuals do not run their assets down to zero when they die, but rather leave assets as bequests to their heirs?

6   Under the LCH would you expect to observe the same marginal propensity to consume out of a one-time temporary $5000 increase

in income for an individual at age 30 as for the same individual at age 50? Explain.

7   Why should consumer durable expenditures be considered as separate from nondurable expenditures? How does this distinction alter the appearance of saving and consumption behavior?

8   How do permanent as opposed to temporary tax changes alter saving and consumption behavior? Can you account for the observed use of temporary tax changes in stabilization policy?

9   Can you calculate the behavior of consumption and saving in Table 13-1 for this assumption about the behavior of actual income?

Period	Actual income
0	10,000
1	10,000
2	6,000
3	6,000
4	6,000

14

Instability in the Private Economy: Investment

The economy is always straining to get to the full employment limit, but by the mere fact of being there for a time, it is projected downward again.[1]

—Richard M. Goodwin

14-1 INVESTMENT AND ECONOMIC STABILITY

We found in Chapter 13 that the permanent income and life cycle hypotheses of individual consumption behavior explain the partial insulation in the short run of aggregate consumption spending from changes in other types of spending. But what are the sources of changes in these other types of spending? The 1976 real GNP was divided among the major types of real expenditures as follows:

Personal consumption expenditures	64.4%
Gross private domestic investment	13.6
Government purchases of goods and services	20.7
Net exports	1.3
	100.0

In addition to consumption, the major types of expenditures are investment and government spending. Postponing our discussion of government spending and other aspects of fiscal policy to Chapter 17, we concentrate here on private investment.

The instability of private investment spending (together with that of consumer durable purchases treated in Chapter 13) forms the essential core of the nonmonetarist case for policy activism. The private economy can be blown off course by too much or too little investment. Even if the permanent income hypothesis temporarily insulates consumption spend-

---

[1] "A Model of Cyclical Growth" in E. Lundberg, ed., *The Business Cycles in The Post War World* (London: Macmillan, 1955).

ing on nondurable goods and services from the effect of unstable investment, there is no tendency for investment itself to come promptly back on
course. Sooner or later households begin to incorporate into their permanent income the change in actual income caused by the altered output
of investment goods. Nonmonetarists emphasize that the Depression
was made more severe by the 86 percent decline in real private investment between 1929 and 1932 and by the failure of domestic investment
to rise higher than 60 percent of the 1929 level even a decade later in
1939. In postwar recessions and expansions investment has maintained
its record of instability. These are the changes in real gross private domestic investment during postwar business cycles:

	Quarters		Percentage change	
Peak	Trough	Peak	Peak to trough	Trough to peak
1948:Q3	1949:Q2	1953:Q2	−26.0	44.5
1953:Q2	1954:Q2	1957:Q3	−10.4	25.1
1957:Q3	1958:Q2	1960:Q1	−19.0	46.1
1960:Q1	1961:Q1	1969:Q4	−20.8	71.6
1969:Q4	1970:Q4	1973:Q4	− 5.2	38.7
1973:Q4	1975:Q2		−38.2	−

In this chapter we review a very simple theory that explains why investment spending is more likely to exhibit pronounced fluctuations than
to remain constant. In so doing, we confirm an important nonmonetarist
criticism of the monetarist platform. Aggregate private spending, although
partially insulated by the permanent income hypothesis of consumption,
exhibits marked and persistent fluctuations as a result of the instability
of private investment. Nevertheless, the nonmonetarist demonstration
of the tendency of the private economy to exhibit business cycles does
not by itself cement the case for an activist stabilization policy. It might
be possible for private spending to fluctuate up and down and yet government intervention designed to stabilize spending could actually make
matters worse by inaccurate forecasting, imperfect knowledge, or political conflicts. The discussion of private investment in this chapter only
justifies a need for activist policy, refuting plank 1 of the monetarist platform in Chapter 12. Nothing here demonstrates that an activist stabilization policy can be successful; nothing here denies plank 3 of the monetarist platform.

The simple **accelerator hypothesis** that explains fluctuations in investment spending received a preliminary introduction in Chapter 13. There,
according to the permanent income hypothesis, households try to maintain a constant ratio of their consumer durable stock to permanent income. This creates sudden bursts of durable purchases when an upward
revision of permanent income causes the desired durable stock to increase. In this chapter the same idea is extended to investment in plant,

equipment, and housing.[2] At first we assume that firms attempt to maintain a constant ratio of their capital stock to expected output. Investment spending spurts when an upward revision of expected output causes the desired capital stock to increase.

After the simple accelerator theory is introduced in the next section, we add amendments that allow variations in the ratio of the desired capital stock (K^*) to expected output (Q^e). Monetary policy can alter the K^*/Q^e ratio by making borrowing more expensive, causing firms to economize on the amount of capital with which they equip each worker. Fiscal policy can also introduce changes that raise or lower the K^*/Q^e ratio. A higher investment tax credit and a liberalization of depreciation allowances are two of the fiscal tools that can raise the K^*/Q^e ratio and thus stimulate investment. The theory of investment developed here lengthens the list of fiscal policy instruments that can be used by policymakers to achieve multiple policy targets.

14-2 THE ACCELERATOR HYPOTHESIS OF NET INVESTMENT

Business firms must continually evaluate the size of their factories and the numbers of their machines. Will they have too little capacity to produce the output that they expect to be able to sell in the forthcoming year, causing lost sales and dissatisfied customers? Or, perhaps, will capacity be excessive in relation to expected sales, causing a wasteful burden of costs to pay maintenance workers and interest expense on the unneeded plant and equipment? The accelerator theory of investment relies on the simple idea that firms attempt to maintain a fixed relation between their stock of capital (plants and equipment) and their expected sales.

Clearly the first key ingredient in a business firm's decision about plant investment is an educated guess about the likely level of sales. Table 14-1 provides an example of how a hypothetical firm, the Mammoth Electric

---

[2] Examples of plant and equipment investment are these:

Nonresidential plant (structures)	Equipment
Factories	Electronic computers
Oil refineries	Jet airplanes
Office buildings	Typewriters
Shopping centers	Cash registers
Private hospitals	Telephone switchboards
Private universities	Tractors

The principles developed in this chapter also apply to investment in residential housing, both single-family homes and multifamily apartment buildings.

TABLE 14-1

Workings of the Accelerator Theory of Investment for the
Hypothetical Mammoth Electric Company (All Figures
in $ Billions)

				Periods			
Variable	0	1	2	3	4	5
1. Actual sales (Q^i)	10.0	12.0	12.0	12.0	12.0	12.0
2. Expected sales						
$(Q^{ei} = 0.5Q^{ei}_{-1} + 0.5Q^i_{-1})$	10.0	10.0	11.0	11.5	11.75	11.87
3. Desired stock of electric generating stations						
$(K^{*i} = 4Q^{ei})$	40.0	40.0	44.0	46.0	47.0	47.5
4. Net investment in electric generating stations						
$(N^i = K^{*i} - K^{*i}_{-1})$	0.0	0.0	4.0	2.0	1.0	0.5
5. Replacement investment						
$(D^i = 0.10K^i_{-1})$	4.0	4.0	4.0	4.4	4.6	4.7
6. Gross investment						
$(I^i = N^i + D^i)$	4.0	4.0	8.0	6.4	5.6	5.2

Company (which can be imagined to supply electricity to the northeastern United States), estimates expected output and determines desired stock of electric generating stations. The estimate of expected sales (Q^{ei}) is revised from the estimate of the previous year (Q^{ei}_{-1}) by any difference between last year's actual sales outcome (Q^i_{-1}) and what was expected:

$$Q^{ei} = Q^{ei}_{-1} + g^i(Q^i_{-1} - Q^{ei}_{-1})$$
$$= g^iQ^i + (1 - g^i)Q^{ei}_{-1} \qquad (14.1)$$

This so-called adaptive or error-learning method of estimating sales expectations is exactly the same as we previously encountered in the formation of expectations of inflation and of permanent income.[3] Once again, the i superscripts stand for a particular economic unit, Mammoth Electric in Table 14-1. Later the i superscripts will be dropped when we talk about the economy as a whole.

The error-learning method is illustrated in Table 14-1 where g^i is assumed equal to 0.5. In period 2 the previous period's sales (Q^{ei}_{-1}) were expected to be $10 billion but turned out actually to be $12 billion (Q^i_{-1}). The revision of expected sales can be calculated from equation (14.1):

$$Q^{ei} = 0.5(Q^i_{-1}) + 0.5(Q^{ei}_{-1})$$
$$= 0.5(12) + 0.5(10)$$
$$= 11$$

---

[3] The formation of expectations of inflation was the subject of section 8-8. The calculation of permanent income was discussed in section 13-3. The only difference between this section and the discussion of consumer durables (section 13-5) is that here expected sales depend on last period's sales, because this year's sales have not yet been observed.

Thus in period 2 expected sales are $11 billion, as recorded on line 2. But then another mistake is made, because in period 2 actual sales turn out to be $12 billion again instead of the expected $11 billion. Once again expectations for the next period are revised.

The next step in the accelerator theory is the assumption that the stock of capital — that is, plant and equipment — that a firm desires (K^{*i}) is a multiple of its expected sales:

GENERAL FORM   NUMERICAL EXAMPLE

$$K^{*i} = v^{*i}Q^{ei} \qquad\qquad K^{*i} = 4.0Q^{ei} \qquad\qquad (14.2)$$

For example, Mammoth Electric in Table 14-1 wants a capital stock that is always four times as large as its expected sales. Notice that the desired capital stock on line 3 of the table is always exactly 4.0 times the level of expected sales on line 2. What determines the multiple v^{*i}, which relates desired capital to expected sales? As we will see, in calculating v^{*i} firms pay attention to the interest rate and tax rates. Their chosen value of the multiple v^{*i} reflects all available knowledge about government policies and the likely profitability of investment.

Net investment (N^i) is the change in the capital stock (ΔK^i) that occurs each period:

$$N^i = \Delta K^i = K^i - K^i_{-1} \qquad\qquad (14.3)$$

In the example in Table 14-1, we assume that Mammoth Electric always manages to acquire new capital quickly enough to keep its actual capital stock (K^i) equal to its desired capital stock (K^{*i}) in each period:

$$N^i = K^i - K^i_{-1} = K^{*i} - K^{*i}_{-1} \qquad\qquad (14.4)$$

Line 4 in the table shows that net investment (N^i) is always equal to the change in the desired capital stock in each period, which in turn from equation (14.2) is 4.0 times the change in expected sales:

$$N^i = K^{*i} - K^{*i}_{-1}$$
$$= v^{*i}(Q^{ei} - Q^{ei}_{-1}) = v^{*i}\Delta Q^{ei} \qquad\qquad (14.5)$$

The accelerator theory, first proposed by J. M. Clark in 1917, says that the *level* of net investment (N^i) depends on the *change* in expected output (ΔQ^{ei}). When there is an acceleration in business and expected output increases, net investment is positive, but when business decelerates and expected output stops increasing, net investment actually falls. And if expected output were ever to decline, net investment would become negative.

Total business spending on plant and equipment includes not only net investment — purchases that raise the capital stock — but also replacement purchases that simply replace old decaying plant and equipment or plant

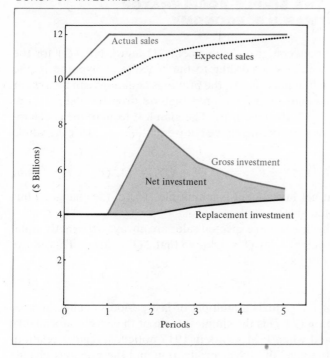

FIGURE 14–1

The Behavior of Actual Sales, Expected Sales, Gross Investment, Net Investment, and Replacement Investment for the Mammoth Electric Company Described in Table 14–1

In period 1 actual sales increase, but expected sales do not begin to respond until period 2. Net investment shoots up in period 2, as Mammoth Edison purchases equipment needed to service the higher expected level of sales. Expected sales continue to grow in periods 3, 4, and 5, but more slowly. Thus net investment actually declines from its peak in period 2.

and equipment that has become obsolete. Line 5 of Table 14-1 assumes that each year 10 percent of the previous year's capital stock needs to be replaced. The total or gross investment (I^i) of Mammoth Electric, the amount recorded in the national income accounts of Chapter 2, is the sum of net investment (N^i) and replacement investment (D^i), and is written on line 6 of the table.

Figure 14-1 is an illustration of the Mammoth Electric example from Table 14-1. The level of actual sales is plotted as the top red line. Underneath, total gross investment is shown as the zigzag line that rises from $4 billion to $8 billion, only to fall in period 3 and afterward back toward the original level. Replacement investment is initially at the level of $4 billion, rising gradually as the capital stock increases. Net investment is the pink shaded area which first increases in size and then shrinks. Overall, the accelerator theory explains why a firm's gross investment is so unstable, at first rising and then falling even when actual sales increase permanently.

The Accelerator Hypothesis of Net Investment **399**

14-3 CASE STUDY: THE SIMPLE ACCELERATOR AND THE POSTWAR U.S. ECONOMY

The relation between gross investment (I) and GNP (Q) for the economy as a whole is, according to the accelerator hypothesis, the same as for an individual firm. All the previous equations can be written for the total economy, requiring only that we drop the i superscript (which denotes an individual firm). The simplest form of the accelerator hypothesis can be obtained if we copy equation (14.5) for the whole economy:

$$N = K^* - K^*_{-1} = v^*(Q^e - Q^e_{-1}) = v^*\Delta Q^e \qquad (14.6)$$

This states that net investment is a multiple (v^*) of the change in this period's expected sales.

In the special case when expected sales are always set exactly equal to last period's actual sales $Q^e = Q_{-1}$, so that $\Delta Q^e = \Delta Q_{-1}$. This allows us to rewrite (14.6) as:

$$N = v^*\Delta Q_{-1} \qquad (14.7)$$

Net investment (N) equals a multiple of last period's change in sales (ΔQ_{-1}). Equation (14.7) is the simplest form of the accelerator theory and was invented when J. M. Clark in 1917 noticed a regular relationship between the level of boxcar production and the previous change in railrold traffic.[4]

> *Perhaps no other equation in this book summarizes so succinctly the inherent instability of the private economy. Any random event —an export boom, an irregularity in the timing of government spending, or an upward revision of consumer estimates of permanent income—can change the growth of real sales and alter the level of net investment in the same direction.*

Figure 14-2 compares real net investment (N) with the change in real output (ΔQ) in the postwar U.S. economy.[5] Unfortunately equation (14.7) appears to be much too simple a theory to explain completely all historical movements in U.S. net investment. True, most peak years in net investment coincided with (or followed by one year) peak years in real GNP growth—1950, 1956, 1960, 1966, 1973. And

---

[4] J. M. Clark, "Business Acceleration and the Law of Demand," *Journal of Political Economy,* vol. 25 (March 1917), pp. 217–35.

[5] To adjust for the steady growth in the size of the economy, both N and ΔQ are divided by real GNP (Q). Thus the actual variables plotted are the share of real net investment in real GNP (N/Q) and the percentage growth rate of real GNP ($\Delta Q/Q$).

THE UPS AND DOWNS OF NET INVESTMENT ARE NOT
PERFECTLY RELATED TO CHANGES IN REAL GNP

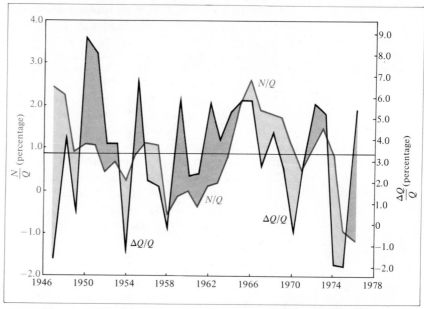

FIGURE 14–2

The Relation of the Net Invest-
ment Share (N/Q) to the Growth
Rate of Real GNP $(\Delta Q/Q)$ in the
U.S. Economy, 1947–76

The net investment share does not
have a perfect or simple relationship
with the growth rate of real GNP.
But the period when the net investment share was high, during 1965–69,
followed five years of high average
output growth. The period when the

net investment share was very low,
during 1958–63, followed a period of
low real output growth, averaging
only 2.7 percent, between 1952 and
1961.

Source: Net investment share (N/Q) is
real nonresidential fixed investment divided
by real GNP minus capital consumption
allowances divided by nominal GNP. All
figures are from the *Economic Report of
the President,* 1977.

trough years in net investment coincided with (or followed by one year)
trough years in real GNP growth — 1949, 1952, 1954, 1958, 1961,
1971, 1976. Furthermore, five years of high net investment (1965–69)
followed seven years (1962–68) in which real GNP growth dipped
below average only once.[6] Also, six years of low net investment (1958–
63) followed eight years (1954–61) during which real GNP growth

---

[6] Average real GNP growth over the 1947–76 period plotted in Figure 14-2 is 3.33 percent. This rate is somewhat below the average growth rate of natural output, because in
1976 the economy was operating at a rate considerably below natural output.

rose above average only twice. But overall, Figure 14-2 reveals quite an imperfect relationship.

There appear to be two main problems with the simple accelerator theory of equation (14.7), judging from the historical U.S. data plotted in Figure 14-2:

1. Net investment does not appear to respond to accelerations and decelerations in real GNP growth with a uniform speed. For instance, the response of net investment was much faster to the 1974–75 drop in real GNP than to the slowdown in GNP growth in 1967–70. It is as if an automobile's engine responded in a split second to some movements of the accelerator pedal, but took minutes to respond to other movements of the pedal.

2. The overall level of net investment relative to real GNP (N/Q) does not have a consistent historical relationship to real GNP growth $(\Delta Q/Q)$. In the following three periods, real GNP growth was quite similar but the net investment ratio (N/Q) was quite different:

Average over period	$\Delta Q/Q$	N/Q
1947–54	3.29%	1.15%
1955–64	3.63	0.30
1965–76	3.07	1.06
Total postwar, 1947–76	3.33	0.83

In the middle period output growth was fastest but N/Q was much lower than in the other periods. If N/Q instead had achieved the average level of the other periods, investment during the 1955–64 period (taken as a whole) would have been $79.2 billion higher and the multiplier would have raised expenditures by an even higher number, perhaps $150 billion.[7]

14-4
THE FLEXIBLE ACCELERATOR

The simple accelerator theory of equation (14.7) depends on several restrictive and unrealistic assumptions. A more realistic version of the theory called the **flexible accelerator** can be obtained if we loosen several of these restrictive assumptions:

---

[7] Any change in investment has a multiplier effect on total expenditures, just as does an increase in government spending. Formulas for the investment multiplier in a simple model are given in section 3-5. Estimates of the size of the multiplier in the U.S. economy are presented in Figure 12-4. The $79.2 billion figure in the text is expressed in 1976 prices.

1. The simple accelerator assumed that this period's expected output was always set equal to last period's actual output. But the error-learning or adaptive hypothesis states that in general only a fraction of expected output is based on last period's output, and the rest conservatively carries over whatever was expected last period.
2. The simple accelerator assumes that the desired capital stock (K^*) is set equal to a constant (v^*) times expected output (Q^e). But actually the desired capital-output ratio (v^*) may vary substantially, depending on the cost of borrowing, the taxation of capital, and other factors; we will postpone until the next section a detailed consideration of the factors that make v^* change.
3. The third assumption made by the simple accelerator is that firms can instantly put in place any desired amount of investment in plant and equipment needed to make actual capital this period (K) equal to desired capital (K^*). Actually, some kinds of capital take a substantial period to construct. Buildings sometimes take two or three years between conception and completion. Some types of electric utility generating stations can take as long as eight years to complete.[8] Further, installing too much new investment at one time would be excessively costly, because firms supplying capital goods might raise their prices and the installation activity might disrupt the flow of production.

Thus net investment in the real world does not always close the whole gap between desired capital and last year's capital stock, but only a fraction of it.

To summarize, the relationship between economy-wide gross investment and output is fairly complex and depends on at least four major factors:

1. *The fraction of the gap between desired capital and last period's actual capital that can be closed in a single period.* The higher this fraction, the more current investment responds to an acceleration in last period's output.
2. *The response of expected output to last period's error in estimating actual output.* The higher this response is, the more expected output and hence investment responds to any unexpected acceleration in last period's actual output.
3. *The proportion of the capital stock that is replaced each year.* For long-lived types of capital, such as office buildings, only a fraction of buildings is replaced each year, and so total investment in office buildings is very sensitive to changes in output. When output stagnates, as in the late 1950s, few new office buildings are needed and there is little

---

[8] At the other extreme, a shop that opens for business today in a large city could probably obtain delivery of needed equipment—cash register, calculating machine, typewriter, postage meter, furniture—in a day or two.

need for replacement, so that gross investment is low. But in years of booming output, as in the mid-1960s, the large net investment in new office buildings swamps the small replacement investment, and gross investment may rise by a factor of five or ten. Exactly the opposite effect works for short-lived types of capital.

A further complication is that the proportion of the capital stock replaced may not remain the same from year to year. The assumption that the replacement fraction is constant has been used in much econometric research.[9] But more recent studies have confirmed the obvious fact that firms are not forced to replace old capital on a fixed schedule.[10] Often new equipment or buildings come most economically in large sizes that lead firms to concentrate their replacement investment during the same periods as their net investment — when output is growing rapidly. Experts in the history of central business districts know, for instance, that old office buildings are rarely torn down except in prosperous periods when land is needed for the construction of new and larger office buildings.

4. *The desired ratio of capital to expected output* (v^*). Investment responds more to changes in expected output in capital intensive industries (those with a high v^*, such as electric utilities, oil refining, and chemicals) than in labor intensive industries (those with a low v^* such as textiles, apparel, and barber shops).

In the next section we investigate the determinants of the desired capital-output ratio and the policy instruments with which the government can affect the size of v^*.

14-5 THE COST OF CAPITAL AND THE DESIRED CAPITAL-OUTPUT RATIO

From the previous discussion of the accelerator theory, a monetarist might conclude that investment spending does not add any extra instability not already present in the economy. If actual output were maintained at a steady pace, business firms would be able to form accurate expectations about future sales, and investment would not exhibit the pronounced up-and-down cycles observed in the past. Thus, the monetarist might conclude, investment spending does not add anything to the case for activist government policy intervention.

But, the nonmonetarists might respond, this sanguine attitude ignores

---

[9] See especially the work of Dale Jorgenson, beginning with his "Capital Theory and Investment Behavior," *American Economic Review,* vol. 53 (May 1963), pp. 247–57.

[10] A study that confirms the procyclical behavior of replacement investment is Martin S. Feldstein and David Foot, "The Other Half of Gross Investment: Replacement and Modernization Expenditures," *The Review of Economics and Statistics,* vol. 53, no. 1 (February 1971), pp. 49–58.

the fact that v^*, the desired capital-output ratio, may vary and can have just as powerful an effect on investment as an acceleration of real output. A given percentage increase in v^* can raise the desired capital stock, and hence investment, by as much as the same percentage increase in expected output.[11] We will see that a deterioration in business confidence can reduce v^* and cause investment to drop, but several government policy instruments are available that can stimulate v^* to offset the decline in confidence.

A business firm is willing to undertake an investment project only when it expects that a profit can be made. Just as we learned in Chapter 7 that an extra unit of labor will not be hired unless its marginal product — the extra output it produces — equals or exceeds its real wage, the same principle applies to capital equipment. An extra unit of capital will not be purchased unless the expected **marginal product of capital** (MPK) is at least equal to the real **user cost of capital** (u):

GENERAL FORM   NUMERICAL EXAMPLE

$$MPK = u \qquad\qquad 14 = 14 \qquad\qquad (14.8)$$

Both the marginal product (MPK) and the real user cost are fractions, which can be expressed as percentages. The marginal product of capital consists of the dollars of extra output each year produced by an extra piece of plant or equipment, divided by the cost of the equipment. If the purchase of an extra machine costing $100,000 allows a firm to produce $14,000 extra output each year, then MPK would be 14 percent.[12]

The user cost of capital is the cost to the business firm of using a piece of capital for a period of time, expressed as a fraction of the machine's purchase price. The user cost might be 14 percent, consisting perhaps of a 4 percent annual real interest rate and a 10 percent depreciation rate.[13]

What does equation (14.8) have to do with the profitability of a business firm? When MPK is 15 percent and user cost is only 14 percent, then the extra revenue generated by a new machine exceeds its cost, and the firm's profits are increased. On the other hand, when MPK is only 13 percent and user cost is the same 14 percent, the extra revenue is insufficient to pay the costs of the new machine, and profits go down if the machine is purchased. Only if policymakers can find some way of reducing user cost to 13 percent will the new machine be purchased.

---

[11] See equation (14.2).

[12] As is always true in economics, the marginal product of a single input measures the extra output produced by an extra unit of that input if the quantity of other inputs is held constant.

[13] Depreciation is part of user cost, because the portion of the machine wearing out must be replaced if MPK is to remain unaffected.

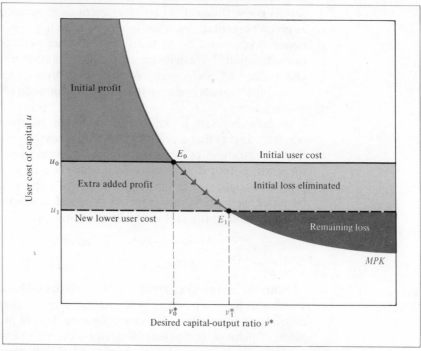

FIGURE 14–3

The Effect of a Drop in the User Cost of Capital (u) on the Desired Capital-Output Ratio (v^*)

Initially the economy is at point E_0. Firms are making a profit on their capital stock indicated by the dark gray area. Any further investment will not be undertaken, because it would create losses indicated by the pink and red areas. But if the user cost can be reduced from u_0 to u_1, the economy will move from point E_0 to E_1. The initial pink area of potential losses is eliminated, and the light gray area of added profit is gained.

The effect of a reduction in user cost on the desired capital-output ratio is illustrated in Figure 14-3. Initially the user cost is u_0; the capital-output ratio v_0^* will be chosen. Why? A smaller amount of capital, to the left of E_0, would mean giving up some of the profits indicated by the dark gray area that measures the difference between the marginal product of capital and the user cost. But to purchase a larger amount of capital, to the right of E_0, would cause losses. The pink and red areas indicate the loss made by purchasing extra units of capital that have an insufficient MPK to pay for their user cost.

Now let us assume that the user cost is cut, perhaps by a new government investment incentive. Additional units of capital will now be purchased to bring the capital-output ratio rightward to v_1^*. The reduction in user cost has made available extra profits, indicated by the light gray area, and it has eliminated the losses indicated by the pink area. Only if the capital-output ratio exceeds v_1^* will the marginal product of capital (MPK) be insufficient to balance the new lower user cost.

> *By using monetary and fiscal policy instruments, the user cost of capital can be cut. Firms can thus be induced to adopt more capital-intensive methods of production and the opposite is true as well. Just as an increase in the wage rate can cause firms to replace marginal workers with extra machines, so that an increase in capital's user cost can cause firms to substitute away from elaborate machines toward more labor-intensive techniques of production.*[14]

14-6 BUSINESS CONFIDENCE AND THE NEED FOR ACTIVIST POLICY INTERVENTION

Remember that any increase in investment caused by a reduction in u is temporary, just as is the increase in investment caused by an increase in output. After the initial burst of investment spending caused by a lower u, firms will find their actual capital stock moving closer to the higher desired level, and they can cut back on their additions to capital.

> **Review:** In Figure 14-1 a permanent increase in actual sales causes only a temporary increase in investment. In exactly the same way for the same reasons, a permanent decrease in the user cost of capital would cause only a temporary boom in investment.

In Chapters 3 and 4 the phrases "business and consumer confidence" were used as a convenient shorthand to refer to factors that could push output in an undesired direction when government spending and the money supply were fixed at a given level.[15] In the flexible accelerator theory of investment summarized here, the confidence of business firms may influence investment spending in three ways:

1. Investment depends on the fraction of an increase in last period's actual output that is incorporated into expected output and hence into desired capital and investment. When businessmen lack confidence in the future, they may refuse to extrapolate a quarter or a year of in-

---

[14] For instance, textile firms in the United States typically use fancier machines and fewer workers to produce given products than those in less developed countries where the wage rate is lower and the user cost of capital is higher.

[15] A highly readable analysis of the factors which have tended to depress business confidence in the late 1970s is presented in Alan Greenspan, "Investment Risk: The New Dimension of Policy," *The Economist* (August 6, 1977), pp. 31–35.

creasing output, believing instead that any increase in output is bound to be temporary.

2. The user cost of capital (u) includes the borrowing costs that business firms expect to have to pay if they undertake an investment project. If businessmen are pessimistic, they may overestimate the true borrowing cost that they are likely to face, making their estimate of u too high and their desired capital stock too low.

3. Perhaps most important, business firms can only guess the likely marginal product of new investment projects. It is the expected marginal product that matters. If business has recently been bad, a condition experienced by many business firms in 1930–33, or as recently as 1975–76, firms may currently have more capital than they may need. Some present capital may presently be underutilized, and future capital investments may be unprofitable, having close to a zero marginal product for the foreseeable future.

Any event, whether political or economic, which causes a drop in business confidence can cause a sharp drop in the level of investment. In the extreme case, the Great Depression of the 1930s, a collapse in business confidence dropped the desired capital stock far below the actual inherited capital stock. Not only did businessmen refuse to add to their capital stock, but they allowed net investment to become negative by refusing to replace worn out and obsolete equipment. Gross domestic private investment plummeted from $55.9 billion in 1929 to $7.9 billion in 1932 (both in 1972 prices), but despite the low levels of gross investment in the 1930s, much capital remained underutilized. The overhang of too much inherited capital depressed investment for a full decade.

Periods of excessive business overoptimism in U.S. history have periodically been followed by overbuilding, underutilized capital, and extensive pessimism. The cycle repeated itself in the late 1960s and early 1970s, leaving the United States in the mid-1970s with a substantial underutilization of some types of capital. The overbuilding of apartments was particularly severe in mid-1976:

> In Chicago, new apartment construction has just about ceased. In Atlanta, where there is at least a three-year supply of unsold condominiums overhanging the market, mortgage companies are auctioning off high-rise units to the public at two-thirds their original asking price. . . . The current problems stem from overbuilding in the early 1970's. . . . Soon the market was saturated and investors were caught in a squeeze. "During the past few years," says a Chicago builder, "there's been no return on investment."[16]

In Atlanta the overbuilding of office buildings had also reached an extreme stage:

---

[16] "The Great High-rise Bust," *Newsweek* (August 30, 1976), p. 5.

> About 9 million of the city's 36 million sq. ft. of office space is vacant. . . . Says architect-developer John C. Portman, . . . "The city has three years' supply of office space, in my opinion. In the case of some of the poorer developments, it may take five years to work out."[17]

When a builder says that his city has "three years' supply" of office buildings, he means that there is no justification for any new construction of office buildings until three years of economic growth has created the demand to fill the previously constructed vacant buildings. If this situation is widespread, the low level of construction investment — working through the investment multiplier of Chapter 3 — may prevent or delay the economic boom that is needed to create the conditions for a future recovery of investment. In the 1930s, investment never did recover to its 1929 level; in 1939 investment was only $33.6 billion in 1972 prices, compared to the $55.9 billion level achieved in 1929. The real problem was nonresidential building for offices and factories; this never exceeded even half its 1929 level throughout the 1930s.

Keynes placed major emphasis on the role of business confidence in determining the level of investment. In the following passage he stresses that investment decisions are based on estimates of the future "yield" (or marginal product) of extra capital, which may be little better than a guess. Faced with identical information, the great uncertainty facing businessmen may lead them to go ahead with an investment project when they feel optimistic but postpone the same project when they feel pessimistic:

> The outstanding fact is the extreme precariousness of the basis of knowledge on which our estimates of prospective yield have to be made. Our knowledge of the factors which will govern the yield of an investment some years hence is usually very slight and often negligible. If we speak frankly, we have to admit that our basis of knowledge for estimating the yield ten years hence of a railway, a copper mine, a textile factory, the goodwill of a patent medicine, an Atlantic liner, a building in the City of London amounts to little and sometimes to nothing; or even five years hence. In fact, those who seriously attempt to make any such estimates are often so much in the minority that their behavior does not govern the market.[18]

14-7 USER COST AND THE ROLE OF MONETARY AND FISCAL POLICY

Government policymakers cannot change the state of business confidence merely by delivering pious speeches. But they can directly determine the user cost of capital (u), one of the major determinants of gross

---

[17] "Atlanta's Building Boom Overshoots Its Mark," *Business Week* (December 13, 1976), p. 92.

[18] Keynes, *General Theory*, pp. 149–50.

investment. The user cost of capital depends on several factors, which can be introduced in two steps. First, let us neglect the effect of taxation. A capital good that is purchased at a given real price imposes three types of cost on its user in the absence of taxation.

1. *An interest cost is involved in buying a capital good.* Either money must be borrowed at the nominal interest rate (i) or else an investor loses the interest (i) he would receive by investing in a savings account the funds that he uses to buy the investment good.
2. *Physical deterioration affects the ability of every capital good to produce, and in addition some capital goods become obsolete.* The **depreciation rate** indicates the annual decline in value of the capital good due to physical deterioration plus obsolescence.
3. *Some used capital goods may depreciate but may simultaneously have a market value that increases.* This paradox can occur when inflation continuously raises the price of new capital goods, "dragging along" the price of used capital goods.

> **Example:** Some readers may have been lucky enough to own a used foreign car during the 1971–75 period when the prices of new foreign cars rose rapidly. In some cases the capital gain due to inflation exceeded the loss in value due to depreciation, so that the used car's price was higher when it was 3 years old than when it was new! The capital gain component can partially offset the positive interest and depreciation costs.

Policymakers cannot alter the relative price of capital goods, which depends on the technical factors that influence innovations and productivity change in capital goods industries compared to the economy as a whole. Similarly, they cannot change the rate of physical decay and economic obsolescence summarized in the depreciation rate. But the real interest rate is under the control of policymakers. As we learned in Chapter 5, a fiscal policy stimulus raises the real interest rate and hence crowds out investment. A monetary policy stimulus, on the other hand, reduces the real interest rate and raises investment. A change in the monetary-fiscal policy mix toward easier monetary policy and tighter fiscal policy cuts the real interest rate and user cost, thus raising investment.

So far taxation has been ignored. But fiscal policy can have a major effect on investment by altering the user cost. Three basic fiscal tools are available:

1. *The U.S. government levies a corporation income tax on corporate profits.* Firms make investment decisions by equating the marginal product of capital with the real user cost of capital *before* taxes. But savers care about the level of their income *after* taxes. Thus to provide savers with a given market return, an investment project must

pay a higher before-tax interest rate (and hence incur a higher user cost) when the corporation tax is high than when it is low.

2. *Firms can cut their corporation tax by deducting the value of depreciation of plant and equipment.* The amount of depreciation they can deduct depends on rules set out by the U.S. Treasury Department. Whenever the Treasury depreciation rules are liberalized, as occurred in 1954, 1962, and 1964, more of corporate profits are protected from tax, thus cutting the user cost of capital.

3. *Since 1962 some investment in the United States has been eligible for an investment tax credit.* In the mid-1970s, business firms could take 10 percent of the value of the equipment investment and deduct that amount from their corporation income tax. Naturally this reduced the user cost of capital, as long as the firm was making profits and was subject to tax.

These three fiscal instruments give the federal government much more flexibility in conducting stabilization policy than would be available if the government were limited to controlling the economy by varying the level of government spending and the personal income tax rate. For instance, government spending can be restrained and the personal income tax rate raised to slow down an economy that is experiencing too much aggregate demand, but at the same time any of the investment-related fiscal instruments can be liberalized if it is believed that the economy has too little investment and too much consumption: (1) the corporation income tax can be cut, (2) business firms can be allowed to deduct a larger fraction of their capital stock in the form of depreciation deductions each year, and (3) the rate of investment tax credit can be raised.

Unfortunately, it is very difficult for policymakers to use monetary and fiscal policy to iron out all fluctuations in investment. A basic problem is the lag in the effect of most policy measures. A reduction in current output caused by the behavior of consumption, exports, or defense spending, or a drop in business confidence, may have an immediate effect on business appropriations for future investment projects. But several quarters may elapse before policymakers decide that a stimulus is necessary, and there may be a further subsequent lag between the policy stimulus and the resulting increase in investment spending. However, if low output or a deterioration in confidence are expected to last for several years, sufficient time may be available for a monetary or fiscal policy stimulus to raise investment and stabilize the economy.

14-8 THE ACCELERATOR AS A SOURCE OF INSTABILITY IN OUTPUT AND INTEREST RATES

The accelerator theory creates a favorite paradox of macroeconomics teachers. We became accustomed in Chapters 4 and 5 to an association of low interest rates with high investment and high interest rates with low investment. This inverse relationship between investment and interest rates has been confirmed in this chapter, because a low level of the real interest rate reduces the user cost of capital, which in turn raises the desired capital stock and hence the level of gross investment (see Figure 14-3). Yet a predominant feature of business cycles in almost every nation is a positive correlation between business investment and interest rates. United States business investment fluctuates procyclically, reaching peaks in years of high output and troughs during recessions or soon after the business cycle trough (Fluctuations of business fixed investment are related to recessions in Figure 12-1.) But at the same time, interest rates also fluctuate procyclically, so that years of low interest rates are usually associated with low investment, not high investment.

How can the positive relationship between investment and interest rates be explained? The accelerator theory provides the answer. Figure 14-4 repeats the *IS-LM* analysis of Chapter 5. The *LM* curve maintains an unchanged position whenever the real money supply (M/P) is fixed. The *IS* curve fluctuates whenever there is a change in the investment purchases that business firms choose to make at a constant real interest rate.

A long list of factors can make the level of gross investment, and hence the *IS* curve, change for a given interest rate. Included are (1) an increase in actual output due to some factor unconnected with the investment process, (2) a change in the extent to which a current output change is predicted to continue in the future, (3) a previous episode of overbuilding that makes the actual capital stock high relative to the current desired stock, (4) a shift in demand toward shorter-lived equipment, (5) a change in the relative price of capital goods, and, finally, (6) an alteration in fiscal incentives that alters the before-tax user cost of capital. A change in any of these elements shifts the level of investment that occurs at a given interest rate and, through the multiplier, shifts the level of total output.

Figure 14-4 illustrates two *IS* curves, IS_0 and IS_1. The movement back and forth between the two *IS* curves reflects any of the elements in the previous paragraph that change the desired capital stock (for a given real interest rate) and thus cause an increase or decrease in gross investment. The positive relationship between investment and interest rates is explained in Figure 14-4 by the constant level of the real money supply, which keeps the *LM* curve fixed at LM_0. Anything in the previous paragraph that cuts the demand for investment goods and shifts *IS* leftward to IS_0 reduces the transaction demand for money, requiring a reduction in the interest rate to maintain the overall real demand for money equal to the fixed real supply of money. Similarly, a boom in the demand for investment goods that shifts *IS* rightward to IS_1 raises the transaction demand for money, requiring an increase in the interest rate

WHY THE INTEREST RATE AND INVESTMENT
OFTEN MOVE IN THE SAME DIRECTION

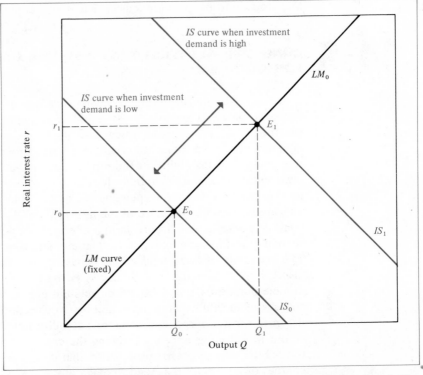

FIGURE 14–4   Effect on Output and the Interest Rate of a Shift in the Level of Investment Relative to the Interest Rate

Shifts in business confidence or in user cost can shift the red *IS* curve back and forth between IS_0 and IS_1. As a result, the interest rate will be high when investment is high, and vice-versa. This conclusion assumes that the real money supply, which fixes the position of the *LM* curve, remains unchanged.

to maintain the overall real demand for money equal to the fixed real supply of money.

The positive relationship between investment and the interest rate illustrated in Figure 14-4 suggests that the depressing effect of low output on investment, working through the accelerator, dominates the stimulative effect of low interest rates on investment, at least in the short run. As recently as 1976 the United States experienced a year in which both investment and interest rates turned out to be lower than most people had expected. In 1976 fixed investment (plant, equipment, and residential construction) had fallen 15 percent from the level of 1973, whereas the average short-term interest rate (3-month Treasury bills) had dropped from 7.0 percent in 1973 to 4.9 percent in 1976.

14-9 CONCLUSION: INVESTMENT AND THE CASE FOR ACTIVISM

A major source of disagreement between monetarists and nonmonetarists is the need for an activist stabilization policy. Monetarists argue that the private economy is basically stable if freed from the destabilizing influence of government intervention, whereas nonmonetarists emphasize sources of instability in the private sector that require government intervention to maintain stability in total output. We concluded in Chapter 13 that consumption spending on nondurable goods and services appeared to bolster the case of the monetarists. Both the permanent income hypothesis and life cycle hypothesis suggested that consumption spending on those items tends to fluctuate less than disposable income. The instability of household saving behavior that appears from a surface inspection of the data actually is caused by (1) variations in consumer durable purchases, which would be stable if policy could eliminate other sources of instability in income, and by (2) variations in tax rates, often designed for the purpose of economic stabilization.

But this chapter appears to swing the case in the opposite direction, toward the nonmonetarist proposition that the private economy contains sources of instability that tend to make any equality between actual and natural output an infrequent coincidence rather than a frequent occurrence. The basic problem is summarized by the accelerator theory of investment. Any event that causes a *permanent* increase in the desired capital stock—whether an increase in expected output or a reduction in the user cost of capital—causes only a *temporary* burst of investment spending. Added to the simple accelerator is the realistic complication of lagged adjustment. In a single year extra investment can close only a fraction of the gap between desired and previous actual capital, because some types of investment (particularly structures) require a long delay between conception and completion. A period when business firms are overoptimistic may lead to excessive overbuilding, followed by many years when vacant apartments and office buildings are the rule and new projects are the distinct exception. Making matters worse, households may begin to incorporate into their permanent income a slump in actual income caused by a prolonged deterioration in investment spending.

Summary: Investment spending may experience sustained booms or slumps lasting several years resulting from fluctuations in confidence and lags between the conception and completion of investment projects. Policymakers can resist a destabilizing recession in total output, but only by introducing an activist policy stimulus. Left alone, the private economy is prone to long booms and slumps in private investment, leading either to accelerations of inflation (as in the mid-1950s and mid-1960s) or to long periods of wasteful unemployment (as in the 1930s, early 1960s, and mid-1970s).

SUMMARY

1. The major source of instability in consumption spending is contributed by consumer expenditures on durables, which can exhibit large fluctuations in response to income changes. This chapter adds private investment spending as an additional source of instability, with the potential of causing major changes in GNP in response to small shocks.

2. The simple accelerator theory of investment relies on the idea that firms attempt to maintain a fixed relation between their stock of capital and their expected sales. Thus the level of net investment—the change in the capital stock—depends on the change in expected output. The accelerator theory explains why the gross investment of most firms is relatively unstable, at first rising and then falling in response to a permanent increase in actual sales.

3. The flexible accelerator theory recognizes that net investment in the real world usually closes only a portion of any gap between the desired and actual capital stocks. Furthermore, the desired capital-output ratio may change, altering investment with a powerful accelerator effect.

4. The accelerator theory implies that any event that causes a permanent increase in the desired capital stock, whether arising from an increase in expected output or from a reduction in the user cost of capital, causes only a temporary rise in investment spending. Thus investment spending may experience sustained booms or slumps lasting several years, resulting from fluctuations in business confidence and lags between the conception and completion of investment projects.

5. Government policymakers can directly alter the user cost of capital. Fiscal and monetary policy can change the real interest rate component of user cost. Taxation can affect the user cost of capital through changes in the corporation income tax, depreciation deductions and the investment tax credit. But the use of these policy instruments cannot eliminate all fluctuations in investment expenditures because most policy measures operate only with lagged effects.

A LOOK AHEAD

In this chapter and the last we have examined sources of instability in the private economy originating in the commodity market—that is, in the market for goods and services. Another potential source of instability is in the money market. Is the private demand for money stable and predictable, or unstable and hard to predict? This is the subject of Chapter 15.

CONCEPTS AND QUESTIONS

IDENTIFICATIONS

Simple accelerator hypothesis
Flexible accelerator hypothesis
Actual capital stock versus desired capital stock
Net investment versus replacement investment

Desired capital-output ratio
User cost of capital
Marginal product of capital
Depreciation deductions
Investment tax credit

QUESTIONS FOR REVIEW

1 How do changes in the user cost of capital alter net investment?

2 How can monetary and fiscal policy alter the user cost of capital?

3 Why is business and consumer confidence important? In what way(s) does it enter the flexible accelerator analysis?

4 There is an asymmetry in the adjustment of the inherited capital stock to the desired capital stock. This is a result of the lower limit of zero on gross investment, which prevents net investment from falling below the amount by which depreciation causes the actual capital stock to shrink. Can you explain how this factor might influence the economy's ability to recover from a depression without government stimulus?

5 Can you explain why gross investment in short-lived types of capital is more stable than gross investment in office buildings? Try to write down an explanation for gross investment in truck tires.

6 "Stable monetary and fiscal policy would eliminate output fluctuations caused by the government. Thus there would be no shocks causing investment to fluctuate." Evaluate this statement.

15 The Demand for Money and the Choice of Monetary Instruments

Unemployment develops . . . because people want the moon;—men cannot be employed when the object of desire (i.e., money) is something which cannot be produced and the demand for which cannot be readily choked off. There is no remedy, but to persuade the public that green cheese is practically the same thing, and to have a green cheese factory (i.e., a central bank) under public control.
—John Maynard Keynes[1]

15-1 THE DEMAND FOR MONEY AND THE EFFICACY OF FISCAL POLICY

The basic theory of income determination developed in Chapters 3–7 was based on a simple economic model consisting of two markets: a commodity market in which goods and services are bought and sold, and a money market in which the interest rate adjusts to induce households and firms voluntarily to hold the supply of money provided by the government. In those earlier chapters the demand functions for commodities and money were taken to be stable and predictable, so that stabilization of real output at the desired level was a simple matter of setting the monetary and fiscal policy instruments at particular values. But now we have seen (in Chapters 13 and 14) that the demand for the two major types of commodities demanded by the private sector—consumption goods and investment goods—depends on a wide variety of factors, including the state of consumer and business confidence, and thus the demand for commodities may not be completely stable or predictable.

In this chapter we shift from the commodity market to the money market and study the determinants of the demand for money. In Chapter 5 we were first introduced to the relationship between the efficacy of policy changes and the sensitivity of the demand for money to changes in the interest rate. We can review our conclusions with the aid of Figure 15-1, which reproduces the *IS* and *LM* curves that were used extensively earlier in the book. Once again the (real) interest rate is on the vertical axis and the level of real output is on the horizontal axis. The *IS* curve

---

[1] *General Theory*, p. 235.

shows all the combinations of the interest rate and real output that maintain equilibrium in the commodity market, that is, that keep output equal to planned expenditures. The position of the IS curve depends on the level of government spending. The curve is at the position IS_0 when government spending equals the fixed value G_0. But when government spending is increased to G_1, the IS curve shifts rightward to IS_1.[2]

The LM curve shows all the different combinations of the interest rate and real output that maintain equilibrium in the money market, that is, that keep the real demand for money equal to the given real supply of money $(M/P)_0$. Two LM curves are illustrated in Figure 15-1. The curve labeled LM_0 has the normal positive slope and assumes that the demand for money is sensitive to the interest rate. The curve labeled LM_1, on the other hand, has the extreme vertical slope and assumes that the demand for money is completely insensitive to changes in the interest rate.[3]

Will the boost in government spending that shifts the IS curve rightward from IS_0 to IS_1 raise the level of real output? In the long run the higher level of government spending will just succeed in raising the price level without any effect on real output. But in the short run the effect of the fiscal stimulus on real output depends on the interest sensitivity of the demand for money. When the demand for money is interest sensitive, the LM_0 curve is valid, and the fiscal stimulus raises real output from Q_0 to Q_1. When money demand is completely independent of the interest rate, however, the LM_1 curve is valid, and then the fiscal stimulus has no effect on real output even in the short run. In this case the economy moves from A to C (not from A to B), and the fiscal stimulus succeeds only in raising the interest rate.

Not only would a vertical LM curve destroy the effectiveness of fiscal policy, it would also eliminate its rationale. Shifts in private spending that move the IS curve would no longer alter real output. The IS curve would just move up and down a fixed vertical LM curve. There would no longer be any need for an activist fiscal policy. Because both the need for policy intervention and the short-run efficacy of fiscal policy depend on an interest sensitive demand for money, economists since Keynes have placed major emphasis on refining the theory of why the demand for money depends on the interest rate, as well as on empirical estimates of the size of the interest response. A major purpose of this chapter is to review the most important explanations of money demand to determine whether or not the dependence of money demand on the interest rate is solidly grounded in theory.

---

[2] The position of the IS curve depends also on anything other than the interest rate that affects the level of planned expenditures in the commodity market, including tax rates, investment tax incentives, real wealth, and the state of business and consumer confidence. To review the determinants of the slope and position of the IS curve, turn back to sections 4-3 and 4-4.

[3] To review the relationship between the interest sensitivity of the demand for money and the slope of the LM curve, turn back to section 4-5.

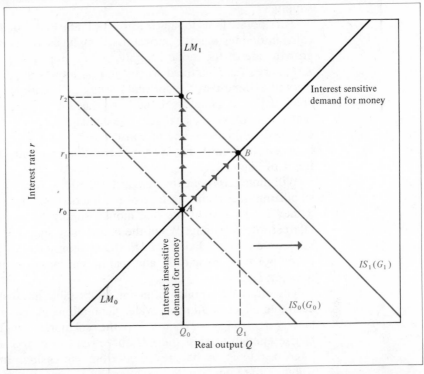

FIGURE 15–1

Two Alternative Responses of Real Output and the Interest Rate to an Increase in Government Spending from G_0 to G_1

An increase in government spending from G_0 to G_1 shifts the IS curve rightward from IS_0 to IS_1. The economy's movement in the short run (while real money balances are fixed) depends on the slope of the LM curve. When money demand is sensitive to changes in the interest rate, the economy moves from A to B. When money demand is completely insensitive to changes in the interest rate, the economy moves from A vertically up to C.

15-2 THE DEMAND FOR MONEY AND THE INSTRUMENTS OF MONETARY CONTROL

A firm understanding of the determinants of money demand is necessary not only for the conduct of fiscal policy but also for the management of monetary policy. Policymakers attempting to maintain a stable level of real output are aided if the demand for money at that desired output level is stable and predictable, because then they need only set the actual supply of money equal to that predicted level of money demand.

If, on the other hand, money demand is unstable and hard to predict, policymakers may do better to stabilize the interest rate than the money supply.

This point, first popularized by William Poole of Brown University, calls into question the monetarist emphasis on achieving a constant growth rate of the money supply.[4] In the top frame of Figure 15-2 the LM_0 curve remains fixed when the real money supply is fixed.[5] At first we will assume that the demand for money is entirely stable and predictable, just as in Chapters 4 and 5, so that the LM curve shifts only if the real supply of money changes. The demand for commodities, however, is assumed to fluctuate and to cause the IS curve to move back and forth between the right-hand IS_1 curve and the left-hand IS_0 curve in the top frame of Figure 15-2.

Will monetary policymakers at the Federal Reserve do a better job of stabilizing output, in the face of the fluctuations in commodity demand, if they hold constant the real money supply or, alternatively, hold the interest rate constant? When the real money supply is held constant, the LM curve remains fixed at LM_0, the economy moves back and forth between positions B_0 and B_1, and real output moves over the limited range between Q_0' and Q_1'.

The alternative policy of maintaining stable interest rates has the undesirable effect of allowing wider fluctuations in real output. When commodity demand is high (along IS_1), the real money supply must be allowed to rise enough to shift the LM curve rightward from LM_0 to LM_2 if the interest rate is to be prevented from increasing. In other words, to stabilize the interest rate in the face of an unstable commodity demand, the Fed is forced to accommodate the additional demand for money that occurs when commodity demand is high. The stable interest rate policy causes the economy to fluctuate between points A_0 and A_1, and it allows real output to vary over the wider range between Q_0 and Q_1.

The top frame of Figure 15-2 demonstrates that when commodity demand is unstable, a constant money supply policy, which keeps movements in real output between the bounds of points B_0 and B_1, is more stabilizing than the alternative constant interest rate policy, which allows output to vary between points A_0 and A_1. But a third alternative is also available. The Fed can pursue an activist countercyclical policy, reducing the money supply and shifting LM leftward to LM_1 when commodity demand is high and raising the money supply to shift LM rightward to LM_2 when commodity demand is low. Now the economy will

---

[4] William Poole, "Optimal Choice of Monetary Policy Instruments in a Simple Stochastic Macro Model," *Quarterly Journal of Economics*, vol. 84 (May 1970), pp. 197–216. A little-known earlier reference is M. L. Burstein, *Economic Theory* (New York: Wiley, 1966), Chapter 13.

[5] A fixed real money supply (M/P) and a fixed LM curve can be achieved either with a constant nominal money supply (M) and a fixed price level (P) or with the money supply growing at the same rate as the price level $(m = p)$.

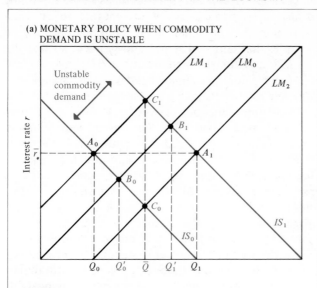

(a) MONETARY POLICY WHEN COMMODITY DEMAND IS UNSTABLE

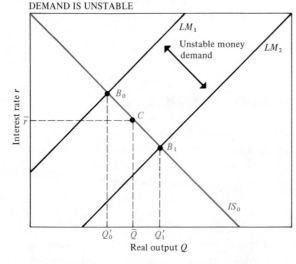

(b) MONETARY POLICY WHEN MONEY DEMAND IS UNSTABLE

FIGURE 15–2

Effects on Real Output of Alternative Policies That Stabilize the Interest Rate or the Real Money Supply When Either Commodity Demand or Money Demand Is Unstable

In the top frame the demand for commodities is unstable, fluctuating between IS_0 and IS_1. A policy that maintains a fixed real money supply and a fixed LM_0 curve leads to smaller fluctuations of output than an alternative policy that stabilizes the interest rate at $\bar{r}$ by shifting LM from LM_1 to LM_2. The contrary is true in the bottom frame, where the demand for money is unstable. In this case a policy of stabilizing the interest rate at $\bar{r}$ will keep real output more stable than an alternative policy that stabilizes the real money supply. When the real money supply is held fixed, shifts in the LM curve from LM_1 to LM_2 are caused by unstable money demand, causing output to fluctuate between Q_0' and Q_1'.

fluctuate vertically between points C_0 and C_1, and real output will not change at all. One disadvantage of a countercyclical monetary policy is evident in the diagram: The interest rate fluctuates more between C_0 and C_1 than between B_0 and B_1. Other possible limitations of a countercyclical monetary policy are the subject of the next chapter.

Not only is a constant money supply policy inferior to a counter-cyclical policy when commodity demand is unstable, as in the top frame of Figure 15-2, it is also inferior to a constant interest rate policy when money demand is unstable, as illustrated in the bottom frame of the diagram. Now we assume that commodity demand is fixed, so that the IS curve remains at IS_0, and the demand for money is unstable and unpredictable. The LM curve does not remain fixed when the money supply is constant, as we have assumed throughout the book, but instead the LM curve moves around unpredictably between LM_1 and LM_2 even when the real money supply is constant. Thus the constant money supply policy recommended by the monetarists leads to fluctuations in the economy between points B_0 and B_1, with output varying between Q_0' and Q_1'. A policy of changing the money supply to maintain a constant interest rate, however, keeps the economy pinned to point C, with a fixed interest rate $\bar{r}$ and a fixed output level $\bar{Q}$.

Figure 15-2 further justifies our interest in the demand for money. If the demand for money is a stable function of output and the interest rate, as in the top frame, the Fed will do better to stabilize the real money supply than to stabilize the interest rate (although it is better still to pursue a countercyclical policy). But if the demand for money is unstable and commodity demand is stable, as in the bottom frame, the Fed will do better to stabilize the interest rate.

15-3 THE QUANTITY THEORY OF MONEY

The dominant analysis of macroeconomics before Keynes' *General Theory* was based almost entirely on the assumption of a stable demand for money. Not only was the demand for money assumed to be stable, but little or no attention was given to the dependence of the demand for money on the interest rate. Thus the entire subject of fiscal policy was neglected, as justified in the context of Figure 15-1 in the extreme case when the LM curve has the vertical slope at LM_1.

The **quantity theory of money** begins with the famous quantity equation, which is called a tautology because it is true by definition:

$$MV \equiv PQ \tag{15.1}$$

Here M as before is the money supply, P is the price level (GNP deflator), Q is real output, and V is the **velocity** of money, the average number of times per year that the money stock is used in making payments for final goods and services. Equation (15.1) is a definition for the simple reason that velocity (V) is defined as (PQ/M). The right side of the equation corresponds to the transfer of goods and services between economic units, and the left side to the matching monetary payment for those goods and services.[6]

As it stands, the quantity equation is not a theory. But we can convert it into a theory by postulating that individuals hold money because their receipts and purchases are not synchronized. A household may receive all its receipts (wages) from the sale of its labor on the first of each month but spend the receipts gradually throughout the month. A business firm may have steady receipts throughout the month but make most of its wage payments at the end of the month. For both households and firms, the major reason for holding money is as a "temporary abode of purchasing power" to bridge the time between receipt and purchase.

The next step is the assumption that people choose to hold a constant fraction $(1/V^*)$ of their nominal income (PQ) in the form of money (M):

$$M = \frac{PQ}{V^*} \qquad (15.2)$$

As written, (15.2) appears merely to be a transformation of (15.1) that divides both sides of the earlier equation by V. The definition becomes a theory when we assume that the fraction of income that people desire to hold in the form of money $(1/V^*)$ is a constant. Starting from an initial situation in which the money supply is M_0, the price level is P_0, output is Q_0, and velocity is at the desired level, any increase in the money supply will raise nominal income. Why? The initial supply of money was the desired fraction $(1/V^*)$ of income, so that any additional money will be considered excess by households and firms and will be spent. Spending (PQ) will rise until the new higher money supply (M_1) is the desired fraction $(1/V^*)$ of the new higher level of spending.

In its original pre-Keynesian version, prices were generally assumed to be relatively or completely flexible, so that almost all the adjustment of nominal income (PQ) would take the form of price changes and almost none the form of quantity changes.[7] We can distinguish two versions of

---

[6] In this discussion we limit our attention to the income version of the quantity theory and ignore for lack of space the transactions version, which replaces Q in equation (15.1) by the total of transactions in the economy, including not only current goods and services, but also transactions in capital assets and intermediate goods. In that version velocity (V) is interpreted as the current value of annual transactions divided by the money supply, or the total turnover of money per year. A more complete discussion of the quantity theory, and a summary of the limitations of the transaction version, are contained in Milton Friedman, "A Theoretical Framework for Monetary Analysis," *Journal of Political Economy,* vol. 78 (March/April 1970), pp. 193–238, reprinted in Robert J. Gordon (ed.), *Milton Friedman's Monetary Framework* (Chicago: University of Chicago Press, 1974), pp. 1–62. See also Milton Friedman, "Money: Quantity Theory," in *International Encyclopedia of the Social Sciences* (New York: Macmillan, 1968).

[7] Milton Friedman has recently published a debate with Don Patinkin (of the Hebrew University in Jerusalem) on the degree to which the pre-Keynesian quantity theorists al-

(continued)

the quantity theory. The weak version states that, because the desired fraction of income held in the form of money ($1/V^*$) is constant, a change in the money supply causes a proportional change in nominal income in the same direction. The strong version adds the assumption that all or almost all the adjustment of nominal income takes the form of changing prices and none or almost none the form of changing output.

The earlier quantity theorists did not believe that the fraction $1/V^*$ was rigidly fixed forever. They discussed a wide variety of factors that could alter $1/V^*$. Some writers emphasized that the amount of money needed for conducting transactions would change as the technology of transactions changed. In the modern era the credit card has reduced the need for money, because households can better synchronize their receipts and payments by making all their credit card payments on payday. In the pre-Keynesian era, quantity theorists discussed other changes in payments practices, the financial and economic arrangements for effecting transactions, and the speed of communication and transportation (payments are made faster by railroad than by stagecoach).

In addition to these mechanical aspects of the technology of transactions, other writers placed emphasis on important economic determinants of $1/V^*$. Money was one of many assets, and the willingness of people to hold money depended on its costs and returns as compared to those on other assets. The pre-Keynesian economist Alfred Marshall of Cambridge University, England, recognized that individuals would calculate not only a fraction of their income to hold as a "temporary abode of purchasing power" but also a fraction of their total wealth to hold in the form of money rather than in other assets:

> Let us suppose that the inhabitants of a country . . . find it just worth their while to keep by them on the average ready purchasing power to the extent of a tenth part of their annual income, together with a fiftieth part of their property.[8]

One of the main costs of holding money is the interest that is lost by not investing the same funds in a bond or savings account. Although the dependence of the demand for money on the interest rate was implicit in the pre-Keynesian quantity theory, the meaning of this assumption was neither fully appreciated nor incorporated into formal analysis. As we have learned, a decline in the demand for commodities, as in the movement from IS_1 leftward to IS_0 in Figure 15-2, cuts real output as

---

lowed real output to vary in the short run. No one appears to dispute the interpretation that in both the earlier and present-day versions of the quantity theory, money is neutral in the long run, that is, money affects only nominal variables (nominal income and the price level), but not real variables. For the debate, see Robert J. Gordon (ed.), *Milton Friedman's Monetary Framework* (Chicago: University of Chicago Press, 1974), pp. 114–18 and 158–62.

[8]Quoted in Gordon (ed.), *op. cit.*, p. 170.

long as the LM curve is positively sloped, and as long as a constant real money supply (M/P) holds the LM curve in a fixed position. The decline in real output can be avoided only by a decline in the price level (P) or by an increase in the nominal money supply (M), both of which raise M/P and thus shift the LM curve rightward, as long as the commodity market stays at the depressed position IS_0.

15-4 THE KEYNESIAN TRANSACTION AND SPECULATIVE MOTIVES

Just as Marshall divides the demand for money into two portions, a fraction of income to be used for transaction purposes and a fraction of property to be used as a form of asset holding, Keynes in the *General Theory* also divided the demand for money into two compartments. The first portion of money was held to satisfy the "transactions motive," the need to hold cash to "bridge the interval between the receipt of income and its disbursement."[9] Individuals with high incomes would need more money for this bridging than people with low incomes, and so the total demand for money for transactions purposes depended on total income (PQ) and was written $L_1(PQ)$.

The second portion of money was held to satisfy the "speculative motive," based on the assumed role of individuals as speculators who were continually trying to make themselves richer by switching their asset holdings back and forth between money and bonds. Imagine a bond that promises to pay the holder $1.00 per year forever. An individual would be willing to pay a price of $1/r$ dollars for that bond. For instance, when the interest rate is 5 percent or 0.05, the price of the bond would be $20.00. Why? Simply because the interest rate (0.05) is the ratio of the return on an investment ($1.00) to its price ($20.00).[10]

If the normal interest rate is 5 percent or 0.05, then the normal bond price is $20.00. Now let us ask what would happen to the willingness of speculators to hold bonds if the actual interest rate were to drop to 0.04 and the bond price were to rise to $25.00. Some investors might feel that a $25.00 bond price is too far above normal and that bond prices are likely to fall. To avoid the risk of capital loss, the speculators might sell their bonds and hold money instead. Thus when the interest rate is low and bond prices high, the demand for money tends to be large.

---

[9] Keynes, *General Theory*, pp. 195 and 199. The first portion, labeled M_1 by Keynes, also included the "precautionary motive," the need to have ready cash available for emergencies.

[10] The simple inverse relationship between the bond price and the interest rate is strictly valid only for a perpetuity, a bond which pays interest forever but which never pays off its principal. For bonds with finite maturities, say 30 years or less, the relationship between bond prices and the interest rate is slightly more complicated.

General Functional Forms

To simplify our exposition, we have so far used only "specific linear" forms for the behavioral equations. For instance, the demand for money in the Appendix for Chapter 5 was written as:

$$\left(\frac{M}{P}\right)^d = eQ - fr$$

This equation can be stated as: The real demand for money $(M/P)^d$ is equal to a positive number (e) times real output (Q) minus another number (f) times the interest rate (r). The equation tells us the specific way in which the real demand for money depends on real output and the interest rate.

But often in economics we are interested only in the general fact that one economic variable, say real money demand, depends on other variables, in this case real output and the interest rate. This general fact can be written:

$$\left(\frac{M}{P}\right)^d = L(Q,r)$$

This equation can be put into words: The real demand for money $(M/P)^d$ depends on real output (Q) and the interest rate (r). The capital letter L and the parentheses represent the words "depend on," and any alphabetical letter can be used.

Why is it interesting to know simply that one variable depends on others? Figure 15-1 provides a clear example. The consequences of a shift in the IS curve differ depending on whether the real demand for money depends both on output and on the interest rate, as assumed along the positively sloped curve LM_0 in Figure 15-1, or whether

$$\left(\frac{M}{P}\right)^d = L(Q)$$

which states that real money depends only on real output (Q) and not on the interest rate, as assumed along the vertical LM curve labeled LM_1.

Without further information one cannot look at these general functional forms and learn whether the assumed relationship is positive or negative. The positive relationship between real money demand and real output and the negative relationship with the interest rate can be written in either of two ways:

Method 1:

$$\left(\frac{M}{P}\right)^d = L(Q, \; r)$$
$$\phantom{\left(\frac{M}{P}\right)^d = L(}(+) \; (-)$$

Method 2:

$$\left(\frac{M}{P}\right)^d = L(Q, \; r); \; L_Q > 0, \; L_r < 0$$

The terms to the right of the semicolon in method 2 can be put into these words: The response of the real demand for money to a change in real output (L_Q) is positive (>0), holding the interest rate constant. The response of the real demand for money to a change in the interest rate (L_r) is negative (<0), holding real output constant.

Conversely, consider a high interest rate of 0.10 and a correspondingly low bond price of $10.00. Now many speculators will be eager to hold bonds instead of money, because they will believe that there is a good chance of a capital gain when bond prices go up. Thus when the interest rate is high and bond prices low, the demand for money is small.[11]

---

[11] In Chapter 5 we studied the effects of an extreme condition called the liquidity trap, which would occur if all speculators were to agree that the interest rate is too low and bond

The behavior of speculators as outlined here is the only reason put forth by Keynes to explain the sensitivity of the demand for money to the interest rate. The portion of money demand held to satisfy the speculative motive was called $L_2(r)$. Thus the total demand for money (M) was the total of the transaction demand $L_1(PQ)$ and the speculative demand $L_2(r)$:[12]

$$M = L_1(PQ) + L_2(r) \qquad (15.3)$$

Keynes' equation has been criticized on several grounds. First, it is artificial to split the demand for money into two parts. In reality, as will be seen in the next section, the transactions demand depends both on real output and the interest rate. Second, Keynes' version erroneously implies that when the price level (P) doubles but real output (Q) and the interest rate (r) remain unchanged, the demand for money goes up by less than the price level—this error occurs because Keynes remembers to include P only in the first portion of the demand for money $L_1(PQ)$ but not in the second speculative portion $L_2(r)$.

Finally, the speculative motive itself has been criticized. The main problem is with the basic idea that speculative money holding occurs only because some investors believe that the interest rate is below normal and bond prices are above normal. This idea, however, cannot explain why the demand for money remains high over an extended period of low interest rates, such as the 1930s, because as time goes by, speculators should begin to revise downward their idea of the normal interest rate. Thus the deviation between the actual and normal interest rate should gradually disappear and speculative money holding should disappear as well.

15-5 THE INTEREST RESPONSIVENESS OF THE TRANSACTION DEMAND FOR MONEY

Since Keynes wrote more than forty years ago, his speculative motive for money holding has drifted gradually out of favor. Why should a speculator hold money during those periods when he is trying to avoid a capital loss? Other assets, particularly savings deposits, are both free from the risk of capital loss and pay interest as well, whereas money (currency and demand deposits) does not pay interest. Surely the main

---

prices are too high. The Fed would be unable to reduce the interest rate in such a situation, because all speculators would refuse to buy bonds with new money created by the Fed. All the available bonds would already have been sold to the Fed. To review the effects of the liquidity trap, see section 5-3.

[12] This is exactly the equation Keynes used, *General Theory*, p. 199. This chapter neglects the distinction between the nominal and real interest rates. Actually the demand for money should depend on the nominal interest rate, for reasons set out in Chapter 10.

feature of money that explains its use in preference to savings accounts is its acceptance in transactions.

But the abandonment of the speculative motive does not mean that the demand for money is independent of the interest rate, nor that the *LM* curve is vertical. In the early 1950s both William J. Baumol (of Princeton and New York University) and James Tobin of Yale (one of the major nonmonetarists) demonstrated that the transactions demand for money depends on the interest rate. Therefore, the *LM* curve is positively sloped even when there is no speculative demand.[13] The basic idea is that the funds people hold for transactions, to "bridge the interval between the receipt of income and its disbursement," can be placed either in *M*1 (currency and demand deposits, which pay no interest) or in savings deposits. The higher the interest rate, the more individuals will tend to shift their transactions balances into interest-bearing savings accounts.

Baumol analyzes the money-holding decision of a hypothetical individual who receives income at specified intervals but spends it gradually at a steady rate between paydays. An example is illustrated in the left frame of Figure 15-3, where the person is assumed to be paid $900 per month ($Q$) on the first of each month. How will the person decide whether to convert all of the paycheck into currency and demand deposits (M1), which bear no interest, or whether to deposit part of the paycheck in a savings deposit that pays a monthly interest rate r?

As in any problem in economics, the individual compares the costs and benefits of holding M1 instead of the savings deposit. The main cost of M1 is the interest rate on savings (r) lost when M1 is held instead of savings deposits. The main benefit of holding M1 is the avoidance of what Baumol calls the "broker's fee" of b dollars charged every time (T) cash is obtained either by cashing the original paycheck or by obtaining cash at the savings bank. The broker's fee in real life includes the time and transportation expense required to make an extra trip to the savings bank to obtain cash from a savings deposit.

The number of times the broker's fee is incurred is equal to the size of the paycheck (Q) divided by the average amount of cash (C) obtained on each trip. For instance, the left frame of Figure 15-3 involves no savings account; the paycheck of $900 ($Q$) is cashed at the beginning of the month ($C = 900$), and so the broker's fee is incurred only one time ($T = Q/C = 1.0$).

In the middle frame half the paycheck is cashed on the first of the month ($C = 450$), and the other half is deposited in a savings account. Interest is lost by holding cash in an amount equal to the interest rate times the value of the average amount held in cash, which is half the value

[13]William J. Baumol, "The Transactions Demand for Cash: An Inventory Theoretic Approach," *Quarterly Journal of Economics* (November 1952). James Tobin, "The Interest-Elasticity of the Transactions Demand for Cash," *Review of Economics and Statistics* (August 1956), pp. 241–47.

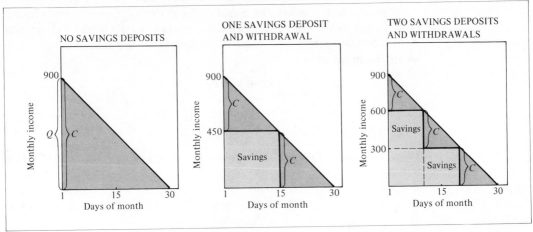

FIGURE 15–3 Alternative Allocations of an Individual's Monthly Paycheck between Cash and Savings Deposits

In the left frame the individual holds all his paycheck in the form of cash, indicated by the gray triangle, which shrinks as the paycheck is spent on consumption purchases. In the middle frame only half as much cash is held because the individual finds it advantageous to hold half the paycheck in his savings deposit for half the month. In the right frame even less cash is held, because initially two-thirds of the paycheck is deposited into a savings account.

of the cash withdrawal $(rC/2)$. Why? In the first half of the month the individual starts with $450 in cash and winds up with zero on the fifteenth of the month, so that his average holding is $225. Then he converts his savings deposit into cash, incurring a second broker's fee. His $450 of cash dwindles again to zero on the last day of the month, so that his average cash holdings during the last half of the month is again $225. Total interest lost is the interest rate times $C/2$, or $225 in this example.[14]

In the right frame only one-third of the paycheck is initially cashed $(C = 300)$, while the other two-thirds is deposited in saving. On the tenth and on the twentieth again withdrawals are made, so that the

---

[14]What is the area of the gray triangle in the left frame? The formula for the area of a triangle is one-half times the height times the length, or 1/2(900)(1), where the length is expressed in months. This equals 450. In the middle frame there are two gray triangles, each with an area 1/2(450)(1/2), or 1/2(450)(1) for both triangles taken together. This equals 225. In the right frame are three triangles, each with an area 1/2(300)(1/3), or 1/2(300)(1) for the three triangles taken together. This equals 150.

broker's fee is incurred three times ($T = Q/C = 900/300 = 3$). The interest rate lost by holding cash is once again $rC/2$.

How should the individual behave? As in the left frame, middle frame, right frame, or should even more trips be made to the bank? The answer is that the combined cost of broker's fees (bT) and interest lost ($rC/2$) should be minimized:

$$\text{Cost} = bT + \frac{rC}{2}, \quad \text{or}$$

$$= b\frac{Q}{C} + \frac{rC}{2} \tag{15.4}$$

It can be shown that the average value of the cash withdrawal (C) that minimizes cost is:[15]

$$C = \sqrt{\frac{2bQ}{r}} \tag{15.5}$$

This equation says in words that the average cash withdrawal is equal to the square root of the following: 2 times the broker's fee times income divided by the interest rate. A higher broker's fee (b) raises cash holdings by discouraging extra trips to the savings bank. But a higher interest rate (r) does just the opposite, reducing cash holdings as individuals shift more funds into savings deposits to earn the higher interest rate.

The Baumol (and Tobin) contributions are of major importance. They show that the interest sensitivity of the demand for money is based not on a flawed theory of speculation but on a transactions motive that is shared by almost everyone so long as money bears no interest and is the only asset that can be used for transactions. The theoretical underpinnings of the positively sloped LM curve are solid, implying that changes in either private spending desires or in fiscal policy will change both real output and the interest rate, at least in the short-run.[16]

---

[15] Here elementary calculus is required. Cost is minimized by changing C to make the derivative of cost with respect to C equal to zero:

$$\frac{\partial(\text{Cost})}{\partial c} = \frac{-bQ}{C^2} + \frac{r}{2} = 0$$

When this is solved for C, we obtain the square-root expression shown as equation (15.5) in the text.

[16] The Baumol theory has the extra advantage of being specific, since the result in equation (15.6) provides a square-root hypothesis of money holding that can be tested against the data. Both the output elasticity and interest rate elasticity of real money demand should be one-half. Why? Let us rewrite (15.6) in exponential form:

$$C = (2bQ)^{1/2}(r)^{-1/2}$$

Thus a one-percentage-point change in Q raises C by 1/2 percent. The most recent empirical tests for the United States have derived an income elasticity of about 0.56 and interest elasticity of -0.19. See Stephen M. Goldfeld, "The Case of the Missing Money," *Brookings*

15-6 THE GENERALIZED PORTFOLIO APPROACH AND THE QUANTITY THEORY RESTATED

TOBIN'S PORTFOLIO APPROACH

At about the same time as the Baumol-Tobin contributions, several articles rehabilitated the asset demand for money from the criticisms aimed at the Keynesian analysis of the speculative motive.[17] In particular James Tobin showed that most people prefer to hold a balanced portfolio with several types of assets.

Some assets, particularly $M1$ (currency and demand deposits) and savings accounts, maintain the nominal value of their principal and are thus "safe" or "riskless."[18] Other assets, particularly stocks and long-term bonds, have a market value (principal) that varies in price every day, and these are called risky assets. If investors are averse to risk, which means that they do not like risk in the form of variations in asset prices, they will be unwilling to hold risky assets at all unless they are "bribed" by a higher average interest return on risky assets than on riskless assets. Otherwise, if the average interest return on a risky asset were no higher than on a riskless asset, why should they be willing to hold a risky asset at all and needlessly expose themselves to risk?

Faced with various safe and risky assets, with the former paying less interest than the latter, most investors make a compromise, diversifying their portfolios of assets. To choose a portfolio consisting only of risky assets would yield a high average interest return but would expose investors to too much risk. With such a risky portfolio, investors might lose most of the value of the principal of their assets (as did so many in the stock market crash of 1929). To choose entirely safe assets would eliminate risk completely, but it would force an investor to settle for a low average return. A mixed diversified portfolio would usually be the best approach, and each person would choose a slightly different balance between risk and return. People of modest means who are saving for their retirement would tend to stay on the safe side by holding mainly savings deposits or the stocks and bonds of solid "blue chip" companies. At the

---

Papers on Economic Activity, vol. 7, no. 3 (1976), pp. 683–730. For more advanced treatments that allow the theoretical elasticities to differ from 1/2, see Edi Karni, "The Transactions Demand for Cash: Incorporation of the Value of Time into the Inventory Approach," *Journal of Political Economy,* vol. 81, no. 5 (September/October 1973), pp. 1216–25 and Herschel I. Grossman and Andrew J. Policano, "Money Balances, Commodity Inventories, and Inflationary Expectations," *Journal of Political Economy,* vol. 83, no. 6 (December 1975), pp. 1093–1112.

[17] The most important of these articles was James Tobin, "Liquidity Preference as Behavior Towards Risk," *Review of Economic Studies,* vol. 25, no. 67 (1958).

[18] "Riskless" is placed in quotes because $M1$ is not free of risk when prices are flexible, since unanticipated inflation causes an unexpected capital loss on holdings of $M1$.

opposite extreme, a young, rich single person with no family responsibilities could afford to take risks in order to earn a high average return.

Although the portfolio approach is very appealing as an explanation for diversifying individual portfolios, it does not explain why anyone is willing to hold $M1$ (currency and checking accounts). Investors can achieve the goal of safety by holding savings deposits, which share with $M1$ a fixed nominal principal, but which dominate $M1$ by paying interest while $M1$ pays no interest. The major contribution of the portfolio approach is to explain why most households desire a mixture of both safe time deposits and risky stocks and bonds rather than a portfolio consisting wholly of either one or the other.

An additional contribution of the portfolio approach is the prediction that savings deposits and variable price securities—both stocks and bonds—are substitutes. This means that investors will shift from savings deposits into stocks and bonds when there is an increase in the interest return on the latter. To maintain their savings deposits intact, both commercial banks and savings banks are likely to raise the interest rate they pay to holders of savings deposits as their response to an increase in the yield on stocks and bonds. As a consequence, any government regulation such as the U.S. Federal Reserve's Regulation Q, which sets a ceiling on the time deposit interest rate paid by commercial banks, prevents the desired matching increase in the interest rate on savings deposits and allows a shift away from savings deposits to take place.

Those types of investment spending which rely heavily on loans from institutions specializing in savings deposits—especially investment in residential housing—tend to be severely hurt when there is an increase in the interest return on stocks and bonds. This is one of the major disadvantages of a countercyclical monetary policy that allows episodes when the interest rate on bonds rises considerably above normal.

FRIEDMAN'S RESTATEMENT OF THE QUANTITY THEORY

An interesting feature of the development of monetary theory in the 1950s was the simultaneous appearance of similar theories by James Tobin, a leading nonmonetarist, and Milton Friedman, the chief monetarist. Tobin's portfolio approach first introduced the role of risk aversion as an explanation for the willingness of investors to hold a portion of their portfolio in the form of safe assets. At about the same time Friedman proposed a general version of the older quantity theory, in which he treated money as one among several assets. According to Friedman's restatement of the quantity theory, the real demand for money can be written:[19]

---

[19] Friedman's approach is explained in more detail in his "The Quantity Theory of Money—a Restatement," in Friedman (ed.), *Studies in the Quantity Theory of Money* (Chicago: University of Chicago Press, 1956), pp. 3–21. A briefer version is contained in his "Theoretical Framework" in Robert J. Gordon (ed.), *Milton Friedman's Monetary Framework* (Chicago: University of Chicago Press, 1974), pp. 10–15.

$$\frac{M}{P} = L(Q, w, r_m, r_b, r_e, p) \qquad (15.6)$$

Looking back at the box in section 15-4, we notice that our money-demand equation differs from Friedman's in several ways. The equations are similar in that ours also contains real income (Q) and the interest rate (r) as independent variables. The main differences are that:

1. Friedman's version splits the interest rate variable into three parts. First is the interest rate paid on money (r_m), an increase in which naturally makes people *more* willing to hold money. The second interest rate variable is r_b, the interest rate paid on bonds, which corresponds to the r variable that appears in our version (equation 15.4) of the demand for money function. An increase in r_b *reduces* the demand for money. The third Friedman interest rate is the interest paid on equities (r_e). Although equities are more risky than money, the portfolio approach suggests that investors will strike a balance between risky and high-yielding equities versus safe and low-yielding savings deposits. Thus an increase in the yield on equities should *reduce* the demand for money.
2. Friedman views money as one way of holding wealth, including not only "nonhuman" financial wealth (bonds, stocks, money) but also "human capital" (the value of an individual's present and future earnings). He recognizes, however, that wealth held in nonhuman (financial) form is more likely to be held partially in the form of money (including savings deposits) than is human capital. Thus the fraction of nonhuman to human wealth (w) appears as an independent variable in the Friedman demand for money function.
3. Perhaps the most important difference between Friedman and Tobin is the former's emphasis on the substitution between money and commodities. When the rate of commodity inflation (p) is high, households will do well to "beat the higher prices" by purchasing goods sooner than usual. Because a reduction in holdings of money is one main way in which individuals can obtain the funds to purchase commodities early, a high rate of inflation (p) reduces the demand for money and appears in Friedman's demand for money function in equation (15.6).

IMPLICATIONS OF TOBIN AND FRIEDMAN APPROACH

Tobin's approach, reflected in many of the large-scale econometric models used for forecasting in the past decade, limits the effect of an increase in the money supply to those categories of spending which depend directly on reductions in the interest rate, particularly the amount of fixed investment and, perhaps, the amount of spending on consumer durables. In Friedman's approach any category of expenditures on GNP may be a substitute for money and may be stimulated by an expansion in the real money supply, even consumer nondurables and services.

Example: An increase in the money supply engineered by the Fed may make banks more willing to make loans of all types. For instance, banks may become willing to lower their standards for the granting of BankAmericard and Mastercharge credit cards and in addition may raise credit limits for existing borrowers. As a result, a monetary expansion may stimulate consumer spending on nondurables and services, such as airline vacations, without any reduction in the interest rate charged on that type of borrowing.[20] Thus current estimates of the interest-responsiveness of autonomous spending may be too low if they take account only of fixed investment and consumer durable spending. As a result, the *IS* curve estimated in many econometric models may be too steep.

The portfolio approach pioneered by both Tobin and Friedman makes the demand for money a function of both income and wealth. The idea that the demand for money depends at least partly on wealth is not new, having been mentioned explicitly by Marshall in the late nineteenth century. But the major implications of a wealth-dependent demand for money have been explored only in the past few years.

The major implication is for fiscal policy. An expansive fiscal policy tends to raise either the supply of money, the supply of government bonds, or both. In general, an increase in either asset raises the value of real wealth and raises the level of commodity demand through the real balance or Pigou effect, shifting the *IS* curve to the right.[21] But now we realize, from our study of the portfolio approach to the theory of money demand, that the demand for money depends on total wealth. Thus any stimulative fiscal policy by raising people's real wealth may raise the demand for money, shift the *LM* curve to the left, and cut back on the fiscal policy multipliers calculated in Chapters 4 and 5.

In principle, the effect of increased wealth resulting from stimulative fiscal policy can reduce the fiscal policy multiplier, although in reality the effect is likely to be small. Why? Because most of the effect of increased wealth is likely to be felt by savings deposits, there being no reason other than the transactions motive that would explain the holding of checking deposits as a form of wealth when savings deposits are available, offering the same safety but paying an interest return as well.[22]

---

[20] The interest rate charged on credit card borrowing has been fixed in most states for many years at 1.5 percent per month, or 18 percent at an annual rate.

[21] The real wealth effect in the commodity market raises the effect on real output of either a decline in prices or a stimulative monetary policy measure. See section 6-6.

[22] A formal analysis of the wealth effect in the demand for money function is the subject of Alan S. Blinder and Robert M. Solow, "Analytical Foundations of Fiscal Policy," in *The Economics of Public Finance* (Washington, D.C.: Brookings, 1974), pp. 45–57. Their paper is the subject of an exchange between the two authors and Ettore F. Infante and Jerome L. Stein in the *Journal of Monetary Economics* (November 1976), pp. 473–510.

15-7 CASE STUDY: THE 1974–76 MONEY DEMAND PUZZLE

The main conclusion of Figure 15-2 is that an unstable demand for money may shift the *LM* curve about unpredictably even if the real supply of money (*M/P*) is held constant. Until a few years ago most studies had found that the demand for money could be quite reliably predicted if one knew only (1) the value of real income, (2) the interest rate on Treasury bills, and (3) the interest rate on savings deposits.[23] But in the last few years the confidence of economists in the stability of the demand for money has collapsed. For the first time the hypothetical example depicted in the bottom of Figure 15-2 has become a reality:

If the demand for money is sufficiently unstable compared to the demand for commodities, a monetary policy that maintains a constant interest rate may do a better job of stabilizing real output than a policy that maintains a constant real money supply.

The quantity theory of money in equation (15.2) was based on the idea that people want to hold a constant fraction (1/*V*) of their income in the form of money. The more modern theories all predict that the fraction 1/*V* will decline when there is an increase in the interest rate — the major cost of holding money. And indeed this has occurred during the postwar years, a time of rising interest rates (a graph illustrating the postwar increase in interest rates is presented in Figure 10-1). In the top frame of Figure 15-4, the downward sloping line labeled 1/*V*1 plots the ratio of the money supply concept *M*1 to nominal income (*PQ*) and confirms the downward drift of money holding relative to income.[24]

The downward drift in 1/*V*1 was not uniform each year. In years of rapidly rising interest rates, the decline in 1/*V*1 was faster than normal, as in 1966. In recession years of falling interest rates, the decline in 1/*V*1 appears to have been interrupted, as in 1954, 1958, and 1961. Indeed Stephen M. Goldfeld has succeeded in explaining almost all the movements in *M*1 and 1/*V*1 during the 1952–73 period with an equation relating the real demand for *M*1 (currency and checking deposits) to real output, the interest rate paid on time deposits, the

---

[23] Stephen M. Goldfeld, "The Demand for Money Revisited," *Brookings Papers on Economic Activity*, vol. 4, no. 3 (1973), pp. 577–638.

[24] Since *V*1 is defined as *PQ/M*1, it follows that 1/*V*1 = *M*1/*PQ*.

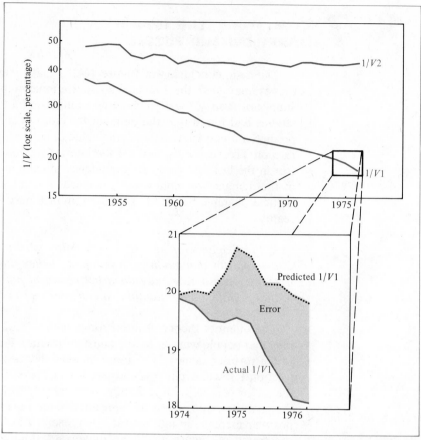

FIGURE 15–4

Actual Ratios of Money to Nominal Income (1/V) for both M1 and M2, 1952–76, and Predicted Value for M1, 1974–76

Notice in the top frame the stability of 1/V2 for the entire period between 1960 and 1976, in contrast to the irregular decline in 1/V1. The bottom frame magnifies the 1974–76 experience for 1/V1. The sharp drop was not expected on the basis of historical behavior.

Source: Actual 1/V from Appendix B. Predicted 1/V1, 1974–76, from Stephen M. Goldfeld, "The Case of the Missing Money," *Brookings Papers on Economic Activity,* vol. 7, no. 3 (1976), Table 2, p. 687.

market interest rate on commercial paper, and last quarter's value of the real demand for M1.

How does the Goldfeld equation explain the postwar decline in 1/V1? First, both interest rates (r_D and r_C) have increased through most of the postwar period, reducing the demand for money. Second, a one-percent increase in output raises money demand in his equation by only about half of one percent in the long run, causing $M1/P$ to grow more slowly than Q.[25] In a recession in which interest rates and Q both decline temporarily, one would expect $1/V1$ to increase temporarily.

THE CASE OF THE MISSING MONEY

The bottom frame of Figure 15-4 is a blow-up of the top frame for the years 1974–76. Goldfeld's equation predicts a substantial increase in $1/V1$ in the worst part of the 1974–75 recession, resulting from the decline in interest rates and in Q. But the predicted behavior did not occur. During the recession $1/V1$ did not exhibit the predicted rise; then during the 1975–76 recovery $1/V1$ declined much faster than predicted. Overall, households and businesses were holding much less money than predicted in relation to their incomes and prevailing interest rates, an unpredicted shortfall of about $30 billion.[26]

Some of the shortfall can be explained by changes in banking rules that allow individuals in some states to pay for transactions with checks written on their savings accounts, thus partially eliminating the need for checking accounts. But some of the prediction error remains a mystery. And if the demand for $M1$ cannot be predicted accurately, then the case for a constant monetary growth rate rule, as recommended by monetarists, is weakened.

Example: Imagine that in late 1973 the Fed had determined that its target value of nominal income (PQ) for mid-1976 was $1527 billion. Based on the prediction of $1/V1$ ($= M1/PQ$) plotted in Figure 15-4, the Fed could have calculated that $M1$ should rise from $269 billion in late 1973 to $302.5 billion in mid-1976 to achieve that target.[27] The Fed did its job perfectly, achieving a level of $M1$ of $302.5 billion in mid-1976. But people mysteriously decided to hold less $M1$ per dollar of income, so that the desired level of $M1$ supported $1675 billion of nominal income ($302.5 divided by actual $1/V1$ of 0.1806) instead of the hypothetical target of $1527 billion ($302.5 divided by predicted $1/V1$ of 0.1981).

In short, the $M1$ prediction error would have caused nominal

---

[25] When M/P grows more slowly than Q, then there is a decline in three ratios, which are equal by definition:

$$\frac{M1/P}{Q} \equiv \frac{M1}{PQ} \equiv \frac{1}{V1}$$

[26] Goldfeld's equation is statistically estimated for the period 1952–73, and so the numerical estimates of the elasticities in his equation do not "use" any information about what happened in 1974–76. The 1974–76 predictions in Figure 15-4 are called out-of-sample or past-sample forecasts.

[27] All mid–1976 figures refer to 1976:Q2.

income to overshoot its target by $148 billion if the only criterion of policy had been to achieve the target growth in $M1$. Considering the theoretical point made in the bottom frame of Figure 15-2, if the Fed had aimed at point C in the diagram, the money demand prediction error would have caused the economy to wind up at point B_1 instead.

The hypothetical example may not ring true to some readers. With the unemployment rate above 7.5 percent in mid-1976, how could the Fed possibly have aimed at a target value of nominal income (PQ) $148 billion below that which actually occurred? Would not achievement of the Fed's hypothetical target have resulted in a mid-1976 unemployment rate that was much higher than the real one, perhaps even over 10 percent? Precisely this danger worried nonmonetarist policy advisers during late 1974 and early 1975 and led them to recommend much faster rates of $M1$ growth than did occur. In contrast to the 5.0 percent annual growth rate of $M1$ achieved between 1973:Q4 and 1976:Q2, nonmonetarist policy advisers recommended rates of 10–12 percent *for a temporary period* to help the economy recover. In fact one prominent forecast made in September 1974 by the MPS econometric model predicted that in 1976:Q2 the unemployment rate would reach 9.6 percent even with 6.0 percent annual $M1$ growth.[28]

Ironically, the economy was "saved" from the adverse effects of the monetarist policy recommendation of slow $M1$ growth thanks to the unpredicted shortfall of the demand for $M1$ illustrated in Figure 15-4. The unemployment rate during 1976:Q2 turned out to be only 7.4 percent, not 9.6 percent, even though $M1$ growth turned out to be lower than in the MPS model forecast. Part of the credit for the lower unemployment rate is due to the tax cuts of 1975. But most of the prediction error in the MPS forecast can be attributed to the overprediction of money demand.

15-8 CONCLUSION: VERDICT ON MONETARY POLICY INSTRUMENTS

A basic theme of this chapter has been that the monetarist prescription of a **constant-growth-rate rule** (CGRR) for the money supply is generally not the optimal approach to monetary policy. If the demand for

---

[28] The forecast is taken from an unpublished release entitled "MPS Model Forecasts, September, 1974, Experiment V." Numerous forecasts are presented, of which the one reported in the text is the first forecast presented for 6.0 percent $M1$ growth and no fiscal action. The MPS initials stand for MIT-Penn-SSRC, a model that is an offshoot of the Federal Reserve-MIT-Social Science Research Council Econometric Model Project initiated in 1965–66 by nonmonetarists Franco Modigliani of MIT and Albert Ando of the University of Pennsylvania, under the financial support (until 1971) of the Federal Reserve Board.

money is stable and predictable but the demand for commodities is unstable, as in the top frame of Figure 15-2, then a countercyclical money supply policy will achieve greater stability of real output than will a CGRR policy. On the other hand, if the demand for commodities is stable and the demand for money is unstable, then a constant interest-rate policy will outperform the CGRR policy.

No clear verdict emerges from our study of the theory and evidence. The flexible accelerator theory of investment almost guarantees that the demand for investment commodities will frequently drift away from its average level (or share in GNP). In this chapter we have demonstrated that the demand for $M1$ dropped drastically during 1974–76 compared to predictions. Because the demand for both commodities and money appears to be less than perfectly predictable, it seems the Fed should adhere rigidly neither to a simple CGRR formula for $M1$ nor to a constant interest rate policy.

The data for $1/V$ presented in Figure 15-4 suggest an intriguing possibility. Although $M1$ has not been easy to predict over the last few years, the velocity of $M2$ ($M1$ plus commercial bank time deposits) displays an incredible constancy in the top half of Figure 15-4. For 17 straight years (1960–76) $1/V2$ (which equals $M2/PQ$) never fell below 0.41 nor rose above 0.43. During the six years 1971–76 the range was even narrower, between a minimum of 0.421 and a maximum of 0.428. In the same paper in which he failed to explain the mysterious drop in the demand for $M1$, Goldfeld found that the 1974–76 behavior of $M2$ could be explained quite accurately using information from the pre-1974 period.

Since $M2$ includes both $M1$ and time deposits, and since $M2$ behaved predictably during 1974–76, the puzzle of too low a demand for $M1$ has been almost exactly balanced by the offsetting puzzle of too high a demand for time deposits. The two puzzles cancel each other out and allow $M2$ to be predicted accurately.

Thus it might appear that a good first approximation for the Fed would be to take advantage of the constancy of $1/V2$ and set the growth of the supply of $M2$ equal to the target desired growth rate of nominal income ($Y = PQ$). Writing rates of growth in lowercase letters, the Fed would set the growth of $M2$ ($m2$) equal to target growth in nominal income ($y' = p' + q'$):

$$m2 = y' = p' + q'$$

For instance, if the Fed predicted that inflation next year was likely to be 5 percent ($p' = 5$) and wanted to reduce unemployment by achieving rapid real output growth (say $q' = 6$), then the $m2$ target should be:

$$m2 = y' = 5 + 6 = 11$$

This all seems very simple, but it cannot be carried too far. An important lesson from *IS-LM* curve analysis in the first part of this book is that monetary expansion tends to reduce velocity (V) and thus to raise $1/V$.

For instance, the value of $1/V2$ in 1972, following a year of fast $M2$ growth, rose to a relatively high value of 42.8 percent. In contrast, the value of $1/V2$ in 1970, following a year of slow $M2$ growth, fell to a relatively low 41.3 percent.[29]

Similarly, the value of $1/V2$ depends on all the determinants of the IS curve, the level of government spending, tax rates, and the strength of investment and consumption demand. Even though the variation in $1/V2$ during the 1971–76 period appears slight, the difference between annual average values of 0.421 and 0.428 is enough to account for a difference in nominal income of about $30 billion at today's prices. Thus a monetary policy that achieves a constant growth of $M2$ may be only a second best policy. The first best stabilization policy may require a mixture of monetary and fiscal policy instruments to achieve simultaneously the target rates of income growth, desired interest rate levels, and the optimal division of total GNP among consumption, investment, and government spending.

SUMMARY

1. The smaller the interest responsiveness of the demand for money, the less real output varies in the short run in response to changes in fiscal policy and in business and consumer confidence. A zero interest response not only destroys the effectiveness of fiscal policy but also eliminates its rationale by insulating real output from variations in private spending decisions.

2. When the demand for money is stable and predictable, a monetary policy that maintains a constant money supply is preferable to one that stabilizes the interest rate. But an even better alternative is a counter-cyclical monetary policy, which reduces the money supply when the demand for commodities is high, and vice versa.

3. When the demand for money shifts about in an unpredictable and random fashion, but the demand for commodities is stable, a policy of maintaining a stable interest rate is preferable to maintaining a constant money supply.

4. Several theories have been developed to explain the relation between the demand for money, income, wealth, and the interest rate. The demand for money for transaction purposes depends on the interest rate, because people will take the trouble to make extra trips to the bank and keep more of their income in savings accounts (and other interest-earning assets) when the interest rate is high.

---

[29] The 1972 value followed a period of 11.4 percent growth of $M2$ between December 1970 and December 1971. The 1970 value followed a period of only 2.6 percent growth of $M2$ between December 1968 and December 1969.

5. The portfolio approach emphasizes the household decision to allocate its wealth among money, savings accounts, bonds, and other assets. Any event that raises wealth, such as a stimulative fiscal policy, will tend to raise the demand for money. This theory suggests that fiscal policy multipliers may be smaller than in the simple theory of Chapter 5, in which the demand for money depends only on income, not on wealth.

6. In 1974–76 the demand for money declined mysteriously compared to the predictions of most economists. As a result, the very small rate of growth in demand deposits and currency ($M1$) allowed by the Federal Reserve was adequate to finance a much faster growth rate of aggregate demand than had been expected.

7. The demand for the $M2$ money concept (including demand deposits, currency, and time deposits) has been easier to predict. Thus a monetary policy that aims at a stable growth rate of $M2$ appears to be preferable to one that attempts to stabilize $M1$. But a coordinated monetary and fiscal policy approach may be better yet.

A LOOK AHEAD

The demands for consumer durables, investment goods, and money ($M1$) exhibit fluctuations and appear to call for an activist government stabilization policy. But the need for an activist policy approach does not guarantee that activism is desirable. On the contrary, the lags between policy actions and the economy's response may be so long and variable that countercyclical policy turns out to make fluctuations worse. Further, the response of the economy to given policy changes may be highly uncertain. In the next part of the book we will form a judgment on plank 3 of the monetarist platform, the claim that an activist countercyclical government policy may do more harm than good.

CONCEPTS AND QUESTIONS

IDENTIFICATIONS

Constant money supply policy versus countercyclical monetary policy
Quantity theory of money
Transaction motive

Speculative motive
Portfolio approach
Velocity of money
$M1$ versus $M2$

QUESTIONS FOR REVIEW

1   What does the interest responsiveness of the demand for money have to do with the potency of fiscal policy? With the effect on real output of changes in business and consumer confidence?

2   When the demand for commodities (*IS* curve) fluctuates widely but the demand for money is stable, explain why it is undesirable for the Federal Reserve to try to maintain a fixed interest rate.

3   The quantity equation is true by definition. Why?

4   What assumptions convert the quantity equation into the quantity theory?

5   Why did the quantity theorists pay little or no attention to fiscal policy?

6   If people believe that the interest rate is unusually low, will their demand for money be high or low according to the Keynesian theory of the speculative motive?

7   Relate your answer to (6) to the concept of the liquidity trap (review section 5-3).

8   If banks were to charge a fixed fee for withdrawals from savings accounts, would this increase or decrease the demand for *M*1 (currency and demand deposits)? Explain.

9   Can you explain in words why people diversify their portfolios by holding a mixture of safe and risky assets?

10 Do you regard the portfolio approach as a convincing explanation of the demand for *M*1?

11 Explain what would have happened to nominal GNP if *V*1 in Figure 15-4 had behaved as predicted in early 1976. How would this difference in the behavior of nominal GNP have been divided between real output and the price level?

Part V

The Control of Aggregate Demand

16 Federal Reserve Monetary Control and Its Limitations

There is a strong presumption . . .
discretionary actions will in general be
subject to longer lags than the automatic
reactions and hence be destabilizing even
more frequently.

—Milton Friedman[1]

16-1 INTRODUCTION

The last three chapters have developed a persuasive case against the proposition that precise control over the money supply guarantees precise control of aggregate demand. The money supply can be completely fixed, and yet aggregate demand can vary whenever anything occurs — whether an economic or political event — to change households' estimates of their permanent income and thus their consumption. Changes in investment tax incentives or business firms' expectations about the future course of output can alter business investment. The *IS* curve can also be shifted by changes in government spending or tax rates. Changes in consumption, investment spending, and fiscal policy alter the *IS* curve when the money supply is constant; in addition, changes in the amount of money demanded at a given level of income and the interest rate can shift the *LM* curve even though the money supply is fixed.

Thus the achievement of stable growth in aggregate demand (nominal income) appears to require an activist countercyclical monetary policy. When either rightward shifts in the *IS* curve due to higher commodity demand or rightward shifts in the *LM* curve due to a drop in the demand for money threaten to push aggregate demand higher than desired, there is a case for a reduction in the money supply (or in the growth rate of the money supply) to shift the *LM* curve back to the left by the desired amount. But this recommendation brings us up against plank 3 of the monetarist platform in Chapter 12: An activist monetary policy may do

---

[1] *Essays in Positive Economics* (Chicago: University of Chicago Press, 1953), pp. 44–45.

more harm than good. Why? The effects of a change in the money supply on aggregate demand do not occur immediately. Economists cannot perfectly forecast future events in the economy, so that a reduction in the money supply today to cut aggregate demand because of excessive current spending might have its major restraining effects next year, by which time conditions might have changed and spending might be weak.

Until now we have assumed that the money supply can be set at any desired value. We examine in this chapter the methods by which the Fed controls the money supply. How quickly can the Fed change the money supply? How long does it take for changes in the money supply to alter spending? Finally, what are the disadvantages of an activist counter-cyclical monetary policy?

16-2 PRINCIPLES FOR CREATING MONEY ON A DESERT ISLAND

Readers may recall from a course in the principles of economics that the banking system can create money and that Federal Reserve actions have a multiplier effect on the total supply of money. The basic ideas of bank money creation can be illustrated here for a hypothetical community of unlucky individuals stranded on a desert island. Although many individuals are stranded, only five take part directly in our drama: the Miser, the Banker, Horace, the Used Raft Dealer, and the Economist.

Initially, the supply of money on the island is 100 gold coins held by the Miser. The Miser is afraid that someone might steal his coins and persuades the strongest man on the island to guard his coins in return for a receipt (IOU) entitling the Miser to have the coins back when desired. Starting from nothing, the strongest man has become the Banker. The balance sheet of his First Desert Island Bank can be written down in the form of a T account, which lists assets on the left side and liabilities on the right side.

First Desert Island Bank (FDIB): Stage 1

Assets		Liabilities	
Gold coins	100	IOU to Miser	100
Total assets	100	Total liabilities	100

At first the Banker simply is doing the Miser a favor. He cannot really be said to have entered the banking business, because he has no income. He cannot spend the gold coins, because the Miser might come in at any time and claim the coins. After months of careful observation, however, the Banker concludes that the Miser never draws out more than 20 percent of the coins at any one time. The Banker separates the gold coins into two piles. The first pile contains the 20 coins needed for the Miser's withdrawals and is labeled by the Banker required reserves. The second pile contains the unneeded coins and is labeled excess reserves. It suddenly occurs to the Banker that he can use the unneeded excess coins to make a loan to someone, can charge interest on the loan, and thus indirectly can earn money from the coins deposited by the Miser. No longer is the Banker doing the Miser a favor; now the Miser is doing a favor for the Banker so long as the Banker fails to pay interest on the Miser's deposit.

Now the Banker's balance sheet can be written:

FDIB: Stage 2

Assets		Liabilities	
Gold coins:		Deposit (IOU)	
Required reserves	20	Owed to Miser	100
Excess reserves	80		
Total assets	100	Total liabilities	100

After questioning the other people on the island, the Banker finds that Horace is eager to borrow 80 gold coins to make a purchase from the Used Raft Dealer. When the loan is made, the Banker has succeeded in converting his unneeded excess reserve of 80 gold coins into an interest-paying loan, that is, a piece of paper stating that Horace owes the Banker 80 gold coins plus future interest payments.

FDIB: Stage 3

Assets		Liabilities	
Gold coins:		Deposit owed to Miser	100
Required reserves	20		
Loan owed by Horace	80		
Total assets	100	Total liabilities	100

After the Used Raft Dealer (URD) has sold the island's only raft to Horace, he faces the same problem as the Miser. He needs a secure place to keep his 80 gold coins and brings them to the Banker. But now the Banker, much to his surprise, finds that his loan to Horace has not succeeded in getting rid of all his excess reserves! If the Banker sets aside 20 percent of the URD's 80 coin deposit, or 16 coins, as a reserve against withdrawals, his balance sheet now looks like this:

Assets		Liabilities	
Gold coins:		Deposit owed to Miser	100
Required reserves	36	Deposit owed to URD	80
(20% of deposits)			
Excess reserves	64		
Loan owed by Horace	80		
Total assets	180	Total liabilities	180

The Banker has failed in his effort to get rid of all his excess reserves. At Stage 3 the Banker converted 80 of his excess reserves into a loan, but yet the 80 coins came right back. The crucial move was the decision of the URD to redeposit his 80 gold coins in the bank. After 16 of the 80 coins (20 percent) are set aside as required reserves, 64 remain.

Just as the Banker is scratching his head, wondering how to get rid of his 64 excess coins, along comes the clever Economist. "I can solve your problem," the Economist asserts confidently. "If you give me a loan of 320, I guarantee that your problem of excess reserves will disappear." "But," asks the astonished Banker, "how can I give you a loan of 320 when I only have 64 excess coins?" "Just trust me," answers the Economist.

And so the Banker follows the Economist's instructions. The Economist is given a loan of 320, which appears on the Banker's balance sheet as an asset. Because the Banker does not have enough excess reserves to give gold coins to the Economist as the proceeds of the loan, instead the Economist is given a deposit of 320:

Assets		Liabilities	
Gold coins:		Deposit owed to Miser	100
Required reserves	100	Deposit owed to URD	80
(20% of deposits)		Deposit owed to Economist	320
Loan owed by Horace	80		
Loan owed by Economist	320		
Total assets	500	Total liabilities	500

The gold coins remain in the bank. Whereas previously only 36 coins were needed as required reserves to support the 180 of deposits at Stage 4, now all 100 coins are needed to back up the 500 of deposits.

REQUIRED CONDITIONS

The money supply is conventionally defined as cash held outside banks plus demand deposits (checking accounts). Initially, the island's money supply consisted only of the 100 gold coins originally held by the Miser.

But now the money supply has expanded to 500, all in the form of bank deposits. The Desert Island Bank has succeeded in creating $5.00 of money for every $1.00 of cash that it initially received. Five conditions were necessary for this to occur.

1. Paper receipts claiming ownership of bank deposits must be accepted as a means of payment on a one-for-one basis — that is, a deposit representing a claim to one gold coin is accepted by sellers as equivalent to payment of one gold coin. Because people almost always want to spend an amount smaller than the total of their deposit, they must be able to spend a portion of their deposit by writing a check or withdrawing a part of their deposit in the form of cash (gold coins in the example).
2. Any seller who receives a cash payment from the proceeds of a loan must redeposit the cash into his own account. Thus the Used Raft Dealer redeposited 80 gold coins in stage 4 above.
3. When sellers receive payment in the form of checks written on bank accounts, they must redeposit the check in their own bank account in the same bank. Although the Economist may write checks on his account of 320 held at stage 5 of the above example, the bank's deposits will not change if each recipient of a check from the Economist brings the check back to the bank and starts his own account.
4. The Bank must hold some fraction of its reserves in the form of cash (20 percent in gold coins in this example).
5. Someone must be willing to borrow from the bank at an interest rate that at least covers the bank's cost of operation. If the bank could find no appropriate lending opportunities at either stage 3 or stage 5 — that is, if neither Horace nor the Economist had been willing to borrow — the bank could not have created money.

THE MONEY-CREATION MULTIPLIER

If all five conditions are met, then the entire process of money creation can be summed up in a simple equation. We let the symbol H denote **high-powered money,** that is, the quantity of the type of money that is held by banks as reserves. In the example, H consists of the 100 gold coins, which are high-powered because they generate the multiplier expansion of money by the First Desert Island Bank. The symbol D represents the total of bank deposits. The symbol e represents the fraction of deposits that banks decide to hold as reserves. The demand for high-powered money to be held as reserves (eD) is then equal to the supply of high-powered money (H):

GENERAL FORM   NUMERICAL EXAMPLE

$$eD = H \qquad\qquad 0.2(500) = 100 \qquad (16.1)$$

The same equation can be rearranged (dividing both sides by e) to determine the size of the stock of deposits (D) relative to the quantity of high-powered money (H) and the bank reserve-holding ratio (e):

GENERAL FORM   NUMERICAL EXAMPLE

$$D = \frac{H}{e} \qquad\qquad 500 = \frac{100}{0.2} \qquad (16.2)$$

The money-creation multiplier is $1/e$, or $1/0.2 = 5.0$ in the numerical example. This is the second usage of the word multiplier in this book. In Chapters 3–6 we examined the factors determining the income-determination multiplier. In its simplest version, that multiplier in Chapter 3 was written:

$$\frac{\text{Income determination}}{\text{multiplier}} = \frac{\text{Autonomous planned spending } (A_p)}{\text{Marginal propensity to save } (s)}$$

An increase in autonomous planned spending (A_p) is multiplied in Chapter 3 because spending creates income, a fraction of which *leaks out* into saving and taxes and the remainder of which goes into additional spending. The multiplier process ends only when the total of extra induced leakages has become equal to the original increase in A_p.

The intuitive reasoning behind the money-creation multiplier is the same. An increase in high-powered money (H) is multiplied here because the initial deposit of H becomes reserves of the bank, a fraction of which *leaks out* into required reserves and the remainder of which is lent out and comes back as additional deposits of the stores and business firms that receive the loan proceeds. The money-creation multiplier process terminates only when the total of extra induced leakages into required reserves has used up the original increase in H.

Now it is time to recognize that some of the five conditions describing money creation on the desert island may not be accurate descriptions of the real world.

Condition (2) required that any seller receiving a cash payment from the proceeds of a loan must redeposit the cash into the bank, as did the Used Raft Dealer at stage 4. If the cash does not come back to the bank, the multiplier process of money creation cannot occur at that bank. If the cash is redeposited at another bank, then the second bank will find itself with excess reserves, allowing the multiplier process to proceed. For instance, if Horace takes his 80 gold coins, stuffs them into a bottle, and sends it off to buy a new raft from the Sears Roebuck catalog, Sears will take the coins and deposit them in their bank (the Sears Bank in the Sears Tower in downtown Chicago). A fraction of the 80 coins will leak into the required reserves of the Sears Bank, but the rest will be available to be lent out.

Conditions (2) and (3) can be revised to apply to any group of banks, say all the banks within the United States. As long as sellers receiving loan proceeds in the form of either cash or checks redeposit the funds in a U.S. bank, then the money-creation multiplier in equation (16.2) remains valid for the U.S. banking system as a whole.

CASH HOLDING

The money-creation multiplier is changed, however, if everyone wants to hold not only demand (checking) deposits at banks, but wants some pocket cash as well. Imagine that everyone wants to hold a fixed fraction (c) of his deposits, say 5 percent, in the form of cash.[2] Then this source of cash holding adds an extra amount (cD) to the total demand for high-powered money. In a revised desert island example, the demand for gold coins, the only form of high-powered money, might be 20 percent of deposits for bank reserves ($eD = 0.2D$), and in addition 5 percent of deposits for pocket cash ($cD = 0.05D$).

The total demand for high-powered money ($eD + cD$) can be equated to the total supply (H):

GENERAL FORM			NUMERICAL EXAMPLE		
Demand	*Supply*		*Demand*	*Supply*	
$eD + cD$	$=$	H	$0.2D + 0.05D = 100$		(16.3)
or $(e + c)D =$		H	or $\quad 0.25D = 100$		

Dividing both sides by $(e + c)$, we can solve for deposits:

$$D = \frac{H}{e + c} \qquad\qquad D = \frac{100}{0.25} = 400 \qquad (16.4)$$

In words, the total of deposits is equal to the supply of high-powered money (H — gold coins in the desert island example) divided by the fraction of deposits that leaks into reserves (e) plus the fraction that leaks into pocket cash (c).

Although specialized courses in monetary economics develop complicated formulas that relate the U.S. money supply to high-powered money and numerous other factors, for our purposes equation (16.4) is an entirely adequate explanation.[3] We can modify (16.4) slightly by recognizing that the total money supply (M) includes not only deposits (D) but also cash (including currency and coins) held in an amount equal to the cash-holding ratio times deposits (cD):

$$M = D + cD = (1 + c)D \qquad (16.5)$$

Substituting for D in (16.5) from (16.4), we obtain:

$$M = (1 + c)D = \frac{(1 + c)H}{e + c} \qquad (16.6)$$

---

[2] The cash fraction c has nothing whatsoever to do with the marginal propensity to consume (c) of Chapter 3. At this stage we have run through the alphabet once and are requiring some letters to perform double duty.

[3] Students interested in the money supply process should consult Albert E. Burger, *The Money Supply Process* (Belmont, Calif.: Wadsworth, 1971).

The supply of money depends only on the three terms that appear here in (16.6): the supply of high-powered money (H), the cash-holding ratio (c), and the ratio of deposits that the banks hold in the form of reserves (e). In an economy in which all high-powered money (H) consists of gold, then the rate of increase in the total supply of money may depend on the economics of gold mining. Because in the long run a sustained acceleration in monetary growth causes an acceleration in inflation, some historical episodes of inflation have been caused by gold discoveries. The inflow of gold into Spain following the discovery of America caused prices to double in the sixteenth century. More moderate price increases followed the gold discoveries in California in 1848 and Alaska in 1898.

Before the establishment of the Federal Reserve in 1914, the U.S. economy was at the mercy of capricious changes in the money supply stemming not only from the influence of gold discoveries on the growth of H, but also from episodes in which the cash-holding ratio (c) and the reserve ratio (e) fluctuated dramatically. During banking panics, which occurred about once a decade and culminated in the serious panic of 1907, depositors began to fear for the safety of their deposits and began withdrawing their deposits, converting them into cash. This raised the cash-holding ratio (c) and cut the money supply. To deal with the tide of withdrawals, banks in turn began to try to bolster their reserves, raising the reserve ratio (e) and further cutting the money supply.[4] In the pre-Federal Reserve era, there was no way for the government to raise H to offset panic-induced increases in c and e. Panics caused a drop in the money supply and in aggregate demand, cutting both output and prices.

16-3 DETERMINANTS OF THE MONEY SUPPLY IN THE UNITED STATES

The Federal Reserve System (the "Fed") was established in late 1913 upon the recommendation of a commission set up to study the causes of the 1907 banking panic and to recommend solutions to prevent future panics.[5] Banks now were to hold most of their reserves in the form of

---

[4] Notice in equation (16.6) that any increase in e reduces the quantity of money (M). Although c appears both in the numerator and the denominator, an increase in c reduces the money supply as long as the reserve-holding ratio (e) is less than 1.0.

[5] A spirited narration on the establishment of the Fed is in John Kenneth Galbraith, *Money* (Boston: Houghton Mifflin, 1975), Chapter 10. See also Milton Friedman and Anna J. Schwartz, *A Monetary History of the United States, 1867–1960* (Princeton, N.J.: Princeton University Press, 1963), pp. 168–72 and 189–96.

TABLE 16-1

Simplified Depiction of the U.S. Money Supply Process

All figures are monthly averages for October, 1976 in $ Billions

FEDERAL RESERVE				COMMERCIAL BANKS			
Assets		Liabilities		Assets		Liabilities	
Gold stock	11.6	Bank reserves	34.3ᵃ	Bank reserves	34.3ᵃ	Deposits (D)	646.0ᶜ
Government securities	99.5	Currency held by public	69.0	Loans and investments	611.7ᵇ		
Loans	0.1						
Other assets, net of other liabilities	−7.9						
Total Fed assets	103.3	Total Fed liabilities	103.3	Total assets	646.0ᵈ	Total liabilities	646.0ᵈ
		Treasury currency	10.8				

High-powered money (H) = 114.1

Money supply (M) = 725.8

ᵃ Bank reserves include both deposits by banks at the Fed as well as currency and coin held by banks as vault cash.

ᵇ Loans and investments are calculated as deposits minus bank reserves. Since total liabilities include several other items not shown here, this method understates loans and investments.

ᶜ Deposits are calculated as M2 minus the currency component of M2 and include both demand deposits and time deposits of all banks, not just banks that are members of the Federal Reserve System. Since nonmember banks are not required to keep reserves at the Fed, the reserve ratio calculated in the text understates the true reserve ratio of member banks.

ᵈ Excludes negotiable time certificates of deposit issued in denominations of $100,000 or more by large weekly reporting commercial banks. Also excludes capital surplus, interbank and U.S. government deposits, and borrowings.

Source: Federal Reserve Bulletin (December 1976), pp. A2, A3, and A12.

---

deposits at the Fed. High-powered money now consisted of two major portions: (1) cash as before and (2) bank deposits at the Fed.

The exact details of monetary control by the Fed have changed in minor ways since 1913, but the basic structure has remained intact and is illustrated in Table 16-1. The table is a simplified representation of the elements of the money supply process, with numerical examples for October 1976. The right half of the table shows the balance sheet of the nation's commercial banks. Just as in the First Desert Island Bank, bank liabilities consist of deposits owed to the depositors, with a total amount of $646.0 billion in October 1976.[6]

Bank assets are of two types. First, banks hold reserves to back up

---

[6] Deposits include both demand deposits (checking accounts), which in most cases pay no interest, and time deposits, which pay interest at varying rates depending on the withdrawal restrictions attached to the deposit.

their deposits, just as the desert island bank kept gold coins on hand to meet withdrawals by depositors. United States bank reserves include vault cash and deposits at the Fed, both of which the banks accept as equivalent, because they can use their deposits at the Fed to obtain more vault cash if they need to accommodate an unusually large withdrawal. The other portion of bank assets consists of loans to households and business firms and investments in various types of federal, state, and local government short-term and long-term bonds.

The new element in Table 16-1, which was not present on the desert island, is the balance sheet of the Federal Reserve. The Fed's balance sheet has some similarity to that of the commercial banks, because a portion of the Fed's liabilities consists of deposits (the bank reserves that the Fed "owes" to the banks). The asset side includes both loans and investments, a tiny $0.1 billion in loans to commercial banks and a much larger $99.5 billion of investments in government bonds.

But there are differences. The Fed can issue currency, unlike the commercial banks, which are prohibited by law from doing so. The Fed's major liability item consists of currency held by the public (take a dollar bill and examine it—above George Washington's picture are the words "Federal Reserve Note" and to the left is a circle indicating the regional Fed bank responsible for issuing the note). Second, a portion of the Fed's assets consists of gold, which the commercial banks are prohibited from holding. Third, unlike the banks, which are required to keep a specified fraction of their deposits on hand in the form of reserves, the Fed does not have to maintain any fixed relation among its assets. Formerly, a fraction of the money supply had to be backed by gold, but this requirement was abandoned by Congress after growth in the money supply outstripped the supply of gold.

Equation (16.6) is just as useful for studying the determinants of the U.S. money supply as of the desert island's money supply. The U.S. money supply concept, which includes all commercial bank deposits, is called $M2$ and includes these components that appear in Table 16-1:

Currency held by the public:

Federal Reserve currency	69.0	
Treasury currency	10.8	
Total currency		79.8

Deposits at commercial banks:

Demand deposits	230.0	
Time deposits	416.0	
Total deposits		646.0
Total money supply ($M2$)		725.8

The currency component of $M2$ appears in Table 16-1 in two places. The major portion is a liability of the Federal Reserve and consists entirely of the paper currency. Treasury currency is issued by the U.S. Treasury, not the Federal Reserve, and consists mainly of coins.

Other concepts of the U.S. money supply are frequently used in policy discussions. $M1$ is equal to $M2$ minus time deposits. $M3$ is equal to $M2$ plus deposits at mutual savings banks and savings and loan institutions. The $M2$ concept is emphasized here because it includes all commercial bank deposits and is thus easiest to present in a simplified fashion in Table 16-1 and also because we discovered in Figure 15-4 that the demand for $M2$ appears to be a more stable fraction of total nominal income than that for $M1$.

Equation (16.6) makes the total supply of money depend on the quantity of high-powered money (H), the bank reserve ratio (e), and the public's cash-holding ratio (c). The three components of high-powered money listed in Table 16-1 are:

Currency held by the public:

Federal Reserve currency	69.0	
Treasury currency	10.8	
Total currency		79.8
Bank reserves		34.3
Total high-powered money (H)		114.1

The bank reserve ratio (e) is the ratio of bank reserves to total deposits:

$$e = \frac{\text{Bank reserves}}{\text{Total deposits}} = \frac{34.3}{646.0} = 0.0531$$

The public's cash-holding ratio (c) is the ratio of currency held by the public to total deposits:

$$c = \frac{\text{Currency}}{\text{Total deposits}} = \frac{79.8}{646.0} = 0.1235$$

Now all the ingredients that determine the money supply can be inserted into equation (16.6):

$$M = \frac{(1+c)H}{e+c} = \frac{(1.1235)114.1}{0.0531 + 0.1235} = 725.8.$$

16-4 THE THREE INSTRUMENTS OF FEDERAL RESERVE CONTROL

Decisions by three types of economic units enter into the determination of the money supply in equation (16.6). The job of the Fed is to calculate the total M that it desires, based on its current target for aggregate demand. The Fed must also predict the public's desired cash-holding ratio (c), over which the Fed has no control. Then the Fed can adjust the two remaining variables in equation (16.6), H and e, to make its desired M consistent with the public's chosen c. The Fed has three main instruments to accomplish this task, the first two of which can be used to control H and the last of which influences e.

FIRST TOOL: OPEN-MARKET OPERATIONS

The first tool is by far the most important. The Fed can change H from day to day by purchasing and selling government bonds. In Table 16-1 the Fed's liabilities are the major component of H, and government bonds are the major asset of the Fed. By purchasing bonds, the Fed raises its assets and liabilities at the same time, thus increasing H. By selling bonds, the Fed reduces its assets and liabilities, lowering H. Any change in H caused by Fed open-market operations causes an even larger change in M through the money creation multiplier.

Federal Reserve policy is decided on the third Tuesday of each month at a meeting of the Federal Open-Market Committee (FOMC) held in a large and imposing room in Washington and attended by the seven Governors of the Fed and the presidents of the 12 regional Federal Reserve Banks.[7] Each meeting results in a directive sent to the Fed's open-market manager in New York, a position held for many years by Alan R. Holmes.

Let us say that Mr. Holmes' directive from the FOMC calls for continued moderate growth in the money supply, and that he has decided that the time has come for a $100 million increase in high-powered money (H). All Mr. Holmes has to do is to pick up the phone and place an order with a New York government bond dealer, say Salomon Brothers, for $100 million in U.S. government bonds. The act that creates H "out of thin air" occurs when the Fed writes a $100 million check on itself to pay for the bonds. Salomon Brothers deposits the check in its account at a commercial bank, say Chase Manhattan. Just as the Desert Island Bank decided to hold 20 percent of its new deposits in the form of gold-coin reserves, so Chase Manhattan holds a portion of its new deposit, say $10 million, in its reserve account at the Fed. The only difference at this stage is that the Fed requires all commercial banks that are members of the Fed System to hold a specified fraction of deposits as reserves.

The Chase Manhattan does not let Salomon Brothers' remaining $90 million deposit sit idly as excess reserves. Why? Because reserves earn no interest. To earn interest, the Chase loans out the $90 million immediately, say to Sears Roebuck, which needs money temporarily to restock its inventories. Sears takes its $90 million check from the Chase and deposits it immediately in the Sears Bank in Chicago, which must put $9 million into its reserve account at the Fed. But now the Sears Bank has

---

[7] All 12 regional presidents attend, but only five (chosen on a rotating basis) may vote.

$81 million remaining to be lent out or invested and decides to buy $81 million in new bonds just issued by the City of Chicago. And the process continues, creating bank deposits again and again at each stage, just as on the desert island.

Thus Mr. Holmes has "created money," not just the original $100 million, but a sizable multiple of $100 million. Yet at no stage has he made anyone wealthier, nor has he given anyone a gift. Salomon Brothers has $100 million more in its bank account, but owns $100 million less in government bonds. Sears has $90 million more in its bank account, but now owes $90 million to the Chase. The City of Chicago has $81 million more in its bank account, but now owes $81 million to the Sears Bank, which holds its bonds.

Holmes' action influences not only the total supply of money but also the interest rate. When he buys the original $100 million in bonds, his action tends to raise bond prices and reduce the interest rate on bonds, just as an increased demand for stocks on the New York Stock Exchange raises stock prices and reduces the yield on the stock (the ratio of the fixed dividend to the higher price).

> **Review:** An important lesson in Figure 15-2 is that the Fed cannot simultaneously control both the interest rate and the money supply. Mr. Holmes' bond purchase that raises the money supply shifts the *LM* curve to the right, moving the economy's equilibrium position southeast down the *IS* curve and thus reducing the interest rate. Similarly, the Fed cannot sell a bond and reduce the money supply without raising the interest rate. The Fed can reduce the money supply without increasing the interest rate only if fiscal policy (by cutting spending or raising tax rates) moves the *IS* curve to the left at the same time.

Sometimes the Fed must engage in open market operations even when it has no desire to raise or lower the money supply. For instance, during Christmas shopping season the public needs more cash for transactions and raises its desired cash-holding ratio (c). Without Fed action this increase in the denominator of the money-supply equation (16.6) would reduce the money supply. Banks would use the reserves to provide cash to the public and would have fewer reserves left over to support deposits, so that the money supply would shrink by a multiple of the public's cash withdrawals. The Fed can avoid this shortage by conducting a defensive open-market purchase of bonds, providing banks with the extra reserves they need to handle the public's cash withdrawals.[8]

---

[8] For further discussion see William Poole, "The Making of Monetary Policy: Description and Analysis," *Economic Inquiry*, vol. 13 (June 1975), pp. 253–65.

SECOND TOOL: REDISCOUNT RATE

Notice in Table 16-1 that in October 1976 the Fed had a small out-standing amount of loans to the banking system, only $0.1 billion. Banks decide how much to borrow from the Fed by comparing the interest rate charged by the Fed, the **rediscount rate,** with the interest rate the banks can receive by investing the funds received from the Fed. Federal Reserve loans tend to be high when the interest rate on short-term investments, such as the interest rate on Treasury bills, is substantially above the Fed's rediscount rate, as in August 1974. And Fed loans tend to be low when the Treasury bill rate is low relative to the rediscount rate, as in October 1976.

	Treasury bill rate	Fed rediscount rate	Fed loans to banks
August 1974	9.0	8.0	$3.351 Billion
October 1976	4.8	5.5	$0.066 Billion

Because $100 million in Fed loans provide banks with $100 million in bank reserves, as does a $100 million open-market purchase, the Fed can control high-powered money (H) either by varying the rediscount rate or by conducting open-market operations. Monetary control can be achieved with either instrument and does not require both. In the first two decades after the Fed was established in 1913, the rediscount rate was the main instrument used by the Fed, whereas in the postwar years open-market operations have been the central instrument. The only justification for continuing the practice of lending by the Fed is the possible need for help by individual banks suffering from an unexpected rush of withdrawals, although these cases are rare and could be handled individually. Many economists have criticized the Fed for continuing its lending, because in periods of high interest rates the Fed tends to keep its rediscount rate low enough to induce substantial borrowing by banks and this in turn reduces the precision of the Fed's day-to-day control over H.

THIRD TOOL: RESERVE REQUIREMENTS

Unlike the desert island, where the Banker chose voluntarily to keep 20 percent of his deposits on hand in the form of gold-coin reserves, in the United States, commercial banks that are members of the Fed must keep a specified fraction of their deposits as **required reserves.** Bank reserves can be held in the form of reserve accounts at the Fed or as vault cash (currency and coin). **Reserve requirements** vary with different types of deposits and with the size of the member bank.[9]

---

[9] The power to change reserve requirements came in 1933, two decades after the establishment of the Fed.

As is evident in equation (16.6), the Fed can raise the money supply by reducing bank reserve requirements (e), or vice versa. Thus a reduction in e accomplishes just the same increase in the money supply as an open-market purchase of the appropriate amount. Why does the Fed need to retain its control over reserve requirements? The only real justification is that a high level of reserve requirements can come in handy in wartime when the government needs to run a large budget deficit. In World War II, for instance, the government would have been required to pay very high interest rates to induce the public voluntarily to finance its entire deficit. To avoid this tactic, the government sold a large quantity of bonds to the Fed, causing H to double between 1940 and 1945.[10] To minimize the inflationary pressure created by the large wartime increase in H, the Fed maintained bank reserve requirements at a level much higher than at present.

Compare the components of equation (16.6) at the end of World War II with the situation in October 1976:[11]

	Percentage		$ Billions	
	c	e	H	$M2$
September 1945	24.88	16.11	43.0	131.0
October 1976	12.35	5.31	114.1	725.8

From 1945 to 1976, H increased by 165 percent, whereas $M2$ increased by 454 percent. This growth was made possible by a sharp increase in the money-creation multiplier, because of a decline in both components (e and c) of the denominator of the money supply equation (16.6). The reserve ratio (e) dropped by two-thirds from 16.11 to 5.31 percent. In addition the cash-holding ratio dropped by half, from 24.88 to 12.35 percent.

An increase in reserve requirements not only allows the government to raise H relative to $M2$ when it wishes to sell extra bonds to the Fed, but it has the second effect of cutting into bank profitability. Because banks receive interest income on their loans and investments, but no interest income on their reserve accounts at the Fed, they prefer to have

---

[10] Imagine that the government writes a $100 check during the war to pay a soldier's wages. The Fed actually writes the check and debits the government's account at the Fed (part of the Fed's liabilities). To restore the previous balance in its account at the Fed, the government sells the Fed a $100 bond, for which the Fed "pays" by adding $100 to the government's balance.

[11] Source for 1945: Milton Friedman and Anna J. Schwartz, *A Monetary History of the United States, 1867–1960* (Princeton, N.J.: Princeton University Press, 1963), Tables A-1 and A-2. Division between required and excess reserves from *Historical Chart Book* (Federal Reserve, 1967), p. 6. Data for 1976 from the same source as Table 16-1.

reserve requirements as low as possible. Thus the postwar decline in reserve requirements has pleased bank stockholders and has increased the value of their stock.[12]

16-5 CASE STUDY: MONETARY CONTROL IN THE 1930s

It appears from the preceding section that the Fed has more policy instruments than it really needs. Because any desired change in $M2$ can be achieved by raising or lowering H through open-market purchases or sales, the rediscount rate and reserve requirement tools appear to be unnecessary. Yet possession of three policy instruments does not guarantee effective monetary control.[13] The Great Depression of the 1930s illustrates two problems: (1) the need during 1929–33 for defensive open-market operations to protect the money supply from undesirable changes in e and c, and (2) the difficulties of interpretation and management introduced by **excess reserves** of banks during 1934–40.

In a previous case study we found that the collapse in aggregate demand during 1929–33 caused a decline in both the price level and in real output. After 1933 real output recovered, but not by enough to reduce unemployment below 14 percent during the entire period 1934–40. The top line in Figure 16-1 plots the dramatic 1929–33 decline in nominal income (Y) and the partial recovery that left Y in 1940 below the 1929 level.[14]

The 46 percent decline of Y during 1929–33 was accompanied by a 35 percent reduction in $M2$, as illustrated in Figure 16-1. The great irony of these years is that the Fed, originally created in 1913 to provide an elastic supply of bank reserves to protect against massive increases in the cash-holding ratio (c) during banking panics, completely failed in 1929–33 to accommodate the increased demand for H by the banks and the public. Although both components of the denominator of the money supply equation, the bank-reserve ratio (e) and the pub-

---

[12] Only part of the decline in reserve requirements listed above has been due to explicit Federal Reserve actions. Part has come from the relatively fast growth of time deposits, which have always had lower reserve requirements than demand deposits.

[13] The Fed has other instruments, the power to set interest rate ceilings on bank deposits and to set minimum down payments and maximum repayment intervals for installment loans.

[14] A 1940 level of Y well above the 1929 value would have been necessary in 1940 to attain a 5 percent unemployment rate, because both the labor force and productivity had grown in the interim. The gap between actual and natural output in 1940 was about 18 percent.

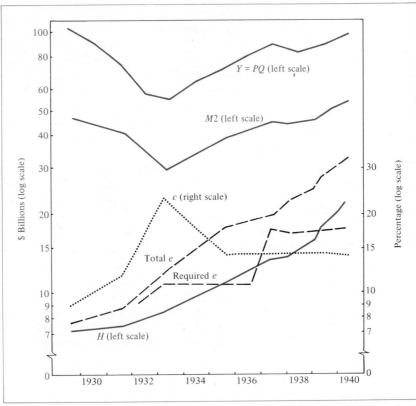

RADICAL CHANGES IN CASH-HOLDING AND RESERVE-HOLDING
BEHAVIOR INFLUENCED THE MONEY SUPPLY IN THE 1930s

FIGURE 16–1

Nominal Income (Y) Annually, and the Money Supply ($M1$) and Its Determinants (H, e, and c) for Selected Months, 1929–40

The 35 percent collapse in $M2$ between September 1929 and March 1933 cannot be blamed on the behavior of high-powered money (H), which actually increased over the same interval. Instead the explanation lies in the massive drain of high-powered money into cash and bank reserves, as signified by the increase in the ratio of currency to deposits (c) and reserves to deposits (e). In the late 1930s, much of the increase in high-powered money (H) went into excess reserves, represented by the distance between the total e and required e lines.

Source: Friedman and Schwartz, *op. cit.,* statistical appendix.

lic's cash-holding ratio (c) increased dramatically, H was only slightly higher at the 1933 trough of the Depression than at the 1929 peak. Compare the situation in September 1929 and March 1933 in Figure 16-1, where the following numbers are plotted.

	Percentage		$ Billions	
	c	e	H	M2
September 1929	8.99	7.65	7.1	46.3
March 1933	22.52	11.88	8.4	30.0

Massive open-market purchases would have been necessary to prevent the 1929–33 decline in $M2$, given the radical increase in e and c. But the observed behavior of e and c would not have occurred if the Fed had more vigorously purchased bonds. The public's higher cash-holding ratio (c) was mainly due to fear induced by several waves of bank failures that began in 1930. In turn, a part of the higher bank reserve ratio occurred as banks attempted to bolster their liquidity to lower the risk of failure. Had more high-powered money been available, fewer banks would have failed, and both c and e would have been lower. The Fed's performance during the 1929–33 period can only be described as inept, for reasons that Milton Friedman attributes to passivity in the absence of strong political or intellectual pressure from outside the Fed and of a strong leader inside the Fed.[15]

After 1933 the money supply grew almost continuously through 1940, the final year plotted on Figure 16-1. By June 1940 the money supply ($M2$) was 17 percent higher than in September 1929, although nominal GNP still fell short of its 1929 peak. The individual components of the money supply equation were quite different in 1929 and 1940, however:

		Percentage			$ Billions	
			e			
	c	Required	Excess	Total	H	M2
September 1929	8.99	7.65	—	7.65	7.1	46.3
June 1940	13.85	17.81	14.05	31.86	21.8	54.3

High-powered money more than tripled between 1929 and 1940, but $M2$ increased by only 17 percent. Why? Only a small part of the discrepancy is explained by the increase in the public's cash-holding ratio. Much more important is the quadrupling of the bank reserve ratio. Although the Fed directly caused a portion of the increase in e through its increase in reserve requirements (its third tool) in 1936 and early 1937, almost half the bank reserves in 1940 were excess, that is, more than required by the Fed as a backing for deposits.

Why did the banks hold such a huge quantity of excess reserves? Figure 16-1 suggests that developments can be separated into three

---

[15] Milton Friedman and Anna J. Schwartz, *A Monetary History of the United States, 1867–1960* (Princeton, N.J.: Princeton University Press, 1963), pp. 407–19.

stages. Between 1933 and 1936 the total e ratio increased while the required e ratio remained constant, a discrepancy that Milton Friedman attributes to the voluntary demand by banks for excess reserves to protect themselves against future failure, as a reaction to the failures of 1930–33. In 1936 the Fed attempted to eliminate excess reserves in the belief that they were truly excess and not desired by the banks. In Friedman's interpretation the banks reacted by attempting to reestablish their previous levels of excess reserves, causing a slight contraction of the money supply in 1937 and a sharp recession in 1937–38. The increase in excess reserves between 1938 and 1940 is attributed by Friedman to a "second shift in preferences" by banks to favor excess reserves.[16]

Friedman's position is not universally held. An alternative interpretation of the 1938–40 episode is that banks did not have enough profitable lending opportunities to use all the reserves provided by the Fed.[17] Since short-term investments were yielding virtually nothing, banks had nothing to lose by holding excess reserves. The importance of the disagreement is central to a proper interpretation of the 1938–40 period. In Friedman's view, excess reserve holdings were desired, so that any extra increase in H engineered by the Fed would have raised the money supply proportionately. In the opposing view, banks could not find attractive lending opportunities, and so any extra increase in H would have further raised excess reserves rather than the money supply. Monetary policy would have been "pushing on a string," impotent to return the economy to full employment without the aid of fiscal policy. So far no study has convincingly reconciled the two views.

16-6 CASE STUDY: MONETARY CONTROL IN SELECTED POSTWAR EPISODES

Since World War II no problems of monetary control have been as serious as those in the Great Depression. The public's cash-holding ratio (c) has remained relatively stable, except for seasonal bulges at Christmas, and the public has been protected from the fear of bank

---

[16] Friedman and Schwartz, *op. cit.*, pp. 538–40. Recent studies of reserve holding in the 1930s include John L. Scadding, "An annual money demand and supply model for the U.S.: 1924–1940/1949–1966," *Journal of Monetary Economics,* vol. 3 (January 1977), pp. 41–58. Also Karl Brunner and Alan Meltzer, "Liquidity Traps for Money, Bank Credit, and Interest Rates," *Journal of Political Economy,* vol. 76 (January/February 1968), pp. 1–35. See also Peter A. Frost, "Banks' Demand for Excess Reserves, *Journal of Political Economy,* vol. 79 (July/August 1971), pp. 805–25.

[17] During the entire 1933–41 period the Fed was entirely passive with the single exception of the 1936–37 increase in reserve requirements. All the increase in high-powered money between 1933 and 1940 is from an increase in U.S. gold holdings, built up mainly by the flight of capital from Europe connected with the outbreak of World War II.

failures by the Federal Deposit Insurance Corporation (FDIC), which guarantees holders of deposits against loss in case of bank failure.[18] Excess reserves have also disappeared, because the interest rate obtainable by banks on short-term investments has been significantly above the zero return on excess reserves, quite unlike the 1938–40 situation when the U.S. Treasury bill rate ranged between 0.05 and 0.01 percent! Thus the Fed has been able to predict e and c with relative accuracy, allowing any target for the money supply to be achieved by altering H through appropriate open-market operations.

The Fed's main problem in the postwar era has not been in setting the money supply at a target level, but in deciding what that target should be. We learned in Chapter 15 that there are at least three monetary variables the Fed may choose to control—the interest rate, the money supply excluding time deposits ($M1$), or the money supply including time deposits ($M2$)—but that in most situations the Fed cannot control all three monetary variables simultaneously. Once a control variable has been chosen, a further choice must be made: whether to maintain stability (a constant interest rate level or steady growth in $M1$ or $M2$) or to use the control variable countercyclically.

We limit this case study to the behavior of $M1$ during two important postwar periods. The first is the 1957–61 interval during which actual output (Q) continuously remained below natural output (Q^*) and the actual unemployment rate remained above the natural rate of unemployment. The second interval is the long 1964–71 period during most of which actual output (Q) exceeded natural output (Q^*), causing the acceleration in inflation that has bedeviled policymakers ever since. In each episode our aim is to determine whether the Fed's control of $M1$ was procyclical, moving $M1$ in the same direction as the deviation of Q from Q^*, and thus aggravating the instability of the economy, or countercyclical, moving $M1$ in the opposite direction as the deviation of Q from Q^*, and thus helping to moderate the instability of the economy.

The red line in Figure 16-2 shows the ratio of actual to natural output (Q/Q^*) for the 1956–61 period. Since inflation tends to accelerate when Q/Q^* is above 100 percent and to decelerate when Q/Q^* is below 100 percent, one test of Fed policy is how close was Q/Q^* maintained to 100 percent? In evaluating the conduct of monetary policy, we are taking advantage of hindsight. Policymakers in 1956 were not familiar with the concept of the natural rate of output, which we calculated earlier with full knowledge of all accelerations and decelerations of inflation during the entire postwar period.[19] They knew

---

[18] FDIC insures deposits up to a ceiling, currently $40,000.

[19] The data for Q and Q^* were originally displayed in Figure 1-2. The relationship between accelerations of inflation and the gap between the actual and natural unemployment rates is displayed in Figure 9-1.

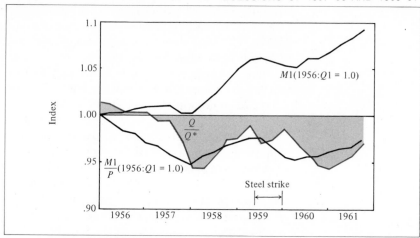

FIGURE 16–2   The Behavior of the Nominal and Real Supplies of Money ($M1$ and $M1/P$) Compared with the Ratio of Actual to Natural Real GNP (Q/Q^*), 1956–61

Actual output was below natural output continuously from early 1957 through 1961 and beyond, as shown by the gray shading. The Fed made the recession of 1957–58 worse by allowing the nominal supply of money ($M1$) to fall in the last half of 1957. Then again the nominal supply of money was allowed to fall from mid-1959 to mid-1960, aggravating the recession that started in early 1960.

Source: Appendix B

only that during 1956 inflation was proceeding and that monetary restriction was appropriate. Thus during 1956 $M1$ was allowed to grow only very slowly and the real supply of money ($M1/P$) declined steadily.

It was in 1957 that the Fed made a serious mistake. The Q/Q^* ratio began to drop, as the monetary tightness of the previous year began to take effect. But instead of moderating the downward pressure, the Fed intensified it. Nominal $M1$ was actually allowed to fall between 1957:Q3 and 1958:Q1, and the decline in real $M1/P$ continued even though a precipitous decline in the output ratio was under way. Thus the Fed appears to have acted procyclically in 1957, aggravating the 1957–58 recession.

This perverse behavior was repeated in 1959–60. After allowing $M1$ and $M1/P$ to increase fairly rapidly during 1958 to stimulate the economy's recovery, monetary growth came to a halt in mid-1959. In retrospect we can see that the Q/Q^* ratio did rise fairly close to 1.0 during mid-1959 and might have continued to increase if the economy's progress had not been interrupted by a steel strike. Thus the Fed's shift to moderate monetary growth is understandable, but the intensity of its mid-1959 policy reversal is not. For three quarters (1959:Q4 to 1960:Q2) the Fed allowed both $M1$ and $M1/P$ to decline, even though the output ratio never rose above 98.5 percent. Throughout 1960 the real money supply ($M1/P$) was below its mid-1959 level, aggravating the 1960–61 recession and helping John F. Kennedy to squeeze by Richard M. Nixon in the election of 1960.

Summary: During the 1956–61 period, the Fed allowed the money supply to move procyclically, aggravating both the 1957–58 and 1960–61 recessions. It is hard to dispute the monetarist argument that a steady growth rate of $M1$ would have resulted in more stable behavior of Q/Q^* than the policies actually followed. On the other hand, as pointed out in our discussion of Figure 15–2, a counter-cyclical policy that achieved fastest $M1$ growth during late 1957 and during 1960 would have been even better.[20]

Another example of procyclical Fed money supply policy is illustrated in Figure 16-3 for the period 1964–71. Twice during this period the Fed allowed both nominal and real money to accelerate while the economy was operating well above the natural output level, that is, when Q/Q^* substantially exceeded 100 percent. In Figure 16-3 the red Q/Q^* line rose above 100 percent in early 1965 and remained at a very high level until early 1970. Yet the Fed allowed both real and nominal money to accelerate in two stages, first between mid-1965 and early 1966 and then between early 1967 and late 1968. Instead of achieving further increases in Q/Q^* and reductions in unemployment, the Fed's excessive monetary expansion caused inflation to accelerate from a rate of about 1.0 percent in 1964 to about 5.0 percent in 1970.[21]

The 1964–71 period was punctuated by two periods of monetary tightness, each causing a temporary decline in the real money supply ($M1/P$). Why did the first period of monetary tightness during late 1966 fail to reduce Q/Q^* back to the desired ratio (1.0), whereas the 1969 period of tightness more than succeeded? Two fundamental differences between these episodes stand out:

1. The 1966 reduction in $M1/P$ was short-lived. By 1967:Q3 $M1/P$ had exceeded its previous high reached in 1966:Q2. In contrast

---

[20] In Figure 15-2 a countercyclical policy causes the economy to move between points C_0 and C_1 when the IS curve shifts back and forth, as compared to movements between points A_0 and A_1 caused by a procyclical money supply policy.

[21] In Chapter 11 we discuss the difficulties faced by policymakers, such as Nixon's advisors during 1970–71, who attempt to reduce an inflation inherited from a previous period when the Q/Q^* ratio was allowed to remain above 1.0.

MONETARY GROWTH ACCELERATED IN 1965 AND AGAIN IN
1967–68, EVEN THOUGH THE ECONOMY WAS OPERATING
ABOVE ITS NATURAL OUTPUT LEVEL

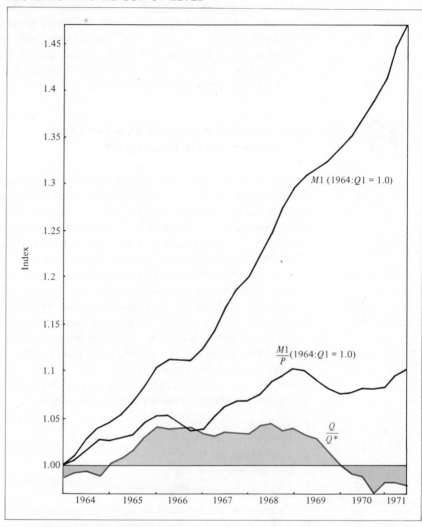

FIGURE 16–3   The Behavior of the Nominal and Real Supplies of Money ($M1$ and $M1/P$) Compared with the Ratio of Actual to Natural Real GNP (Q/Q^*), 1964–71

Actual output was above natural output continuously from early 1965 through the end of 1969, as shown by the pink shading. The Fed contributed to the acceleration of inflation during this period by twice accelerating the growth of the nominal money supply, first in late 1965 and again in 1967–68.

Source: Appendix B

the 1969 crunch lasted longer. Real money $M1/P$ remained below its late 1968 peak for 10 quarters.

2. The stance of fiscal policy was completely different. In 1966–67 real government expenditures were rising very rapidly, whereas in 1968–71 they were falling.[22] In terms of our previous theoretical analysis, in 1966–67 the IS curve was moving rightward up the LM curve, causing the crowding out of investment.[23] During 1969–70, however, both the IS and LM curves were moving to the left.

16-7 LIMITATIONS OF COUNTERCYCLICAL MONETARY ACTIVISM: LAGS

How can we choose between the monetarist recommendation that the money supply be fixed by a constant-growth-rate rule (CGRR) and the nonmonetarist preference for an activist countercyclical policy? According to the analysis of Figure 15-2, countercyclical movements in the real money supply can achieve a more stable path of real output than a CGRR at the cost of greater fluctuations in the interest rate. The two main objections to countercyclical activism are (1) that lags prevent the monetary changes from influencing the economy until it is too late and (2) that the extra fluctuations in the interest rate caused by activism are undesirable. Monetarists have generally emphasized only the first objection.[24]

Several types of lags intervene that prevent either monetary or fiscal policy from immediately offsetting an unexpected shift in the demand for commodities or money. There are five main types of lags, some of which are common to both monetary and fiscal policy and the rest of which are more important for one or the other:

1. The data lag
2. The recognition lag
3. The legislative lag
4. The transmission lag
5. The effectiveness lag.

To explain the meaning of each lag and to estimate its length, let us take the example of the "pause" in the U.S. economic recovery that began in mid-April 1976 and extended until October.[25]

---

[22] You can trace the behavior of real government spending during 1965–71 in Figure 12-1.

[23] A case study of this period was presented in section 5-7.

[24] See Milton Friedman, "The Lag in Effect of Monetary Policy," *Journal of Political Economy,* vol. 69 (October 1961), reprinted in his *The Optimum Quantity of Money and Other Essays* (Chicago: Aldine, 1969), pp. 237–60.

[25] The Department of Commerce "index of four coincident indicators" increased by 9.9 percent between March 1975 and April 1976, but then by only 0.2 percent between April and October 1976. Source: *Business Conditions Digest* (December 1976), Series 920.

1. *The data lag.* Policymakers do not know what is going on in the economy the moment it happens. Although a few industries have sales reports with a lag of only a few days, the first sign of the 1976 pause did not appear until mid-June, when the news of a decline in employment and in real manufacturing and trade sales became known.[26] It was not until mid-July that the quarterly GNP figures revealed that the growth rate of real GNP had dropped from an annual rate of 9.2 percent in 1976:Q1 to only 4.5 percent in 1976:Q2.

2. *The recognition lag.* No policymaker pays much attention to reversals in the data that occur for only one month. The usual rule of thumb is to wait and see if the reversal continues for three successive months. A three-month continuous decline in industrial production or in payroll employment causes policymakers to think about the possibility of a recession. In 1976, industrial production declined for only September and October, although one employment series did decline slightly for three months. If the 1976 pause had been more serious, three months of data would not have been available until late August, and a second reading on quarterly GNP growth would not have been available until mid-October.

3. *The legislative lag.* Although most changes in fiscal policy must be legislated by Congress, an important advantage of monetary policy is the short legislative lag. Once a majority of the Federal Open-Market Committee (FOMC) decides that an acceleration in monetary growth is needed, only a short wait is necessary until the next meeting of the FOMC, which occurs once every month. It was possible to detect a modest response of monetary policy to the 1976 pause. Growth in *M*2 accelerated in early September and averaged 12.8 percent in the subsequent four months, compared to 10.1 percent in the previous five months. Short-term interest rates were allowed to drop continuously from early June to Christmas, although the major drop occurred in two stages in October and late November.

4. *The transmission lag.* This lag is the time interval between the policy decision and the subsequent change in policy instruments — the money supply, government spending, or tax rates. Again, it is a more serious obstacle for fiscal policy. Once the FOMC has given its order for the open-market manager to make open-market purchases, the expansion in the money supply begins almost immediately, although the full multiple money-creation process may require one or two months.

5. *The effectiveness lag.* Almost all the controversy about the lags of monetary policy concerns the length of time required for an acceleration or deceleration in the money supply to influence real output.

---

[26] The two promptest pieces of economic news are reports of auto sales for each 10-day period, available only three days later, and large chain-store sales, almost always published on the fourth day of the following month. Weekly retail sales and railroad freight traffic are published with a lag of about 10 days.

Milton Friedman is on record, from his extensive historical studies of U.S. monetary behavior between 1867 and 1960, as arguing that the effectiveness lag is both "long" and "variable."

Many estimates of the lag of monetary policy are available. Let us first develop an informal estimate of the average lag between the month of maximum monetary tightness and the subsequent onset of recession in the four major post-Korean recessions, recognizing that each recession was influenced by factors other than monetary policy.

Business cycle peak of	Month/year of peak in:		Average lag (months)
	M1/P	Coincident indicators (CI)	
1957	4/56	2/57	10
1960	7/59	1/60	6
1969	2/69	10/69	8
1973	1/73	11/73	10
Average	–	–	8.5

Here the dates of cyclical peaks are indicated for the real money supply excluding time deposits $(M1/P)$—the same variable plotted in Figures 16-2 and 16-3. Our measure of real economic activity is taken to be the government's index of coincident indicators (CI).[27] In each business cycle the peak in $M1/P$ has occurred before that in CI. The lag between the peaks in $M1/P$ and CI ranges from 6 to 10 months. Thus the label "short but variable" would appear to be a better description of the monetary effectiveness lag than Friedman's "long but variable."

A vast amount of statistical and econometric research has been conducted to determine the timing of the economy's reaction to an increase or decrease in the money supply. Ironically, the econometric model built by the Federal Reserve Bank of St. Louis, a monetarist bastion, has a much shorter effectiveness lag of monetary policy than does the MPS (MIT-Penn-SSRC) model, designed by Franco Modigliani of MIT and other leading nonmonetarists. Thus the St. Louis results support the nonmonetarist case for countercyclical activism, whereas the MPS model supports the "long lag" monetarist argument against activism and in favor of monetary rules.

As an example, the St. Louis results indicate that virtually all the ultimate effect of a monetary change on spending has occurred by the end of four quarters. The MPS model indicates that less than half the ultimate effect has occurred by then. Thus the St. Louis results are more con-

---

[27] This is an average of these four series: (1) employees on nonagricultural payrolls, (2) real personal income less transfer payments, (3) index of industrial production, and (4) real manufacturing and trade sales.

sistent with our crude timing table. Why do the models disagree? Unfortunately the subject is much too complicated to be summarized here. My own suspicion is that the MPS model, despite its elaborate structure, still is overly restrictive and does not capture all the channels by which monetary policy directly influences personal consumption expenditures, thus forcing the influence of money on the economy to follow an overly roundabout and indirect route.[28]

To summarize this section on lags, let us add up the total delay between an unexpected economic pause and the arrival of stimulus from a reaction to that event by the Fed:

Time of lag	Estimated length (months)
1. Data	2.0
2. Recognition	2.0
3. Legislative	0.5
4. Transmission	1.0
5. Effectiveness	8.5
Total	14.0

Thus a pause beginning in mid-April 1976 could not be counteracted by by the Fed until June 1977, although the variability of the effectiveness lag might shorten or lengthen the lag by two or three months. By the time the Fed's stimulus arrived, the economy might not need additional stimulus. Or, looking at the problem in another way, the Fed would have had to forecast the 1976 pause as early as July 1975, an unlikely event because the major forecasters failed to foresee the pause.[29]

16-8 LIMITATIONS OF COUNTERCYCLICAL MONETARY ACTIVISM: VARIATIONS IN INTEREST RATES

No one disputes that an activist countercyclical monetary policy generally causes increased fluctuations in interest rates, just as a CGRR policy causes interest rates to fluctuate more than an accommodating policy that attempts to stabilize interest rates.[30] Possible harm done by

---

[28] The best recent study of the differences between the St. Louis and MPS models is Franco Modigliani and Albert Ando, "Impacts of Fiscal Actions on Aggregate Income and the Monetarist Controversy: Theory and Evidence," in Jerome L. Stein (ed.), *Monetarism* (Amsterdam: North-Holland, 1976), pp. 17–42. For one example of a study that finds an additional channel of monetary influence on consumption not present in the MPS model, see Frederick S. Mishkin, "Liquidity, and the Role of Monetary Policy in Consumer Durable Demand," *New England Economic Review* (November/December 1976), pp. 31–42.

[29] Forecasts for the 1970–76 period are displayed in Figure 12-3.

[30] In Figure 15-2 the accommodating policy holds the interest rate constant, the monetary rule causes fluctuations between B_0 and B_1, and the countercyclical policy causes greater fluctuations in the interest rate between C_0 and C_1.

variable interest rates is an important consideration for proponents of an activist monetary policy.

Throughout this book we have referred to *the* interest rate, ignoring for the most part differences among the interest rates available on different assets. Yet a major factor bearing on the costs of monetary activism is the existence of ceilings set by the Fed that limit some interest rates but not others. The Fed's **Regulation Q** fixes ceilings on the interest rate that can be paid on commercial bank demand deposits (zero) and time deposits (a set of ceiling rates).[31] Similarly, the Federal Home Loan Bank sets ceiling rates for savings and loan institutions that are almost identical to those set by the Fed's Regulation Q.

Although ceilings are set on savings accounts, there is no interest-rate ceiling on short-term and long-term bonds or on stocks (equities). Thus during a period when the Fed, conducting a policy of countercyclical activism, reduces the supply of money while the demand for commodities is strong, the interest rates on bonds and stocks may substantially exceed the ceiling rates available on savings deposits.[32]

DISINTERMEDIATION

Naturally, many holders of savings deposits are likely to find irresistible the higher yields on bonds and stocks, say 8 or 10 percent, when the yields on their savings accounts are limited by Regulation Q ceilings to the range of 5 to 7.5 percent.[33] Any substantial downward shift in the demand for savings deposits has a disproportionate deflationary effect on the housing market, because savings intermediaries other than commercial banks (SI's) are required by law to hold almost all their assets in the form of mortgages. The supply of mortgage finance declines, for purchasers of both new and used homes. The shift toward bonds and stocks away from SI's is called **disintermediation.**

In principle disintermediation does not require a countercyclical monetary policy. A CGRR monetary policy might also lead to disintermediation. Imagine that the price level (P) and the money supply (M) were both rising at a steady rate of 5 percent, maintaining a constant real money supply (M/P) and fixed LM curve. A sufficient rightward shift in the IS curve caused by an upsurge in investment or government spending, or a drop in tax rates, could cause the interest rate to rise and funds to flow into bonds and stocks from the SI's. But whatever the dislocations caused by disintermediation resulting from a CGRR policy,

---

[31] Since July 1973 the ceiling rate on passbook savings deposits at commercial banks has been 5.0 percent. Higher rates are available on certificates, depending on maturity and minimum denomination.

[32] Such a situation is illustrated at point C_1 in Figure 15-2.

[33] In this discussion we have lumped together time deposits of commercial banks with deposits at mutual savings banks and savings and loan institutions. In the subsequent discussion both of the latter institutions are referred to as SI's.

TABLE 16-2 Magnitude and Timing of Episodes of Disintermediation: 1966, 1969, and 1973–74

Date of Treasury bill interest rate peak (month/year)	Decline in monthly change in mortgage debt between peak and trough month		Decline in real housing expenditure between peak and trough quarter	
10/66	−64.6%	(12/65 to 12/66)	−25.9%	(1965:Q2 to 1967:Q1)
12/69	−48.9	(11/68 to 11/69)	−15.3	(1969:Q1 to 1970:Q2)
8/73, 7/74	−67.0	(11/72 to 11/74)	−45.1	(1973:Q1 to 1975:Q1)

Sources: Treasury bill rate and change in mortgage debt from *Business Conditions Digest,* series 114 and 33. Real Housing Expenditure from *Survey of Current Business.*

the dislocations caused by a countercyclical monetary policy will be even greater.

An outflow of funds from the SI's, a drop in mortgage finance, and a decline in housing expenditure, have all occurred in every postwar episode of high interest rates. Of the three most recent episodes of disintermediation—in 1966, 1969, and 1973–74—Table 16-2 indicates that the most recent was also the most severe. The twin peaks in interest rates on Treasury bills reached in the summers of 1973 and 1974 pulled billions out of SI's and forced the growth of mortgage debt to drop from an annual rate of $60 billion in late 1972 to a mere $20 billion in late 1974. With a one-quarter lag, housing expenditure also dropped precipitously, from $64.5 billion to $35.4 billion in 1972 prices.

Some economists have argued that during a period of excess demand for commodities the brunt of a monetary crunch must fall on someone, and that new houses are a logical candidate because they are very long-lived and are thus postponable purchases. A drop in new housing construction is accommodated by a delay in the destruction of old buildings and by a postponement of new household formation as young people are forced to live for another year or two with their parents. But the damage done by disintermediation spreads out much wider than that. Construction firms are forced to declare bankruptcy. Construction workers are laid off (the unemployment rate for construction workers exceeded 18 percent in 1975). Sales of old houses come almost to a halt as buyers are refused mortgage funds, and moves must be postponed.

THE NEED FOR REGULATORY REFORM

Why does the brunt of tight money fall on housing? The ceilings on deposit rates at SI's are the apparent cause of the massive outflow of funds into bonds and other securities, so why can't the Fed and other government regulators lift the ceilings? Unfortunately, government regulations prevent savings banks from lending for purposes other than housing. Because mortgage loans have long maturities, many savings banks are stuck with low-yielding 5 and 6 percent mortgages lent out years ago. With this limit on the income from their assets, savings banks cannot afford to pay higher interest rates on their deposits. On the other hand commercial banks can raise their time deposit rates in a period of high interest rates on bonds, because they have assets with shorter maturities. Thus without further reforms an end to all interest rate ceilings would cause savings banks to go out of business as funds flow out to bonds and to commercial banks.

Elimination of disintermediation requires a whole set of regulatory changes. Savings banks must be allowed to lend for purposes other than housing. Mortgage loans with variable interest rates should be introduced in order to sustain the flow of mortgage funds during periods of high interest rates. These and other reforms were recommended in the 1971 report of the President's Commission on Financial Structure and Regulation (the Hunt Commission) but have not yet been put into effect. Why? The story is an old and familiar one that afflicts almost all proposals for government regulatory reform: Businessmen loudly condemn government regulation in general but then raise their voices unanimously in protest at any proposal to lift the particular regulations that shield them from competition. Commercial banks and savings banks are simply afraid of the new competition that the Hunt Commission recommendations would have fostered.

The construction industry, potential home buyers, and sellers of existing homes are the main victims of high interest rates on bonds when ceilings are set on savings bank deposit rates. But there are other losers as well. The very fact that savings banks lose only a portion of their deposits means that households continue to hold hundreds of billions of savings deposits at relatively low interest rates. Why doesn't everyone switch from savings banks to Treasury bills and other high-yielding but risk-free securities? The three main reasons are ignorance, transactions costs, and minimum purchase requirements for securities. All three together imply that *affluent savers* benefit from higher interest returns available on bonds, but *small savers* are stuck with low returns on savings accounts. Small borrowers may also be refused loans as banks struggle to provide the credit needs of their large corporate customers.

Summary: When interest rate ceilings on savings deposits are in effect, a countercyclical monetary policy has undesirable side effects. The right solution is to reform the undesirable regulations and ceilings, as proposed by the Hunt Commission, not to abandon countercyclical policy. A side effect of such reforms would be to reduce the welfare costs of inflation, which in Chapter 10 included the redistribution of income from savers to borrowers when inflation pushes up the nominal interest rate on bonds, and to reduce the need for periodic recessions as an anti-inflation measure.

16-9 CONCLUDING ARGUMENTS ON MONETARY RULES VERSUS ACTIVISM

The postwar case study in section 16-6 provided convincing evidence that the Fed destabilized the economy during the 1950s and 1960s, aggravating the recessions of 1957–58 and the acceleration of inflation in 1965–69. Partly as a reaction to these events themselves, and partly in response to sustained criticism by Milton Friedman and other monetarists, the Fed in January 1970 substituted monetary growth for interest rates as the primary target of monetary policy. Later, in early 1972, growth in bank reserves was substituted for "credit conditions" (interest rates) as the primary week-to-week instrument of policymaking. Nevertheless, monetary policy has continued to contribute to instability in the 1970s.

The evidence in favor of this proposition is clear-cut. First, let us examine the growth rates of the two money concepts, $M1$ and $M2$, during the 1970s.

GROWTH RATES IN 12 MONTHS ENDING
IN DECEMBER

Year	M1	M2
1970	6.1	8.4
1971	6.3	Peak → 11.2
1972	Peak → 8.7	11.1
1973	6.1	8.8
1974	4.8	Trough → 7.2
1975	Trough → 4.2	8.8
1976	5.7	11.1
1977*	7.6	10.5

*Twelve months through October 13, 1977.

The two major episodes of economic instability in the 1970s were excessive real spending in 1973 and a severe recession that touched bottom in March 1975. Clearly the Fed's behavior aggravated both episodes. Monetary growth of $M1$ reached its peak rate in 1972 and of $M2$ in 1971–72, raising spending in 1973 (because of the lag in the effect of monetary policy). Then monetary growth of $M1$ dropped off just as the economy was collapsing, with trough rates of growth of $M1$ during 1975 and $M2$ during 1974. With the Fed's performance in the 1970s as poor as during 1957–60, it would indeed be hard to argue that the Fed has learned much from the research that monetarist and nonmonetarist economists have published in the interim.

What should we conclude on monetary activism? Milton Friedman has recently summarized his case in favor of the CGRR (constant-growth-rate-rule) monetary policy:[34]

1. The past performance of the Fed
2. The limitations of our knowledge
3. The promotion of confidence
4. Neutralization of the Fed.

Clearly the past performance of the Fed has been abysmally procyclical, and a CGRR would be an improvement. Adherence to a CGRR would promote confidence and prevent the Fed from succumbing to the temptation to influence election results by preelection monetary acceleration.

But all these arguments are also merits of a countercyclical policy as well. The fact that the Fed has failed to act countercyclically in the past does not prevent economists from urging it to adopt an activist counter-cyclical policy in the future. While there are limitations to our knowledge (Friedman's second reason) that prevent the Fed from knowing precisely how much of a change in the money supply is needed and at what exact time, nevertheless we can do better than a CGRR.[35] A stabilizing policy which temporarily slows monetary growth when forecasters predict unemployment at or below the natural rate for next year, and which temporarily accelerates monetary growth when unemployment above the natural rate is predicted, appears to be feasible with present knowledge. Lags in the effect of monetary changes appear to be less than a year in length, and forecasters in the 1970s have been able to predict accurately a year in advance the direction of most changes in unemployment, even though they failed badly in predicting the magnitude of the increase in unemployment following the 1973–74 supply shock episode.

SUMMARY

1. A set of banks in a closed economy – one with no transfers of funds to the outside – can "create money" by a multiple of each dollar of cash that is initially received. This is true for a single bank on a desert island or for all banks in the United States taken together.

2. Among the assumptions necessary for money creation to occur are that only a fraction of the initial cash receipt is held as reserves by banks or as pocket cash by depositors and that banks loan out excess reserves to willing borrowers.

3. The deposit-creation multiplier is 1.0 divided by the fraction of an

---

[34] "The Case for a Monetary Rule," *Newsweek* (February 7, 1972).

[35] In studies of past episodes using both the monetarist St. Louis econometric model and the nonmonetarist MPS model, J. Phillip Cooper and Stanley Fischer have confirmed that an activist policy, in which monetary growth responds to the real rate of change of unemployment, would have outperformed a CGRR. See their "Stabilization Policy and Lags: Summary and Extension," *Annals of Economic and Social Measurement* (October 1972), pp. 407–18.

initial cash receipt that is held as bank reserves or pocket cash. The money-creation multiplier is then the deposit-creation multiplier times 1.0 plus the pocket cash-holding fraction. The money supply is equal to high-powered money times the money-creation multiplier.

4. The Federal Reserve can change high-powered money by conducting open-market operations or adjusting the rediscount rate. The Fed can also alter the required reserve ratio for banks. The final determinant of the money supply, the public's cash-holding ratio, is not under the control of the Fed but depends on the behavior of individual households and firms.

5. During the 1930s a dramatic collapse in the money supply was caused not by a decline in high-powered money, but by increases in the reserve-holding ratio and cash-holding ratio caused by a widespread and correct fear of bank failures. The Fed's control over the money supply in the late 1930s was loosened by the unwillingness of banks to loan out their excess reserves.

6. In the late 1950s and again in the 1960s, the Fed destabilized the economy by reducing the money supply when the economy was weak and by accelerating monetary growth when the economy was strong.

7. There are five sources of lags between an initial change in the economy and the minimum interval before which monetary or fiscal policy can influence spending. The total length of the five lags taken together is about 14 months for monetary policy in the United States.

8. A major disadvantage of countercyclical monetary policy is the dislocation in the economy caused by significant shifts in interest rates. An increase in the interest rate on bonds caused by restrictive monetary policy leads to an outflow of funds from savings institutions, a decline in mortgage lending, and a drop in housing starts.

A LOOK AHEAD

Having studied some of the advantages and disadvantages of an activist countercyclical monetary policy, we now turn to consider fiscal policy. Some of the issues are the same, particularly the question of lags. But fiscal policy also raises new issues, because of the wide variety of alternative expenditure categories and types of taxes that might be chosen as fiscal policy instruments.

CONCEPTS AND QUESTIONS

IDENTIFICATIONS

Required reserves
Excess reserves
Demand deposits
Money-creation multiplier
High-powered money
Cash-holding ratio

Reserve ratio
Federal Reserve System
Open-market operations
Rediscount rate
Regulation Q
Disintermediation

QUESTIONS FOR REVIEW

1 Because banks can make profits by increasing their interest-earning loans and granting the borrower a noninterest-bearing demand
   deposit, what prevents banks from increasing their loans without
   limit?

2 Starting from the situation of the First Desert Island Bank at
   Stage 5, when its assets and liabilities are both equal to 500, calculate the effect on the bank of the following events (in each case,
   indicate the ultimate level of the bank's reserves, loans, and deposits after the full money-creation process has taken place):
   a. Discovery by the Miser of an additional 100 gold coins, which he
      deposits in the bank.
   b. The decision by the Banker to reduce his voluntary reserve ratio
      from 20 percent—the example used in section 16-2—to 10 per-
      cent.
   c. The decision by all holders of demand deposits at the bank to
      hold 5 percent of their deposits in the form of gold coins as
      pocket cash.
   d. Withdrawal by the Miser of all his deposits in the form of gold
      coins, followed by his departure from the island.

3 Explain in words what happens when the Federal Reserve conducts an open-market sale of $100 million in bonds. What does the
   open-market manager do? How do banks respond? What is the ultimate effect on high-powered money and the money supply?

4 Does a reduction in the Fed rediscount rate tend to raise or lower
   the money supply? Is your answer affected if initially the outstanding loans from the Fed to the banks are zero, as in October 1976?

5 Using the figures in section 16-5, what actions by the Fed would
   have succeeded in doubling the money supply in 1939? How much
   of an increase in high-powered money do you think would have been
   required? What conclusions do you reach about the Fed's power
   to end the Great Depression by itself, without any help from
   fiscal policy?

6 Why do you think the Fed allowed the money supply to accelerate
   in 1967–68 (see Figure 16-3). Using *IS-LM* analysis, can you spec-
   ulate what would have happened if the Fed had succeeded in keeping *M*1 constant?

7 What are some of the disadvantages of a monetary policy that
   allows interest rates to rise significantly in an effort to restrain the
   economy? Are these disadvantages inevitable, or can you suggest
   reforms that might alleviate some of the harmful side effects of high
   interest rates?

17 The Government Budget and the Public Debt

As to deficits, a new distinction was drawn between "deficits of weakness" that arise out of backing into a recession and "deficits of strength" that arise out of measures to provide fiscal thrust to a lagging economy.

—Walter W. Heller[1]

17-1 INTRODUCTION

If a countercyclical stabilization policy is to be pursued to offset an undesirable decline or increase in the private demand for commodities, should an activist monetary policy, an activist fiscal policy, or some combination of the two be used? The last chapter distinguished several possible disadvantages of an activist monetary policy—lags, fluctuating interest rates, overconcentration of policy's effects on housing, and the poor historical record of the Fed. How does fiscal policy compare? We will see in the next chapter that an activist fiscal policy is subject to criticism for some of the same reasons, particularly lags, and for quite different reasons as well.

First, this chapter introduces important concepts frequently used in discussions of fiscal policy, including the natural employment surplus, fiscal dividend and fiscal drag, and automatic stabilization. Before the limitations of fiscal policy are confronted in the next chapter, we need to know how to measure the degree of fiscal stimulus. As is true in most discussions of macroeconomics, our attention is limited to the federal government; it ignores state and local governments. Why? First, because state and local governments are limited in the fiscal deficits they can run, and none can print money to cover their deficits. Second, because state and local finance involves issues regarding the migration of labor and capital among states that are best covered in courses on public finance.

---

[1] *New Dimensions of Political Economy* (New York: Norton, 1967), p. 40.

17-2 THE FULL-EMPLOYMENT AND NATURAL-EMPLOYMENT BUDGETS

For years the guiding motto of fiscal policy was to "maintain a balanced budget." Pursuit of a balanced-budget policy was considered by some politicians to constitute fiscal responsibility, and deficits were fiscally irresponsible. But this old-fashioned doctrine did considerable harm to the economy and has since been abandoned by all economists, monetarists and nonmonetarists alike. Why? Because in a recession when GNP declines, the taxable incomes of individuals and firms decline, the government's tax receipts fall, and a budget deficit emerges even if government expenditures and tax rates remain constant. To achieve a balanced budget in a recession requires an increase in tax rates or a reduction in government spending, either of which tends further to depress the economy. From the present perspective it seems unbelievable that in order to balance the budget, the Hoover administration actually raised tax rates by a major amount in 1932, when the unemployment rate was 24 percent!

The government budget surplus in real terms, as we learned in Chapter 2, is defined as real tax revenue net of transfer payments (T), minus real government spending on goods and services (G):

$$\text{Surplus} \equiv T - G \tag{17.1}$$

Tax revenues net of transfers (T) can be redefined as total real GNP (Q) times the average ratio of tax revenue net of transfers to GNP (t):

$$\text{Surplus} \equiv tQ - G \tag{17.2}$$

It is convenient to make one more change, both multiplying and dividing tQ by the same thing, the natural level of output (Q^*):[2]

$$\text{Surplus} \equiv tQ^* (Q/Q^*) - G \tag{17.3}$$

The purpose of writing the surplus in the form of (17.3) is to distinguish three sources of change in the surplus: (1) **automatic stabilization** through changes in Q/Q^*, (2) **discretionary fiscal policy** through changes in t and G, and (3) economic growth that raises Q^*.

AUTOMATIC STABILIZATION

When output (Q) goes up in an economic boom, the output ratio Q/Q^* rises as well and automatically boosts the government surplus by generating more tax revenues. Federal revenues from the personal and

---

[2] Earlier we defined the natural level of output (Q^*) as the amount of output the economy can produce without any tendency for inflation to accelerate or decelerate.

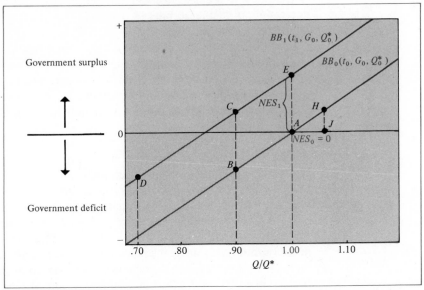

FIGURE 17-1

The Relation between the Actual
Government Surplus, the Natural
Employment Surplus (NES), and
the Ratio of Actual to Natural
Output (Q/Q^*)

The lower budget line BB_0 shows all
the levels of the government budget
surplus (or deficit) that are compatible
with a given level of government expenditures (G_0), tax rates (t_0), and
the level of natural output (Q_0^*). The

BB line slopes upward to the right,
because as we move rightward the
higher output ratio (Q/Q^*) raises
government tax revenues (tQ), thus
increasing the government surplus in
a vertical direction. The upper BB_1
line indicates a higher government
surplus at every level of output than
the lower line BB_0, because the tax
rate has been raised from t_0 to t_1,
thus raising government revenues and
hence the government surplus.

corporation income taxes are very responsive to higher income levels.
The higher surplus helps to stabilize the economy, since the higher tax
revenues leak out of the spending stream and restrain the boom. Similarly,
tax revenues drop in a recession, cutting the leakages out of the spending
stream and helping to dampen the recession.

The automatic stabilization effect of Q/Q^* on the surplus is illustrated
in Figure 17-1. The horizontal axis is the output ratio Q/Q^*, and the vertical axis is the surplus. In the gray area above the zero point on the
vertical axis, the government runs a positive surplus, with tax revenues
exceeding expenditures. In the pink area below zero the surplus is negative, meaning that the government is running a deficit. The red upward

sloping BB_0 budget line illustrates the automatic stabilization relationship between the surplus and the output ratio Q/Q^* when the other determinants of the surplus in equation (17.3) are constant—t, Q^*, and G.

The budget line BB_0 is drawn so that the government runs a balanced budget (surplus = 0) at point A, when output is at its natural level ($Q/Q^*=$ 100 percent). If the economy were to enter a recession and the output ratio were to fall from 100 to 90 percent, the economy would move from point A to point B, where the government is running a deficit.[3]

DISCRETIONARY FISCAL POLICY

The second source of change in the surplus comes from alterations in the tax rate (t) and government spending (G). It is evident from equation (17.3) that an increase in the average tax rate (t) raises the surplus, whereas an increase in government expenditures (G) reduces the surplus.[4] How are such discretionary changes illustrated in Figure 17-1? An increase in the tax rate shifts the red budget line upward for any given output ratio, since at a given level of output the government can collect higher tax revenues when tax rates are increased. If the original budget line BB_0 is drawn for an initial assumed tax rate t_0, then an increase in the tax rate to a higher level t_1 causes the budget line to shift upward to the new position BB_1.

> **Example:** Let us imagine that in 1931 the economy was at a point like B in Figure 17-1, with a government deficit and an output ratio of 90 percent. Herbert Hoover was sufficiently distressed by the deficit at point B to raise tax rates, shifting the budget line upward from BB_0 to BB_1. If the higher tax rates had no depressing effect on private spending, Hoover would have achieved his goal, a budget surplus at point C along the new budget line BB_1. But our theory of Chapters 3–5 suggests that a tax increase depresses output. If the tax multiplier were large enough, and the output ratio Q/Q^* were to fall far enough, it is conceivable that the government might run a larger deficit at point D than it was previously running with lower tax rates at point B!

This example illustrates the basic flaw in using the actual budget surplus or deficit as a measure of fiscal policy's effect on the economy. Use of the actual budget ignores the two-way interaction between the budget and the economy: *the budget affects the economy and the economy affects the budget.* First, the budget affects the economy through dis-

---

[3] At the trough of the most recent recession in 1975:Q1, the output ratio Q/Q^* was 90.1 percent.

[4] We ignore here the automatic changes in the average tax rate caused by progressivity in the tax structure.

cretionary fiscal policy, changes in G or t. But the state of the economy feeds back into the budget through automatic stabilization, the dependence of the government's tax revenues on output.

Given the inadequacies of the actual budget, what other single number can we use to summarize the effect of fiscal policy on the economy? In the diagram the fact that BB_1 is a more restrictive budget is evident from the fact that its vertical position is higher than that of BB_0. Therefore its restrictive effect can be summarized by describing the height of the budget line at some standard agreed-upon output level, say when the output ratio is at 100 percent. The budget surplus at this output ratio can be called the **natural employment surplus** (NES) and is defined as the value of the government surplus when actual output (Q) equals natural output (Q^*). When we substitute $Q/Q^* = 1.0$ into equation (17.3) we obtain:

$$\text{NES} = tQ^* - G \qquad (17.4)$$

The natural employment surplus changes whenever there is a change in any of the three components on the right side of (17.4). An increase in the average tax rate (t) or in natural output itself (Q^*) raises the natural employment surplus, whereas an increase in government spending (G) has the opposite effect.

In Figure 17-1 the two budget lines BB_0 and BB_1 correspond to the two hypothetical tax rates, t_0 and t_1. The respective values of the natural employment surplus are denoted at NES_0 and NES_1 in the figure. The natural employment surplus in the diagram corresponding to each budget line is simply the vertical distance between that budget line and zero, measured at $Q/Q^* = 100$ percent on the horizontal axis. Along the lower budget line NES_0 equals zero because tax revenues just balance government expenditures when the economy is operating with an output level (Q) equal to natural output (Q^*). Along the higher budget line tax rates are higher, allowing the government to run the natural employment surplus NES_1 corresponding to the vertical distance AE.

"Natural employment surplus" (NES) is a phrase coined for this book, corresponding to the natural rate hypothesis developed in Chapter 8, which states that any attempt by policymakers permanently to maintain the unemployment rate below the natural unemployment rate leads to acceleration in inflation. Other textbooks and government publications feature an identical concept called the Full employment surplus (FES), which differs only in that it is defined for a lower unemployment rate and an output level higher than Q^*. At this more ambitious output level, hypothetical government revenues are higher than at Q^*, and so the full employment surplus along the BB_0 budget line in Figure 17-1 is the positive amount measured by the vertical distance HJ, not the zero value NES_0. The FES target is unrealistically optimistic because it calculates government tax revenues at a high output level, which if achieved and maintained permanently, would cause an accelerating inflation. Thus we reject the unrealistic FES target and concentrate in the rest of this chapter on the natural employment surplus (NES).[5]

17-3

FISCAL DIVIDEND AND FISCAL DRAG

FISCAL DIVIDEND

We have examined two sources of change in the budget surplus as defined in equation (17.3), automatic stabilization through changes in Q/Q^* and discretionary fiscal policy through changes in t and G. The final element in (17.3) is the natural output level itself (Q^*), which tends to grow steadily from year to year, currently at a rate of about 3.5 percent annually in the United States, as a result of increased productivity and growth in the labor force. Even if the government succeeds in achieving a stable output ratio of 100 percent, the government surplus will grow from year to year when the tax rate (t) and government spending remain fixed.

The automatic growth in the surplus that occurs as growth in Q^* raises tax revenues is called the **fiscal dividend.**

In Figure 17-2 the initial red budget line BB_0 has a natural employment surplus (NES_0) of zero, as indicated at point A. The BB_0 line differs in one important respect from BB_0 in Figure 17-1. In the U.S. tax system tax rates are progressive—rich households pay a larger fraction of their income in tax than do poor families. If we now interpret t_0 to be a fixed structure of tax rates, we must draw the BB_0 budget line corresponding to the tax structure t_0 as a curved line. An increase in the output ratio (Q/Q^*) raises incomes and pushes some people into higher tax brackets, thus raising the share of government revenue in GNP, even if the tax rate in each tax bracket is left unchanged. Thus as Q/Q^* increases along a given budget line, government tax revenues rise proportionately more than output, accounting for the curvature in the budget line BB_0.

Automatic growth in revenues occurs if the structure of tax rates (t_0) and the level of government spending (G_0) are held fixed, while the natural output level is allowed to increase over one year, say from the initial level Q_0^* to a new higher level Q_1^*. The budget line shifts leftward, from the initial line BB_0 to the new line BB_1, and as a result the natural employment surplus has risen from zero ($NES_0 = 0$) along the old line

---

[5] Finally, after many years of featuring the obsolete FES concept, the *Economic Report of the President* in January 1977 recognized explicitly that the budget concept had to be defined for a less ambitious output target. But its new estimates of attainable or "potential" output and the FES are still too ambitious (at least until policymakers manage to reduce the natural rate of unemployment along the lines discussed in Chapter 9).

ECONOMIC GROWTH IN Q^* BOOSTS THE NATURAL EMPLOYMENT SURPLUS IF
TAX RATES AND GOVERNMENT SPENDING REMAIN CONSTANT

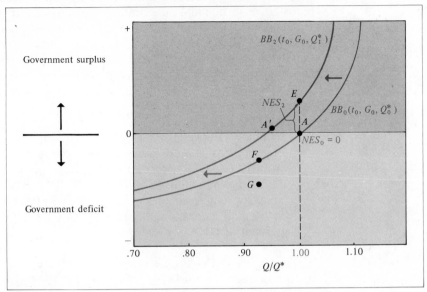

FIGURE 17–2

The Effect on the Budget Line
of an Increase in Natural Output
from Q_0^* to the Higher Level Q_1^*

Economic growth in Q^* raises the
amount of revenue that the government can collect a given output ratio

(Q/Q^*) and at a given level of government spending (G_0) and tax rates
(t_0). The higher level of revenue
raises the natural employment surplus
from $NES_0 = 0$ to NES_2 (the distance EA).

to the positive value NES_2 along the new line.[6] The fiscal dividend is the
increase in NES, represented in the diagram by the distance EA, caused
by the increase in natural output (Q^*).

The fiscal dividend can be created not only by an increase in natural
output (Q^*), as illustrated in Figure 17-2, but by inflation. An increase
in the price level (P) that raises all incomes has exactly the same effect
on tax revenues as an increase in Q^* of the same proportion. Because of
the progressivity of the tax system, an increase in either Q^* or P raises
nominal income, pushes people into higher tax brackets, raises tax rev-

---

[6] Why does the budget line shift leftward when Q^* rises? Because federal revenues and
the federal surplus are constant if output (Q) is constant while the tax structure and government expenditures remain unchanged. An increase in Q^* reduces the output ratio
(Q/Q^*) at which the zero surplus occurs from point A, where Q/Q^* equals unity, leftward
to point A' at the new lower level of Q/Q^* caused by the increase in Q^*. For instance, if Q^*
rises by 5 percent, then Q/Q^* declines from an initial 100 percent to 95 percent, and the
point of zero surplus moves leftward from point A to point A' in the figure.

enues by a larger proportion than income, and thus increases the share of government revenue in GNP. Although an increase in P (unlike Q^*) tends to raise nominal government spending automatically, there is no increase in the share of real government spending in output. Thus inflation makes the natural employment surplus increase automatically, since the share of revenue in GNP is increased but the share of spending in GNP is not changed. In diagrammatic terms, an increase in the price level (P) shifts the budget line leftward, although not by as much as the same percentage increase in Q^*.

> **Example:** Between 1973:Q3 and 1974:Q4 the share of natural-employment federal government revenue in Q^* was pushed up from 19.6 to 20.6 percent, mainly as a result of a rapid inflation rate. Federal expenditure as a fraction of Q^* hardly changed at all, increasing only from 20.3 to 20.4 percent. The result was an increase in the real natural employment surplus from -0.7 percent to $+0.2$ percent of Q^*.

Thus a fiscal dividend emerges automatically as a result of growth in natural output (Q^*) or in the price level (P) if adjustments are not made in tax rates or in real government spending. Policymakers can react to the automatic growth of the NES and the emergence of a fiscal dividend in three basic ways:

1. The first alternative is to allow the NES to remain positive, as at NES_2 in Figure 17-2, by holding government spending and tax rates constant. This, as we will see later in the chapter, tends to encourage private investment.
2. The second alternative is to reduce the average tax rate, cutting revenues and shifting the budget line back down toward BB_0.[7]
3. The third alternative is to raise real government spending (G_0). If G were raised by the full amount of the fiscal dividend, the budget line would shift back down from BB_1 to BB_0, and the natural employment surplus would return to zero.

THE FISCAL-MONETARY MIX AND THE CARTER CAMPAIGN PROMISES

If this set of choices sounds familiar, we encountered it once before at the end of chapter 5, when we discussed the mix of monetary and fiscal policies. If monetary policy is adjusted to keep the economy operating

---

[7] Many economists recommend indexing the tax system to prevent people from being pushed into higher tax brackets by inflation (see Section 11-8). This would have the effect of automatically reducing tax rates levied on a given level of nominal household income. Under this proposal an increase in prices would no longer generate a fiscal dividend.

at its natural output level, then fiscal policy must make the decision each year as to how the fiscal dividend should be allocated. To reduce the real interest rate and encourage private investment, the natural employment surplus should be kept high. To encourage private consumption, tax rate reductions can use up the fiscal dividend. Finally, government spending can be expanded if tax rates are maintained and the fiscal dividend is used up in spending increases.

During the 1976 election campaign, candidate Jimmy Carter was criticized as inconsistent when he promised to revive the economy, introduce new government programs, and balance the government budget, which in mid-1976 was running a deficit of about $50 billion (at an annual rate). Figure 17-2 shows how all three promises could be consistent in principle if the economy started in a recession at point F with a government deficit. First, the budget could be balanced along the initial budget line BB_0 if output could be stimulated enough to move the economy from point F to point A. Then the fiscal dividends produced by the growth in Q^* over the years would provide funds for new government programs while maintaining a balanced natural employment budget at point A.

Unfortunately, Carter's actual problem was more difficult. The natural employment budget was not balanced, as at A, but was in deficit. The economy was actually operating not at F, but at the lower point G. Thus part of the fiscal dividend could not be used for new government programs, but had to be left untouched in order to allow the NES to rise from a negative number to zero. Furthermore, how was Carter to get output back up from recession levels at point G to the desired level at A? Permanent tax cuts could not be used to stimulate the economy, because they would use up the fiscal dividend needed to raise the NES and to provide for new government programs. Temporary tax reductions had the defect that they might not stimulate the economy, but might merely be tucked away under mattresses and in savings accounts. The best way out of the dilemma was a temporary increase in the rate of monetary expansion, but the Federal Reserve was an independent agency and would not necessarily do Carter's bidding.[8]

FISCAL DRAG

One man's investment stimulus is another man's fiscal "drag." In Figure 17-2 the upper budget line BB_2 has a natural employment surplus NES_2. In a sense the surplus NES_2 acts as a drag on the economy because between points A' and E along the budget line BB_2, as the output

---

[8] Carter's solution, proposed in January 1977, was a mixed package, consisting mainly of temporary tax rebates. Carter's well-trained economic advisers recognized that a large share of the rebates might go into saving, but they hoped that the 1977 episode would differ from 1975 and 1968. Soon thereafter the tax rebate plan was withdrawn, partly because of Congressional opposition and partly because the economy appeared to be reviving by itself.

ratio expands toward 100 percent, the government surplus rises toward NES_2, siphoning more and more funds out of the economy in the form of tax leakages. Walter W. Heller coined the term fiscal drag in the early 1960s when he was chairman of the Council of Economic Advisers.

> **Fiscal drag** *describes the emergence of a fiscal dividend that is not used up in either tax cuts or increases in expenditure.*

How can we reconcile the views of Heller, who viewed a positive surplus like NES_2 as a drag on the economy, and those who today recommend a large natural employment surplus like NES_2 to stimulate investment? Clearly the difference is that the second group trusts monetary policy to maintain a high output ratio, whereas Heller either ignores this possibility or is so dubious of the potency of monetary expansion that he fails to mention it.[9] A policy mix of "tight fiscal, easy money" can keep the NES high but maintain an output ratio of 100 percent by keeping the money supply at a reasonably high level. Heller was right in the early 1960s that a tight fiscal policy with a high NES can be a drag on the economy if monetary policy fails to provide the necessary stimulus.

17-4 FISCAL STIMULUS AND FISCAL RESTRAINT

The natural employment surplus concept is useful for two primary purposes. First, the NES tells whether at natural employment private investment exceeds or falls short of private saving. When the NES is positive, the government takes in more than it spends if the economy is operating at natural employment, compelling private investment to exceed private saving.[10] The opposite occurs when the NES is negative — the government's full-employment tax revenue falls short of government spending, so that some private saving is required to buy government bonds, thus partially crowding out private investment.

The second major use of the NES concept is to measure discretionary fiscal policy changes. In a particular episode, did discretionary fiscal policy act to stimulate or restrain the economy? The NES falls and the economy is stimulated when government spending rises or tax rates decline. The NES rises and the economy is restrained in the opposite situation, when government spending declines or tax rates are raised. Thus it seems appropriate to define fiscal stimulus and restraint as follows:

---

[9] Walter W. Heller, *New Dimensions of Political Economy* (New York: Norton, 1966), p. 65.

[10] In section 2-6 we learned that by definition the surplus $(T - G)$ equals private investment (I) minus private spending (S).

1. Fiscal stimulus occurs when the NES falls (ΔNES is negative).
2. Fiscal restraint occurs when the NES rises (ΔNES is positive).
3. Fiscal neutrality occurs when the NES is constant (ΔNES $= 0$).[11]

A brief review of sections 3-6 through 3-8 should convince the reader that $-\Delta$NES (minus the change in the NES) is a very crude measure of the effect of fiscal policy on total spending. If policymakers decide to stimulate the economy by raising government expenditures by $1.00, that full $1.00 flows directly into GNP. Then the $1.00 is "blown up" by the multiplier effect.[12] In contrast, if the same $1.00 stimulative reduction in the NES is achieved by cutting taxes by $1.00, the initial increase in income will not be the entire $1.00, but the fraction of that $1.00 that is spent. Any portion of the tax cut that is saved leaks out of the spending stream, cutting the multiplier.

The conclusion? A $1.00 change in the NES stimulates the economy more if it takes the form of a $1.00 increase in G than a $1.00 decrease in taxes. Thus a given fiscal stimulus, as measured by $-\Delta$NES, is only a crude measure of the effect of fiscal policy on the economy—a true measure would have to be weighted by the fraction of the budget change that flows directly into GNP (100 percent for spending changes, less than 100 percent for permanent tax cuts, and only a small fraction for temporary tax cuts).

The same point can be made in another way. Recall from section 3-7 that an increase in government spending balanced by an increase in taxes still can stimulate the economy. Thus $-\Delta$NES is flawed as a measure of fiscal stimulus, since the economy can be stimulated by balanced-budget discretionary fiscal changes that leave the NES constant.

Despite the defects of the natural employment surplus we will treat its changes ($-\Delta$NES) as our measure of fiscal stimulus and restraint in the case study presented in the next section. A better measure of fiscal stimulus would be changes in the weighted standardized surplus, which differs from $-\Delta$NES by placing weights of less than 100 percent on changes in NES caused by tax rate changes and by evaluating the effect of tax rate changes at today's output, not natural output.[13] But we prefer for expositional clarity to concentrate on the NES itself.[14]

---

[11] Each of the three sentences should be qualified: "and Q^* remains fixed." If Q^* and G or t change together, then the value of ΔNES mixes up discretionary fiscal changes with the automatic fiscal dividend.

[12] See section 3-6.

[13] The best exposition of the arguments for changes in the weighted standardized surplus are in Alan S. Blinder and Robert M. Solow, "Analytical Foundations of Fiscal Policy," in *The Economics of Public Finance* (Washington, D.C.: Brookings, 1974), pp. 11–33.

[14] We are interested in the NES not only because its changes represent fiscal stimulus or restraint, but also because its level measures the influence of government on the balance between natural employment saving and investment. For this second purpose the weighted standardized surplus of Blinder and Solow is useless. Fortunately, Blinder and Solow's own data suggest that $-\Delta$NES captures all the main episodes of fiscal stimulus or restraint that they measure by changes in their weighted standardized surplus. See their Table 4, p. 26.

17-5

CASE STUDY: DISCRETIONARY FISCAL POLICY IN THE POSTWAR UNITED STATES

Figure 17-3 illustrates the level of the real natural employment surplus and real actual budget surplus during the entire postwar period between 1950 and 1976 measured as a percentage of real GNP. The actual surplus (black line) lies below the NES (red line) during depressed years such as 1958 and 1975–76 when output fell well below its natural level. In very prosperous years, such as 1966–69, the black actual surplus line lies above the red NES line. The maximum level of the NES was about 6 percent in late 1950, and the largest negative value was about 4 percent in 1975:Q2.

EPISODES OF FISCAL RESTRAINT

The NES line enters into surplus territory on six separate occasions illustrated in Figure 17-3. Of the six occasions, three represent increases in the NES caused by discretionary fiscal restraint and the remainder represent higher values of the NES created by an unspent fiscal dividend—that is, an increase in tax revenues generated from growth in natural output (Q^*) that was not dissipated in the form of higher spending or lower tax rates. The six occasions of an increasing NES were:

1. *1950.* Tax increases were legislated very rapidly after the outbreak of the Korean War, but it took time for the Defense Department to spend the money. Thus the NES rose temporarily in 1950 but then fell in 1951 as the bills came in.
2. *1953–56.* At the end of the Korean War, there was a major discretionary move toward fiscal restraint in the form of a decline in defense expenditures much greater than the accompanying decline in tax rates.
3. *1958–60.* The NES was allowed to move into a record peacetime surplus in 1960 through the failure of the Eisenhower administration to spend the fiscal dividend. The Eisenhower advisers tried to keep the *actual* surplus at zero. As a result they neglected the burgeoning value of the NES. The combination of tight fiscal policy with tight monetary policy aborted the economy's recovery in 1959–60 and caused a recession in 1960–61. The high value of the NES in 1959–62 was the ammunition that Walter Heller's Council of Economic Advisers under President Kennedy used in 1962–63 to convince Congress that a permanent tax reduction was needed.
4. *1965.* Finally Walter Heller's dream came true, and tax rates were cut in 1964. But the NES was sent only briefly into deficit, for the fiscal dividend pulled the NES back into surplus in early 1965. A

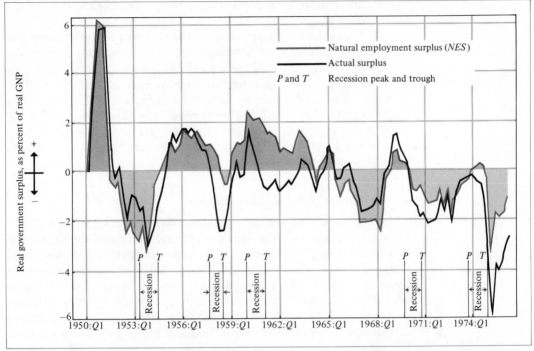

FIGURE 17-3 A Comparison of the Actual Budget Surplus and the Natural Employment Surplus (NES) for the U.S. Federal Government, 1950–76

The red NES line lies above the black actual budget line in years when the economy was weak, with actual output below natural output. The pink-shaded regions reflect periods when the NES was negative — in deficit — whereas the gray-shaded regions reflect quarters of a positive NES. Notice the movement of the NES into deficit during the 1965–67 escalation of the Vietnam War, followed by the movement to a positive NES as a result of the tax surcharge of 1968. The large NES deficit of 1975 reflects the tax rebate of that year.

Source: Appendix B.

second round of tax reductions in 1965, combined with Vietnam War expenditures, worked to plunge the NES into deficit for most of the rest of the 1960s.

5. *1968–69.* The most important economic event of the 1960s was the Vietnam War, which caused the economy to overshoot the natural rate of unemployment and achieve too-high levels of employment and output during 1966–69. One aggravating factor was the delay in legislating tax increases to pay for the Vietnam War. Finally, in mid-1968 government revenues were raised substantially by a 10

percent personal and corporate income tax surcharge. The NES increased from −2.6 percent of GNP in 1968:Q2 to 0.7 percent in 1969:Q2.

6. *1974.* The final episode was the emergence of a small natural employment surplus in 1974 through the effect of inflation on the fiscal dividend. Between 1972 and mid-1974 the natural employment ratio of tax revenues to GNP was allowed to increase without any offset in the form of tax-rate reductions or increases in the natural employment share of government spending in GNP. Although fiscal restraint in this episode was automatic rather than discretionary, nevertheless the timing of the restraint helped to push the economy into recession in late 1974.

EPISODES OF FISCAL STIMULUS

Just as there are six major episodes of fiscal restraint in the 1950–76 period, there are six major episodes of fiscal stimulus when the natural employment surplus declined substantially, in each case moving from positive to negative territory in Figure 17-3. Unlike the episodes of restraint, half of which were discretionary and half of which represented the automatic emergence of the fiscal dividend, all the episodes of fiscal stimulus were discretionary. In other words, since natural output and the price level always tend to increase, natural employment tax revenues always grow automatically and never shrink when tax rates are left unchanged.

Any automatic change in the NES must be in the direction of restraint; any movement toward stimulus must be discretionary.

1. *1951–53.* Tax rates were increased immediately in 1950 at the beginning of the Korean War. Then for three straight years spending (mainly for defense) increased much faster than natural employment tax revenues.

2. *1958.* Tax rates remained unchanged between 1954 and 1964. All the 1958 stimulus, which reduced the NES by 1.5 percent of GNP, was caused by an increase in expenditures. Notice that although the Eisenhower administration can be credited with an admirable achievement of countercyclical fiscal policy in 1958, it promptly discredited itself by imposing a sharp movement toward restraint in 1959 and 1960, helping to abort the 1959 recovery and cause the 1960–61 recession.

3. *1964.* After more than a year of debate, a permanent reduction in individual and corporate income tax rates was passed by Congress four months after the assassination of President Kennedy; it was promptly signed into law by President Johnson in March 1964. The reduction in the NES amounted to almost 2 percent of GNP.

4. *1965–67*. In 1965 the fiscal dividend was once again used to reduce income taxes, and in addition federal excise tax rates were reduced. Then, after a brief interlude, an additional fiscal stimulus was applied in the form of higher defense expenditures connected with the Vietnam War. The combined effect of the stimulus applied between mid-1965 and early 1968 amounted to 3 percent of GNP, a highly undesirable procyclical policy action, given that in mid-1965 output had already risen above its natural rate.
5. *1969–71*. Most of the stimulus applied during the 1970–71 recession did not consist of new fiscal actions, but rather the undoing of a previous restraining policy. The income tax surcharge that had been introduced in 1968 was allowed to end in early 1970.
6. *1975*. Alarmed by the steep decline of the economy into a serious recession in late 1974 and early 1975, Congress acted promptly to cut taxes. The 1975 stimulus consisted both of a temporary tax rebate and permanent tax reductions. The rebates were actually paid in May 1975, the month when unemployment reached its postwar peak, 9.0 percent.

Summary: The natural employment budget alternated over the postwar years between stimulus and restraint. In at least half the episodes fiscal policy was destabilizing, either applying stimulus when output was at or above its natural level (1951–53, 1965–68), or applying restraint while the economy was slipping into recession (1959–60, 1974). The major stabilizing fiscal policy actions were stimuli applied when unemployment was high, in 1958, 1964, and 1975. Discretionary restraining tax increases occurred at the right time in 1950, but three years too late in 1968.

17-6 CASE STUDY: AUTOMATIC STABILIZERS BEFORE AND AFTER WORLD WAR II

The extent of automatic stabilization is measured simply by the percentage of any change in GNP that automatically leaks out of the spending stream into government tax revenue plus the percentage that is automatically injected back into the spending stream in the form of income-contingent transfers, such as unemployment benefits and welfare payments. The higher this marginal tax rate ($\bar{t}$), adjusted for transfers, the steeper is the *BB* budget line in Figures 17-1 and 17-2 and the greater is the change in the natural employment surplus (NES) when the output ratio (Q/Q^*) rises or falls.

When we ask what fraction of a shortfall of actual output (Q) below natural output (Q^*) is offset by a reduction in government tax revenues (T) below natural employment revenues (T^*), we have the following expression for the marginal tax rate ($\bar{t}$):

$$\bar{t} = \frac{T - T^*}{Q - Q^*} = \frac{\Delta T}{\Delta Q} = \left(\frac{T^*}{Q^*}\right)\left(\frac{\Delta T/T^*}{\Delta Q/Q^*}\right) \qquad (17.5)$$

The first term in the right-hand expression, T^*/Q^*, is the natural employment share of real tax revenues in real GNP. The second term is the elasticity of tax revenues to changes in the output ratio.[15]

The revenue share (T^*/Q^*) depends on the overall size of government and is much larger now than before World War II. The elasticity term depends on the progressivity of the tax schedule. If tax rates are proportional, then government tax revenue tends to remain at a constant fraction of GNP as long as tax rates are fixed and the elasticity term equals 1.0. But if tax rates are progressive, like those of the U.S. federal government, then government tax revenues rise by more than 1 percent for every percentage point increase in output, and the elasticity term in equation (17.5) exceeds unity.

The much higher marginal tax rate in the postwar years, which has steepened the budget line and contributed so much to automatic stabilization, has been mainly due to the larger size of government, and only to a much smaller extent due to an increased revenue elasticity:

	Percentage		
	$\bar{t}$	T^*/Q^*	Revenue elasticity
1932	5.5	3.9	1.41
1975	36.9	20.1	1.83
1976	36.3	20.4	1.78

The difference between the 1932 and 1975–76 situations is illustrated by the two budget lines in Figure 17-4. Since we are interested in this section in the slope of the budget line rather than its vertical position, both budget lines plot on the vertical axis the difference between the actual surplus and the natural employment surplus, expressed as a ratio to natural output. Once again the horizontal axis is the ratio of actual output to the natural level of output (Q/Q^*). In 1932 the output ratio had fallen to a mere 67 percent, much lower than in any postwar year, and yet the actual surplus had fallen by only 1 percent of natural output. Why the small decline in the surplus? The federal government was such a minor part of the economy that its expenditures in 1932 were only 3.6 percent of Q^*. Even if tax collections had fallen to zero, the actual surplus could not have fallen to more than -3.6 percent of Q^*.

---

[15] This elasticity is simply the shortfall of T below T^* as a percentage of T^* divided by the shortfall of Q below Q^* as a percentage of Q^*:

$$\text{Elasticity} = \frac{\Delta T/T^*}{\Delta Q/Q^*} = \frac{(T - T^*)/T^*}{(Q - Q^*)/Q^*}$$

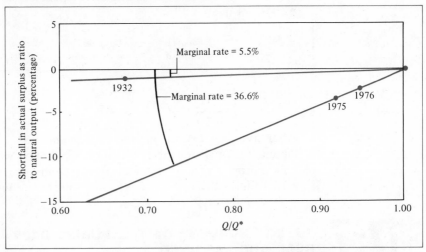

FIGURE 17–4

Change in the Federal Budget Surplus Caused by the Reduction of Actual Output below Natural Output in 1932 and in 1975–76

The vertical axis measures the difference between the actual surplus and the natural employment surplus, expressed as a ratio to natural output. The horizontal axis is the output ratio Q/Q^*. Notice that in 1932 output was one-third below natural output, but the actual surplus had fallen by only 1.25 percent of natural output. In 1975 and 1976 the recession was much milder, and yet the actual surplus fell by more than in 1932.

Sources: For 1932, see (1) Difference between actual surplus and natural employment surplus, from E. Cary Brown, "Fiscal Policy in the 'Thirties': A Reappraisal," *American Economic Review,* vol. 46 (December 1956), Table II, p. 873; (2) Actual and natural output from Appendix B converted to 1947 prices (the basis used by E. Cary Brown). For 1975 and 1976, see Appendix B.

In 1975 and 1976 the budget line was much steeper. The output ratio fell by much less than in 1932, yet the recession caused a major shortfall in the actual surplus, equal to 3.0 percent of Q^* in 1975 and 2.1 percent of Q^* in 1976. In 1975–76 the fiscal system did a much better job of automatic stabilization, insulating the economy against much of the shock of the decline in spending that occurred in the recession. The Great Depression would have been considerably less severe if the high postwar marginal tax rate ($\bar{t}$) and associated lower multiplier had been in effect during 1929–32.

The same conclusion has been reached by Bert G. Hickman of Stanford and Robert M. Coen of Northwestern, who have built a large and complex econometric model of the U.S. economy spanning the entire period between 1921 and 1966. They have calculated the following multipliers, which show the change in real GNP resulting from a $1.00 change in real autonomous spending, after the designated number of quarters.[16]

Quarters elapsed	Multipliers for 1926–40	Multipliers for 1951–65
1	3.23	1.88
5	5.09	2.10
9	3.54	2.25

After five quarters, for instance, a sustained $1.0 billion drop in the autonomous component of private consumption would lead to a $5.1 billion drop in real GNP under prewar conditions, as opposed to only a $2.1 billion drop in real GNP under postwar conditions.

17-7 FUTURE BURDENS OF THE PUBLIC DEBT— REAL AND IMAGINED

An important virtue of the natural employment surplus concept is that it helps government officials to avoid Herbert Hoover's 1932 mistake— a major increase in tax rates designed to bring the actual budget into surplus in the face of a rapidly growing deficit caused by a collapsing economy.[17] If the economy starts out with its output ratio at 100 percent

---

[16] Bert G. Hickman and Robert M. Coen, *An Annual Growth Model of the U.S. Economy* (Amsterdam: North-Holland, 1976), Table 9.6, p. 194.

[17] In the following table notice the effect of Hoover's mid-1932 tax increases and also the major Roosevelt tax increase in 1936–37 caused by the introduction of the Social Security system. Notice also that Roosevelt allowed government spending to fall substantially in 1937, despite a major output gap. In fact Roosevelt's 1937 move toward fiscal restraint was even greater than Hoover's in 1931–33.

	T^*/Q^*	G/Q^*	NES/Q^*	Q/Q^* (%)
1929	3.68	2.52	1.16	101.4
1930	3.60	2.71	0.89	89.5
1931	3.06	4.34	−1.28	80.3
1932	3.89	3.59	0.30	67.3
1933	6.00	4.45	1.55	64.2
1934	6.13	6.43	−0.30	67.4
1935	6.24	6.29	−0.05	71.4
1936	6.83	8.15	−1.32	78.9
1937	8.14	6.46	1.68	80.4
1938	8.27	7.39	0.88	75.0
1939	7.89	7.55	0.34	78.6

Sources: Same as Figure 17-4.

and a balanced natural employment budget, then the deficits that emerge as the output ratio falls below 100 percent reflect the automatic stabilizers in action. Any attempt to interfere with the automatic stabilizers through discretionary fiscal actions like Hoover's which eliminate deficits in recession situations, or which eliminate surpluses in boom situations, destabilizes the economy and undermines the automatic stabilizers.

A defender of Hoover's policy might not, however, be convinced that it is legitimate for a government to pursue a deficit spending policy. "Surely the increase in the government debt caused by the government's failure to 'pay its bills' creates a burden on the future taxpayers who must pay interest on the debt," he might assert. How are we to assess the argument that government deficits create an extra burden of the public debt, thus mitigating their virtues as devices to stabilize the economy?

THE BURDEN OF THE AT&T DEBT

The burden of the public debt is a topic that has taken up a vast amount of space in the economic literature, and yet the most important ideas are very simple.[18] When the government fails to collect sufficient tax revenues to pay for its expenditures, it finances its deficit by selling bonds to the public. The government must pay interest on these bonds for many years in the future. Extra taxes must be levied on future taxpayers to cover these interest payments. At first glance government deficit spending appears to be similar to deficit spending by the telephone company AT&T, which fails to collect sufficient revenues from telephone service to pay for all its new plant and equipment. It finances its deficit by selling bonds to the public. What is the difference between the "burden of the AT&T debt" and the "burden of the public debt"?

No one has ever accused AT&T of creating a burden on future generations by issuing bonds, and for good reason. Like any other corporation, AT&T is in business to make a profit for its stockholders, and it tries to avoid borrowing money to finance loss-making investment projects. To avoid this, AT&T attempts to estimate the future rate of return on each planned investment project (telephone exchanges, new installation equipment, and so forth), that is, the annual future profit likely to be contributed by each project divided by its cost.[19] When each project is ranked in order of its rate of return, AT&T is ready to make its investment decisions. Projects with rates of return greater than the interest rate that

---

[18] The most accessible collection of articles is contained in J. M. Ferguson (ed.), *Public Debt and Future Generations* (Chapel Hill: University of North Carolina, 1964). Undergraduates are warned that delving into the complexities of this book is best undertaken by those working on an advanced senior thesis or independent study.

[19] See the example of the ranking of investment projects in Figure 4-1. The fact that AT&T is a regulated monopoly that can cover the expenses of an additional investment project by raising prices is not important for the example in the text. We choose AT&T because in an average year it singlehandedly accounts for more than half the U.S. corporate bond issues.

AT&T must pay to sell bonds (AT&T's borrowing rate, say r_0) are approved. Projects with a rate of return below the borrowing rate (r_0) are rejected, since interest payments on the bonds floated to finance the projects would exceed the funds generated by the projects to pay interest, and thus the projects would lose money. Finally, projects with a rate of return equal to the borrowing rate (r_0) are just barely approved, since they neither contribute to profits nor create losses.

The contribution to revenue and expenses of the marginal AT&T project is summarized on the first line of Table 17-1. Net of all operating expenses (labor, materials, fuel, and so forth), the marginal project generates a rate of return (r_0) just equal to the borrowing rate (r_0), and thus it contributes zero to net profit.[20] There is no burden on present or future generations. Individuals currently living make voluntary purchases of AT&T bonds without compulsion. Workers and firms voluntarily build AT&T telephone exchanges and new installation equipment because they are paid with the money that AT&T raises from the bond purchasers. Thus in the present generation everyone acts voluntarily in his own best interests and there is no burden on anyone.

In future generations the bondholders receive the interest payments that induced them to purchase the bonds in the first place. Where does AT&T obtain the money to pay the interest payments? By definition the marginal investment project creates exactly enough revenue (over and above operating costs) to pay the interest costs. Thus in future generations everyone is acting voluntarily. The investment projects create extra revenue for AT&T that pays the interest to keep the bondholders happy.

THE BURDEN OF THE PUBLIC DEBT

If AT&T bonds do not create a burden for present or future generations, what is meant by the burden of the public debt allegedly created when the government issues bonds? The entire discussion depends on the way the government spends the proceeds of the bond floated to finance its deficit. If the government spends the proceeds on an investment project that yields a return to society sufficient to pay the interest costs on the bonds, then there is no future burden. In this case the government is acting exactly as does AT&T. But if the government spends the proceeds on consumption (for example, ammunition that is used up in a war), then there is no future benefit to pay for the future interest payments, leaving future generations with a net burden.

Government investment projects, such as the construction of government hospitals, schools, and public universities, generate a future rate of

---

[20]This discussion neglects explicit consideration of corporation and personal income taxes. The AT&T rate of return on line 1 can be calculated after payment of corporate income taxes. Although personal income taxes must be paid on interest payments to individuals by both AT&T and the government, this factor makes no essential difference in the discussion.

TABLE 17-1   Comparison of Consequences of AT&T Debt
with that of Public Debt

	(1) Rate of return	(2) Interest payment	(3) Net of interest return
1. AT&T marginal investment project	r_0	r_0	0
2. Government marginal investment project	r_0	r_0	0
3. Government deficit-financed consumption expenditure	0	r_0	$-r_0$

return. The return does not take the form of a monetary profit, since the government is not in business to make a profit; rather the return consists of the benefits to future society created by the project. Assuming that a hospital is utilized to cure sick patients, society is better off to have the hospital than to let patients go uncured in the absence of the hospital. The hospital's rate of return is the annual stream of benefits to society (net of the hospital's operating costs) divided by the cost of the hospital.

If the government chooses only to invest in projects yielding future benefits to society that on an annual basis equal or exceed the government's borrowing rate, then the bonds floated to finance government investment projects are exactly analogous to AT&T bonds. As illustrated on line 2 of Table 17-1, the marginal government investment project generates a future rate of return in the form of future benefits to society that just suffice to pay the interest on the government bonds. If the interest rate on government bonds—like that on AT&T bonds—is r_0, and the social rate of return of the government investment project is the same rate r_0, then there are no future burdens on society. The AT&T bond and the government bond are identical.[21]

The main difference between AT&T bonds and government bonds is that people pay voluntarily to receive telephone service, automatically generating revenue to pay the interest on AT&T bonds without compul-

---

[21] Problems involved in the choice of the interest rate ("the social discount rate") that should be used in evaluating government investment projects have been elegantly analyzed by A. C. Harberger in "Our Measuring the Social Opportunity Cost of Public Funds," in his *Project Evaluation* (Chicago: Markham, 1972), Chapter 4, pp. 94–122.

sory taxation, whereas the government must raise taxes to pay the interest on its bonds.[22] No burden on future taxpayers exists if they are the same individuals who benefit from the government investment project. For a local road or rapid transit project financed by local property taxes, there is a presumption that the beneficiaries and the taxpayers are the same people. For federal projects this assumption may be invalid. Benefits may be concentrated on certain constituencies (the often-publicized flow of federal dollars to the sunbelt) whereas taxes are widely dispersed across all households. In this case no aggregate burden is created by government deficit spending to finance investment projects but rather a redistribution from some members of future generations to others.

The true and unambiguous burden on future generations is created by government deficit spending that pays for goods that yield no future benefits, for example, current maintenance of parks and streets. As illustrated on line 3 of Table 17-1, absolutely nothing is generated in the future as a rate of return; all benefits accrue in the present and none in the future. The government must pay interest to keep bondholders happy, just as AT&T must pay interest, yet in current government deficit-financed consumption, there is no future benefit or income to pay the interest. Future taxpayers are forced to hand over extra payments to the government to cover the interest cost on the debt, and the taxpayers receive no benefit in return.

> **Example:** In the fiscal year 1978 (ending September 30, 1978), interest on the public debt is estimated at $39.7 billion, or about $520 per household.[23] Unless the government uses deficit financing to cover these interest payments, it must cover them by raising taxes. Thus 1978 taxpayers are turning over to the federal government $520 per household. What is their benefit in return? Part of the deficit was incurred to build post offices in the Great Depression of the 1930s, and other public buildings in recent years, but most of the present benefits of past deficits are intangible—present freedom here and in some foreign countries as a result of deficits incurred in past wars.

If the federal government is running a balanced natural employment budget (NES = 0), then a recession period with low output and employment is characterized by an actual federal deficit and growth in the public debt. What is the burden of the public debt thus created? The answer

---

[22] The alternative of floating more bonds to pay the interest cost on the original bonds is ignored. If the growth rate of real income exceeds the real interest rate on the government debt, then the government can finance its interest cost by issuing new bonds without raising the ratio of the value of outstanding bonds to GNP.

[23] Estimate of fiscal 1978 interest from *Economic Report of the President,* January 1977, Table B-68, p. 267. Households (families plus unrelated individuals) is for 1975 from *ibid.,* Table B-25, p. 216.

depends on the extra investment generated by the fiscal stimulus. In the simple model of Chapters 3–5, extra government spending or tax cuts raise the interest rate (when the real money supply is held fixed) and crowd out investment spending. In the more realistic investment theory developed in Chapter 14, the fiscal stimulus applied when the economy is in recession not only raises the interest rate (which raises the cost of capital and hence cuts the desired capital stock) but also raises expected output and hence increases the desired capital stock. It is conceivable, although not at all guaranteed, that a fiscal stimulus in a recession will not create any burden for future generations because extra public and private investment will be generated to provide sufficient future income to pay for the extra interest on the public debt.

Example: Imagine that taxes are cut and that the tax multiplier (extra dollars of output per dollar of tax cut) is 3.0, consisting of 2.0 of extra consumption and 1.0 of extra investment spending. Then each dollar of government debt generated to pay for the tax cut would be balanced by an extra dollar of investment, which would yield future returns to pay for the tax burden of the future interest payments on the government debt. If the extra investment generated through the tax multiplier is less than $1.00 per dollar of government deficit, then future generations will suffer a burden.

THE MONETARY-FISCAL MIX DURING PERIODS OF HIGH UNEMPLOYMENT

The possibility that fiscal stimulus during a recession will create a burden for future generations raises an obvious question: Why not stimulate the economy via tax cuts or increased government expenditure financed not by a higher public debt but by a higher money supply? In terms of Chapters 4–5, why not shift the LM and IS curves rightward at the same time, rather than shifting the IS curve alone rightward, with the resulting increase in interest rates? Government deficits financed by money creation create no burden for future generations, because no interest is paid by the government on the high-powered money that it creates. In this situation the government bonds issued by the Treasury are purchased by the Federal Reserve. The Federal Reserve earns the interest on the bonds and returns it to the Treasury, so that no taxes need to be levied to pay the interest cost.[24] In terms of our discussion in Chapters 15 and 16, this constitutes just one more argument in favor of coun-

---

[24] Economists always hope that a small portion of the extra interest payments earned by the Fed will be siphoned off to pay for the employment of more economists in the research divisions of the Fed, before the large remaining portion of the interest is returned to the Treasury. The large demand for economists by the Fed and other U.S. and international agencies in Washington explains why the job market for Ph.D. economists is so much better these days than in most other fields.

tercyclical monetary policy. A given economic stimulus delivered during a recession by monetary policy has more favorable consequences for future generations than the same stimulus delivered by fiscal policy through tax cuts or expenditure increases.

17-8 THE U.S. CAPITAL SHORTAGE

How should we react to the frequent statements that the United States faces a future capital shortage, that is, a shortfall of private investment below a desirable level? These statements are based on calculations of future saving with the total amount of future investment that is felt to be needed or desired. Some proponents of this view recommend that the government should consistently run a positive natural employment surplus to raise the total supply of saving available to finance private investment.[25] If total private saving is sensitive to the after-tax return to savers, the taxation of income from capital reduces saving below its optimal level. Thus we could concur with the capital shortage advocates (CSA) and recommend a positive natural employment surplus, if taxation of income from capital were the only relevant factor. Yet there are virtues of deficit financing of some government investment projects—analogous to the virtues of deficit financing of some AT&T investment projects—that are generally ignored by the CSA group.

Most of the complaints of the CSA group really call not for a natural employment surplus but for reform in the United States tax laws to end undesirable distortions. For instance, inflation causes overtaxation of income from capital because the tax laws ignore numerous effects of inflation on real income.[26] Reform of the tax laws would allow more investment without requiring a government surplus, by raising the quantity of private business and household saving.

---

[25] The specter of capital shortage was raised in The New York Stock Exchange, *The Capital Needs and Savings Potential of the U.S. Economy, Projections through 1985* (New York: September 1974). A full analysis of the capital shortage problem cannot be attempted within the limited space of this chapter. For a brief skeptical view see Robert Eisner, "Capital Shortage: Myth and Reality," *American Economic Review,* vol. 67 (February 1977), pp. 110–15.

[26] For instance, all interest earnings on corporate and government bonds are taxable, both the real return and the inflation premium of Chapter 10, which compensates savers for the loss of purchasing power on the principal of their investments. As the inflation rate increases, the after-tax real return on saving automatically decreases as a fraction of the real marginal product of capital. Similarly, the tax laws allow corporations to deduct from income only the historical cost of depreciation on their capital rather than the true replacement cost. Result? Depreciation deductions that are too low, and corporation income taxes that are too high, as a result of inflation. Eisner, *op. cit.,* discusses other distortions involving investment in residential construction, research, and education.

SUMMARY

1. The actual government surplus can change for three reasons. First, changes in the output ratio Q/Q^* alter the government's tax collections even if tax rates are fixed. This response of the actual budget to the economy is called automatic stabilization. Second, the actual surplus can change through discretionary fiscal policy actions that raise or lower tax rates and government spending. Finally, the actual surplus can change through economic growth, which raises natural output (Q^*) and creates a fiscal dividend.

2. The response of the budget to the economy is called automatic stabilization because the positive response of tax collections to changes in total output raises leakages out of the spending stream when the economy is expanding, thus dampening the expansion. Similarly, leakages out of the spending stream fall when the economy is shrinking in a recession, thus helping to limit the decline in output.

3. The natural employment surplus concept (NES) eliminates changes in the budget due to the automatic stabilization response of the budget to the state of the economy. The NES can change either through discretionary fiscal policy actions or through the fiscal dividend created by economic growth.

4. The NES budget concept is useful for two main purposes. First, the level of NES tells whether or not the government is running a surplus when the economy is operating at natural employment. Second, changes in the NES with the sign reversed ($-\Delta$ NES) are a crude measure of the degree of fiscal stimulus and restraint.

5. In the postwar United States there were six episodes of fiscal restraint (an increase in NES), in half of which the cause was discretionary policy and in the remaining half the cause was the emergence of a fiscal dividend caused by economic growth and inflation. In contrast, all the episodes of fiscal stimulus (a decline in NES) were discretionary.

6. The government budget has helped to stabilize the economy to a much greater extent since World War II than before the war. The main reason is that the government is much bigger, collecting more of GNP in the form of taxes and accounting for more of total spending on goods and services. Combined with the high responsiveness of tax revenues to changes in the state of the economy, this means that more than one-third of any change in the output ratio (Q/Q^*) leaks out of the spending stream, cutting the spending multiplier far below its prewar value.

7. Government deficits raise the public debt and increase the amount of taxes that must be collected in the future to pay the interest on the public debt. This imposes a burden on future taxpayers if today's government deficit is incurred to finance government consumption but not if it finances government investment projects that yield a benefit to future society.

A LOOK AHEAD

The next chapter completes the discussion of monetary and fiscal policy and of the possibility of controlling aggregate demand through activist countercyclical policy. We examine the advantages and disadvantages of discretionary fiscal policy as compared to countercyclical monetary policy. The lags and side effects of fiscal policy raise issues different from those considered in Chapter 16 for monetary policy.

CONCEPTS AND QUESTIONS

IDENTIFICATIONS

Actual government surplus
Natural employment surplus
Automatic stabilization
Discretionary fiscal policy
Fiscal dividend

Fiscal drag
Fiscal stimulus and restraint
Burden of the public debt
Capital shortage

QUESTIONS FOR REVIEW

1 Explain why the budget line in Figures 17-1 and 17-2 slopes upward. What factors determine the steepness of the line? Can you explain why the actual U.S. budget line in Figure 17-4 was steeper in 1976 than in 1932?

2 Explain how each of the following would affect the budget line: increase in government spending to build the B-1 bomber; a higher federal gasoline tax; growth in real natural output; an increase in the price level.

3 A 1 percent change in nominal income generates a change in federal tax revenues of about 1.8 percent. Using this information, explain what would happen to the NES if the federal government were to keep all tax rates constant while maintaining a fixed fraction of government spending in nominal income.

4 Turn back to Figure 17-3. Explain in words why the actual budget line drops so much more than the NES line between early 1974 and early 1975. Why does the actual budget line lie above the NES line in 1966?

5 Consider a hypothetical government program to fight a recession by creating government jobs for unemployed teenagers, with the payments to the teenagers financed by running a deficit. What information would you need to decide whether this type of deficit spending imposes a burden on future society? Can you think of ways in which such programs may create future benefits that par-

tially or completely outweigh the need to collect taxes in the future to pay interest on the public debt?

6 Is the change in the natural employment surplus (NES) an accurate measure of fiscal stimulus or restraint when the government conducts a balanced budget expansion that raises government spending and tax collections by the same amount?

APPENDIX TO CHAPTER 17
The Optimal Natural Employment Surplus

Current deficits incurred to finance government consumption impose a burden on future generations, as indicated in Table 17-1. Can an argument be made that to avoid this burden the government should consistently run a positive natural employment surplus relying on monetary stimulus to maintain output at the natural level and prevent fiscal drag? If a desirable or optimal level of private investment is defined as that which would occur without interference of the government, how can the natural employment surplus be adjusted to allow society to attain its optimal level of investment?

TAXATION OF CAPITAL AS AN ARGUMENT FOR A POSITIVE NATURAL EMPLOYMENT SURPLUS

The basic argument for a positive natural employment surplus appears in Figure 17-5.[1] The horizontal axis measures the amount of investment and saving, and the vertical axis measures the interest rate. The downward sloping I line illustrates the dependence of the demand for investment goods on the interest rate. A reduction in the interest rate increases the demand for investment goods as firms find that additional investment projects can earn a future return sufficient to cover reduced interest costs. The upward sloping S line illustrates the dependence on the interest rate of the supply of saving. An increase in the interest rate induces individuals to sacrifice consumption now and raise saving in order to obtain more consumption goods in the future.

In the absence of any government spending or taxation, the private economy operates at point A, with a level of investment and saving (I_0) that maximizes welfare. Why? At point A the future return on investment (the vertical distance r_0) exactly compensates savers for their sacrifice of current consumption, measured as the vertical height of the S line. Investment projects made possible by saving produce a future

---

[1] The diagram in Figure 17-5 and the entire argument of this section relies heavily on Martin J. Bailey, "The Optimum Full Employment Surplus," *Journal of Political Economy*, vol. 80 (July/August 1972), pp. 649–61.

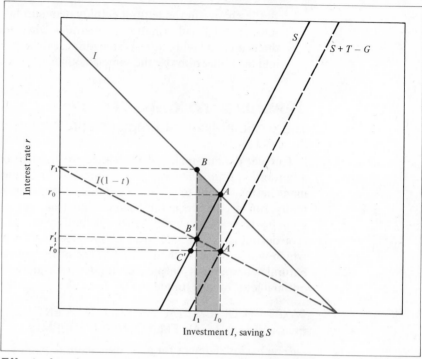

FIGURE 17-5

Effect of an Income Tax and of a Government Surplus on Investment and Saving

In the absence of taxation the amount of saving and investment is determined at point A, where the solid black saving schedule (S) intersects the downward sloping red investment schedule (I). The introduction of an income tax cuts the after-tax return on invest-ment projects to the lower dashed red $I(1-t)$ line, and the amount of investment is now determined at point B'. The effect of taxation is thus to cut investment from I_0 to I_1. A government surplus generates additional saving which raises the economy's total supply of saving to the black dashed $S + T - G$ line, and this extra saving allows investment to return to its initial level I_0 at point A'.

return just high enough to provide the extra future consumption goods that "bribe" savers to sacrifice current consumption.

What is wrong with an alternative position, say the investment level I_1? At I_1 the return on the marginal investment project is the vertical distance r_1, but the value to savers of sacrificing current consumption goods for future consumption goods is the smaller vertical distance r_1', the height of the saving line S at point B'. An additional \$1.00 of saving and investment produces future consumption goods in an amount that substantially exceeds the value placed by savers on the sacrifice of a dollar from current consumption and society can gain by shifting current consumption into additional saving and investment.[2]

> **Example**: Imagine that individuals currently receive an interest rate (r_1') of 5 percent on their saving. This means that they are willing to sacrifice $1.00 of current consumption for a return of $1.05 in future consumption goods obtained one year later. If the return on investment (r_1) is 10 percent, then an extra dollar of current saving produces $1.10 in extra consumption goods next year, enough to pay savers the $1.05 they require and still leave $.05 as a net gain for society. In this situation society will be better off if it continues to cut back current consumption and add extra dollars of saving and investment until the return on investment equals the return required by savers.

Taxation of income from capital interferes with the economy's ability to obtain the optimal investment level I_0 in Figure 17-5. Savers do not obtain the entire profit produced by investment projects. Instead, the government siphons off a substantial portion of capital income through the corporation income tax and the individual income tax on income from dividends, interest, and rent. The after-tax income from added investment is measured in Figure 17-5 by the line labeled $I(1 - t)$, which lies below the I line by a fraction equal to the tax rate (t). If the tax rate is 50 percent, the vertical position of the $I(1 - t)$ line is everywhere exactly 50 percent of the I line. Now only a fraction of the return on capital is available to reward savers, and the level of investment cannot exceed I_1, the amount savers are willing to provide for an after-tax return of r_1'.

Since I_0 is the optimum amount of investment, and only I_1 takes place because of taxation, the best government policy is to run a natural employment surplus equal to the shortfall of investment below the optimum

---

[2] In the jargon of economists, the amount of future consumption next year (C_{+1}) required by savers voluntarily to sacrifice $1.00 of consumption today, is 1.0 plus the rate of time preference (ρ). Thus:

$$1 + \rho = \frac{C_{+1}}{C}$$

or

$$\rho = \frac{C_{+1}}{C} - 1$$

This investment is at an optimal level in Figure 17-5 at point A where the marginal return on investment (r_0) equals the rate of time preference (ρ), the vertical height of the saving line.

$(I_1 - I_0)$. The dashed line labeled $S + T - G$ illustrates the total supply of private saving plus the government surplus required to return investment to the optimum level I_0. Now at point A the before-tax rate of return on capital is r_0, yielding an after-tax return to savers of r_0'. Private saving induced by the return r_0' is indicated at point C' along the original S saving schedule. The government surplus, the distance $C'A'$, provides the extra saving needed to achieve the optimum level of investment I_0.

THE BALANCE-OF-IGNORANCE PRINCIPLE
AS AN ARGUMENT FOR DEFICIT SPENDING

This argument indicates that the government should run a natural employment surplus, in contrast to the natural employment deficits actually achieved in 1975–76 (see Figure 17-3). Is there any offsetting argument for a full employment deficit? A government investment project financed by deficit spending, requiring a bond issue, creates no burden if those who benefit from the future payoff of the project are exactly the same people who have to pay the future taxes required to finance the interest payments on the bonds. If a current government investment project creates future benefits for a known group, say a sewer improvement project for a town, then financing the project by current taxation of town residents or by a bond issue paid by future town residents creates no impact on the saving or consumption behavior of anyone. Town residents voluntarily pay taxes in return for the higher standard of living made possible by better sewers.

In contrast to the sewer example, in which the recipients of future benefits are known and certain, Martin J. Bailey[3] of the University of Maryland points out that some government projects have future benefits whose recipients are unknown and uncertain, for example, veterans' hospitals.[4] If the government runs a balanced budget, then every government investment project with uncertain benefits must be financed by current taxation. Today's taxpayers pay their tax bills by reducing current consumption below the optimal amount, because uncertainty prevents them from being able to foresee the future benefits of the project. The government can avoid the undesirable current reduction in consumption by financing such projects by deficit spending, financing the interest on the bonds by future taxes whose incidence is uncertain.

Bailey labels his conclusion the "balance-of-ignorance" principle. Government projects that yield a stream of future benefits should be

---

[3] Bailey, *op. cit.*

[4] Current veterans do not know how sick they will be in future years. Also, young members of the population do not know whether they will be future veterans because future wars and the likelihood that the military draft will be reinstated are highly uncertain.

financed by issuing a bond whose interest payments are paid by taxes having the same time profile as the project's benefits. The government deficit each year would equal the increase in the stock of projects eligible for deficit finance, that is, those with uncertain benefits. Future consumers would pay taxes balanced by the enjoyment of benefits received from the government projects, while present consumers would be unaffected either by project benefits or current taxation.

Thus the balance-of-ignorance principle argues for a natural employment deficit in direct contrast to the capital taxation argument that supports a natural employment surplus. If the two opposing arguments were of exactly the same practical importance, their net effect would cancel out and the optimum natural employment surplus would be zero. Indeed in Bailey's own numerical example, the net recommendation is for a natural employment surplus close to zero.[5]

---

[5] Bailey, *op. cit.*, p. 659.

18 Contributions and Limitations of Fiscal Policy Instruments

Economists can't make us follow the
sensible paths they've laid out, but they'd
like to. Sometimes in frustration they swat
us with a tax.

—Eliot Marshall[1]

18-1 CRITERIA FOR EVALUATING FISCAL POLICY

Countercyclical monetary and fiscal policy are engaged in a contest in this book, both against each other and against do-nothing policy rules. First, in Chapter 12 we debated whether or not countercyclical activism is to be preferred to fixed policy rules. We concluded in Chapters 13–14 that variations in the user cost of capital and in business confidence can stimulate or depress business fixed investment for a considerable length of time, resulting in a substantial period during which output deviates from its natural level if policy remains set according to a fixed monetarist rule. In addition, fluctuations in consumer durable expenditures can amplify the effect of a destabilizing drop or increase in private or government spending. Thus a case can be made for countercyclical fiscal and monetary activism, which may help to stabilize output when demand is depressed in a recession or overly stimulated in a boom.

If a countercyclical activist policy is to be used, should primary emphasis be placed on monetary or fiscal tools? Two major issues are involved: (1) which tools are more efficient, altering output in a rapid and predictable manner with a minimum of side effects and (2) can monetary and fiscal policy be coordinated so that their differing side effects do more good than harm for society?

In Chapter 16 we judged countercyclical activist monetary control by two main criteria, lags and side effects. The overall lag of changes in monetary policy appears to be relatively short, a total of little more than a year between an unpredicted surprise change in economic con-

---

[1] "False Prophets," *New Republic* (October 1, 1977), p. 50.

ditions and the earliest possible countervailing change in output induced by monetary policy. The major side effect of countercyclical monetary policy—the wide amplitude of fluctuations in housing caused by the movement of funds in and out of savings institutions as monetary policy reduces and increases market interest rates on bonds—appears to be a consequence of government ceilings on the interest rates savings institutions can pay.

Our discussion of fiscal policy in this chapter begins in parallel with that of monetary policy and includes consideration of both lags and side effects. Fiscal policy lags are more uncertain than those of monetary policy because they involve both political and economic factors. Most important is the highly unpredictable time period taken by Congress to consider fiscal policy initiatives in contrast to the regular frequent meetings of the Federal Open Market Committee. As for fiscal side effects, a major consequence shared in common by all types of fiscal policy stimulus is an increase in interest rates, which tends to crowd out an amount of private spending that offsets at least part of the fiscal stimulus. In this sense countercyclical fiscal and monetary policy share a parallel disadvantage: Monetary restraint and fiscal stimulus both raise the real interest rate, while monetary stimulus and fiscal restraint both lower the real interest rate.[2]

There is one important aspect of fiscal policy, however, that distinguishes it from monetary policy. Unlike monetary policy, which consists of only a single tool (control of the money supply combined with side effects on interest rates), fiscal policy embraces a multitude of alternative specific proposals—changes in many types of expenditures and tax rates. Because these alternative changes in expenditures and tax rates have differing side effects, some influencing consumption, some investment, some the natural rate of unemployment, and some inflation, a set of fiscal policy proposals can be designed to tackle a wide variety of policy goals. For instance, investment can be stimulated via changes in the investment tax credit, while the natural unemployment rate may be reduced by a fiscal incentive plan that subsidizes employers to hire disadvantaged individuals and train them for skilled jobs.

18-2 LAGS IN THE EFFECT OF FISCAL POLICY

Lags weaken the case for any countercyclical policy, whether monetary or fiscal because they may prevent activist policy changes from influencing the economy early enough to help offset destabilizing shifts in

---

[2] These statements refer to the short run. Monetary stimulus reduces the real interest rate in the short run but may raise the nominal interest rate in the long run by increasing the expected rate of inflation (Review section 10-2.)

spending. A stimulus designed to dampen a recession may wind up influencing the economy a year or two later, when the problem may have changed to one of restraining a boom. As in monetary policy, several types of lags intervene that prevent any fiscal policy change from immediately offsetting an unexpected shift in the demand for commodities or money. The first two types of lags are shared by monetary and fiscal policy:

1. The data lag
2. The recognition lag

In section 16-7 we conclude that these lags introduce a delay of about four months between a change in economic conditions and the earliest feasible response of the policy authorities. An initial wait occurs as data are collected, and a subsequent delay interferes as analysts wait for several months to pass so that they can determine whether a reversal in the behavior of an important data series represents a transitory "blip" or a lasting alteration.

LEGISLATIVE LAG

The third source of delay, the legislative lag, is much more important for fiscal than for monetary policy. Not only the Congress, but also the President, are involved. President Kennedy's economic advisers recognized the need for a permanent income tax reduction almost immediately when they arrived in Washington in 1961, but the President did not finally agree to propose the change until mid-1962, and the Congress did not enact the necessary legislation until March 1964. In that episode Congress had a hard time accepting the radically different "New Economics" of the President's economic advisers. As summarized in sections 17-2 and 17-3, Walter Heller and associates in the 1961–63 period dropped any appeal for fiscal responsibility and emphasized instead the fiscal drag caused then by a high natural employment surplus in the absence of stimulative monetary policy.

Similarly, there was a long lag between the date when in early 1966 economic advisers realized that a tax increase was needed to offset expanding government expenditures on the Vietnam War and the final enactment of the income tax surcharge in mid-1968. The first problem of the advisers was to persuade President Johnson, who did not want to raise taxes and aggravate opposition to the war before the Congressional elections of November 1966. Finally, in January 1967, Johnson recommended a tax increase, but final enactment by Congress was delayed a full 18 months.

Legislative lags have been much shorter in recent episodes. Although policymaking in the 1974–75 recession was marred by President Ford's Hoover-like plan to raise tax rates in the fall of 1974, finally in January 1975 the collapse of real GNP led the President to propose a $16 billion tax reduction. Congress responded with alacrity, passing a $21 billion tax cut only two months later. In 1977 the legislative lag was four months between President Carter's January proposal of a $31 billion two-year stimulus package and the passage by Congress in May of a $20 billion package. The legislative lag would probably have been longer if the administration had not in April withdrawn part of its stimulus proposal—an $11 billion tax rebate—which had generated considerable opposition in the Senate.

TRANSMISSION LAG

The fourth source of delay, the transmission lag, varies in length for different types of fiscal policy. A change in income tax rates can alter paychecks within weeks, as soon as new withholding tax tables are printed and mailed to employers. But an increase in government spending (for example, public works expenditures), is subject to a long transmission lag because of delays necessary for designs to be created, plans to be drawn, bids to be submitted, contracts to be signed, and work to begin. The desire to minimize the transmission lag for public works projects has led to proposals for an "ever-ready" shelf of projects for which all these preliminary steps have been completed. For example, Congress appropriated $2 billion for local public works in the fall of 1976, but no money had been expended (except for administrative bureaucrats) as of February 1977.

EFFECTIVENESS LAG

The final delay, the effectiveness lag, varies among alternative types of fiscal policy. Further, econometric models differ in their estimates of the multipliers associated with individual types of policy change. For instance, in the first quarter following a $1 billion increase in government spending, estimates of the resulting increase in nominal GNP range between $0.7 and $1.8 billion. After three quarters have elapsed, the estimates range between $1.2 and $2.7 billion.[3] Thus policymakers who want to raise spending by, say, $25 billion have no firm guidance on the exact size of the fiscal stimulus that is required.

A discussion of this subject written a few years ago would have carefully balanced the advantage of the short legislative lag of monetary policy against the short effectiveness lag of fiscal policy instruments. Monetary policy was thought to influence aggregate demand only through a roundabout process. The lag between changes in the interest rate and investment was estimated by some economists in the late 1960s to be at least eight quarters, as compared to only about two quarters for fiscal tax reductions or expenditure increases.[4]

---

[3] Source: see Figure 12-4.

[4] Charles W. Bischoff, "The Effect of Alternative Lag Distributions," in Gary Fromm (ed.), *Tax Incentives and Capital Spending* (Washington, D.C.: Brookings, 1971), pp. 61–130. See especially Figure 3-6, p. 114.

But the evidence examined in Chapter 16 suggests that the effectiveness lag of monetary policy is much shorter, only around two to three quarters and is thus fully comparable with that of fiscal policy. One factor that had been overlooked was credit rationing. Because of interest-rate ceilings on savings bank interest rates and on the interest rates paid by consumers on installment loans, mortgage and consumer credit tends to be rationed when banks can lend funds profitably for other purposes at high rates.[5] In a situation when consumer credit is rationed, banks can raise consumer loans and stimulate consumer spending quite rapidly when the Fed allows the money supply to increase. Another source of rapid response is the influence of changes in money on stock prices and then of stock prices on consumption. This channel of monetary influence was neglected in earlier research. In Section 16-7 the average lag between the onset of monetary restraint and cyclical peaks in real output appeared to be only 8.5 months. On this subject there appears to have been a lag in the ability of the econometric model builders to understand the underlying behavior of the economy!

Should we conclude that countercyclical monetary policy is superior to fiscal policy because its legislative lag is shorter and more predictable, while its effectiveness lag is not appreciably longer? Such a verdict appears premature for two reasons. First, the much more rapid response of Congress in the 1970s than in earlier decades suggests that the legislative lag, although uncertain, may not be a major obstacle to the use of fiscal policy, at least when the economy is widely agreed to be operating too far away from the natural unemployment target as in 1975. Second, the side effects of monetary and fiscal stimulus are different and must be considered in light of other policy objectives, for instance, those of promoting investment and economic growth and of minimizing inflation.

18-3 FISCAL DISCRETION VERSUS FORMULA FLEXIBILITY

Convinced that long lags, caused in particular by the unpredictable legislative lag, prevent discretionary fiscal policy changes from stabilizing the economy at the time when stimulus or restraint is needed, some critics would abandon discretionary policy entirely. Sole responsibility for stabilization would rest with the automatic stabilizers, and discretionary policy changes would be reserved for infrequent increases in expenditures or reductions in tax rates required to allocate the fiscal dividend automatically generated by economic growth. One of the proponents of this view, that discretionary "fine tuning" of the economy should be

---

[5] D. M. Jaffee and Franco Modigliani, "A Theory and Test of Credit Rationing," *American Economic Review*, vol. 59 (December 1969), pp. 840–73.

avoided, was Wilbur Mills, former Chairman of the House Ways and Means Committee, who declared that "taxes should not be raised and lowered from season to season like the hemlines of women's skirts and dresses."[6]

An alternative to a do nothing reliance on automatic stabilizers would be to replace the present U.S. system, in which each tax rate and expenditure change must be separately approved by Congress, with an automatic formula. Under **formula flexibility,** for instance, the marginal personal income tax rate might be reduced by a fixed number of percentage points for each percentage point by which the actual unemployment rate exceeds the natural rate. A plan that would automatically reduce tax rates when real output declines would amount to an increase in the degree of automatic stabilization in the economy. The government deficit would increase by a larger share of any decline in GNP than is now the case — absorbing say 50 percent of any change in income rather than the present 36 percent.[7] Similarly, tax rates would rise automatically during a period of booming demand and low unemployment. Formula flexibility would have automatically resulted in higher tax rates during the period of low unemployment during the Vietnam War and would have prevented at least some of the acceleration of inflation that occurred during 1966–69.

Formula flexibility could be adopted also as a technique of monetary control. The rate of growth of the money supply could be automatically decelerated by some predetermined amount if unemployment were to fall below the natural rate, or vice versa. In computer experiments with several different econometric models, J. Phillip Cooper and Stanley Fischer have shown that a formula flexibility rule that varies the growth of the money supply in response to changes in unemployment and in the inflation rate would stabilize the economy more effectively than a monetarist constant-growth-rate-rule for the money supply.[8] Several kinds of formulas are available for both monetary and fiscal policy operating on the level of unemployment relative to some target, on the rate of change of unemployment, or on the cumulative deviation of unemployment from its target. And other policy targets, for example, the inflation rate, might be included in the formula.[9]

---

[6] *The New York Times,* April 20, 1967, p. 1. Mills' opposition to tax changes was a major factor in the long 1967–68 legislative lag in enactment of the temporary income tax surcharge proposed by President Johnson to help pay for Vietnam War expenditures.

[7] The effective 1975–76 marginal leakage rate contributed by taxes and transfer payments is plotted in Figure 17-4.

[8] See J. Phillip Cooper and Stanley Fischer, "Simulation of Monetary Rules in the FRB-MIT-Penn Model," *Journal of Money, Credit, and Banking* (May 1972), pp. 384–96.

[9] The classic theoretical contribution on formula flexibility is a pair of articles by A. W. Phillips. See "Stabilization Policy in a Closed Economy," *Economic Journal,* vol. 64 (June 1954), pp. 290–323, and "Stabilization Policy and the Time-Forms of Lagged Responses," *Economic Journal,* vol. 67 (June 1957), pp. 265–77. A theoretical analysis of the effects

(continued)

Formula flexibility for fiscal policy shades gradually into discretionary action. For instance, Congress might reserve for itself the veto right over any change in tax rates or spending called for automatically by the operation of the formula. Or Congress could change the formula itself if there were widespread opposition to the direction of the automatic fiscal change. Or the discretion for initiating a change in taxes could be left to the President subject to a possible Congressional veto. The latter proposal was made by President Kennedy in 1962 and received a cold reception by Congress, which is jealous of its authority over tax rates and expenditures, its "power of the purse."

The disadvantage of formula flexibility is, ironically, its inflexibility. Every economic situation is different, and it would be impossible to design an ironbound formula that would be just right for every circumstance. One recession might be economy-wide and call for reductions in the personal income tax, but the next might be exclusively concentrated in the investment sector and might call for a temporary increase in the investment tax credit. An advantage of the present system is that planners can design a separate policy package for each economic situation. In the end, one's verdict on formula flexibility comes down to one's trust in the ability of Congress and the administration to act promptly and wisely when the economy is blown off course.

18-4 CHOICE OF FISCAL INSTRUMENTS: LIMITATIONS OF TAX RATE CHANGES

If a countercyclical activist fiscal policy is to be pursued, which fiscal tools should be used? The number of possibilities is almost endless. Any of the following tax measures could be introduced: temporary tax credits, rebates, or surcharges; permanent changes in personal and/or corporate income tax rates; changes in the investment tax credit; liberalization of depreciation allowances; extensions of unemployment compensation; and employment subsidies. Or any one of several types of government spending can be altered: public works, grants to state and local governments, manpower training programs, and others.

The efficiency of a fiscal tool can be defined as its bang per buck, the dollars of extra nominal GNP created per extra dollar of budget deficit. If we assume that the natural employment surplus (NES) is initially at its desired level, then any discretionary fiscal change will push the NES away from its desired level. If, for instance, the objective is a $20 billion increase in GNP required to reduce unemployment, an efficient policy

---

on formula flexibility of long and variable lags is Stanley Fischer and J. Phillip Cooper, "Stabilization Policy and Lags," *Journal of Political Economy*, vol. 81 (July/August 1973), pp. 847–77.

stimulus is one with a large multiplier effect, achieving the policy objective with, say, only a $5 billion decrease in the NES. A less efficient policy with a smaller multiplier might require a $40 billion decrease in the NES to raise GNP and reduce unemployment by the same amount.

As we first learned in Chapter 3, the multiplier effect of any change in tax rates or government spending depends on (1) the fraction of each initial dollar of deficit that is spent immediately on the first round rather than saved, and (2) the fraction of the income created from the first-round extra spending that is spent again rather than leaking out of the spending stream into saving, income taxes, and imports.[10] Component (2) is roughly the same for all types of fiscal changes, but component (1) may differ widely.

For instance, any extra dollar of budget deficit caused by a dollar of extra government expenditures results in a spending fraction on the first round of 100 percent.[11] At the opposite extreme, an extra dollar of budget deficit incurred when a tax rebate is given to rich people may have a spending fraction on the first round of only 2 or 3 percent. Rich people may have all the consumption goods they want and may put almost all the tax rebate into savings. An extreme example of an inefficient fiscal stimulus would be extra government spending on Japanese-made television sets. On the first round the spending fraction within the United States would be zero, because all the extra income would flow to Japanese firms and workers.[12]

INEFFICIENCY OF PERSONAL TAX RATE CHANGES

Changes in personal income tax rates in 1964, 1968, and 1975 designed for stabilization purposes were largely absorbed by offsetting changes in saving. In these instances the average spending fraction on the initial round, that is, the marginal propensity to consume out of a change in taxes, was only about 14 percent, according to a recent study by F. Thomas Juster of the University of Michigan.[13] Of each dollar of tax change 86 percent went directly into saving. Somewhat surprisingly, Juster finds no evidence that the response of saving to tax changes announced as temporary (the 1968 surcharge and 1975 rebate) was significantly different from the permanent 1964 tax rate reductions.

Thus inefficiency is the fundamental limitation of changes in tax rate

---

[10] If the money supply is fixed, a higher demand for money will raise the interest rate and cause a crowding out effect on private spending. See section 5-6.

[11] Recall that total GNP (Q) = Consumption (C) + Investment (I) + Government spending (G). Thus each dollar of any change in G causes a first-round change in Q of $1.00, or 100% as much.

[12] The long-run effect would be slightly positive, because the Japanese workers would spend part of their higher incomes on products made in the United States.

[13] F. Thomas Juster, "A Note on Prospective 1977 Tax Cuts and Consumer Spending," unpublished manuscript (January 1977), Table 2, equation 1.

as a tool of discretionary fiscal policy. Very large shifts in the natural employment surplus (NES) may be necessary to achieve significant changes in total spending and unemployment. To achieve a given unemployment target through tax policy alone, the NES may have to be shifted from its desired level by four or five times more than if the same unemployment target is reached through changes in government spending.

Tax rate changes present other less important difficulties. First, members of Congress tend to differ on the desired form of tax rate changes, some favoring the limitation of the impact to one or another economic group. Past tax proposals designed for stabilization have become mixed up with the continuing debates on the desirability of redistributing income from the rich to the poor, on closing tax loopholes, and on opening new loopholes to encourage particular activities (energy-saving, plant and equipment investment, and others).

Tax policy differs from the use of government spending for stabilization by temporarily shifting the short-run Phillips curve. In a recession, when a reduction in unemployment is desired, a cut in income taxes tends to shift the short-run Phillips curve downward temporarily because tax cuts enable firms to reduce the selling price of their products while maintaining intact both after-tax wages and profits. The same phenomenon works in reverse in a boom when an increase in unemployment and reduction in inflation is desired; a tax rate increase may shift the Phillips curve upward and thus have a perverse effect, increasing the inflation rate instead of reducing it. Why? Higher taxes will sooner or later be incorporated into business costs and prices. This upward shift in costs may outweigh the anti-inflationary contribution of the reduction in aggregate demand achieved by the tax increase.[14]

The fiscal policy tool that has most often been used for countercyclical stabilization policy—changes in personal income tax rates—thus appears to be severely flawed. It is a poor stimulus for use in recessions because so much of each dollar of extra federal deficit leaks out into saving. And it is a poor anti-inflationary device for use in booms because tax increases raise business costs and prices. Should tax policy be abandoned as a stabilization tool?

OTHER TAXES

Several tax instruments are available besides the personal income tax. Any tax or subsidy on spending, such as a sales or excise tax or an investment credit, is ideally suited for stabilization if legislative lags are sufficiently short. Imagine that a U.S. national sales tax of 5 percent were levied on all products and that in a recession the sales tax were eliminated for six months. The temporary nature of the tax cut would aid in stimu-

---

[14] For a theoretical analysis demonstrating that the final outcome may go either way, see Alan S. Blinder, "Can Income Tax Increases be Inflationary? An Expository Note," *National Tax Journal*, vol. 26 (June 1973), pp. 295–301.

lating economic recovery, because it would induce households to make their purchases of durable and semi-durable goods (autos, clothing) earlier than would otherwise have occurred.

The major disadvantages of temporary changes in sales taxes are practical. First, the effect will be perverse during Congressional debate of the measure; households will delay spending during a recession if they think that proposed tax cuts will make goods cheaper in the future after Congressional action. Second, there is no national sales tax in the United States that can be used for countercyclical stabilization. The federal government could subsidize state and local governments to reduce their own sales taxes during recessions, but this proposal has the disadvantage of inequity, since some states (albeit a minority) do not have a state sales tax and thus would be unable to take advantage of the federal subsidy.

Because of these limitations, sales tax changes in U.S. stabilization policy have been limited to alterations in the investment tax credit (ITC), first introduced in 1962 as a permanent stimulus to investment. Unfortunately, past attempts to use the ITC as a countercyclical stabilization tool have been ill-timed and counterproductive. The ITC was repealed in the spring of 1969, too late to offset the excessive spending and too-low unemployment of the 1966–69 period. The decline in investment spending induced by the repeal of the ITC served only to amplify the decline of spending in the 1969–70 recession. Then the credit was reintroduced in late 1971, and it contributed to the excessive spending that occurred in late 1972 and early 1973. This sad experience has led Harvard's Dale W. Jorgenson to conclude:

> The investment tax credit cannot be used as a short-run stabilization or countercyclical measure because the time lags involved are too long. Instead, it should be kept on permanently at a relatively high rate to foster the long-run goal of stimulating the growth of the capital stock.[15]

Despite his opposition to using the ITC for stabilization, Jorgenson himself has shown that a properly timed elimination of the ITC in 1964 and reinstatement in 1969 – precisely the reverse of what actually happened – would have eliminated almost half the deviation of output from its target during the 1959–72 period.[16]

Another conflicting piece of evidence is the success in Sweden of a somewhat different stabilization tool, a countercyclical investment fund. The Swedish plan uses a powerful fiscal stick and carrot to shift investment from booms to recessions.[17] The stick is the corporation income

---

[15] "A Tax Credit to Check Inflation and Recession," *Business Week* (November 16, 1974), p. 118.

[16] Roger Gordon and Dale W. Jorgenson, "Policy Alternatives for the Investment Credit," unpublished, February 1975.

[17] See Hans Brems, "Swedish Fine Tuning," *Challenge* (March/April 1976), pp. 39–42.

tax, which corporations naturally try to avoid. The government encourages avoidance by allowing firms in boom years to put aside up to 40 percent of pretax profits in a special fund. Investment in booms is reduced, since firms have immobilized part of their profits, which, after paying tax, they could have used for investment.

The carrot to firms is the availability of all the fund—including the profits that otherwise would have gone to the government in tax—for specific types of investment projects during certain specified recession periods. From the firm's point of view, the plan amounts to an extreme liberalization of depreciation that allows taxes to be written off even before an investment is made.[18] Although firms are not forced to invest in the fund, they are eager to do so. In 1970, the accumulated fund amounted to 57 percent of annual private manufacturing investment.[19]

18-5 CHOICE OF FISCAL INSTRUMENTS: LIMITATIONS OF EXPENDITURE CHANGES

Changes in government expenditures are more efficient than changes in tax rates because 100 percent of the extra spending automatically becomes extra GNP. The main disadvantages of spending changes are (1) delays in timing and (2) the possibility that the social value of the extra output produced may be relatively low. The timing problem is most acute. In early 1977, for instance, President Carter's advisers did not include major spending increases in the first year of their two-year stimulus package because they did not believe that it was administratively possible suddenly to spend extra billions productively. Even after the legislative lag is surmounted, there are usually long delays while projects are planned and funds allocated. In our federal system of government, there may be a further delay if the spending increase takes the form of a federal government grant that is actually spent by state and local governments.

Just as questions of equity cloud any discussion of tax rate changes, changes in spending on public projects raise the same questions of fairness. Spending on what? Cleaner parks for Grand Rapids? A new city hall for Plains? City mayors in February 1977 criticized a $2 billion public works program appropriated by Congress in the fall of 1976. Not only had no money yet been spent, complained the mayors, but some cities had received too large an allocation and some too little. One mayor claimed that "45 out of the 100 largest cities in America were excluded,"

---

[18] In the United States depreciation deductions—which cut a corporation's tax bill—are made over the life of an investment after it is installed.

[19] Brems, op. cit., p. 40.

and that more money went to cities with low unemployment rates than to those with above average unemployment.[20]

Another disadvantage of spending changes is that they are not easily reversible. Let us imagine that money was allocated even-handedly in 1977 both for cleaner parks in Grand Rapids and a new city hall for Plains. Then let us suppose that a rapid economic expansion in 1978 requires fiscal restraint. The choice of cutbacks in public works projects as a fiscal tool is bound to cause unhappiness and waste. Grand Rapids residents will complain about the mess in their parks. Plains residents will complain about their half-finished city hall. Frequent changes in government spending plans can lead to a lack of confidence in the promises of goverment officials and considerable difficulties in hiring employees who may fear subsequent dismissal when economic conditions change.[21]

THE THREE BRANCHES OF GOVERNMENT

It is possible to go beyond the practical disadvantages of cyclical changes in government spending to argue that in principle government expenditures should not be varied countercyclically. Richard A. Musgrave of Harvard has suggested the useful device of dividing the government into three imaginary branches.[22]

1. *The allocation branch* would decide on the division of natural employment output between private expenditures and public goods purchased by the government. It is also a function of the allocation branch to attempt to achieve the optimum division between present consumption of both private and public goods, as opposed to private and public investment to provide additional consumption in the future.
2. *The distribution branch* designs a system of taxes and transfers that alters the distribution of income achieved by the private economy toward a more just or fair distribution. In most countries, including the United States, it is felt that the pretax earnings differentials between the rich and poor that the private economy tends to generate are excessive, and so the rich pay relatively high marginal tax rates,

---

[20] James C. Hyatt, "The Public Works Controversy," *Wall Street Journal* (February 14, 1977).

[21] In an early study, S. J. Maisel found a delay of about one year between the authorization of certain federal public works projects and the awarding of contracts. See S. J. Maisel, "Timing and Flexibility of a Public Works Program," *Review of Economics and Statistics,* vol. 31 (May 1949), p. 149. A more recent study by Albert Ando and E. Cary Brown suggests that an attempt by the federal government during the 1957–58 recession to accelerate spending on construction projects did not succeed in stimulating the economy during the period when it was needed. See Albert Ando and E. Cary Brown, "Lags in Fiscal Policy," in *Stabilization Policies* (Englewood Cliffs, N.J.: Prentice-Hall, 1963).

[22] Richard A. Musgrave, *The Theory of Public Finance* (New York: McGraw-Hill, 1959), Chapters 1 and 2.

whereas the very poor pay no tax but receive transfer payments of various types (welfare, food stamps, medicaid).

3. *The stabilization branch* is concerned with the main problem of this book, achieving a stable output level equal to the natural level of output with a minimum of inflation. Changes in government spending (G) for the purpose of stabilization policy have the disadvantage in Musgrave's framework of interfering with the optimal level of G chosen by the allocation branch. Changes in the structure of tax rates or transfers would interfere with the decisions of the distribution branch. Thus the stabilization branch must either do nothing (which would please the monetarists), or they must pursue countercyclical policy by simply adding proportional tax surcharges to the existing tax rate structure, or by granting a proportional tax credit.

GOVERNMENT INVESTMENT AS AN ANTI-RECESSION TOOL

Martin J. Bailey has constructed an example that has the effect of denying Musgrave's contention that the allocation and stabilization branches can be so neatly separated.[23] In Figure 18-1 the left frame illustrates a red downward sloping demand curve for private investment (I_0). In the right frame is plotted a hypothetical black downward sloping curve showing the marginal return on government investment projects (G_I), ranked by their productivity.

> *The economy is most efficient when scarce resources are allocated to their most productive use.*

This rule of efficiency calls for funds to be moved between private and government investment until the marginal product of the two types of investment is equalized. If the marginal return on private investment is below that on government projects, society can gain future income by reallocating funds to the higher-yielding government projects until marginal returns are equalized.

In Figure 18-1 an efficient equilibrium is represented at points A and A', where the returns on private and government projects are both equal to r_0. The amount of private investment is I_0, and of government investment is G_{I_0}. Now let us assume that a collapse in business confidence, as during the Great Depression, reduces the expected return on business investment and shifts the private investment schedule down from the red I_0 line to the lower red I_1 line. How should policy be used to maintain the original level of output and employment?

One possibility would be sufficient monetary expansion to allow main-

---

[23] The following discussion of Figure 18-1 is based on Martin J. Bailey, *National Income and the Price Level* (New York: McGraw-Hill, 1971), pp. 187–89. Bailey does not mention Musgrave's three-branch distinction.

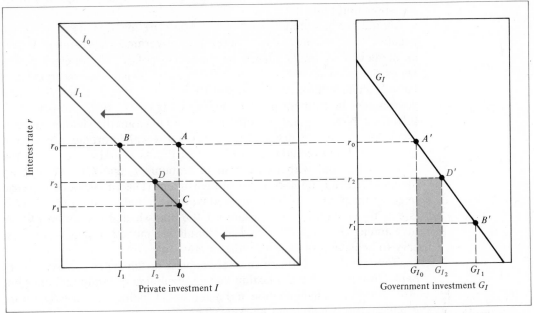

FIGURE 18–1 Optimal Stabilization Policy When a Recession Is Caused by a Drop in Private Investment

Initially the economy is at point A in the left frame, with private investment I_0, and A' in the right frame, with government investment G_{I_0}. A recession now reduces the return on private investment, shifting the red investment schedule in the left-hand frame from I_0 to I_1, moving the economy to point B. The Fed can attempt to cure the problem of low investment by reducing the interest rate from r_0 to r_1, attaining the original level of private investment (I_0) at point C in the left frame. But this is inefficient, because the yield on private investment projects has been reduced below that on government investment (still r_0). If some investment – shown by the pink shading – is shifted from private to government projects, the economy moves to point D in the left frame and D' in the right frame, with the same return (r_2) on both private and government investment.

tenance of the original level of investment I_0. This would require a reduction in the interest rate from r_0 to r_1, in order to induce private firms to invest in less productive projects yielding only r_1. This solution would be inefficient because government investment would continue to have the original return r_0, so that society's future income could be raised by shifting funds from private to government investment. Musgrave is wrong in suggesting a complete separation of allocation and stabilization issues, as he does when he opposes the use of public works projects for stabilization. Why? Because the need to stabilize the economy requires an increase in government investment over the amount originally chosen by the allocation branch.

Should use of stimulative monetary policy be abandoned entirely? No, because total reliance on an increase in government investment is just as inefficient as total reliance on monetary policy. If monetary policy keeps the interest rate constant at the original level r_0, the assumed collapse in confidence cuts investment from I_0 to I_1 (the distance BA), and government investment must be increased from G_{I_0} to G_{I_1} to provide a full offset. Now at point B' in the right-hand diagram the yield on government investment has dropped to r'_1, much lower than private investment at point B, again resulting in inefficiency. Points D and D' represent the efficient solution, with investment in amounts I_2 and G_{I_2} and with an identical return r_2 on both types of investment. The pink-shaded increase in government investment compared with the initial situation $(G_{I_2} - G_{I_0})$ is exactly enough to compensate for the pink-shaded decline in private investment $(I_0 - I_2)$. Notice that stimulative monetary policy is necessary to achieve a reduction in the interest rate from r_0 to r_2.

Government investment projects consist of the types of government expenditures that have a lasting impact, including not only buildings but also investments in education and manpower training that raise the future productivity of individual workers. The classic example of the effective use of public investment for countercyclical stabilization is represented by President Roosevelt's Works Progress Administration, which between 1935 and 1943:

> spent $11 billion to give work to 8.5 million Americans ranging from laborers, clerks, and plumbers to painters, writers, and actors. WPA crews constructed 651,000 miles of highways and roads, 78,000 bridges, 125,000 buildings and almost 600 airports. They built or improved 8,000 parks, 12,800 playgrounds and 1,000 libraries and erected 5,900 schools. They also constructed power lines in rural areas, planted millions of trees, put up privies, worked on flood-control projects, drained malarial swamps, exterminated rats in slum areas, organized nursery schools, produced garments for needy families and taught thousands of illiterate adults to read and write.[24]

Bailey's case for countercyclical fluctuations in government investment projects is persuasive. The big problem is administrative—how to allocate funds rapidly and fairly. The Swedes solve this problem by keeping a large inventory of projects ready to be mobilized on short notice, in say one or two months. The Japanese have also developed a system of countercyclical public works expenditures that avoids lags in starting new projects and the dislocations and inefficiency caused when projects

---

[24] "It Wasn't All Leaf-Raking," *Newsweek* (January 20, 1975), p. 57.

are cancelled. The technique is simple—increase or decrease the speed with which a given project is completed. For instance, the 115-mile Tokyo Coastal Bay Expressway has been under construction since 1962. The Japanese central government decides each year how much money should be allocated to it, depending on the stabilization needs of the economy. No one knows when the project will be completed, because "that depends on the economy and how we control spending."[25]

18-6 USING FISCAL POLICY TO REDUCE THE NATURAL RATE OF UNEMPLOYMENT

Employment is another area of overlap between the tasks of the government's allocation and stabilization branches. The major theme of Part III was that the reduction of unemployment and inflation involves far more than the traditional task of activist stabilization policy—the manipulation of aggregate demand to keep actual unemployment (U) close to the natural rate of unemployment (U^*). Any excessive expansion of aggregate demand pushes U below U^* only temporarily and leads to an acceleration of inflation. Permanent reductions in unemployment require actions that reduce the natural unemployment rate (U^*) itself, a major task that is beyond the capability of monetary policy and of aggregative fiscal measures.

The high level of U^* in the United States was attributed in Chapter 9 to three major factors: (1) temporary layoffs, (2) a large amount of job turnover that occurs when individuals quit jobs and take their time looking for better jobs, and (3) worker-job mismatch, the fact that many unemployed individuals lack skills required to be eligible for available job slots or they are in the wrong geographical location.

How might fiscal policy reduce the mismatch between workers and jobs? Unlike monetary policy and aggregative fiscal policy measures, which influence total spending without reducing worker-job mismatch, targeted fiscal measures can be designed to improve the matching of workers and jobs. Two basic approaches have been proposed: (1) direct government hiring of disadvantaged job seekers and (2) government subsidies to subsidize private firms to hire the disadvantaged. What are the relative merits of the two alternative types of targeted fiscal policy?

DIRECT GOVERNMENT HIRING

The first approach, direct government hiring, usually is called public service employment (PSE). General government hiring, without careful

---

[25] The speaker is a Mr. Ito, who oversees the Japanese Construction Ministry's financial planning, as quoted in Andrew H. Malcolm, "Japan Is Battling Economic Slump with Public Works Projects," *The New York Times* (May 12, 1976), p. 57.

limitation to the relatively disadvantaged subgroup of the unemployed, is just another form of aggregative fiscal policy. The only difference between an aggregate PSE program and Japanese-style accelerated public works is the particular mix of government goods and services produced. A public works program creates long-lasting government investment projects—post offices, roads, parks—and tends to generate jobs for the more highly skilled of the unemployed. An aggregate PSE program leads to extra spending on the particular goods and services chosen by the state and local governments that do the actual hiring—often the projects are a mixture of government consumption and investment. Examples from one existing PSE program include maintenance work on public buildings and housing projects, the repair of motor vehicles for local agencies, the provision of security for government buildings, and the cleaning up and landscaping of parks.[26]

But PSE does not reduce the natural unemployment rate unless it is designed as a targeted program that hires disproportionately large numbers from demographic groups with high unemployment rates—blacks, women, and teenagers—and individuals from cities suffering from above average unemployment. To make a permanent contribution, a targeted PSE program should be designed to equip disadvantaged workers with skills that will qualify them for job vacancies in the private sector. Otherwise, the PSE employees are likely to return to unemployment if the program were eventually to be terminated. Any permanent reduction in the natural rate of unemployment would require a permanent targeted PSE plan.

So far, U.S. experiments with PSE have not been encouraging. A recent study finds that the PSE job slots funded under the Comprehensive Employment and Training Act have been relatively high in skill requirements and that undereducated workers have not benefited.[27] On the other hand, some small individual programs have hired very "undesirable" individuals—ex-criminals, drug addicts, and welfare mothers—and have succeeded in providing useful services and training for private jobs. In one case there was no net cost to the taxpayer because the wages paid to the employees were fully covered by reduced welfare payments and unemployment compensation, income taxes paid by the employees, and other benefits.[28]

GOVERNMENT SUBSIDIES

An alternative to PSE would be a subsidy or voucher plan to bribe private firms to hire disadvantaged workers. The government would pay

---

[26] Allan L. Otten, "Jobs for the 'Unemployables,'" *Wall Street Journal* (April 1, 1976), p. 18.

[27] Michael Wiseman, "Public Employment as Fiscal Policy," *Brookings Papers on Economic Activity,* vol. 7, no. 1 (1976), pp. 67–104.

[28] Allan L. Otten, "Jobs for the 'Unemployables,'" *op. cit.*

private firms some fraction of the wage cost of eligible employees for some specified period. A firm could offer a wage of $3.00 per hour to an unemployed disadvantaged individual whose productivity (at least initially) is only $1.50, receiving the $1.50 difference in the form of a subsidy from the government. The main problem with the subsidy plan is to devise a way to determine eligibility so that only deserving individuals benefit. Otherwise, firms will receive subsidies for hiring the "normal" people whom they would have hired anyway. Also, the subsidy plan will have to be permanent rather than temporary unless firms can somehow be required to provide training and to upgrade workers as they develop skills, rather than simply to place disadvantaged workers in dead-end jobs (dishwasher, busboy) for which they would have qualified even in the absence of the subsidy.

A consensus seems to be developing, at least among some nonmonetarist economists, that a subsidy for disadvantaged individuals, available either to private firms or to state and local governments, would allow both private and public activities to use disadvantaged workers.[29] Provision of productive activities for these individuals provides valuable job experience and contributes to the formation of good work habits, even if initial productivity is low. This subsidy approach is preferable to the pure waste of idle unemployment supported by welfare and unemployment compensation. Further, reducing the natural rate of unemployment through a mixture of private and public activities is consistent with Bailey's efficiency rule, summarized in Figure 18-1, which states that economic stimulus in the form of a mixture of private and public investment projects will usually be superior to a stimulus limited exclusively to one or the other.

18-7 USING FISCAL POLICY TO REDUCE THE INFLATION RATE

Monetary policy and aggregative fiscal policy influence the rate of growth of aggregate demand, which in turn alters the inflation rate in the short run. A monetary stimulus and a deficit-financed expenditure increase that both raise aggregate demand (nominal income) by the same amount share the same effect on inflation.[30]

But tax policy differs. Virtually every tax change, in addition to its effect on the growth of aggregate demand, has a separate effect that shifts the short-run Phillips curve, altering the rate of inflation associated with

---

[29] See the discussion of Wiseman, *op. cit.*, pp. 111–14.

[30] This statement is true only in a closed economy. In an open economy under flexible exchange rates, monetary stimulus raises the inflation rate more than fiscal stimulus, by causing the exchange rate to depreciate and the prices of imported goods to rise.

a given unemployment rate. *In short, tax changes have not only a demand effect but also a supply effect.*

It is easiest to understand the supply effect in the simple example of a state sales tax. Imagine that the state of Illinois were to eliminate its present 5 percent sales tax. The retail price (including tax) of all goods sold in Illinois would fall by 5 percent. The consumer would find that the price level had dropped by 5 percent, while firms would be able to maintain unchanged both their own profits and the wages of their workers.[31]

The supply effect is not limited to state sales taxes. Virtually every tax can be treated as part of the "wedge" between the market price paid by consumers and the after-tax income of labor and capital (take-home pay in the case of labor, after-tax dividends and retained earnings in the case of capital). For instance, a reduction in social security or income tax rates would allow firms to reduce retail prices and the before-tax pay of their workers while maintaining intact the take-home after-tax wage rates. I have estimated that the increases in personal income and social security tax rates that took place in the last half of the decade of the 1960s caused an increase in the price level of about half a percentage point purely through the supply effect.[32] Since the federal government has no sales tax that it can control directly, probably the most powerful way to reduce the price level through the supply effect would be a reduction in social security payroll tax rates.

Tax reductions can cause a permanent downward shift in the economy's price index at a given level of aggregate demand, but a permanent reduction in the level of prices represents only a temporary reduction in inflation, that is, in the rate of change of prices. This distinction can be illustrated as follows if the tax reduction causes the price level to drop from one position before time period 0 to a new lower level after time period 1:

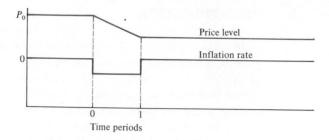

[31] In terms of the aggregate supply and demand curves of Chapter 7, the tax reduction not only raises the aggregate demand curve (*DD*) but also shifts the supply curve (*SS*) downward by 5 percent. The net effect on the rate of inflation depends on the tax multiplier (determining how far *DD* shifts), the response of monetary policy, and the adjustment, if any, of worker expectations of the future price level.

[32] Robert J. Gordon, "Inflation in Recession and Recovery," *Brookings Papers on Economic Activity*, vol. 2, no. 1 (1971), pp. 105–58.

Since the price level is constant both before time period 0 and after time period 1, the rate of inflation is exactly the same (zero) both before and after the effect of the tax reduction. Nevertheless, the temporary reduction in the inflation rate may help permanently if worker expectations of future inflation are reduced.

Other fiscal measures are available to provide at least a temporary reduction in inflation. Like tax reductions, each of these measures increases government spending and thus raises the government deficit. The choice among the alternative programs should be based on the "bang per buck" criterion for efficiency: Which program generates the largest slowdown in inflation at the smallest budgetary cost?

1. *A temporary output subsidy in response to a supply shock.* A crop failure or other temporary event that causes a short-term increase in commodity prices can be prevented from influencing the overall price level, and hence worker expectations of future inflation, if an offsetting subsidy is provided to reduce the price of those goods which are not in short supply. The entire subsidy would not be a net drain on the federal treasury. First, the subsidy would prevent the crop failure from reducing overall personal income and hence personal income tax collections. Second, in years of above-average crops an offsetting tax could be levied; in principle, subsidy payments in bad years would cancel out tax payments in good years.

2. *Buffer stocks.* If the government had purchased stocks in years of bumper harvests, then crop failures would cause no price increases or other economic disruption because the government could make up for the missing supply by selling off part of its stockpile. In light of the fear that economic expansion in the late 1970s may be blocked by bottlenecks in the form of inadequate capacity to produce raw materials, the government could build up supplies of the "problem" raw materials during years of slack demand.

3. *Targeted investment incentives.* The United States may face two kinds of bottlenecks in its attempt to reduce the unemployment rate below the range of 5 to 6 percent in the late 1970s and early 1980s. Not only may skilled labor be in short supply, requiring government subsidies to help train unskilled workers, but also crucial raw materials may be scarce. As an alternative to government accumulation of buffer stocks, which would provide relief from commodity shortages for only a year or two, I have suggested that the government might build the steel, aluminum, and paper plants that will be needed later. Then the plants could be resold to business firms when total aggregate demand rises to the point required to make use of them.[33]

---

[33] See my comment on Barry Bosworth, "Capacity Creation in Basic Materials Industries," *Brookings Papers on Economic Activity,* vol. 7, no. 2 (1976), pp. 342–45.

Why should the government become involved in building plants? Such action would not be necessary (1) if no time delay occurred between the need for plant capacity and the minimum time required to construct it, and (2) if private firms were willing to construct sufficient capacity on their own without skepticism either of the government's ability to maintain actual unemployment close to the natural rate, or of the government's promises not to reimpose price controls. But in fact neither (1) nor (2) appears to be valid, leaving open a possible role for government intervention.

18-8 FISCAL POLICY AND THE SOURCES OF ECONOMIC GROWTH

The mix of monetary and fiscal policy, and the choice of the particular fiscal tools for the conduct of countercyclical stabilization policy, have side effects not only on unemployment and inflation – the main concerns of this book – but also on the U.S. rate of economic growth. During the past 20 years Japan and most European nations have experienced rates of output growth more rapid than that of the United States, and by some measures Sweden and Switzerland have now caught up to the United States in real output per capita.

Figure 18-2 illustrates the historical performance of actual real output in some of the main industrialized countries for selected years during the last century. The data, compiled for this book, are based on a careful attempt to control the comparisons between countries for differences in prices and in the provision of free services (health, education) by the government.[34] All nations appear to have enjoyed substantial growth in output; in the United States, real output per capita increased from $980 in 1870 to $7,855 in 1976 (both in 1976 prices).

Growth has been faster in some eras, particularly 1953 to 1973, and some nations have grown faster than others. Over the last 106 years, Japan has grown most rapidly, with 1976 real output per capita 14.5 times higher than in 1870. In order, the seven countries multiplied their real output per capita by the ratios in Table 18-1.

The increase in Japan's relative position, and the decline in the United Kingdom's, have been particularly dramatic since 1953. If the postwar trend were to continue, by 1985, the Japanese would have the world's highest real output per capita.

Although not as important in the present as the rates of unemployment

---

[34] The source of the price comparisons is the major international study headed by Irving B. Kravis of the University of Pennsylvania. See Irving B. Kravis *et al., A System of International Comparisons of Gross Product and Purchasing Power* (Baltimore: John Hopkins, 1975).

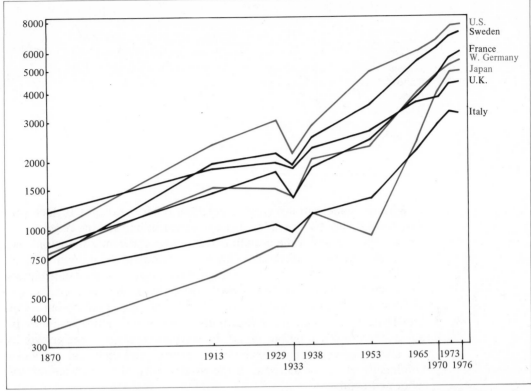

FIGURE 18–2   Per-Person GNP in 1976 U.S. Prices for the Main Industrial Countries, 1870–76

Notice that the United Kingdom had the highest per-person income level in 1870, but its slow growth during the past century now places it second from the bottom, just above Italy. In 1976 the United States ended in a dead heat with Sweden, while the up- ward surge of Japan during the post- war era was halted by the recession of 1973–75. Note also how France and West Germany, neighbors and longtime rivals, have remained almost tied for most of the past century, and that both have raced past the once- mighty, but now faltering United Kingdom.

Source: See Appendix C.

and inflation, the rate of output growth profoundly influences our future and that of our children. If real GNP per person grows at an average annual rate of 3 percent, the U.S. output per capita will be almost twice as high in constant dollars in the year 2000 as in 1976: $16,137 instead of $7,855. But if the average annual growth rate between 1977 and 2000 instead were 5 percent, the real output per capita in the year 2000 would be a much higher $25,542.

TABLE 18-1

Nation	Ratio of real output per capita in 1976 to that in 1870
Japan	14.5
Sweden	10.0
United States	8.0
France	7.1
West Germany	7.0
Italy	4.9
United Kingdom	3.6

Why do some nations grow faster than others? Edward F. Denison has, for the past two decades, been engaged in painstaking research to identify the sources of the growth in real output of the main industrialized countries. Denison's method is simple: (1) calculate the growth rates of factor inputs, both labor and capital; (2) then calculate the contribution to output growth of total input growth, computed as the weighted average of labor growth and capital growth; and (3) study the possible sources of growth in the productivity of the inputs (the growth in input productivity equals the growth in output minus the weighted average of the growth in the factor inputs). As an example, inventions and technical advances continually allow an increase in the productivity of a given amount of labor and capital.

Table 18-2 illustrates Denison's calculations for the United States and the two next largest economies in the Western world, West Germany and Japan. Total output growth per annum in the United States was only two-thirds that of West Germany and less than half that of Japan. Why? First Denison computes the growth in the contribution of labor input, taking account of increases in employment due both to population growth and to the increased labor force participation, of changes in hours of work, and in the contribution of education. The growth rate of labor input is converted into labor's contribution to output growth by applying a fractional weight equal to the estimated response of output growth to changes in labor input. For instance, total growth of labor input in the United States might have been 2.00 percent per annum, which when multiplied by a response of 0.65 equals the 1.30 percent contribution of labor listed in the table in the U.S. column, on the line labeled Labor.

Although differences among the three countries in the contribution of labor appear to have been minor, both West Germany and Japan experienced substantially faster growth in capital than did the United States. The United States also lagged badly behind in the contribution of input productivity, labeled Output per unit of input in the table. The other two benefited from a substantial movement out of agriculture and

TABLE 18-2
Sources of Economic Growth,
United States Compared to West Germany and Japan

	United States, 1948–69	West Germany, 1950–62	Japan, 1953–71
OUTPUT GROWTH RATE	4.00	6.27	8.81
TOTAL FACTOR INPUT	2.09	2.78	3.95
Labor	1.30	1.37	1.85
Employment	1.17	1.49	1.14
Hours of work	−0.21	−0.27	0.21
Education	0.41	0.11	0.34
Other	−0.07	0.04	0.16
Capital	0.79	1.41	2.10
OUTPUT PER UNIT OF INPUT	1.91	3.49	4.86
Decline of agriculture and self-employment	0.30	1.01	0.95
Residual (mainly economies of scale and contribution of advances in knowledge)	1.61	2.48	3.91

Source: Edward F. Denison and William K. Chung, *How Japan's Economy Grew So Fast* (Washington: Brookings, 1976), Table 4-8.

self-employment (small shopkeepers), a phenomenon that occurred earlier in the United States.

How might fiscal policy be used in the United States to raise the rate of economic growth? The major government lever that influences the long-run rate of growth is fiscal investment incentives, of the types described in section 14-7, and the monetary-fiscal policy mix, as described in section 5-10. More generous investment incentives and a movement toward easier money in the form of lower real long-term interest rates, combined with heavier taxation of consumption goods, might help to narrow the gap between the ratio of investment to GNP in the United States as compared to West Germany and Japan:[35]

	Ratio of investment to GNP, 1970
United States	19
West Germany	35
Japan	39

[35] See footnote 34 for source.

Another possible area for government policy intervention is the quality and effectiveness of labor input. Government training programs and subsidies to private firms are alternative techniques for equipping presently unskilled workers with the knowledge and abilities they need to qualify for job openings. If successful, such programs would raise U.S. input productivity. For instance, someone working as a skilled lathe operator for $10.00 per hour, which is counted as the same number of hours of labor input as an unskilled dishwasher who earns only $2.50 per hour. But the output produced by the lathe operator is four times the amount produced by the dishwasher (since the wage is four times as high), and so any government program that succeeds in allowing ex-dishwashers to qualify for lathe operator jobs will raise output per man-hour, that is, the productivity of American labor, and will thus contribute to an acceleration in U.S. economic growth.

Another method of increasing productivity would be to raise the pace of invention and innovation. What can the government do to stimulate research and development (R&D) of new processes and products? Individual firms evaluate investments in R&D continuously as possible alternatives to investments in new plants and equipment. Anything the government does to stimulate conventional investment, such as reducing the corporation income tax or increasing the investment tax credit, is likely to boost R&D spending as well. Recently, however, there has been some concern that the federal government has been forcing R&D into unproductive directions. General Motors, for instance, estimates that 20 percent of its R&D spending goes to meet federal safety and emissions standards. New Federal fuel-economy rules could push the total of R&D spending devoted to compliance with government regulations closer to 40 percent. *Business Week* recently editorialized:

> There is no reason to abandon the health and safety programs or the efforts to protect the environment. . . . But preempting the R&D budget for compliance studies is the road to economic stagnation, not the path of sustained, noninflationary growth the nation has sought so long. The U.S. is in danger of losing the future by asking too much in the present.[36]

CONCLUSION TO PARTS IV AND V
Verdict on Monetary and Fiscal Policy

Two main themes have been our focus in Parts IV and V. The first is the monetarist-nonmonetarist debate on the relative merits of policy activism as opposed to fixed policy rules, particularly a constant-growth-rate-rule for the money supply. The second theme is a comparison of the

---

[36] The Drain on R&D," *Business Week* (June 28, 1976), p. 120.

relative merits of alternative policy instruments that might be used to pursue an activist countercyclical policy.

VERDICT ON ACTIVISM

In an imaginary world in which all private spending consisted of consumer expenditures on services, the case for countercyclical activism would be relatively weak. Consumers would tend to keep their consumption of services equal to a fixed (or very slowly changing) fraction of their permanent or lifetime income. Since only a small fraction of any transitory shock would be incorporated into permanent income, consumer spending and hence total private spending would be stable. If the government could manage to avoid sudden accelerations or decelerations in the growth of government spending, then total GNP could grow fairly smoothly.

This imaginary world lacks one crucial feature of the real world, the accumulation of capital, both by businessmen and by consumers in the form of durable goods.[37] The decision to accumulate durable goods is a two-stage process. First, numerous factors, including monetary and fiscal policy, influence the total stock of capital goods that each firm desires to hold. Second, firms may vary the speed at which they adjust their actual capital stock to the level that they desire. Both stages can contribute to highly unstable rates of annual spending on durable goods, resulting in aggregate economic instability when durable goods industries suffer from stretches of inadequate demand followed by years of excess demand. The basic rationale for an activist countercyclical policy is that society is better off if these swings in durable goods expenditures, and the accompanying fluctuations in employment and unemployment, are smoothed out by countercyclical policy.

Monetarists do not deny that private investment tends to be unstable. In fact, they almost never mention the instability of investment inherent in the accelerator process.[38] Instead, the opposition of monetarists to countercyclical activism is mainly based on the poor past performance of the government, the inability of economic forecasts to look accurately far enough ahead to overcome long policy lags, and, perhaps more fundamentally, a deep distrust of government. Most proponents of activism do not deny these accusations, except the last. Nor do they insist that every small wiggle in the growth rate of output must be smoothed out. But

---

[37] Consumer nondurable goods are a hybrid, mixing the characteristics of services and durable goods. Some nondurable goods are like durables, yielding a flow of services lasting for several years (clothing, shoes, tires). Other nondurables must be purchased continuously (food, drugs).

[38] For an example of a monetarist analysis of the sources of the Great Depression that does not once mention the contribution of the durable goods accelerator, see Allan H. Meltzer, "Monetary and Other Explanations of the Start of the Great Depression," *Journal of Monetary Economics,* vol. 2 (November 1976), pp. 455–72.

they argue that society wastes huge amounts of resources, in the form of idle people and machines, when it pursues fixed policy rules during long slumps of investment (1930–41, 1958–63, and 1975–?). In a symmetric fashion, long booms of the 1966–69 Vietnam variety should be avoided as well. Lags between the initiation of a countercyclical policy action and the economy's response do not appear to be more than a year in duration, certainly a short enough delay to allow ample room for an activist policy to counter a three- or four-year investment slump, even if not enough room to counter a six-month economic pause.

CHOICE OF TOOLS

The second theme of Parts IV and V is the choice of tools for an activist policy. Since society has a multitude of goals, no one policy instrument is adequate. The evidence accumulated in Chapters 15–18 points to the following as desirable policy tools to achieve the principal goals, although many economists would be able to construct their own list differing somewhat in components and emphasis:

1. *Keep the actual unemployment rate close to the natural rate of unemployment.* This target is best left to countercyclical variations in the growth rate of the money supply. Aggregative fiscal measures suffer from serious defects as countercyclical tools, particularly the low efficiency of personal tax changes and the problems of administering and allocating sudden spurts in government spending. The major qualifications to this argument are the Bailey approach, which recommends expanding both private and public investment projects during a recession, together with the Japanese success in administering accelerations and decelerations in government public works projects.

2. *Minimize the rate of inflation.* In the short run, aggregative tools cannot move the economy off the short-run Phillips curve determined by current expectations of future inflation, which in turn depend on the rate of inflation inherited from the past. Two approaches to inflation fighting are emphasized in this book. First, the social cost of an inherited inflation can be reduced by institutional reforms, particularly indexing of the tax system, issuance by the government of an indexed bond, and termination of restrictive government regulations on the financial system that limit the returns available to savers. Second, the danger that accelerating inflation may emerge as a consequence of stimulative policies, due to a shortage of skilled workers and plant capacity needed to produce critical raw materials, can be mitigated by targeting fiscal and manpower policies to overcome these shortages.

3. *Reduce the natural rate of unemployment.* Some of the schemes discussed in Chapter 11 and in this chapter, such as reform of the unemployment compensation system, training subsidies for low-skill workers, and buffer stocks of scarce raw materials, would help to reduce the natural rate. If successful, these programs might allow

U.S. policymakers to pursue an expansive policy that might be able to reduce actual unemployment to 4.0 or below, as compared to an attainable minimum of 5.0 or 5.5 percent in the absence of such programs.

4. *Promote economic growth.* The United States saves less, invests less, and grows slower than most advanced industrialized countries. Most economic researchers agree that U.S. saving and investment can be increased by specific targeted investment incentives, either an increase in the present investment tax credit, a liberalization of depreciation allowances, or a Swedish-type countercyclical investment fund. Application of the Bailey principle would suggest pursuit of a balanced program to shift private resources from consumption to private investment and at the same time to fund high-yielding government investment projects.

Some investment incentives may worsen the inequality of the distribution of income in the United States, since rich people would benefit disproportionately from any measure that reduced the taxation of income from capital. How then can we resolve the paradox that the United States not only has a less equal distribution of income than Sweden, Japan, or Germany, but also saves and invests less? To avoid making inequality worse, a delicate fiscal reform will be required that raises transfers to the poor and increases incentives to investment, while at the same time paying the bill by an increase in taxation on the consumption of nonpoor individuals. One proposed reform that would accomplish all these objectives would be to shift from our present income-tax system to a progressive consumption tax, that is, a tax that taxes people only on their consumption, in contrast to the present income tax system that taxes all income, whether it is consumed or saved.[39]

SUMMARY

1. Fiscal policy lags are more uncertain than monetary policy lags. Unlike monetary policy, in which decisions are made in a single meeting, fiscal policy changes usually require debate in Congress that may extend over many months. This legislative lag is a crucial disadvantage of using fiscal policy for short-run stabilization.

2. Fiscal policy shares with monetary policy additional lags between a turning point in the economy and the earliest possible effect of countercyclical policy. The transmission lag differs among types of fiscal policy and is long for government investment projects, but short for tax changes. The effectiveness lag likewise varies among policies.

---

[39] Martin S. Feldstein, "Taxing Consumption," *The New Republic* (February 28, 1976), pp. 14–17.

3. An alternative to countercyclical *discretionary* fiscal activism is formula flexibility. Under this approach fiscal policies change automatically in response to conditions in the economy. The main advantage of a formula is that it eliminates the legislative lag; the main disadvantage is inflexibility.

4. The variety of fiscal policies is almost limitless. An efficient fiscal tool generates a relatively large change in output for a given change in the natural employment surplus. Temporary changes in income tax are inefficient compared to permanent ones, and temporary subsidies or indirect taxes on goods and services may be more efficient than permanent changes. For instance, a temporary increase in the investment tax credit may lead to a desirable stretching out of an investment boom.

5. To permanently lower unemployment without accelerating inflation, the natural rate of unemployment must be lowered. Targeted fiscal measures can be designed to improve the matching of available skills and job requirements, either by tailoring jobs to people or people to jobs. Even if the government pays as much to provide employment or training as the jobless presently receive in unemployment benefits, society is better off by the amount of output produced by those who were previously idle.

6. Although both monetary and fiscal policy can be used to raise aggregate demand, tax changes also have supply effects that generally are absent when there is a change in the money supply or government spending. Tax changes can make firms and workers want to produce more or less; they can *permanently* alter the price level, but can only *temporarily* alter the inflation rate. To steady the inflation rate in the face of supply shocks, selective tax reductions that offset the supply shock can be introduced.

7. During the last century industrial nations have experienced impressive increases in their standards of living. In the long run output grows with increases in labor and capital inputs and with advances in technology and knowledge. Net investment, the change in capital input, can be altered by the government through its tax policy. The government can also encourage growth by fostering education, manpower training, and research and development.

A LOOK AHEAD

This chapter concludes our study of macroeconomic policy in a closed economy. We will examine in Chapter 19 the constraints on domestic policy imposed by foreign trade and capital movements. Economic policy in an open economy greatly depends on whether the foreign exchange rate is fixed or flexible.

CONCEPTS AND QUESTIONS

IDENTIFICATIONS

Formula flexibility   Tax wedge

Efficiency of a fiscal tool   Buffer stocks

Countercyclical investment fund   Public works projects

Targeted fiscal measures   Sources of economic growth

QUESTIONS FOR REVIEW

1. Since either monetary or fiscal policy can alter output, why do we not rely exclusively on one or the other?

2. What are the main side effects of fiscal policy, other than altering total spending? Of monetary policy?

3. In what sense are formula flexible policies inflexible?

4. What factors help explain why the efficiency of various fiscal policies differ?

5. Even after it has been decided that increased (or decreased) government spending is the appropriate way to eliminate a difference between actual and natural output, what decisions must still be made? What do these decisions depend on?

6. Give examples of targeted fiscal measures that improve worker-job matching. How do these measures differ?

7. Why can't sales tax reductions be used to reduce the rate of inflation permanently? How could output subsidies and buffer stock plans help stabilize the rate of inflation?

8. What factors influence the growth rate of natural output?

9. How do government policies influence the growth rate of natural output?

Part VI

The Open Economy

19 Policy in an International Setting

Business fortunes are made on the ability to forecast such changes in the values of national currencies, while political futures become frayed as a result of these changes.

—Robert Z. Aliber[1]

19-1 INTRODUCTION

In most discussions of macroeconomic policy in the United States, it is possible to ignore the outside world and treat the economy as an island. For this reason, little attention has been paid in this book until now to the interactions of the domestic economy with the rest of the world.

With only a few exceptions, the rest of the book has covered macroeconomic theory and policy for a closed economy, one that has no flows of goods, capital, or money to or from other nations. This chapter, though, treats special problems of formulating policy in an open economy, one that trades goods, capital, and money. Our attention to the closed economy in previous chapters is justified by the orientation of this book toward the United States, where the massiveness of the domestic economy and relatively unimportant foreign trade give policymakers the luxury of ignoring the outside world.[2] In very small countries where foreign trade makes up a large share of domestic production and consumption, much of our closed-economy analysis is irrelevant. In extreme cases there is virtually no role for domestic macroeconomic policy because the price level and real output depend almost completely on what happens in other nations.

---

[1] *The International Money Game* (New York: Basic Books, 1973, p. 4.)

[2] According to government data, the U.S. economy is more dependent on international trade than is commonly believed: (1) One out of six manufacturing jobs produces for export. (2) One out of three acres of U.S. farmland produces for export. (3) Nearly one out of three dollars of U.S. corporate profits derives from the international activities, exports, and investments of corporations. Source: *The New York Times* (June 13, 1977), p. 46.

Most industrialized nations face an intermediate situation between the closed-economy autonomy of U.S. policymakers and the pure open-economy helplessness of policymakers in very small countries. In this intermediate case, domestic policy decisions matter, but at the same time the domestic policy environment is strongly influenced by events in the rest of the world. In the 1970s, for instance, all nations have faced the problem of world inflation, which has fed into each domestic economy by raising the prices of imports, of exports, and of the domestic goods that are closely competitive with imports and exports. Despite this common external environment, however, the economic performance of individual nations has varied widely, partly as a result of different domestic policy reactions. In West Germany the price level (GNP deflator) increased by 27.6 percent between 1972 and the fourth quarter of 1976, a much better performance than the 86.7 percent increase in the price level registered over the same period by the United Kingdom.

In this chapter we introduce some of the main themes of open-economy macroeconomics, sometimes called international monetary economics. Goods, services, and capital flow among nations. Problems arise when inflows do not balance outflows. If a nation buys more imports than the combined value of the exports it sells and capital it borrows, how is it to pay for the difference, called the deficit on its **balance of payments**? It must pay in a form of money that other nations find acceptable, such as gold or U.S. dollars, of which it keeps a stock, called its **international reserves,** to be used as a contingency when there is a balance-of-payments deficit. Problems arise when the stock of international reserves runs low, just as a family faces difficulties when it runs out of money.

The theme of this chapter is that there are two main methods of adjustment to an imbalance between international receipts and expenditures. The most straightforward is a system with a flexible **foreign exchange rate,** the amount of another nation's money that residents of a country can obtain in exchange for a unit of their own money. In late 1977 a resident of the United Kingdom (U.K.) could obtain $1.80 in U.S. dollars for one unit of its own money, the pound sterling. If the United Kingdom faces a balance-of-payments deficit, without enough dollars to pay for its international expenditures on imports and capital outflows, its foreign exchange rate tends to drop to bring the demand and supply for the pound sterling back into balance.

The second method of adjustment occurs if the foreign exchange rate of the pound is held fixed and prevented from dropping. The U.K. policymakers must find some other way of inducing foreigners to raise their demand for pounds and to induce British citizens to reduce the supply of pounds that they are offering to foreigners to pay for imports. The prices of British products must be made cheaper, and so the British inflation rate must be reduced, raising all the problems of inflation adjustment that we examined in Chapter 11.

Just as we learned in Part III that the sluggish adjustment of wages and prices makes it difficult to slow down inflation in a closed economy such as that of the United States, we will find here that sluggish price adjustment inhibits the adjustment of open economies to a balance-of-payment surplus or deficit under a system of fixed exchange rates. Partly as a result, the world has shifted from the fixed exchange rate system that was in effect between the end of World War II and early 1973 to a new system in which exchange rates are flexible and change every day. We will see that the flexible exchange rate system does not solve all problems of balance-of-payments adjustment or completely insulate individual economies from the rest of the world.

19-2 FLOWS OF GOODS, SERVICES, CAPITAL, AND MONEY

Not only does the U.S. Department of Commerce keep track of the total flows of goods and services in the U.S. domestic economy in its national income and product accounts (reviewed in Chapter 2), but it also is the official record keeper for U.S. international transactions. Table 19-1 summarizes international inflows and outflows during 1976, including goods and services sold by Americans to foreigners and purchased from foreigners, income earned on foreign assets, gifts and transfers, loans and borrowing, and the flows of international reserves that "pay" for any imbalance. The data in Table 19-1 are sometimes called the balance-of-payments (BOP) statistics, even though they include not only the net balance between inflows and outflows, but also the individual components of the flows.

THE CURRENT ACCOUNT

Table 19-1 is divided into three sections. The top (white) section is the **Current Account,** including flows of goods, services, and transfer payments. The middle (gray) section is the **Capital Account,** including borrowing and lending by banks and purchases of U.S. private assets by foreigners and foreign assets by U.S. individuals and by the U.S. government. The bottom (pink) section of Table 19-1 shows how the balance-of-payments (BOP) surplus or deficit is financed. The table is arranged so that the sum of all the items in the right-hand Balance column is zero. If the total of the items in the Current Account and Capital Account sections is negative, then the United States is running a BOP deficit (see line 9) and there must be an exactly equivalent positive financing item to cover the deficit (see line 12).

Every figure in Table 19-1 is preceded by a plus or minus. Plus items are credits, any transactions that provide the United States with an additional supply of foreign money. Examples of current account credits

TABLE 19-1   U.S. International Transactions, 1976 ($ Millions)

Line number	Items	Credits (+)	Debits (−)	Net credit (+) or debit (−)	Balance
	CURRENT ACCOUNT				
1.	Exports and imports of goods and services				
	a. Goods	+114,692	−123,916	− 9,224	
	b. Current services	+ 26,856	− 23,769	+ 3,087	
	c. Income on foreign assets	+ 22,654	− 12,116	+10,538	
	d. *Balance on goods and services*	+164,202	−159,801		+ 4,401
2.	Net transfers				
	a. Government grants			− 3,139	
	b. Government pensions and private remittances			− 1,866	
	c. *Net unilateral transfers*				− 5,005
3.	**Balance on current account**				− 604
	CAPITAL ACCOUNT				
4.	Long-term borrowing (+) or lending (−)	+ 12,394	− 23,767	−11,373	−11,373
5.	**Basic balance on current account and long-term capital**				−11,977
6.	Nonliquid short-term private capital flows			− 9,818	− 9,818
7.	**Liquidity balance**				−21,795
8.	Liquid foreign capital flows			+11,231	+11,231
9.	**Official reserve transactions balance**				−10,564
	METHOD OF FINANCING				
10.	Reduction in U.S. official reserve assets (+)			− 2,530	
11.	Increase in foreign official assets in the United States (+)			+13,094	
12.	**Total financing of deficit**				+10,564

Note: Line 6 includes the statistical discrepancy.
Source: Adapted from *Survey of Current Business* (March 1977), p. 44.

are exports of wheat, travel by foreigners on U.S. airlines and ships, and income earned by U.S. holdings of assets abroad (for example, the Ford Motor Company, Heinz Soup, and many other firms own factories in foreign countries). Examples of capital account credits are investments by Arab sheiks in the U.S. stock market and construction of a German-owned Volkswagen assembly plant in Pennsylvania. In each of these cases, U.S. households or firms are paid in foreign money—British pounds sterling, German marks, and many others—and a demand for dollars is created as the U.S. recipients take the foreign money they have received to their banks and turn it in for the U.S. dollars they want.

Minus items are debits, the opposite of credits, and are any transactions that provide foreigners with an additional supply of dollars. Examples of current account debits are imports of Scotch whiskey and French wine, travel by Americans on foreign-owned airlines and ships, and dividends paid to Arab sheiks who own stock in U.S. companies. Capital account debits occur when General Motors builds a factory abroad or when an American deposits funds in a Swiss bank account.

What was the situation of the United States in 1976? Total debits exceeded total credits, so that the United States ran a balance-of-payments (BOP) deficit. After we examine the main sources of the deficit, we will learn how in the bottom pink part of Table 19-1 how the United States managed to finance the excess of its supply of dollars (debits) over the demand for dollars by foreigners (credits).

The first line of Table 19-1 states that U.S. exports of goods (a credit that supplies the U.S. with foreign money) were $114,692 million, or $114.7 billion. Imports of goods exceeded exports of goods by $9,224 million. Two of the reasons the United States imported so much in 1976 were our heavy dependence on imported oil (more than $34,000 million) and automobiles ($16,400 million). The deficit in the trade of goods was more than offset by a surplus on services and income on foreign assets. Despite the large debit caused by U.S. travel abroad, a surplus was earned on current services, thanks to fees and royalties for foreign use of U.S. inventions and patents and to foreign customers of U.S. banks, insurance companies, lawyers, and other services. A surplus of more than $10 billion was earned from income on foreign assets, because U.S. investments abroad are much higher than foreign investments in the United States.

The sum of the first three lines (1a, 1b, and 1c) is called the balance on goods and services (line 1d), sometimes called **net exports** of goods and services. This balance is a component of GNP and directly contributes to production and employment.[3] The $11.9 billion deterioration in this balance that occurred between 1975 and 1976 (from $16.3 to $4.4 billion) caused just as serious a decline in production and employment as would have been caused by a drop of $11.9 billion in private investment or government spending.[4]

The United States did not retain the excess of foreign money earned from its surplus on goods and services, but gave it away in the form of transfer payments. Most of this (line 2a) was in the form of government grants, or foreign aid. The remainder consisted of a variety of items (line 2b), including government pensions to employees who have retired abroad and private remittances, including gifts from Americans to their

---

[3] Net exports were introduced as a component of GNP in section 2-5. The total amount of net exports (foreign investment) recorded in Figure 2-6 differs slightly from the balance on goods and services in Table 19-1 because of minor differences in definitions.

[4] The statement in the text needs to be qualified, because the BOP figures cited are nominal (stated in current dollars), whereas production and employment depend on real shifts in the balance on goods and services. Expressed in 1972 dollars, the real balance on goods and services deteriorated by $6.6 billion between 1975 and 1976.

children and other relatives living overseas. Transfers are flows of money without any corresponding return flow of goods and services and hence make no contribution to GNP.

The total balance in the white portion of Table 19-1 is called the balance on current account, and it summarizes all the current transactions, those which do not involve the transfer of assets or liabilities. In 1976 the U.S. current account balance was a relatively small minus number, −$604 million, in contrast to the surplus of $11,697 million earned in the previous year. Any surplus or deficit on current account must be exactly balanced by capital transactions in the gray block of the table or by financing items in the pink area. For the United States in 1976, the current account was almost in balance, so that almost all the financing was made necessary by a capital account outflow.

THE CAPITAL ACCOUNT

Foreign lending by the United States is a debit item, because we supply dollars to foreigners as we buy assets in other nations, whereas investment by foreigners in the United States is a credit item. The United States has traditionally incurred a deficit on long-term capital account (line 4) because the United States is a relatively wealthy country that is better endowed with capital than with labor. It is quite natural that the return on capital investments should be higher in other countries that have less capital and that U.S. firms would be attracted to send capital abroad to earn these high returns.[5]

Short-term capital movements refer to lending and borrowing of short duration. Examples are investments by foreigners in U.S. 90-day treasury bills (a credit) and loans by U.S. banks to finance U.S. exports (a debit). Combining lines 6 and 8, the United States in 1976 ran a slight surplus on short-term capital movements, so that the overall BOP deficit on line 9 was slightly smaller than the basic balance on line 5. Why the split between lines 6 and 8? Some experts prefer to tally up the BOP deficit excluding the effect of line 8's short-term foreign deposits in U.S. banks on the argument that these deposits are volatile and may be withdrawn at any time. A counterargument is that these deposits should not be counted as part of the U.S. BOP deficit, because they are already treated as debit items in the accounts of foreign nations, preventing the total world BOP from netting out to zero. Further, these deposits are not necessarily volatile and subject to immediate withdrawal; many are needed for commercial transactions by foreigners.

---

[5] Both free trade and free capital movements cause a redistribution of income between domestic labor and capital and between different types of U.S. workers. The nature of these redistributions is beyond the scope of this book and is treated in courses on international trade. See Richard E. Caves and Ronald Jones, *World Trade and Payments,* second ed. (Boston: Little, Brown, 1977).

SIGNIFICANCE OF THE OFFICIAL RESERVE TRANSACTIONS DEFICIT

These considerations lead to the choice of line 9 as the fundamental U.S. BOP deficit. The name **official reserve transactions** (ORT) **balance** refers to the fact that only movements of international reserves by governments and official agencies are excluded from the components of the ORT balance on lines 1 through 8. Thus any changes in international reserves serve as a means of financing the ORT deficit, as illustrated for 1976 in lines 10 and 11.

The United States holds its international reserves in two main forms, (1) gold, and (2) its reserve position at the International Monetary Fund (analogous to reserves that banks hold at the Federal Reserve). One way for the United States to cover a deficit is to draw down its holdings of gold; this method was the dominant means of financing deficits between 1957 (when the U.S. gold stock was $22.8 billion) and 1968 (by which time the gold stock had fallen to $10.9 billion). In 1976 U.S. reserve assets increased because the United States raised its reserve account at the International Monetary Fund (IMF), so that we must look elsewhere to learn how the United States financed its deficit.

The United States has an advantage over other nations, which all hold U.S. dollars as part of their international reserves. The demand for international reserve dollars by other nations allows the United States to finance its deficit in a year like 1976 without drawing down its own reserve assets. How? On line 11 foreign nations demanded $13,094 million as an addition to their official international reserves. This extra demand for dollars exceeded the excess supply of dollars created by the ORT deficit (line 9), allowing the United States to increase its own international reserves by $2,530 million (line 10).

COLLAPSE OF FIXED-EXCHANGE-RATE SYSTEM

During the last years of the fixed exchange rate system, the period between 1968 and 1973, the United States was able to run virtually any ORT deficit it desired. How? Foreign governments that had an excess supply of dollars received from the U.S. deficit, as a result of the excess of U.S. debits over credits, were prevented from cashing in their dollars for gold, because the United States in 1968 and thereafter refused to pay out any more of its gold stock. Japanese merchants could sell their excess dollars to the Japanese Central Bank in return for yen, but the Japanese Central Bank could not get rid of its excess dollars because the United States refused to accept them. To make matters worse for Japan, the increased supply of yen now held by Japanese merchants constituted an increase in the domestic money supply and added to domestic Japanese inflation.

Adjustments were necessary to eliminate the Japanese BOP surplus that provided the excess dollars. The two basic alternatives, examined later in this chapter, were to change the exchange rate between the Japanese yen and the U.S. dollar or to allow the Japanese economy to experience a higher inflation rate (which would make its exports more expensive and induce higher Japanese imports as well).

The Japanese and the Germans (they were in similar situations) attempted to postpone the necessity of changing their exchange rate with the dollar. Eventually in 1971 and 1972 these countries were so inundated with unwanted U.S. dollars that they allowed their exchange rate to appreciate.[6] By early 1973 the fixed-exchange rate system had collapsed and a new system of flexible exchange rates was introduced, which allowed exchange rates to change considerably more from day to day and month to month than previously had been acceptable. The current system does not, however, allow the exchange to fluctuate by enough to eliminate all changes in international reserves. Most countries still experience either a surplus or deficit in their balance of payments, as exhibited by the United States situation for 1976 in Table 19-1.

IS THE DEFICIT HARMFUL?

Is the U.S. BOP deficit (ORT version on line 9) harmful to the economy in any way? The very large deficits incurred in 1971–72 clearly exceeded the demand for added dollar reserves by foreign nations and had the effect of forcing extra inflation on them. But surprisingly enough, a modest BOP deficit like that incurred in 1976 is a healthy and natural phenomenon and could continue for a long time without adverse consequences. Why?

1. The method of computing the BOP statistics is misleading because the U.S. capital outflow is treated as a debit but there is no offsetting credit for the assets that U.S. individuals and firms acquire overseas. Thus at the end of 1975 the U.S. owned $304.1 billion in assets abroad, swamping the $210.5 billion of foreign holdings of U.S. assets (including dollars held as reserves).
2. Foreign holdings of U.S. dollars as international reserves can grow only if the United States runs an ORT deficit. Yet most of these deficits are caused fundamentally by the acquisition of foreign factories, stocks, and bonds by U.S. investors. Thus the United States for many years has been operating as a giant bank or financial intermediary, simultaneously borrowing from the foreign governments that hold their international reserves in the form of bank deposits and short-term government securities in the United States and lending back to foreign nations by buying up long-term foreign assets. The United States

---

[6] Japanese official holdings of dollars leaped from $3.2 billion at the end of 1970 to $16.5 billion at the end of 1972.

comes out ahead in this operation if it earns a higher rate of return on its foreign assets than it pays out in interest on its reserves.[7]

Summary: In 1976 the United States ran a deficit in its official reserve transactions balance. But this was almost entirely accounted for by a long-term capital outflow, financed by increased foreign holdings of the U.S. dollar as international reserves. This deficit did not change the net wealth of the United States, but simply its liquidity, because it involved the acquisition of long-term assets in trade for short-term liabilities.

19-3 THE MARKET FOR FOREIGN EXCHANGE

When an American tourist steps into a taxi at the London airport, the driver will expect to be paid in British currency, not American dollars or German marks. To obtain the needed British currency, the tourist must first stop at a bank (in his original U.S. airport or at the London airport upon arrival) and buy British pounds in exchange for U.S. dollars. Banks that have too much or too little of given types of foreign money can trade for what they need on the foreign exchange market. Unlike the New York Stock Exchange or the Chicago Board of Trade, where the trading takes place in a single location, the foreign exchange market consists of hundreds of dealers who sit at desks in banks, mainly in New York and London, and conduct trades by phone. In London, 256 banks are authorized to deal in foreign currencies.

The results of the trading in foreign exchange are illustrated for four foreign nations in Figure 19-1. Each section of the figure illustrates the exchange rate, expressed in terms of the price of U.S. cents per unit of foreign currency. The data expressed are quarterly, and thus they conceal additional day-to-day and month-to-month movements. Major changes occurred during the years plotted; there is a dramatic contrast between the appreciation (increased dollar price) of the West German mark and Japanese yen as compared with the depreciation (reduced dollar price) of the British pound.

Most foreign exchange trading is quoted in terms of the price of each foreign currency in dollars. It is not necessary for separate prices to be

---

[7] The hypothesis that the United States plays the role of a financial intermediary, borrowing at short term and lending at long term, was first proposed in Emile Despres, Charles P. Kindleberger, and Walter S. Salant, "The Dollar and World Liquidity: A Minority View," *Economist* (London), vol. 218 (February 5, 1966). See also Walter S. Salant, "Capital Markets and the Balance of Payments of a Financial Center," in William Fellner, Fritz Machlup, Robert Triffin, *et al., Maintaining and Restoring Balance in International Payments* (Princeton, N.J.: Princeton University Press, 1966), Chapter 14.

SINCE 1970 THE POUND HAS DEPRECIATED AGAINST THE U.S. DOLLAR;
THE MARK AND YEN HAVE APPRECIATED; AND THE CANADIAN DOLLAR
HAS FLUCTUATED WITHIN A NARROW RANGE

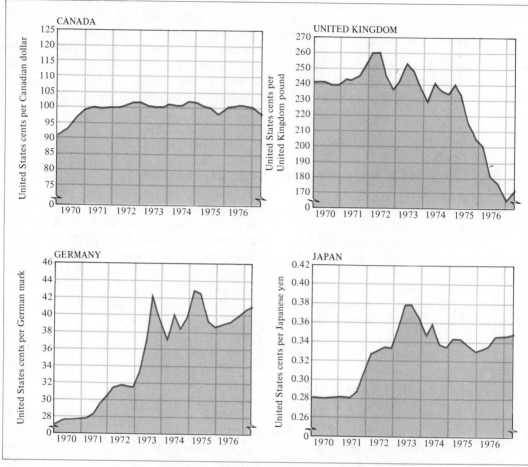

FIGURE 19–1   Foreign Exchange Rates of Four Major Industrial Nations Expressed as U.S. Cents per Unit of Foreign Currency, Quarterly, 1969–77

Each foreign exchange rate displays jagged quarter-to-quarter fluctuations, together with an overall downward or upward trend. The Canadian dollar has fluctuated within a fairly narrow range, but the other three currencies have not. The British pound plum-meted in 1975 and 1976 by about 30 percent of its 1974 value. In contrast the German mark appreciated by about 50 percent between 1970 and mid-1973, although little happened be-tween mid-1973 and early 1977. The Japanese yen followed the German pattern, although somewhat more moderately.

Source: International Financial Statistics, various issues.

set for other combinations, such as the price of pounds in terms of marks, because traders will quickly eliminate any potential profits to be made from inconsistent quotations. Can you calculate the price of marks in terms of pounds at the beginning and end of the interval shown in Figure 19-1? What was the percentage change in the mark-per-pound price?

THE DEMAND FOR AND SUPPLY OF FOREIGN EXCHANGE

The factors that determine the foreign exchange rate and influence its fluctuations can be summarized on a demand-supply diagram like that used in elementary economics to analyze many problems of price determination (for instance, the explanation of the price of wheat, real wage rate, return on capital, and other microeconomic problems). In Figure 19-2 the vertical axis measures the dollar price of the British pound, exactly the same price as is plotted in the upper right frame of Figure 19-1 for the actual 1969–77 behavior of the pound. The horizontal axis shows the number of pounds that would be demanded or supplied at different prices.

Currencies such as the U.S. dollar and the British pound are held by foreigners who find dollars or pounds more convenient or safer than their own currencies. For instance, sellers of goods or services may be willing to accept payment in dollars or pounds, but not in the Finnish markka or the Malaysian ringgit. Thus a change in the preference by holders of money for a currency such as the British pound will shift the demand curve for pounds and influence the pound's exchange rate.

All currencies, whether or not they are demanded as a means of money holding, have a demand that is created by a country's exports and a supply generated by a country's imports. Figure 19-2 and Table 19-1 are connected. The British have a balance of payments statement that contains entries for the same items as the American BOP statement in Table 19-1. British credits for exports create a demand for the pound. So too do credits generated by foreigners who invest in British factories, who repay previous loans, who send to Britain dividends and interest payments on British overseas investments, and who are attracted by high British interest rates to put money into British savings accounts and government securities. Thus the demand curve for pounds D_0 in Figure 19-2 is labeled with two of the credit items that create the demand (British exports, capital inflows). In the same way, the supply curve of pounds S_0 depends on the magnitude of the debit items—mainly British imports and capital outflows.

What explains the slopes of the demand and supply curves as drawn in Figure 19-2? Imagine that a British automobile costs 2,000 pounds. If the exchange rate is $2.00 per pound, as at point A, an American would have to pay $4,000 for the automobile. A decline in the exchange rate from $2.00 to $1.50, however, would cut the dollar price from $4,000 to $3,000 if the British domestic price remained fixed at 2,000 pounds.

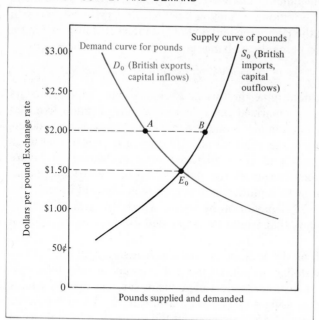

FIGURE 19–2

An Illustration of the Determination of the Price in Dollars of the British Pound Sterling

The demand curve D_0 slopes downward and to the right, reflecting the increased demand for pounds induced by depreciation (a lowering in the pound's price). The supply curve S_0 is assumed to slope upward, although this does not always occur (see text). The equilibrium price of the pound in the diagram is assumed to be $1.50, at the crossing point of the D_0 and S_0 curves.

If the demand for British automobiles in the United States is price elastic, so that a decline in price raises the quantity purchased, the demand for British pounds will rise as the exchange rate falls and the number of British automobiles purchased goes up. The demand curve D_0 would be vertical only if the price elasticity of American demand for British imports is zero, that is, completely insensitive to changes in price.

The supply curve of pounds S_0 depends on the price elasticity of British demand for imports from the United States. First, imagine that the price elasticity is zero. Will the supply curve be vertical? The answer, surprisingly, is no. Imagine that a U.S. auto sells for $3,000, and the British always buy one auto regardless of its price. Then at an exchange rate of $2.00 per pound, the British will spend 1,500 pounds on the auto (1,500 = $3,000/$2.00 per pound). But at the lower exchange rate of $1.50, an expenditure of 2,000 pounds will be necessary to obtain the same automobile (2,000 = $3,000/$1.50 per pound). Thus with a completely inelastic demand for imports, the British supply curve of pounds would have a negative slope, opposite that depicted in Figure 19-2. The supply curve will be vertical if the price elasticity of demand for imports is −1.0, so that expenditures in pounds are independent of the exchange rate.[8] Only if the price elasticity is greater than unity (in absolute value) will the supply curve slope positively, as drawn in Figure 19-2.

DETERMINATION OF FOREIGN EXCHANGE RATE

The foreign exchange rate is determined where the demand curve D_0 crosses the supply curve S_0 in Figure 19-2. As the curves are drawn, the equilibrium exchange rate is $1.50 per pound at point E_0. At a higher exchange rate, say $2.00, the supply of pounds exceeds demand by the the distance AB. British imports and capital outflows exceed the demand for pounds created by British exports and capital inflows. In order to induce foreigners to accept their pounds, the British will have to accept a lower exchange rate, $1.50. If the British government wants to maintain the higher exchange rate of $2.00, it can do so only by exchange market intervention. It must buy up the excess supply of pounds from the foreigners who have received payments in pounds from British purchasers of imports. What does the government use to obtain these pounds from foreigners? This is the purpose of its international reserves (holdings of gold and U.S. dollars). If the government does not intervene, or if it runs out of international reserves so that it cannot intervene, the foreigners holding excess pounds will sell them on the foreign exchange market, driving the price down to $1.50.

There is a possibility that the exchange market is unstable, if the supply curve is negatively sloped and flatter than the demand curve. Imagine as an example that the demand curve is vertical and the supply curve has a negative slope. At the crossing point of the two curves demand and supply are equal, but the equilibrium is not stable. Why? If the exchange rate falls slightly below the crossing point, supply will exceed demand, driving the exchange rate down continuously. In the same way an increase in the exchange rate above the crossing point will cause demand to exceed supply, driving the exchange rate up continuously.

The condition required for a decline in the exchange rate to raise the demand relative to the supply is called the Marshall-Lerner condition. It states that (ignoring the negative signs of the elasticities) the sum of

---

[8] The price elasticity of demand, a concept used in most elementary economics courses, is defined as:

$$\text{Elasticity} = \frac{\text{Percentage change in quantity}}{\text{Percentage change in price}}$$

When the elasticity is -1.0, the percentage change in quantity is equal to and opposite in sign to the change in price, so that revenue ($=$ price $\times$ quantity) does not change. For the American automobile, a drop in the exchange rate from $2.00 to $1.50 would raise the price of the car from 1,500 to 2,000 pounds, an increase in price of 33 percent and would cause a reduction in quantity purchased from 1.0 to 0.67 autos. Total British expenditure originally was 1,500 pounds (1.0 autos times 1,500 price) and in the new situation is still 1,500 pounds (0.67 autos times 2,000 price).

TABLE 19-2

	American demand elasticity for British exports	Slope of demand curve for pounds	British demand elasticity for imports	Slope of supply curve for pounds	Sum of demand and supply elasticities	Effect of drop in exchange rate on trade balance
1.	−1.0	−1.0	0.0	−1.0	−1.0	None
2.	0.0	Vertical	−1.0	Vertical	−1.0	None
3.	0.0	Vertical	0.0	−1.0	0.0	Worsens
4.	−1.0	−1.0	−1.0	Vertical	−2.0	Improves

the elasticities of the demand and supply curves must exceed 1.0.[9] If the sum of the elasticities is less than 1.0, a decline in the exchange rate will raise the supply relative to the demand and worsen the trade balance. Table 19-2 shows some examples with different combinations of elasticities of the demand and supply curves for the British case.

On line 1 both the demand curve and supply curve have the same negative slope, so that a change in the exchange rate alters supply and demand by exactly the same amount and thus has no effect on the trade balance (balance on goods and services). On line 2 the borderline situation again occurs, this time with elastic import demand and inelastic export demand. On line 3 the Marshall-Lerner condition is not satisfied; both demand elasticities are zero and the supply curve slopes negatively while the demand curve is vertical, so that a depreciation in the exchange rate raises the supply of pounds more than demand, worsening the trade balance. Finally, line 4 exhibits the favorable situation with a sum of elasticities of −2.0, so that an exchange rate depreciation raises the demand more than the supply and improves the trade balance. According to most estimates, the sum of the two elasticities does in fact exceed 1.0, so that line 4 can be considered the normal case.

Since balance of payments deficits cannot occur if governments allow the foreign exchange rate to float freely, the fact that most countries run deficits or surpluses demonstrates that their governments actively intervene in the exchange market to moderate exchange rate fluctuations. For instance, in the year ending in mid-1976 the United Kingdom ran a balance-of-payments deficit of 3,132 pounds. This means that the British government bought up 3,132 pounds by using its reserves because it was

---

[9] The Marshall-Lerner condition is named after Alfred Marshall, *The Pure Theory of Foreign Trade* (1879) and Abba P. Lerner, *The Economics of Control* (Macmillan, New York, 1946). The condition given in the text ignores the possibility of changes in the domestic prices charged by the producers of exports. For more complicated versions of the condition, see Joan Robinson, "The Foreign Exchanges," in *Essays in the Theory of Employment* (Oxford: Blackwell, 1947).

unwilling to allow the precipitous drop in the exchange rate that would have occurred without its intervention.[10] In terms of Figure 19-2, it was government intervention that caused the British to have a $2.00 exchange rate during this period, together with a balance-of-payments deficit like AB. Without government intervention, the exchange rate would have fallen well below $2.00, perhaps as far as $1.50 at point E_0, but there would have been no balance-of-payments deficit.

19-4 CASE STUDY: DETERMINANTS OF EXCHANGE RATES IN THE LONG RUN

The most important factor determining the level of exchange rates is the fact that in open economies the prices of traded goods *should be the same everywhere,* after adjustment for customs duties and the cost of transportation. This is called the **purchasing power parity (PPP) theory** of the exchange rate. It can be written as follows:[11]

GENERAL FORM

$$\text{Domestic price } (P) = \frac{\text{Foreign price } (P')}{\text{Foreign exchange rate } (F)}, \quad \text{or} \quad P = \frac{P'}{F} \quad (19.1)$$

As an example of a situation when PPP is satisfied, consider a bushel of wheat selling for $3.00 on the world market and for 2.00 pounds in Britain, with an exchange rate (F) of $1.50 per pound:

NUMERICAL EXAMPLE

$$P = \frac{P'}{F} = \frac{\$3.00}{\$1.50/\text{pound}} = 2.00 \text{ pounds}$$

If PPP were not satisfied, an unsustainable situation would be created. For instance, if the British price of wheat were only 1.50 pounds, then foreigners would be able to obtain wheat in Britain cheaper than the $3.00 world price. They would pay:

---

[10] *Economist* (London), October 16, 1976, p. 21. The deficit was financed as follows, in millions of pounds:

Reduction in international reserves	502
Borrowing from other governments, international agencies, and other sources.	2,630
Total financing of deficit	3,132

[11] A review of the theory, limitations, and applications of the PPP approach is contained in Lawrence H. Officer, "The Purchasing-Power-Theory of Exchange Rates: A Review Article," *International Monetary Fund Staff Papers,* vol. 23 (March 1976), pp. 1–60.

Price of British wheat to foreigners

$$= PF$$

$$= (1.50 \text{ pounds})\left(\frac{\$1.50}{\text{pound}}\right) = \$2.25$$

Foreigners would rush to Britain to buy up all the cheap British wheat, and the higher demand would push up the British price into equality with the $3.00 world price.

As written in equation (19.1), the PPP approach is a theory for determining the domestic price, given foreign prices and the exchange rate. But the same equation can be turned around to state the PPP theory of exchange rates:

$$F = \frac{P'}{P} \tag{19.2}$$

This states that if the world price level (P') increases faster than the domestic price level (P), there is an increase in P'/P and the exchange rate appreciates. In the wheat example, if a worldwide inflation were to raise the price of wheat from $3.00 to $4.00, but there were no inflation in Britain to alter the fixed 2.00 pound price of British wheat, the British exchange rate would increase from $1.50 per pound to $2.00 per pound:

$$F = \frac{P'}{P} = \frac{\$4.00}{2.00 \text{ pounds}} = \$2.00 \text{ per pound}$$

Exactly the opposite would occur if British prices were to rise faster than foreign prices. If British inflation were to double the price of British wheat from 2.00 to 4.00 pounds, whereas foreign prices remained fixed at $3.00, the British exchange rate would depreciate from $1.50 per pound to $0.75 per pound:

$$F = \frac{P'}{P} = \frac{\$3.00}{4.00 \text{ pounds}} = \$0.75 \text{ per pound}$$

PPP IN ACTION: 1966–76

Another way of writing (19.2) is to express the exchange rate and the two prices in terms of rates of growth, written as a lower-case letter for each variable:[12]

$$f = p' - p \tag{19.3}$$

In words, this states that the rate of change of the foreign exchange rate (f) equals the difference between the foreign inflation rate (p') and

---

[12] The growth rate of a ratio like P'/P is equal to the growth rate of the numerator (p') minus the growth rate of the denominator (p).

the domestic inflation rate (p). For Britain and the U.S., this relationship is almost exactly correct for the decade between 1966 and 1976:

	Annual rate of change of British-U.S. exchange rate		Annual rate of change of U.S. GNP deflator		Annual rate of change of British GNP deflator
Theory:	f	$=$	p'	$-$	p
Actual for U.K.:	-4.4	$\cong$	5.7	$-$	9.9

The relation does not hold exactly in each year, partly because the balance of trade is not in long-run equilibrium each year.

The PPP theory contains an essential kernel of truth, that nations that allow their domestic inflation rate (p) to exceed the world rate will experience a depreciation of their exchange rate, and vice versa. But there are numerous exceptions to the relationship, because the demand for and supply of foreign currency depends on factors other than the simple ratio of domestic and foreign aggregate price indexes. Consider the same relationship of (19.3) for Japan and the United States over the 1966–76 interval.

	Annual rate of change of Japan-U.S. exchange rate		Annual rate of change of U.S. GNP deflator		Annual rate of change of Japanese GNP deflator
Actual for Japan:	$+2.5$	$\neq$	5.7	$-$	7.4

How can we explain the appreciation of the Japanese exchange rate (dollars per yen) knowing that Japanese inflation was 7.4 percent per annum, faster than U.S. inflation? At least three crucial factors can cause the behavior of the exchange rate to differ from the simple difference between foreign and domestic inflation rates:

1. *Technology and natural resources.* Imagine that the Japanese and U.S. inflation rates were absolutely identical over some time period. Then, according to PPP, there should have been no change in the Japanese exchange rate over the same period. But imagine also that over this period the Japanese produced several new products that U.S. firms and households imported in great numbers, such as color television sets and videotape recorders, without any similar addition of new products sold by U.S. exporters. As a result there would be an increased U.S. demand for the yen to pay for the color television sets and videotape recorders and no change in the supply of yen. The price of the yen would have to increase (appreciate) to keep the foreign exchange market in equilibrium.

Discoveries of natural resources have the same effect on the exchange rate as applications of new technology. With identical inflation rates in Britain and the United States, the British exchange rate would be bound to appreciate as a result of the discovery of oil in the North Sea. British oil imports would fall, cutting the supply of pounds, and Britain might eventually be able to export some of its oil, raising the demand for pounds.

2. *Capital movements.* The exchange rate depends not just on the products exported and imported by a country, but also on the demand for its money by foreigners. Customers from all over the world send funds to Switzerland for deposit in anonymous numbered bank accounts. Why? Because tax authorities cannot identify the owners of the accounts, making such deposits attractive to criminals, tax evaders, and other individuals who are eager to keep their financial operations secret. Partly as a result, Switzerland enjoyed a substantial appreciation of its exchange rate over the 1966–76 decade, despite a rate of inflation approximately equal to that of the United States:

	Annual rate of change of Swiss-U.S. exchange rate		Annual rate of change of U.S. GNP deflator		Annual rate of change of Swiss GNP deflator
Actual for Switzerland:	+5.7	≠	5.7	−	6.4

A nation with an attractive currency, such as Switzerland, can enjoy a low rate of domestic inflation because the higher prices of imports charged by foreigners is offset by exchange-rate appreciation, which makes a growing number of dollars available per Swiss franc. But problems are created for exporters, such as producers of Swiss watches. Export prices in dollars will tend to increase at the Swiss domestic inflation rate (6.4 percent per annum between 1966 and 1976) plus the growth rate of the exchange rate (a 5.7 percent change per annum in the dollars needed to purchase one Swiss franc).

3. *Government policy.* Even if there are no changes in technology, no discoveries of natural resources, and no capital movements, the PPP relationship of equation (19.3) still may not hold. Governments can interfere in several ways. First, a trade surplus generated by low domestic inflation may not cause an appreciation if the government gives the surplus away by supporting a large defense establishment overseas or by making large grants of foreign aid to other nations. Such government actions partly explain why the United States ran an overall balance-of-payments deficit in the early 1960s despite a large trade surplus and a low domestic in-

flation rate. Second, a government facing a trade surplus may decide to stimulate the domestic demand for imports by cutting customs duties. Third, a government may try to prevent the exchange rate from appreciating by barring or taxing capital inflows, a tactic used by Germany in the early 1970s. In contrast, the United States in the 1960s tried partially to offset a balance-of-payments deficit, caused mainly by Vietnam war spending, by taxing capital outflows.

All these factors can interfere with the operation of the PPP relationship, but they do not change the basic validity of its prediction that, under a *flexible* exchange rate system, a nation that allows its domestic inflation rate to accelerate relative to foreign inflation will experience a depreciation in its exchange rate. Under a *fixed* exchange rate system, a nation that allows its domestic inflation rate to accelerate relative to foreign inflation will experience a growing deficit in its balance of trade. Eventually the government will be unable to sustain the exchange rate at an artificially high level and a devaluation will be forced, like that of Britain in 1967 when the pound was allowed to drop from $2.80 to $2.40.

19-5 DETERMINANTS OF EXCHANGE RATES IN THE SHORT RUN

INELASTIC SHORT-RUN SUPPLY AND DEMAND

Why do governments intervene to limit the fluctuations of their exchange rates rather than allowing the exchange rate to adjust freely according to PPP? The basic problem is that without government intervention drastic up-and-down movements in exchange rates may be necessary to equate demand and supply in the short run, and these fluctuations in turn can cause undesirable movements in domestic prices and output. The most important cause of large fluctuations in exchange rates is the low elasticity of demand for imports and exports, particularly in the short run.

A nation may face two sets of demand and supply curves for foreign exchange. In the short run the supply and demand elasticities may be close to zero, but in the long run the elasticities may be substantial. The transition from the short run to the long run is illustrated in Figure 19-3. The demand and supply curves indicated by the solid lines, D_1 and S_1', are valid in the long run. At an initial exchange rate of $1.50, Britain is running a trade deficit shown by the distance between the D_1 and S_1' curves, the distance $E_0 F$. After enough time has passed, the British trade deficit can be eliminated at point E_1 if the exchange rate is allowed to decline to $1.25.

But what happens in the short run, before British producers have time to increase their production of exports and import substitutes? The rele-

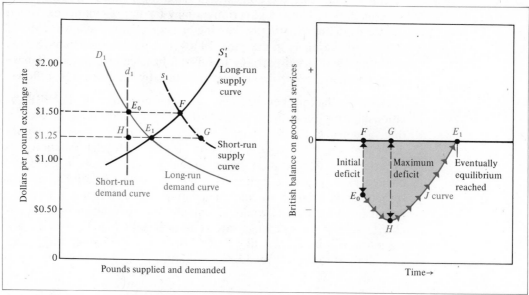

FIGURE 19-3   Response of the Balance on Goods and Services to a Devaluation in the Exchange Rate from $1.50 to $1.25, in Both the Short Run and the Long Run

Initially we assume that intervention by the British government holds the exchange rate at $1.50 in the left frame. The trade deficit will be the distance between the solid red demand curve D_1 and the solid black supply curve S_1', or the distance E_0F. In the long run an equilibrium with a zero trade balance can be obtained at an exchange rate of $1.25, but, in the short run, the trade balance will get worse when the exchange rate drops from $1.50 to $1.25. Because demand and supply are inelastic, the short-run curves are the dashed lines d_1 and s_1, and the trade balance widens to the distance HG. The right frame shows the evolution of the trade balance over time, at first widening from E_0F (now plotted in the vertical direction) to HG, and then disappearing at point E_1.

vant schedules reflecting inelastic short-run demand and supply are the dashed red d_1 and dashed black s_1 curves. A decline in the exchange rate to $1.25 will widen the trade deficit to the distance HG, the distance between d_1 and s_1. No reduction in the exchange rate, no matter how drastic, can bring the trade deficit into balance in the short run. The British government will be forced to intervene to keep the exchange rate from falling below $1.25 by buying up the excess pounds that foreigners have obtained from the import purchases of British firms. Only by patient waiting will the needed improvement in the trade balance occur. If the exchange rate is held at $1.25 by the government, the demand and supply curves will slowly change their shape. The s_1 curve will pivot clockwise until it becomes the S_1' curve. The d_1 curve will pivot counterclockwise until it becomes the D_1 curve. And the trade balance will gradually shrink from the large amount HG to zero at point E_1.

The right frame of Figure 19-3 illustrates the evolution of the trade balance as time passes. Now the trade balance is plotted in a vertical rather than in a horizontal direction. The initial trade balance is the distance E_0F. After the exchange rate depreciates to \$1.25, at first the trade balance widens to the distance HG, and then it narrows to eventually reach zero at E_1. The red line running between E_0, H, and E_1 has the shape of the capital letter J, tipped over on its side. Thus the situation of a trade balance that deteriorates in the short run following a depreciation in the exchange rate is called the **J curve phenomenon.**[13]

Summary: The J curve phenomenon partly explains why the world-wide flexible exchange rate system in the 1970s has exhibited such sharp short-run changes in exchange rates. Small changes in the supply and demand curves for foreign exchange may require drastic changes in exchange rates in the short run. The actual value of the exchange rate then depends on the extent of government intervention. Since governments quite frequently may change their idea of the correct long-run equilibrium exchange rate, the rate at which they intervene is likely to be quite variable. Finally, private speculators also form expectations about the exchange rate, and they will raise their demand for a currency that they think is about to appreciate.

MAJOR EXCHANGE RATE MOVEMENTS IN THE 1970s

The major sources of long-run changes in exchange rates are: differences among countries in the development of technology and natural resources; differences in inflation rates; and the differing attractiveness of various currencies for investors of funds. Since each of these three sources tends to change gradually over the course of time, why can't governments simply intervene and peg the exchange rate to the slowly evolving long-run equilibrium rate? Were the wide swings in the exchange rates depicted in Figure 19-1 for the 1970s really necessary?

The trouble is that no one, either inside the government or in the private sector, has discovered a reliable way to figure out what the exchange rate should be. Expectations of future exchange rates, as reflected in the forward exchange rate negotiated for future sales and pur-

---

[13] Recent evidence on the J curve is presented in Rudiger Dornbusch and Paul Krugman, "Flexible Exchange Rates in the Short Run," *Brookings Papers on Economic Activity,* vol. 7, no. 3 (1976), especially on pp. 558–66. The authors conclude that "there is a significant price responsiveness, but adjustment lags are important and run to years, not quarters" (p. 566).

chases of foreign exchange 90 or 180 days in the future, have been extremely inaccurate estimates of the actual outcome. The main theories of exchange-rate determination do not seem to work. The purchasing-power parity (PPP) theory states, for instance, that when the German inflation rate is one percentage point slower than the U.S. inflation rate, the German mark should appreciate at a rate of 1 percent per year. Yet Figure 19-1 reveals fluctuations in the dollar-mark rate of 15–20 percent in one direction, followed by a reversal.

If the government cannot estimate the right equilibrium value of the exchange rate, it does not know how to conduct a policy to stabilize the exchange rate in the short run at the correct equilibrium rate. Nor do private speculators who buy and sell foreign currencies appear to have any better idea. As Henry Wallich, a Governor of the Federal Reserve System, described the problem:

> The market certainly knows a wrong rate when it sees one. As for the "right rate," there seems to be a rather wide range upon which views are quite loosely held. This is evidenced, for instance, by the way in which spot and distant forward rates often move together, although the facts affecting the spot rate today might seem to be irrelevant to the spot rate in a distant future. There seems to be little of the stabilizing speculation that theoreticians have relied upon to push rates back to equilibrium after they have been knocked off balance.[14]

The failure of private speculators to maintain the day-to-day exchange rate at the equilibrium value does not constitute an automatic argument for intervention by government. Governments appear to be no better at forecasting than private dealers. Further, heavy intervention tempts governments to maintain a disequilibrium exchange rate to try to achieve other policy goals. In early 1977, for instance, both Germany and Japan attempted to keep their exchange rates from appreciating, despite massive trade surpluses. Then in the summer of 1977, under pressure from U.S. officials, the value of the German mark and Japanese yen was finally allowed to rise. Three economists associated with the U.S. Treasury Department have recently concluded:

> Historical experience clearly demonstrates the relevant choice is neither between imperfect markets and ideal government speculation nor between ideal private market speculation and misguided government intervention, but between imperfect private and imperfect government speculation.[15]

---

[14] Henry Wallich, "What Makes Exchange Rates Move?" *Challenge*, vol. 20 (July/August 1977), p. 40.

[15] Dennis Logue, Richard Sweeney, and Thomas D. Willett, "Speculative Behavior of Foreign Exchange Rates During the Current Float," U.S. Department of the Treasury, Assistant Secretary for International Affairs Research Office, Discussion Paper 77/2, p. 19.

19-6 BALANCE-OF-PAYMENTS ADJUSTMENT WITH FIXED EXCHANGE RATES

So far we have examined determinants of the foreign exchange rate in the long run and short run, but we have not paid any attention to interactions between the exchange rate, the balance of payments, and the domestic level of output and employment. For this analysis it is useful to return once again to the *IS-LM* curve diagrams developed in Part II. It is possible to superimpose on the *IS-LM* diagram a balance-of-payments line (*BP*), which shows the relationship of the balance of payments to the domestic interest rate and real output. This allows us to analyze the effects on the economy and balance of payments of changes in monetary policy, fiscal policy, and the foreign exchange rate.

THE *BP* CURVE

The U.S. balance of payments is divided in Table 19-1 into three sections: (1) the current account, (2) the capital account, and (3) financing items. The balance of payments (BOP) is said to be in equilibrium when the financing items equal zero, implying that the balance on current account exactly cancels the balance on capital account. For instance, the overall BOP can be in equilibrium when there is a current account surplus and equivalent capital account deficit, or vice versa. When the current account and capital account do not cancel each other, there is an overall BOP surplus or deficit. An overall BOP surplus is financed by an inflow of international reserves, which consist of gold and certain important foreign currencies, particularly the U.S. dollar. An overall BOP deficit is financed by paying out reserves or by borrowing from other countries or from international agencies.

How are the current account and capital account related to the domestic economy?

The current account consists of exports and imports of goods and services and unilateral transfers. Three of the most important determinants of the current account balance are the level of domestic output (Q), the domestic price level relative to the foreign price level (P/P'), and the foreign exchange rate (F). When the price ratio P/P' and the exchange rate (F) are fixed, then an increase in domestic output causes the current account to deteriorate. Why? Export sales depend on output in other countries and are thus independent of domestic real output. But purchases of imports depend on domestic real output, because people buy more of all types of goods, both domestic and imported, when their real income (Q) increases.

The capital account includes both long-term and short-term capital flows. Many firms and individuals have a choice about the location of

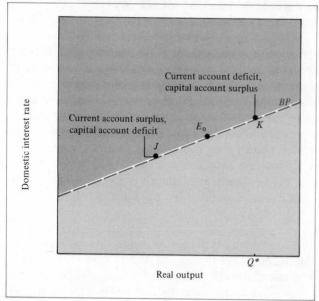

FIGURE 19–4   The BP Curve, Showing Different Combinations of Domestic Output (Q) and the Domestic Interest Rate (r) Where the Balance of Payments Is in Equilibrium

In the gray area the balance of payments is in surplus, and in the pink area, there is a deficit. Points J, E_0, K, and every other point along the red dashed BP line represent situations of balance-of-payments equilibrium. At point J real output is low, depressing imports and leading to a current-account surplus. To offset this, the capital account must be in deficit, which can occur if the domestic interest rate is low and funds flow abroad seeking a higher interest return. At point K real output is high, raising imports and causing a current-account deficit. To offset this, a high domestic interest rate is required to attract sufficient foreign funds to generate a capital-account surplus.

their bank accounts and holdings of short-term securities. If no changes in foreign exchange rates are expected, then investors will shift their funds to countries that have the highest interest rates.

The dashed red BP curve drawn through points J, E_0, and K in Figure 19-4 shows all the combinations of the interest rate (r) and real output (Q) consistent with overall balance-of-payments equilibrium. In the gray area above the BP line, the balance of payments is in surplus because an increase in the interest rate causes an increased capital inflow. In the pink area below the BP line, the balance of payments is in deficit, because a decrease in the interest rate leads to a smaller capital inflow or increased outflow. If policymakers want to avoid losing their international reserves, they must keep the economy out of the pink area. But if they want to avoid building up extra reserves that are not needed, they must keep the economy out of the gray area.

Everywhere along the BP line the balance of payments is in equilibrium. At point J real output is relatively low, so that imports are low and the current account is in surplus. To offset this, and keep the overall balance (the sum of the current and capital account) equal to zero, the capital account must run a deficit. This adjustment requires a relatively low interest rate, so that funds will flow abroad to seek a higher return. Point K illustrates the opposite situation. Relatively high real output pulls in imports and causes the current account to run a deficit. To offset the deficit, the capital account must run a surplus, requiring a relatively high interest rate to attract funds from abroad. At point E_0, an intermediate situation, both the current and capital accounts are balanced, as is the overall balance of payments.

As with any market equilibrium curve in this book, we must ask several questions about BP to understand it fully:

1. *What makes BP slope upward?* The BP line has a positive slope because higher interest rates improve the capital account, requiring higher income to make the current account deteriorate by the offsetting amount needed to keep the overall balance of payments in equilibrium. If capital is perfectly mobile, all of it flows out of the country if the domestic interest rate should fall even slightly below the foreign interest rate, say r'. And if the domestic interest rate rises even slightly above the foreign interest rate r' when capital is perfectly mobile, the country is flooded with capital inflows. Thus in the case of perfect capital mobility, the BP line would be horizontal and lie at the level of the foreign interest rate r'.

   At the other extreme, if capital is completely immobile, there is no capital account at all. The overall balance of payments can be in equilibrium only when the current account is balanced. In this case the dashed red BP curve will be a vertical line running through E_0.

2. *What causes the BP curve to shift its position?* As is true of all diagrams, the BP equilibrium curve will shift if there is a change in any variable other than those plotted on the axes in the upper right frame, the interest rate (r) and real output (Q). For instance, the BP line in Figure 19-4 is drawn on the assumption that both the ratio of domestic to foreign prices (P/P') and the exchange rate (F) are fixed. A decline in P/P' will make domestic goods cheaper and improve the trade balance for any given level of output, thus moving the BP line to the right. This shift in BP increases the size of the gray surplus area and raises the payments surplus at every level of output. In the same way, a depreciation in the exchange rate will shift the BP line rightward.[16] And an appreciation of the exchange rate will shift BP to the left.

Government intervention can also cause the BP curve to shift. Anything that improves the current account for a given value of real output

---

[16] The rightward shift in BP will occur only after the temporary J curve deterioration in the current account has ended and the current account has begun to improve.

(Q) will shift the BP curve to the right. In addition to a reduction in the price ratio (P/P') or the exchange rate (F), a rightward shift in BP can be caused by an increase in customs duties on imports or subsidies to exports. Similarly, anything that improves the capital account at a given interest rate will shift the BP line rightward. Examples are taxes or prohibitions on capital outflows.

BALANCE-OF-PAYMENTS ADJUSTMENT WITH A FIXED PRICE LEVEL AND EXCHANGE RATE

Figure 19-4 provides no information on precisely what the economy's level of real output, interest rate, and its balance of payments will be. The BP equilibrium curve merely shows numerous possible combinations of output and the interest rate that are compatible with balance-of-payments equilibrium. Which of these combinations will occur? In Chapter 4 we learned that the economy's level of real output and interest rate occurs at the intersection of its commodity market and money market equilibrium schedules, the IS and LM curves. Now in Figure 19-5 we combine the new BP curve with IS and LM curves to determine where the economy will operate and how it will adjust to balance-of-payments surplus or deficit.

The BP equilibrium curve from Figure 19-4 is drawn again in the left frame of Figure 19-5 and is labeled BP_0. The red IS_0 line shows all the combinations of real output and the interest rate compatible with equilibrium in the commodity market. Earlier we learned that expansive fiscal policy can move the IS curve to the right. In addition, because the balance of payments on current account (net of transfer payments) is part of the demand for commodities, or expenditures on GNP, anything that improves the current account balance for a given level of real output will shift the IS curve to the right. One such event would be a decrease in domestic prices relative to foreign prices (P/P') — this would raise the domestic production of export goods and cut imports. Similarly, a depreciation in the exchange rate would stimulate the current account balance and shift the IS curve rightward.[17]

In Figure 19-5 three LM curves are drawn. Each shows different combinations of real output and the interest rate at which the demand for and supply of money are equal. Recall that the position of the LM curve depends on the size of the real money supply, that is, on the ratio of the nominal money supply (M^s) to the price level (P). An increase in M^s/P shifts the LM curve to the right, and vice versa. Whereas in earlier chapters the money supply was determined solely by decisions of the Federal Reserve, now in addition the size of the money supply and hence the position of the LM curve depend on the balance of payments.

---

[17] The elementary theory of income determination in an open economy with exports and imports is reviewed in the Appendix to Chapter 3.

IN AN OPEN ECONOMY MONETARY POLICY MAY BE UNABLE TO ACHIEVE NATURAL OUTPUT
WITHOUT THE COOPERATION OF FISCAL POLICY

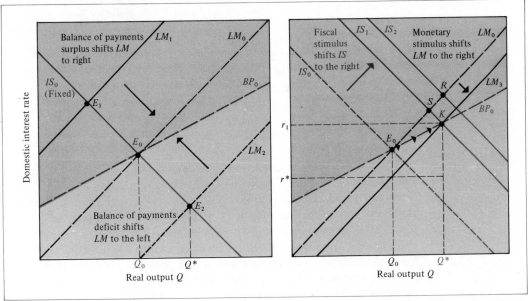

FIGURE 19–5   Adjustment of the Balance of Payments with a Fixed Price Level and Exchange Rate

In the left frame the economy automatically gravitates to point E_0, where the balance of payments is in equilibrium along the BP_0 line and the money and commodity markets are also in equilibrium along LM_0 and IS_0. The money supply will adjust automatically through gains or losses of international reserves to reach E_0 from any other starting point like E_1 or E_2. In the right frame a coordinated monetary and fiscal expansion can keep the balance of payments in equilibrium and at the same time achieve the natural level of output Q^* at point K.

Let us assume that the economy is initially at point E_1 in the left frame, at the intersection of the fixed red IS_0 line and the black LM_1 money market line. Because E_1 lies in the gray area above the BP curve, the balance of payments is in surplus, and the central bank adds to its holdings of international reserves. For the United States, these extra international reserves might be in the form of gold. For other countries, the extra reserves might be in the form of gold or dollars. Either way, the assets of the central bank are increased, which tends to increase the money supply and thus shift the LM curve to the right.[18] The rightward shift in LM

---

[18] In Chapter 16 we learned that the money supply is a multiple of high-powered money, which with a few minor adjustments equals the assets of the central bank (the Federal Reserve in the United States). The assets of the central bank consist mainly of domestic

(continued)

will continue until the balance-of-payments surplus is eliminated, which occurs when the *LM* curve crosses the *BP* line at point E_0.

Exactly the opposite shift in *LM* occurs if the economy begins at point E_2 (the crossing point of IS_0 with LM_2), which lies in the pink area where the balance of payments is in deficit. The central bank finances the deficit by supporting the current foreign exchange rate of its own currency, using up some of its international reserves. The loss of reserves cuts the assets of the central banks and thus reduces the money supply, shifting the *LM* curve leftward from LM_2 back toward LM_0. The shift in *LM* continues until the drain of international reserves stops, which occurs only when the balance of payments returns to equilibrium along the *BP* line at point E_0.

The shift in the *LM* curve that achieves balance-of-payments equilibrium occurs automatically, without policymakers doing anything. What remains for policymakers to do? The noteworthy fact about the equilibrium position E_0 is that output Q_0 is undesirably low, lying well below the natural output level Q^*. How can expansive monetary or fiscal policy simultaneously achieve the high level of output Q^* together with balance-of-payments equilibrium along the *BP* line? Clearly, monetary policy is impotent. Starting from equilibrium at point E_0 along the LM_0 curve, any expansion in the money supply will push *LM* to the right toward LM_2. But this will just cause a loss in international reserves that will push *LM* back leftward to LM_0 again.

> *In an open economy with fixed prices and exchange rates, monetary expansion is impotent to achieve natural output (Q^*) from a starting point like E_0 for more than a short transition period. Open-market purchases by the central bank will raise the money supply only temporarily, but then will lead to losses of international reserves that brings the money supply back to its original value.*[19]

government bonds and international reserves (gold in the United States, gold and dollars elsewhere). In principle a central bank can prevent the money supply from rising in response to an inflow of international reserves resulting from a balance of payments surplus. How? There are several methods of "sterilizing" a reserve inflow, of which the most obvious is an open-market sale of government bonds. If reserves increase by $1 billion, then a $1 billion sale of bonds cancels any effect on high-powered money or the money supply. Another method would be for the central bank to raise legal reserve requirements of the commercial banks, which tends to cut the number of dollars of money supply that can be created per dollar of high-powered money. Many foreign central banks are limited in their ability to sterilize by open-market sales because their portfolios of government bonds are relatively small and they have been reluctant to change bank reserve requirements.

[19] A corollary is that any country with a balance of payments problem has only itself to blame. Just as an expansion in holdings of domestic bonds by the central bank (accomplished through open market purchases) causes a loss of reserves, so a country can accumulate extra reserves by reducing its holdings of domestic bonds. An extreme version of this theory with perfect capital mobility and instantaneous equality between foreign and domestic prices implies that the central bank has no control at all over its own money

If monetary policy cannot achieve an increase in output because of the leak of international reserves abroad, then economic expansion requires a fiscal stimulus. In the right frame of Figure 19-5 we continue to assume that the price level and the exchange rate are fixed. Nevertheless the natural output level Q^* can be achieved at point K, where the balance of payments is in equilibrium.[20] It is not enough for fiscal policy alone to stimulate the economy. A rightward shift in the IS curve to position IS_2 will achieve the desired increase in output to point R, where real output is at its natural level Q^*. But R lies in the gray area above the BP line, indicating a balance-of-payments surplus. Point K is superior because not only is natural output achieved, but the balance of payments is in equilibrium as well. Point K lies at the intersection of the IS_1 and LM_3 schedules and can be reached from a starting point of E_0 by a combined fiscal stimulus that shifts the IS curve from IS_0 to IS_1, together with a monetary stimulus to shift the LM curve from LM_0 to LM_3.[21]

Although expansive fiscal policy is essential for the simultaneous achievement of natural output (Q^*) and a balance-of-payments equilibrium, nevertheless point K in Figure 19-5 may not be the best possible situation. The fiscal policy stimulus requires some combination of a cut in tax rates or an increase in government expenditure, raising the government deficit. The higher government deficit (an increase in the supply of government bonds relative to the demand for them) pushes up the interest rate and allows the economy to enjoy a higher level of output without a deterioration in the balance of payments. But at the same time some private investment may be crowded out, leading to a situation at point K with too much government spending and private consumption or both and too little private investment.

In drawing our positively sloped BP line, we have assumed that capital is only imperfectly mobile between nations. The BP curve is a horizontal line at the level of the world interest rate if capital is perfectly mobile because a domestic interest rate even a fraction higher than the world interest rate would cause an infinite amount of capital to flood in. This result is illustrated by the BP_1 line in Figure 19-6. In this case a fiscal expansion from IS_0 to IS_1' can push the economy to natural output (Q^*) along the horizontal BP line. The money supply will be lifted automati-

---

supply. See Harry G. Johnson, "The Monetary Approach to Balance-of-Payments Theory," in Jacob A. Frenkel and Harry G. Johnson (eds.), *The Monetary Approach to the Balance of Payments* (Toronto: University of Toronto Press, 1976). See also Harry G. Johnson, "The Monetary Approach to Balance of Payments Theory: A Diagrammatic Analysis," *The Manchester School,* vol. 43 (September 1976), pp. 220–74.

[20] Turn back to Figure 19-4, where an identical point K is plotted.

[21] If monetary and fiscal expansion are applied simultaneously, then the economy can move immediately from the initial position E_0 to the desired point K. If fiscal policy is applied alone, K is reached in two stages. First fiscal policy expands the economy to point S, where a balance-of-payments surplus causes international reserves to flow in; this in turn gradually raises the money supply and shifts the economy from S to K.

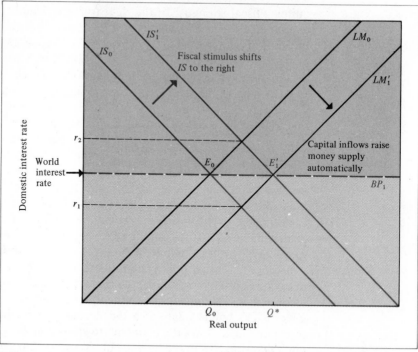

FIGURE 19–6

Effect of a Fiscal Stimulus on Real Output and the Interest Rate When Capital Is Perfectly Mobile

Now the BP line is horizontal. Why? With perfectly mobile capital even the slightest increase in the domestic interest rate above the world interest rate causes capital to flood in. The balance of payments can be in equi-librium only when the domestic interest rate is exactly equal to the world interest rate, as along the flat BP_1 line. Now a fiscal stimulus which moves IS rightward from IS_0 to IS_1' can raise real output without increasing the interest rate. Inflows of capital provide international reserves which boost the money supply, shifting LM rightward from LM_0 to LM_1'.

cally by capital movements from LM_0 to LM_1' to prevent any increase in the domestic interest rate. As a result there is no crowding-out effect and the full Chapter 3 investment multiplier occurs.

In the case of imperfectly mobile capital illustrated in the right frame of Figure 19-5, the interest rate at point K increases compared to the initial interest rate at E_0. In the case of perfectly mobile capital (Figure 19-6) with a horizontal BP line, the interest rate is not affected by a fiscal expansion designed to raise output to the natural level at E_1'. But what if a lower interest rate is desired? Let us assume that the interest rate designated r^* in Figure 19-5 is necessary to achieve the right blend of consumption, investment, and government spending. How can the lower interest rate r^* be reached, while maintaining natural output (Q^*) and an equilibrium in the balance of payments?

BALANCE-OF-PAYMENTS ADJUSTMENT WITH FLEXIBLE PRICES AND A FIXED EXCHANGE RATE

The first method of improving the situation should be familiar. As in many areas of macroeconomics, problems tend to disappear if the price level is perfectly flexible. The beneficial effects of a drop in the domestic price level relative to foreign prices (P/P') are illustrated in Figure 19-7. Once again we assume that capital is only imperfectly mobile, so that the BP curve slopes upward. Each of the three curves (IS, LM, and BP) is affected by the drop in prices. First, lower prices make exports more attractive to foreigners and also cause domestic purchasers to switch from imports to domestically produced goods. The balance on goods and services (part of GNP) improves. This extra injection of spending shifts the IS curve rightward from IS_0 to IS_0'. Similarly, the improvement in the current account shifts the BP line rightward from BP_0 to BP_0'. Finally, the position of the LM curve depends on the ratio of the nominal money supply (M^s) to the price level (P). With lower prices M^s/P rises and the LM curve shifts rightward from LM_0 to LM_0'.

The economy's new equilibrium position is at point E_0', with a higher output and lower interest rate than at the initial E_0. Two automatic mechanisms guarantee that the three curves will all cross at the new position E_0'. First, the phrase price flexibility means that the price level will continue to fall until the economy reaches its natural output level Q^*. This makes the IS_0' and BP_0' curves shift rightward until they cross at the natural output level Q^*. Second, the LM curve must cross point E_0'. If not, the balance of payments will be in surplus or deficit and the nominal money supply will expand or contract until the LM curve reaches E_0'.

Thus flexible prices can achieve natural output automatically, without any need for a coordinated monetary-fiscal expansion, as was necessary in the right frame of Figure 19-5. This is the same conclusion reached in Chapter 6 for a closed economy: When the price level is perfectly flexible, policymakers can "go fishing" with the assurance that the price level will automatically adjust to keep actual real output at the natural level Q^*. The only remaining role for policymakers is to choose the desired interest rate. If the optimal interest rate is r^* in Figure 19-7, but flexible prices push the interest rate to r_0', a combination of fiscal restraint and monetary stimulus can push the economy to the best position of all, E^*. Price flexibility will work to keep the balance of payments in equilibrium at E^*.

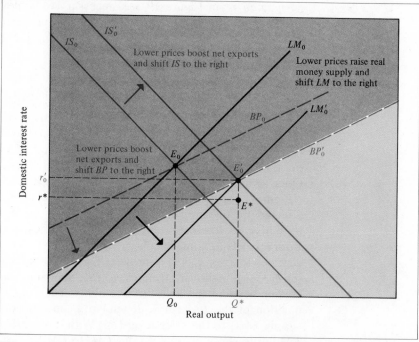

FIGURE 19–7   Effect on Real Output, the Interest Rate, and the Balance of Payments of a Decline in Domestic Prices Relative to Foreign Prices (P/P')
Lower prices cause all three curves to shift to the right. More exports will be sold, and fewer imports bought, which raises the current account balance. This shifts both IS and BP rightward. And the lower price level raises the real money supply (M^s/P), thus shifting the LM curve rightward.

In contrast, if capital is perfectly mobile and the BP curve is a horizontal line, as in Figure 19-6, there is no role for policymakers at all. The interest rate is fixed at the level of the world interest rate. Starting out from the lower output level at point E_0, flexible prices by themselves will guarantee that the economy will reach natural output (Q^*) at point E_1'. The drop in prices will shift the IS curve right as export sales are stimulated and import sales are inhibited. And the reduction in the price level will raise the real money supply and shift LM rightward until the economy reaches E_1'.

19-7 THE ROLE OF POLICY UNDER FLEXIBLE EXCHANGE RATES

EFFECTS ON REAL OUTPUT

If we continue to assume perfect capital mobility, Figure 19-6 is equally relevant for an analysis of the economy's adjustment when the foreign exchange rate is flexible. Whereas previously a monetary expansion was impotent, because a rightward shift from LM_0 to LM_1' would cause a capital outflow and a loss of international reserves, this no longer happens under flexible exchange rates. There is no automatic influence of a balance-of-payments deficit or surplus on the money supply because the flexibility of exchange rates keeps the balance of payments in equilibrium at all times.

On the contrary, monetary policy becomes a potent policy tool with flexible exchange rates. Initially, an increase in the nominal money supply shifts LM rightward from LM_0 to LM_1'. But this in turn induces a capital outflow, because the interest rate is pushed down in the short run to r_1 by a monetary expansion. The capital outflow cuts the exchange rate, which in turn stimulates the balance on goods and services; this increase in exports relative to imports shifts the IS curve rightward from IS_0 to IS_1'.

Although flexible exchange rates make monetary policy more potent than under fixed exchange rates, fiscal policy becomes less potent. In Figure 19-6 a fiscal expansion will initially shift the IS curve to the right. But the temporary increase in the interest rate to r_2 will induce a capital inflow and an appreciation of the exchange rate. Exports will become more expensive and their sales will fall. Imports will become more attractive. This decline in net exports (exports minus imports) will shift the IS curve backward toward IS_0. Since this process will continue as long as the interest rate is above the world interest rate, we conclude that in an open economy with a flexible exchange rate fiscal policy loses control of the IS curve.

The only effect of a fiscal expansion is on foreign countries, which enjoy an increase in net exports and domestic income as a result of the appreciation in the currency of the country illustrated in Figure 19-6. In the same way, the potency of monetary expansion under flexible exchange rates is offset by the negative effect on net exports and domestic income in foreign countries. The influence of a monetary expansion will be transmitted abroad if foreign nations react by raising their own money supplies. Thus the effect of monetary expansion, taking into account the reaction of other nations, may be to induce a worldwide expansion of the money supply. Since the world is a closed economy, a worldwide monetary expansion would then have exactly the same effects as those analyzed in Chapters 7 and 8. There would be an expansion in both output and the price level if the worldwide economy were initially below the natural level of output (Q^*); but a monetary expansion that occurs when the economy is initally at Q^* would have only an inflationary effect with only a transitory boost to real output.

THE OPEN-ECONOMY PHILLIPS CURVE

How does a system of flexible exchange rates affect the choice of policymakers in the United States and other large countries between monetary and fiscal expansion in situations when output is low and unemployment is high? In the real world fiscal expansion is not completely impotent. Though a rightward shift in the *IS* curve does tend to raise the real interest rate, attract foreign capital, and thus lead to an appreciation of the exchange rate, it may take a substantial length of time for the appreciation to cut net exports by enough to offset the effect of the fiscal expansion. Just as the *J*-curve phenomenon in Section 19-5 suggests that a nation's trade balance may improve temporarily following a depreciation in the exchange rate, so it also implies that a fiscal expansion, which causes an exchange-rate appreciation, may temporarily improve the trade balance.

Because fiscal expansion tends to cause the exchange rate to appreciate and monetary expansion causes a depreciation, domestic policymakers find that the short-run Phillips-curve relationship between inflation and unemployment now depends on the type of stimulus chosen. Previously in the closed-economy analysis of Chapter 8 the short-run increase in inflation associated with a given reduction in unemployment did not depend on the choice of policy instruments. Consider in Figure 19-8 an economy starting at point A, with an unemployment rate well above the natural unemployment rate. The black short-run Phillips curve corresponds to our previous analysis of the closed economy and shows the short-run increase in inflation that will be induced by a policy stimulus that reduces unemployment by a given amount, say to point B.

The same reduction in unemployment will have a different inflationary effect in an open economy with flexible exchange rates. A fiscal expansion, which causes the exchange rate to appreciate, will tend to moderate the inflationary effect of the same reduction in unemployment. Why? An appreciation means that domestic residents have to pay fewer units of their own currency to buy an imported good selling for a given number of units of foreign currency. A Mercedes-Benz selling for 45,000 marks costs an American $22,500 if a dollar buys only 2 marks, but the dollar price drops to $15,000 if suddenly the dollar appreciates to a rate of 3 marks per dollar. The effect of the appreciation alters not only the prices of imports, but also the dollar prices of some exports and some domestically produced goods that compete with imports. A reduction in unem-

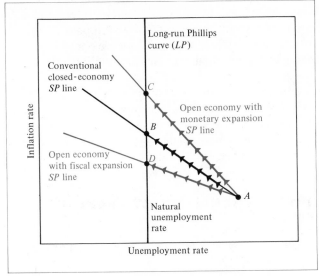

FIGURE 19–8   Comparison of Conventional Closed Economy Short-run Phillips Curve with Two Alternative Curves for an Open Economy with Flexible Exchange Rates

In a closed economy a reduction in unemployment starting from point A causes inflation to increase along the path marked by the arrows between A and B. In an open economy with flexible exchange rates a reduction in unemployment generated by fiscal expansion causes the exchange rate to appreciate and the inflation rate to be moderated by smaller price increases of imports and exports. A monetary expansion has the opposite effect, causing the exchange rate to depreciate, prices of exports and imports to rise, and domestic inflation to accelerate relative to the closed-economy case.

ployment now in the short-run pushes the economy along the red path from A to D in Figure 19-8.

A monetary stimulus has just the opposite effect. The exchange rate tends to depreciate, because of the increased supply of domestic money. Prices of imports, exports, and import substitutes go up. A reduction in unemployment now in the short run pushes the economy along the red path between A and C in Figure 19-8. And the situation may be even worse than indicated by the red path between A and C, which describes the short-run inflation-unemployment tradeoff while holding constant people's expectations of future inflation. If individuals learn that monetary expansion implies more domestic inflation, caused by a currency depreciation, their inflation expectations will shift the short-run Phillips curve up above the red line running through A and C.

Combined with the J-curve phenomenon, which states that following an exchange-rate depreciation the trade surplus (part of GNP) temporarily deteriorates, monetary expansion may not only make inflation worse, but may cause real output to fall and unemployment to become worse as well. The disadvantages of monetary policy are paralleled by corresponding advantages of fiscal policy, which can temporarily moderate the inflation rate with a possible temporary improvement in the trade surplus. Many economists believe that it is important to insulate domestic inflation from the disruptive influence of exchange rate movements and that any policy stimulus consists of a balanced monetary and fiscal expansion while holding the exchange rate constant. A tax cut or spending increase should therefore be accommodated by faster monetary growth, a recommendation that would conflict with the monetarist preference for a constant monetary growth rate rule.

19-8 CONCLUSION: INTERNATIONAL POLICY PROBLEMS OF THE LATE 1970s

HAS NATIONAL MONETARY INDEPENDENCE BEEN ACHIEVED BY THE FLEXIBLE RATE SYSTEM?

The old system of fixed exchange rates collapsed in 1971–73 when nations having a surplus, particularly Germany and Japan, lost their monetary independence. To keep their currencies from appreciating, they had been forced to buy massive amounts of dollars. These dollars tended to raise the domestic money supply of Germany, Japan, and other nations more than the amount desired by their domestic central banks, thus contributing to a worldwide acceleration of inflation in 1973. Flexible exchange rates were attractive to these countries as a way of untying their money supplies from the influence of the United States. If American monetary growth was excessive, the dollar would depreciate while the mark and yen appreciated, allowing Germany and Japan to maintain lower inflation rates than the United States. This monetary independence had previously been stymied by massive inflows of reserves that their central banks had been forced to accumulate to keep their exchange rates fixed.

In the long run a flexible exchange rate system does permit a country to choose an inflation rate that differs from that of its main trading partners. The contrast between the low inflation rate enjoyed by Germany since 1973, compared to the much higher inflation rates of Italy and the United Kingdom, provides evidence of the advantages of flexible rates for nations attempting to avoid inflation. If there were a permanent long-run tradeoff between inflation and unemployment, other nations might be able to use their monetary independence in a flexible exchange rate system to achieve less unemployment at the cost of higher inflation. But because the long-run Phillips curve in fact appears to be vertical, it may not be possible for nations to buy lower unemployment for more than a short transition period by their willingness to suffer high inflation, leaving no obvious advantages of flexible rates for countries with high inflation.

If the flexible exchange rate system is advantageous to those nations with a taste for low inflation rates, what are the offsetting costs? We have seen that, in the short run, exchange rates tend to fluctuate widely around their long-run equilibrium levels. Such fluctuations may inhibit the growth of foreign trade and capital movements, although as yet there is little evidence that the post-1973 flexible exchange rate system has had any such effect. Another problem is that adjustment may eventually be costly when a country allows its currency to become overvalued or undervalued relative to long-run equilibrium. Depreciation for an overvalued currency requires that resources be shifted toward export industries, and also may cause transitional unemployment in other nations. But these adjustment costs are probably not as serious under the flexible rate system as under the old system of fixed exchange rates, which by the late 1960s had allowed exchange rates to become badly out of line.

VICIOUS AND VIRTUOUS CIRCLES

The adjustment lags summarized as the *J*-curve phenomenon pose a dilemma for countries with weak economies, as for Britain and Italy in the mid-1970s, which were both experiencing high unemployment and above-average inflation simultaneously. High inflation leads speculators to expect that the long-term equilibrium exchange rate is declining according to the purchasing-power parity theory, and accordingly the actual value of the exchange rate is bid down. This depreciation aggravates the inflation problem by raising the prices of imports, exports, and import substitutes, and may even temporarily worsen unemployment, if the *J*-curve phenomenon is strong. Thus a vicious circle develops, with inflation causing depreciation, which causes further inflation, all without any major stimulus to real output or employment.

Strong countries with below-average inflation rates benefit from a corresponding virtuous circle, with low inflation causing appreciation, which causes inflation to slow still further. Eventually changes in the exchange rate do help to improve a depreciating country's trade performance. But economists have been gradually raising their estimates of the adjustment lags and of the importance of factors other than prices alone, which influence the success of a nation's export sales performance or its ability to compete with imports. In early 1977 Germany still enjoyed a massive surplus of exports over imports, despite an effective appreciation of the mark of more than 30 percent between early 1973 and early 1977. Apparently German suppliers provide goods of high quality with prompt delivery and have a sufficient monopoly of these desirable talents to be able to sell goods even at the higher prices forced by appreciation. British suppliers do not appear able to take advantage of their price advantage in many important industries and, in addition, the vicious circle of inflation and depreciation often makes foreign buyers fearful to enter into contracts with British firms, because high inflation may require future price increases.[22]

AN ERA OF WORLD STAGNATION?

By allowing other nations to pursue independent monetary policies, the flexible exchange rate system has reduced the ability of the United States to impose its tastes. United States officials in 1977 generally believed that the pace of economic expansion was too slow in the other major industrial nations and particularly in the two strong nations enjoying large export surpluses, Germany and Japan. Under the old fixed exchange rate system the United States, whose currency is widely held as international reserves, could force other nations to expand their money supplies by increasing its own rate of monetary growth. Now, however, Germany and Japan are able to resist this pressure by allowing their exchange rates to appreciate. Ironically, instead of stimulating economic growth in these countries, U.S. monetary expansion may actually retard their growth of real output as the effects of appreciation gradually reduce the German and Japanese export surplus.

The basic problem remains — the primary importance placed by these nations, and particularly Germany, on achieving a continued deceleration of inflation. Anti-inflation policy retains its dominant role in Germany despite the achievement of only a 4.2 percent increase in consumer prices in the year ending in June 1977, a figure considered enviable by most other nations. In Japan policymakers appear unwilling to raise their fiscal deficit, as would be required to boost the rate of growth of Japanese aggregate demand and real output through fiscal expansion.[23] An acceleration of Japanese monetary expansion, on the other hand, would not contribute to economic growth elsewhere — except perhaps during a transitional J-curve period — and in fact would tend to dampen economic activity elsewhere by making Japanese goods more competitive.

In a different category are the oil-exporting nations, which are limited in their ability to increase their import purchases from industrial nations by inadequate port facilities and other constraints. Taken together Germany, Japan, and the oil-exporting nations exported $80.4 billion more than they imported in 1976, as indicated in column (3) of Table 19-3. In contrast most of the other nations experienced trade deficits in 1976 amounting to very substantial fractions of their imports.

The imbalance summarized in the table can be eliminated in three main

---

[22] A further assessment of the vicious circle problem is contained in William J. Fellner, "The Payments Adjustment Process and the Exchange Rate Regime: What Have We Learned?" *American Economic Review,* vol. 55 (May 1975), pp. 148–151.

[23] "Japan can't start its engine," *The Economist,* vol. 264 (August 20, 1977), pp. 78–79.

TABLE 19-3   Exports, Imports, and Net Exports In Surplus and Deficit Nations, 1976 (U.S. $ Millions)

	(1) *Exports*	*(2)* *Imports*	*(3)* *Net exports*	*(4)* *Net exports as percentage of imports*
Surplus countries				
Germany	101,977	88,209	13,768	15.6
Japan	67,167	64,748	2,419	3.7
Oil Exporters[a]	131,800	67,600	64,200	95.0
Total	300,944	220,557	80,387	
Deficit countries				
United States	114,977	129,565	−14,568	−11.2
Italy and U. K.	83,224	99,401	−16,177	−16.3
Other Industrial[b]	252,975	273,187	−20,212	−7.4
Other European[c]	36,320	58,750	−22,430	−38.2
Less Developed	118,330	146,200	−27,870	−19.1
Total	605,846	707,103	−101,257	
Worldwide Total[d]	906,790	927,660	−20,870[e]	

[a] Algeria, Indonesia, Iran, Iraq, Kuwait, Libya, Nigeria, Oman, Qatar, Saudi Arabia, United Arab Emirates, and Venezuela.
[b] Canada, Austria, Belgium, Denmark, France, Netherlands, Norway, Sweden, and Switzerland.
[c] Faeroe Islands, Finland, Greece, Iceland, Ireland, Malta, Portugal, Romania, Spain, Turkey, Yugoslavia
[d] Includes only members of International Monetary Fund, and excludes most communist nations.
[e] Total worldwide exports and imports do not add up to the same amount, because of differences among countries in methods of counting, and differences of timing.
Source: Adapted from *International Financial Statistics* (June 1977), pp. 38–39.

ways. First, the deficit countries can allow their exchange rates to depreciate, but this may trap them in a vicious circle. This is particularly likely if the oil exporting countries do not respond by purchasing more imports because of their limited capacities to absorb industrial products. Second, deficit countries may be forced by exhaustion of their international reserves to introduce import controls and restrictive domestic policy (or both) aimed at reducing the income their citizens have to buy imports. Third, the trade imbalances may be offset by capital movements. The oil exporters tend to invest their hoards of foreign currency in the industrial countries, providing bankers needed funds to lend to the deficit nations. The main problem of recycling these petro-dollars is that bankers may refuse to lend to some of the weaker nations. To some extent this gap has been filled by the International Monetary Fund, which has provided loans to weak nations such as the United Kingdom, on the condition that they restrain their monetary policies in order to bring inflation under control.[24]

As long as the oil exporters are limited in their ability to absorb imports and Germany and Japan refuse to stimulate real output growth in their own economies to a greater extent, the world faces a dilemma. The scope for antirecession policy measures in most of the deficit countries is limited. Speculators would react to larger budget deficits and faster monetary expansion in nations such as Britain and Italy by causing a further depreciation, aggravating their vicious circle. All these weak countries can do is patiently await an export-led recovery stimulated by economic growth elsewhere. But where is that rapid growth going to originate?

This unique situation places a heavy burden of responsibility on the United States. Since a return to fixed exchange rates is not feasible because of the large differences among national inflation rates, a continuation of the flexible rate system seems inevitable. The United States can help in two ways. First, it can encourage international facilities for borrowing by deficit nations. Second, and perhaps more important, U.S. policymakers have an unusually large constituency in the outside world with an interest in seeing rapid U.S. real output growth stimulated by a balanced monetary and fiscal expansion.

Because of the limitations of fiscal stimulus explored in Part V and the strong political pressure within the United States for maintaining moderate rates of monetary growth, it may be difficult for the United States by itself to lead the world to full economic recovery. We have learned that time lags and uncertainty make precise control of aggregate demand elusive at best. Fiscal policy stimulus within the United States inevitably is sensitive to the political environment as Congress debates the form the stimulus is to take. And now the political environment in Germany, Japan, and other nations matters as well. It is fitting that we end our book about macroeconomics on this humbling note. Despite our improved understanding of the economic factors that brought the world to its mid-1970s situation of unprecedented inflation and unemployment, the design of a solution cannot be extricated from political factors of which economists have only a modest understanding and over which they exercise even less control.

It is also humbling for U.S. citizens to realize that we no longer have the power by ourselves to guide the world economy along the path we choose. The United States role as the world's monetary engine, along with the fixed exchange rate system, was a casualty of the late 1960s monetary expansion that can be linked indirectly to U.S. fiscal deficits in the Vietnam War period. For the United States now to engineer a world-

---

[24] During the late 1970s the United Kingdom is making the transition from an oil importer to an oil exporter. Its situation may no longer be "weak" by the time you read this.

wide recovery on its own is a highly problematical undertaking. As Wilson Schmidt of Virginia Polytechnic Institute has observed:

> Fine tuning with an international orchestra requires a strong conductor: fixed exchange rates. But, for better or worse, that conductor has passed from the scene.[25]

SUMMARY

1. The international transactions of any nation are divided into the three categories—*current* transactions involving the export or import of goods and services, together with unilateral transfer payments; *capital* transactions involving long-term and short-term borrowing and lending; and *financing items* required to offset any deficit or surplus on the current and capital accounts taken together.

2. If governments allowed the exchange rate of their currency to fluctuate from day to day to eliminate any imbalance on current and capital account, no financing items would be necessary. But if a government intervenes to maintain a fixed exchange rate, then there is likely to be a surplus or shortage of foreign exchange, which in turn causes an increase or decrease in the government's stock of international reserves (or, when the reserves run low, borrowing from abroad).

3. In the absence of government intervention, the foreign exchange rate tends to appreciate when there is an increased demand for a currency due to higher exports or capital inflows. The rate tends to depreciate when there is an increased supply of a currency due to higher imports or capital outflows.

4. In the long run, the main determinants of the exchange rate between the currencies of two nations are their relative inflation rates, their comparative rates of innovation and technological change, their comparative rates of discovery of natural resources, and the balance of flows of capital and government transfer payments between them.

5. In the short run, the exchange rate can fluctuate widely around the long-run equilibrium exchange rate, because the price elasticities of imports and exports may be smaller in the short run than in the long run, and because neither the government nor private speculators have enough knowledge to stabilize the exchange rate at its long-run equilibrium level.

6. When the exchange rate is fixed, monetary policy by itself cannot stimulate real output, if the balance of payments is initially in equilibrium. Fiscal and monetary policy must be used together to achieve simultane-

---

[25] Quoted in "The flaws in U.S. world economic strategy," *Business Week* (March 28, 1977), p. 14.

ously the natural level of real output together with equilibrium in the balance of payments.

7. When prices are flexible and the exchange rate is fixed, the economy tends to arrive automatically at natural real output with its balance of payments in equilibrium, and changes in fiscal policy are necessary only if a change in the interest rate is desired.

8. In a system with flexible exchange rates, monetary policy becomes more potent by causing a depreciation which reinforces a monetary stimulus, while fiscal policy becomes less potent by causing an appreciation which works to offset a fiscal stimulus.

9. While monetary policy becomes more potent under a system of flexible exchange rates, the short-run inflation-unemployment tradeoff becomes worse for monetary than for fiscal policy.

CONCEPTS AND QUESTIONS

IDENTIFICATIONS

Open economy versus closed economy

Balance of payments surplus or deficit

Foreign exchange rate

Appreciation versus depreciation

International reserves

Current account versus capital account

Official Reserve Transactions Deficit

Purchasing-power-parity theory of the exchange rate

J-curve phenomenon

BP line

Fixed exchange rate system

Flexible exchange rate system

QUESTIONS FOR REVIEW

1   In which of the categories of Table 19-1 would you classify the following international transactions of the United States?

    a. Purchase of a $100,000 Caterpillar tractor from the Peoria, U.S.A. factory by an Italian road building contractor.

    b. Short-term loan to the Italian contractor by the First National Bank of Chicago to finance the tractor.

    c. Purchase of a $450 round-trip ticket to London on British Airways by a student at Pennsylvania State University.

    d. A $100 gift sent by a recent Irish immigrant in the United States by mail to his mother in Dublin.

    e. Purchase of an old Chrysler factory at New Stanton, Pennsylvania by the Volkswagen company of Germany for $40 million.

    f. A $100 million increase in the holdings of short-term U.S. government bonds by the Bank of England (the central bank of the United Kingdom).

2   What method of financing its balance-of-payments deficit is avail-

able to the United States, but not to other countries? Does the availability of this special method make U.S. citizens better off?

3   Explain the nature of the dilemma of a nation facing a balance-of-payments deficit, when the sum of its import and export price elasticities is less than 1.0. How does this problem help to explain exchange rate movements in the 1970s?

4   Explain why the exchange rate of the Japanese yen appreciated in the 1966–1976 decade relative to the U.S. dollar, despite the higher inflation rate in Japan than in the United States.

5   Explain in words why the *BP* line in Figure 19-4 slopes upward to the right. Under what circumstances would it be horizontal?

6   When exchange rates are fixed, is monetary or fiscal policy a more potent method for controlling real output? Why?

7   When exchange rates are flexible, is monetary or fiscal policy a more potent method for controlling real output? Why?

8   If a nation operating under flexible exchange rates desires to cut its excessively high unemployment rate by a given amount, will its inflation rate increase more if it chooses monetary policy to achieve its economic expansion or if it chooses fiscal policy?

9   In mid-1977 economic growth in many industrialized nations appeared to be stalled at rates well below the 4 to 5 percent growth rate of natural output. What are some of the reasons for this world-wide economic stagnation?

10 In your library try to find out what has happened to the growth rate of real output in Japan, Germany, and other countries since mid-1977. See sources such as: *International Financial Statistics* (International Monetary Fund), or *Main Economic Indicators* (OECD). Both are published every month.

Appendixes

Appendix A
Conceptual Problems in the Measurement of Income and Prices

Introductory Note: This supplement can be read either immediately after Chapter 2 or else after the rest of the book. It is designed to deepen the student's understanding of the differences between GNP as currently measured and national welfare and to introduce the student to problems in achieving a better measure of welfare as well as to problems in measuring prices. Although these are interesting questions currently under active investigation by economists inside and outside the federal government, they are not crucial to the understanding of the rest of the book, and so this discussion has been placed here at the end. For instance, an improved measure of economic welfare may decline less during a recession than the current official measure of GNP, but improved measurement does not eliminate our need for a good theory of recessions and how to avoid them. Similarly, the annual increase in our price indexes may be somewhat overstated as a consequence of measurement error. However, this has been true for many decades and does not lessen our need for an explanation of the much faster inflation rate of the past decade compared to previous eras.

A-1 FROM NET NATIONAL PRODUCT TO NET NATIONAL WELFARE

WELFARE CONCEPTS OF CONSUMPTION AND INVESTMENT

The U.S. National Income and Product Accounts (NIPA) are the official data on Gross National Product (GNP), Net National Product (NNP), and all the other magnitudes depicted in Figure 2-6 and described in the main part of Chapter 2. The NIPA are widely admired for their detail, consistency, and timeliness compared to the national accounts of other nations. Nevertheless, the accounts have been subject to criticism for many years as inadequate measures of economic welfare. For instance, real NNP as currently measured is the same in two different years, if the net quantity of currently produced goods and services sold on the market is identical, even when pollution has increased between the two years and as a result true welfare has decreased. Similarly, an increasing crime rate from the first year to the second may be accompanied by higher market purchases of guard dogs, burglar screens, and more comprehensive insurance policies as well as higher government expenditures for larger and better equipped police forces—all of which raise NNP even if true welfare has remained the same or declined. In fact, some critics have claimed that NNP is so irrelevant a measure of welfare that economic growth (growth in NNP) actually does more harm than good.

Recall that total final product (GNP) includes all currently produced goods and services that are sold on the market, but not resold. Net National Product (NNP) differs from GNP only in its exclusion of currently produced investment goods that replace obsolete and worn-out capital goods. To achieve a better approximation to the annual increase in the nation's well-being or welfare, it has been suggested that we switch from the current NNP concept to "Net National Welfare" (NNW). The concept NNW is defined as consumption and net investment, but differs from NNP because consumption and net investment are treated differently.

The consumption part of NNW measures the enjoyment of services by households. Some household expenditures that do not provide enjoyment are included in NNP, but excluded from NNW. For instance, commuting is a necessary evil that helps to produce household income, but is not enjoyed itself. Purchases of durables (houses, autos, TV sets), now included in NIPA consumption, are instead counted as gross investment in the NNW approach. TV sets only contribute to consumption or enjoyment as they produce services, that is, as they are used. Finally, NNW consumption includes several important intangible items that are not sold on the market and are not in NNW, but that add to welfare (leisure time) or reduce welfare (congestion and pollution).

The net investment part of NNW includes all net additions to the stock of assets that yield goods and services. This includes not only business structures, equipment, residential housing (which are already in NNP), also several extra items: additions to the stock of consumer-owned assets (autos, TV sets, education, health) and government-owned assets (schools, national parks). Net investment equals gross purchases of assets minus capital consumption, the portion of the existing capital stock that is used up or consumed due to obsolescence or physical wear and tear.

STEP-BY-STEP FROM NNP TO NNW

William D. Nordhaus and James Tobin of Yale University have attempted to calculate a rough measure of net national welfare, NNW.[1] Table A-1 sets out the main components of NNP and NNW side-by-side for the year 1965, measured in the constant prices of 1958.[2] Look first at columns (3) and (4) of the table, which list the major components of the official NIPA concept of GNP (consumption, investment, and government spending), adding up to $617.2 billion in 1958 prices. The deduction of capital consumption allowances yields a total value of NNP of $563.1 billion, at the very bottom of column (4).[3]

Step 1: Identical Items. More than half the dollar value of NNP is treated identically in the welfare measure, NNW. On line 1 the pure consumption portion of NNP, for example food and haircuts, is listed as $243.2 billion as a component of NIPA final product in column (3) and as part of NNW consumption in column (6). Gross private domestic investment, for example, factories and residential housing, is listed as $99.2 billion on line 11 both as a component of NIPA final product and as part of NNW investment. The same goes for net foreign investment on line 12 and for capital consumption allowances on line 20. In addition, both NIPA final product and NNW include an imputed estimate of the services that homeowners receive from the houses they own (line 2). This imputation is calculated by government statisticians, since it does not represent something bought or sold in the market. An imputation is a transaction that does not actually take place on the market, but nevertheless represents a service that increases or decreases consumer well-being.

Step 2: Intermediates and Regrettables. The conventional NIPA measure of final product excludes intermediate goods, items that are

---

[1] William D. Nordhaus and James Tobin, *Is Growth Obsolete?* (Washington, D.C.: National Bureau of Economic Research, General Series 96, 1972). Nordhaus-Tobin call their concept Measure of Economic Welfare, or MEW. Our NNW total in Table A-1 is identical to their sustainable MEW, except that we do not concur in their deduction from net investment of a large growth requirement to be set aside to guarantee continued steady future growth.

[2] A good term paper project for an interested student would be to construct an estimate of NNW for a recent year, using Appendix A in Nordhaus-Tobin *op. cit.* as a guide to sources.

[3] Compare these totals with Figure 2-6. Notice the tremendous growth in all the magnitudes between 1965 and 1976, due both to real economic growth and to inflation.

TABLE A-1 Relation of NIPA Net Income Product (NNP) to a Measure of Net National Welfare (NNW)

(1965 Totals in 1958 Prices)

	Sources of data		National income and product (NIPA)		(5) Extra intermediates and regrettables excluded from NNW	Components of welfare (NNW)	
	(1) Market purchases	(2) Imputations	(3) Components	(4) Totals		(6) Consumption	(7) Investment
1.	Pure consumption		243.2			243.2	
2.	Consumer durables		60.9				60.9
3.	Education and health		30.1				30.1
4.	Commuting and personal business		30.9		30.9		
5.		Dwelling services	32.0			32.0	
6.		Other capital services				62.3	
7.		Leisure time				626.9	
8.		Nonmarket work				295.4	
9.		Urban congestion				−34.6	
10.				Total consumption = 397.1			
11.	Gross domestic investment		99.2			99.2	
12.	Net foreign investment		6.2			6.2	
13.				Total investment = 105.4			
14.	Government consumption		1.2			1.2	
15.	Government gross investment		50.3				50.3
16.	Government regrettables and intermediates		63.2		63.2		
17.		Government capital services				16.6	
18.				Total government = 114.7			
19.				Gross nat. prod. = 617.2			
20.	NIPA capital consumption		−54.7	−54.7			−54.7
21.	Extra capital consumption						−92.7
22.							99.3
23.				Net nat. prod. = 563.1		1243.0	
24.						Net national welfare = 1342.3	

Source: Author's rearrangement of William D. Nordhaus and James Tobin, *Is Growth Obsolete?* (Washington, D.C.: National Bureau of Economic Research, General Series 96, 1972. Tables A.1, A.4, A.5, A.16, and A.17.

ingredients in final goods purchased by households, business firms, and the government (recall the discussion of Figure 2-2). Our NNW measure excludes some additional items, which, although purchased by consumers or government and not resold, nevertheless are mere ingredients in producing the services that households enjoy and are not the objects of enjoyment themselves.

One easy example consists of consumer purchases made only because they are tools necessary to earn an income, including uniforms and the costs of commuting. They are listed on line 4 of Table A-1 as a component of NIPA final product and again to the right as an intermediate good excluded from NNW. Other consumer expenditures that are not separated out in the table, but which might be excluded from NNW include the costs of anticrime devices and insurance. These purchases are not made because they are enjoyed, but only because they are viewed as necessary to protect the consumer assets (houses, cars, boats, TV sets) that do yield services or enjoyment.[4]

Somewhat more controversial is the exclusion from NNW of the majority of government purchases. Just as consumer expenditures on locks and other anticrime devices can be viewed as necessary evils that do not add to welfare, so government expenditures on police and fire protection can be viewed as intermediate goods useful only as a means of protecting consumer assets.[5] And if police are a necessary evil, so are defense expenditures. The increased level of international tension in the postwar world has required a much higher level of military spending than in 1890 or 1925, even though our level of national security (a component of welfare) is no higher than before. Just as an increase in the crime rate requires greater expenditures on locks and police to maintain the same level of welfare as before, in the same way a deterioration in the international political atmosphere requires higher military expenditures than before just to keep welfare constant. The item labeled Government regrettables and intermediates on line 16 of Table A-1 isolates the $63.2 billion counted as part of final product in the NIPA accounts, but is shown again to the right as excluded from NNW. Only a small portion

---

[4] In this case, and in several others that follow, the Nordhaus-Tobin estimates summarized in Table A-1 represent only a partial and incomplete attempt to calculate NNW. A more comprehensive approach is the Total Income System of Accounts (TISA) currently being developed by Robert Eisner and his students at Northwestern. Preliminary estimates of TISA are available for 1959 and 1969, but were judged too complex for textbook presentation. Another source, already published, is Nancy Ruggles and Richard Ruggles, *The Design of Economic Accounts* (Washington, D.C.: National Bureau of Economic Research, 1970).

[5] Here is an example of government purchases that are substitutes for consumer purchases. If the government spends more on police and fire protection, the consumer may spend less on locks and fire insurance. If so, our income determination multipliers developed in Chapters 3 and 4 are reduced.

of government expenditures are included in the consumption part of NNW on line 14, basically government provision for cheap postage stamps (through financing of the postal service deficit) and for cheap recreation (through below-cost or no-cost charges for national, state, and city parks).

Step 3: The Treatment of Capital. Net national welfare includes the consumption of enjoyable services and net additions to capital. Why? Compare two nations, say Britain and West Germany, which have had roughly the same level of real consumption per person in 1970. Since West Germany added about twice as much to capital as Britain in that year, that is, its net investment was twice as high, West Germany should be regarded as being better off, because higher additions to capital will allow it to enjoy a higher level of consumption in the future. Nations that shift resources from the provision of present consumption to net investment, which provides future consumption, should not be regarded as making themselves worse off. For this reason both consumption and net investment are included in both NNP and NNW.

The main difference in the welfare approach is the much broader class of goods treated as investment. Investment in business structures and equipment, residential construction, and net foreign investment (lines 11 and 12) all are included as investment in both NNP and NNW, with capital consumption subtracted in the same way in both approaches (line 20). In addition, consumer purchases of autos, TV sets, and other durable goods are treated as investment in NNW (line 2). Once purchased and in operation, consumer durables provide a flow of services (the annual enjoyment provided by an automobile or TV set), which is included as part of NNW consumption on line 6.

Many consumer expenditures on education and health (line 3) should also be treated as investments. Teenagers go to college and some adults go to night school with the expectation that their expenditures on books, tuition, and lab fees will provide them with additional knowledge and will allow them to earn higher incomes in the future. These expenditures add to the nation's stock of human capital and are just as valid a component of national wealth as our stock of factories and machines. Health expenditures either cure present illnesses or prevent future illnesses and can be treated as raising the level of health capital, thus raising the future level of production and consumption (although some health expenditures admittedly have no effect on either current or future health).

The government makes many expenditures that add to the nation's wealth and allow more production and consumption to be enjoyed in the future. Examples are federal support of school, hospital, highway, and mass transit construction, as well as expenditures for the development of nuclear power for electricity generation and for agricultural research. This portion of government expenditures, presently counted as part of

GNP, but not as an addition to wealth, is listed as Government gross investment on line 15.

We cannot count all expenditures on investment goods as additions to wealth. If $500,000 worth of machinery is purchased, but half the new machinery simply replace $250,000 of old machinery that had become obsolete or worn out, the net addition to the nation's capital stock or net investment is $250,000.[6] In the case of machinery, the total expenditure of $500,000 is entered as part of Gross domestic investment on line 11 of the table and the consumption of capital as old machines become obsolete and wear out is entered as a minus item on line 20. The welfare approach simply adds in an extra entry on line 21 for depreciation on those goods that are considered investment in the NNW accounts — consumer durables, consumer expenditures on education and health, and government gross investment.

The Nordhaus-Tobin approach to the measurement of NNW in Table A-1 does not exhaust the possibilities for treatment of items as investment and capital. Additional items that might be included are child-rearing expenses of parents, since better education of children at home raises their achievement at school and ultimately their income-earning potential. Another possible category is consumer and business expenditures for moving employees from city to city. These moves in many cases are part of the process by which individuals find jobs better suited to their own capabilities and the economy-wide matching of jobs and workers is improved (see Chapter 9). Since this process increases future incomes, it should in principle be treated as investment.[7] Finally, business expenditures on research and development develop new products that consumers value (jet airlines) or that increase the potential (or natural) level of attainable production (computer-controlled machine tools) and should be considered as investment adding to the nation's stock of research and development capital.

Step 4: Addition and Subtraction of Intangibles. One of the most important components of consumer enjoyment is never bought or sold on the marketplace. Yet without it consumers would have little incentive to work hard and accumulate possessions. Puzzled? This mysterious component is leisure time, the portion of the week spent in activities other than work, sleep, and housework. What fun would boats and fishing poles provide if there were no time to enjoy them? The production of leisure

---

[6] This sentence is correct if the values are measured in constant prices and if the measurement of prices adequately takes account of all differences in quality between new and old machines. More on the problems of price measurement follows.

[7] In the NIPA accounts, consumer expenditures on moving are counted as pure consumption (line 1), while business reimbursements of moving expenses are treated as an intermediate good and are excluded from NNP.

services can be viewed as a production activity requiring the input of two basic ingredients, a durable good (boat, fishing pole) and household leisure time.

How much is this time worth? Ask yourself why most people only have one job requiring roughly 40 hours per week of work. Why don't they take an extra job requiring another 20 or 30 hours of work? Leaving aside the possibility that they can't find such an extra moonlighting job because the economy is weak, the basic reason for the refusal to work an extra job is the value of the leisure time that would be sacrificed. Since we observe that most people refuse second jobs, we deduce that their leisure time must be worth at least the wage rate on such jobs. Hence the best simple estimate of the value of each hour of leisure time is the wage rate. The imputation of the 1965 value of leisure time in Table A-1, line 7, is an immense $626.9 billion, larger than the entire NIPA concept of GNP of that year!

But we are not finished. In most households a great deal of time is spent on housework, predominantly still performed by women and to a small extent by men. Many women are on the borderline between staying at home and making the decision to accept a job and more and more each year enter the labor force to work. The borderline nature of the decision suggests that the work women do in the home is valuable and should be considered part of NNW—after all, if housework and child rearing did not produce something of value, all women would long since have entered the labor force. Line 8 in Table A-1 registers the value of housework, with each hour (as in the case of leisure) valued at the wage rate.[8]

Finally, one last correction must be made that reduces welfare. On average, inhabitants of cities and metropolitan areas earn more than those who live in the country. When people migrate from the farm to the city, as they have done throughout our history, conventionally measured GNP is raised by the increase in market wages received in the city. But at least part of the higher urban wage is a payment made to offset unpleasant aspects of city life—congestion, pollution, noise, litter, and lack of access to nature. Line 9 in Table A-1 subtracts an estimate of this cost of urban living based on a statistical study by Nordhaus and Tobin of wage rates in urban and rural areas.

Step 5: NNW and Its Historical Growth. The grand total of the components of NNW for 1965 consists of $1243.0 billion of consumption

---

[8] This overstates the value of housework, since a housewife compares the value of staying at home not with the before-tax wage rate (assumed in Table A-1), but rather with the wage rate after subtraction of all taxes and commuting expenses. I estimate the value of home time for married women to be only 40 percent of the average hourly wage in my "Welfare Cost of Higher Unemployment," *Brookings Papers on Economic Activity,* vol. 4, no. 1 (1973).

and $99.3 billion of net investment or a total NNW of $1342.3 billion.[9] This is much more than double the total official estimate of NNP for the same year. As the table shows, most of the difference is due to the huge imputations for the value of leisure and housework time. This source of difference explains why between 1929 and 1965 per-person NNW grew so much more slowly (0.98 percent per year, compounded) than did per-person NNP (1.75 percent per year).

The largest difference between the two concepts, leisure time, is not assumed to grow at all in value per person. Yet an argument could be made that leisure time is now more valuable, because recreational equipment is better and more widely owned and, in particular, air and auto travel have opened access to vacation and weekend locations that have made leisure more pleasant. Thus the growth rate of NNW is probably an underestimate.

The Nordhaus-Tobin method of calculating the leisure and housework component of NNW uses the current wage rate to value each hour of leisure time and housework. Thus, during the Great Depression when millions were out of work, their increased hours of leisure are treated as just as valuable to them as the income that they received from work! This is unreasonable and fails to explain why everyone was so unhappy during the Great Depression. An improved concept of NNW would value hours of leisure caused by involuntary unemployment at an hourly rate much below the current wage rate.

CONCLUSION ON THE WELFARE MEASURE

When can we look forward to official NIPA estimates that come closer to a measure of welfare? A long-planned major revision of the NIPA concepts was published in early 1976, but every single change was minor. Not one of the changes in treatment outlined in Table A-1 was adopted. Why? Because traditionally the Bureau of Economic Analysis in the U.S. Department of Commerce, which is the branch of the federal government responsible for compilation of the NIPA estimates, has emphasized precision at the expense of conceptual merit. Since many of the major changes in the NNW measure of Table A-1 involve imputations for services that are not bought and sold on the market, they must of necessity involve reliance on economic theory and some guesswork. Accountants who specialize in the careful transcription of figures on market transactions will naturally balk at the prospect of working with

---

[9] The close reader of Nordhaus-Tobin will notice that their deduction for the investment growth requirement has been omitted. This is the portion of investment needed to sustain the inherited rate of output growth. Taking aside the question of population growth, their procedure is peculiar. Why should Japan be penalized by a growth requirement deduction for its additions to capital that allow it to grow faster and enjoy a higher level of future consumption than other countries that invest less?

a welfare concept (NNW) that actually includes a larger value of imputations than of market transactions.

Another argument can be made in favor of the retention of the present concept of NNP based on market transactions: NNP is a better indication than NNW of the total amount of job-creating economic activity. For instance, when the nation fights a war, NNP goes up and extra jobs are created, but NNW does not increase because military expenditures are treated as regrettable intermediate goods excluded from NNW. Even if economists can eventually convince the federal government to begin compiling an official set of data on NNW, most would nevertheless recommend that publication of NNP statistics be continued as well.

A-2 PROBLEMS IN THE MEASUREMENT OF PRICE DEFLATORS

As outlined in the last section of Chapter 2 and in the numerical example of Table 2-3, the price deflator for GNP is simply a weighted average of many different individual price indexes. If the individual component price indexes increase on average between two successive years, then the GNP deflator will increase and indicate that inflation has occurred between the first year and the second. While the procedure for weighting causes minor difficulties, most of the serious problems involved in price measurement involve the accuracy of the individual price indexes themselves. The basic flaw is that the goods and services whose prices are being compared in two different years should be identical in quality. Yet it is difficult and sometimes impossible to hold quality constant when measuring price change.

HOLDING QUALITY CONSTANT

The basic principle to be observed is that price comparisons between two different years are to be made for goods that are identical in quality. When a newer, higher quality model is introduced at a higher price, as when refrigerators were first equipped with automatic defrosting, we do not want to treat the entire price increase as contributing to inflation, because the higher quality of goods and services (the automatic defroster) is something real that raises real GNP. In many cases it is easy to hold quality constant when measuring the prices of individual products because exactly the same models with exactly the same specifications are sold in two successive years. But in other cases the attempt to hold quality constant raises significant and sometimes even insurmountable problems.

Quality Change in Existing Products. For some products, for instance washing machines, refrigerators, and automobiles, there are years in which all models change in quality. How then can prices be compared? Economists have developed techniques for measuring the value of changes in quality. Unfortunately, these new techniques for quality adjustment have been used only recently and sporadically by the Bureau of Labor Statistics, the branch of the federal government responsible for the compilation of most of the individual price indexes on which the GNP deflator is based.[10] For instance, a great effort appears to be made to correct automobile prices for the effect of quality change, but much less is done for office machinery and machine tools. Thus the official data that show that the prices of automobiles have increased less over the postwar era than the prices of machines may not reflect actual facts, but rather inconsistent techniques of measurement. Further, methods of measurement are steadily improving, which suggests that the price data for earlier historical periods are less accurate than those for recent years. If so, and if quality on balance has been improving rather than deteriorating, then the acceleration of inflation in the period since 1965 is understated in the official data (that is, the bias in the official inflation rate measure overstates inflation more before 1965 than since).

When New Products Are Introduced. Some new products perform the same function as an older product, in which case a price comparison can be made. For instance, the electronic calculators introduced in 1970 for about $200 can multiply and divide, just as did the old rotary electric calculators sold in 1970 for $1000. This appears to represent a price decline of 80 percent. Actually the true price decline was much more, because the new electronic calculators perform given operations much faster than the older models and also perform operations that formerly had to be done by hand (for instance, placement of the decimal). Incredibly, despite the occurrence in this case of a price decline of 90 percent or more, the official government price data failed to register any price decline at all![11]

Other cases where a large price decrease occurred, but was ignored by government statisticians, include the replacement of piston airliners by jets and the development of more durable synthetic fibers. Unfortunately, some kinds of new products are so different that a measurement of quality change is impossible. How can television be compared to radio?

---

[10] A wide variety of techniques for the measurement of quality change are reviewed and utilized in my book, *The Measurement of Durable Goods Prices,* National Bureau of Economic Research, forthcoming. An earlier collection of essays is Zvi Grilichus (ed.), *Price Indexes and Quality Change* (Cambridge, Mass.: Harvard, 1971).

[11] In the official jargon, the new price index for electronic calculators was linked to the old one for rotary electric calculators. In the month of the linkage no price change was assumed to occur, although since then the official index has mirrored the rapid decline in the prices of electronic calculators.

Color television to black and white TV? How can the freedom allowed by the automobile be compared to the limitations of train travel?

TRANSACTION VERSUS LIST PRICES

Most price indexes of consumer products are compiled from the reports of government field agents who go out and record the actual selling prices of individual items. But the prices of investment goods, both structures and equipment, may not fully reflect actual selling prices. In the case of structures, the government indexes are not (with a few exceptions) based on actual price quotations at all, because it is all but impossible to find structures that are identical in quality. Instead, the prices of structures are taken to be averages of wage rates and the prices of construction materials, a procedure that ignores improvements in labor productivity and fluctuations in the profits of construction contractors. Thus government price indexes for structures do not reflect the price reductions that occur in periods of weak demand when contractors are willing to slash profit margins to stay in business.

The price indexes for machines are collected from mail reports sent in by manufacturers. Unfortunately, firms report the list prices of equipment; rarely do they report the discounts that they allow in recessions and premiums that they sometimes charge in prosperous periods. (Often the discounts and premiums take the form of the changing availability of free delivery and other services.) This flaw in the government's price collecting procedures implies that the overall GNP deflator understates the true decline in transaction prices during recessions and exaggerates the true decline in real output. Nevertheless, this deficiency is relatively minor and it does not lessen the importance of gaining an adequate understanding of the causes of inflation and recession.

Appendix B
Time Series Data for U.S. Economy, 1900-1977

Introductory Note: All data in this appendix have been revised through the second quarter of 1977 and incorporate the July 1977 revisions of the National Income and Product Accounts. These revisions create very minor differences for the most recent years (1974–76) between the data printed here and the data used in some of the figures in the first half of the book.

TABLE B-1   Annual Data, 1900–1977

	Nominal GNP (Y)	GNP deflator (P)	Real output (1972$) (Q)	Natural output (1972$) (Q*)	Unemployment rate (U)	Natural unemployment rate (U*)	Money* supply (M1)	Money supply (M2)
1900	19.5	15.78	123.3	129.3	5.0	3.4	0.0	6.6
1901	21.5	15.60	137.6	134.7	4.0	3.4	0.0	7.5
1902	22.5	16.18	138.9	140.2	3.7	3.4	0.0	8.2
1903	23.8	16.30	145.8	146.1	3.9	3.4	0.0	8.7
1904	23.8	16.51	144.0	152.1	5.4	3.4	0.0	9.2
1905	26.2	16.92	154.7	158.4	4.3	3.5	0.0	10.2

Note: M1 data are not available before 1915.

	Nominal GNP (Y)	GNP deflator (P)	Real output (1972$) (Q)	Natural output (1972$) (Q*)	Unemployment rate (U)	Natural unemployment rate (U*)	Money supply (M1)	Money supply (M2)
1906	29.9	17.32	172.6	165.0	1.7	3.5	0.0	11.1
1907	31.7	18.07	175.4	171.9	2.8	3.5	0.0	11.6
1908	28.9	17.95	160.9	177.4	8.0	3.5	0.0	11.4
1909	33.5	18.55	180.5	183.0	5.1	3.5	0.0	12.7
1910	35.4	19.07	185.6	188.9	5.9	3.5	0.0	13.3
1911	35.9	18.86	190.4	194.9	6.7	3.5	0.0	14.1
1912	39.5	19.63	201.2	201.2	4.6	3.5	0.0	15.1
1913	39.7	19.55	203.1	207.6	4.3	3.5	0.0	15.7
1914	38.7	19.94	194.1	212.9	7.9	3.5	0.0	16.4
1915	40.1	20.85	192.4	218.3	8.5	3.5	12.5	17.6
1916	48.4	23.34	207.6	223.9	5.1	3.5	14.7	20.9
1917	60.6	28.99	208.9	229.5	4.6	3.5	17.1	24.4
1918	76.6	32.66	234.6	235.4	1.4	3.6	19.0	26.7
1919	84.2	37.23	226.3	241.4	1.4	3.6	21.8	31.0
1920	91.8	42.41	216.4	247.5	5.2	3.6	23.7	34.8
1921	69.8	35.34	197.5	253.8	11.7	3.6	21.5	32.8
1922	74.3	32.49	228.8	260.3	6.7	3.6	21.7	33.7
1923	85.3	33.28	256.4	266.9	2.4	3.6	22.9	36.6
1924	84.9	33.21	255.8	273.7	5.0	3.6	23.7	38.6
1925	93.4	33.68	277.2	280.6	3.2	3.6	25.7	42.0
1926	97.3	33.13	293.7	287.8	1.8	3.7	26.2	43.7
1927	95.2	32.45	293.3	295.1	3.3	3.7	26.1	44.7
1928	97.3	32.97	295.0	302.6	4.2	3.7	26.4	46.4
1929	103.4	32.86	314.7	310.3	3.2	3.7	26.6	46.6
1930	90.7	31.80	285.2	318.8	8.9	3.7	25.8	45.7
1931	76.1	28.90	263.3	327.6	16.3	3.7	24.1	42.7
1932	58.3	25.71	226.8	336.6	24.1	3.8	21.1	36.0
1933	55.8	25.12	222.1	345.9	25.2	3.8	19.9	32.2
1934	65.3	27.28	239.4	355.4	22.0	3.8	21.9	34.4
1935	72.5	27.80	260.8	365.2	20.3	3.8	25.9	39.1
1936	82.7	27.93	296.1	375.2	17.0	3.8	29.5	43.5
1937	90.7	29.28	309.8	385.5	14.3	3.9	30.9	45.7
1938	85.0	28.61	297.1	396.1	19.1	3.9	30.5	45.5
1939	90.8	28.40	319.7	407.0	17.2	3.9	34.2	49.3
1940	100.0	29.10	343.6	418.2	14.6	3.9	39.7	55.2
1941	124.9	31.49	396.6	429.7	9.9	3.9	46.5	62.5
1942	158.3	34.82	454.6	441.5	4.7	3.9	55.4	71.2
1943	192.0	36.41	527.3	453.6	1.9	4.0	72.2	89.9
1944	210.5	37.13	567.0	466.1	1.2	4.0	85.3	106.8
1945	212.3	37.98	559.0	479.0	1.9	4.0	99.2	126.6

	Nominal GNP (Y)	GNP deflator (P)	Real output (1972$) (Q)	Natural output (1972$) (Q*)	Unemployment rate (U)	Natural unemployment rate (U*)	Money supply (M1)	Money supply (M2)
1946	209.6	43.94	477.0	492.1	3.9	4.0	106.5	138.7
1947	232.8	49.70	468.3	505.6	3.9	4.0	111.8	146.0
1948	259.1	53.13	487.7	519.6	3.8	4.1	112.3	148.1
1949	258.0	52.59	490.7	533.8	5.9	4.1	111.2	147.4
1950	286.2	53.64	533.5	548.5	5.3	4.1	114.1	150.8
1951	330.2	57.27	576.5	566.4	3.3	4.1	119.2	156.4
1952	347.2	58.00	598.5	584.7	3.0	4.2	125.2	164.9
1953	366.1	58.88	621.8	603.8	2.9	4.2	128.3	171.2
1954	366.3	59.69	613.7	623.5	5.5	4.2	130.3	177.2
1955	399.3	60.98	654.8	643.8	4.4	4.3	134.4	183.7
1956	420.7	62.90	668.8	664.7	4.1	4.3	136.0	186.9
1957	442.8	65.02	680.9	688.2	4.3	4.3	136.7	191.8
1958	448.9	66.06	679.5	712.6	6.8	4.3	138.4	201.1
1959	486.5	67.52	720.4	737.8	5.5	4.3	143.6	210.5
1960	506.0	68.67	736.8	763.9	5.5	4.4	143.5	212.6
1961	523.3	69.28	755.3	791.0	6.7	4.4	146.5	223.7
1962	563.8	70.55	799.1	818.9	5.5	4.4	149.7	236.7
1963	594.7	71.59	830.7	847.9	5.7	4.5	154.1	252.0
1964	635.7	72.71	874.4	877.9	5.2	4.6	160.2	267.8
1965	688.1	74.32	925.9	909.0	4.5	4.7	167.1	289.2
1966	753.0	76.76	981.0	941.1	3.8	4.8	174.7	311.6
1967	796.3	79.02	1007.7	974.4	3.8	4.9	181.5	335.5
1968	868.5	82.57	1051.8	1010.9	3.6	4.9	194.3	365.5
1969	935.5	86.72	1078.8	1048.7	3.5	5.0	206.4	389.8
1970	982.4	91.36	1075.3	1088.0	4.9	5.1	214.5	406.0
1971	1063.4	96.02	1107.5	1128.8	5.9	5.2	228.9	453.1
1972	1171.1	100.00	1171.1	1171.0	5.6	5.3	245.0	501.0
1973	1306.6	105.80	1235.0	1214.9	4.9	5.4	263.3	549.1
1974	1412.9	116.02	1217.8	1259.5	5.6	5.4	277.7	595.3
1975	1528.8	127.18	1202.1	1300.6	8.5	5.4	289.5	641.0
1976	1706.5	133.88	1274.7	1344.9	7.7	5.4	304.2	703.8
1977	1890.4	141.32	1337.6	1390.6	7.0	5.4	324.5	777.6

TABLE B-2   Quarterly Data, 1947–1977

	Nominal GNP (Y)	GNP deflator (P)	Real GNP (1972$) (Q)	Natural output (1972$) (Q*)	Unemployment rate (U)	Natural Unemployment rate (U*)	Money supply (M1)	Money supply (M2)	Actual federal surplus	Natural employment surplus
1947.Q1	224.9	48.5	464.0	502.5	3.9	4.0	109.8	143.3	39.5	37.3
1947.Q2	229.1	49.0	467.6	503.9	3.9	4.0	111.6	145.4	27.8	36.2
1947.Q3	233.3	49.9	467.9	507.3	3.8	4.0	112.6	147.0	20.1	30.5
1947.Q4	243.6	51.4	473.7	510.8	3.8	4.0	113.1	148.3	29.6	37.5
1948.Q1	249.6	52.3	477.3	514.2	3.7	4.1	113.1	148.7	26.0	34.5
1948.Q2	257.1	52.9	486.0	517.7	3.7	4.1	112.1	147.9	19.8	26.0
1948.Q3	264.0	53.8	490.8	521.2	3.8	4.1	112.2	148.1	10.8	16.8
1948.Q4	265.5	53.5	496.0	524.8	3.8	4.1	111.8	147.8	6.2	12.1
1949.Q1	260.1	53.0	490.9	528.3	4.7	4.1	111.2	147.3	1.1	9.6
1949.Q2	256.6	52.5	488.9	531.9	5.9	4.1	111.4	147.7	−5.9	5.9
1949.Q3	258.6	52.4	493.2	535.5	6.7	4.1	111.0	147.4	−7.8	4.8
1949.Q4	256.5	52.4	489.1	539.2	7.0	4.1	111.0	147.4	−7.8	7.2
1950.Q1	267.4	52.3	511.5	542.8	6.4	4.1	112.0	148.6	−9.0	−3.6
1950.Q2	276.9	52.7	525.2	546.2	5.6	4.1	113.7	150.5	14.8	12.2
1950.Q3	294.5	54.3	542.4	550.9	4.6	4.1	114.9	151.6	30.6	18.6
1950.Q4	305.9	55.2	554.6	555.3	4.2	4.1	115.9	152.5	31.4	21.7
1951.Q1	319.9	56.9	562.3	559.7	3.5	4.1	117.1	153.8	32.2	28.8
1951.Q2	327.7	57.2	573.1	564.2	3.1	4.1	118.2	155.0	14.7	9.5
1951.Q3	334.4	57.2	584.6	568.8	3.2	4.1	119.7	157.1	1.7	−3.9
1951.Q4	338.5	57.8	585.6	573.3	3.4	4.1	121.9	159.9	−2.9	−5.9
1952.Q1	341.1	57.7	591.3	577.9	3.1	4.2	123.5	162.2	.3	−2.8
1952.Q2	341.3	57.6	592.1	582.5	3.0	4.2	124.5	163.8	−6.4	−8.9
1952.Q3	347.0	58.0	598.3	587.2	3.2	4.2	125.8	165.8	−12.9	−15.2
1952.Q4	359.2	58.7	612.4	591.9	2.8	4.2	127.1	167.9	−6.3	−12.9
1953.Q1	365.4	58.7	622.2	596.6	2.7	4.2	127.6	169.2	−7.7	−16.4
1953.Q2	368.8	58.9	626.4	601.4	2.6	4.2	128.4	170.8	−10.5	−18.4
1953.Q3	367.8	59.1	622.5	606.2	2.7	4.2	128.6	171.8	−9.8	−14.9
1953.Q4	362.6	58.8	616.6	611.1	3.7	4.2	128.7	172.9	−20.1	−14.8

1954.Q1	362.0	59.5	608.0	616.0	5.3	4.2	129.1	174.3	−17.8	−13.9
1954.Q2	361.8	59.7	605.6	621.0	5.8	4.2	129.4	175.9	−11.2	−5.8
1954.Q3	366.2	59.6	614.3	625.9	6.0	4.2	130.6	178.3	−8.6	−4.2
1954.Q4	375.0	59.9	626.0	630.9	5.3	4.2	132.0	180.2	−3.2	−1.2
1955.Q1	387.5	60.4	641.1	636.0	4.7	4.3	133.5	182.2	3.0	2.1
1955.Q2	395.4	60.8	650.8	641.1	4.4	4.3	134.3	183.4	8.1	6.3
1955.Q3	404.0	61.2	660.3	646.2	4.1	4.3	134.9	184.3	7.8	5.1
1955.Q4	410.2	61.5	667.0	651.4	4.2	4.3	135.1	185.0	10.6	7.7
1956.Q1	411.9	62.0	664.0	656.6	4.0	4.3	135.6	185.5	10.6	9.3
1956.Q2	417.4	62.5	667.4	661.9	4.2	4.3	135.9	186.4	9.3	8.2
1956.Q3	422.4	63.2	667.8	667.7	4.1	4.3	136.0	187.2	8.2	8.2
1956.Q4	430.9	63.8	675.7	673.5	4.1	4.3	136.6	188.4	9.9	9.5
1957.Q1	438.9	64.5	680.4	679.4	3.9	4.3	136.9	190.0	7.1	6.9
1957.Q2	441.0	64.8	680.9	685.3	4.1	4.3	136.9	191.4	4.3	5.6
1957.Q3	448.2	65.4	685.6	691.3	4.2	4.3	137.0	192.7	4.3	6.7
1957.Q4	442.8	65.4	676.7	697.3	4.9	4.3	136.2	193.2	−2.0	5.5
1958.Q1	435.8	65.7	663.4	703.4	6.3	4.3	136.1	195.2	−11.4	3.4
1958.Q2	439.9	65.8	668.2	709.5	7.4	4.3	137.6	200.0	−18.1	−1.5
1958.Q3	453.1	66.2	684.3	712.7	7.3	4.3	139.0	203.5	−18.3	−5.7
1958.Q4	466.3	66.4	702.2	722.0	6.4	4.3	140.7	205.9	−15.1	−7.1
1959.Q1	476.0	67.0	710.7	728.3	5.8	4.3	142.6	208.8	−4.3	1.7
1959.Q2	489.9	67.4	726.3	734.6	5.1	4.3	143.8	210.5	2.4	5.1
1959.Q3	486.5	67.7	718.6	741.0	5.3	4.3	144.5	211.6	−2.7	4.9
1959.Q4	493.5	67.9	726.3	747.5	5.6	4.3	143.6	211.0	−2.2	5.7
1960.Q1	506.6	68.4	740.4	754.0	5.1	4.4	143.0	210.1	11.3	16.2
1960.Q2	506.5	68.5	738.9	760.6	5.2	4.4	142.8	210.3	6.1	13.8
1960.Q3	506.2	68.8	735.6	767.2	5.5	4.4	143.9	213.4	2.0	13.2
1960.Q4	504.6	68.9	731.9	773.9	6.3	4.4	144.2	216.4	−1.6	13.2
1961.Q1	507.1	68.8	736.5	780.7	6.8	4.4	144.8	219.2	−6.2	10.4
1961.Q2	518.2	69.2	749.1	787.5	7.0	4.4	146.0	222.4	−7.4	7.1
1961.Q3	527.2	69.5	758.8	794.3	6.8	4.4	146.9	225.2	−5.6	7.3
1961.Q4	540.7	69.6	777.0	801.3	6.2	4.4	148.3	228.0	−3.2	5.6
1962.Q1	553.0	70.2	788.1	808.3	5.6	4.4	149.2	231.8	−8.0	−.5
1962.Q2	562.1	70.4	798.3	815.3	5.5	4.4	149.8	235.8	−5.8	.8
1962.Q3	567.8	70.6	804.2	822.4	5.6	4.4	149.5	237.7	−4.5	2.4
1962.Q4	572.3	71.0	805.7	829.6	5.5	4.4	150.4	241.4	−5.8	1.4

TABLE B-2   Quarterly Data, 1947–1977 (continued)

	Nominal GNP (Y)	GNP deflator (P)	Real GNP (1972$) (Q)	Natural output (1972$) (Q*)	Unemployment rate (U)	Natural Unemployment rate (U*)	Money supply (M1)	Money supply (M2)	Actual federal surplus	Natural employment surplus
1963.Q1	580.2	71.3	813.5	836.8	5.8	4.5	151.8	245.9	−2.7	4.9
1963.Q2	587.9	71.4	823.7	844.1	5.7	4.5	153.3	250.0	2.7	8.7
1963.Q3	600.5	71.6	838.9	851.5	5.5	4.5	154.8	253.8	1.7	5.8
1963.Q4	610.4	72.1	847.0	858.9	5.6	4.5	156.4	258.2	−.3	3.2
1964.Q1	622.4	72.3	861.1	866.4	5.5	4.6	157.3	261.1	−4.2	−2.8
1964.Q2	632.4	72.5	871.9	874.0	5.2	4.6	158.8	264.6	−9.2	−8.9
1964.Q3	642.1	72.9	880.4	881.6	5.0	4.6	161.4	270.0	−3.3	−3.0
1964.Q4	646.0	73.1	884.0	889.3	5.0	4.6	163.4	275.4	−1.4	−.7
1965.Q1	665.4	73.7	903.1	897.0	4.9	4.7	164.5	281.0	6.2	2.3
1965.Q2	678.7	74.1	916.4	904.9	4.7	4.7	165.8	285.5	5.3	−.6
1965.Q3	695.1	74.6	932.3	912.8	4.4	4.7	167.7	291.3	−4.0	−11.9
1965.Q4	713.3	74.9	952.1	920.7	4.1	4.7	170.5	299.0	−4.5	−15.9
1966.Q1	733.7	75.7	969.5	928.8	3.9	4.8	173.2	305.3	.8	−13.1
1966.Q2	747.6	76.6	976.4	936.9	3.8	4.8	175.3	310.8	1.7	−12.3
1966.Q3	759.0	77.0	985.5	945.0	3.8	4.8	175.0	313.8	−4.2	−17.9
1966.Q4	771.7	77.7	992.8	953.3	3.7	4.8	175.2	316.7	−7.6	−20.8
1967.Q1	777.5	78.2	994.4	961.6	3.8	4.9	176.9	323.2	−16.4	−27.3
1967.Q2	785.8	78.5	1001.3	970.0	3.8	4.9	179.5	330.1	−16.8	−27.1
1967.Q3	803.1	79.2	1013.5	979.0	3.8	4.9	183.5	339.2	−17.2	−27.6
1967.Q4	818.7	80.1	1021.5	988.0	3.9	4.9	186.2	349.6	−16.2	−27.3
1968.Q1	837.3	81.2	1031.4	997.1	3.7	4.9	188.7	353.8	−11.9	−24.0
1968.Q2	861.8	82.1	1049.4	1006.4	3.6	4.9	192.2	360.7	−14.6	−29.0
1968.Q3	880.0	82.9	1061.8	1015.6	3.5	4.9	196.2	368.8	−2.8	−18.9
1968.Q4	894.7	84.0	1064.6	1025.0	3.4	4.9	200.2	378.9	.8	−14.0
1969.Q1	913.0	84.9	1074.7	1034.5	3.4	5.0	203.9	386.4	13.2	−1.3
1969.Q2	929.0	86.0	1079.6	1044.1	3.4	5.0	206.1	390.5	13.9	.7
1969.Q3	946.9	87.4	1083.4	1053.7	3.6	5.0	207.3	390.6	7.7	−2.4
1969.Q4	953.3	88.5	1077.4	1063.4	3.6	5.0	208.5	391.7	4.7	−.1

1970.Q1	964.2	89.8	1073.6	1073.8	4.2	5.1	210.4	393.2	−1.2	−.4
1970.Q2	976.5	90.9	1074.1	1083.7	4.7	5.1	213.1	400.2	−14.1	−11.8
1970.Q3	992.6	91.7	1082.0	1093.8	5.2	5.1	215.8	410.3	−15.9	−12.5
1970.Q4	996.3	93.0	1071.4	1104.0	5.9	5.1	218.7	420.2	−21.6	−11.3
1971.Q1	1034.0	94.4	1095.3	1114.2	5.9	5.2	222.4	434.6	−19.6	−13.8
1971.Q2	1056.2	95.7	1103.3	1124.6	5.9	5.2	228.0	450.4	−24.9	−18.7
1971.Q3	1072.4	96.5	1110.9	1135.0	6.0	5.2	231.8	459.3	−24.2	−17.1
1971.Q4	1091.2	97.4	1120.6	1145.5	6.0	5.2	233.3	468.0	−22.8	−15.6
1972.Q1	1127.0	98.8	1141.2	1156.2	5.8	5.3	237.5	481.9	−13.6	−13.8
1972.Q2	1156.7	99.4	1163.1	1166.9	5.6	5.3	242.3	494.1	−20.1	−20.3
1972.Q3	1181.4	100.3	1178.0	1177.7	5.6	5.3	247.4	507.4	−10.8	−11.1
1972.Q4	1219.4	101.4	1202.1	1188.7	5.4	5.3	252.9	520.5	−24.5	−27.3
1973.Q1	1265.3	102.9	1229.8	1199.7	4.9	5.4	257.6	532.5	−9.4	−15.7
1973.Q2	1288.4	104.7	1231.2	1210.9	4.8	5.4	261.7	543.4	−6.3	−10.5
1973.Q3	1317.5	106.6	1236.3	1221.6	4.8	5.4	265.3	554.1	−4.9	−8.2
1973.Q4	1355.1	109.0	1242.6	1231.8	4.8	5.4	268.7	566.5	−5.3	−7.7
1974.Q1	1369.0	111.3	1230.2	1242.2	5.0	5.4	272.7	580.1	−5.5	−2.7
1974.Q2	1400.1	114.3	1224.5	1252.6	5.1	5.4	276.5	590.9	−7.6	3.0
1974.Q3	1430.1	117.5	1216.9	1263.1	5.6	5.4	279.4	600.4	−8.0	9.1
1974.Q4	1452.4	121.1	1199.7	1273.7	6.7	5.4	282.2	610.0	−21.7	6.2
1975.Q1	1453.0	124.2	1169.8	1284.4	8.1	5.4	282.6	618.6	−48.5	−7.0
1975.Q2	1496.6	126.0	1188.2	1295.2	8.8	5.4	287.8	634.3	−99.2	−58.0
1975.Q3	1564.9	128.2	1220.7	1306.0	8.6	5.4	292.9	650.3	−65.5	−30.9
1975.Q4	1600.7	130.2	1229.8	1317.0	8.4	5.4	284.6	660.7	−67.6	−34.3
1976.Q1	1651.2	131.5	1256.0	1328.1	7.6	5.4	296.7	677.0	−60.3	−31.5
1976.Q2	1691.9	133.1	1271.5	1339.2	7.5	5.4	302.8	694.8	−46.2	−19.6
1976.Q3	1727.3	134.6	1283.7	1350.5	7.8	5.4	306.1	710.6	−53.5	−26.5
1976.Q4	1755.4	136.4	1287.4	1361.8	7.9	5.4	311.1	732.8	−55.9	−30.0
1977.Q1	1810.8	138.1	1311.0	1373.2	7.5	5.4	314.4	751.0	−38.8	−16.7
1977.Q2	1869.7	140.5	1330.7	1384.7	7.1	5.4	321.1	768.3	−40.0	−18.0
1977.Q3	1915.9	142.2	1347.4	1396.3	6.9	5.4	328.5	788.0	−59.3	−37.9
1977.Q4	1965.1	144.3	1361.4	1408.0	6.6	5.4	334.1	802.9	—	—

Appendix C
Data Sources
and Methods
for Appendix B

C-1 ANNUAL VARIABLES

1. Nominal GNP *(Y)*:

   1900–08: *Long-term Economic Growth, 1860–1970,* (Washington, D.C.: U.S. Department of Commerce, 1973), series A7, linked in 1909 to:

   1909–28: *Long-term Economic Growth, 1860–1970,* series A8, linked in 1929 to:

   1929–45: *Economic Report of the President 1972,* (Washington, D.C.: U.S. Government Printing Office, 1972), Table B1.

   1946–76: *Survey of Current Business,* (Washington, D.C.: U.S. Department of Commerce, January 1976 and July 1977), Table 1.1.

2. Implicit GNP deflator *(P)*:

   1900–76: Obtained by dividing nominal GNP *(Y)* by real GNP, 1972 $ *(Q)*, then multiplying by 100, that is, $P = 100 \times (Y/Q)$.

3. Real GNP, 1972 $ *(Q)*:

   1900–08: *Long-term Economic Growth, 1860–1970,* series A1, linked in 1909 to:

   1909–28: *Long-term Economic Growth, 1860–1970,* series A2, linked in 1929 to:

   1929–45: *Economic Report of the President, 1972,* Table B2.

   1946–76: *Survey of Current Business,* January 1976 and July 1977, Table 1.2.

4. Natural output, 1972 $ *(Q*)*:

1900–55: Q^* is calculated as the geometric interpolation between the Q^* values of the benchmark years of 1902, 1907, 1913, 1929, and 1950. Thus, between benchmark years 1902 and 1907, the one year growth rate of Q^*, q^*, is calculated as

$$q^* = \left(\frac{Q^*1907}{Q^*1902}\right)^{\frac{1}{5}} - 1.0$$

Benchmark values for 1902, 1907, 1913, 1929, and 1950, are estimates of output producible at an adjusted unemployment rate, UA, of 5 percent. Q^* for the benchmark years is estimated as: $Q^* = (Q) \times [1.0 + 2 \times (UA - 0.05)]$ where Q is actual real output, the parameter 2 is an approximation of the relationship between changes in the unemployment rate and actual output during the 1900–1929 period, and UA, the adjusted unemployment rate, is obtained by dividing the number of unemployed persons by the civilian labor force net of self-employed persons.

1956–73: Q^* is calculated as the geometric interpolation between the Q^* values of the benchmark years of 1956, 1967, and 1973. Q^* for those years is estimated as: $Q^* = (Q) \times [1.0 + 3 \times (U - U^*)]$ where Q is actual real output, the parameter 3 is an approximation of the relationship between changes in the unemployment rate and capacity output during this period, U is the published unemployment rate, and U^* is the natural unemployment rate (see following).

1974–76: Q^* is calculated to grow at an annual growth rate of 3.4 percent from the 1973 benchmark. Source: Otto Eckstein *et. al.*, *Economic Issues and Parameters of the Next 4 Years*, Economic Studies Series (Lexington, Mass.: Data Resources, Inc., 1977), Table 1, p. 10.

5. Unemployment rate *(U)*:

1900–39: *Long-term Economic Growth, 1860–1970*, series B1.
1940–70: *Long-term Economic Growth, 1860–1970*, series B2.
1971–76: *Economic Report of the President, 1977*, Table B29.

6. Natural unemployment rate *(U*)*:

1900–56: U^* is calculated as the linear interpolation between the U^* values of the benchmark years of 1902, 1907, 1913, 1929, 1950, and 1956.

U^* for the benchmark years of 1902, 1907, 1913, 1929, and 1950 is calculated as $U^* = 5.0 \times (U/UA)$ where U is the published unemployment rate and UA is an unemployment rate that adjusts for self-employment. UA equals the number of unemployed divided by the civilian labor force net of self-employed persons. The assumed 5.0 rate for UA, assumed to be consistent with long-run equilibrium, reflects the value of UA observed in late 1950, when the economy was operating at its natural rate of unemployment.

Changes in U^* before 1950 reflect only changes in the U/UA ratio.

1956–76: As estimated by Robert J. Gordon, "Structural Unemployment and the Productivity of Women" in K. Brunner and A. Meltzer (eds.), *Stabilization of Domestic and International Economy*, vol. 5 of a supplementary series to the *Journal of Monetary Economics*, 1977, p. 189–191 (line 5).

7. Money supply ($M1$):

1915–46: Historical Statistics of the United States, *Colonial Times to 1970*, (Washington, D.C.: U.S. Department of Commerce, 1975), series 414.

1947–76: *Federal Reserve Bulletin*, various issues.

8. Money supply ($M2$):

1900–46: Historical Statistics of the United States, *Colonial Times to 1970*, series 415.

1947–76: *Federal Reserve Bulletin*, various issues.

C-2 QUARTERLY VARIABLES

1. Nominal GNP *(Y)*:

1947:Q1–1977:Q2: *Survey of Current Business*, January 1976 and July 1977, Table 1.1.

2. GNP implicit price deflator *(P)*:

1947:Q1–1977:Q2: Obtained by dividing nominal GNP *(Y)* by real GNP, 1972 $ *(Q)*, then multiplying by 100, that is, $P = 100 \times (Y/Q)$.

3. Real GNP, 1972 $ *(Q)*:

1947:Q1–1977:Q2: *Survey of Current Business*, January 1976 and July 1977, Table 1.2.

4. Natural output, 1972 $ *(Q*)*:

1947: Q1–1977:Q2: The quarterly values are derived by linear interpolation between the annual values.

5. Unemployment rate *(U)*:

1947:Q1–1977:Q2: *Business Conditions Digest*, (Washington, DC.:), U.S. Department of Commerce; April 1976 and various issues, series 43.

6. Natural unemployment rate *(U*)*:

1947:Q1–1977:Q2: The quarterly values are derived by linear interpolation between the annual values.

7. Money supply ($M1$):

1947:Q1–1977:Q2: *Federal Reserve Bulletin*, various issues.

8. Money supply ($M2$):

1947:Q1–1977:Q2: *Federal Reserve Bulletin*, various issues.

9. Actual federal government surplus, 1972 $:
   1947Q.1–1977Q.2: *Survey of Current Business,* January 1976 and July 1977, Table 3.2.
10. Natural employment surplus, 1972 $:
   1947Q.1–1977Q.2: The natural employment surplus is calculated as the difference between natural output expenditures (E^*) and natural output revenues (R^*). E^* is a weighted average of actual (E) and high-employment expenditure (E^H):

$$E^* = (1 - \alpha)\ E + \alpha E^H$$

R^* is calculated as the product of natural output (Q^*) and the ratio of revenue to output, evaluated at natural output. That ratio is a weighted average of the ratios of revenue to output, evaluated at high-employment and actual output:

$$R^* = (Q^*)\ [(\alpha)\left(\frac{R^H}{Q^H}\right) \times (1 - \alpha)\,(R/Q)]$$

where:

$$\alpha = \frac{Q^* - Q^H}{Q - Q^H} \quad \text{if} \quad 0 \leq \alpha \leq 1$$

$$\alpha = \quad 0 \quad \text{if} \quad \frac{Q^* - Q^H}{Q - Q^H} < 0$$

$$\alpha = \quad 1 \quad \text{if} \quad \frac{Q^* - Q^H}{Q - Q^H} > 1$$

Sources: *Q, E, R: Survey of Current Business,* January 1976 and July 1977, Tables 1.2, 3.2, 5.1. Q^H, E^H, and R^H: 1955:Q1–1976:Q3, unpublished data provided by the Council of Economic Advisors. 1947:Q1–1954:Q4, supplied by the Federal Reserve Bank of St. Louis.

C-3   VARIABLES USED IN FIGURES BUT NOT LISTED IN APPENDIX C

Figure 8-11. For the methodology used to "strip" food and energy prices out of the GNP deflator, see Robert J. Gordon, "The Impact of Aggregate Demand on Prices," *Brookings Papers on Economic Activity,* vol. 6, no. 3 (1975), Appendix A, pp. 656–60.

Figure 9-1. The expected rate of inflation is a weighted average of past quarterly rates of change of the GNP deflator "stripped" of food and energy prices (see above note to Figure 8-11). The weights are derived from a regression of the nominal Moody's Aaa bond rate on the quarterly rate of change of this stripped deflator. For more details on the estimation of the expected rate of inflation and the natural unemployment rate, see the source cited above in Appendix section C-1, regarding the construction of U^* for 1956–76.

Figure 11-4. The wage rate series is the Bureau of Labor Statistics index of private nonagricultural average hourly earnings adjusted for changes in overtime and the interindustry mix of employment, available quarterly since 1964. Pre-1964 data were derived in Robert J. Gordon, "Inflation in Recession and Recovery," *Brookings Papers on Economic Activity,* vol. 2, no. 1 (1971), Appendix C, pp. 153-4.

Figure 18-2. This comparison of real income per capita across nations is not based on market exchange rates, which can be misleading. Instead, the comparison for 1970 is based on an extremely careful study which involved traveling to each nation to collect data on their prices for goods identical in quality to those in each other nation. Adjustments were made for services provided free by the government in some countries but not in others, e.g., free national health care in the United Kingdom. See Irving Kravis *et al., A System of International Comparisons of Gross Product and Purchasing Power* (Baltimore: published for World Bank by Johns Hopkins, 1975). The 1970 comparison for Sweden, a country not covered by the Kravis study, is based on the assumption that Swedish prices are identical on average to those in Germany, an assumption which probably leads to overstatement of comparative Swedish real income per capita. Figures for other years were obtained as follows:

1953–76. The 1970 dollar figures were extrapolated forward and back by real GNP per capita data obtained from *International Financial Statistics.*

1870–1938. The postwar figures were linked in 1953 to those compiled for 1870–1960 in Angus Maddison, *Economic Growth in the West* (New York: The Twentieth Century Fund, 1964), Appendixes A and B.

Table 2-1. Same as Figure 18-2 for 1970.

Glossary of Major Concepts

Note: Numbers in parentheses indicate the chapter and section where each term is first introduced. Words and phrases in the text set in boldface type are those defined in this list. The glossary does not include every word listed in the Identification section at the end of each chapter, particularly those whose use is confined to a single chapter.

Accelerator hypothesis (14–1). The theory that the level of net investment depends on the change in expected output, because firms are assumed to attempt to maintain a fixed ratio of desired capital to expected output.

Adaptive expectations (7–4, 8–8). A hypothesis that claims economic units base their expectations for next period's values on an average of actual values during previous periods.

Adjusted demand growth (8–6). The growth rate of actual aggregate demand (nominal income) minus the growth rate of natural output. In the long run, must equal the inflation rate.

Adjusted output growth (8–6). The difference between the growth rates of actual and natural real output.

Aggregates (1–4). The total amount of an economic magnitude for the economy as a whole. Example: **GNP** is an economic aggregate.

Aggregate demand (1–5). Total (nominal) spending on goods and services by all economic units in the economy. See **nominal GNP.**

Aggregate demand curve (6–2). The schedule that indicates the combinations of the price level and output at which the money and commodity markets are simultaneously in equilibrium.

Aggregate supply curve (6–8, 7–3). A short-run schedule that indicates the amount of output supplied at any price level, given a fixed expected price level.

Appreciation (10–8, 19–3). A rise in the value of one nation's currency relative to another nation's currency. Example: The appreciation of the American dollar relative to the British pound in the 1970s means one dollar buys more British pounds than before.

Automatic stabilization (3–appendix, 17–2). A feature of any economy in which tax receipts depend on income; the economy is stabilized by the leakage of tax revenues from the spending stream when income rises or falls.

Autonomous (3–2). A magnitude which is independent of the level of income. Example: Autonomous consumption spending.

Autonomous spending (3–4). Categories of spending which do not depend on income in the simple model of Chapters 3–7, including a portion of consumption (Autonomous consumption) and all of private **investment.**

Average propensity to consume (3–4). The ratio of consumption expenditures to disposable income. See **Marginal Propensity to Consume.**

Average propensity to save (3–4). The ratio of personal saving to disposable income. See **Marginal Propensity to Save.**

Balanced budget multiplier (3–7). The ratio of the change in equilibrium real income to the change in government expenditure when government expenditure and tax revenues are raised by an equal amount.

Balance of payments (10–8, 19–2). The total of an economy's external trade in goods, securities, and money. When the balance of payments runs a surplus, a nation gains foreign-exchange reserves. With a deficit the nation loses reserves.

Balance of trade (19–2). The difference between exports and imports. When a nation's exports exceed its imports, it has a balance of trade surplus; when its imports exceed exports, it has a balance of trade deficit. Also called **net exports.**

Base year (1–2, 2–9). The year with which a magnitude is compared in the calculation of an index. Example: The **implicit GNP deflator** is a price index which currently is calculated using 1972 as the base year.

Bears (5–3). Individuals who think stock and bond prices are likely to decline. In the liquidity trap, everyone is a bear.

Budget constraint (8–6). The sum of the inflation rate and adjusted output growth must always equal the adjusted demand growth rate ($p + \hat{q} = \hat{y}$).

Capital account (19–2). The portion of the balance of payments which includes direct investment and trade in both long-term and short-term securities.

Capital consumption allowances (2–8). Amount of capital stock used up in the process of production due to obsolescence and physical wear. See **depreciation.**

Capital gain (10–3). Any increase in the value of a physical or financial asset. If you buy a share of stock for $20 and sell it six months later for $25, your capital gain is $5.

Closed economy (1–5). Economy in which there are no flows of labor, goods, bonds, or money to and from other nations.

Commodity market (3–1). The aggregate market for goods and services (GNP).

Comparative statics (7–1). A technique of economic analysis in which a comparison is made between two equilibrium positions, ignoring the behavior of the economy between the two equilibrium positions, either the length of time required or the route followed during the transition between the initial and final positions.

Constant growth rate rule (15–8). A policy (recommended by many monetarists) which advocates a constant percentage rate of the money supply in order to prevent the Federal Reserve from destabilizing the economy.

Constant unemployment line (8–6). The schedule along which adjusted demand growth is equal to the inflation rate. When the economy is on this schedule, the growth rates of real and natural output are the same, leaving the unemployment rate unchanged.

Consumption expenditures (2–3). Purchases of goods and services by households for their own use.

Consumption function (3–2). The relationship between the amount households desire to consume and their disposable income.

Cost-push (7–7). An autonomous decision by workers to demand a higher wage rate or by firms to raise their profit margins. The effect of a cost push on output and the price level depends on the behavior of the central bank.

Countercyclical (13–5). An adjective describing any economic variable which fluctuates in the opposite direction as real output over the business cycle. See **Procyclical.**

Cross section (13–2). Data which covers several categories, each at the same point in time. Example: Cross-section studies of the income-consumption relation often gather consumption data for the various income classes, during a single year.

Crowding-out effect (5–6). A term which describes the decrease in one component of spending when another component of spending rises. Example: When government expenditure rises, the interest rate rises depressing investment spending. This fall in investment is the amount which has been crowded-out.

Current account (19–2). The portion of the balance of payments which includes exports and imports of goods and services, as well as transfers and gifts.

Deflation (1–3). A sustained downward movement of the aggregate price level.

Deflator (1–2, 6–1). See **Implicit GNP deflator**.

Demand-pull inflation (7–7). Inflation caused by a continuous rightward shift of the aggregate demand curve.

Depreciation (2–8). The annual percentage decline in the *value* of a piece of capital due to physical deterioration and obsolescence. Example: If your new car purchased for $5,000 is worth only $4,000 after one year, then its depreciation rate over that year is 20 percent.

Depreciation (10–8, 19–3). A decline in the value of one nation's currency relative to another nation's currency. Example: The depreciation of the American dollar relative to the German mark in the 1970s means one dollar buys fewer marks than before.

Discretionary fiscal policy (17–2). A deliberate policy which alters tax rates (and/or) government expenditure in an attempt to influence real output and unemployment.

Disintermediation (16–8). The term used to describe the shift of funds out of savings banks when the interest rate on stocks and bonds increases. An important cause of disintermediation is the **Regulation Q** ceiling which prevents savings banks from raising their interest rate on deposits to compete with the higher returns available on bonds.

Dynamic multipliers (12–7). The amount by which output is raised during each of several time periods after a one-dollar increase in autonomous spending. Example: The econometric

models discussed in section 12–7 have dynamic multipliers for a change in government spending, which generally rise through the first year peak in the second year and decline steadily thereafter.

Econometric models (12–7). A group of equations, each one representing a different relation in the economy, in which the parameters are estimated by the statistical study of past historical episodes. All the equations of an econometric model can be solved simultaneously to determine the levels of inflation, unemployment, other variables of interest, and what changes would occur with differing economic policies.

Economic model (5–Appendix). A graphical or mathematical representation of an economy, usually consisting of two or more graphical schedules or algebraic equations. Example: The *IS* and *LM* curves of Chapters 3–6 combine to form an economic model which determines the equilibrium levels of real income and the interest rate. The same information is contained in the algebraic version in the Appendix to Chapter 5.

Equilibrium (3–4). A state in which there exists no pressure for change. Example: The commodity market is in equilibrium when the demand for commodities equals the supply of commodities.

Ex ante (3–4). A term that describes planned expenditures (before they actually take place); before the fact. Example: Ex ante inventory accumulation is planned inventory accumulation. See **ex post**.

Excess reserves (16–2). The amount of reserves held by a bank in excess of its **required reserves**.

Exchange rate. See **Foreign exchange rate**.

Expectations effect (6–6). The decline in commodity demand during a price deflation due to the expectation that future prices will be lower, leading to a postponement of purchases to take advantage of lower prices in the future.

Expected real interest rate (10–2). The real rate of return which people expect to pay on their borrowings or earn on their savings after deduction of the expected rate of inflation from the nominal interest rate. Example: If people receive a 10 percent nominal return on their savings and expect a 7 percent inflation rate, the expected real interest rate is 3 percent. See **Real interest rate.**

Exports (2–5, 19–2). Exports of country A are goods and services produced in country A and shipped to residents of another country. See **imports.**

Ex post (3–4). A term that describes the actual expenditures that have resulted after the fact. Example: Ex post inventory accumulation is actual inventory accumulation. See **Ex ante.**

Extra convenience services (10–6). The convenience of money compared to bonds and other assets for conducting transactions. Money is immediately and universally accepted for purchases and payments, whereas bonds and other interest-bearing financial investments are not, forcing bondholders to convert their bonds into money before making transactions.

Final product (2–3). All currently produced goods and services that are sold through the market but are not resold. Same as **Gross national product.**

Final good (2–3). Part of final product. See **Intermediate good.**

Fiscal dividend (17–3). The automatic growth in the federal government surplus generated by growth in the natural rate of output.

Fiscal drag (17–3). A fiscal dividend which is not eliminated by tax cuts or expenditure increases.

Fiscal policy (1–4). Government policy that attempts to influence target variables by manipulating government expenditures and tax rates.

Fixed investment (2–4). All final goods purchased by businesses which are not intended for resale. Example: Buildings, machinery, office equipment.

Flexible accelerator (14–4). The theory that the desired ratio of capital to expected output may be affected by the user cost of capital. The flexible accelerator hypothesis also usually maintains that only a portion of any gap between the actual and desired capital stock will be made up in any one period.

Flow magnitude (2–2). Economic magnitude which moves from one economic unit to another at a specified rate per unit of time. Examples: **GNP, personal income.**

Foreign exchange rate (10–8, 19–3). The amount of another nation's money that residents of a country can obtain in exchange for a unit of their own money. For instance, in November, 1977, residents of the United Kingdom could obtain .$1.74 in U.S. dollars for one pound sterling.

Formula flexibility (18–3). An automatic procedure for adjusting stabilization policy (tax rates or the money supply) in response to changes in unemployment, inflation, or other variables specified in advance, without any need for legislative deliberation.

General equilibrium (4–7). A situation of simultaneous equilibrium in all the markets of the economy.

GNP gap (5–3). The difference between natural output and actual output.

Government deficit (2–6). Excess of government expenditures over tax revenues.

Gross (2–8). An adjective which usually refers to magnitudes which include capital consumption allowance. Example: Gross national product. See **Net.**

Gross national product (1–2). The market value of all currently produced goods and services during a particular time interval which are sold through the market, but are not resold.

High-powered money (16–2). The sum of currency held by the nonbank public and bank reserves. This money is high-powered, because it is capable of supporting bank deposits equal to a multiple of itself, when held by banks as reserves.

Implicit GNP deflator (1–2, 2–9). The economy's aggregate price index. Defined as the ratio of nominal GNP to real GNP.

Implicit price deflator (1–2). See **Implicit GNP deflator.**

Imports (2–5, 19–2). Imports of country A are goods and services consumed in country A, but produced elsewhere. See **Exports.**

Indexation (10–1). The tying of wages, tax brackets and/or government bond yields to the overall average inflation rate so that real values are maintained.

Indexed bond (11–8). A bond which pays a fixed real interest rate to its holder by nominal interest rate equal to the fixed real interest rate plus the actual inflation rate.

Indirect business taxes (2–8). Taxes on business levied as a cost of operation. Examples: Sales, excise, and property taxes.

Inflation (7–6). A sustained upward movement in the aggregate price level which is shared by most products.

Inflation rate (1–3). The rate of change of an economy-wide price per unit of time.

Inflation tax (10–3). The extra revenue which the Federal government receives when it raises the nominal money supply in response to higher prices.

Inflationary recession (1–1). See **Stagflation.**

Injection (2–6). That part of income which is spent on nonconsumption goods. Example: Private investment, government spending. See **Leakage.**

Intermediate good (2–3). Any good which is resold by its purchaser either in its present or in altered form. See **Final good.**

International reserves (19–2). The internationally acceptable assets which each nation maintains to pay for any deficit in its balance of payments. The main types of international reserves are gold, the U.S. dollar, and special drawing rights.

Inventory investment (2–4). Changes in the *stock* of raw materials, parts, and finished goods held by business.

Investment (2–4). The portion of final product which adds to the nation's stock of income-yielding assets (inventories, structures, and business equipment) or which replaces old worn-out assets.

IS **line** (3–4). The schedule that identifies the combinations of income and the interest rate at which the commodity market is in equilibrium: everywhere along the *IS* curve, the demand for commodities equals the supply of commodities.

J-**Curve phenomenon** (19–5). The tendency for a nation to run a larger excess of imports over exports in the short-run following a depreciation of its exchange rate, followed later by reduced trade deficit.

Job vacancy rate (9–4). The ratio of the number of total job vacancies to the civilian labor force. Unfortunately no data are collected in the United States to correspond to this concept.

Keynes effect (6–6). The stimulus to aggregate demand generated by a decline in the rate of interest caused by the rise in the real money supply (caused in turn either by a higher nominal money supply or lower price level).

Law of diminishing returns (7–2). The principle that the extra output (such as wheat) produced by the addition of a unit of one input (such as labor), declines as more of that input is added, as long as there is at least one other input which is fixed in amount (such as land).

Leakage (2–6). That part of income which leaks out of the spending stream and is not available to be spent on consumption goods. (See **injection**). Examples: Income taxes, personal savings.

Life-Cycle hypothesis (13–4). The theory that people try to stabilize their consumption over their entire lifetime. The life-cycle hypothesis predicts that young and old households will consume in excess of their income and that those in the middle-aged groups will save to support themselves during their retirement.

Liquidity trap (5–3). A situation in which the interest rate is believed by all to be at its minimum possible value and the price of bonds is as high as it is likely to go. Because people uniformly expect that bond prices will fall, they hold no bonds and there is no one from whom the Federal Reserve can purchase bonds in order to lower the interest rate and stimulate the economy.

LM **curve** (4–5). The schedule that identifies the combinations of income and the interest rate at which the money market is in equilibrium; everywhere along the *LM* curve the demand for money equals the supply of money.

Long-run equilibrium (7–5). A situation in which aggregate demand equals aggregate supply and in addition expectations turn out to be correct. See **Short-run equilibrium.**

M1 (15–7). The narrowly defined money supply; the public's holding of currency and checking accounts.

M2 (15–7). The broadly-defined money supply; the sum of currency and checking accounts held by the public (*M*1) plus savings deposits held at commercial banks.

Macroeconomics (1–4). The study of the major economic totals or aggregates.

Man-hours (7–2). The product of the number of employees and their average number of hours worked. Example: The number of man-hours employed per year is the average number of employees per year times their average number of hours worked per year.

Marginal leakage rate (3 – appendix). The fraction of income which is not spent on consumption; the fraction of income that flows into savings, income tax payments and import purchases.

Marginal product of capital (14–5). The dollars of extra output in constant prices which a firm can produce over a specified period by adding an extra unit of capital, divided by the total cost of that capital. The marginal product, like the user cost of capital, is expressed as a percent. Example: If an extra $1,000 machine produces an extra $150 worth of output in a year when no additional labor is hired, the marginal product of that piece of capital is 15 percent.

Marginal product of labor (7–2). The dollars of extra output in constant prices which a firm can produce over a specified period by adding an extra man-hour of labor.

Marginal propensity to consume (3–2). The change in **consumption expenditures** that results from an extra dollar of income; the fraction of an extra dollar of **personal disposable income** that households spend on consumption goods and services.

Marginal propensity to save (3–2). The change in **personal saving** induced by a one dollar change in **personal disposable income.**

Market (4–7). The process in which producers supplying a good or group of goods come to-gether with the purchasers demanding that good. The interaction of supply and demand determines the market price. The market for assets (such as government bonds) determines the price of the asset and hence its yield or interest rate.

Monetarists (1–7). A group of economists who are opposed to government intervention in the economy and who disagree with nonmonetar-ists on several major issues. See also sections 12–2 and 12–3.

Monetary policy (1–4). Government policy conducted in the United States by Federal Reserve Board that attempts to influence target variables by changing the money supply and/or interest rates. See **Fiscal policy.**

Money supply (1–7, 4–5). The main policy instrument of monetary policy. The money-supply concept *M*1 consists of currency held by the public and all checking accounts (demand deposits). *M*2 includes in addition savings accounts at commercial banks.

Multiplier (3–1). The ratio of the change in income to the change in **autonomous spending,** which causes the change in income.

Multiplier uncertainty (12–7). The uncertainty about the exact numerical values and timing of spending multipliers; used as an argument against an activist stabilization policy. Example: Since each **econometric model** produces different estimates of policy multipliers, policy-makers are uncertain as to the time value of each multiplier and therefore of the actual effect of policy changes.

National income (2–8). The income that originates in the production of goods and services; net national product less indirect business taxes.

National income and product accounts (2–3). The official United States government economic accounting system which keeps track of GNP and its subcomponents.

Natural employment surplus (17–2). The difference between tax revenue and government expenditure which would be generated if the economy were operating at the natural rate of output.

Natural rate of unemployment (1–3). The minimum sustainable level of unemployment below which inflation tends to accelerate. At this rate of unemployment, there is no tendency for inflation to accelerate or decelerate.

Natural real output (1–3). Estimate of the amount the economy can produce when actual unemployment is equal to the **natural rate of unemployment.** In this situation, there is no tendency for inflation to accelerate or decelerate.

Net (2–8). An adjective which usually refers to magnitudes that exclude the capital consumption allowance. Net investment is the amount by which the capital stock changes over a specified period. See **Gross.**

Net exports (2–5). Excess of exports over imports.

Net foreign investment (2–5). Excess of exports over imports or net exports.

Net national product (2–8). Net market value of goods and services produced, per unit time; GNP less **capital consumption allowances.**

Net tax revenue (2–6). Taxes collected minus transfer payments.

Nominal (1–2). An adjective which modifies any economic magnitude measured in current prices. Example: **Nominal GNP** is the current dollar value of GNP.

Nominal GNP (1–2). The value of **Gross national product** in current (actual) prices.

Nominal interest rate (10–2). The interest rate actually charged by banks and earned by bondholders; the market interest rate. Example: When a customer pays 12 percent interest on an auto loan, the nominal interest rate is 12 percent.

Nonmonetarists (1–7). See **monetarists,** and Sections 12–2 and 12–3.

Normative economics (1–6). An individual's recommendations regarding an optimal or desirable state of affairs. (See **Positive economics**)

Official reserve transactions balance (19–2). The balance-of-payments surplus or deficit concept which includes all trade in goods and securities; any such deficit must be offset by an outflow of international reserves.

Okun's law (8–4). The name given to the close relationship in the postwar United States between the unemployment rate (U) and the ratio of actual to natural real output (Q/Q^*). According to Okun's law, a one percentage point rise (drop) in the unemployment rate is associated with roughly a three percent decrease (increase) in (Q/Q^*).

Open economy (1–5). Economy in which there are flows of labor, goods, bonds, and/or money between nations.

Open-market operations (16–4). Purchases and sales by the Federal Reserve selling of government bonds used to influence the supply of high-powered money the money supply and interest rates. When the Federal Reserve wishes to raise the money supply, it buys bonds, paying with high-powered money, resulting in a higher money supply.

Optimum quantity of money (10–6). The stock of money which minimizes the costs in terms of fees and inconvenience of conducting transactions.

Parameters (5 – appendix). A parameter is taken as given or known within a given analysis. Example: In the consumption function, ($C = a + cQ_D$), autonomous consumption (a) and the marginal propensity to consume (c) are parameters. Many exercises in economics involve examining the effects of a change in a single parameter.

Permanent income (13–3). The average income which people expect to receive over a period of years, often estimated as a weighted average of past actual income.

Permanent income hypothesis (13–3). The theory that consumption spending depends on the long run average (permanent) income which people expect to receive. Example: If people's incomes rise and fall with the business cycle, then their actual incomes will be above their permanent income in booms and below in recessions. Their saving will rise and fall with their actual income.

Personal disposable income (2–8). The income available to households for consumption and saving; personal income less tax payments.

Personal income (2–8). The income received by households from all sources (interest, wages, transfers); national income less corporate undistributed profits, corporate income taxes and social security taxes, plus transfer payments.

Personal saving (2–4). That part of personal income which is neither consumed nor paid out in taxes.

Pigou effect (5–5, 6–6). The direct stimulus to Autonomous consumption spending that occurs when a price deflation raises the real money supply and thus wealth. Also called the real balance effect.

Policy instruments (1–4, 12–5). Elements of government policy which can be manipulated to influence target variables. Examples: Personal income tax rate, money supply.

Positive economics (1–6). The attempt scientifically to describe and explain the behavior of the economy.

Price controls (8–10, 11–5). Government imposed restrictions on nominal wages and prices.

Price index (1–2). A weighted average of prices in the economy at any given time, divided by the prices of the same goods in a base year. Example: The consumer price index is the ratio of an average of the prices of consumer goods in each month to the average prices of the same goods in 1967, the base year.

Procyclical (13–5). An adjective describing any economic variable which fluctuates in the same direction as real output, rising during a boom and declining during a recession. See **Counter-cyclical.**

Productivity (11–2). A general term which most often means the average amount of output (real GNP) produced per employee or per man-hour. New machines and inventions tend to raise productivity by helping workers to produce more.

Purchasing power parity theory (19–4). The theory that the prices of identical goods should be the same in all countries, differing only by the cost of transport and any import duties.

Pure fiscal policy shift (5–6). A shift in policy that involves changes in government spending and/or tax rates while the money supply is held constant.

Pure monetary policy shift (5–6). A shift in policy that involves changes in the money supply while government spending and tax rates are held constant. See **Pure fiscal policy.**

Quantity theory of money (15–3). The theory that money is demanded to conduct transactions and that to facilitate these transactions people hold a constant fraction of their nominal income in the form of money. The strong version of the theory assumes also that real output is fixed, so price changes are proportional to changes in the money supply.

Rate of return (4–2). The annual dollar earnings of an investment good divided by its dollar cost.

Real (1–2). An adjective which modifies any economic magnitude measured in the constant prices of a single base year. Opposite of Nominal.

Real balance effect (5–5, 6–6). See **Pigou effect.**

Real GNP (1–2). The value of gross national product in constant prices.

Real interest rate (10–3). The interest rate people actually pay on their borrowings or receive on their savings after allowing for inflation rate. This equals the nominal interest rate minus the actual inflation rate. Example: When the nominal interest rate is 12 percent and actual inflation is 10 percent, the real interest rate is 2 percent.

Real output (1–3). Same as real GNP, total production measured in constant prices. Also the same as real income.

Real wage (7–2). The value of the nominal wage in terms of the goods and services it can purchase, the nominal wage divided by the price level. A competitive firm will tend to hire workers up to the point where the marginal product of labor equals the real wage.

Rediscount rate (16–4). The interest rate which the Federal Reserve charges banks when they borrow funds.

Redistribution effect (6–6). The effect on commodity demand caused by the redistribution of income from debtors to creditors during a price deflation. If debtors cut their consumption more than creditors raise theirs, then aggregate consumption falls.

Regulation Q (16–8). The Federal Reserve Board requirement which sets an upper limit on the nominal interest rate commercial banks can pay to holders of time deposits. A similar regulation limits the allowable interest rates payable on deposits by savings and loan institutions.

Required reserves (16–2). The reserves banks must hold according to Federal Reserve regulations, banks' deposits times the reserve ratio. Example: A bank with $100 million in deposits has required reserves of $10 million when the reserve ratio is 10 percent. In the U.S., reserves can be held either as cash in the vault or as reserve deposits at the Federal Reserve.

Reserve requirements (16–2). The rules which stipulate the minimum fraction of deposits that banks must maintain as required reserves.

Saving. See **Personal saving.**

Self–correcting forces (6–1). Inherent forces in the economy, particularly price flexibility, that propel it toward the natural output level without any government intervention.

Short-run equilibrium (7–5). A situation in which Aggregate demand equals short-run Aggregate supply, given the current state of expectations (expectations do not have to be realized in short-run equilibrium, as is required for long-run equilibrium).

Short-run Phillips curve (8–2). The schedule relating unemployment to the inflation rate achievable given a fixed expected rate of inflation.

Spending responsiveness (4–4). The dollar charge in planned autonomous spending divided by the percentage point charge on the interest rate which causes it.

Stabilization policy (1–5). A general term for monetary and fiscal policies. Any policy that seeks to influence the level of aggregate demand.

Stagflation (1–1). A situation which combines stagnation (zero or negative output growth) with inflation.

Stock (2–2). An economic magnitude in the possession of a given unit or aggregate at a particular point in time. Examples: The capital stock, the money supply.

Supply shock (1–7). A change in the amount of output which firms are willing to produce at a given price level. Examples: Crop failures caused by droughts and the 1973–74 increase in oil prices. See also sections 7–7 and 8–10.

Target variables (1–4, 12–5). Aggregates whose values society cares about; society's economic goals. Examples: Inflation, unemployment.

Time-series (13–2). Data which cover a span of time. Example: The behavior of consumption and income since 1900 constitutes time-series evidence that income and consumption are related.

Total labor force (9–2). The total number of those employed and unemployed. Excludes those not working who do not seek work.

Transfer payments (2–6). Payments made for which no goods or services are produced in return. Examples: Welfare and social security.

Unanticipated inflation (10–3). That portion of actual inflation which people did not expect; actual inflation minus expected inflation. Example: If people expect inflation to be 10 percent per year, but the actual rate is 12 percent, the unanticipated inflation rate is 2 percent.

Undistributed corporate profits (2–8). That portion of corporate profits that remains with firms after stockholder dividends and corporate income taxes are paid. Also called retained earnings.

Unemployment rate (1–3, 8–1). The number of jobless individuals who are actively looking for work (or are on temporary layoff), divided by total employment plus unemployment.

Unintended inventory investment (2–4). The amount by which businesses are forced to accumulate inventories above their plans when the economy's planned expenditures fall short of production and income.

User cost of capital (14–5). The cost to the firm of using a piece of capital for a specified period, expressed as a percent of the total cost of the capital. The user cost is influenced by the interest and depreciation rates and by the tax treatment of investment, depreciation, and corporate profits.

Value added (2–3). The increase in value of inputs which is imparted by a particular stage of the production process.

Variables (1–6). Magnitudes that can change. Consumption, GNP, and the money supply are all variables.

Velocity (4–6, 15–3). The ratio of nominal income (PQ) to the money supply (M); the average number of times per year that the money stock is used in making payments for final goods and services. The inverse of velocity (M/PQ) is the amount of money held relative to nominal income.

Guide to Symbols

Symbol	Chapter where introduced	Explanation
0 or 1	3	When used as subscript, 0 and 1 distinguish an initial situation from a new situation after some parameter or exogenous magnitude has changed. Example: $r_0 =$ original real interest rate, $r_1 =$ new real interest rate.
Δ	3	The change in a magnitude. Example: ΔQ is the change in real income between one period and another.
a	3	Autonomous real personal consumption expenditure.
$\bar{A}$	4	Planned real autonomous expenditure at a zero interest rate.
A_p	3	Planned real autonomous expenditure: $A_p = a + I_p + G - c\bar{T}$
b	5–Appendix	Response of real autonomous planned expenditure to a one percent change in the interest rate.
BC	8	The Budget Constraint line.
c	3	Marginal propensity to consume.
c	16	Fraction of bank deposits held as cash by the public.
C	2	Real personal consumption expenditures.
C_D	13	Real personal consumption expenditures on durable goods.
C_{ND}	13	Real personal consumption expenditures on nondurable goods.
CU	8	The Constant Unemployment line.

Symbol	Chapter where introduced	Explanation
D	16	Total demand deposits (checking accounts).
DD	6	Aggregate demand curve.
e	5–Appendix	Response of money demand to a one dollar change in income at a fixed interest rate.
e	16	Fraction of deposits which banks hold as reserves.
E	2	Real expenditures: $E = C + I + G$
E_p	3	Planned real expenditures: $E_p = C + I_p + G$
ECS	10	Extra convenience services of money.
f	5–Appendix	Response of money demand to a one percent change in the interest rate.
f	19	Rate of change of foreign exchange rate.
F	19	Foreign exchange rate.
F	2	Real government transfer payments.
F_G	2	Real government transfer payments.
F_p	2	Real interest paid by consumers to business.
g	7	Coefficient of adjustment of expectations.
G	2	Real government purchases of goods and services.
GNP	1	Gross National Product, either nominal or real.
h	3–Appendix	Marginal propensity to import.
H	3–Appendix	Real imports.
H	16	High-powered money.
i	13,14	When used as a superscript, i denotes a magnitude for an individual, not an aggregate magnitude.
i	10	Nominal or market interest rate.
I	2	Real gross private investment.
I_p	3	Planned real gross private investment.
I_U	3	Real unintended inventory investment: $I_U = E - E_p$
IS	4	Commodity market equilibrium curve.
k	3	Spending multiplier.
K	14	Capital stock of investment goods.
K_D	13	Desired stock of consumer durable goods.
K^*	14	Desired capital stock
LM	4	Money market equilibrium curve.
LP	8	Long-run Phillips curve.
$M1$	15	Money supply concept, includes currency held by public and commercial bank demand deposits.

Symbol	Chapter where introduced	Explanation
M2	15	Money supply concept, includes currency held by public, and all commercial bank deposits (M2 = M1 + time deposits).
M3	16	Money supply concept, includes currency held by public, commercial bank deposits, and deposits at savings institutions (M3 = M2 + deposits at savings institutions).
M^d	4	Nominal money demand.
M^s	4	Nominal money supply.
MPK	14	Expected marginal product of capital.
MPL	7	Marginal product of labor.
n	11	Growth rate of employment.
N	14	Net real private investment.
N^D	7	Labor demand curve.
N^S	7	Labor supply curve.
NNP	2	Real net national product: $NNP = GNP - S_D$
p	8	Inflation rate.
p'	19	Foreign or world inflation rate.
p^e	8	Expected inflation rate.
P	2	Implicit price deflator for Gross National Product: $P = \dfrac{Y}{Q}$
P'	19	Foreign or world price level.
P^e	7	Expected level of a price index.
q	8	Growth rate of real output.
q^*	8	Growth rate of natural real output.
$\hat{q}$	8	Deviation of actual from natural output growth: $\hat{q} = q - q^*$
Q	2	Real income or real GNP.
Q_D	2	Real disposable personal income.
Q_N	2	Real national income: $Q_N = NNP - R_B$
Q_P	2	Real personal income: $Q_P = Q_N - S_B - R_C - R_S + F_G$
Q^e	14	Real expected sales.
Q^p	13	Real permanent income.
Q^*	5	Real natural output.
QQ	6	Real natural output line.
r	4	Real interest rate.
r_b	15	Nominal interest rate paid on bonds.
r_e	15	Nominal interest rate paid on equities.
r_m	15	Nominal interest rate paid on money.

Symbol	Chapter where introduced	Explanation
r_{min}	5	The minimum real interest rate.
r^e	10	Expected real rate of return.
$\hat{r}$	5	The real interest rate at which the IS curve intersects natural output.
R	2	Real government tax revenue.
R_B	2	Real indirect business taxes.
R_C	2	Real corporate profits taxes.
R_P	2	Real personal tax payments.
R_S	2	Real corporate contributions for social insurance.
s	3	Marginal propensity to save.
S	2	Real saving.
S_B	2	Real undistributed corporate profits.
S_D	2	Real capital consumption allowances.
S_P	2	Real personal saving.
SP	8	Short-run Phillips curve.
SS	6	Short-run aggregate supply curve.
t	17	Average ratio of tax revenue to GNP.
$\bar{t}$	3–Appendix, 17	Marginal personal income tax rate.
T	2	Real government tax revenue net of transfers: $T = R - F_G$
T^*	17	Tax revenue when the economy is operating at the natural rate of unemployment.
u	14	Real user cost of capital.
U	8	Unemployment rate.
U^*	8	Natural unemployment rate.
v^*	14	Desired capital-output ratio.
V	4	Velocity ($V = PQ/M$).
w	11	Growth rate of nominal wages.
w	15	Ratio of nonhuman to human wealth.
W	7	Nominal wage.
X	2	Real exports.
y	8	Growth rate of nominal income: $y = p + q$
$\hat{y}$	8	Adjusted demand growth; deviation of the growth rate of nominal output from growth rate of natural output: $\hat{y} = y - q^*$
Y	2	Nominal income or gross national product: $Y = PQ$

Index

Research and development (R&D), 534

Reserve requirements
  historical data in 1930s, 461
  monetary control instrument, 458–459

Retirement age
  life-cycle hypothesis, 380

Risk
  money, demand for, 431–432

Robinson, Joan, 556n

Robock, Stefan H., 326n

Roosevelt, Franklin D., 496n, 524

Rosen, Sherwin, 258n

Ross, Leonard, 3

S

St. Louis
  econometric model, 358–359, 476n
  Federal Reserve Bank, 341
  lag in monetary policy, 470–471

Salant, Walter S., 551n

Sales, expected, 396–399

Saving
  autonomous, 54–62
  case study, 56–57
  determination of, 52–65
  historical data, 57, 370
  induced, 52–65
  inflation, effect of, 279–284, 300–302
  measurement, 27–30
  taxation of capital, 505–508
  U.S. circular flow in 1976, 37–43

Saving rate (see Average propensity to save)

Savings accounts
  demand for money and, 427–430, 432
  payment of interest, 471–474
  reform proposals, 470–471
  regulation Q ceiling, 281, 323–324, 432
  taxation of interest, 323n

Scadding, John L., 121n, 370n, 463n

Schwartz, Anna J., 340, 459n, 462n, 463n

Search unemployment (see Turnover unemployment)

Sharpe, Myron E., 315n

"Shoe-leather" costs of inflation, 291–295

Shortages of goods
  in U.S., 318–320
  in U.S.S.R., 321–322

Short-run aggregate supply curve (see SS curve)

Short-run equilibrium
  SP and BC curves, intersection of, 220–223
  SS and DD curves, intersection of, 186–187

Short-run Phillips curve (see SP curve)

Siegert, Alice, 283n

Skills
  higher education, 260
  incentive for training, 257, 266–268
  lack, solutions for, 266–268
  mismatch unemployment, 256–260, 266–268
  training in school, 259, 267

Solow, Robert M., 240n, 358n, 434n, 489n

SP curve
  controls, effects of, 229–232
  derived, 202–206
  expectations of inflation, cause of shifts, 206–210
  Friedman, Milton, use by, 18n
  open-economy analysis, 576–578
  recession, shifts in, 304–311
  SS curve, relation to, 202–206
  supply shocks, effects of, 229–232

Speculative motive (see Money, demand for)

SS curve
  characteristics of, 177–184
  cost push inflation and, 191–192
  demand-pull inflation, 187–191, 202–206
  fiscal and monetary expansion, 184–187
  fiscal and monetary stimulus, 202–206
  Great Depression (case study), 163–165
  inflation, sources of, 187–194
  slope and shifts, 177–182
  SP curve, relation to, 202–206

Stabilization policy
  government action, scope for, 95–96

role in controlling economy, 11–12
(See also Monetary policy, Fiscal policy, Policy activism)

Stagflation
  defined, 4
  problem introduced, 4
  shifting expectations, caused by, 225–228
  supply shocks, caused by, 232–235
  termination of controls, caused by, 231–232, 236–238
  U.S. experience, 1970–1971, 226–228
  U.S. experience, 1971–1976, 235–238

State and local government
  public service employment and, 269–270
  sales taxes, 528

Stein, Jerome, 359n, 434n, 471n

Stephenson, James B., 287

Stock magnitudes
  flows, compared to, 23–24

Stock market
  demand for money and, 97
  dividend yield, 106
  interest rate and, 106
  life-cycle hypothesis of consumption, 380–381
  poor performance, 289n

Subsidies
  supply shocks, response to, 529
  U.S.S.R., 322

Supply curve, aggregate (see SS curve)

Supply of labor (see Labor supply)

Supply shocks
  cost-push inflation and, 191–198, 232–235, 250
  permanent, 234–235
  role in U.S., 1973–1975, 239–242, 250
  subsidies to offset, 529
  temporary, 234
  wage indexation and, 326

Sweden
  countercyclical investment fund, 519–520
  real output per capita, historical data, 531

Sweeney, Richard, 564n